Ahead of the Game

Brentford FC's
2014/15 Season

Greville Waterman

Published in 2015 by Bennion Kearny Limited.

Greville Waterman has asserted his right under the Copyright, Designs and Patents Act, 1988 to be identified as the author of this book.

ISBN: 978-1-910515-14-3

Published by Bennion Kearny Limited
6 Woodside
Churnet View Road
Oakamoor
ST10 3AE

www.BennionKearny.com

Foreword

It's a great pleasure for me to write a foreword to this history of a season, written, not in retrospect but as it happened. No rose-tinted look back or facts reordered to fit a theme, but rather a week-by-week or even day-by-day record of Brentford FC in action, on and off the field, in real time.

I'm sure many of us have considered doing such a diary, or may even have started one, but saw early enthusiasm wane quite quickly. So I am rather in awe of Greville's ability to keep his blog going over the last eleven months. And of the way he managed to find new perspectives on the regularity of the matches home and away to retain his readers' interest.

His recruitment and inveigling of his many contacts to add their own contributions also kept it fresh and thought-provoking. We owe him a real debt of gratitude for sticking to the task.

As I discovered very soon after taking up my role at BFC, one of the defining characteristics of our club is the very real involvement of the supporters, and this well before the arrival of social media made it easier for fans of all clubs to have their views heard. And I feel my enthusiastic endorsement of Greville's blog and this collection of extracts is entirely consistent with that history and tradition of us all being in it together.

And what a season he chose to record, our first at this level for over twenty years and one that is surely going to remain long in the memory. It would be easy to pretend now that we had no apprehension following promotion to the Championship and that we foresaw our securing early safety and a challenge for playoffs or better. But as the blog testifies, it was never as straightforward as all that - it seldom is for Brentford fans.

I hope Greville keeps it going because I sincerely believe that this season is just the start and the best is yet to come.

Next year's edition will no doubt prove me right or wrong. In the meantime, enjoy reflecting on this amazing season in the pages that follow.

Thanks Greville!

Cliff Crown.
Chairman of Brentford FC

About Greville Waterman

Greville and son Nick, Elland Road, Feb 2015

Greville Waterman is a long-term Brentford supporter who has enjoyed all the good and bad times at Griffin Park and who can finally see light at the end of a very long tunnel.

He was a director of the club for a brief spell in 2005 (don't ask) and is currently on the board of Bees United.

Greville owned a sponsorship consultancy for many years and now teaches Autogenic Therapy, a Mind/Body relaxation technique that helps people who are suffering from anxiety, stress and mild depression (see *www.howtobeatstress.co.uk*). Greville needed the help of AT after suffering the trauma of watching the Bees over a fifty year period!

He is also Chief Executive of The Institute, a long-established adult education college in North London. Greville is married to his long-suffering and beautiful football widow, Miriam, and has two wonderful children, Nick and Rebecca; this book is dedicated to the three of them.

Greville will be making a contribution to Brentford FC out of his royalties.

About Mark Fuller

The images in this book are the work of **Mark D. Fuller**. Mark is Brentford FC's Official Photographer, and the season featured in this book was his eighth season fulfilling the role. He has covered in excess of 500 games during that time. Shooting around a thousand frames each game, each season he racks up 100,000 shots and 18,000 miles of travel. To keep up with these demands he uses an ever-expanding collection of Canon professional photography equipment and a battered Audi A6.

Mark's Brentford FC work can be viewed at: *officialbfcpics.co.uk*. Official Brentford Pictures updates are on Twitter: *@BFCPics*.

Mark also undertakes product photography for a number of clients including Premier League and Championship football clubs. Other photography work undertaken includes Corporate & PR work along with the occasional wedding.

If you need a photographer then Mark can be contacted by email: *mark@markdfuller.co.uk* and followed on Twitter: *@TheMarkFuller.*

JUNE

Why Am I Doing This? – 19/6/14

My name is Greville Waterman and way back in 1965 my Dad, a transplanted Scouser making his way in London, decided it was time for me to be indoctrinated into the mysteries of football. Over the course of a few months he took me to Stamford Bridge, Craven Cottage, Loftus Road and then finally to the ground nearest to our home in Richmond - Griffin Park. A team in red and white stripes pulverised a team in blue and white hoops by five goals to two and when, on the first day of the following season, I was given the option of returning to Griffin Park, the seemingly invincible Bees thrashed their patsies, Queens Park Rangers, by six goals to one.

I was hooked. This football lark was going to be enjoyable and stress free! Soon, surely, I would be following the mighty all-conquering Bees as they took on the might of Mars and Jupiter in some Intergalactic competition of the near future. Well, in the near-fifty years since my indoctrination the success that I expected has somehow eluded me. My loyalty and devotion has been rewarded by one season in the second tier of English football, six promotions, five relegations, seven heartbreaking and draining playoff campaigns, three Associate Member Final losses, a run to the sixth round of the FA Cup, giant killing victories over two top-flight teams, and a moral victory over Champions League winners Chelsea.

Pretty thin beer, you might agree, particularly when compared to the glory hunting supporters of the Premiership teams. So, when promotion to the Promised Land of the Championship was finally achieved in April 2014 I thought that I would commemorate our first season there since 1992/93 by compiling a fans-eye view of what happened and how we coped with this rise in status. Let's begin…

The Excitement Mounts – 20/6/14

So what has happened over the past week at Griffin Park? Not a lot really if you want to ignore the end of the early-bird season ticket sale (which left us with a club record number of nearly five thousand season ticket holders), the Capital One Cup draw away at our East London neighbours, Dagenham & Redbridge, the publication of the new league fixture list, and far too much unsettling speculation about the future of club legend and hero Clayton Donaldson.

It will be great to see a Griffin Park packed to the gills (that's *gills* NOT *Gills* who we have hopefully left behind for evermore) at most games next season. Of course, we are all excited at the imminent prospect of Lionel Road and recognise that progress and finances dictate that we have to move, but I have had nearly fifty years of Griffin Park and it is seared into my soul. There is a magic about watching games at a real, old-fashioned football stadium hidden in the back streets surrounded by terraced houses – not forgetting the pubs on each of its four corners. Night matches are something else, with a packed and raucous crowds on the Ealing Road terrace (yes, that's still a terrace) sucking the ball into the net as our boys rampage forwards towards that end, ideally in the second half. Goalkeepers have learned to dread being serenaded with that raucous cry of *It's all your fault* as the crowd rejoices in their errors – not that most opposition goalkeepers have been anything other than inspired when they come to play us.

I feel a personal slight and insult when we are turned around at the coin toss and forced to attack the Ealing Road end in the first half. What are the opposition playing at? They can't do that! We always kick that way in the second half! But you know what, in an idle few minutes I looked at the facts – never let the facts get in the way of a good story – and the truth is that last season in our twenty-three home league games we attacked Ealing Road in the first half six times (against Shrewsbury, MK Dons, Port Vale, Wolves, Notts County and Crawley) and won five of them. Indeed, I remember Tony Craig, to my utter bemusement, choosing to play that way against MK Dons just after Christmas and my bellows of anger were answered in the best possible way by Clayton scoring a second minute gift goal when nemesis Dean Lewington lost David Button's howitzer kick forward in the low setting sun. Shows what I know.

As for the opposition goalkeepers, I think I just said how good they generally were against us and it is hard to remember any total Ashley Bayes-esque disasters and gifts coming our way. Well, Crewe's Alan Martin did considerately dive over Clayton Donaldson's far from fulminating twenty-yarder, but we were four up at the time. Ironically, the biggest and most helpful blunder and cock-up of the season came at the Brook Road end when Paul Jones somehow managed to pat-a-cake Jonathan Douglas's less than bullet header into the net to settle the nerves and win that crucial late season game against Crawley.

Tuesday, April 8th, the night of that aforementioned Crawley game, had to be one of the best nights of the season. The nerves were audibly jangling as the elusive goal failed to arrive until Jones's *faux pas*. The three points calmed the nerves and brought our promotion dreams ever closer to fruition particularly after Nigel Clough's Sheffield United team of reserves and kids did the business over their hated rivals Rotherham thanks to a glorious last minute penalty. As for Paul Jones, he was rewarded for two seasons as an ever-present with the tin-tack and has joined Portsmouth where he replaces another flapper in ex-Bee loanee Trevor Carson. For all his Dracula-like propensities, Jones was unbeaten in four penalty kicks in a row against the Bees. Billy Clarke, Myles Weston and Kevin O'Connor were foiled by him when he was at Exeter and Clayton Donaldson shot horribly wide at Crawley in 2013 before Adam Forshaw finally got one right earlier last season to give us a narrow away win. Just writing about clinching promotion makes me come out in goosebumps and I cannot wait for the new season to start – not too long now!

Does He Stay Or Does He Go? – 21/6/14

I spent a few moments on YouTube this morning watching a montage of some of the goals that Clayton Donaldson scored for the Bees last season. There were eighteen in all, and over the past three seasons he has scored a total of fifty-three goals in one hundred and fifty-five appearances. At a time when having a hangnail seems a plausible enough excuse to miss a game it's worth having another look at his appearance record. Clayton is seemingly indestructible and has averaged almost fifty-two appearances per season – an incredible record.

He never hides, always puts in a shift, does more than his fair share of defensive donkey work, has pace and power, can play down the middle or down either wing and scores goals with his left foot, right foot and his head. And yet for all the recognition of his magnificent talent and achievements – and believe me, without Clayton we would be opening our new season against the likes of Chesterfield rather than in the Championship against Charlton – he has been subjected to many grudging comments over the past three years:

Can't score in a brothel. Scores one in every five chances. The worst penalty taker ever. Totally wasted out on the wing.

There might well be a modicum of truth in some of those assertions but we are not talking about Alan Shearer or Luis Suarez here, but a thirty year-old striker who had never played above the Third Division in England, plus a few games in Scotland with Hibernian (about the same level in my biased opinion) before he joined Brentford on a Bosman free in 2011. He took some time to find his feet and I remember his first home goal against Colchester, which was a typical Clayton finish, running onto a Myles Weston through ball, bursting past his defender, brushing him off, outpacing friend and foe alike and striding into the penalty area before curling the ball perfectly past a helpless keeper. How many times was that beautiful cameo repeated? Remember Swindon in the playoff's in 2013, or MK Dons away the year before when he silenced a vociferous home crowd pretty much single-handed?

He always played with a smile on his face and seemed to genuinely enjoy himself on the pitch – perhaps pinching himself at just how far he had come from his humble beginnings in Hull City (NOT Tigers) reserves. Reading the message boards of opposing teams there was always a grudging admiration of his ability, or in the case of Swindon Town, against whom he scored five goals in two seasons, a sense of abject terror at the prospect of Clayton turning out against them.

So why do I find myself writing in the past tense? Simply because Clayton's contract expires in less than a fortnight and there is currently no sign of him extending his stay at the club. He has received some stick on *The Griffin Park Grapevine* fans' messageboard and Facebook from some supporters who feel that his behaviour is selfish and traitorous and that he is letting us down.

Where do I stand on this issue? We have been good for Clayton and he has been equally good for us. His goals and performances have put him in the shop window and he has certainly been in the sights of many avaricious Championship managers who see the opportunity of signing a proven striker on a free transfer. But look at that statement more carefully. At thirty, Clayton is at the peak of his career and for a player who relies to a great extent on his pace and power he is perhaps unlikely to get much better, stronger or faster as he enters his fourth decade. He is unlikely to ever have any resale value and, most importantly, he is an educated gamble because he has never before been tested at Championship level.

We have certainly made him a more than decent offer and that, linked with the guarantee of Championship football and the convenience of not having to uproot himself or disrupt his home life, made me feel that we were favourites to retain his services – and maybe we still are. Clayton returns from his honeymoon this weekend and is shortly due to make public his decision about his future, with Birmingham City reputed to have agreed terms with his agent, who has certainly been *busy* on his client's behalf. Despite my concerns about whether he can hack it at the higher level, I would be very upset should Clayton decide to go elsewhere even though he came for nothing, gave us three years of magnificent service and would leave for nothing, as he is quite entitled to do.

From our perspective, we have a paucity of strikers with the enigmatic (I suspect some less charitable supporters could find another adjective to describe him!) Will Grigg the only firmly contracted forward remaining at the club. Clayton has been a talisman for Brentford, the one true match winner that we possess and he will be hard to replace. Let's just hope that we don't find ourselves in a position where we have to do so. But if we do, Clayton would leave with my total respect, thanks, gratitude and best wishes for the future.

Except, of course, when he plays against us.

Help Needed – Is There a Statto In The House? – 22/6/14

Yesterday's article on Clayton Donaldson brought about an interesting question from Andrew Potter who asked where he currently stands on Brentford's all time list of top goal scorers. So, I undertook what used to be called *desk research* and which has now translated into cribbing stuff from Wikipedia. Brentford's Top Ten all time goalscorers:

1. Jim Towers 163 (153 lge 9 FAC 1 LC)
2. George Francis 136 (124 lge 12 FAC)
3. Jack Holliday 122 (119 lge 3 FAC)
4. Gary Blissett 105 (79 lge 7 FAC 9 LC 10 other)
5. Dave McCulloch 90 (85 lge 5 FAC)
6. Bill Lane 89 (79 lge 10 FAC)
7. Lloyd Owusu 87 (76 lge 4 FAC 3 LC 4 other)
8. Billy Scott 86 (83 lge 3 FAC)
9. Jack Lane 86 (74 lge 12 FAC)
10. Idris Hopkins 80 (77 lge 3 FAC)

Clayton, with his fifty-three goals for the club is nowhere near the top ten, but I still fervently hope that he will remain with the club and start shooting higher up the charts over the course of the next few seasons. All will, I am sure, be revealed over the next few days. I was lucky enough to see two of the top ten play in Gary Blissett, and Lloyd Owusu, and many others still around would, of course, have seen the *Terrible Twins* Jim Towers and George Francis in action.

There is no way of comparing them in terms of their ability and style of play, given the differences in the game over the decades but I would love to somehow create a Brentford FC *Back To The Future* and be in a position to see Jack Holliday and Dave McCulloch in action. What were they like, were they big and relied on their strength, were they great in the air, how fast were they, were they goal-hangers or did they have defensive responsibilities too, what was the quality of the goalkeeping and defending like? So many questions and so few answers, as so little newsreel film remains. The newspaper accounts of the time don't really help either as, despite being packed full of wordy and flowery descriptions of the action and atmosphere, they are frustratingly short of tactical information regarding how teams and individual players performed.

On an aside, I was fortunate enough recently to pick up a copy of Mark Chapman's fascinating book of facsimile editions of the 1935/36 Brentford FC First Division match programmes, and what staggered and amazed me was how small footballers were in those distant days. You think of some half-remembered heroes from that period and your imagination (or certainly mine) conjures up images of giants striding the pitch like veritable colossi. In reality, think again! Stanley Matthews – 5ft 9ins and 10 stone 10 lbs, Arsenal legend and hard man Wilf Copping – 5ft 7ins, England centre forward Ted Drake a whopping 5ft 10ins, immortal international goalkeeper Harry Hibbs – a mere 5ft 9ins tall, and most amazing of all, goalscoring legend from Everton, Dixie Dean, also only 5ft 10ins. These were by no means the exceptions, it was rare to find a goalkeeper or centre half in those days who was over six feet tall.

Does anyone remember the Bantam Divisions in the First World War in which the normal minimum height requirement for recruits was reduced from 5ft 3ins to a mere 5ft? I don't want to divert into a sociological study of height and diet in Edwardian Britain but, as you can see, times were different and things have to be judged in isolation; comparisons are pretty meaningless.

Who's Coming In? – 23/6/14

If ever I want to make myself laugh or simply while away a few moments of downtime I log onto the Football Rumours website – you all know the one I'm talking about – and don't tell me you haven't looked at it too. Giving it my normal cursory glance – Oh, OK, I admit it, I read it religiously from top to tail every day – the following names are apparently on their way to join us:

- Calvin Zola – sorry gone to Stevenage
- Callum Wilson – hmmm, surely we would never be in a position to spend the money needed to get him
- Marvin Sordell – good shout as he would be well known to Mark Warburton, but again…. the wages

- Sean Scannell – hope he is better than his brother who had an anonymous loan spell with us aeons ago
- Emmanuel Frimpong – please noooooo
- Korey Smith – another good call, an excellent young player with a bright future
- Dean Cox – a bit too much like Sam Saunders but a proper footballer with a great left foot
- Alan Judge – well they had to get one right
- Billy Paynter and Julian Alsop – methinks it's someone from the GPG playing games again

The website is total fiction and absolute rubbish but it provides hours and hours of harmless fun for us fans who aren't *in the know* about impending transfers to and from Brentford FC. And, in passing, can I just make the point that under the new regime at the club, secrets no longer seep out as if by osmosis. In past years, speculation was rife and there was always someone - totally on the money - with the name of the next signing well in advance of his arrival. Well, those days have gone, new security systems and a policy of *omertà* are in place, and not before time. The success of ongoing negotiations are no longer compromised by a series of embarrassing and costly leaks. More evidence indeed of the club's professionalism in the way it conducts its business.

Matthew Benham's tried and tested transfer blueprint has been to bring in a series of precociously talented youngsters, ideally on an initial try-before-you-buy basis, leavened with some experienced tried and tested professionals. Adam Forshaw and Jake Bidwell would best sum up the first category with Jonathan Douglas and Alan McCormack the latter. So what is in store for us as Mark Warburton and Frank McParland aim to build a squad ready and able to take on the unknown challenge of Championship football? What really concerns me is that I am finding it hard to assess what the required standard is, and whether the calibre of player we have signed (or scouted) in the past will be of the requisite standard.

There will certainly be several holes to fill given the departure of loanees Marcello Trotta and George Saville as well as squad players Shaleum Logan, Scott Barron and Farid El Alagui. As well as out of contract Clayton Donaldson.

We will certainly need two or maybe three new strikers, and given how difficult and expensive it is to find them, I am totally in the dark as to where we will be prospecting. Will we splash the cash in a totally un-Brentford manner and spend serious money on a proven goalscorer? Highly unlikely in my mind, given the cost and impact upon our existing wage structure. My money is on a high quality but unproven loanee, a gamble from the lower leagues, and perhaps a signing from abroad. Maybe we will be able to make our money go further in Eastern Europe or even Spain. I also suspect we will sign one very experienced striker who knows the ropes at this level.

Elsewhere we are in pretty good shape with Messrs. Dallas, Judge, and the fit again Sam Saunders available on the flanks, together with the emerging pace and promise of Josh Clarke and Charlie Adams. We will probably sign another loanee in midfield to cover the loss of George Saville and perhaps a left sided utility defender who can provide cover at left back and centre-half. Nico Yennaris will also have to prove that he can make the right back berth his own. Otherwise the squad seems primed and ready to go. I am deliberately writing this before the players return to training and before any signings, with the exception of the exciting Alan Judge, have been made. I fully expect to have egg all over my face when every prediction of mine is proved incorrect – but that is what being a fan is all about!

A Bite To Remember! – 24/6/14

Well sometimes you just have to go with the flow and be topical. My new article containing a detailed, cogent and hopefully witty review of the brand new (and pithily titled) Brentford FC DVD *We're Going Up!* was all ready to go when Luis Suarez changed the script.

I fully realise that Italian defenders make a meal of challenges they receive from opponents but Georgio Chiellini certainly did not appreciate being made THE meal by the snaggletoothed striker or should that be biter?

So how do I put a Brentford spin on tonight's appalling event? The best that I can do is go back through the memory banks and briefly recall some of the worst fouls committed by, or perpetrated on, Brentford players in recent years. Does anyone remember Pat Terry, a frighteningly tough journeyman centre forward from the sixties, who looked like a middleweight boxer and saw out his long career with a final season at Brentford punctuated by goals and red cards? Never mind red cards, it was the red mist that descended one autumn evening in 1968 when over seventeen thousand packed into Griffin Park to see if we could send Norwich City the same way as Hull City who we had pulverised in the previous round of the Football League Cup (no sponsors in those days). A Hugh Curran inspired Norwich were strolling to an easy victory when Terry, frustrated at the way his evening had gone, launched himself into a maniacal two-footed kick into the chest of the gormless but totally innocent Laurie Brown who collapsed like a felled oak.

Those were violent times and earlier that season the bald assassin, Chesterfield's Keith Kettleborough, had to be smuggled out the side door of Griffin Park with his head hidden in a blanket after his assault on star winger Allan Mansley left the star winger crocked and never the same player again. Walsall's Paul McShane will never be forgiven by the Griffin Park faithful after young striker Alex Rhodes, just blossoming into a dangerous and skilful attacker, never fully recovered his pace or confidence after being clattered into the Braemar Road Paddock and suffering serious injury as a result. Let's also give a well-deserved namecheck to Chelsea's David Luiz for his cynical, mean-spirited and cowardly shoulder barge on young Jake Reeves – an assault that tarnished a wonderful day out at Stamford Bridge.

It's not always the Bees who end up as the victims as Cambridge United's Mick Heathcote and Paul Raynor's spat over defensive responsibilities led to the former seeing red in more ways than one. Not that we are immune to such behaviour as Darren Powell and Karleigh Osborne demonstrated at Bournemouth one Easter. Nasty and unpleasant as all these incidents were, tonight's assault took the biscuit. I was unable to take another bite of my meal.

Say It Isn't So Clayton – 25/6/14

Well that was a bit of a letdown. Today should have been one of the most exciting days of the season, one that I had been looking forward to for weeks… The Brentford players returned to training this morning preparatory to their trip to a swanky US training camp next week. All should have been great, as indeed it was, until I opened the Birmingham City website and was greeted by the sickening sight of our hero and talisman Clayton Donaldson being paraded around the St. Andrew's pitch.

I thought that I had prepared myself in a calm and rational manner to face life at Griffin Park PC, post-Clayton. Well I was wrong.

He really has gone. I know I have to face this fact, however hard it is to accept. We won't see those lung-bursting runs any more. He won't score any more of those match winning goals for us that seemingly snatch victory from certain defeat. Remember Portsmouth and Peterborough and the countless other times when he almost singlehandedly carried us over the line? We won't ever see that infectious smile and pure joie de vivre. We will really miss his unheralded and much appreciated work for the Community Sports Trust.

True, we also won't see him screw up any more one-on-ones, and certainly no more penalty kicks, and I suppose for that we should be grateful. Today though is a day of mourning. Clayton came with high expectations and more than fulfilled them. Now he has gone and I am very, very sad.

Bienvenido A Marcos – 26/6/14

Brentford yesterday announced the arrival of new Spanish midfielder Marcos Tebar Ramiro and on first examination (via the tried and tested fan scouting resources of Wikipedia, YouTube and FIFA Soccer) the former Real Madrid player appears to be an exciting prospect. He is not the first Spaniard to play for the club as Javi Venta had a short spell at Griffin Park last season and winger Jose Gallego made six appearances way back in 1946. Born in the Basque Country, Gallego's family fled to Britain to escape the ravages of the Spanish Civil War and he has the distinction, as far as I'm aware, of becoming Brentford's first overseas player. I know I've set myself up with that last statement and fully expect some anorak statto will pedantically correct me if I neglected to mention some long-forgotten Lithuanian fullback who played a few reserve games before the war – and just in case anyone thinks otherwise, Cyril Toulouse was born locally in Acton!

Brentford's track record with foreign players has been fairly up and down in recent years with some magnificent successes tempered by some dismal failures – Hermann Hreidarsson and Jide Olugbodi everyone? Hermann's arrival in 1998 came totally out of the blue. Since when did *Little Old Brentford* ever pay seven hundred and fifty thousand pounds for a player and how could they afford such a sum? Later on, during Ron Noades's reign, that and many other similar questions would be answered! Hermann bestrode the pitch like a titan, light years ahead of team mates and opponents alike in terms of his speed of thought and pure ability, although his early appearances were littered with costly errors as his seemingly casual approach was at odds with the hustle and bustle of the fourth tier of the English game. He soon settled and scored a classic and staggeringly confident winning goal against promotion rivals Cardiff. Hermann was far too good for us and was soon off to Wimbledon for a massive two-and-a-half million pound fee – a sum we have since come nowhere near matching, until perhaps the sad day when Adam Forshaw eventually leaves us.

Iceland has provided a fertile hunting ground and the peerless Ivar Ingimarsson went through the entire 2001/02 season as an ever present without once picking up a yellow card – a record I sorely wish he had tarnished by kicking Jamie Cureton up in the air just before our nemesis broke our hearts when his late goal cost us promotion. Polish midfielder Detzi Kruszynski was a massive influence in helping us win the last six games of our promotion-winning season of 1991/92 but he soon faded away. Dutch defender Pim Balkestein also started well as a loanee but seemed to lose focus and interest after signing permanently and drifted out of the reckoning. I was a massive admirer of sweeper John Buttigieg, winner of over one hundred caps for Malta, who was signed by Steve Perryman (seemingly oblivious to the fact that the sweeper system was totally unsuited to his squad).

Others also flattered to deceive. American striker Mike Grella fired nothing but blanks apart from one amazing never-to-be-repeated night when, touched by genius, he put AFC Bournemouth to the sword with a four-goal performance. He now attempts to repeat the feat with the Carolina RailHawks. Marcello Trotta was also on an emotional rollercoaster during his two loan spells at the club. Thankfully, it all ended well with promotion after the trauma of the previous season.

Let's end with the truly bonkers Jean-Phillippe Javary. Signed from the mighty Raith Rovers despite rumours of a previous involvement with Barcelona, the midfielder was much hyped by Ron Noades but turned out to be a total damp squib and left in ignominy after strange goings on during a reserve match at Cheltenham. We all hope that Marcos has a longer and more successful stay at the club than Javary and maybe, just maybe, there is a plan afoot for the arrival of a previously unknown twenty goal foreign striker – hopefully somebody more potent than the late unlamented Clyde Wijnhard or Lorenzo Pinamonte.

Too Excited To Sleep! – 27/6/14

It's late – or rather, very early in the morning – and it is well past my normal bedtime. So what's keeping me up? It is the prospect of Brentford signing a couple of players later today. We supporters need a fillip after the disappointment of losing Clayton Donaldson earlier in the week and more importantly, we need to sign some forwards given that Will Grigg – rumoured to be leaving himself – is currently the last man standing. So who might be coming in?

Many names have been bandied about on Twitter and *The Griffin Park Grapevine* including Callum Wilson and Patrick Bamford, but according to social media the likely prospects have now been narrowed down to two. Namely Moses Odubajo of Orient and Andre Gray of Luton Town.

A youth team product from Greenwich, Moses took the division by storm last season, scoring a dozen goals and making many more from his berth on the right wing. He beat players with guile and pace, was brave, worked hard and had a real eye for goal. His precocious talent, so reminiscent of another Orient favourite from the past, the late lamented Laurie Cunningham, was evident and once Orient lost so cruelly in that torrid penalty shootout at Wembley it was obvious that Moses, who had lit up Wembley with an outrageous volleyed goal in the first half, would be on his way to bigger and better things. Bigger and better surely than Brentford, with many Premiership clubs rumoured to have run their eyes over a player valued by his club at well over a million pounds. For those with a taste for *schadenfreude*, I can only begin to think how sick Orient fans will feel should they lose their star player to a club they erroneously perceive to be their inferior.

Andre Gray's signing would also turn heads as he is a pacy, lithe, sinuous striker and clinical finisher who came late onto the scene having blown his early chance at Shrewsbury. He rehabilitated himself at Hinckley before signing for Luton two years ago where he has averaged one goal in every two games, and proved far too quick and sharp for Conference defenders. He celebrated his twenty-third birthday yesterday and hopefully he will be receiving another wonderful present later today.

Goodnight!!

What A Wonderful Day! – 28/6/14

Well some days are just perfect and yesterday was really up there with the best of them. I cannot tell you how many times I visited the Brentford FC website on Friday morning hoping to find confirmation of our new signings, until the great news was finally confirmed – Orient's Moses Odubajo and Luton striker Andre Gray were now Brentford players!

There have been many murmurings about Rotherham's trolley dash with ten players already signed, but in comparison to the Bees's new arrivals, it really seems a case of quality over quantity. You can't really say a word against the Millers given the two tonkings they gave us last season when they were the only team to do the double over us, but I know whose squad I prefer. The good news just didn't stop coming with goalkeeper David Button signing a new three-year contract and, judging by the tone of the players in their Bees Player interviews, it really seems a happy and confident camp.

It is rare that transfer fees are announced nowadays and yesterday was no exception, but figures of around one million pounds for Moses and five hundred thousand pounds plus for Andre have been bandied about on social media. Who knows how accurate these figures are but it would appear that Brentford have comfortably smashed their transfer record (for the aforementioned Hermann Hreidarsson).

The last time Brentford went on a similar spending spree was at the beginning of Chairman Jack Dunnett's reign back in 1962. It all ended in tears and almost the demise of the club itself, but that is a story for another day. The club caused a sensation when it brought in an all-international strike force of Johnny Brooks, John Dick and Billy

McAdams and their goals ensured that the Fourth Division Championship was won at a relative canter with a massive ninety-eight goals scored. The difference between then and now (and really let's not try and compare Jack Dunnett with Matthew Benham – please) is that we were signing excellent proven players whose best days were well behind them. Their impact was short term and none of them had any resale value given that they were dead assets. Things are different now as the club is stuffed to the gills with players who are coveted by other teams. Let's just hope that they can fulfil their ambitions at Griffin Park – and indeed, Lionel Road, and that we have no need to cash in on the likes of Adam Forshaw, James Tarkowski and Jake Bidwell, to say nothing of the plethora of young kids with enormous potential nicely coming to the boil in the Academy.

Talking of Johnny Brooks brings me onto the only truly sad part of this article, as The Times reported on Friday that eighty-two year old Brooks is now suffering from vascular dementia, which brings to the surface yet again the issue of concussion and the repeated effects of heading what was more like a cannonball than a football. There is much in terms of research and indeed disclosure that needs to be done in this area given that Johnny Brooks is by no means an isolated example. Indeed, Jeff Astle died of chronic traumatic encephalopathy (CTE), a degenerative brain condition that has affected countless American footballers. Footballers should not, and must not, be allowed to die of *industrial injuries*. So at a time of great joy, hope and optimism for all Brentford fans let's end by remembering and rejoicing in the huge talent of Johnny Brooks and the enormous pleasure he gave fans of Spurs, Chelsea, Brentford and Crystal Palace alike, and send him our best wishes.

JULY

We're Going Up! – 1/7/14

It's okay, you can all breathe more easily now – you didn't dream it and it wasn't a fantasy! It's absolutely true – we really *are* going up! Last season was so incredible, enjoyable and fantastic that sometimes I find it hard to accept that it really happened. As a tried and tested Brentford fan of many years' vintage I am reconciled and inured to things going wrong; defeat seized from the jaws of achievement and success. Those horrid, negative expressions *It's Brentford Innit* and *It's the hope that kills you* have ruled the roost at Griffin Park for far too long and become self-perpetuating prophesies. Last season proved that we could dispense with this negativity once and for all.

And why is that? Because with a lot of hard work, a clear strategy, highly talented personnel across the club, and the support and vision of owner Matthew Benham, we have become an ambitious and amazingly well run, organised and structured club that has laid the correct foundations from top to bottom. Given these circumstances you actually make your own luck and last season proved that we are now a force to reckon with.

All of the above is reinforced by the Brentford promotion DVD *We're Going Up!* which provides a comprehensive and high quality record of the best season in living memory. You can revel once again in all of the goals we scored and my Top Ten quickly became a Top Twenty-Five. How can you possibly choose between the long range Exocets of Alan Judge, Kadeem Harris, George Saville and Adam Forshaw; Marcello Trotta's trickery and quick feet; Clayton Donaldson's power and strength and the many examples of high quality, pacy interchanges when the team turned defence into attack in the blink of an eye?

The contentious moments are all featured and Toumani's disallowed goal against Carlisle still looks like an awful decision by an inept referee. There is also Jonathan Douglas's farcical moment of high dudgeon with that bounce up after the penalty-that-never-was at Sheffield United. It's all there, so sit back and enjoy it once again. The commentary doesn't pull punches either with a certain Brentford goalkeeper's *faux pas* at Stevenage aptly described as *a moment of madness*. I would have like to have seen Tony Craig's heroic one-against-five defending against Oldham, but that's a minor quibble.

A couple of my Premier League team supporting mates came round the other night, ostensibly to watch the World Cup but bribed and liberally plied with alcohol, they agreed to forgo the dubious pleasure of Brazil versus Chile and were instead treated to twenty minutes worth of Brentford at their best. Their reaction was indeed gratifying: *I never realised they were so good, Football like it should be played, They didn't play like that when you dragged me to Stevenage, Can I come and see them with you next season?*

Proof indeed that the tom toms are sounding loud and clear and many others are also finally beginning to recognise and acknowledge our progress and prowess!

5,000 And Counting! – 2/7/14

Brentford have just announced that they have finally broken the five thousand season ticket sales barrier. What a fantastic achievement and well done to everyone who has bought one! This milestone really demonstrates just how popular our club is becoming as news spreads far and wide about the sheer quality and excitement of the football that the team produces.

The five thousand figure is apparently an all-time club record and is almost double the total figure sold last season. Indeed, the average attendance when the Bees reached the second tier of English football back in 1992/93 was just over eight thousand and the last time the club had a five figure average home attendance was over forty years ago. Maybe we can repeat that feat next season?

Something will have to give this coming season, and what is beyond any doubt is that supporters and casual visitors alike will have to change the match day habits and routine and superstitions honed and perfected in many cases over many years. No longer will the average supporter be able to enjoy a leisurely pint or three in one of the four pubs surrounding the ground and then rock up to the turnstiles, cash in hand, at five minutes to three. Not if they expect to get in to watch the match!

Many Hands – 3/7/14

How many of you died-in-the-wool Brentford supporters remember dear old Jimmy Sirrel? For those of you who don't recognise that wonderful buck-toothed grin, Jimmy was chief cook and bottle washer at Griffin Park way back in the late sixties. A tenacious Scottish inside forward at Celtic, Bradford, Brighton and Aldershot, Jimmy eventually ended up at Brentford as trainer. A trainer in those days was generally a medically unqualified loyal retainer whose job was to run onto the pitch and squeeze a freezing cold wet sponge onto any injured part of a player's body. Some did more harm than good but Jimmy progressed beyond that role when, in September 1967, after the departure of Billy Gray as last man standing, he became team manager.

But with the parsimony that Brentford was justifiably renowned for in those difficult financially strapped days, soon after the abortive QPR takeover, he was not allowed to relinquish his old post and for a couple of years a miniscule first team squad was led by the doughty Sirrel who combined the roles of manager, coach, scout, physio and trainer. It was an immense challenge but one that the taciturn Scot, a man of few words who actively discouraged media attention (not that anyone could ever understand or decipher what little he said), rose to with flying colours.

He had just seventeen players, no reserve or junior team and a back-up staff which consisted of Club Secretary Denis Piggott, and Ann Lamb on the administrative side, a few dedicated volunteers – and that was it. As Sirrel stated at the time: *Griffin Park was like a ghost town some days, so few people were around. I even had to turn my hand to washing the kit at times.*

Eventually he had had enough and quite understandably Jimmy Sirrel rejoined former Brentford Chairman Jack Dunnett at Notts County where he totally justified his move by eventually leading the Magpies into the top division and becoming a Meadow Lane legend. Jimmy Sirrel was a true footballing great, but his versatility was by no means unique and I remember stories about the mid-fifties Hartlepool manager, Fred Westgarth, who in quiet moments used to pot pigeons with his shotgun from the roof of the main stand at Victoria Park!

So why mention Jimmy Sirrel today? His name came back to me when I read the announcement on the Brentford FC website of Matt Springham who joined the club from Brighton as Head of Conditioning, replacing Chris Haslam who followed Uwe Rösler to Wigan. Matt will head up a three-man conditioning team incorporating Tom Perryman and James Perdue and will be working with Neil Greig, Head of Medical and the Medical Department. I thought then that I would check upon the number of support staff currently employed at the club. The list is long and varied comprising such titles as: Sporting Director, Manager, Assistant Manager, Goalkeeper Coach, Academy Director, Development Squad Manager, Youth Team Manager, Assistant Youth Team Manager, Head of Academy Operations, Head of Academy Recruitment, Education and Welfare Officer, Head of Performance Analysis, Head of Medical, Head of Conditioning, Conditioning Coaches, Team Doctor, Academy Doctor, First Team Physiotherapist, Academy Physiotherapist, Academy Conditioning Coach, Sports Therapist, Masseur, Kit Man, Assistant Kit Man, and Player Liaison Manager.

The list is endless and boggling to us traditionalists, and emphasises the total professionalism of the club nowadays. Cynics might say that, as in Parkinson's Law, *Work expands so as to fill the time available* for its completion, but despite the numbers this is a close-knit team where everybody knows his role and pulls his weight and there is a development pathway for everyone.

Jimmy Sirrel is probably looking down enviously from above, wishing that he had received similar levels of support but those were different times when football was far less scientific and the club was run on a shoestring. But for all their defined roles and professionalism, one question remains unanswered at Griffin Park – who is responsible for shooting the pigeons?

Gillingford – Part 1 – 4/7/14

So it is farewell to Luke Norris who has decided to accept a two-year deal from Gillingham rather than remain at Brentford. And who can blame him as he is twenty-one now and at an age where he feels that he needs to play regularly and start making a name for himself. Luke was another youth team product who spent four years at the club. He got his chance to show what he could do at first team level last season when he spent two productive loan spells at Northampton Town and Dagenham and Redbridge in League Two where he scored nine goals including some real crackers. He also made his first start for Brentford's First Team and scored with a clinical finish for The Bees in the

Johnstone's Paint Trophy against AFC Wimbledon where he linked up well with Farid El Alagui.

Given the choice of joining a League One team in Gillingham who are likely to offer him regular first team football at a decent level or biding his time at Griffin Park it is hardly surprising that he has decided to leave. The Gills have also shown their faith in him by offering Luke a two-year contract rather than the one-year extension that he has been offered by Brentford. Luke showed that he has a keen eye for goal and clinical finishing ability so it is not beyond the bounds of possibility that he will come back to haunt us in the future. Indeed to a large degree I hope that he does as I am sure that we have included a decent sell-on clause into the deal with Gillingham.

Luke's departure is merely the latest in a long conveyor belt of moves between the two clubs and it is interesting to examine some of them in more detail and decide who got the better end of the deals. The standout name is Nicky Forster who to my utter amazement joined the Bees in 1994 when he was being talked about as a future Premiership star. His agent *Monster, Monster* Eric Hall saw Brentford as a suitable stepping stone and the pacy striker gave us two and a half seasons of excellent service terrifying opponents with his pace and anticipation and horrifying us supporters with his utter inability to score from one-on-one opportunities.

In a moment of true and typical Brentford folly and madness he was sold to Birmingham City in January 1997 at a time when we were miles ahead at the top of the league and looking like a shoo-in for promotion. The fact that his replacement was a total nonentity in QPR loanee Steve Slade spoke volumes for the club's ambitions at the time. Talk about shooting yourself in the foot, as we blew automatic promotion (and can David Webb please tell us why top scorer Carl Asaba was moved out to the left wing) and limped into the playoffs where we were summarily despatched by Crewe in another Wembley non-event and abject surrender.

Tony Funnell, the diminutive striker who looked more like the mascot than a player, was pretty much a waste of sixty thousand pounds but his late goal against Millwall did preserve our third tier status when relegation looked on the cards. Billy (The Pitbull) Manuel cost us a similar fee and was converted from an adequate left back into an excellent midfield ball winner who starred in our ill-fated season in the second tier. Simon Royce was also foisted on us by Gillingham but he came predominantly as our goalkeeper coach and only played in an emergency after Richard Lee was sent off against Yeovil. He proved to be so far over the hill that he was coming down the other side and his first touch of the ball was to pick Paul Wotton's fulminating free kick out of the net. His static and rickety goalkeeping also did little to help Andy Scott's failing cause as we stumbled to a four goal to one thrashing at Dagenham in Royce's only full appearance. Luckily he has proved to be an excellent coach! Do as I say rather than as I do might well be his motto!

Gillingford – Part 2 – 5/7/14

Previously, I had a look at the players who have signed for the Bees from Gillingham over the past few years – and a pretty motley crew they mostly are! Nicky Forster apart, none of them really made a lasting impression on the club or supporters and, if truth be told, we have not really been the recipients of too much quality from the Medway.

But it is when you look at the moves that have been made in the opposite direction that you can see that there is a totally different story to tell and one that has subtly changed over the years. The first thing to remark upon is how many players have left us to join the Gills. Without taking too much time to think, I came up with the following names over the past twenty or so years: Neil Smillie, Simon Ratcliffe, Barry Ashby, Paul Smith, Robert Taylor, Brian Statham, Myles Weston, Leon Legge, Antonio German and Luke Norris.

This list also doesn't take into account Carl Asaba, Stuart Nelson and Alan Julian who made the same journey but by a more circuitous route via Reading, Orient and Stevenage respectively.

In the mid to late 1990's Gillingham, managed by the combative Tony Pulis and then Peter Taylor, were ambitious, well funded by Paul Scally and on the rise. They saw Brentford, holed beneath the water line, as easy pickings and a fertile hunting ground for proven talent. In seemingly no time at all, several of our best and most established players left Griffin Park for Gillingham, some on Bosmans, others via tribunal rulings and transfers and the talent drain encompassed such talent as Paul Smith, Barry Ashby, Brian Statham, Robert Taylor and Carl Asaba. Brentford supporters were left sickened and horrified by these moves, which were seen as proof of our own lack of ambition as well as asset stripping on a large scale. We felt bereft and denuded as so many of our favourites were allowed to leave the club and generally for far less than we felt they were worth.

Asaba and Taylor in particular formed a lethal twin spearhead that lit up Wembley in that never-to-be-forgotten playoff Final classic against Manchester City. Paul Smith played over three hundred games for Gillingham as their midfield powerhouse and dynamo and Barry Ashby proved to be an impassable barrier at the back. The thought remained that they should still have been performing in a red and white striped shirt rather than the blue of Gillingham!

Eventually we rebuilt under Ron Noades after suffering relegation to the bottom division with a side of makeweights and nonentities, but the bitterness remained and Gillingham were seen as nouveau riche and deadly rivals purely out of our envy and jealousy. Now the boot is very firmly on the other foot. Gillingham eventually fell on hard times and are only now re-establishing themselves in the third flight. We, on the other hand, are on the crest of a wave. Instead of losing our best and brightest assets we are now sending Gillingham what we could unkindly term as our rejects. That is not to say that they are anything other than very decent established third division footballers, but for the most part they have outlived their use and are not really up to the magic carpet ride that we are currently on.

Leon Legge, in particular, was a firm fan favourite and there were certainly times last season when his height, strength and physicality - not forgetting his threat in opposing penalty areas - would have come in very useful. But, for the most part, as an old-fashioned stopper, he was struggling to play with the ball at his feet – a pre-requisite in the new Brentford style of play. Myles Weston, too, ran into one blind alley too many and was jettisoned despite being a match winner on his somewhat infrequent good days. Stuart Nelson was a firm favourite at Brentford under Martin Allen who also installed him as his first choice at Gillingham where he has been impressively consistent, managing to minimise the mad rushes of blood and poor kicking that so marred his spell at Griffin Park.

The road to and from Gillingham has been well trodden and perhaps there will be more moves over the next year or so. Maybe more of our squad players will end up plying their trade at the Priestfield Stadium and I certainly would not be unhappy if bright young talent such as Bradley Dack ended up coming in our direction. Let's wait and see but in the meantime the Gillingford connection is as strong as ever.

Turning My Back On The Premier League! – 6/7/14

There are some teams like Fulham and QPR who we Brentford fans see as deadly rivals; others, such as the appalling MK Dons, that we cordially detest. On the other hand I have never heard a Brentford fan have a bad word to say about Dagenham & Redbridge who we will be visiting in the first round of the Capital One Cup next month.

So why is that? Because we recognise that they are a true blue collar club, punching way above their weight and massively overachieving to even remain in the Football League. In John Still, they had a miracle worker as manager who every year seemed to produce yet another rabbit from the hat whose eventual transfer fee would help keep the club solvent for another season. Dwight Gayle anyone?

I have never had much luck on my visits to Victoria Road – or the London Borough of Barking & Dagenham Stadium to give it its full title. Back in March 2009 I decided to give the game a miss as it was due to be televised live on Sky TV but when I arrived home that evening I was bemused to discover that the match had been postponed owing to a floodlight failure. By the time the game was eventually played in April, we were a win away from the title and we all thought that we would be holding a promotion party after the match.

How wrong can you be? Hubris was invented for moments such as this as we were taken apart on the night as two tricky wingers in Matt Ritchie and a certain Sam Saunders created chance after chance for the goal-hungry partnership of Paul Benson and Ben Strevens. Future Bees goalkeeper David Button played for Daggers that night but I have no memory of his performance given that he was totally untested. The score could and should have been in double figures but we limped away after a 3-1 mauling with our tail firmly between our legs and grateful that it was only three. Promotion would have to wait for another few days.

Our final visit to East London came two years later after the Daggers had achieved the minor miracle of getting promoted to the First Division. We arrived there one night in the dog days of the Andy Scott regime. His time had surely come and he duly went immediately after the inept 4-1 defeat - or abject surrender - in a game notable for the utter lack of effort from a Brentford team who sleep-walked through the entire ninety-minute horror show.

Our last meeting came in the Capital One Cup last season when Uwe Rösler introduced us to his new and totally bonkers squad rotation principle and a severely weakened team scraped home 3-2 thanks to Farid El Alagui's injury time winner.

We also made a triple transfer swoop on *The Dagenham Three* five years ago bringing Danny Foster, Ben Strevens and Sam Saunders to Griffin Park. Foster was a sound and totally undemonstrative right back whose one amazing feat was to be arrested for vandalism after allegedly dancing in the streets of Aviemore, in the Scottish Highlands, wrapped in some lager advertising banners!

He soon drifted off to Wycombe where Strevens, who had been plagued by injuries at Griffin Park, joined him. Sam Saunders though proved to be a keeper. He managed to overcome a slow start when he fell out of managerial favour but has since proved to be a crucial squad member. Fitter and sleeker, the skilful perma-tanned winger played a vital role in last season's promotion both as starter and super-sub and his incredible pratfall free kick goal against Swindon last season still brings tears of laughter to my eyes!

It is good to know that we have also helped the Daggers out on occasion too. Luke Norris had a productive loan spell there last season, Alan Connell played for them yesterday, and goalkeeper Liam O'Brien – the invisible man at Griffin Park who went through the entire season playing one Development Squad match, will be trying to establish himself as the Daggers keeper next season. Despite the good feeling between the clubs, let's hope that we put them firmly in their place when we meet them in August.

Preseason Comparisons: 1992 v 2014 – 7/7/14

I have been enjoying Peter Gilham's daily description of the cutting edge fitness facilities available at Brentford's training camp in Florida. So, when I saw a recent thread on the subject on *The Griffin Park Grapevine*, my thoughts turned to how the squad prepared themselves last time they were promoted to the second tier of English football, back in 1992 and how it compares to this preseason.

Brentford came up on the rails to snatch the Third Division title by winning their last six matches of a pulsating 1991/92 season. A team turbocharged by the goals of Dean Holdsworth and Gary Blissett held off the challenge of rivals Birmingham City and sent their supporters into delirium. I have just gone through the local papers and also *The Big Brentford Book of the 90s* in order to confirm my memories of that summer of 1992.

Brentford's preparation for their first season back in the second tier of English football since 1954 differed not one iota from what was customary at that time. There was no preseason tour and certainly no special training camp. Instead, the team prepared for their new challenge with lung-bursting runs and stamina training in Richmond Park as had been the case for many years beforehand.

Surely some big name foreign team was enticed to play us in a preseason friendly? Indeed, that was the case, as we travelled to a foreign land to meet the might of Merthyr Tydfil and came away chastened after being hammered by four goals to one.

The only consolation from that defeat was that new signing, and Dean Holdsworth's replacement, Murray Jones paid off the first instalment of his £75,000 transfer fee from Grimsby by notching our consolation goal. That was, incredibly, his only goal in our colours, ignoring a one-on-one he scored against David Seaman in a behind-closed-doors friendly against Arsenal.

Our opponents that preseason were Chesham, Merthyr Tydfil, Windsor & Eton, Queens Park Rangers, Slough, Uxbridge, Woking and Harrow Borough. Eight non-league teams (Oh alright then, seven non-league teams plus QPR). This was considered sufficient preparation for us to face the might of Newcastle United and West Ham United in the coming season!

The fans did their bit too with over five thousand attending the *Fun Day* in May and a record 2,200 season tickets were sold. The average attendance was almost 8,500, a figure since unequalled.

As for the team, we were holed beneath the waterline when Dean Holdsworth was transferred with unseemly haste to Wimbledon soon after the 1991/92 season ended. There are claims and counter claims about how hard the club tried to keep him or whether they were reconciled to his departure, or indeed wished to cash in on their star asset. What is certain is that the inadequate fee we received for him was not wisely invested and the fact that we failed to insist on a sell-on clause sums up the haphazard way in which the club was run back in those days.

Not much came in to strengthen what was thought to be a pretty decent squad. As part of the Holdsworth deal, Wimbledon unloaded Detzi Kruszynski and Mickey Bennett onto us. When on loan the previous season, Detzi had played a key role in our late promotion surge as his calmness on the ball and passing ability made him stand out in what was a very direct team, who got the ball forward quickly and without fuss. Unfortunately, he proved to have an aversion to training and time keeping and he soon drifted away from the club – a real waste of talent.

As for Mickey Bennett, he started out like a house on fire as a direct and goal hungry right winger and we thought we had discovered a new star, but he too flattered to deceive and perhaps his most accurate shot was on the jaw of team mate Joe Allon after a training ground spat the following season. We all waited agog for Dean Holdsworth's replacement, tried and failed to sign John Goodman from Millwall and finally, one sultry Summer's day, the news broke, we had signed Murray – Who? Murray Jones was apparently a friend of our star defender Keith Millen and a journeyman striker who counted Exeter City and Grimsby amongst his previous teams. His goalscoring record was non-existent and to add insult to injury we forked out seventy-five thousand pounds on a player that Grimsby supporters gleefully told us was about to be released on a free transfer.

Not one of our proudest moments as Jones proved to be totally inept and never scored a competitive goal for the club. To put things into context, Manager Phil Holder was allowed to spend no more than ten to fifteen percent of the money brought in for Holdsworth on his replacement – and this was to strengthen a team about to compete in a higher standard of football.

That surely speaks for itself and eerily echoes 1972, when the club, newly promoted to the Third Division, shamefully sold star striker John O'Mara against the wishes of manager Frank Blunstone, greedily accepting the first offer of £50,000 from Blackburn Rovers, and replaced him with the utterly appalling Stan Webb and deservedly suffered relegation. Anyone see a pattern emerging?

The most interesting newcomer was midfielder Grant Chalmers who came on trial from the Channel Islands, but his vision and passing ability didn't fit in with how manager Holder wanted his team to play. The squad totalled twenty-five, but that figure included a number of youngsters and first year professionals who were hardly to figure in the first team, if at all.

It is interesting to look at the team photograph and count the support staff. They totalled five, with Manager Phil Holder backed up by Player-Coach Wilf Rostron, Graham Pearce, Joe Gadston and physio, Roy Clare. Now contrast that situation with today.

- Over five thousand season tickets sold.
- A large and ever improving squad packed full of emerging young talent.
- Again, we have lost our top scorer straight after promotion, but I confidently expect that the ghosts of Stan Webb and Murray Jones will be fully allayed when Clayton's replacement eventually arrives at the club.
- Training facilities to die for in Florida.
- Top level foreign competition in Nice and Espanyol who will provide a stern test to our squad in forthcoming friendly matches
- A first class and growing support team of fitness experts, analysts, nutritionists and specialist coaches.

The comparison with 1992 is boggling. As golfer Gary Player memorably stated: *The harder I practice, the luckier I get.* Let's just hope that Brentford's incredible organisation and preseason planning this summer bears fruit and that the season ends far more positively than in 1993.

Can We Take Any More Excitement? – 10/7/14

Somewhere in the dark recesses of YouTube I am sure you can find some long-forgotten, blurred and faded, black and white footage of a Watney Cup tie forty-four years ago between Hull City and Manchester United. That game from a short-lived preseason tournament heralded the first ever penalty shoot out in a professional match in England.

The first player to take a kick was George Best, and the first to miss was Denis Law. Ian McKechnie, the rotund Hull goalkeeper who Brentford fans still have clear memories of from *that* FA Cup tie in 1971, saved Law's kick, and was also the first goalkeeper to take a kick; but his shot hit the crossbar and deflected over, putting Hull City out of the Cup.

The penalty shoot out has become recognised as perhaps the best, the fairest, the most heartbreaking, and certainly the most exciting way to settle a drawn cup-tie.

Brentford fans are no strangers to the horrors and delights of the penalty shoot out and whilst it has been unpleasant, if perhaps cathartic, to dredge up some of the memories, there have also been some triumphs. Perhaps the most painful shoot out was in 1995 when a Brentford team finished second in the Second Division in the only season that saw just one automatic promotion place (owing to Premier League restructuring) – it's Brentford Innit!

We should have won comfortably in the playoff semi-final at Huddersfield where Bob Taylor's open goal miss still rankles and amazes and the referee missed Andy Booth's climb all over Kevin Dearden for their equaliser at Griffin Park. So penalties it was and Denny Mundee, who ironically had scored two penalties against Huddersfield the previous season, managed to outguess himself and miss. Subsequently, Jamie Bates' weak effort was easily saved by Steve Francis and the Bees had lost. I can still hear the eerie quiet that descended like a blanket of fog around Griffin Park as we filed out, after the match, struck dumb by shock and disbelief.

Richard Lee had a wonderful penalty shoot out record for the club back in 2010/11. He needed something to go right as his start at his new club had not gone well and he fell out of favour with manager Andy Scott. A succession of loan keepers came in but Lee played in the cup-ties and his overall performance and then penalty save in the shoot out from Jermaine Beckford won Brentford the match against Everton.

Better was to come in the Johnstone's Paint Trophy as, touched by genius, Lee saved three successive spot kicks in a shoot out victory against Charlton, a feat only previously achieved by Graham Benstead against Wrexham in 1991. Richard's account of how he prepared and psyched himself up makes for fascinating reading in his book *Graduation*.

Brentford's last penalty shoot out remains fresh in the memory as victory over Swindon in the dreaded playoffs was secured after five perfect penalties from Sam Saunders, Paul Hayes, Harlee Dean, an emphatic thump from skipper Tony Craig (followed by a wild-eyed celebration) and Adam Forshaw's cool *coup de grace*. Simon Moore too played a match winning role by saving Swindon's fourth effort and the side taking their penalties second won the day, a feat only achieved in 40% of all penalty shoot outs. Love them or hate them, penalty shoot outs are here to stay but penalty kicks have proved to be Brentford's nemesis on so many occasions recently. I am sure that we will return to this subject as soon as I can face it!

Stepping Stone – 11/7/14

One of my real pleasures in life during the football season is to lie in bed on a Sunday morning reading the sports section of *The Sunday Telegraph* counting how many former Brentford players I can spot in the line-ups of the other teams in the Premiership and Football League. Does anybody else do the same as me or am I just a total sad sack who needs to get a life? On second thoughts please ignore that question as I think I know the answer without being told.

I generally set myself a goal of discovering a set number of ex-Bees, generally around fifty, split between permanent signings and loanees. With the rapid turnover of players over the past three years there is an increasing number of our former favourites now plying their trade elsewhere, even though sometimes I have to cheat to reach my target and include Shay Logan and Farid El Alagui from the Scottish Premier League.

The Premier League team sheets last season produced pretty slim pickings with Michael Turner and very occasionally Simon Moore the only candidates, bolstered by former loanees in Steve Sidwell, Saido Berahino and the wonderful Wojciech Szczęsny. Oh, and Lewis Price too. Their numbers will be boosted by Liam Moore and Jeffrey Schlupp next season and hopefully the names of Adam Forshaw, James Tarkowski and Jake Bidwell will not be added to that list until our dreams and fantasies are answered by the Bees reaching the promised land of the Premier League under their own steam.

Some of the names in the Championship bring back happy and even wistful memories, and will hopefully be revisiting Griffin Park in the near future. The fawn-like promise that Jordan Rhodes demonstrated at the tender age of eighteen, culminating in his perfect hat trick at Shrewsbury and the thought that our current regime certainly would not have allowed him to leave Ipswich for Huddersfield without putting up a fight for his signature. We might not have been able to hold onto him for long but we would have made a fortune when he left us.

What about the enigma that is Lewis Grabban? He had outstayed his welcome at Millwall and he had two in-and-out loan spells at Griffin Park where he shone fitfully and seldom demonstrated his true potential. He was generally played down the right wing but in his last game for the club he partnered the speedy Schlupp up front in a pacy combination that terrified a static and cumbersome Huddersfield defence and shared four goals between them – a feat of generosity matched by our own porous back four! Not too many complained when he was shown the door by the time that Uwe Rösler arrived at the club but his subsequent conversion to a devastating central striker who recently changed clubs for a three million pound fee has proved that perhaps our judgement could have been better – easy though it is to be wise after the event.

Tom Adeyemi made a massive impact in his one season on loan at the club with his hard tackling and powerful lung-bursting box-to-box runs. Our loss has proved to be Birmingham's gain although hopes persist that we might not have seen the last of him in a Brentford shirt. Ben Hamer couldn't seem to stay away from Griffin Park and had four loan spells with us, becoming a firm fan favourite. He finally established himself in the Charlton goal and now has the opportunity to play in the Premier League with Leicester City. Harry Forrester's name barely appeared on the Doncaster team sheet last season as his injury jinx struck with a vengeance and only time will tell whether his move was ill-judged. He has talent to burn but he needs nursing and I can only hope that he recovers the sizzling form that he showed us spasmodically. Maybe it's also time for us to let go and stop sticking pins in his effigy?

Two massive favourites played on and off for Ipswich in Jay Tabb and Steve Hunt and I am full of admiration for their determination to make the most of their talent and have long and fruitful careers. The Alex McCarthy who starred in goal almost every week for Reading can only be the twin brother of the hapless keeper who fumbled and stumbled through a desperately unimpressive and tentative loan spell at Brentford four seasons ago. He conceded a gift goal early in his debut against Walsall and never really recovered – but look at him now – a prime example of the old adage that the game is as much about confidence as ability.

Cheer Or Boo? That Is The Question – 12/7/14

Previously, I wrote about some of the ex-Bees who are now playing for other clubs in the Premier League and Championship and how much pleasure it gives me to pick out former heroes (and a few villains) from the weekly team lists. Whilst former Bees are in fairly short supply at the top level of the game, that is not the case lower down the pyramid where they abound. Colchester, for example, fielded Ryan Dickson and Marcus Bean in our 4-1 thumping late last season. Dickson, whose presence was blithely ignored by the Brentford fans, had filled out and seemed to have lost some of the pace and verve that had made him stand out a few short years back. Despite how well he played on the day, I felt a bit sad that he had lost his way and rather missed the boat. His much heralded move to Southampton ended in as many tears as Paul Smith's had done previously and he now seems to be just hanging on when, at one time, he threatened to become a star.

Marcus Bean was as combative as ever, gave his all, played the simple pass well and scored a brave and decisive goal which, given that the game meant nothing for Brentford supporters but pride, was roundly applauded by the entire ground. Bean represents everything that is good about football and footballers. He plays with an obvious joy, relish and commitment and gives everything to his cause. He has made the most of his ability and has served every club he has played for with pride and passion. All true supporters identify with Marcus as he plays in the manner that they surely would if they could swap places with him on the field.

Leon Legge also served us well as a strong, traditional centre half, unbeatable in the air and also blessed with a turn of pace, but not so comfortable with the ball at his feet. He too received a warm welcome when he returned with Gillingham, as did keeper Stuart Nelson, another who gave the club good service.

Some ex-Bees cannot expect the same treatment. Brian Statham was so unnerved by the poor reception he received when returning with a Gillingham team packed with our former players that he panicked, reacted, conceded a game-clinching penalty kick, and simultaneously earned himself an early bath – welcome back, Brian! Gary Alexander has just announced his retirement so, unfortunately, we Bees fans will not have another opportunity to express our anger and disgust at the shabby way in which he left the club for Crawley two years ago at a crucial phase of the season, an action that might well have guaranteed his future for another couple of seasons but one that contributed greatly to our playoff charge being derailed. Let's just say that he is probably not on Uwe Rösler's Christmas card list. Alexander did return to Griffin Park a couple of times with Crawley and was unsurprisingly greeted like a pantomime villain. On each occasion he played like a man with lead in his boots and was totally peripheral to the action. Conscience perhaps, or maybe the incessant booing and jeering got to him?

So how should you behave towards a former player returning with his new club? What advice does the etiquette book give, or is this a topic where no hard and fast rules apply? I think it depends largely upon how popular the player was, whether he gave everything to the cause, and the manner in which he left.

I still feel hopelessly compromised about Clayton Donaldson who is due to return to the scene of his past glories, with his new club, the hated Birmingham City. It almost felt like a dagger to my heart when he decided to leave us and I know that it will hurt to see him in the Brummie Blue. That being said, I will certainly applaud him given his magnificent service and I really hope and indeed expect that everyone else does the same. Whether I will still be feeling so indulgent should he score is another matter. Good manners can only extend so far. Given his past history Clayton won't celebrate. He scored four times in total against his former club Crewe on their last two visits to Griffin Park and each time he marched po-faced back to the halfway line like a man suffering from a severe case of haemorrhoids.

I personally find this new-fangled non-celebration pact as meaningless and annoying as the trend towards kissing the badge, and whilst Emmanuel Adebayor might conceivably have taken things a tad too far with his provocative celebration when scoring for Manchester City against his former team Arsenal, I really see nothing wrong with celebrating – after all, that's what a striker is there for, isn't it?

The weirdest return to Griffin Park was surely that made by journeyman striker Leon Constantine when playing for his new club, Torquay United on Boxing Day 2004. He had played a few uneventful games for the Bees the previous season and never threatened to break his scoring duck – the number 65 bus trundling down Ealing Road outside the stadium was at more risk than the goalkeeper so wild was his shooting. Totally out of character, he followed the immutable law of the Ex, scored a clinical and match-winning second half hat trick, celebrated wildly, and got away scot-free given that no Brentford supporter even recognised or remembered him. Sometimes former players can take unfair advantage of their reception and abuse their host's hospitality.

A case in point was goalkeeper Paul Smith who was a firm fan favourite during his spell at the club and his much needed transfer fee from Southampton helped keep the club afloat at a time when creditors were beating on the door. He returned to Griffin Park with Southend United for a Third Round FA Cup replay last year with the reward of a plum home tie with Chelsea awaiting the winners. Smith milked the generous applause that rang around the ground and was so inspired that he held the Bees to a narrow 2-1 victory on a night when he faced an incredible thirty shots and he even saved a Harry Forrester penalty kick. He played Brentford on his own that night and almost deprived us of our prize. So the moral of the story is to be nice to your returning heroes – but just not too nice!

Cricketing Bees – 14/7/14

I spent some of Sunday afternoon watching the Test match between India and England fizzle out into a bore-draw. In a quiet moment – and believe me, there were quite a few to choose from – I started thinking about the time when sportsmen were able to combine careers in professional football and cricket. The seasons didn't overlap to the extent that they do now and there was a clear demarcation between the two. In many cases, it was cricket that took precedence over football for players who saw the summer game as a safer and even more lucrative career option given that a cricketer could earn a tax-free benefit after ten years as a regular first teamer.

Now the situation has changed with football being pretty much a year-round affair and the wages differential has made football an easy choice for most youngsters equally talented at both sports. Growing up in the 60s and early 70s footballing cricketers were the rule rather than the exception and quite a few have stuck in my memory.

Jim Standen had a pretty good year and busy time back in 1964, winning an FA Cup winner's medal with West Ham against Preston before hurrying off to play for Worcestershire where he topped the bowling averages with his medium pace seamers for a team that won the County Championship. Let's hope he earned a bonus from both teams – and the following season he was also in goal as West Ham won the European Cup Winners' Cup at Wembley Stadium.

If I can be allowed to digress for a moment, the Preston centre forward in that 1964 Cup Final was the formidable Alex Dawson, also known as *The Black Prince* who boasted an impressive goalscoring record with over two hundred goals in a wonderful career that started at Manchester United. He was a gnarled veteran of thirty with a rugged, chiselled look, a prominent broken nose and a face that surely only a mother could love, but he had an inspirational loan spell at Griffin Park in 1970, scoring seven times in eleven games including the winner in that amazing late, late show FA Cup victory against Gillingham. Typical of the times at Griffin Park, he departed after his loan spell as apparently the club was unable to agree personal terms with him. A classic example of both parties suffering, given that Dawson never played another Football League game and Brentford lacked a focal point in their attack until the arrival of John O'Mara later that same season.

Standen wasn't alone and I remember stalwarts such as Ted Hemsley, Phil Neale, Ian Buxton, Jimmy Cumbes and Graham Cross. Cricketing legend Ian Botham also spent part of his winter as a lumbering centre forward with Scunthorpe United! Brentford's most recent experience of facing a footballing cricketer came about in September 1975 when Chris Balderstone made history by taking part in a County Championship match and a Football League game on the same day. Balderstone was fifty-one not out against Derbyshire at the end of day two of Leicestershire's match at Chesterfield. After close of play he changed into his football kit to play for Doncaster Rovers in an evening match 30 miles away. He helped Donny to a 1-1 draw with Brentford. Undaunted, and obviously not having been made to run about too much by the Bees, he returned to Chesterfield the following morning to complete a century and take three wickets to help wrap up Leicestershire's first ever County Championship title. Pretty impressive, I'm sure you would agree!

The only first class cricketer to play for the Bees in recent times was defender Sid Russell who made fifty-four appearances back in the late 50s. He had far more success as a stalwart batsman for Middlesex and Gloucestershire. Future Middlesex and England wicketkeeper John (JT) Murray played for Brentford Juniors in the FA Youth Cup against Manchester United but ultimately made the decision to concentrate on cricket. As a youngster he was one of my favourites as his grace, elegance and metronomic efficiency behind the stumps inspired me to take up wicketkeeping. I used to wear a pair of his autographed gloves but his magic certainly didn't rub off on me! England Test batsman Bill Athey was also a reserve team regular in the early 80s but this was more of a fitness exercise than a serious attempt to launch a dual career.

By far Brentford's most famous cricketer was the immortal Patsy Hendren. He was a prolific batsman for England averaging nearly fifty in his fifty-one Test matches. At a time when fielding acrobatics were frowned upon, he carried on playing until he was forty-eight and he amassed over fifty-eight thousand runs and one hundred and seventy First Class centuries. What was equally amazing was that he also managed to sustain a long and successful football career with spells at Brentford, Queens Park Rangers, Manchester City and Coventry City. A truly staggering career record; the diminutive Patsy Hendren was a true giant of English sport. Other Brentford players to play first class cricket included goalkeeper Jack Durston, centre half Jack Chisholm, and the amazing Bill Caesar who made one appearance for the Bees at Fulham in 1929 but is best remembered for his unusual cricket career.

He played one game for Surrey back in 1922 and following a gap of twenty-four years he turned out three times for Somerset in 1946 aged forty-six.

Thanks to the inimitable Paul Briers for his help; his incredible website is packed full of Brentford memorabilia. It is well worth a visit at brentfordfcmemorabilia.wordpress.com/

Farewell To Farid! – 15/7/14

So it is farewell to Farid El Alagui who completed his transfer to Hibernian yesterday. Like many Bees fans, I was sorry to see him go, but he fully deserved the opportunity to play first team football every week and that was not going to be the case for him at Griffin Park. A return to his old stamping ground across the border made sense for all parties. Farid's stay at Brentford will always be filed in the *Might Have Been* category as injury totally ruined his chance to establish himself at the club. He arrived in the Summer of 2012 on the crest of a wave as the Scottish First Division Player of the Year after scoring twenty-seven goals for Falkirk and he seemed exactly what Brentford needed, a strong target man with a real eye for goal. He was seen as the replacement for the departed Gary Alexander and it was anticipated that his partnership with Clayton Donaldson would spearhead Brentford's promotion challenge.

The fans loved his *kissing the coin* ritual after every goal that he scored and his warm and sunny personality ensured that he was instantly welcomed and accepted by players and supporters alike. Unfortunately, we were to be short-changed, as after a promising start including a classic last-minute diving header winner against Colchester, the injury hoodoo hit. Characteristically chasing down a lost cause, he collided with Crawley keeper Paul Jones with a sickening thud, and suffered a serious knee injury, which ended his season – and pretty much his Brentford career. Bravely he fought his way back to fitness at the start of last season and onto the Brentford substitutes' bench, but his days as a first choice were over.

Typical of the man, he shrugged off his disappointment and contributed mightily from the bench, with a crucial ninety-sixth minute equaliser at Gillingham, as well as playing a significant role in Clayton Donaldson's goals against Peterborough – a vital late winner, and Crewe. Just to emphasise that he was as sharp as ever, he also scored five goals in the various cup competitions. His all-action, bustling approach and power in the air did not fit in with the patient passing style adopted by Brentford last season, but he provided an incredibly valuable option off the bench which allowed us to go seamlessly to *Plan B* with every likelihood of success.

In January the decision was made by Manager Mark Warburton to allow Farid to move on loan for the rest of the season to Dundee United where he scored three times. This was a surprising and more than magnanimous gesture as it allowed a player coming to the end of his contract the opportunity to put himself in the shop window and ideally secure a new deal elsewhere. The gamble paid off both for Farid and ourselves but there were certainly times when we missed him and the impetus he gave us, but all's well that ends well.

Farid's transfer is the most recent of a series of moves between Brentford and Hibernian. Eddie May, a Scottish Under 21 International, was signed by Steve Perryman from Hibernian for a club record fee of £167,000 as Andy Sinton's replacement, but he never settled in London. May was skilful with a good eye for goal but was also lightweight and often peripheral to the action and soon returned North of the border.

Clayton Donaldson also had a fairly indifferent spell at the Edinburgh club before finding his feet – and his goal touch – at Crewe. Remarkably, Brentford also signed two goalkeepers from Hibernian; the eccentric Olafur Gottskalksson, who started off so well and tailed off so dismally, and the ineffable Simon Brown who started off badly at Griffin Park and got worse. Hibs fans will probably not want reminding of the final link between the two clubs – Manager Terry Butcher, whose dismal spell at Griffin Park was surpassed by his exploits at Hibs last season where he was at the helm for their disastrous relegation from the Scottish Premiership.

I am sure every Brentford supporter will join me in wishing Farid *bon chance* for the future as I cannot think of another player who deserves it more given what he has gone through, and yet he has emerged smiling from the other side of the abyss. I shall certainly look out for Farid throughout next season and my regular Sunday morning forensic examination of team line-ups for ex-Bees will require more attention now to the Scottish game.

Experienced Help Arrives – 15/7/14

Today, I heard that Brentford had signed the former Watford and Cardiff winger Tommy Smith on trial and it's likely that the thirty-four year old will see some action in the forthcoming series of friendly matches. The initial reaction to his arrival has been fairly muted on *The Griffin Park Grapevine* where he has been harshly, and I believe erroneously, described by some as an over-the-hill journeyman.

This really sells him short, as Smith is a tried and tested winger or striker who has proved himself over the years to be just short of Premiership calibre. Maybe the legs have gone to an extent but he didn't play much last season, he has a wealth of experience at Championship level, and is recognised as an excellent pro and positive influence in the dressing room.

I think this is a win/win situation for both parties. If Smith is still up to the job he will be offered a contract, if he isn't, then he goes. We are still lacking players who have played at this level, which will be new to many of the squad. We have talented youngsters aplenty but currently have no experienced forwards and Smith could fill that gap. He can also play out wide or down the middle, which suits our current style of football.

Players like Smith can act as teachers and mentors by setting the right example both on and off the pitch and Tommy will be well-known to Mark Warburton from his time at Watford. So welcome to Tommy and here's hoping that he proves to be a success. Let's just keep it between ourselves that he had a recent spell with Queens Park Rangers –we won't hold that against him!

Rivalry Resumed! – 16/7/14

Sky Sports announced today that the eagerly awaited derby match between Brentford and local rivals Fulham has been selected for live television broadcast on 21st November. Proof indeed that the fixture's appeal extends far beyond West London. As soon as the fixtures were released last month the first dates I looked for were for the two matches against Fulham. I also decided to delve more deeply into the rivalry between the clubs and, to my surprise, I found that it is of a very recent vintage.

In fact, the paths of the two clubs have rarely crossed and it was not until Brentford were relegated from the First Division soon after the war that they played against each other regularly. Brentford's further relegation in 1954 meant that hostilities were not resumed until 1980 and it was that decade that saw the rise of the current rivalry between the two clubs. The Eighties saw a series of ding-dong battles between two fairly evenly-matched third tier teams.

We can start with Dean Smith's volley off the underside of the crossbar, which was ludicrously ruled to have not crossed the goal line, and denied us a late equaliser in a tight FA Cup tie. I recall a memorable Sunday morning 3-3 draw played on a Griffin Park skating rink when the kick off was delayed by an hour in an optimistic but unsuccessful attempt to allow the pitch to thaw. Fulham colossus Roger Brown once scored a perfectly sliced own goal to equalise a Gordon Davies long range cracker at Craven Cottage before an ice cool Barry Tucker penalty gave us a rare win at Craven Cottage. Referee Kelvin Morton was also at his eccentric best in another tussle, disallowing a perfectly taken Andy Sinton penalty for some unknown reason in a 3-1 Bees victory.

Then came the notorious Jim Stannard/Gary Blissett incident that resulted in a red card for the Brentford striker after he struck the keeper. Why did he do it? Well I think you'd have to ask Gary that question as many rumours abound.

How about Roger Stanislaus's long-range howitzer equaliser that gets further away from the goal in the telling? It is now generally described as a forty yarder and I have no intention of re-watching the video and allowing the truth to get in the way of a great story. I remember Graham Benstead's world-class display in a 1-1 draw at Craven Cottage in 1990 and our wonderful double over Fulham in our 1992 promotion season. A smash and grab 1-0 away win earned by a towering Terry Evans header and Benstead's penalty save from Gary Brazil on a day when we kept loanee Andy Cole quiet, was followed by that Sunday morning 4-0 thrashing where the Bees touched perfection. Four up at the interval with the goals all scored in front of the disbelieving Fulham fans, we toyed with the visitors after the break and the thrashing set us up for the last day of the season title win at Peterborough.

Boosted by Al Fayed's investment, Fulham left us far behind them after the end of the 90s and this will be our first encounter since Bob Taylor limped off in a lame 2-0 home defeat in 1998 that saw Fulham promoted and the Bees relegated. Oh, there was also that disastrous meeting in Kevin O'Connor's Testimonial Match in 2010 when Fulham emphasised their superiority, strolling to an effortless 5-0 victory.

The tables have finally been turned and we will meet again this coming season on equal terms. That is to say that we are both in the same Division but hardly competing on an even playing field, given that Fulham have been buttressed by their enormous Parachute Payment after relegation from the Premier League and that has allowed them to splash out a reported £11 million for Ross McCormack from Leeds. But, as they say, it's not necessarily how much you've got, it's how well you spend it that counts. Marcello Trotta is another recent link between the two clubs but I suspect he will have found a new team and will not be involved once hostilities resume.

The Brentford/Fulham rivalry is neither as deep seated nor as long lasting as that between the Bees and our real deadly enemies in Queens Park Rangers, but its resumption is still something that we are all looking forward to with relish and I cannot wait until the 21st November. I suspect I will have no problem finding a suitable home for my spare season ticket that night!

Ambition Personified – 18/7/14

Brentford FC media guru Mark Chapman totally nailed it with his tweet yesterday: *It wouldn't be a proper Summer unless we signed Swindon's best player from the season before.* Cutting – certainly, maybe even a bit cruel, but totally true. For Jonathan Douglas read Alan McCormack. For Alan McCormack now read Alex Pritchard. No wonder the Swindon message boards are beside themselves and drowning in vitriol.

What is more ironic is that Swindon, who rejoiced in being seen as Tottenham Hotspur's nursery team last season are now fast becoming Brentford's feeder team! For all their demeaning comments, most Swindon fans bemoaned the loss of both Douglas and

McCormack and the drive, skill and passion that they had provided the Robins over the years. The disappointment they felt over the loss of the two Irishmen is nothing compared to their fury at losing their star player from last season to a team that Swindon supporters resolutely refuse to accept has overtaken and far surpassed them in terms of infrastructure, financial solidity and prospects for the future.

Alex Pritchard was a shining star at The County Ground last season. On a season-long loan from Spurs he rapidly proved himself to be one of the most exciting prospects in the division and finished with eight goals and an identical number of assists. He terrorised opponents with a combination of pace, skill and directness and was a danger from long range with his ability from set pieces and eagerness to shoot with either foot. His temperament let him down on occasions and he had some disciplinary issues but hopefully he is maturing and can be handled by Mark Warburton and David Weir. Pritchard caused the Bees problems last season with a live wire display at Griffin Park where he helped set up the first goal and forced a wonderful late save from David Button and at the County Ground he led Alan McCormack a merry dance, forcing a penalty kick and being a constant danger.

The news of his arrival on a season long loan has been welcomed with enthusiasm by Bees fans who see another missing link being filled. Pritchard will bring pace and guile to Brentford's left flank and he and Jake Bidwell are certain to combine effectively to provide a constant left-sided threat to all opponents. Pritchard is Brentford's fifth preseason arrival and the gulf in quality between all of them and say, Rotherham's *Dirty Dozen* is boggling. Rotherham have mainly brought in experienced journeymen and some gambles. Fair play to them, maybe that is all that their budget allows.

Brentford, for their part have signed proven La Liga experience in Marcos Tebar and he is expected to add tackling ability and vision to the midfield. There have also been unsubstantiated rumours both on the Transfer Rumours website as well as our old friend and comfort blanket, *The Griffin Park Grapevine*, that concerted efforts continue to be made to bring in other foreign players. Personally I hope that these stories are true as I believe that there is more value for money shopping abroad and we can potentially find and afford players of a calibre that are beyond our reach in the UK.

That being said we haven't done too badly so far with our other new additions! We have succeeded in signing proven talent at First Division level in the anticipation that they can continue to develop and thrive in The Championship. In Alan Judge, Moses Odubajo, Alex Pritchard, not to mention Adam Forshaw, James Tarkowski and Jake Bidwell, Brentford now possess six of the best players from last season's First Division and the signing of Andre Gray, probably the best player in The Conference, further reinforces Brentford's approach in the transfer market which is to identify the best affordable young talent in the lower leagues and hope that we can develop them further as we progress through the divisions. There is talk of Scott Hogan, Rochdale's emerging young striker joining the Brentford project, and given his growing reputation and burgeoning talent, he would also fit the bill should he eventually sign for the club.

Hogan's Heroes! – 21/7/14

Well he's finally arrived! After a week of rumour and speculation, our sixth preseason signing put pen to paper and was announced to the supporters this morning. Striker Scott Hogan has been signed from Rochdale for an unannounced fee thought to be in the region of £750,000. If this figure is anywhere near correct then it will have taken our spending to a figure well in excess of two million pounds – a truly staggering sum and one unprecedented in the club's history. The signing further reinforces Matthew Benham's determination to cement Brentford's status in The Championship and ensure that we remain in that division when the time comes to move to our new stadium in Lionel Road. The club's blueprint, so effectively created and put into practice by the Benham, Warburton and McParland think tank is to bring in young emerging, developing and to a degree, unproven talent and see them improve and their value appreciate over the coming season.

In Hogan, we have obtained a twenty-two year old striker of immense talent and potential who scored nineteen goals for a promoted Rochdale team and in the process bullied and terrified a disjointed Leeds United team – who were anything but – in an FA Cup giant killing. Under the astute Keith Hill, Rochdale play football in the right way with short passing to feet and Scott has had a good grounding in the game, is eager to improve and impress, and will relish the opportunity to play at a higher level. Rochdale have a justified reputation for developing and selling on good young strikers and Scott is following in the footsteps of such luminaries as Rickie Lambert, Grant Holt, Adam Le Fondre and Glenn Murray. If he does half as well as those four, and hopefully better than their last major striker sale in Bobby Grant, who has struggled at a higher level, then everything should be fine.

Brentford now possess a squad that is surely the envy of many of their rivals and Peterborough Chairman, Darragh MacAnthony today acknowledged our transfer success and saw us as an outside bet for a successful season in The Championship. We now have a member of the PFA Division Two Team of The Year in Hogan, the First Division Player of The Year for both 2013 and 2014 in Alan Judge and Adam Forshaw plus two members of the PFA Team of The Year in Forshaw and Jake Bidwell not forgetting Andre Gray, the top player in The Conference last season. Add in Alex Pritchard, short-listed for Division One Player of The Year, Moses Odubajo, James Tarkowski and Harlee Dean and you can see we are awash in young talent.

Jonathan Douglas, Alan McCormack and Tony Craig will provide the necessary experience and here we are with just under three weeks to go before the big kickoff with a squad that looks lean, mean, strong and ready to do the business. I suspect that there will be one more striker to come in and perhaps some defensive cover on loan but this strikes me as potentially the best Brentford squad that I can recall. Roll on the ninth of August. I can hardly wait!

Higgy! – 22/7/14

Amongst all the euphoria and optimism surrounding Brentford FC, today is tinged with a little sadness. It is the second anniversary of the death of Tom Higginson or Higgy, as he was universally known or referred to with genuine affection. You don't find too many like Higgy anymore. He gave Brentford eleven years of committed service and is regarded as a true Bees legend. Signed by Manager Malcolm MacDonald from Kilmarnock in 1959, Higgy forced his way into what was a settled team firstly as an inside forward and then as a wing half.

For Brentford to make any signing at that time was a rarity as through parsimony and policy the club relied on a constant conveyor belt of local talent from the Juniors. When the supply ran dry, MacDonald went back to his Scottish stomping grounds and brought in youngsters such as John Docherty, John Hales and Tom Higginson. Some sank without trace, others flourished and Higgy kept hold of his shirt and fought off the competition from many players more technically gifted than him. Why? Because he was a winner who gave everything for the cause and never knew when he was beaten.

He was a true hardman, impervious to pain, who gave and took tough knocks without complaint or recrimination. The key to his game was to win the ball off an opponent and then play a simple pass to a player in a red and white shirt who was more capable of doing something positive with it. No frills, nothing fancy, just pure effort and commitment and nonstop running and tackling for the entire ninety minutes. Tough but fair, apart from one day when he and Shrewsbury's hard man Eric Brodie went head to head and took things too far and were both dismissed – Brentford's first sending off since the War. It certainly was a different game in those days!

He played his role so well that opponents actively avoided him on the pitch and he blotted out many International forwards who went missing against Brentford. I don't want to sell him short though, as a couple of times each season Higgy would unleash a twenty-yard screamer into the net, or score following a lung-bursting box-to-box run. No histrionics, no over-celebrating, he would trot back to the centre circle with a shy grin on his face as if embarrassed that the spotlight had fallen on him.

In all, Higgy played 433 times for Brentford and was second only to Ken Coote when he left the club and he is now fifth in line after Coote, Peter Gelson, Jamie Bates and Kevin O'Connor. Even at thirty-three his legs had enough left in them to inspire Hillingdon Borough, the elephant's graveyard for ex-Bees, to reach a Wembley FA Trophy Final. Higgy won a Fourth Division Championship medal in 1963 but more than that he won the admiration, respect and affection of every Brentford supporter. In the dark days of 1967, when the very future of the club hung on a precipice, it was Higgy, a former Powderhall sprinter, who led a Brighton to London fundraising walk from start to finish, despite getting lost and covering several extra miles.

That was Higgy in a nutshell. He gave everything for the cause and hopefully his massive contribution will be recognized by him being inducted into the Brentford Hall of Fame. After retiring from football he became a butcher, a career choice not without its sense of irony and he played local football well into his fifties. He died far too young after Alzheimer's took its toll. I wonder if he is another to add to that ever-growing list of former footballers who suffered the fatal consequence of repeated heading of what was more akin to a cannonball on wet days? Higgy, today and everyday we salute you. RIP.

What Price Loyalty? – 26/7/14

I spent some time yesterday looking at a wonderful photograph of the Brentford team that won promotion from the Fourth Division in 1972. Why? Because it gives me goose bumps and makes me feel nostalgic for a lost age. Oh, and just look at those haircuts and sideburns too!

It was also the first time since I started supporting them (six years earlier) that a Brentford team actually won anything. Led by the wily Frank Blunstone, Brentford became a team to reckon with. Hard, tough and mean at the back. Nonstop running and harrying in midfield and real quality and vision up front plus the aerial threat and battering ram that was John O'Mara. What a team, and but for the club's decisions to cash in on Roger Cross and a year later, John O'Mara, who knows how high we could have climbed rather than crashing and burning and returning immediately to the bottom division.

Amazingly given today's move towards squad rotation Brentford only used eighteen players throughout the entire season of whom four made a mere twenty-four appearances between them. In fact, eleven of the squad played over thirty times so there was a consistency of selection and a determination to grit your teeth and play though injuries. Brentford supporters of a certain age will relish recalling the names of those who played in that momentous season: Peter Gelson, Alan Nelmes, Gordon Phillips, John O'Mara, Alan Hawley, John Docherty, Bobby Ross, Jackie Graham, Paul Bence, Stewart Houston, Roger Cross and Mike Allen.

All names to conjure with, and okay, I will admit it, they are still heroes to me. No wonder that team was successful given the grit, character, determination and, of course, skill that it possessed. But they also possessed another quality, something intangible, that no amount of money could buy – loyalty allied with their love of the club.

Between them, the twelve players mentioned above played a total of 3,338 games for the club and stayed at Griffin Park for 94 years. These are truly staggering figures and by way of comparison only eight current Bees players have played over one hundred times for the club and the entire squad has played no more than 1,750 times for Brentford. Remember too that that figure is boosted by Kevin O'Connor's incredible five hundred game record and three substitutes being allowed per game, whereas only one was permitted back in 1972. Another surprising statistic is that no current Brentford player with the exception of Kevin O'Connor – who truly deserves to be ranked amongst some of the greats mentioned earlier, and Toumani Diagouraga, has been with the club for more than five years.

Of course, the game has changed beyond recognition from what it was forty years ago, and in many cases for the better. The modern day player is far more likely to move on quickly given freedom of contract and the desire to better himself both professionally and financially, whereas in those days there was generally no financial incentive to do so. When I helped compile *The Big Brentford Book Of The 70s* three years ago, Dave Lane, Mark Croxford and I invited some of our heroes to a launch event at the club. Knowing how awkward and difficult some present day players are reputed to be, we were all very concerned about whether anybody would show up. We really shouldn't have worried as the bush telegraph started working and it proved remarkably easy to get Alan Hawley, Jackie Graham. Peter Gelson, Paul Bence, Terry Scales, Pat Kruse, Andy McCulloch and Paul Bence to attend. Even the reclusive John O'Mara, who generally keeps himself to himself, was there and had a great time. In fact, we had players asking us if they could come!

What struck me was how grounded, modest and pleasant all of them were – and how much Brentford meant to them. They were, without exception, proud, surprised and delighted to be remembered and were happy to talk with supporters and remember past times. Alan Hawley even came up at the end of the evening and thanked us for inviting him. He really didn't realise that the honour was all ours and that we were privileged to be in the same room with him. What a gentleman!

It was a night that made me proud to be a Brentford supporter and reminded me, yet again, of what a great club we have. Togetherness off the pitch and a strong team spirit generally translate to success on it and they're both traits that we have in abundance today. Kevin O'Connor is as much a hero to me now as were some of those immortal names from the past. Given that he has much in common with - and shares the same values as - icons such as Peter Gelson and Alan Hawley, transmits them to his team mates, and is a living embodiment of what Brentford represents, I feel as confident about the future of this club as I am proud of its past.

Formidable! – 27/7/14

It really doesn't seem so long since we were cheering ourselves hoarse after celebrating promotion and here we were back at Griffin Park less than three months later for the first home friendly match of the new Championship season. The message seemed to have got out about the new ticketing system and several friends reported no more than a few minutes' wait before they were able to purchase a ticket at the Sales Booth. You can install all the technology and new fangled systems that you like, but they are only as good as the human beings that operate them and my turnstile operator was banana-fingered and totally flummoxed and needed five tortuous goes before my ticket was duly swiped and entrance allowed.

I hurried inside impatiently but I needn't have worried. Griffin Park was resplendent, glistening and glinting in the baking July sunshine and you could see that massive and painstaking efforts had been made on a makeover to upgrade the facilities for the larger crowds ahead. The Matchbook logo now adorned the New Road roof, the TV Gantry also boasted a *Welcome to Griffin Park* sign and there was spanking new directional signage everywhere. Griffin Park really looked at its best and the pitch, freshly tended and reseeded, was a sea of verdant green.

What about the football you might well ask? Well that was pretty good too and the Bees saw off their toughest challenge yet by defeating OGC Nice of Ligue 1 in France by three goals to two. The new boys all impressed. Marcos Tebar dovetailed perfectly with Jonathan Douglas with one sitting and the other marauding forward and he was strong and relentless in his tackling and pressing as well as confident on the ball with an excellent range of passing. He looks like he could be the fulcrum for the entire team and he really excited me.

Moses Odubajo was a human dynamo on the right, terrifying his wingback with his sheer pace and persistence. He made clever runs, darting inside and out and he got behind the defence several times. His final delivery was quick and incisive. No *parting like the Red Sea* jokes here but he will shine in the Championship and mesmerise defenders. I would also put him down for ten goals too. I never really thought I would ever see the day when my Brentford, once the pauper of London football, surviving on begging bowls and handouts, were going to be in the position to spend one million pounds on a player but Moses is the real deal and deserves all the accolades he will receive.

We played a 4-2-3-1 formation with Judge and Pritchard rotating in the middle and down the left like effervescent balls of fire. Pritchard is a game changer with the ability to open up a defence at will and he scored with a perfect Saunders-esque 25 yard free kick dinked over the wall, as well as a close range finish when the Nice defence, not for the first time, evaporated and self-destructed.

Andre Gray looked like a welterweight, all honed muscle allied to real pace and ability on the ball. He sprinted into the gap between two immobile central defenders to score coolly and immaculately in the first minute and he looked a real prospect, revelling in his lone striker role. Scott Hogan also showed that he was no slouch before limping off after a worrying blow to his ankle.

It has to be said that, at times, Nice defended naively and their gross overplaying at the back cost them the crucial third goal but coming forward they attacked with vim and gusto and provided our defence with a gruelling challenge which they met with flying colours.

So overall a good day all round with optimism unbounded. The Bees won, played well and with a confident swagger with nary a long ball in sight. They certainly lack height in key areas and it remains to be seen whether the intricate ball skills of Judge and Pritchard prove effective against some of the Neanderthals we will come up against over the coming nine months. In Odubajo and Gray we certainly possess two match winners and it looks like we have bought wisely and well.

Yet today was about far more than the actual football. It was the renewal of a right of passage. Football is back at Griffin Park and everything is right with the world.

Friends And Families – 28/7/14

What can be better or more fun than meeting your mates at a football match? I described Saturday's match and the start of a new season as a *resumption of a rite of passage* and one of the best things about the day was catching up with so many people at the ground who I hadn't seen, or spoken to, since the curtain went down on last season after the Stevenage game. I fully realise that, at my age, memory loss is beginning to kick in but it is remarkable how many people I saw yesterday and exchanged greetings and snippets of news with, without actually knowing their name, or they mine. You know who I am talking about – the bloke from the Press Room (not you Dave!) and the guy in the Programme Shop to highlight just two of many.

We all have that one thing in common – an absolute and unshakeable love for Brentford FC and an insatiable interest in everything that surrounds it. I am sure that everyone reading this would have a similar tale to tell too. Would it therefore be a revolutionary idea if I suggested that instead of just saying *hello* in future when we see characters such as the ones that I have mentioned, that we actually take the time to find out who we are talking to, as well as a bit more about them?

I remember having a season ticket back in the late 1970s and despite exchanging pleasantries at every match with the guy sitting next to me I never took the trouble to discover who he was, and this is something that I have always regretted. It is the British reserve that is ingrained into us from childhood and it is time that we did something about it! It was also heart-warming and quite moving to see so many families at the match, sometimes encompassing three generations of supporters.

That wonderful writer Duncan Hamilton wrote so memorably and movingly about his relationship with his father in *The Footballer Who Could Fly*. His Dad, a former miner, and a man of his times, found it impossible to express or show his feelings and emotions and it was only through their shared passion for Newcastle United that the two of them were ever able to communicate. *Without football we were strangers under a shared roof. Without football we'd have had nothing to say to each other. The game alone pushed us into one another's orbit.*

My Dad started taking me to Brentford when I was ten but he soon cried off given his work and golfing commitments at the weekend and from then on I was pretty much on my own. Sad, but that is just the way it was. I remember, as a twelve year old, fighting my way through what seemed an impassable snowdrift and somehow making it through the blizzard to Kew Bridge where, frozen and with teeth chattering, I finally got onto a number 27 bus after the Guildford FA Cup tie was abandoned.

Neither of my kids have ever shown much interest in football although they will come with me from time to time when they are around and they think that I need humouring. My wife was far too discriminating to come regularly and was turned off by some of the poor football on display on the rare occasions that I could inveigle her to accompany me. Having given up on trying to change her mind during many years of non-achievement at Griffin Park, things changed a couple of years ago. I had been burbling on to her for months about the revolution taking place at Brentford under Matthew Benham and Uwe Rösler, but my words had fallen on deaf and sceptical ears. I went down on bended knee to beg her to come to the Chelsea FA Cup tie and the scales finally fell away from her eyes. I wouldn't go as far as to say that she was hooked, but she enjoyed the theatre of the occasion and was very pleasantly surprised by the calibre of our football.

I have just taken the bull by the horns and bought her a season ticket and hopefully she will come to a few games with me over the coming months. It has been a long and hard road but hopefully I can now come to the games with my family, something that has long been an unfulfilled wish of mine. So look out for me in Block B304 in the Braemar Road stand, and if I am on my own, you will know that I have become Billy No Mates!

So We Lost…. It Was Only A Friendly! – 30/7/14

Sometimes you learn more from a defeat than a victory and last night was certainly a case in point as Brentford went down by four goals to nil to Osasuna at Griffin Park. Make no mistake about it, Osasuna were no mugs and despite their relegation from La Liga at the end of last season they looked a highly impressive team – particularly that is in the second half when they made eleven substitutions and brought on pretty much their entire first team. Skilful on the ball with slick passing and impressive running off the ball, the visitors took total control after the break, cut Brentford apart on countless occasions and ran in four goals in a victory that looked by no means certain at the halftime interval. I would be surprised if we meet many teams better than them next season.

So why am I sanguine about things even after so heavy a defeat? Simply because preseason is when you learn about your squad. Who is good enough, who isn't and who, in time, might be. Certainly Brentford would have come away with a closer scoreline had they fielded a line-up similar to the one they put out on Saturday against Nice. But what would that have proved and what would Mark Warburton have learned had that been the case? Absolutely nothing, in my opinion.

As it was, he made sure that most of the squad now have ninety minutes of match action under their belt and most importantly, talisman and inspiration, Adam Forshaw made his first appearance of the preseason and played all of the second half. He was tentative and showed little, but in the great scheme of things last night is simply a pathway leading towards the big kick off on August 9th and Mark Warburton's objective is to have a full squad, fit, ready, eager and fully prepared in time to face Charlton Athletic.

There were many positives last night. Alan McCormack returned from injury and was his normal robust and competitive self and came closest of any Bee to scoring when his overlapping run ended with a cross-shot just wide of the far post when the game was still goalless. Harlee Dean too played the full ninety minutes and was probably our best player. He looks to have slimmed down and was everywhere in defence as well as making some storming runs upfield. He knows he faces a stern fight for a first team place and looks like he is well up for the challenge. Richard Lee too was calmness and competence personified and we have two excellent goalkeepers to choose from.

Mark Warburton was delighted with our first half display when we matched our illustrious visitors, mainly, in my view, thanks to Marcos Tebar who pulled all the strings in midfield. Always looking for the ball, always available, always using the ball accurately and with imagination and also, very gratifyingly, prepared to press and challenge and win the ball back. On the evidence of the last two games we have a massively impressive asset there and his partnership with Jonathan Douglas augurs well for the long season ahead.

We rested ten of the eleven starters from Saturday with Andre Gray the only exception, and his presence was only due to the ankle injury suffered by Scott Hogan against Nice. Again, good management, as Hogan could have been strapped up and sent out to play, but what would have been the point? Andre hustled and bustled, had a good shot which hit the keeper and, as always, looked dangerous, but he lacked support and given Scott's likely absence for a fortnight, we need more help and an extra body up front and I am certain that there will be moves in that direction within the next few days. Tommy Smith is also on the injured list but will hopefully play some part on Saturday against Crystal Palace and his experience would be really useful at the moment. The match also demonstrated to the younger and more inexperienced players exactly how high is the standard that is required of them if they are to make their way at this level of the game and Raphael Calvet, Josh Clarke, Jake Reeves, Montell Moore, Charlie Adams and trialist Daniel O'Shaughnessy will have learned much from last night's experience.

Last night was a learning curve and taught us far more about the entire squad than would a run out against a local non-league team. I am sure that on Saturday we will see all of the players who were rested last night. It is all about being ready and prepared first for Crystal Palace and then for Saturday week against Charlton Athletic, and I have no doubt that we will be.

The Brentford squad and the team behind the team.

AUGUST

The Seventies Revisited – 1/8/14

As the years go by, your memory seems to fade and incidents seem to merge into each other or get lost completely into the mists of time. Whilst faces, appointments and names are forgotten and my glasses and mobile phone remain permanently lost, there is still one decade that remains sharply in focus to me – namely the seventies. Why should that be when so many other years have gone totally blank? Maybe because it was my formative years, the time of my teens, O and A levels, learning to drive, going to University (or in my case, three of them!), leaving home, my first job – even my first girlfriends. It was the time of Abba, M*A*S*H, Monty Python, Fawlty Towers, the first colour televisions, decimal currency, the Three Day Week, flared trousers, loon pants, sideburns, the baking hot Summer of 1976, the Queen's Silver Jubilee, Punk Music, The Winter of Discontent and the election of Margaret Thatcher.

Bringing matters back to football, who can forget Brazil and The Beautiful Game in the 1970 World Cup? The Gordon Banks save from Pele, Mavericks such as Peter Osgood, Stan Bowles, Tony Currie, Alan Hudson and Frank Worthington, the Chelsea versus Leeds FA Cup Final replay kicking match at Old Trafford. And, for me, most evocative of all, Barry Davies's iconic commentary: *Lee.... interesting....very interesting. Look at his face, just look at his face,* as Francis Lee's twenty-yarder screamed into the roof of the Manchester City net.

As for Brentford, the Seventies saw two promotions, a relegation, and an FA Cup run to the Fifth Round – a bit tame perhaps for a normal Brentford decade given the excitement and non-stop action of subsequent years! I can still vividly picture great talents such as Roger Cross, John O'Mara, Pat Kruse and Andy McCulloch, the moody genius of Steve Phillips, the loyalty of characters such as Peter Gelson, Paul Bence, Bobby Ross, Alan Hawley, Gordon Phillips and Alan Nelmes and the steely determination, skill and commitment of the man who, for me, best symbolised what being a Brentford player is all about – the immortal Jackie Graham.

As for individual moments that encapsulated the decade, what better than Bobby Ross's coolness-personified penalty against Exeter that clinched promotion in 1972? Any goal by John O'Mara, Roger Cross, Gordon Sweetzer, Andy McCulloch or Steve Phillips, beating Cardiff in the mud bath at Ninian Park, Alex Dawson's last gasp winner against Gillingham in the FA Cup, Paul Priddy's Superman impersonation at Vicarage Road (saving those two Watford penalties) and poor Stan Webb attempting the impossible by trying to replace the legend that was John O'Mara – a real Dean Holdsworth/Murray Jones scenario. How about Bob Booker's legendary hat-trick against Hull, Lee Holmes riding pillion on the motorbike on the way to his wedding after defeating Southend, Bill Glazier literally throwing away the chance of an historic League Cup win at Old Trafford, the exciting smooth-as-silk attacking football of the Bill Dodgin promotion team and winning the first set against Crewe by 6-4? One other name to conjure with – John Bain – has there been another midfielder (bar Stan Bowles) as cultured and skilled at the club since his short stay came to such a premature end?

There was a real sense of togetherness between the players and the supporters with many memorable trips to distant away games at such far-flung and uncharted territories as Workington, Southport and Darlington. Most poignantly, who can forget the packed Royal Oak, the two 18,000+ crowds in 1971-2, a triumphant promotion season when we attracted crowds of more than 10,000 to fifteen Football League games and wonder where they have all disappeared to now?

I still bemoan the lost opportunity, the last one for some considerable time, when lack of vision, ambition and investment saw the club crash straight back into the bottom division in 1973, a calamitous fall which saw us hit the bottom of the entire Football League the very next season. Let's not hark back on sad memories, instead we should concentrate on the things that gave us all so much joy.

Three Into Two Doesn't Go – 2/8/14

So, it is a warm welcome to Daniel O'Shaughnessy who signed for Brentford yesterday on a two-year contract, subject to international clearance. The young central defender has looked solid and impressive whilst on trial over the past three weeks and, no wonder, as he has already packed a vast amount of experience into his tender nineteen years. He spent three years at FC Metz and is a Finnish Under 21 International who played against England Under 21s last season. He came on for the last few minutes on Tuesday against Osasuna when the cause was already lost but he played with energy, strength and commitment and looked highly promising – another talented youngster to add to the coterie already at Griffin Park.

His arrival means that we are now immensely strong and well covered in central defence with Tony Craig, James Tarkowski and Harlee Dean competing for the starting positions by playing their own version of three into two doesn't go, with Alfie Mawson and now Daniel all in support as back ups. It has been a competitive and evenly matched battle for the first team shirts and is one that is just symptomatic of the quality of our strength in depth in most areas.

It will be interesting to see who starts in today's final friendly match against Crystal Palace as that should provide a strong hint as to which central defensive partnership Mark Warburton will favour come the big kick off next Saturday. Tony Craig and James Tarkowski finished the season as the men in possession and, apart from that disastrous afternoon at Colchester when, in fairness, the entire team sleep-walked through the ninety minutes, looked a dominant partnership who dovetailed well together. Tarkowski was a revelation after his arrival from Oldham in January as he combined strength and anticipation with a level of quality on the ball and passing ability unseen at the club since the heady days of Hermann Hreidarrson. Tony Craig remains, well – Tony Craig – a rock and total inspiration to all who play with him. Nobody dares to hide or shirk when the skipper is around and he serves as the ultimate example of the skill, dedication and character required to be a successful professional footballer. Unlike many of his teammates, he has plenty of Championship experience at Millwall and his knowledge of what is required at this higher level will be of immense value to the entire squad.

Harlee Dean is a man on a mission after recovering from the long-term injury, which hindered his progress last season. He played hurt for many months without complaint and took some criticism from supporters for doing so when, understandably, he was unable to summon up the pace to reach balls that he would normally have eaten up and cleared with comfort. He deserves praise and not brickbats for his bravery and dedication to the cause. Remember how well he played at Leyton Orient when he replaced Tarkowski after his stupid red card? He was a colossus and inspiration. He looked sleek and fit on Tuesday and was our best player against Osasuna.

One last thought. Let's hope that our central defenders chip in with their fair share of goals next season. Tarky managed to score twice in his thirteen games, an impressive record, but Tony and Harlee drew blanks. Tony has yet to open his account for us, ignoring, of course the three he has stuck into his own net, but will long be remembered for his wonderful rip-roaring penalty kick and even more dramatic celebration, in the pulsating Swindon shoot out. Harlee hasn't managed a goal since the Yeovil playoff final and is long overdue. It is a week until the season starts in reality and there is still much to play for as the squad jockey for their places. Interesting times!

Just another day…… – 3/8/14

Where do you start after an afternoon that was packed so full of action, excitement and talking points? In football terms the day was a total success as Brentford finished their preseason with a flourish by outplaying Premier League opposition in Crystal Palace and totally deserved their victory by three goals to two. Brentford's smooth passing style totally bamboozled a big, hard and tough Palace team that provided a stern challenge, but were unable to deal with the pace and movement of Brentford's midfielders and attackers who interchanged to marvellous effect. Having faced the tippy-tappy possession-based style of Nice and Osasuna in their previous two friendlies, Brentford wanted to face a high quality team which played in a traditional English style in their last preseason game and Palace totally fitted the bill. The score by no means flattered the Bees who could and should have scored six had it not been for some desperate last gasp defending and some shoddy finishing.

Andre Gray was a revelation, pulling the defenders out of position, holding the ball up, and providing a constant goal threat. As for Moses Odubajo, he scored a winning goal that lit up Griffin Park and has merited countless repeats on Sky Sports News. Taking a long diagonal ball from the impressive Tommy Smith on his chest, he flicked the ball effortlessly over the left back, retained full control at top speed and roared into the penalty area where he dipped his shoulder, left Damien Delaney for dead and had enough composure to keep his balance and slot home a goal that defied both gravity and belief.

The Tebar/Douglas partnership also played its part in the win with both players dovetailing perfectly and the way Jonathan took Marcos's flick in his stride, waltzed into the penalty area, rounded his man and contemptuously curled the ball into the far corner had to be seen to be believed and demonstrated his growing confidence. It isn't often that a player shows signs of real improvement to his game after the age of thirty but Jonathan seems to be bucking the trend.

Matthew Benham has just started his game of posting cryptic clues about new arrivals which given that his brain seems to work in a totally different dimension to mine, are totally above and beyond me. However, I assume that a new striker will be arriving next week to fill the major gap in the squad. All sorts of names, some close to home and others more exotic are being bandied about on the message boards and social media and I am sure that all will be revealed shortly.

After Adam Forshaw failed to appear on the team sheet and was, indeed, absent from Griffin Park, Mark Warburton confirmed that a second and still unacceptable bid had been received from a *rival Championship club* (or Wigan, as we all know) and that Adam had been given a couple of days off to consider his future. Candidly, I still feel that Adam would be best served by playing another season at Brentford where he would be an automatic first choice and a major driving force in the team. The extra experience and profile he would gain would make him an even more enticing prospect for clubs far higher in the food chain than Wigan. I await the next act with bated breath!

The End Of The Day – 4/8/14

With all the talk over the last few days concentrating upon the future of Adam Forshaw and, to a lesser degree, the identity of Brentford's latest transfer targets it is very easy to lose sight of what are, in reality, far more serious and important matters. Yesterday Scott Barron announced his retirement from the game after failing to recover from a chronic hip injury that he incurred at Southend in an otherwise unremarkable and frankly, unimportant, Johnstone's Paint Trophy match back in December 2012. He fought his way back to action and even managed a few appearances last season but he was released by Brentford in May and he has finally been forced to admit defeat and is now looking for a fresh start and a new career.

Yet, looking at the statistics, you could say that Scott was one of the lucky ones. According to the PFA, the average career span for a professional footballer is eight years and Scott managed to last in the game for over ten, making one hundred and fifty first team appearances in a career that took him from his North West home to Ipswich Town and their famed academy. From there he was transferred to Millwall and spent five successful years there and established himself as their first choice left back, making over one hundred and thirty appearances before moving to Griffin Park in August 2012. A figure that would have been far higher had the injury gremlins not struck.

Ironically it was an injury to a team mate that provided Scott with the opportunity to play, and star in Millwall's 2010 playoff final victory over Swindon. His appearance at Wembley was undoubtedly his career highlight but his progress was hindered by a series of groin and knee injuries even before his career-ending and recurring hip problem. He did everything possible to recover full fitness including undergoing hip surgery but it wasn't to be.

He was brought to Brentford by Uwe Rösler at the start of the 2012/13 season when it appeared unlikely that Everton would release Jake Bidwell for another loan spell, but – Sod's Law – almost before the ink on Scott's contract was dry, Everton relented and Scott went from first choice to the bench in the blink of an eye. Such is the way of football. He always gave of his best and played well when given the chance. He even managed a substitute appearance against Chelsea in the FA Cup. But for all his passing ability and skill on the ball he was never going to replace Jake Bidwell given his greater power, strength and defensive ability. Scott also made the odd impressive appearance on the left side of midfield but for the most part he became a member of the Bomb Squad and swiftly faded from the scene.

Even when injured or not picked, Scott remained a positive influence in the dressing room and around the club and was highly popular with his team mates. He also grew an astonishingly full beard, which was the subject of much comment and hilarity. His eventual free transfer came as little surprise, but what did make me stand up and take note was the searing honesty of his comment whilst he was twisting in the wind at the end of last season, waiting for the bad news: *I haven't spoken to the club yet but I don't think I've warranted a new contract. I don't deserve it. I haven't performed well enough and it hasn't gone particularly well for me.* I was impressed by what he said and how he neither felt sorry for himself nor bemoaned his fate. He just accepted what life had to bring and tried to move on and get on with things. For that attitude and approach he has my deepest respect.

I asked Mike Calvin, author of *Family* – that wonderful book where he described a year spent behind the scenes with Millwall FC – for his view on Scott, and this is his verdict on him, and what a lovely epitaph it is: *By usual standards, Scottie would be patronised, and easily overlooked. He wasn't a regular when I knew him at Millwall, and fate has conspired against him at Brentford. Let's, though, look beyond appearance statistics and concentrate on the man. He is the type who makes a dressing room tick: fully committed, unflinchingly honest and good-humoured. Those qualities will hold him in good stead for the future.* Scott Barron personified the *good pro* in everything he did and like all Brentford supporters, I would like to thank him for his time at the club and wish him well for the future.

The Brentford Oscars – Part 1 – 5/8/14

Following on from my recent overview of the Seventies, I got to thinking about the Brentford players from that decade and I thought that I would open up a veritable hornet's nest by highlighting some of them as follows.

1. MOST RELIABLE GOALKEEPER

- Chic Brodie – Calmness and competence personified
- Steve Sherwood – Player of the Year in 1975 when he was an ever-present during his loan spell from Chelsea
- Len Bond – One of my all-time favourites

2. GOALKEEPERS WHO MOST DROVE SPECTATORS TO VALIUM – OR ONE OUT OF THREE AIN'T BAD

- Paul Priddy – Although I still remember that incredible Easter Saturday at Watford in 1977 when he turned into Superman and saved those two penalty kicks
- Garry Towse – Garry – who?
- Bill Glazier – Never to be forgiven for his costly howler at Old Trafford
- Paul McCullough – The Kamikaze Kid
- Graham Cox – The Ashley Bayes of his time?

3. MOST INSPIRATIONAL CAPTAIN

- Bobby Ross – What a servant to the club. A genuinely good and pleasant man as well as being a born leader
- Jackie Graham – Nothing really to say. A total inspiration and would YOU ignore his instructions – I know I wouldn't dare

4. MR 100% EFFORT

- Tom Higginson – No contest
- Jackie Graham – Non-stop dynamo

5. THEY SHALL NOT PASS – DEFENDERS WHO TOOK NO PRISONERS

- Dick Renwick – The donor of cinder rash to many a winger
- Mick Brown – Three games on loan from Brighton in 1973. Was he booked in every match?

6. BLAZING METEORS – WHY DIDN'T THEY MAKE THE GRADE?

- Allan Mansley - Such potential, such ability, but it never really happened as it should have done. But what memories…
- Andy Woon – When you score a hat trick on your full debut there is really only way left for you to go
- Nigel Smith – A calm, gifted defender, yet he was finished by the time he was twenty-one. Why?
- Willie Graham – Too much too soon? A lot of skill but something was missing

7. WET PAPER BAGS – STRIKERS WHO DIDN'T

- Bill Brown – Four eminently forgettable games in 1969/70
- Micky Cook – Ran around a lot and got nowhere
- David Jenkins – A tremendous shot – or so we were told. Off to the knacker's yard
- Stan Webb – Vilified ever since he left and on a total hiding to nothing trying to replace the legend that was John O'Mara; always just too late on the scene to score

- Garry Rolph – Scored on his debut but did nothing much afterwards
- Lee Frost – Great winger but terrible striker
- Micky French – More potential unrealised

8. BEST HEADERS OF THE BALL

- John O'Mara – Annus Mirabilis in 1971/72
- Dave Simmons – Would have taken penalties with his head
- Andy McCulloch – Simply the best

9. MOST "GENTLEMANLY" STRIKERS

- Roger Cross – Physical contact wasn't his game, but what a player
- Gordon Neilson – So skilful but always peripheral to the action

10. BEST FINISHERS

- Willie Brown – Will someone please explain to me why after scoring for fun he was replaced by Micky French and sold to Torquay, where he continued to score regularly
- Gordon Sweetzer – Brave and clinical – if only his knees hadn't given up on him
- Steve Phillips – Who can forget those goals he scored for us in 1977/78. An arrogant pest on the field – but so much talent

11. BEST PENALTY TAKER

- Terry Johnson – seven out of seven isn't bad

12. MOST SKILFUL PLAYERS

- Dave Metchick – Over the hill but a lovely touch on the ball
- Roger Cross – A beacon of hope during some bleak times. Oh, and those white boots too!
- Stewart Houston – an International in the making
- Pat Kruse – A cultured ball-playing centre half
- John Bain – What if – a truly wonderful player who made his name in Portland, Oregon, rather than West London
- Barry Lloyd – The fans never gave him a chance
- Dean Smith – So much talent but not enough commitment or hunger. He should have become a star but drifted out of the game far too early

13. BEST BARGAINS

- Jackie Graham – Nothing more needs to be said
- Paul Bence – Mr. Versatility
- Paul Shrubb – Never properly appreciated – a really good player
- Doug Allder – Revitalised us in 1977

- Steve Phillips – All those goals for only £5,000!
- John Fraser – Consistent and versatile
- Barry Tucker – The final part in the promotion jigsaw. Calmness personified

14. UNFULFILLED PROMISE – YOUNGSTERS WHO DESERVED MORE OF A CHANCE

- Roy Cotton
- Richard Poole – Tall, lanky and gangling – but a real talent
- Gary Smith
- Dave Silman – Giant centre half – one game and out
- Iori Jenkins
- Billy Stagg
- Billy Eames – Fantastic goal on his debut but not kept on by Bill Dodgin

15. BEST LOANEES

- Gerry Baker
- Alex Dawson – A real hero who made a massive impact
- Steve Sherwood
- Steve Scrivens – Impressive loan spell but he never played another League game after leaving us. Why?
- Lee Frost – Brilliant, pacy winger, but never a striker

One Out Of Three IS Bad – 7/8/14

Who can tell me what the following figures refer to? Sorry there are no prizes on offer though!

- 33%
- 69%
- 54%
- 57%

No ideas? OK, I will put you all out of your misery. These figures represent the percentage of penalty kicks that we have actually managed to score over the past four seasons. Woeful aren't they? To put a bit of flesh on the bones: In 2010/11 we managed to score a princely three out of the nine penalties we were awarded. I really cannot bring myself to say anything more about that pathetic record. The following season we scored eight of our first nine, and even when Gary Alexander missed, Niall McGinn managed to score from the rebound away at Colchester. Then it all went pear-shaped and we missed two of the next four kicks including the fiasco at Stevenage where we threw away our last chance to reach the playoffs when Donaldson and Saunders both hit the woodwork rather than the back of the net. Overall, though, nine out of thirteen (plus McGinn's effort) represented an adequate, if not startling success rate.

The last two seasons have been appalling. We managed to score only seven out of thirteen in 2012/13, culminating in Marcello Trotta's epic failure in the promotion decider against Doncaster. Last season we actually improved, and scored eight out of fourteen penalty kicks, a figure that was indelibly tarnished once Alan Judge took over the job late in the season and missed three out of his four efforts.

Confusingly enough what also has to be taken into consideration is our perfect record of six out of six successes in the promotion playoffs and shootout in 2013 – where we excelled in high-pressure situations. Go figure! There really is no rational explanation.

What is also interesting is just how many penalty kicks we have been awarded since Uwe Rösler and Mark Warburton have taken charge at the club. Forty penalty kicks coming our way in the past three seasons just highlights how attacking we are and the success we have in getting quick players to run at the opposition in their penalty area.

Some of the individual penalty records of our players also merit comment. Kevin O'Connor has scored nineteen times in twenty-four attempts and has taken more penalties than any other Brentford player since 1970. Pretty decent, but still only a 79% success rate. Stephen Hunt was very reliable and but for a great save from Kuipers would have notched an almost unprecedented hat trick of penalties against Brighton and in total scored twelve out of fifteen. Steve Phillips started well but incredibly missed his last four kicks yet somehow managed to keep hold of the job until he left the club. Paul Evans only missed once and memorably scored an arrogant dinked *Panenka* kick against Oldham back in 2001. Stan Bowles had the most casual approach, swaggering up to the spot, before dummying the keeper as well as the crowd behind the goal with nonchalant ease and rolling the ball into the corner. I never worried when Stan took the kicks and what amazes me is that he actually missed one of his twelve kicks. Class, total class.

Back in the 70s Terry Johnson was a perfect seven out of seven and Roger Cross never missed either. Bobby Ross, my first Brentford hero won us promotion in 1972 with a perfect penalty kick against Exeter. I remember Bill Dodgin going ballistic on the touchline when Andy McCulloch was invited by his team mates to notch his hat trick with a late penalty kick against Tranmere. Hubris triumphed as the keeper smothered his weak effort. Also, Peter Gelson blasting a vital last minute spot kick against Aldershot into Brook Road and Steve Butler almost hitting the corner flag against Chesterfield. Horrid, horrid memories!

How about Andy Sinton who was entrusted with a last minute penalty kick on his Brentford debut against Bury and showed nerves of steel by slotting in the winning goal? In more recent times Adam Forshaw scored five out of six last season by varying his approach yet he always looked like missing his second attempt at Peterborough where it was patently obvious to all observers that he had no plan for how to take a second kick in the same game. Clayton Donaldson started with a successful kick at Preston before his crucial miss at Stevenage. He also totally failed to hit the target with his last two gruesome efforts at Scunthorpe and Crawley where his pathetic first minute attempt that skewed wide of Paul Jones's post earned me an immediate red card from our living room as my barrage of choice epithets was not well received by my wife or, indeed, the dog. One of them growled menacingly at me, and – no – it wasn't the dog.

Some missed penalties have a knock-on effect on the player's career. Who can say how Will Grigg's season would have turned out if he had managed to mark his home debut with a hat trick against Sheffield United – maybe he would have scored twenty goals and would now be looking forward to starting a new season in the Championship at Griffin Park instead of slumming it at the Moo Camp? What about Paul Hayes? Would he have gained some much-needed confidence had he scored that penalty he missed against Yeovil soon after he came on as a substitute on his debut? Maybe he too would have gone on to justify Uwe Rösler's faith in him?

The margin between success and failure in football is so narrow. In these cases, no wider than the length of a goalkeeper's arm. Sam Saunders too, for all his dead ball prowess, obviously finds it easier to score from twenty-five yards out rather than twelve as his meagre 40% penalty kick success rate indicates. His costly miss at Sheffield United in 2013 also seems to have slipped under the radar and escaped censure given the euphoria after our last minute equaliser.

I really do not know whether the best approach is the side foot, as exemplified by Bowles, or the Martin Grainger thunderbolt. Both were highly successful. As for why our recent record is so poor, heaven only knows as players like Trotta, Saunders, Forrester and Judge are all excellent strikers of a ball – sorry Clayton, but anyone on the Ealing Road terrace who was forced to spend much of the pre-match shooting practice ducking your misdirected slices as they screamed into the crowd would agree that you are – on occasion – not the cleanest striker of a football.

I predict that the number of penalty kicks we receive next season with be less than half that of last year, but given that I am sure that every goal will count next season, we will score a far higher proportion of them. Let's hope that this is not a jinx! In passing many, many thanks to my friend and fellow Bees author, Mark Croxford for providing all the facts that I have mangled in this article!

You Have To Dream, Don't You? – 9/8/14

Today is the day we have been looking forward to, and dreaming about, since the beginning of May. It is the first day of what I fully expect to be the most momentous and exciting season I can remember since I first started supporting Brentford way back in 1965. Today for me is the reward for all those freezing days in midwinter with the icy wind chilling my bones, watching and groaning as inept journeymen like Eddie Hutchinson, Jide Olugbodi, Paul McCullough, Clyde Wijnhard and Fola Onibuje stuttered and fumbled their way to inevitable defeat. Today is payback time for those seven playoff failures and pathetic capitulations at places like Cheltenham, Peterborough and Macclesfield – grounds that we hope never to have to visit again.

Today makes up for all the smug comments I have had to endure over the years from all my patronising Premier League supporting friends and workmates. Today is the day we take our first step along the road to what we hope and indeed expect, will be a highly successful season in the Championship. We are ready for the challenge that awaits us. Our preparation has been sharp, focused and committed. The new players are bedding into the squad. The squad is strong and of a quality unsurpassed almost in living memory.

How will the opening game with Charlton go? Will we win and get off the mark with our confidence boosted to an even greater degree? Will we perform to the best of our ability and put on a show and prove that we are no longer *Little Old Brentford* and we fully deserve to be where we are? Will we freeze on our big day in front of a packed Griffin Park and get off to a faltering start and have to play catch-up? No wonder I cannot sleep – and I am sure that I am not alone. All around the country there are supporters with similar thoughts in their heads as mine – and yours too, I am sure!

To prove my point, I am going to quote a passage from one of my favourite football books. *Only A Game?* was written over forty years ago by the then Millwall and Eire International midfielder Eamon Dunphy. I will allow him to explain in his own words, far better and more lyrically and lucidly than I can ever dream about, what the eve of the new season really means to players and supporters alike:

Tomorrow, the first game. I am confident. Not certain, for that is impossible. The season begins tomorrow and for nine months our lives are committed to the business of winning games. This is a very special day for football people. Small children lie restless in bed dreaming of the conquests they and their heroes will make tomorrow. Their dads, pints in hand, talk cynically in pubs – "They will be just as bloody terrible this year." But in a small corner of their hearts, they too nurture a dream that this will be "our year".

More than anyone, the pro dreams tonight. He is more than a dreamer, he is a dream maker. No matter how long you have been in the game, how cynical you have become, or how terrible you know your team to be, tonight you push the past and present behind to dream of the future, which for you is nine months long.

This year I am confident. There are no certainties, but when I look rationally at Millwall, I cannot see us failing. We have everything. Skill, character, experience, a good crowd. We only need the luck. We should not fail, but we might.... I believe in what we now have at Millwall.... Of course I have my reservations. Yet I still believe.

Millwall finished the season in twelfth place and Dunphy was dropped, transfer listed, and sold by the end of November – but you have to dream don't you?

Off And Running – 10/8/14

Well it wasn't a win and we didn't start the season off with the three points that we wanted, but there was much to be positive about in our 1-1 draw with Charlton yesterday as well as several lessons that need to be learned. Football was back and we basked in the sun. We were playing in the Championship after eons in the nether regions of the Football League and there were many differences to remark upon. The Griffin was heaving from midday and new replica shirts were stretching alarmingly over well-developed paunches. The queue to get into the Club Shop snaked around The Princess Royal. In fact, there were queues everywhere, something that we will have to get used to on a regular basis as Griffin Park struggles to cope with the higher crowds. It was rumoured that ticket touts were also seen around the ground taking advantage of the match being designated as all ticket. All that was missing was pirate programmes and those blasted half-and-half *friendship* scarves.

Fleet Street's finest, including such luminaries as Nick Szczepanik and the doyen of the press box, Brian Glanville, were seen reacquainting themselves with the whereabouts of TW8. Peter Gilham, MC Extraordinaire, showed that he realises we are in the big time now by deigning to announce the name of Charlton's goal scorer instead of blithely ignoring him, as has always been his wont. What's more *The Football League Show* featured extended match highlights at a time well before the watershed – and by the way, Leroy, Adam Forshaw isn't injured!

As for the actual football, with Adam Forshaw still in purdah, manager Mark Warburton sprung a surprise by relegating Marcos Tebar to one of the plush newly refurbished and stuffed substitutes' seats. We started well, an incisive 4-5-1, with Pritchard, Judge and Dallas interchanging and weaving their spells as Charlton sat back and absorbed our early pressure. Pritchard's fast and clever feet created space and his curling twenty-five yarder inched past the post with the keeper struggling to make up the ground. Pritchard then performed a perfect balletic *pas de deux* with the ball glued to his feet as he slalomed past three defenders before being scythed down.

We played the Brentford way, with the ball thrown short every time by Button, keeping possession and switching the play as we probed for openings. But that was the main difference between Division One and the Championship – the paucity of actual chances created. Charlton covered well and packed their own half and Gray was left isolated and alone in the penalty area. Charlton finally awoke from their slumbers and broke fast. One defence-splitting diagonal pass and Tucudean was left clean through but Button was quick, brave and positive and saved our bacon. Judge then forced an excellent save with a deflected long ranger.

We were well ahead on points at the break but the scoreline remained blank. The second half was a different matter. Tebar replaced Moses who was apparently not fully fit and whilst he helped us keep the ball better, our game slowed down, and we weren't making the quick, incisive runs needed to create space and gaps. Our game is all about *pass and move* and we forgot about the crucial second part of the equation. Charlton took over and slowly adopted a formation less defensive than the Maginot Line and our defence creaked as we began to be put under pressure. Vetokele was strong and mobile and his movement was too much for us. Button made two more saves, one quite exceptional from a close range header, turning it onto the post before we broke away and Pritchard's beautifully flighted cross found Gray in space and he headed it back the way it came, but too close to Henderson.

Eventually Charlton's pressure told and Jackson's in swinging corner found the ever-willing Vetokele who beat Button to the ball when he shouldn't have done, and headed home almost from on the goal line – a really poor goal to concede. The game drifted as we sought a spark to reignite our fading challenge, and then came the turning point. We brought on experience and fresh legs in Nick Proschwitz and Tommy Smith and it was the latter who produced the best pass of the day that totally split the defence and left a clear run on goal – unfortunately it was our defence he split and Button was forced to rush well out of his goal to try and clear the danger. He failed, a quick sideways pass and

Harriott faced an empty goal twenty yards out but he obligingly crashed the ball onto the underside of the bar. Tebar dived in to sweep away the loose ball, and we had somehow survived. We were still in the game – just!

We took full advantage and after Craig had volleyed over from a corner – high and not very handsome, we finally scored our first Championship goal just at a time when we had gone longer in our approach, and started chasing the game. McCormack's long diagonal pass into the penalty area found Smith who used what suspiciously looked like an arm to control it before turning, cutting inside and finding the bottom corner with a powerful shot that kissed the lunging defender before finding its way perfectly inside the near post. Silence for a second, we were taken by surprise as a goal really hadn't looked much like coming, and then Griffin Park erupted and became a cauldron of noise for the remaining few minutes.

Relief and joy as Tommy Smith equalises late on against Charlton Athletic.

The players were visibly lifted and raised their game as Charlton wilted and funnelled back to protect what they had. Judge almost won it with a gorgeous curling free kick that clipped the bar on its way over before Smith shot high and wide with the last chance.

So, a point. A decent start and we showed that we can cope with the higher level. There was much to take out of yesterday, but equally, a lot that we have to take on board very quickly as the games will now start coming thick and fast. It's a squad game now and our substitutes all made a crucial difference. In the second half, the midfield played too deep and never got forward enough to support the lone striker. In preseason, Tebar and Douglas dovetailed perfectly with one sitting and the other going forward. Douglas played too deep in the first half and after the break we conceded the initiative with neither of them attacking enough. We need to make better runs off the ball, which will open up gaps in the opposition defence. We have to get more players into the box as Gray was often left on his own, vainly competing against the tag team pair of Bikey and

Ben Haim. We need to, in the words of Mark Warburton, *Look after the ball*, and not give it away so cheaply. Too often we were careless in possession, and in this division you have to work far harder and longer to get it back. We also looked a bit small and lightweight and lacked physical presence.

The overriding feeling after the game was one of relief. We hadn't been embarrassed or shown up, we had played well in patches and proved that we could compete. We had got the opening match out of the way and notched our first point of the season after it had looked, for a while, like we were about to start with a demoralising home defeat. The Bees are off and running but the road will be a long and testing one.

Button It! – 11/8/14

The Brentford crowd has been remarkably supportive to their team over the past couple of seasons – and why shouldn't they be given the quality of football they have witnessed, the high entertainment levels provided, and the overall success of the team? After all, nineteen home wins and promotion last season is pretty good going in anyone's language. There are still murmurings from time to time when the ball is patiently played from side to side across the back four as we probe for openings and attempt to pull the opposition out of position. But I think that is understandable as we have been used to a far less cerebral and patient (and much more blood and thunder) approach over the years, and it is hard to change the habits of a lifetime.

For my part I have to continually blink and remind myself that this is really Brentford that I am watching and not some figment of my hopes and dreams. Fred Callaghan's 1982 team contained the best footballers I have seen at Brentford up until the present day. It boasted the finest midfield I have ever seen at the club. Terry Hurlock, Chris Kamara and Stan Bowles provided a perfect blend of competitiveness, hard tackling, aerial strength, nonstop running and of course, Stan's ability to mesmerise and open up a defence with one pass. The front three, which comprised the rejuvenated Tony Mahoney, as well as the pace and finishing ability of Francis Joseph and *Gasping* Gary Roberts were far too good for the plodding, pedestrian defences we faced. Unfortunately, we were poor at the back, gave up too easily away from home and were finished off by Mahoney's cruel injury.

Today's squad will need to adapt to the higher level but I have every confidence that they will be able to do so. There is, however, one player who the supporters seem ambivalent about. Goalkeeper David Button is still fairly inexperienced in the game. At twenty-five he is young for a goalkeeper, has only played just over one hundred and fifty first team matches and was loaned out to ten clubs whilst still developing and learning the game at Spurs. No slouch as a youngster, he was picked to play for England thirty-one times from Under 16 to Under 20 level. He did manage to replace ex-Bee Ben Hamer for a while at Charlton but was regarded as the back up there and Brentford is the first club that has really offered him the chance to cement his place and establish himself as the first choice keeper.

If you look at the figures, he played forty-two league games last season, conceded only thirty-seven goals and kept nineteen clean sheets. He saved two penalties and contributed greatly to wins over Notts County, Preston, Leyton Orient, Walsall and Gillingham. Of course, he played behind an excellent defence but you don't rack up those kinds of numbers without having real ability. A huge man, Button presents a massive barrier in goal and his shot stopping is beyond reproach. He is agile and narrows the angle well. He dropped a long-range effort at the feet of Wilson against Coventry but it is difficult to remember any goal he conceded where he really should not have been beaten by the shot. His reflexes are excellent and he moves his feet quickly for such a big man; his save from a close-in header on Saturday was world class. He was caught in no-man's land against Notts County which contributed to a late goal, but he times his approaches towards onrushing forwards exceptionally well, stands tall, and made a crucial save before half time against Charlton on Saturday when a striker was clean through.

He can be tentative on crosses and does not impose himself enough and often punches when the opportunity is there to catch the ball but this comes with experience. He really should not have been beaten to the ball from a near post corner for Charlton's goal. He was hesitant and slow to react. He gave a clear shout of *keeper* but didn't get there first as he should have done. More work is needed to improve this vital part of his game. What really divides the fans is his distribution. The Brentford way is to build up from the back with patient passes and Button is key to that, kicking or throwing the ball short to his back four or Douglas at every opportunity. It can go wrong, as it did so disastrously at Stevenage and Swindon last season and he will learn from those mistakes.

When he is forced to kick by opponents closing us down he is remarkably consistent, pinging passes fifty to one hundred yards with almost unerring accuracy and composure. Again, some fans find this approach hard to get used to and Button is the fall guy for their anger and concern. He also hasn't been forgiven for not being Simon Moore, the immensely popular and gifted keeper who Button replaced when Moore left for Cardiff last season. That isn't his fault and as much as I rated Simon, I believe that David offers us more in terms of his shot stopping ability, particularly from long range, where Simon was vulnerable, and in his distribution. Simon on the other hand dealt with crosses far better than David.

We are fortunate to have a goalkeeper in Button whose strengths far outweigh his weaknesses. Richard Lee has also been quick to acknowledge just how talented David is and that is more than just the Goalkeepers' Union talking. Mistakes by goalkeepers are always magnified and are obvious to the eye, and he makes very few. He will get even better as he gets used to weekly first team football and here is where I feel the key to his progress and development lies.

A couple of years ago he described himself as a *journeyman* given that he was always being sent out for short loan spells and had never been given his chance to put down roots or establish himself at any club. That was a telling comment, and I suspect that he is both a late developer and also lacks some confidence in his own ability, given his background and how he has been moved from pillar to post. Finally he has found a club where he can settle and that believes in him. He will respond accordingly, and over the next couple of years I am certain that he will become even better and demonstrate just how good he is. So my message for the doubters is get behind him and please button it!

Dagenham & Redbridge 6 Brentford 6 – Bees Win In Tiebreak! – 13/8/14

You can just imagine Brentford manager Mark Warburton giving his team his final instructions just before this surreal, ridiculous, incredible, unbelievable match kicked off last night. *Keep passing the ball, just support the man in possession and the goals will come. Oh, and make sure you keep it tight at the back – it's about time we kept a clean sheet.* Famous last words as the crowd at Victoria Road were treated to twelve goals plus six more successful penalty kicks in a shoot out finally won 4-2 by the Bees. History was made last night as the 6-6 draw equalled the highest scoring draw in UK football history and it was the first time a Brentford team has ever played in a match that ended with this scoreline. I was one of the lucky ones who saw the unforgettable 5-5 draw with Barnet in the same competition back in 1991 but last night's game was even crazier than that one.

Mark Warburton treated the Capital One Cup with the respect it deserved and fielded a strong team that included Marcos Tebar and Stuart Dallas as well as all seven substitutes from Saturday's match plus Kevin O'Connor and Toumani Diagouraga. Alan Judge and Andre Gray were included amongst the substitutes should they be needed, as indeed they most certainly were. Brentford purred into action with two clinically taken Stuart Dallas goals from short corners – yes, the Bees actually scored twice from corner kicks, with both chances being expertly created by the highly impressive debutant Montell Moore. The football early on was crisp and easy on the eye, and the clumsy home defence was pulled from pillar to post and carved open with embarrassing ease, and it just looked a matter of how many we would win by. Maybe we became complacent as the home team scored with almost their first attack as a driven low left wing cross was expertly finished at the far post. No worries, Brentford regained almost total control of the game with Tebar and Diagouraga imperious in the midfield. A comic cuts mix up allowed the impressive Nick Proschwitz in behind Scott Doe for his first Brentford goal and Tommy Smith was then within inches of making it four.

Dallas was dangerous every time he gained possession of the ball, Smith and Moore combined well and it was a highly impressive first forty-five minutes. Unfortunately, Mr. Hill decided to play three minutes of injury time given that Yennaris had gone off with a dead leg, and in that time our midfield gave the ball away sloppily, and the defence went walkabout as Craig hung back and the others moved forward for a non-existent offside and Lee was left totally exposed as the ball was dinked expertly over him. Schoolboy defending. So a potential 4-1 scoreline became 3-2, and by such narrow margins are football matches decided. Dagenham went into half time re-energised and cock-a-hoop and Brentford had lost the initiative and never really regained it.

The second half was a battle and Boucaud deservedly levelled when he danced around Diagouraga and his swerving twenty-five yarder was too well placed for Lee to get there. The cavalry came on in the form of Judge and Gray but we created little apart from Dean's close in header which was blocked and with Tebar's withdrawal we lost control of the midfield where Dagenham buzzed around us, their confidence high. But then, on eighty-two minutes, Smith and Judge combined perfectly and the latter's low cross was turned in expertly by Gray for the sort of close range poacher's goal that we so rarely score. Game over? Not a chance of it as right on time came a disgraceful equalising goal when a quick throw from well inside the home half went over our entire defence, caught too far upfield and dozing gently, waiting for the final whistle, and Hemmings left O'Connor trailing in his wake before hammering a cross-shot over the arching Lee into the far top corner. Genius or fluke? Who knows but it was extra time.

Montell Moore put us back in front with an excellent angled shot into the far corner, a goal taken with massive composure but then Smith limped off with a groin strain and we were down to ten men. Our nemesis Jamie Cureton responded to his customary warm welcome from Brentford fans with long memories, by slotting in from the edge of the area after we gave the ball away through overplaying and the force was now with the home team. Cureton missed a sitter and then Liam O'Brien made a wonderful save from Dallas to prevent the hat trick and our regaining the lead. The second half of extra time was all Dagenham and it came as no surprise when more gaps in defence occurred as we were over-run and Hemmings slotted home through Lee's dive.

Brentford looked shell-shocked and an embarrassing defeat seemed on the cards particularly when Judge fizzed one just wide, but we summoned up one last surge and Bidwell's near-post free kick tempted the keeper out of goal and Harlee Dean beat him to the ball for an unexpected late equaliser. Even then we almost threw it away as Dean sliced horribly just past his own post and then we allowed a free header from the corner which inched wide of the post.

So it was penalties, taken in the gathering gloom down at the home end. Finally sanity prevailed as we again overcame the disadvantage of taking our kicks second and Dallas, Judge, Craig and O'Connor all scored calmly and expertly whilst Richard Lee did what he does best and made two exceptional saves. We have now scored our last nine penalty shoot out kicks in a row, evidence, indeed, of our ability to keep calm and not let the occasion get the better of us.

We had finally won and scraped through to the next round after a night of almost unbearable excitement. Yes, there was much to be pleased about, in particular our early attacking combinations and clinical finishing but the defensive play and covering were truly laughable – that is if you didn't want to cry. We lacked pace at the back and the midfield stopped tracking back. We were horribly exposed time after time and made catastrophic errors of judgement that would have had any AFC Bournemouth scout rubbing his hands with glee before Saturday's game.

Mark Warburton is not known to be a shouter, but he would have had plenty of reasons to let rip after last night's defensive debacle and shambles. In years to come there will be around five hundred Brentford fans who will be able to say *I was there* at this unforgettable match but there is much talking and work that needs to be done on the training ground before the weekend.

So Near……….. – 17/8/14

Very occasionally you can take almost as much out of a defeat as a victory and Saturday's narrow one-nil loss to AFC Bournemouth was a case in point. Of course, the bottom line is that we lost, and you don't win style points for playing well, but there were so many positives from our performance. We more than matched a team that is seen very much as one that we aspire to be in terms of the quality of their football and how quickly and well they have adapted to the challenge of Championship football.

But first things first. What a pig of a journey. I am totally anal about arriving early wherever I am due (and, indeed, last Tuesday was parked up outside Dagenham's ground punctually at 5.30pm for a 7.45pm kickoff). I fully expected some traffic on the motorway and left North London at 9.45am. I finally pulled up outside the stadium, tired and feeling homicidal after the stop start journey from hell, at 1.30pm.

Not a great start to the day, but things soon got better once the game began. A beautifully original and intricate three man free kick move carved open the home defence only for Andre Gray to turn sharply and hammer the ball onto the underside of the bar from a tight angle – so nearly the perfect start. We funnelled back, pressed hard and, for the most part, kept Bournemouth at bay. Button saved brilliantly after an equally inventive corner kick routine created space for Kermorgant and we coped well with the home team and minimised their goal threat. What became obvious is how crucial ball retention is at this level of the game. Bournemouth held onto it far better than us with their back four all showing instant control and the ability to retain possession. We were far more wasteful and have got to realise that if you give the ball away you might well have to wait quite a while before you get it back.

After weathering an early second half storm culminating with Bidwell heading the ball off our goal line, we came alive, showed far more confidence and self-belief on and off the ball, and finally got our midfield runners up the field to support the isolated Gray. Pritchard and Judge threatened and the Irishman shot inches wide and then Douglas could not control an effort from the edge of the area and shot over. We improved even more after Dallas replaced Tebar who had found the pace of the game too much for him and had been caught in possession too often for comfort. We tested Lee Camp from a Pritchard free kick and a rasping long ranger from the effervescent Judge as we took total control.

A goal looked like it was on the way and it finally came – but for Bournemouth as we again gave the ball away near the halfway line. Bidwell was caught upfield and a swift break saw a man over on their right hand side and Fraser's excellent centre was converted at the far post by Junior Stanislas. It is ironic that I was writing just the other day about Roger Stanislaus and now his near namesake's goal condemned us to defeat. Smith and Proschwitz impressed after replacing Odubajo and Gray who had both worked selflessly and run themselves out and we looked stronger, more forceful and composed up front. Bournemouth funnelled back to protect their lead and wasted time under the eyes of an indulgent referee who seemed to see no evil whenever it was perpetrated by a player wearing red and black. Smith and Dallas roared down the wings, Douglas marauded forward and headed a late chance inches over the crossbar.

Defeat was tough to take given how much we had contributed to the match but there are some hard lessons that need to be learned very quickly about playing in the Championship. Games at this level are decided by very narrow margins. Ball possession is key. Lose it at your peril in your own half of the field. The back four cannot lose concentration and be careless with their passing as was far too often the case. Chances are few and far between and Brentford need to be much more clinical and also get more players up in support of the lone striker. The final ball also needs to be on the money.

A couple of times we broke with pace and had men over but were unable to thread the ball through to the unmarked runner who would have been in on goal. A bit of luck would also be welcome, as the ball invariably broke to a defender in their penalty area and not a Brentford player. Perhaps they anticipated the ball better and quicker than us too? We need to find another out ball when the opposition close down our back four and prevent Button distributing the ball to his defenders. The goalkeeper was often forced to kick the ball long where a home defender gobbled it up and the ball was turned over to the opposition. This is also where I feel we will have problems in future games given the make up of our squad.

Today was a football match in every meaning of the word. Of course the tackles flew in but both teams wanted to play and succeeded in doing so. As such, it was probably the most technically skilful game I have ever seen the Bees play in, with both teams contributing fully to the entertainment. Watching *The Football League Show* last night it is becoming pretty obvious that the Championship is the land of the giants with size, strength and power dominating, and I believe that we run the risk of being out-powered and outmuscled by the opposition in many games. We are a small and gifted bunch but it is possible that we will need to fight fire with fire when we come up against some of the less talented but bigger and stronger opponents.

Proschwitz provided some physical presence up front and it is noticeable that we played higher up the pitch once he came on and his strength and size enabled us to play off him and retain possession in the final third. Gray, though, gives us explosive pace and the ability to get in behind opponents and down the sides and it will be a difficult decision for Mark Warburton to make. Scott Hogan is also rapidly returning to fitness and he remains an unknown quantity. We also have the two exciting Spanish midfielders to look forward to, and I can't wait for my first sight of the exciting José Ignacio Peleteiro Ramallo, or Jota, our recent signing from Celta de Vigo.

Today was so nearly perfect, but ultimately was a disappointment as we could and perhaps should have come away with at least a point. We should derive confidence and self-belief from the performance as we promised much and demonstrated that we both belong at, and can cope with this level of the game. There is much to look forward to, starting hopefully on Tuesday at Blackpool, who will offer an entirely different type of challenge than AFC Bournemouth.

Well Worth Waiting for! – 20/8/14

Well, it's just gone one-thirty in the morning and I'm back home after a long, exhausting but ultimately successful and exhilarating day out. I detoured to *The National Football Museum* in Manchester, which was frankly a bit of a damp squib. The highlight of the afternoon was finding a parking space less than fifty yards from the front door of the museum, which was worth a quick visit but was an ultimate disappointment, filled as it was with far too much Manchester United and City-related ephemera: lots of signed shirts and interactive games and far too few exhibits of real and lasting historical value and interest. Nothing much there to excite Brentford fans either, apart from a Sikh sword awarded to the club by the local community – I wonder if the donors know where their prized gift is now located! That being said the many families and kids (of all ages) seemed to love it – so what do I know?

The evening's entertainment at Bloomfield Road was far more exciting as Brentford broke their duck by winning their first Championship game of the season and, indeed, their first victory at this level of the game since defeating Barnsley at Griffin Park on May 1st 1993. An auspicious night and result which has raised the Bees to the giddy heights of twelfth in the embryonic league table, three points ahead of Uwe Rösler's stuttering Wigan team and a massive four – yes, four – points ahead of Fulham, ignoring, of course that they do have a game in hand. Back to the action: Andre Gray was injured – nothing serious apparently, so Nick Proschwitz started as the sole striker and Stuart Dallas replaced Marcos Tebar in a team that was otherwise unchanged from the one that started the match at AFC Bournemouth on Saturday. Jack Bonham was on the bench instead of the injured Richard Lee and was joined by our two new Spanish signings in Jota and Toral.

Blackpool fielded their usual Rag, Tag and Bobtail assortment of unknown foreigners and slightly tarnished or over-the-hill journeymen; players like Ishmael Miller, Francois Zoko and Peter Clarke with yet another new signing, Nile Ranger – looking like he had enjoyed a Summer without too much hard training, starting on the bench. I felt sorry for their manager, José Riga, for having to work under such constraints, and trying to make bricks without straw, but his team did him proud tonight, keeping possession well and probing at the Brentford defence without really threatening until Zoko found space on the left side of the area and his curling cross was easily headed home by Nathan Delfouneso, who was in splendid isolation.

The goal came at a time when Brentford were beginning to impose themselves on the game and they started to dominate proceedings once they managed to keep tighter watch on the two overlapping full backs who had both caused problems, and with their out balls stifled, Brentford took control. Lots of intricate football, pass and move with Moses Odubajo terrifying the home defence with his pace and directness. As has been the case though, our moves seemed to fizzle out on the edge of their box with few actual shooting chances created – but that will come as confidence grows and the players get more used to each other and the system being employed. You have to score when you are on top and thankfully the goal came with Judge and Moses combining well before Pritchard took a touch and arrowed a low right-footed drive into the far corner beyond the unsighted keeper. There was nearly another just before half time when Pritchard cut inside but fired straight at Lewis. Despite their dominance the Bees were indebted to a wonderful block by Craig to foil Miller right on the halftime whistle.

The force was now with the Bees who took total control and were rewarded when the ever-willing Dallas chased a forlorn hope, dispossessed the dallying defender who was trying to usher the ball out for a goal kick, turned inside and walloped it into the top corner. Dallas has been a revelation this season with his directness, pace, strength and potency in front of goal. There is now huge competition for places and Stuart has reacted well to the challenge. Proschwitz had run himself out as he and Moses were replaced by

Smith and Jota. The Spaniard impressed in his cameo, looking positive and assured in possession and quick on the ball, his pace and dancing feet almost gave Pritchard a tap in, and he will be a massive influence once he settles into the English game. Lesson number one for him, though, is not to dally on the ball and take an extra touch when under pressure forty yards from your own goal. You will lose possession and put your defence under threat, as was the case last night. Tommy Smith was, well, Tommy Smith, cool, calm and composed, settling us down as we attempted to run down the clock.

We dropped deeper as the prospect of that elusive first win affected tired minds and limbs and we gave the initiative back to Blackpool, almost literally at times as we became our own worst enemy, gifting them the ball in dangerous positions through overplaying and casualness. Another crucial lesson that has to be learned quickly if we are not to suffer the inevitable consequences. Our formation veered from 4-1-4-1 to an interesting and probably unique 4-6-0, but thanks to the home team's failings in front of goal, an excellent smothering save from Button and heroics from Douglas and the entire back four, we held on and there was much joy and celebration at the final whistle.

Players, staff and fans alike knew the importance of this victory and how it can provide a platform and springboard towards a successful season. We needed that first win, we fully deserved it, we got it, and the Bees are on the march.

The Eighties Revisited – 21/8/14

The Eighties – what memories does that decade still conjure up for those of us of a certain age? They were probably the most formative years for me as they saw me take on most of the trappings of adulthood such as taking out a mortgage, moving abroad, buying a car, running a business and finally getting married, even though inside I still felt that I was a teenager – as indeed I still do! It was the decade of Pac-Man, Rubik's Cubes, Betamax VCRs, The AIDS pandemic and E.T.

As far as football is concerned, who can forget the pantomime villain Diego Maradona and *that* goal as he slalomed through the entire England defence? The first sponsored football shirts, the tragedies of Heysel and Hillsborough, the introduction of three points for a win and the dreaded playoffs – so long Brentford's nemesis, Holland's Total Football and short shorts. Ricky Villa's mazy run that won the FA Cup for Spurs, Andy Gray's Nat Lofthouse impression against Watford at Wembley and the fantastic Coventry v Spurs FA Cup Final.

As for Brentford, the Eighties were a time of consolidation with the club remaining in the third tier of the Football League. Progress seemed minimal with the club stagnating in the middle part of the decade and looking back now I was surprised at how low many of the home attendances were. The managerial appointment of Steve Perryman revitalised the club, improved its level of professionalism and saw Brentford end the decade on an upward curve with seemingly much to look forward to in the Nineties. Much of the excitement and pride came from the Cup competitions, culminating in the 1985 Freight Rover Trophy Final appearance at Wembley (with many lapsed supporters coming out of the woodwork) and then the incredible march to the FA Cup Quarter Final in 1989, and the humbling of Manchester City and Blackburn Rovers before bowing out bravely at Anfield against the best club in the country. The aforementioned Manchester City and Blackburn games showed how well the team could perform, combining skill, pace, organisation and a tenacious will to win. But rather than thinking about the Brentford teams of that era, I prefer to think back and reminisce about some of the great characters and talents who graced Griffin Park during the Eighties.

Long before the internet, news spread far slower in those days. I remember coming in from playing cricket late one Saturday evening in August 1980 and switching on my television set and seeing to my amazement that Brentford were being featured on ITV's Big Match and, what's more, we had managed an impressive and unexpected 3-2 away win at Walsall. Was this really Brentford wearing an unfamiliar sky blue away kit and if so who was this fearsome long-haired, bearded figure marauding around the midfield leaving bodies prostrate in his wake, with his earring flashing in the late Summer sunshine like a Norse God? That was my introduction to Terry Hurlock who later joined Stan Bowles and Chris Kamara to form the best midfield I have ever seen play for the club.

Watching Brentford take penalties has understandably always been a source of great stress to me over the years and I have never known whether to focus my attention on the goal or fix it on a point five feet over the crossbar where the ball was next likely to appear once it had been struck, yet with Bowles I never worried.

His ability and seeming arrogance meant that a goal was inevitable as he swaggered up to the spot and gently rolled the ball to where the goalkeeper wasn't, and until photographic evidence is produced to prove otherwise, I still refuse to accept that he actually missed a penalty at Wrexham back in 1983! There were many other massive talents like Francis Joseph – how far could he have progressed if the injury demons had not struck? Robbie Cooke, Andy Sinton, Keith Jones, Roger Joseph, Richard Cadette and Gary Blissett. What about Tony Mahoney? Seemingly in the last chance saloon with his career petering out, and on the dole when signed on trial after a undistinguished spell at a club I will not mention, who suddenly transformed himself into the second coming of Roy Race until injury cruelly intervened. Fred Callaghan certainly had an eye for a player and was responsible for bringing great talent to Griffin Park and unearthing non-league gems such as Hurlock, Gary Roberts and David Crown.

Brentford has always been a family club with players showing loyalty and an affinity with the supporters and long-serving heroes such as Gary Phillips, the immortal Bob Booker, Terry Evans, Jamie Bates, Simon Ratcliffe and Keith Millen were all stalwarts of the Eighties. We all have unabashed favourites and mine was Allan Cockram. Those of you who know me will surely snigger and accuse me of total self-delusion and wishful thinking when I say how much I wanted to have hair like Allan's plus a modicum of his footballing ability too – surely not too much to ask for? Of course he was a luxury player but what pleasure he gave with his passing, bamboozling free kicks, his exuberance and obvious love of the game, which transmitted itself to every supporter.

On the other hand, I can remember my sense of frustration at some of the players who tried their best but for whom seemingly nothing ever came off. Paul McCullough, Lee Frost, Graham Wilkins, Keith Bowen, Ian Bolton, Tom Finney, Steve Butler, Ian Holloway, Wayne Turner, the dreaded David Geddis, and even Les Ferdinand – the players we loved to hate. In retrospect I would like to offer them all my belated thanks for all their efforts and apologies for the boos! That being said, poor Ashley Bayes made his debut right at the end of the decade, but maybe it's best if we leave him for the 90s!

There was also a massive development, indicative of the changes in society, one memorable October's day in 1987 when the Brentford team for the first time ever included five black players in Roger Stanislaus, Keith Jones, Roger Joseph, Paul Smith and Paul Williams and I was proud to say that very few supporters even batted an eyelid. A decade of mixed fortunes perhaps, but one that brought me much joy whilst following my favourite club.

Still A Bee! – Part One – 22/8/14

Out of the blue, a few days ago, I started receiving correspondence from Richard Poole, who, for those of you of a more recent vintage, was a Brentford player back in the early 1970s. Richard was a local youngster, who in 1972 was one of the first batch of apprentice professionals taken on by the club. A tall and strong centre forward, he rose through the youth system like a blazing meteorite and made his Football League debut in February 1974 in a 2-1 victory against Lincoln City when at the tender age of sixteen years and five months, he became the second youngest player in the club's history after Alan Hawley. He had a decent run in the side and was full of energy and youthful enthusiasm. The highlight of his time at Griffin Park was scoring a beautifully taken goal against Bradford City from the edge of the penalty area, a goal which extinguished any lingering fears of re-election. Richard signed professional terms with the club and made twenty-one appearances in all but was surprisingly released in 1976 and moved to Watford where he played a handful of times before drifting out of the game.

I asked him to put some flesh on the bones about his spell at the club and why his career seemed to fizzle out so quickly after such a wonderful start, and he has been very open and forthcoming and was keen to share his memories and experiences with fellow Bees fans.

What great memories I have of Brentford, like the day when I joined the club and was right next to stars like John O'Mara, also when I made my first team debut when I was only a sixteen year old apprentice. As Brentford was my boyhood club you can imagine my excitement when I joined them, as well as my disappointment when John Docherty let me go, as I made my first team debut with him and I think one of the reasons I was released, well, that's another subject!

How did you come to join Brentford?

I lived in Heston at 80 Northfields Road and went to Berkeley School then to Spring Grove Central. At twelve years of age I signed schoolboy forms for Brentford and played in the FA Youth Cup First Round for Southall Under 18s when I was only fourteen. I got a rollicking for that from Mr. Blunstone but things really started happening for me when I played for Hounslow Schools Under 15s with some great friends like Kevin Harding and Neil Oliver. We all signed as apprentice professionals at the same time and Kevin and I then played for Hounslow Schools Under 18 team, which got through to a cup final against Hillingdon at Brentford's ground. So, warming up before the game, Kevin and I were told that we could not play as we were too young, even though we had played in all of the qualifying games. Hillingdon had complained so we were very disappointed. We learned why after the game that a certain Under 15 player of theirs could not play as he was injured, so this was their retribution. The Hillingdon player was Butch (Crab) Wilkins, yes the future Chelsea and England player. That stuck in our throat for a long time.

This was the age of David Bowie and Nazareth but as budding apprentices, well, we had a choice to make! There are so many things I could tell you. My grandfather played for Sheffield United and my father played cricket for England Youth before he decided to enlist in the Royal Belgian navy in World War 2 as he was too young and had been rejected by the British navy. I think I could do a book just about being a fifteen year-old apprentice. In 1972/73 with Brentford in the Third Division, I do remember the home friendly when Mr. Blunstone put all the squad on the team sheet for the friendly with Portsmouth, who had in their ranks one of my heroes, Ron Davies, but please do not tell him my real hero was Big John O'Mara! I will always remember him when he came back to play in Alan Hawley's Testimonial. I played the ball to him for a shot at goal and afterwards he said "Richard, next time shoot yourself, always try to score" but sadly I always made more for others than myself.

What happened after you left the club?

I did smile a lot at your comments regarding Paul Priddy's penalty saves at Watford. Did you know I played in that game for Watford and one of those penalties was awarded for a foul on me by Paul Bence and those saves finished Watford's promotion dreams? But I must say that although I was released by them that year, what a great youngster they had in our reserve team in Luther Blissett who was a great pal. I also have fond memories of Keith Mercer and lots of others and I do remember just before a Fourth Division game up North our President Elton John came out in "Rolling Stone" magazine, and I always wonder why he was banned from our dressing room! Well after leaving Watford at the end of the season I signed for the Sporting Club of Toulon in the French Second Division in 1977/78 where I played with Jean Tigana but in April 1978 I suffered a bad knee ligament injury which finished my career when I was still only twenty years of age.

I have been in France for the past thirty-seven years and had two hip and knee replacements before I was fifty and quite a few other health problems too. I do remember my league debut at home to Lincoln City in February 1974 and I still treasure the telegram I received from Alan Hawley that day, such a great man on and off the field. And yes, I scored against Bradford City in the last home game of that season with the other goal being scored by Dave Simmons. He was such a great help to me and I was so sad to learn of his death in 2007. The only thing I do regret was in my third year at Brentford when I refused Frank Blunstone's offer to join Manchester United's youth team.

Richard then went on to talk about his managers and team mates as well as some of the characters behind the scenes at Griffin Park.

There is so much I can say about Mike Everitt and Mr. Blunstone. Well Mr. Blunstone was a great manager for the years before I signed as an apprentice as well as the season when we went down to the Fourth Division. The problem from my view was Mr Piggott, not to slay him, but as apprentices, Kevin Harding and I had to take the first team training kit every Friday to the local laundromat in Brentford High Street and you can just imagine how we felt when we had to walk there! When we were in the Third Division we were given a leather bag marked with "Brentford FC" on it to put our playing kit in. Well when I was released four or five years later he asked for it back!

Anyway Mr. Blunstone used to give Kevin and I extra training sessions in the afternoon with a football, which at that time was unusual. I was so sad when he had his car accident as he used to give the apprentices a lift to the training sessions held away from Griffin Park. Mike Everitt gave me my first team chance and it was not as easy as you might remember. I got injured on my debut and came back on Easter Friday away to Colchester who were then top of the league. I played all the game and the following day we played away to Chester and I played all the second half and the following Tuesday we played Colchester at home, which I think was my best game, and it finished 0-0.

I could go on, but now looking back, there were some differences of opinion between some senior players I think and Mr. Everitt. I prefer not to say who, but I think every Brentford fan could see, in particular, a certain one who became a manager afterwards. Mr. Everitt had to fight the Gods in the Boardroom, for they awarded me appearance money when I played in the first team as well as a bonus like all the rest of the first team players. When I signed professional terms with Brentford I was earning, I think, £20 a week or a bit less, and a year after, when I was at Watford I was on £60 a week.

Yes of course I would have played for nothing for Brentford. When I made my debut that season Mr. Everitt brought some experienced players in like Jimmy Gabriel – well what more can a young sixteen year old at the time ask for? As for Stan Webb, I do think you were hard on him. He was a gentleman, always willing to help us youngsters and he always tried his best in a struggling team getting on in years and I never heard an angry word from him, and us apprentices heard a lot in our time!

When I was in my first year in France Mr. Everitt phoned me as at that time in 1977/78, Southampton wanted to sign me, but Toulon would not let me go and six months later I had my career finished by my cruciate ligament injury. In all my time at Brentford though, I am not sure there was another person who helped me more than the groundsman, John Stepney, who was very important to Brentford behind the scenes. He was always giving us advice – mostly "get off the pitch!" when we were training in the afternoons. He was a really great man.

Well that's enough for now. I've still got lots to tell about my beloved Brentford. I am still living in the Southern French Alps, but always look out for Brentford's result first and I am sorry about my English but after thirty-seven years abroad I muddle things up! Keep up with the good work on Brentford FC. Thanks once more. I'm still a BEE!

Mad Madley! – 24/8/14

Sometimes it is better to wait a little while before putting your thoughts down on paper. Time can indeed provide some perspective and also have a calming influence, so I have therefore waited the requisite cooling off period before providing my more measured thoughts on yesterday's strange happenings at Griffin Park, and you know what – I am even angrier now than I was at the time.

We first came across Robert Madley in the crucial promotion clash at Leyton Orient, late last season, when his eccentric and one-eyed refereeing display bemused and angered every Brentford fan, rabid and fair-minded alike. It was generally accepted that he only got one thing right that day, the decision to send off James Tarkowski for two silly and obvious yellow card offences. Leyton Orient were allowed to steal yards with impunity at every throw and seemed to have been granted immunity from being penalised for any offence committed that day, however cynical or serious, whilst Mr. Madley stamped down ruthlessly on any Brentford infraction.

Well the one thing you can say about Mr. Madley is that he is totally consistent given yesterday's mirror image and reprise of the Leyton Orient horror show. This time it was Birmingham City who were the grateful recipients of his largesse. Another Bees player saw red early on yesterday and you have to say that the referee got it right. Again though, in the eyes of the Brentford fans, it was pretty much his only correct decision as we will discuss later on. Tony Craig committed *hari-kari* with the perfect Triple Salchow combination of appalling defending – let the ball bounce, head it weakly back towards your own goal, and then compound your felony by putting your hands all over the striker streaking in to take advantage of the gift. In this case, Clayton Donaldson, returning to his old stamping ground, went down like the proverbial sack of spuds and Craig and Brentford suffered the ultimate penalty. Jonathan Douglas had enveloped Clayton in a playful bear hug during the pre-match ceremonial handshakes and it appeared that Tony Craig was merely following his example, but unfortunately fifteen minutes too late. Brentford were down to ten men and once Caddis put away the spot kick, they were trailing a tough, large, unsophisticated and direct Birmingham team by a goal and facing an uphill task to get anything out of the match.

Even before the goal, the referee ignored a strong penalty appeal when Gray was manhandled off the ball as a cross came into the area – *see no evil, hear no evil* appeared to be Mr. Madley's mantra – at least as far as Brentford were concerned. Brentford were poor in the latter stages of the first half, over-hitting passes, going too long and generally feeling sorry for themselves. Smith was clipped in the area but retained his balance when he could have given Mr. Madley another decision to make. On second thoughts, he probably knew what the outcome would have been, so he didn't bother to fall over! Birmingham were on top and pinged a series of dangerous crosses into the box.

Harlee Dean seized his opportunity (as indeed he had at Orient when he replaced another Brentford red card victim) and he and Tarkowski defended heroically aided as they were by Birmingham's relentless long ball barrage. The game should have been over by the interval but Thomas headed a gift chance over the bar and Button saved well from

Cotterill's curler and incredibly from a point blank header from Novak – a save that defied gravity and belief.

Harlee Dean winning another aerial challenge against Birmingham.

Birmingham started the second half in the same vein but after their early efforts came to nothing, they retreated into their shell and attempted to hold on to what they had. Manager Lee Clark also went totally Rösler-esque with his tactics, withdrawing both of his central strikers and therefore handing the initiative on a plate to Brentford. The Bees took total control for the last twenty minutes and began to threaten the Birmingham goal. Pritchard and Judge interchanged with balletic grace, half time substitute Dallas threatened with his pace and power and Douglas marauded forward like a man inspired. Gray was tireless with his clever running and forced an excellent smothering save from Randolph. The referee then returned to the spotlight when Bidwell turned in the box and an outrageous chest high tackle from Spector halted his progress. Mr. Madley pointed dramatically – for a goal kick.

Then came another turning point and a managerial masterstroke by Mark Warburton, who, unsurprisingly given the referee's performance, had been unusually animated on the bench, regularly getting into the ear of the Fourth Official. Alan McCormack had been his normal combative self, but he was replaced by Moses Odubajo who immediately stormed forward to heap more pressure on the suddenly stretched Birmingham defence, which began to creak ominously. The pressure eventually told when Grounds lost possession badly on the halfway line and Odubajo streaked away and couldn't be caught. Time seemed to stand still as he bore down on the Birmingham goal but he had the composure to dink the ball over the keeper, and the ground erupted.

One dink or two?
Moses Odubajo's coolly taken equaliser against Birmingham.

Birmingham's heads went down, their manager paced impotently on the touchline, aware that his own tactical shortcomings had hamstrung his team's chances of success. There was now going to be only one winner and the Bees went close when Dallas unleashed a swerving long-range effort that almost deceived Randolph. You could say that Brentford had got out of jail but Birmingham had missed their chances and let the Bees off the hook – and how well they took their opportunity. It was impossible at times to tell who had the extra man as Brentford's beautiful short passing game came into its element in the second half and enabled them to keep possession. This was a topsy-turvy game but the point gained was a golden one and will boost confidence to even higher levels.

The past seven days have provided a tough learning curve but Brentford have come through with flying colours and fans, management and players now know that they truly belong in the Championship. Now Fulham await, and what an enticing prospect that is! As for Mr. Madley, he has justifiably joined the pantheon of iconic horrors and pantomime villains like Norman Burtenshaw, Kevin Lynch, Keith Stroud, Andy D'Urso, Stuart Attwell and Ray Bigger in Brentford's refereeing Hall of Shame. Surely we can't have him inflicted upon us again – once a season is more than enough!

Bob Spicer – RIP – 25/8/14

I was still a bit fed up yesterday morning and kept replaying some of Saturday's key incidents in my mind whilst chuntering on about Robert Madley's refereeing horror show to anyone who would listen to me – in truth, not too many people! So, after lunch I thought it might distract me if I had a quick look through Saturday's Matchday Programme, or *Bees Review*, as it is so catchily titled now. I had stuffed it into my pocket before the kickoff and given all the distractions I had never quite got round to looking at it. When I got to page forty-seven I saw something that shocked and really upset me and rapidly forced me to forget all about Saturday's events and put such minor pinpricks firmly into perspective. There was a picture commemorating the passing of someone who I remembered extremely well and with great fondness; a man whom I had known for the greater part of my time supporting Brentford FC.

Bob Spicer had been a dedicated Brentford fan for well over fifty years and in his time supporting the club he estimated that he had seen over three thousand games involving the Bees. A truly wonderful and remarkable record. Indeed, he used to demonstrate his passion for Brentford by wearing a club badge on the lapel of his jacket. I only wish that I could tell you some interesting and pithy anecdotes about Bob and his life but I just didn't have that sort of relationship with him, and I only wish now that I had done.

I first met him many years ago when we sat near each other in Braemar Road; we would also bump into each other regularly in *Stripes*, both of us desperately trying to keep warm before a match. He was a charming, intelligent, quiet, softly spoken and thoroughly decent man, a real gentleman, in every meaning of the word. He would always ask me how I was doing and took a real interest in my family and my career, even remembering my wife and children. He was inquisitive and interested without prying and would always appear to take great delight in what I had been up to. In particular, we used to talk about New York where I had lived and worked for a few years in the 1980s. It was far harder to get Bob to open up about himself given his natural reticence and modesty but from time to time he would tell me some wonderful stories about some of the heroes and legends he had watched over his many years supporting the club.

Bob and others of his vintage are literally a dying breed and I wonder if the club or perhaps even Dave Lane and Mark Croxford, my fellow authors of *The Big Brentford Book* Series, could make a concerted effort to record some of their wonderful oral memories whilst the opportunity still exists? So Bob, I wish we had become real friends, but it was an honour and a privilege to get to know you, albeit so slightly over the years. Rest In Peace.

No Longer A Soft Touch! – 26/8/14

So Adam Forshaw is about to leave us, which means that we can finally put all this distraction behind us and move on to other matters. Wherever you stand on this issue what cannot be denied is that the Forshaw saga has dragged on interminably for the best part of a month and has undoubtedly proved to be a distraction to everybody and, despite the club's best efforts, may well even have had a detrimental effect on our preparation and unity. The fee will doubtless be *undisclosed* at the request of one or both of the clubs concerned. It will be interesting to see how long it takes before the actual figure leaks out and I can only assume that we have smashed our previous transfer record when we received two and a half million pounds from Wimbledon for Hermann Hreidarsson in October 1999. Wigan fans on social media are already suggesting that we have received an initial fee of three million pounds with another million pounds contingent on performance, plus a large sell on percentage. Inside knowledge or guesswork?

Mark Warburton stated yesterday that Wigan had finally met our valuation of the player and if these figures are anywhere near correct then I believe that we have received a realistic figure for someone who was a class above his peers and was deservedly voted Player of the Year in Division One last season. We also handled a difficult situation perfectly in my opinion and proved that we are no longer going to be a pushover and simply lie down when so-called *bigger* teams come calling coveting our stars. Warburton treated Forshaw sympathetically and with respect but basically set a boundary by putting him on gardening leave and also making it clear that he was going nowhere unless our terms were met and that only players who were fully committed to the club would be selected in the First Team.

In the past, our straightened financial circumstances, combined with our naivety in negotiating, allied to an apparently obscene eagerness to sell our players at the earliest opportunity, frequently resulted in our being short changed and receiving very little or well under market value for our prize assets. Our attitude towards player sales in the 1970s can best be summarised by these telling if resigned comments from former Brentford manager, Frank Blunstone.

Brentford would sell anyone. Ken Furphy was manager at Blackburn Rovers at the time and straight after we'd beaten them four nil at Griffin Park he came up to me and asked if I'd sell them John O'Mara. I laughed and said knowing the Chairman, "I expect so". He rang back on the Monday morning and offered £30,000 for John and off he went. One day Bill Dodgin rang me up and asked if I'd sell Roger Cross, so I had to say those words again, "I expect so, Brentford will sell anybody!"

There is also the apocryphal story that when Sheffield Wednesday manager, Jack Charlton, who coveted our star striker Andy McCulloch, made an initial bid of £60,000 for him, purely as an opening gambit, fully expecting that it would be laughed off, he was amazed when it was accepted with alacrity by the bumbling Brentford board of directors. The list of players sold at apparent knock down fees is endless with Paul Smith and DJ Campbell being just two of the more recent examples. Times have changed, we are no longer a soft touch and we are now fortunate to have the financial clout not to be in a position to have to sell anyone.

Adam Forshaw is simply a case in point. We spotted him in Everton Reserves and took a chance on him when nobody else was prepared to do so. Through the quality of our coaching and training regime and the faith we have placed in him we have helped develop him into the jewel that he has undoubtedly become. Adam will be a star and a likely Premier League starter and the only pity is that he was not prepared to stay another year with us in order to develop his game further. On the face of it his joining Wigan appears to make sense. Wigan is a club who were recently in the Premier League and are based near to his family and friends in the North West. They can afford to pay him an eye-watering salary, bolstered as they are by their Premier League Parachute Payments. He will also be reunited with Uwe Rösler who was his first manager at Brentford.

In my view, however, he is taking a risk on the Rösler regime bearing fruit and restoring Wigan to the promised land of the Premier League. Given their resources his gamble could pay off, but there is the nagging doubt that it could all go pear-shaped and Wigan might not prove to be the stepping stone that he undoubtedly wants it to be. He will also be subject to Uwe's strict rotation policy and for a player who wants and expects to play every week, he might find this frustrating. Maybe if he had been prepared to give us another year he might well have progressed sufficiently to join a Premier League club directly without the need to take this interim step.

In financial terms we have done really well out of Adam Forshaw. He came on a free transfer and whatever the percentage of the fee Everton ultimately receive (and in similar situations it is commonplace for the potential selling club to attempt to renegotiate the previously agreed sell on percentage in order to help grease the wheels for a deal to be completed) we will have made a handsome profit on him. What is more we have done what all sensible and forward thinking clubs do in similar situations and replaced him before we actually sold him.

Jon Toral will be the eventual Forshaw replacement and we will probably start to see him being eased into the team in the very near future. We also have the enticing prospect of Jota who has already impressed in his two short cameo appearances. Now is the time to draw a line under the Forshaw situation. Life goes on – and how!

A Hard Lesson Learned – 27/8/14

It is never a nice feeling when you lose a game, and a defeat to your local rivals is particularly galling. Brentford knocked on the door but were unable to make their first half dominance count, and gradually ran out of steam and ideas before subsiding to a narrow one-nil Capital One Cup defeat to Fulham. I am sure that most fans will be feeling a sense of frustration and disappointment today but it is also important, once emotions cool down, to look at things with more perspective and see the wider picture.

Fulham came into the match reeling from their four consecutive Championship defeats, but in reality their team was sharp and incisive on the night, played some lovely patient football, and created a plethora of chances. Away from the pressures of the league, they played with the shackles off and looked exactly what they are – a team packed with high quality, expensive and experienced footballers, some of whom have extensive Premier League and international experience.

Brentford will have learned much from last night, in particular the overriding need to protect and keep the ball better and to be far more incisive and clinical with their chances. For all Brentford's possession and dominance, particularly in the first half when Fulham's narrow diamond formation allowed them much space to attack down the flanks, they created very little in terms of chances and actual shots on goal and after the break, when Fulham opened up more and gained in confidence, the Bees never tested their keeper at all. The final pass has to improve, and the players need to try something more expansive in the final third of the pitch rather than just take the safe option. Defences are better and more sophisticated at this level and more guile is needed to break them down, as Brentford are beginning to learn.

In truth, whilst understanding how important this game was to the supporters in terms of local pride, Mark Warburton also needed to rest some tired and aching limbs and give much needed minutes of action and match practice to some of his squad players who were chafing at the bit. It was tough to reconcile both requirements and, indeed, something had to give. Brentford missed *big* players like Alan McCormack and in particular, Jonathan Douglas who would have provided a much needed protective barrier in front of the back four, which came under a lot of pressure. We were also denied the midfield prompting, direct running, liveliness on the ball and pure inventiveness of Alan Judge and Alex Pritchard that would surely have opened up the visitor's defence and created chances for Nick Proschwitz, who replaced Andre Gray up front. The Spanish trio of Tebar, Jota and debutant Toral played together for the first time in midfield and, at times, they shone and combined well. Toral grew into the game and his hard running and delicate ball skills look to be an enticing proposition as he gains in experience and confidence. Jota too is a real talent and had our two best efforts on goal last night.

We repeated the AFC Bournemouth three-card trick from a free kick on the edge of the box, with this time Tebar pushing the ball wide to Toral who placed an instant pass into the path of the third-man runner Jota who forced a wonderful save from the keeper. The Olé's rang around the stadium. It was a move touched with genius that deserved a goal. Inspiration matched with perspiration, and testimony indeed to hours well spent on the training ground. A clever short corner routine also opened up the Fulham rearguard on the stroke of halftime but Jota's hard low shot came back off the near post. Toral headed over too but that was really it in terms of clear chances created in the first half despite the hard running of Dallas and Odubajo's energetic overlapping from his new right wing-back position.

Fulham took over after the break. Button was alert in goal and Dean and Tarkowski dealt manfully with everything that was thrown at them. New skipper Bidwell now had his hands full but still managed to break out menacingly down our left flank. The tide was turning though, and after McCormack had a goal disallowed for offside the breakthrough finally arrived following the best move of the game. A fast exchange of low passes culminated in McCormack's one-two with David and a delicate side-footed finish past the stretching goalkeeper Button. In truth it really didn't come as a surprise and was well deserved. It was a move of high quality and the speed and timing of McCormack's run highlighted why he had cost so much money and it left Tarkowski chasing shadows.

The Bees huffed and puffed but constantly gave the ball away in the final third and dillied and dallied on the ball without getting the ball into the box. Two late chances for substitute Scott Hogan, finally making his long-awaited debut after injury, and Tommy Smith were sent narrowly over the bar from the edge of the area and that was that.

The game ended with Fulham cutting us open on the break and fully deserving their win. Had we scored early on when we were on top and Fulham were tentative and still settling into the game, then who knows, maybe we would have taken control and the Fulham heads might have gone down. As it is, the hard facts are that we still await a home win, have yet to keep a clean sheet and have gone behind in every game so far this season. As I said, a tough learning curve.

We could have made it easier for ourselves by fielding a stronger team last night, but it is a marathon and not a sprint and something had to give in terms of using the entire squad. We might be licking our wounds today but in the long run, easing the likes of Jota and Toral into the team is no bad thing. We were beaten, and it hurts to have lost the local bragging rights, but we move on and frankly the Rotherham match, on Saturday, is far more important to our season – and we will still have two more opportunities to gain some element of revenge!

The Nineties Revisited – Part One – 28/8/14

The Nineties – what a wonderful rollercoaster decade jam-packed with incident and activity and an intoxicating mixture of ups and downs. No I am not talking about events at Griffin Park, but for those few who are interested, I am referring to my own life, as it was a decade that saw the birth of my two wonderful children, the launch of my own business as I had finally realised – long after everybody else – that I was totally unemployable, and to my total amazement seeing the company take off and thrive and allow me the opportunity to deal predominantly with a variety of football, cricket and rugby clubs as well as a number of major blue-chip brands – total joy rather than hard work!

Enough of the self-indulgence and back on track – the Nineties saw a similar level of excitement for Brentford, as the club seemingly either climbed a ladder or slithered down a snake pretty much every season throughout the decade. The Nineties saw two promotions, three unsuccessful playoff campaigns and two gut-wrenching relegations, as well as the sporadic highs and lows of the Webb and Noades eras. As fans we were taken to the heights and then dropped down to the depths, and by the end of this momentous decade we ended up pretty much where we had started, back in the third tier of the Football League, but what a journey we had undertaken, one that we both relished and endured throughout this bitter sweet decade. Phil Holder took over the managerial reins after the surprise resignation of Steve Perryman and his legacy should never be diminished or forgotten, as he was the only Brentford manager since Harry Curtis to lead the team to promotion to the second tier of English football – a feat now matched, of course, by Mark Warburton. He changed the image of the club and its playing style and no longer were we a soft touch particularly away from home. He inherited a wonderful platform from his former Spurs colleague but he moulded the team into one that was the antithesis of the diminutive manager, a ball playing midfielder during his own career at Spurs and Crystal Palace.

We were big and tough and very hard to beat and in Dean Holdsworth, Gary Blissett, Marcus Gayle and the immortal Neil Smillie we had a front four to fear. Perhaps the Asaba, Forster, Taylor, Bent axis in those heady early days of the 1996/97 season comes close but for me Holder's Heroes were the best front four we have had in my time supporting the club. Yes, we relied extensively on set pieces and long balls with the midfield often ignored, but we could also play, particularly in the opponents' final third and 1991/92 was a season of total pride, joy and excitement as we timed our late run perfectly, came up on the rails, and took the title on that unforgettable final day of the season at Peterborough. I can still taste the horrendously expensive bottle of Perrier-Jouet champagne that I contentedly glugged down to celebrate this massive achievement. I might not have bothered had I known then what was to happen the following season!

We threw away our hard-earned higher status after a catastrophic season of cock-ups on the pitch, in the dugout and in the boardroom culminating in the final day capitulation at Bristol City which saw a relegation that never should have happened. Everybody was to blame! The memories are still painful as I believe that we had the ammunition but not the vision or foresight to remain and then consolidate in that division. This was a massive opportunity thrown away and I will just touch on the following and allow others to fill in the details:

- Murray Jones
- Bigger
- Buying Joe Allon rather than Stan Collymore
- The opening day injury to colossus Terry Evans, and wasn't it great to see him back on the Griffin Park pitch on Tuesday when he became a worthy member of the Brentford Hall of Fame
- Missing key penalty kicks – now where have I heard that one before?
- Marcus Gayle's season-defining late open goal misses against Newcastle and Sunderland
- Making late, irrelevant panic buys perhaps better suited to Masters Football

I could go on, but I will digress: I heard a story that apparently came from a Charlton Athletic player who performed at Birmingham City on the final day of that calamitous season. Birmingham needed to win to escape the drop and Charlton had nothing to play for. We had long since raised the white flag at Ashton Gate and were relying upon our fellow Londoners to do us a massive favour and save us from relegation. No such luck, as allegedly the Charlton team who had dominated a scoreless first half at St Andrew's were warned by a senior policeman, who came uninvited into their dressing room at the interval, that their safety could not be guaranteed if they won. That was the end of the visitors' threat and a late horrendously offside goal from Paul Moulden allowed by officials perhaps intimidated by the vociferous crowd sent us down. A farcical end to a farcical season, and one that we took years to recover from.

Nearly twenty years on I have just about come through the trauma of Brentford missing out on promotion in 1994/95. The one season that only one team received automatic promotion owing to League re-organisation – and guess who finished second? It's Brentford Innit! Yet we had only ourselves to blame, The FT Index rained goals at Griffin Park but a late season hiccup at home where we allowed relegation-haunted Chester and Bournemouth to snatch vital points and a capitulation at St Andrew's – yes Birmingham again – allowed our arch rivals to snatch the title, much as we had three years earlier. Frankly, we choked and have nobody else to blame except ourselves. I shall draw a veil over Bob Taylor's miss at Huddersfield and the penalties at Griffin Park, as my psyche cannot take it even so long after the event. Shortly I will take a deep breath and continue my review of this tumultuous decade. Now pass me the tranquillisers please!

Still A Bee! – Part Two – 29/8/14

Richard Poole was a local boy made good who succeeded in playing for the team he had supported from childhood. He retains affection for Brentford and fond memories of his spell at the club, to this day. It doesn't really get any better than that does it? And, in truth, isn't it exactly what we all hoped and dreamed would happen to us? Some of us continue to have the same pipe dream to this day, even if youth, a flat stomach and what modicum of football ability we once possessed are all long gone.

For my part, my hopes of football fame and fortune turned to dust and received a firm reality check one unforgettable autumn's day back in 1972. I was a decent young goalkeeper who had played at a reasonable and respectable level for Corinthian Casuals and had trials for the Great Britain Maccabi Games team, but I was small and a bit frail and, if truth be told, a bit too keen on self-preservation so was totally unprepared and unable to cope with the physicality of the massive Scotland International striker Hugh Curran who turned my trial at Oxford United into a personal nightmare. He bashed me around unceremoniously throughout the entire morning and then thumped some twenty-yard howitzers that I barely saw, grateful indeed that I hadn't got a touch to them as they whistled past me. To be honest, he did me a favour as he disabused me totally of any misconceptions that I could compete at this level. It really was a totally different game to the one I was used to! I learned the hard way about the gaping chasm in ability, speed of thought and fitness between a talented amateur and a seasoned professional and I now totally understand why it is that so few of the multitude of faceless trialists who seek their fame and fortune every preseason actually have their dreams realised and fulfilled.

As for Richard Poole, it was very sad to discover that his early promise and enthusiasm were largely unfulfilled as injury cost him the career that he deserved and at one time promised to have. Fate had dealt him some heavy blows as it seemed odds on, at one point, that he would become a star, but it just wasn't meant to be once fate took a hand. Rather than being bitter and twisted as would have been totally understandable, Richard comes over as a positive, modest and well-rounded man who has made a new life for himself abroad, got on with things and ignored everything that life has thrown at him in terms of injury and illness. He sent me a few additional memories of his life and times at Brentford:

I remember like it was only yesterday. Brentford had just gone up to the Third Division and they had this Open Day in July at Feltham Arena. I had my fifteenth birthday and the Friday was my last day at school. The Summer holidays were here and I said good-bye to my school friends (and my girlfriend too) and the following day I was a proud fifteen year old apprentice at my Brentford, and all my schoolboy dreams of playing and scoring for Brentford were coming true. How little did I know that a mere six years later my dreams would be in tatters.

I well remember the photo of Jesse Willard and Mike Everitt consoling me after I was injured on my debut by Ian Branfoot as he clobbered me from behind and it really hurt me. Mr. Blunstone used to tell me that when I was clattered I should just get up and smile, and most of the time I did. I think Mr. Branfoot remembered my first tackle in my debut game where he ended up in the stand. Andy Woon came on after I was hurt and I think Mr. Branfoot will remember the game well as my team mates paid him back, but the only important thing to me was that my Brentford won the game by two goals to one. I loved the comment from another fan who has kept a programme from my debut which is signed by the young man himself – well this young man is now fifty-seven years old, but it does still go to my heart that real fans still remember me.

As I said, I could go on and on. In my few years with the club I had great times as well as some that were not so good.

At the time money was not as important and even now I am sure there are youngsters out there who want nothing more than to play for their local team. I hope their dreams come true. Mine did for a while and that can never be taken from me. To me it was just like being Roy of the Rovers but it was Richard Poole playing for Brentford – yes a Fourth Division team – but my team.

I would like to thank Mr.Brown and Mr.Tyler, two neighbours who took me to Brentford games when I was a young boy, as well as to say sorry to my young brother who, when he was very young, had to come to all those away games when Brentford Reserves played at places like Southend, Peterborough and Cambridge City on cold and wet Wednesday nights because my mother and father followed me everywhere, may they rest in peace. And thank you Mr.Waterman for helping me relive these memories, even the hard ones. So to all true Brentford fans – come on the Bees!

It's Academic Mr Reeves – 30/8/14

So it's farewell to Jake Reeves who has just had his contract terminated by mutual consent after making forty-seven appearances for the club. Personally, I think that this is the correct decision as, at twenty-one years of age, Jake needs to play every week in order to continue his development and prove himself as a football league calibre player. Unfortunately, our progress has left him behind and he was highly unlikely to be anything other than an emergency replacement given our strength in midfield. Taking into account the still awaited departure of Adam Forshaw, Jake was probably our eighth choice central midfielder behind Douglas, Tebar, Toral, Jota, Judge, Pritchard and Diagouraga.

The competition for places is fearsome and he has lost out in the battle. But that is not to say that he has been a failure. Perish the thought! For any youngster to come through the Academy system, sign a professional contract and actually get to play in the Football League is a massive achievement and not one to be denigrated. No more than ten percent of all youngsters who join Academies get to the point where they are offered professional terms, and of those lucky ones, only a tiny fraction ever make it to the First Team.

Jake arrived at Brentford at the age of sixteen from the Tottenham system and found a great supporter in Uwe Rösler. He played well against Stoke City in a preseason friendly back in 2011 and was in the First Team squad for three years. The weight of expectation was on him and he often delivered. Supporters did not take into account his tender years and lack of experience and perhaps expected too much of him too soon. He needed to get into the rhythm of first team football but was rarely given the opportunity of a run in the team when he might have gained in confidence and been able to fully express himself and demonstrate his burgeoning talent. He sometimes looked like he was trying too hard and forcing things in an attempt to influence the game and make an immediate impression when he came on as a substitute. Jonathan Douglas too, a formidable performer, occupied his preferred spot in front of the back four, and was not to be moved or swept aside. Jake, though, more than held his own when given the opportunity.

I well remember his wonderful performance at Sheffield United in that crazy match at the end of the 2012/13 season where he dominated proceedings and pinged any number of defence splitting passes. He was a true quarterback that evening and he looked like an experienced and battle-hardened veteran rather than the inexperienced tyro he really was.

Jake goes to Swindon with the good wishes of all Brentford supporters ringing in his ears. He was one of ours and almost made it with us, but our progress was too much for him to keep up with and the time had come for us to part. Our standards have risen exponentially over the past three years and only the cream of the crop will now have the ability to make it at Griffin Park.

League Table – 30/8/14

Position	Team	P	W	D	L	F	A	GD	Pt	Form
1	Nottingham Forest	5	4	1	0	11	3	8	13	W D W W W
2	Watford	5	4	0	1	13	6	7	12	W L W W W
3	Wolverhampton Wndrs	5	4	0	1	6	2	4	12	W L W W W
4	Norwich City	5	3	1	1	8	3	5	10	L W W W D
5	Millwall	5	3	1	1	6	3	3	10	W W D L W
6	Charlton Athletic	5	2	3	0	9	7	2	9	D W W D D
7	Derby County	5	2	2	1	9	5	4	8	W D L W D
8	**Brentford**	5	2	2	1	6	4	2	8	D L W D W
8	Cardiff City	5	2	2	1	6	4	2	8	D W W L D
10	Sheffield Wednesday	5	2	2	1	5	4	1	8	W D D W L
11	Bournemouth	5	2	1	2	9	6	3	7	W W L L D
12	Wigan Athletic	5	2	1	2	8	5	3	7	D L L W W
13	Brighton and Hove A	5	2	1	2	6	5	1	7	L L W W D
14	Blackburn Rovers	5	2	1	2	8	10	-2	7	D W L W L
15	Reading	5	2	1	2	5	8	-3	7	D W L L W
16	Middlesbrough	5	2	0	3	6	6	0	6	W L W L L
17	Rotherham United	5	2	0	3	2	5	-3	6	L W L W L
18	Leeds United	5	2	0	3	3	8	-5	6	L W L L W
19	Ipswich Town	5	1	2	2	5	6	-1	5	W L D L D
20	Birmingham City	5	1	2	2	4	9	-5	5	L W D D L
21	Huddersfield Town	5	1	1	3	6	13	-7	4	L L W D L
22	Bolton Wanderers	5	0	1	4	4	10	-6	1	L D L L L
23	Fulham	5	0	1	4	3	10	-7	1	L L L L D
24	Blackpool	5	0	0	5	3	9	-6	0	L L L L L

SEPTEMBER

Wake Me Up – I Think I'm Dreaming – 2/9/14

I still sometimes find it hard to believe everything that has been happening at Brentford FC. Is that really my team, little old Brentford, that has, in the space of three short years, been transformed into what is probably one of the best run, most ambitious and progressive clubs in the country? A club that is beginning to establish itself in the Championship, plays a beautiful short passing style of positive, attacking football and possesses a burgeoning Academy system that is the envy of its rivals.

Surely not, and I fully expect to wake up one morning and find out that it was all a dream and a product of my wishful thinking, and that in reality we remain in twelfth place in Division One and are looking forward to our next match at home to Walsall with Charlie MacDonald and Gary Alexander plodding away together upfront. But it is all true, and yesterday's activity simply reinforced how well organised we are at the moment.

Poor Scott Hogan had no sooner managed to get himself fit after his niggling ankle injury when his studs caught in the turf shortly after he made his Championship debut as a substitute late on in Saturday's victory at Rotherham and he went down with nobody else anywhere near him. It looked bad at the time and first reports from the club's Medical Team have confirmed that it is a serious injury to his left knee. This is an awful blow to a young player who was looking to make the most of his opportunity and hopefully he will make a complete and speedy recovery. Even before the loss of Scott I felt we were light in numbers up front.

Andre Gray was establishing himself as first choice as the lone striker employed in our 4-1-4-1 formation, with Nick Proschwitz covering on the bench. Montell Moore had appeared briefly, but despite his raw talent he needs time to develop. At Blackpool we had been reduced to using Tommy Smith as an emergency striker late in the second half. An interesting move that ended up with us adopting a unique 4-6-0 formation as we clung on to our win. We therefore needed to replace Scott Hogan as quickly as possible but, particularly given the international break, I fully expected that we would wait until the loan window reopened next week before making our move. I should have known better! That would have been so *Old Brentford* – instead we went out yesterday and made yet another incredible signing that none of us saw coming.

Betinho, a young Portugal Under 21 international striker from Sporting Lisbon was signed on loan until the end of the season. A player with a boggling 60 million Euro release clause, he was yet another prospect who impressed Mark Warburton in the Next Gen competition and - from what footage you can find on YouTube - he looks like he is an amazing young talent with a real eye for goal. We must allow him time to settle and ideally minimise our immediate expectations, but we might just have hit the jackpot. Congratulations are due yet again to Frank McParland and his recruitment team who acted so swiftly, efficiently, and, most importantly, so quietly. We don't make a fuss about our transfer dealings these days, unlike other clubs, in particular one in the North West that I'm far too polite to mention. We keep things confidential and operate under the radar, and very little seems to leak out in advance. Frustrating that might be for all us fans who love transfer gossip and speculation, but it is the right way to conduct your business. I think it is fair to say that apart from Alan Judge, who was always going to be a prime target, the identity of all our signings remained a secret until they were done deals. In today's world of social media and camera phones that is quite some achievement.

We have managed to secure twelve, yes twelve, new signings of a quality pretty much unheard of since perhaps the mid thirties – and no, my memory does not go back quite that far! We now have three high calibre Spanish players and one Portuguese, and, by the way, doesn't it seem weird to have players who are known by one name only in Jota and now Betinho. We really are in the big time now!

Assuming the new players gel, and some of them might well need some time to settle down in a new environment, I feel that we have every chance of establishing ourselves as a real force in this new division. Alan Judge, Alex Pritchard, Andre Gray, Moses Odubajo, Marcos Tebar, Jota, Jon Toral, Scott Hogan, Nick Proschwitz, Tommy Smith, Daniel O'Shaughnessy and now, Betinho. That is quite an assembly of talent!

The Nineties Revisited – Part Two – 4/9/14

In the first part of my Nineties overview, I had to stop after 1995, as I was still traumatised by the lasting memory of how we first threw automatic promotion away and then compounded matters by blowing it in the playoffs. They say that history repeats itself, and they are words that are never truer when it comes to describing Brentford's fortune, or lack of it, in the Nineties.

After a nothing sort of season in 1995/96, where we suffered a massive hangover after the previous year's disappointment, livened up solely by a magnificent FA Cup victory at Norwich City, the following year saw yet another lost opportunity. In January 1997 we were well clear and comfortable at the top of the league, and looked destined for automatic promotion. Being Brentford, we then shot ourselves in the foot, totally collapsed, and finally limped into the playoffs after a second half of the season downfall following the sale of top scorer Nicky Forster to, where else, Birmingham City, in a transfer that surely merited a stewards' enquiry. David Webb promised an instant replacement of similar pedigree – we are still waiting David – and we ended up with Steve Slade, a journeyman striker from QPR, whose loan spell promised little and produced less. Top scorer Carl Asaba was then mysteriously moved to the left wing from his centre forward berth where he had terrorised the opposition. What on earth was going on? Answers on a postcard please.

The only surprise was that a team seemingly dead on its feet, somehow revitalised itself in the playoffs and beat favourites Bristol City home and away, and looked good in the process. Does anyone else remember Gus Hurdle's beautiful curling cross at Ashton Gate, which was sublimely converted by Bob Taylor with a glancing header? As for the embarrassment of our total non-performance at Wembley, where we had a wonderful first two minutes of total domination, and then gently subsided, with Carl Hutchings playing Crewe seemingly on his own, words almost fail me. We suffered the indignity of the biggest one-nil thrashing in history, had a player sent off in the process and we lost a lot of supporters that sad day, who were totally disillusioned by what they had seen.

The core of the team was immediately dismantled and largely decamped in a fire sale to Gillingham, and the aftermath of the disastrous Webb takeover saw a team of has-beens, journeymen and non-league nonentities bumble its way to inevitable relegation in another season marked by anger, disillusionment and eventual fan revolt. Richard Goddard, Leon Townley, Simon Spencer and Ricky Reina, anybody? Our stars were Charlie Oatway, Kevin Rapley, Graeme Hogg and Glenn Cockerill, which just about says it all. I well remember the fall guys in Eddie May and Micky Adams who were left holding the baby after the heart of the team had been ripped out. They both ended up trying to make bricks without straw given the dog's dinner of a squad they were stuck with, and they were rewarded with the sack. The only surprise is that we took it until the last game of the season before relegation was confirmed. An appalling season both on and off the field, where the only redeeming factor was the action of the supporters who banded together to demonstrate their fury at what was going on, and their determination not to put up with it.

Who was to ride to our rescue on his white charger but Ron Noades, and the decade ended on a high with a promotion based on the acquisition of several young, vibrant, talented youngsters from non-league football and the incredible record purchase of Hermann Hreidarsson. After the sterility of the football in the previous season what a pleasure it was to watch exciting young players like Darren Powell, Lloyd Owusu, Gavin Mahon and Martin Rowlands leavened by the more experienced Warren Aspinall and Paul Evans. At this time of understandable euphoria few looked at the small print, and little did we know how the Noades era was to end and who was actually paying for his *investment*.

It was an exhausting and exhilarating decade where we were blessed to see some of the best and worst players to have graced Griffin Park since the war. Strikers of the calibre of Dean Holdsworth, Gary Blissett, Nicky Forster, Bob Taylor, Carl Asaba and Lloyd Owusu contrasted with the likes of Murray Jones, Matthew Metcalf, Drewe Broughton, Leo Fortune-West and Julian Charles who were perhaps less prolific to say the least! The heroics of Graham Benstead, and, yes, I was one of the few who watched his gravity-defying three penalty saves that frozen night against Wrexham, and the consistency of the amazing Flying Pig Kevin Dearden. And let's also remember Ashley Bayes – *another nonsense from Ashley Bayes* as the feckless, overmatched young keeper committed yet another offence against reason or belief against Brighton, Luton or Spurs. I am glad that the once poor, hapless Ashley Bayes recovered from his traumatic start and became a survivor who had a long and respected career. He even made a decent return to Griffin Park for Conference South Basingstoke in an FA Cup tie three years ago and received a warm welcome as indeed, he fully deserved to.

So many players, so many incidents, so many memories to conjure with, but I will end by briefly touching on the enigma and would-be genius that was Tony Folan and mourn what might have been had he gone some way towards fulfilling his boundless potential. For whatever reason, it was not meant to be. I can still clearly picture in my mind that outrageous long range lobbed winner that settled a key promotion tussle against Cambridge United and his unforgettable slow motion dribble against Peterborough. And yes – I still hate Birmingham City.

Keeping In Touch – 5/9/14

I've been away for the past few days and my wife and I have been fortunate enough to have been sunning ourselves on the beach near Marbella. We normally go there in early October, but needed to reschedule at the last minute when my wife learned that one of her sculptures had been accepted into a forthcoming exhibition at The Mall Gallery. For those of you already losing interest – don't worry, I am about to get back on track.

I naturally went into a panic when she suggested going away in late August instead, as I was desperate not to miss any Brentford home games at such a crucial time in a new season full of hope, excitement and new challenges. Marriage is all about compromise, letting the tiddlers go, and picking your fights extremely carefully. Was missing a Brentford match worth having an argument over? Do I really need to answer that question?

In truth, I was quite prepared to miss the trip to Rotherham, having suffered through that miserable hiding last season, the interminable drive home in the early hours of the morning, and the resultant teasing from a Millers-supporting friend of mine who lives nearby. Actually, he really wasn't in the least bit arrogant or obnoxious after the result, but instead, he was rather apologetic and solicitous – an attitude that I found far more patronising and annoying than if he had jumped up and down in front of me celebrating his team thrashing the Bees. Anyway, it was agreed that I would miss the Rotherham match, but what about the following week? And that's when the advantage of being in the Championship really sank in.

There was going to be an international break immediately after the Rotherham game, and we didn't have a fixture for another two weeks. It honestly took quite a while for this fact to sink in and fully compute, as I am really not used to discussing Brentford FC and international breaks in the same sentence. My first problem was therefore solved.

I wouldn't miss a home match during my holiday and I was prepared to compromise and give up the dubious delights of a trip to Yorkshire for the sake of marital harmony. That led directly to the next obstacle. How best to stay in touch with what was happening at Griffin Park during my absence? Fortunately I was spoiled for choice. Things have certainly changed for the better in recent years given the massive improvements and developments in communication technology.

Back in the early 1980s, I made what turned out to be a life-changing decision to move to New York City. I ended up missing the majority of what were, in truth, three pretty drab seasons, and in those now unimaginable pre-internet days, I was sent carefully folded copies of *The Middlesex Chronicle*, lovingly dispatched by my Mother, to bring me up to speed, about a week or so late, on what was happening at the club. Like all other football loving expats, I had to rely upon the elusive *BBC World Service*, and do my utmost to track down the dulcet and unmistakable tones of Paddy Feeny who hosted *Sportsworld* every Saturday. The problem was it constantly changed frequencies throughout the afternoon and was almost impossible to keep tuned into, even with the expensive shortwave radio I was forced to purchase. The coverage also tended to cut out, invariably at exactly the wrong time, whilst the final scores were being broadcast. I once managed to catch the hardly credible words *Brentford Four* and floated on air until the belated arrival of the English Sunday newspapers two days later confirmed that we had, in fact, only drawn at Scunthorpe.

The arrival and widespread use of the internet around the turn of the century totally revolutionised how we learned how our team had done. I remember many hurried visits to internet cafes in places such as Florida, New York and Cyprus during a variety of family holidays, some with positive outcomes, but given the poverty of our away record, mostly not. Times have changed and I've had a total information overload since I've been in Spain. Luddite that I am, I have yet to get Bees Player to work on my iPad. Frankly, despite the undoubted skill of Mark Burridge, Luis Melville and Billy Reeves I cannot bear to listen to live match commentary of Brentford games. Every time the ball goes into our half I can picture it about to enter our net and it just does my head in.

On Saturday, I managed to keep in touch with the remarkable happenings at Rotherham despite a dodgy Wi-Fi connection, thanks to a combination of *BBC Radio London* via the incredible TuneIn Radio app, and a series of texts from Northampton Bee. Pure agony and totally draining though. Hoping against hope that my phone wouldn't ping, or that the presenter wouldn't announce: *There's been late drama at Rotherham*. In fact he did, and, resigned to my fate, I heard instead the miraculous and totally unexpected news of our second goal. Far better than last year when our stay coincided with three defeats in an horrendous week, to Rotherham, Peterborough and Stevenage respectively. Not, of course, that I allowed this appalling sequence of results to spoil my holiday in the slightest!

All this week I have had the wonderfully opinionated and comprehensive *Griffin Park Grapevine* to provide me with my daily fix of all things Brentford. I have been able to wallow in its unparalleled coverage of match reports, transfer deadline gossip, the signing of Betinho, the departure of Adam Forshaw, moans about the venue and price of tickets for the 125th Anniversary Dinner, injury updates about poor Scott Hogan, the thoughts of trolls, bores, bigots and sages alike, and finally, club owner Matthew Benham participating in a surreal and probably unique Q&A session with supporters. Truly, something for everyone.

In the interests of marital harmony I've had to seriously restrict my time on the GPG over the past week and also barely managed to visit the Beesotted Message Board. Despite my distance from the heart of the action in what was a frenetic week, I was able to keep myself fully informed and up-to-speed thanks to the wonders of modern technology. Tomorrow we are on our way home, tanned and replete, and I am looking forward to a quiet week ahead of total inactivity at Griffin Park. After the week I've just experienced, even from long distance, I think I need a holiday!

How Others See Us – 10/9/14

Yesterday I came across this excerpt from an interview with Mike Calvin about his highly regarded book *The Nowhere Men* which covers the crucial role scouts play in discovering emerging football talent.

Q. Which of the many set-ups discussed in "The Nowhere Men" impressed you most and why?

Personally, I felt the team of Matthew Benham and Miguel Rios at Brentford came across particularly well.

A. Brentford surprised me, because what I discovered defied the perception of the club. I was hugely impressed by the work done at all levels. Interestingly, Miguel and Mark Warburton, who is now manager, come from a City trading background. That makes them more inclined to think laterally and differently. At Academy level, the human chemistry between Shaun O'Connor and Ose Aibangee, who are different characters, really works. This is a club operating to a long term strategy: much of that is down to owner Matt Benham, who is a fan, but also utilises his professional experience and perspective.

Doesn't it just make you feel proud to read about your team described in such glowing terms? In fact, such positive coverage about Brentford has come to be the norm rather than the exception over the past year or so. Just the other day, Mark Warburton and Orient manager Russell Slade were the guests on *Goals On Sunday* on Sky Sports, and the pair of them, looking like a combination of Uncle Fester and the Mitchell Brothers, did their clubs proud, speaking with eloquence, humour, and common sense about their roles and experiences.

Mark Warburton's unique City Trader background and his unusual route into coaching and management, whilst old hat now to us seasoned Brentford fans, continues to be a source of interest, and indeed wonder to the media. Recently Henry Winter wrote a highly perceptive and favourable profile of the Brentford manager in the Daily Telegraph (http://tinyurl.com/onjdkg9) which highlighted Warburton's ethos and how his previous career has really helped him, given the similarities in approach between managing traders and young footballers.

Brentford have suddenly become fashionable, if not actually trendy. I first noticed this around the time of the Chelsea FA Cup tie last January when the newspapers were suddenly filled with articles which recognised our progress under Uwe Rösler. Rösler was portrayed in the media as a well-spoken, intelligent young manager on the move, and I am sure his media presence helped make him better known and more attractive to the bigger fish. Since succeeding Rösler at the helm, Mark Warburton has also become something of a media attraction, and is increasingly being sought out for his well thought out and considered views on the game, and to explain his unique approach to man management. He comes over well on television apart from his annoying tendency to mumble and speak too quickly, but he will improve with more practice. All of this coverage is totally to the benefit of the club, which is now increasingly seen and perceived as forward thinking, ambitious and well run.

How the times have changed! Can you imagine the media of the time trying to get any sense or soundbites out of former managers such as the monosyllabic Malcolm MacDonald or the more loquacious but totally unintelligible Jimmy Sirrel?

Given the way the club has transformed itself over the past three years it is not surprising that it has recently attracted many players who are also highly intelligent, with minds and opinions of their own. Richard Lee has written a well-received book on the psychology of goalkeeping, and his sharp and astute comments receive a regular airing in the local media. Sam Saunders has managed to occupy himself during his long injury layoff by providing expert and pithy analysis for Bees Player, and now Sky Sports too, and Kevin O'Connor always adds value to any match he commentates on.

Things have moved a long way from my time on Bees Player, trying my hardest to coax interesting and coherent comments from the likes of the shy and tongue-tied Leon Legge! Not forgetting media darling Natalie Sawyer, star of Sky Sports News and now their Football League coverage, who is never slow to make her allegiance to the Bees known to viewers or on-screen guests alike.

The one name missing is, of course, that of reclusive and media shy club owner Matthew Benham. To my knowledge has never been the subject of an in-depth profile or interview. Indeed, until recently, it was almost impossible to even find a photograph of him, and the club owner was able to stand on the terraces without fear of being recognised. Brentford has traditionally been a small club, an underdog even, punching above its weight. That will surely change, as the club's success secrets are now becoming common knowledge in and around the game.

International Bees – Part One – 12/9/14

It has been another good week for Brentford as their burgeoning reputation was further recognised on the international front with Alex Pritchard making his debut for the England Under 21 team with two successful substitute appearances. Young reserve central defender, Daniel O'Shaughnessy, also started twice for Finland Under 21s, scoring a well-taken goal against San Marino; Stuart Dallas had to return home early through injury; and Will Grigg gathered splinters, sitting on the bench for Northern Ireland throughout their victory over Hungary.

I fully realise that Alex Pritchard is likely to be our player for only a limited period of time, given how highly he is regarded by Spurs, but it made my heart sing to read the England team sheet for both the Lithuania and Moldova matches and see the words *Pritchard (Brentford)*. This is how far we have come in a short period of time. What is totally beyond doubt is that given our new Championship status, we have totally upgraded the quality of our player recruitment and it is now pretty much the rule, rather than the exception, for most of the squad to have earned international honours at some level or other.

Looking back, I well remember the days when were in awe at the likes of Ashley Bayes, Danis Salman and Marcus Gayle who all won England Youth international caps, and, as a young child, I always used to glow with pride when I read about our former goalkeeper

Gerry Cakebread being twice selected as a reserve for the England Under 23 squad, as it was at the time, way back in the 1950s. It was often said of him that if he hadn't remained a part time professional, spending his workdays poring over charts at the Admiralty, then he might well have won full international honours for his country. Who knows if that was really the truth or merely the exaggerated comments of a supportive local journalist, but it was obvious that Gerry was far more talented than was the norm at the club.

I was far too young to see him play, or indeed the all-star international strike force of Johnny Brooks, Billy McAdams and John Dick from the early sixties, but for all their talent and short term success, it was patently obvious that they were all well over the hill and, indeed, coming down the other side. Mel Scott, I certainly recall as a cultured centre half, who I could well believe had played for the Under 23 team whilst at Chelsea, and there was enough about Ian Lawther, a real favourite of Peter Gilham, to understand why he had previously earned four caps for Northern Ireland as a bustling striker. But, as you can see, internationals were in short supply in those days, as we had to cut our cloth accordingly, and rely on a combination of experienced journeymen professionals and local talent.

Brian Turner does come to mind, a combative attacking midfielder who arrived via Chelsea and Portsmouth and who should be known to all Brentford fans as *The Nearly Man*, as it was his low drive that thumped against the Hull City post and came within a whisker of putting the Bees two goals up, and on their way to the Sixth Round of the FA Cup. Turner won over one hundred caps, and was an integral part of the New Zealand team in the 1982 World Cup Finals.

That fact leads me onto the obvious question, and my quiz for today: How many other former Brentford players have appeared in the final stages of either the World Cup or European Championship? I will be charitable and allow former loanees too. My starter is the recent and obvious one of Wojciech Szczęsny. I hope you can all do better than that!

Other internationals who played for Brentford in the 1970s were Jimmy Gabriel, a combative Scottish midfielder who was coming to the end of the road after a long spell at Everton and Bill Glazier, a former England Under 23 international goalkeeper, although you would never have known it given how awfully he performed in that Football League Cup tie at Old Trafford. Going up the ladder, rather than down the snake, were Stewart Houston, a cultured left back, initially played as a striker alongside John O'Mara, who was soon to become a full Scotland international after his move to Manchester United, and Jim McNichol, who added to his tally of Scotland Under 21 caps whilst at Griffin Park. A mention too for Canadian international striker Gordon Sweetzer, another one who blazed like a meteor across Griffin Park before fizzling out far too early.

The 80s saw former England international and maverick, Stan Bowles, grace Griffin Park and his performances and, indeed, commitment to the cause, live long in the memory. Terry Hurlock, his combative midfield partner, went on to win England B honours after leaving Brentford and was a devastating combination of brains and brawn, and I think he has been underrated even to this day. Winger Gary Roberts earned one Wales Under 21 cap but rather under-performed in his career given his ability to ghost in undetected towards the opposition goal.

Other experienced former internationals such as Ron Harris (England Under 23), Ian Davies (Wales), Ian Stewart (Northern Ireland) and Eire internationals Paddy Roche, Henry Hughton (Under 21) and Jimmy Holmes all played a lesser role in the 80s. Roche was a brilliant keeper on his day and a wonderful shot stopper but his day didn't come along too often and he lacked consistency.

How about a mention for Northern Ireland international Tom Finney, surely one of the most unpopular players ever to play for the club? I can still remember the home fans booing him for his overly-robust tackling against Bishops Stortford in the FA Cup. Paul Merson had a brief loan spell with us whilst he was still a teenager. He looked a class act in the making even if he persisted in missing gilt-edged chances to score. Roger Joseph (England B), and Andy Sinton were truly excellent players who both went on to win international recognition after they left Brentford, and Steve Perryman still looked a class player whenever he decided to pick himself, always finding that yard of space or extra second on the ball.

My personal favourite was Graham Rix, holder of seventeen full England caps, who showed supreme quality and a magic left foot during a highly productive loan spell in December 1987. I have always thought that Dean Holdsworth might have won more than a solitary England B cap given his excellent scoring record over his long career, and the decade ended with several other Bees internationals in sweeper John Buttigieg, who failed to impress Phil Holder despite his ninety-seven caps for Malta, another disappointment in Eddie May (Scotland Under 21) and the emergence of Marcus Gayle. Gayle was capped by England at Under 17 level but later decided to switch allegiance and play for Jamaica who he was eligible to represent through his father. He eventually represented Jamaica at the 1998 World Cup Finals.

As for the worst future international to play for the Bees in the 80s? Without a shadow of doubt it was Les Ferdinand who made three appalling loan appearances in March 1988 and was a shadow of the fearsome striker he eventually became.

Pride! – 14/9/14

I saw a wonderful film last night. *Pride* tells the remarkable true story of how a group of lesbians and gays selflessly raised funds to support the Welsh miners who were suffering from the hardships caused by the knock-on effects of the Miners' Strike thirty years ago. They overcame scepticism, prejudice and downright aggression from all parties, including the very people who they were trying to help, but they persisted, and through a combination of bravery, persistence and sheer bloody-mindedness they were eventually accepted and recognised for all their selfless and incredible efforts. It was a heart-warming film that focused on human endeavour and kindness, and how people can work together to break down barriers, overcome obstacles and eventually triumph. I am not afraid to say that it moved me to tears.

Pride is also the word that I want to use to illustrate exactly how I feel after watching Brentford's victory over Brighton, as there are, I believe, so many parallels between the film and what we witnessed at Griffin Park yesterday. The three-two scoreline and the brief match facts that will follow, in my opinion, go nowhere near to explaining either the significance or indeed symbolism of what yesterday really meant or represented. More of that later though.

The Bees made one change from the team that won at Rotherham last time out with Moses Odubajo replacing Stuart Dallas who had been injured whilst on international duty. This was a massive decision by Mark Warburton and one that was to have a huge influence on the game. For the first fifteen minutes Brighton passed and pressed us to death. We couldn't cope with their movement and skill on the ball and were left chasing shadows. We didn't help ourselves with some sloppiness and one particularly horrendous error when Alan McCormack sent a quick throw in directly across the face of his own goal, beyond the reach of the straining Harlee Dean, and Croft's instant and fulminating volley from twenty yards hit the post and bounced the right way for the Bees. Tarkowski also cleared off the line from Baldock when he had rounded Button and should have scored.

Fortunate not to be dead and buried after a start reminiscent of the one against Birmingham, we woke up and came alive. Douglas dummied and Gray shot through the gap before being manhandled by Dunk just outside the box. Surely a clear goal-scoring opportunity but referee Steve Martin only brandished yellow when everybody, including the Brighton manager, and I suspect the player himself, expected red. Jota's free kick inched past the post but we then took the lead with a goal that personified where we are now as a team.

Judge looked up in the centre circle and picked out Moses Odubajo's run inside the dozing full back with a fifty-yard pass that was truly a Hoddle-esque thing of beauty. The pass deserved a goal and Moses took instant control, held off two challenges and hit a perfect angled shot just inside the far post. We were ahead for the first time at home this season, totally against the run of play, but for the next twenty minutes we took the visitors apart by playing an exuberant brand of one-touch passing football that really had to be seen to be believed. Douglas won everything. Pritchard and Judge worked tirelessly and dribbled and passed to perfection.

Jota for the first time showed us what he will bring to the team. He is a will-o'-the-wisp combining pure skill and vision, and he is not afraid to do his share of hard graft either. He switched flanks with Moses who then put on the afterburners and combined perfectly with Jake Bidwell, whose inviting low cross was converted by Gray at the near post. Brighton were reeling but got back into the match with a soft goal from a flicked on corner and were a whisker away from an equaliser when Greer's volley was disallowed after the referee spotted a push in the area. The next goal was crucial and it was the Bees who scored it. Moses shot just wide after galloping through a terrified defence before Bidwell managed to control a pass that he had no right to reach, and exchanged a one-two with Jota, before crossing the ball into the area where Douglas timed his late run perfectly and scored with a powerful header. For those of you old enough to remember, Douglas resembled no one more than the great Martin Peters, a member of England's 1966 World Cup winning squad, who was renowned for ghosting in undetected and finding space in the area where none seemed to exist.

It was exhibition time again and both Judge and Pritchard came close to a fourth goal before Brighton fought their way back into the game and former Brentford loanee

Teixeira tied the entire home defence in knots with his trickery before setting up Holla for a twenty-five yard curler into the top corner for a goal of stupendous quality. The force was now with Brighton but we kept possession where possible, and aided by three excellent substitutions, in Dallas, Toral and Proschwitz, ran the clock down and, in the end, fully deserved the win.

Button, in truth, never had to make a save but his command of his area and distribution were exactly what was required. The back four were exceptional, and after his early aberration, Alan McCormack never put a foot wrong, defending with strength and passion and combining beautifully with Moses, and later, Dallas. Believe me when I say that he is not out of place in the Championship, as many supporters feared. Gray ran tirelessly and is a real danger who comes alive in the box, and once the paperwork is concluded with the Portuguese FA, hopefully in time for Tuesday, we will also have Betinho to support him to add even more pace and goalscoring threat up front.

So what did yesterday really mean? Yes of course it was three points which took us up to the heady heights of sixth place in the table, in itself an eye watering achievement. But in my opinion it means so much more. Yesterday represents a total mindshift in how Brentford as a club, and, indeed, we supporters should regard ourselves. We have traditionally been, and indeed regarded ourselves, as a small club punching way above our weight and Martin Allen in particular used to promote this as a virtue in order to motivate us to achieve more than we perhaps should have done.

Any victory over a so-called more glamorous or bigger club was hailed as a giant-killing and was generally obtained by a combination of hard work and organisation. Now, those are two crucial virtues that we must never lose, but yesterday, for the first time in my many years watching Brentford, the penny finally dropped – we are now as good as anyone else in our division. There is no need for an inferiority complex any more. Our football is as good, and in many cases, far more impressive, than that of any opposing team we are likely to come up against. Yes, we must always treat our opponents with respect, but we should now go out on the pitch expecting, rather than merely hoping, to win.

We proved that we can play football of a calibre that I never believed that I would ever see Brentford play – and many other supporters said the same thing after yesterday's match. This takes me back to where I came in. *Pride*. Something that we should all possess in abundance today, after what we were privileged to watch yesterday afternoon and yes, I also cried some tears after the match!

Travesty! – 17/9/14

When the normally cool, calm and collected Mark Warburton loses his temper you can be sure it is with good reason. Last night was a case in point when the Brentford manager was left incandescent with rage over referee Tim Robinson's bemusing refusal to award Brentford what appeared to everybody in the stadium, bar one, to be a stonewall penalty when Alex Pritchard was pulled down in the area. The video evidence is even more damning and the body language of the Norwich defenders makes it clear that they expected the worst. Mark Warburton's words speak for themselves:

Pritch gets into the penalty area and if I'm the only one who thinks that's a penalty then maybe I need to go to Specsavers.

Games at this level are decided by fine margins, and none finer than last night, when having gifted Norwich the lead through overplaying, then giving the ball away at the back, at a time when Brentford were well ahead on points, the Bees were denied the chance of an instant reply by the referee's non-decision. It must have been twenty minutes at least before Brentford were even awarded a free kick last night and Robinson's performance clearly reminded me of that of Neil Swarbrick who gave us less than nothing (excuse my understandable bias) when he totally favoured Chelsea in the FA Cup replay a couple of years ago. Another referee suffering from Big Club Syndrome!

Looking objectively at the season to date, it can certainly be said that referees have not done Brentford any favours – very much the opposite, in fact, after Tony Craig's red card and penalty concession against Birmingham, the Bidwell penalty appeal in the same game, and the totally baffling decision not to dismiss Brighton defender Lewis Dunk after his blatant last man foul on Saturday. Tonight though, was the worst and most costly of the lot as, had we equalised, the impetus and force would have been with us, and one point would almost certainly have been our minimum reward. As it was, Brentford were punished with two late breakaway goals that gave the final scoreline a totally unrealistic and misleading appearance.

After their customary slow start, Brentford grew into the game and totally dominated the final thirty minutes of the first half. Their high tempo approach and stiletto-sharp passing carved open the highly rated visitors' defence on several occasions and Brentford really should have gone into the break at least one, if not, two, goals to the good. Ruddy saved miraculously from McCormack's long ranger and more fortuitously from Pritchard's close range poke, after wonderfully persistent play from the industrious Alan Judge, who refused to concede that a long ball was running out of play. Gray also had two close-range efforts deflected just wide then over the bar. Yet you somehow thought that these misses might well come back to haunt Brentford as they have already learned to their cost how imperative it is to score when you're on top, as chances are hard to come by at this level, and must be capitalised upon, particularly against teams of Norwich's calibre,

The second half was closer, although after a nervy start when the ball was given away several times cheaply in dangerous areas, the Bees came again and Ruddy saved well from Gray and Judge whose deliberately placed low twenty-yarder was somehow pushed past the post by Ruddy, who was at full stretch. The first goal came well against the run of play and was a total gift. Tarkowski took possession after a quick kick out by Button but gave the ball away dangerously in midfield. Norwich had men over, took full advantage, and Tettey slotted the ball beneath the keeper. A harsh and totally undeserved blow, but one that Brentford seemed to have recovered from when Pritchard went down in the area straight after the goal – but that is where we came in! Their tails up, Norwich then finished us off with two clinical finishes by Cameron Jerome, the second a long range beauty. Three-nil looks conclusive but it was never that.

John Ruddy was the difference between the two teams for much of the game and saved Norwich on at least four occasions. Highly ironic as I am led to believe that Ruddy was, at one point, on the verge of joining the Bees on a season's loan, when Andy Scott changed his mind and signed Lewis Price instead! However, there are several hard lessons that must be learned by Brentford as quickly as possible, and they are the same ones that have become evident in so many of our previous matches.

1. You have to score when you are on top

2. You cannot afford to waste your chances as they will be at a premium

3. Don't give a sucker an even break

4. You mustn't give the ball away cheaply in dangerous areas

5. It is potential suicide to overplay at the back. Keep playing it short when it is safe to do so, but there is also a time and place to mix it up and go longer

6. Recognise that we are just as good as the opposition and fully deserve to be on the same pitch as them

7. Play the eleven facing you on the pitch and not their name, history, or tradition – they aren't supermen, and can be beaten

8. Moses Odubajo is a match winner and is far too valuable in a more advanced position to play at right back

9. Play some of your Spaniards in every match as they have the ability to turn games in our favour

10. We need a left footed defender to play left-sided centre back

11. Play to the whistle and keep your head up when things go against you

And here is a new one for Mark Warburton and David Weir:

12. Stop being so polite and reticent on the bench. Get in the Fourth Official's face and fight your corner – everyone else does. I am not suggesting for one moment that they become as obnoxious and irritating as Steve Evans and Paul Raynor of Rotherham, but simply that they try and ensure that we get a fair crack of the whip from officials, something that we are patently not receiving at present.

It is so disappointing to lose a match that was balanced on a knife's edge, but there was so much good to take out of last night's performance. We played much better football than our illustrious visitors but we could not match them for size and strength, but nor would we want to do so, as that is not the way we play the game. Their finishing was also more clinical than ours and they took full advantage of what little they created late on in the game. We have to recognise that there will be other such games as this when we get far less than we deserve but last night also demonstrated that we have the ability to match everybody in this league, and also come out on top more often than not.

Another chance goes begging against Norwich City.

Play It Short Or Kick It Long? – 18/9/14

There has been a lively debate within the pages of *The Griffin Park Grapevine*, the main Bees supporters' message board, regarding how we now almost invariably build up slowly from the back. Some love it and see it as further evidence of our progress and development, others are not so keen. The trend started under Uwe Rösler, but it has been developed over the past nine months under the direction of Mark Warburton and David Weir until it is now our default approach. Warburton is always talking about the need to *take care of the football* and is loathe to allow the players to give it away unnecessarily.

Gone are the days when the ball was thumped from end to end by goalkeepers either looking for the head of a giant striker or even seeking to put the ball into touch deep in the opposition half for a set piece restart. Richard Lee is an obvious exception, but most Bees keepers of recent vintage have been blessed with the ability to launch the ball to the other end of the pitch, even if where the ball ended up was pretty hit and miss. Now, it is very much the exception rather than the rule for David Button to kick the ball long either out of his hands or from the ground. Our attacks start from the back with Button encouraged to throw or kick the ball out short (and quickly) to a member of the back four or sometimes midfielders Jonathan Douglas or Alan Judge. It is then up to them to seek out gaps in the opposition formation and ideally move the ball onto one of the other midfielders who can start an attack. Maintaining possession is the key to our footballing philosophy. Patience is a virtue and the players are encouraged to pass the ball across the back four from side to side whilst they probe for openings.

The perfect example of how this approach can work was seen on Saturday against Brighton, when Button threw the ball short to Judge, the opposition backed off and he then hit a wonderful defence-splitting pass inside the left back that allowed Moses Odubajo to do his magic and score a goal that was truly a thing of beauty. All our defenders are skilful on the ball, probably even more so than they ever thought possible; they have developed the confidence to call for the ball when under pressure, secure in the knowledge that they are good enough to either beat or outpace their man or pass the ball quickly to an unmarked team mate. Ninety-nine times out of one hundred all goes well, the ball is moved slickly between players, and we are off and running. It is the hundredth time that causes concern, as that is when disaster strikes.

David Button's inelegant attempted step-over and pirouette fooled nobody, particularly Francois Zoko who managed to stop laughing long enough to charge down the keeper's eventual delayed and inept clearance and score a crucial equaliser for Stevenage, who went on to beat us in a match that had massive repercussions for the team. Button too was mainly responsible for Swindon's winner in a tightly-fought battle late last season. Right on halftime he exchanged passes with Tony Craig and rather than play the ball long, as the situation surely demanded, he played a hospital pass to Jonathan Douglas twenty-five yards out, directly in line with the centre of the goal. Douglas had his back to the opposition, but Button was facing the play and should have noticed the cavalry bearing down on Douglas, who was duly dispossessed, and Louis Thompson ran through a non-existent defence to score the crucial goal. Finally, on Tuesday night, Button played the ball short to James Tarkowski who was in space, but he played a sloppy pass in front of Douglas, the ball was intercepted, Norwich had men over and scored comfortably. The game turned and slipped away from us in a twinkling of an eye.

There have also been some narrow escapes as opposing forwards begin to wise up to our approach and press us high up the field. We played Russian Roulette for much of the second half at Blackpool and on Tuesday, Norwich forced two errors soon after half time but we got away with them. AFC Bournemouth also pressed us and Button was forced to go longer and kick the ball forward.

In David Button we are blessed with a keeper who despite his *faux pas* at Stevenage, is remarkably talented with the ball at his feet and he strikes the ball beautifully with both of them. He reminds me of a golfer as he pings the ball forward. Occasionally he over-clubs and it goes into touch but he is very accurate and more often than not he finds his man. The problem is, though, that in a team comprised mainly of Diddy Men, we have very little aerial ability and also generally only play one striker. We are packed full of speedy, small, ball players who revel in keeping possession of the football. If, and when, Button does kick it long it invariably comes straight back and we lose possession – a cardinal sin. Gray is weak in the air and Proschwitz, who can head the ball, is generally stuck on the bench. Button's interim solution is therefore to look for Jake Bidwell, just over the halfway line. A Plan C is definitely needed.

Whatever we fans think, nothing is going to change for the foreseeable future, and, indeed, we play exactly the same way, with a patient build up, in all of the age group teams too. We are still learning and I see this philosophy as being part of Mark Warburton's desire to empower the players to take responsibility and keep possession at all costs. For the most part the fans have been supportive of this new-fangled approach and there is overall approval, if not amazement at the sight of Brentford players looking so skilful and confident on the ball. This really isn't what we have been accustomed to over the years and we are still getting used to it. But isn't it wonderful!

There are a few reactionaries who scream at Button to *kick the damn thing up the field* and who are not onboard with the new philosophy. When things do go wrong you can hear them tutting in disapproval and saying *I told you so*. My view is that we are still a work in progress. We are getting far better at keeping possession and mistakes are now becoming less common – but will still occur. Within reason, I am happy with that state of affairs as the advantages more than outweigh the negatives. Yes, I do sometimes cringe when we pass the ball around - dangerously - twenty yards from our goal, but it is all part of our progression and development. The club has been turned upside down over the past couple of years and I for one am proud and delighted with what we are now seeing. The odd mishap and accompanying raised blood pressure is surely a small price to pay!

Mark Warburton – The Renaissance Man Of Football – 19/9/14

I have just listened to Brentford manager Mark Warburton's latest interview on Bees Player and he was in typical bullish and confident form. He was still angry about Tuesday's events and felt that the final score was totally misleading and that but for a referee's blatant error our valiant efforts would most likely have received their just reward. He focused on all the positives that came out of what was indeed an excellent team performance and hoped that they would be of benefit when it comes to Saturday's tough challenge at Middlesbrough. It must be wonderful for his squad to have a manager who demonstrates such positivity and encouragement in everything that he says and does.

Football managers have traditionally used a combination of carrot and stick to motivate their players, but management by fear and intimidation is now a totally outmoded concept that is doomed to failure in today's more enlightened times. Mark Warburton is in the vanguard of a much more modern approach where players are treated like adults and are encouraged to buy into a much more collaborative and empowering way of doing things. That is not to say that they do not have to take full responsibility for their actions on and off the pitch, but the players know that if they follow instructions and do as they have been coached to do, then, even if things go wrong, they know that their manager will back them to the hilt.

Tuesday was a case in point as Norwich City's first goal came when our short passing approach broke down close to our goal and our opponents took full advantage of the unforced error. Rather than blast James Tarkowski for playing what was generally accepted to be a sloppy pass that conceded possession in a dangerous position, Warburton instead backed his young defender and made it clear that our style of play would not alter one iota. I suspect that in private he spoke to Tarkowski and reminded him of the need to maintain concentration and exhibit more care in his passing, but that is all part of the learning process. The Brentford squad is packed full of promising young talent who are all comfortable on the ball and in Warburton they have the perfect manager, a patient teacher who is steeped in the development of young players who always encourages them to play and express themselves without fear of failure.

Here is midfielder Alex Pritchard on what it is like to play for Mark Warburton:

Mark Warburton is a very good manager and he is great with the players. He expects a lot from you but I'm really enjoying playing under him. He is always trying to help me improve and I can feel myself learning from him.

His squad also fully understands that beneath the calm exterior, Warburton is neither weak nor a soft touch, and if players do not perform then they will not keep their place in the team. He has also made it perfectly clear, on many occasions, that he is always looking to revitalise and improve the makeup of the squad. Players accept this as a way of life and as long as they are treated fairly then they will respond. Indeed twelve new players of immense talent have come through the door since the end of last season but the nucleus of last year's promotion team has been retained given that players of the ilk of Button, Bidwell, Tarkowski, McCormack, Judge and Douglas have demonstrated that they are fully capable of meeting the tough challenge of playing Championship football. Should they fail to do so in the future and let their standards drop, then they know that they will be replaced, such is the way of football.

Warburton has also emphasised that his office door is always open if players want to discuss why they aren't playing and what is required of them if they are to regain their first team place. In other words, he treats his players like adults and they therefore respond well and behave like adults too. Whilst such a collaborative and open door policy is commonplace in business and industry, that is not necessarily the case in football where dialogue between players and management is often not encouraged and sometimes even frowned upon.

In his recent book, Bees goalkeeper Richard Lee highlighted the fact that the players found it almost impossible to talk to former manager Andy Scott, who would keep things extremely close to his chest, and would never explain the rationale for his selection decisions to his squad. The team was never announced until an hour before the kick off when the unlucky squad players not required for the match would finally learn their fate and then slope off out of the dressing room. You shouldn't treat anybody in that manner, and certainly not highly-skilled professionals who were about to go out and perform on a public stage. How were players expected to prepare, and psyche themselves up, for a match when they did not even know if they were playing until just beforehand? In life, you reap what you sow, and once things turned sour and results deteriorated, I can well understand why Scott was eventually thrown to the wolves after a truly shocking and spineless performance one horrible night at Dagenham.

Mark Warburton is simply treating his players as he would want and expect to be treated himself, and he too had a bad experience in his short playing career when he came under the direction of Jock Wallace, a fearsome man of the old school who had a one-size-fits-all approach to managing his players and whose bark was just as bad as his bite. Warburton learned how not to do things and has also applied the lessons of man management learned during his many years spent working in the city. The way he handled the difficult Adam Forshaw situation, when he put him on gardening leave and made it perfectly clear that unless the player was prepared to commit himself to the club then there was no place for him in the squad, showed great strength of character and determination. Forshaw did indeed leave the club, but only when we were ready for him to do so, on our terms, for a club record transfer fee and after he had been replaced. Good and decisive management yet again.

Personally I feel that Brentford have lucked into having a truly exceptional man at their helm given that Mark only took over the job after Uwe Rösler's unexpected departure to Wigan. He is a man of intelligence and vision, whose fresh approach, open mindedness, positivity and determination that we express ourselves in every match we play and never show fear, has stimulated a fantastic response from his team who totally believe in him – as do we supporters. Mark Warburton is indeed a true Renaissance man of football.

Keep Calm! – Part One – 22/9/14

Well, it was all going so well – an hour gone last Tuesday night and we were in control of the match against Norwich, pressing hard for the opening goal which looked certain to arrive at any moment. One point seemed likely to be the minimum reward for all our efforts and we looked like ending up with a potential four, or maybe even six point return from two really difficult matches against Brighton and Norwich, both sides likely to be promotion challengers. Then the roof fell in. An unforced defensive error, a refereeing howler and the Norwich game slipped through our hands, albeit unjustly, but such are the whims of the footballing Gods.

Brentford travelled to another one of the Championship elite in Middlesbrough on Saturday, hoping to right the ship, but returned with their tail firmly between their legs after suffering a four goal hiding that, from all accounts, could easily have been more. This was also the first time a Mark Warburton team has lost successive matches. So what now, and where do we go from here?

Firstly, we need to put things into perspective. Brighton, Norwich and Middlesbrough were always going to present a tough challenge, and three points out of the nine on offer, and one-and-a-half excellent performances out of three is probably as much as any of us supporters really expected beforehand. That being said, seven goals conceded and none scored in our last two hours of play is a worrying record to say the least. It would be easy to write Saturday off as being simply a bad day at the office, and, indeed, maybe that is all it was. We play a high tempo, energetic, pressing game and two full-on matches followed by a journey to the other end of the country left the squad tired and leggy and lacking their customary verve and brio.

I am sure that there will be a reaction from the players and a much-improved performance next week against a revitalised Leeds United team. This league is totally unforgiving, there really is no such thing as a easy game in the Championship, and next Saturday's match will provide yet another stern test, and if that isn't difficult enough, we then visit neighbours Watford for a keenly awaited local derby against yet another team aiming for promotion. Most importantly, we have to avoid feeling sorry for ourselves at all costs. Even though we can't buy a decision from referees at the moment, we simply have to keep our heads up and continue playing the way that we have been doing as it has brought us sustained success for the past couple of years.

I remember Richard Lee saying in his book that if you keep losing but continue to do exactly the same thing in both matches and preparation, then you cannot expect results to change. That certainly isn't the case with Brentford's situation at present. Yes, there are many things we need to improve upon in terms of defending tighter, protecting the ball better and being more clinical in the final third, but these merely require tweaks to our current system rather than major changes. That well-known philosopher Martin Allen would always warn players and fans alike not to pop the pills when results go badly, or conversely, glug the champagne when you are winning. Sage advice, as it's crucial to keep things in perspective and recognise just how narrow are the margins between success and failure.

Things can change in an instant and it won't take much for Brentford to get back onto the winning trail. Frankly, Saturday's match was the first one all season where the Bees were clearly second best. In the previous seven games, either team could have come out on top as the advantage seesawed and veered dramatically as the minutes unfolded. So what changes will Mark Warburton make for the next match? Very few I suspect, given that the whole team seemed to have a collective off-day on Saturday. Odubajo, Judge, Jota and Pritchard will be expected to be less profligate with the ball, stop turning it over so easily and make things happen. A bit more defensive cover from them would also be appreciated. There could be a return for the hard running of Stuart Dallas, and, if match fit, Betinho might well challenge for his full debut.

I can't see a fundamental change with two strikers starting a match together although I think there will come a time when this needs to be tried out. Teams have to defend from the front and if the ball keeps being given away by the attackers then the defence will come under continuous pressure with the likelihood of drastic results. This is what happened at Middlesbrough and it cannot reoccur next Saturday. Both full backs were left isolated and exposed and need midfielders to track back and provide additional cover.

I do wonder if the manager might decide to play Alan McCormack in midfield alongside Jonathan Douglas, a move that will provide us with far more bark and bite and one that looked very promising against Norwich City. If so, who will play at right back? Moses is surely wasted there but Nico Yennaris is currently unavailable through injury. Jon Toral might also be a decent long shot to start as he is a tireless runner, blessed with great ability, who makes things happen. Perhaps he is seen as the eventual Adam Forshaw replacement as we lack a real box-to-box player at present.

I wrote just before the start of the season that three into two doesn't go and there is yet another decision to be made regarding the two central defenders. Tony Craig has not played since his dismissal against Birmingham a month ago and I think it is time to bring the skipper back. His experience, calmness under pressure and leadership have never been needed more than now. Having a left footed centre half also makes us more balanced. This is certainly no reflection upon Harlee Dean who, as always, has given everything to the cause, but has been guilty of some rash decisions that have proved costly. Harlee wears his heart on his sleeve and his post match interview on Saturday simply demonstrated his passion and hatred of losing. Neither are bad things, but engaging your brain before opening your mouth is always advisable and he came close to making direct criticisms of his teammates which might not have been well received within the dressing room, and it might be expedient to take him out of the firing line for a spell.

The good news is that the squad now has a full week before the next game and can spend quality time on the training field to retrench, recover and regain their strength, shape and confidence. It is not about licking wounds, but much more about tinkering with a few things and reminding players about their responsibilities and, indeed, what they have previously proved that they can do so well. They have already demonstrated that they are more than good enough to compete successfully at this level, but everyone needs to be on form and on top of their game against Leeds United. Roll on next Saturday!

Keep Calm! – Part Two – Richard Poole Has His Say – 26/9/14

I wrote the other day about the need to keep calm and not overreact after the last two defeats and the accompanying jolt to our confidence levels. Well, our former striker from the 70s, Richard Poole, seems to agree as he has just sent me this latest update and his passion and deep-felt love for Brentford FC has moved me deeply, as I hope it will you:

I have just been watching the Liverpool match in the League Cup against Brentford's last league opponents Middlesbrough. This brings back such wonderful memories from September 1974 when we were drawn away to Liverpool in the second round of the League Cup. Although I was still a young apprentice, Mike Everitt took me along as thirteenth man. Only one substitute was allowed back then so I sat on the bench and watched how close we came to beating the mighty Liverpool that night. Yes, us, little Brentford, ran them so very close and took the lead through Roger Cross, nearly made it two-nil when Barry Salvage missed a great chance, and only lost narrowly by the odd goal in three. Although Kevin Keegan did not play that night I remember I was standing outside our team's dressing room when he spoke to me and asked if I would like to take a look around the trophy room with him, and did I jump at this opportunity!

I only really realised recently just how lucky I was to live the dream even for such a short period of time. The thrill of actually sitting on the bench at Anfield and as I went up the tight stairway to the players' tunnel seeing the immortal words "THIS IS ANFIELD" before taking my place on the bench with the rest of the staff. Incredible times! Although we lost the match, we gained the total respect of all the Liverpool players who recognised how close we had come to a massive upset. We did not travel back to London that night, which was rare at that time, and certainly the exception to the rule. After most away matches we travelled back to Brentford on a long coach journey, generally not arriving home until well into the early morning. That night we stayed at a hotel and were invited by the Liverpool players to join them at a night club. Not only were they great stars but they were also great men.

I was fearfully proud to be a Bee, but sometimes it was very hard given the way some people in the football world would denigrate and talk the club down. There was a time just before signing for Brentford when I was selected for England Under 15 Schoolboy trials along with Kevin Harding which took place at Bisham Abbey and lasted for a whole week. We both signed schoolboy forms for Brentford at thirteen or fourteen years old and played for Hounslow schools. So here we were with talented Under 15s like Ray Lewington and Butch Wilkins, and lots of others who were on schoolboy forms with big clubs like Chelsea, Arsenal and QPR. The following year we would play against them all in the South East Counties League.

We had some great players like Roy Cotton but most of our team were non-contract players and we would be up against the likes of Chelsea and Arsenal who would have twelve or fourteen apprentices in their squad but our team, Brentford, at least won their respect. Anyway going back to the England trials, we were all asked by the England training staff who we had signed schoolboy forms for. Well when Kevin and I said "Brentford" we could hear this audible gasp go up around us, but we were always proud to pull on that red and white shirt. From the moment we joined the club as schoolboys under Frank Blunstone, and when we became apprentices at fifteen we were made to feel proud to belong to Brentford FC. This feeling was instilled into all of us by the training staff as well as all the players.

When we signed apprentice forms at the age of fifteen, we played in the South East Counties League Under 18 Championship, which contained a lot of the First Division Under 18 sides which were packed full of apprentices. Our home matches were played at Ruislip Town's ground, not on the their first team pitch but on the one just next to it with a slope worse than the one at the old Yeovil Town ground.

We had a great team who more than defended Brentford FC's name and everyone was proud to pull on that shirt. At the end of the season we were invited to enter a youth tournament in Frankfurt with lots of international teams, which we won after a penalty shoot out. Yes, a Brentford team winning on penalties and we must have been one of the first English teams to win a penalty shoot out. I am proud to say that the last shot was from me and as well as winning the competition, I finished top goal scorer in the tournament and won an award Although we came back with a trophy there was only a little picture in the Middlesex Chronicle! All the playing staff and managers really made you feel part of something and to be proud but upstairs in the Board Room, well that was another story. When we played our youth matches on a day when the first team was at home there were always some of the players cheering us on as we played on the Saturday morning.

One who was always there was Jackie Graham. What a great bloke he was. I remember when I scored my first team goal against Bradford City, I turned and started running back to the centre circle, but then I heard a strong Scottish voice saying "stop running son, enjoy the moment" – it was Jackie Graham. He was so hard and a great competitor on the pitch particularly when we had Scotland versus England matches in training! Now I hope he won't mind me saying this, but he was a man who was not afraid of anything except the dreaded needle when each year we had a flu injection. Please forgive me Mr.Graham!

So, all you Brentford fans just KEEP CALM. You will earn respect and you must never forget where we come from – yes, Brentford, and we should be so proud of Brentford too! I for one will never forget what it meant to me when I was that starry-eyed youngster, to belong to something called BRENTFORD FC. Thanks to everyone who helped me during my time at this great club. I think that at the time I just did not understand quite how lucky I was. I experienced Liverpool, Lincoln and Bradford with Brentford and made my debut in the league cup for Watford at Crystal Palace and in the next round I played against Sheffield Wednesday at Hillsborough. My paths crossed with so many places and so many different people throughout my career. I also met Elton John who was the club president at Watford. Brentford gave me such a good base, which even to this day helps me in my life.

I think that Richard has said it all and he has demonstrated yet again how former players feel about our club, which is a truly special one. Another Brentford supporter, Andre, was similarly moved by Richard's comments:

Whatever ups and downs the next forty years have in store for the club (and I hope there's more of the former), I really hope we never leave behind the essence that prompted Richard's comments and the reason why we continue to follow this club, and that in forty years time some of the current players will be able to write about their time at the club in the same heartfelt and moving fashion. And, for the avoidance of doubt, that's not a tear in the corner of my eye – just a bit of grit. Honest.

The Right Approach! – 27/9/14

It is a big game for Brentford this afternoon when they take on Leeds United at Griffin Park. Well, in truth, every match in the Championship is one to relish. Today's game, though, has even more significance, coming as it does after the Bees have suffered two consecutive defeats, the first a very harsh and undeserved one at the hands of Norwich, whereas last week we were well and truly tonked at Middlesbrough. Confidence must have taken a bit of a jolt after these reverses so what I, and I am sure every Brentford fan is looking for, is a response and a reaction today. Ideally, we won't be feeling nervous or sorry for ourselves but will come out with all guns blazing, be positive and take the game to our opponents. In other words we need to seize the initiative from the first whistle and believe in ourselves and our right to be competing on the same stage as our illustrious opponents.

What makes matters even more intriguing, though, is the identity and reputation of our visitors. This afternoon we take on one of the greats of English football in Leeds United, a team who in the past decade have graced the Premier League and competed for top European honours. Mark Warburton has remarked on many occasions of the need for his Brentford team to concentrate solely on the eleven players facing them out on the field and not on the name, heritage and tradition of the team for whom they are playing. In other words we should ignore the badge on their shirt and simply regard them as just another team that we are looking to beat.

We have already proved against top teams in Brighton, AFC Bournemouth and Norwich City that we belong in the Championship and are there by right and not simply good fortune. Our football has been slick, cohesive and positive and we have always looked, both home and away, to take the game to our opponents rather than merely sit back and absorb their pressure.

It is highly illuminating to look back at the last time we played Leeds United and contrast the situation we faced then with how things are now. Leeds were in Division One after our promotion to that division back in 2009 and our two matches against them were the most keenly anticipated once the fixtures were announced. The first match at Griffin Park in December 2009 came at a time when Brentford were struggling, and Andy Scott reacted to our lack of form, and the strength of the promotion-challenging opposition by setting us up in a totally defensive 4-5-1 formation with Ben Strevens playing on the right hand side of midfield and Charlie MacDonald left to forage alone and totally unsupported up front. We stifled the midfield, defended like heroes and harassed and harried our opponents at every opportunity. In other words, we were totally negative in our approach, made no real effort to win the game and basically gave Leeds the initiative and the message that despite our home advantage we did not believe that we were capable of defeating them, or of even attempting to do so. Andy Scott's approach was rewarded with the nil-nil draw that he was undoubtedly hoping and playing for and the crowd accepted his approach and cheered the result to the echo. We knew our place in the football food chain. Would our supporters have been so forgiving if Leeds had put away one of the many chances that the profligate Jermaine Beckford spurned on an afternoon when Brentford had precisely no efforts on target? Who knows.

The return match at Elland Road in March 2010 saw a brave and more cohesive display by the Bees, which was rewarded with a fully merited one all draw. Again though, our approach was all wrong as the large number of travelling Brentford supporters resembled nothing more than a coach party of country yokels up for a rare day out in the big city. The occasion was all that mattered and the chance to visit a much bigger club, look around the ground and admire the Billy Bremner statue and, as far as the match was concerned, we had few, if any, expectations. Nor was it really the priority for the day. The draw was a massively unexpected bonus and it was certainly an afternoon that will remain long in the memory.

I am, of course, being a bit unfair as Brentford, if not quite run on a shoestring at that time, could not be expected to compete in quality with the Leeds players we were facing and we therefore employed the tactics that we did in an effort to nullify their extra skill and ability. Two draws would say that Andy Scott was totally justified in how he set his team up in both games against far superior opposition, however it is imperative that we employ a totally different mindset today.

We have to go out onto the Griffin Park pitch believing that we are as good as Leeds, if not better, and then do everything within our power to prove it by attacking them rather than give away the initiative, as was the case on the last two occasions we played them, where in truth, we made very little effort to win either game. For all their track record and reputation, we are not inferior to Leeds. They will be trying to impress their new manager and come into the match bang in form following wins over AFC Bournemouth and Huddersfield Town and also as a total mystery to Mark Warburton who has no real idea how his opponents will set up. So what. Let them worry about us.

Hopefully Judge, Pritchard, Jota and Odubajo will give them something to worry about and I am sure that Jonathan Douglas, once an Elland Road hero, will also feel that he has something to prove against a team that dispensed with his services a few years back. Today provides us with the chance to turn things round, but our approach to the game will dictate whether we are successful or not. It's not about Leeds – it's totally about us, so let's be brave and positive and let them worry about us.

What A Response! – 28/9/14

For all the optimism I publicly expressed before yesterday's crunch match against Leeds United I have to admit that I felt pretty nervous before the kickoff. Which Brentford team would turn up? Would it be the confident eleven that had passed Brighton off the pitch and came so close to humbling Norwich City or the no-hopers who capitulated without much of a fight at Middlesbrough last Saturday? The match appeared to be very much a watershed that might well prove to be a lasting indication of how well we were going to do throughout the season. Every match in the Championship is like climbing a mountain and there are no easy points on offer. It would be so easy for the Bees to start feeling sorry for themselves and become overwhelmed at the level of challenges that faces them every week.

As Manager Mark Warburton emphasised in his programme notes yesterday, the overriding difference between Division One and the Championship can simply be summed up in one word – quality. That is not just the quality of the opposition we face on the pitch but, just as importantly, the heightened quality of the opposition's preparation, off field support, analysis and fitness. As we have already learned to our cost, any mistakes, loss of concentration and general sloppiness which would have resulted last year in nothing more than a groan of disappointment, are this season punished ruthlessly at this exalted level, and the few chances that come along cannot be spurned.

Our confidence and self-belief had certainly taken a blow, and we - management, players and supporters alike, had had a whole week to stew over things without the opportunity of a midweek match to prove that this was merely a blip rather than the beginnings of a rapid descent down the league table. The upside of this delay was the squad had been able to get the spring back into their legs and also spend valuable time on the training ground all this week, not merely to lick their wounds, but also to practice all the areas that had let them down at Middlesbrough, in particular, defending from the front and being more penetrative in the final third of the pitch.

Yesterday was therefore a daunting proposition, particularly given that we were playing another of the so-called *big boys* in Leeds United, a team who had graced the Premier League and European competition in recent years and whose tradition and record of success dwarfed our own. On the last occasion we faced the same opposition at Griffin Park we adopted a formation about as aggressive as the Maginot Line and we resembled nothing more than a tortoise with its head withdrawn within its shell, hoping to ward off the blows which would doubtless rain down upon us from our exalted opposition. We were in awe of Leeds and played accordingly and totally ceded the initiative to our opponents.

Would history repeat itself yesterday afternoon or would the team have the strength of character to go out and prove that they truly belong in the Championship? There were so many other questions to answer: Would we be out sung and intimidated by the raucous hordes of Leeds United supporters who flooded Griffin Park? Would our small and slight team be knocked off the ball and their close passing game by the Land of the Giants who emerged from the away dressing room? Well, the team provided an emphatic answer to all their critics and played Leeds United off the park and cruised to a two – nil victory which, had it not been for the acrobatics and gymnastic shot stopping of keeper Silvestri, could have ended up in a five goal thrashing.

The football was slick and effective. We ran at the opposition and pulled them out of position and the interchange of passing was a joy to behold. Pritchard came back to form and threatened the opposition with his ceaseless promptings. Judge was tireless, switching from the middle to the left wing and his dribbling and accurate passing found the gaps in the porous Leeds defence. Jota started quietly but showed his true class with an eye-catching first goal for the club where he showed instant control, found space in a crowded penalty area and his fast and twinkling feet left two defenders on their backside before he found the roof of the net. A goal which arrived at a crucial time, just before the interval, and one of real beauty as it came from a series of wonderful one touch passes under extreme pressure that tore the opposition apart. You get what you pay for and Jota is the real deal and is showing signs that he is beginning to settle down.

Odubajo terrified Leeds with his pace and close control and was two excellent saves away from scoring. Gray played the lone striker role to perfection, worrying the two centre halves with his pace and intelligent running. He turned beautifully early on but his goal-bound effort was blocked. Douglas then threaded him through with a defence-splitting pass. Pearce bundled him over and, miracle of miracles, referee Dean Whitestone pointed to the spot. Craig ran up to the official no doubt to remind him of the red card he received recently for an incident, that in all honesty was far more clear-cut than yesterday's. So yellow it was, and then, to general incredulity, James Tarkowski strode up to the spot. Would he stroke the ball effortlessly into the corner of the net and give us the lead our possession fully merited? Unfortunately not as he joined the pantheon of Brentford defenders such as Peter Gelson, Jason Cousins and Leo Roget when his rising shot screamed over the cross bar and is probably still in orbit. According to his manager, Tarkowski is metronomic in his accuracy from the spot in training at Jersey Road but, as we saw yesterday, there is a massive difference between slotting them away on an empty training ground and attempting to do the same when facing hordes of manic away supporters. Tarkowski unfortunately lost his nerve and for all his manager's post match support, which is no more than you would expect from such a master of man management, I would expect that James might well go to the back of the queue when we are next awarded a spot kick.

Leeds had barely threatened and the Bees fully merited their interval lead. After a brief flurry when Judge and Jota both shot over, the visitors came back in to the game when they started to play through the middle and Button was forced into an excellent stretching save from a Pearce header, but that was almost the only time that Leeds forced him into action. The sign of a good keeper is when he is called upon to make a crucial save after having had nothing to do and Button rose to his challenge. The back four won all their battles. The recalled Tony Craig provided balance and calmness and led his troops well and unobtrusively. His return made a real difference. Tarkowski put his penalty nonsense behind him and played impeccably. McCormack and Bidwell did all that was necessary and took full advantage of the attacking space granted them by the Leeds diamond.

Silvestri saved brilliantly from Gray and Moses and then foiled Tebar when the substitute tried to outguess the keeper with a subtle dink. Douglas then took a quick free kick that put McCormack away and with Moses screaming for the ball on his right, Alan strode on unopposed. Surely he would slip Moses through on goal but Leeds continued to back away and McCormack shot from just inside the area and a deflection took the ball past the keeper who had seemed almost unbeatable. The expression on Moses's face was a picture and had Alan not scored then I suspect that he would have been in for a real mouthful from his colleague.

Alan McCormack scores against Leeds United.

Every player was on his game but the real accolade has to go the former Leeds midfielder Jonathan Douglas who is a new man this season. He led our pressing game and was everywhere on the pitch as he foraged tirelessly to break up the opposition attacks. What has come as a welcome surprise is that with the extra space afforded him in the Championship he has shown a real confidence on the ball and yesterday he played some beautifully weighted and subtle passes that created time, space and opportunities for his team mates. He was a true leader and inspiration.

So, a lot of questions were answered yesterday and we left the ground filled with pride. Brentford had played beautiful football and demonstrated yet again that their positive approach can obtain results. We had made a team coming off two wins look second rate. Today is a day off and the chance for us all to recover and take pleasure in what we were privileged to watch yesterday. Tomorrow the team starts to prepare to face traditional rivals Watford on Tuesday evening. The Championship is relentless and unforgiving, and yesterday proved that we are certainly up to the challenge.

Into The Hornets' Nest – 30/9/14

It's a local derby for Brentford tonight when they visit Vicarage Road to take on a Watford team that has serious promotion aspirations. Watford have made a solid start to the campaign and are a vibrant attacking team jam packed full of extravagant foreign talent brought in by their owner, Giampaolo Pozzo. And yet this just might not be the worst time to play them for a variety of reasons. Watford had a long and exhausting journey back home from Blackburn on Saturday and the Bees will hope that they are still leggy and recovering from all their travelling. Star striker and team fulcrum and inspiration Troy Deeney is still absent through his hamstring injury, not that Watford are short of other excellent striking options, and Oscar Garcia yesterday resigned as Head Coach through health reasons after a stay of less than four weeks, following his recent heart scare. We obviously all wish him a full and speedy recovery and recuperation, and he has quickly and seamlessly been replaced by his assistant, former Fulham coach, Billy McKinlay, who is an experienced and wily old bird.

For those of you too young to remember, there was a keen rivalry between the two clubs, particularly in the mid to late 70s, before Watford motored on ahead on their journey to the top division, under the inspired leadership of Graham Taylor. The last time we won at Vicarage Road was back in April 1977 when Andy McCulloch's majestic header, accompanied by Paul Priddy's two incredible penalty saves gave us a very satisfying one-nil victory. That completed a rare double as the previous month a large and expectant crowd under the floodlights at Griffin Park saw an electrifying three goal burst in the opening quarter of the game, which enabled the Bees to cruise to victory. As always there is a back story and apparently Jackie Graham made it perfectly clear to his team mates just before the match in the tunnel exactly how much it meant to him to beat our local rivals, and, probably more terrified of their own skipper than the opposition, the Bees came out of the traps like scalded cats and hammered their opponents.

Watford took full revenge the following season when they cruised effortlessly to victory by the same score at Griffin Park. The season ended with both teams being promoted from the Fourth Division and an honours-even draw at Vicarage Road. As ITV's *The Big Match* coverage confirms, we then played out a thrilling three-all draw the following season in a match notable for the appearance of the Playboy Bunny Girls and the phantom whistle just before Watford's second goal. Marvellous memories.

In our last brief spell in the second tier of English football, an appalling home team penalty decision for handball when the ball was driven against Billy Manuel from point blank range, settled the match and contributed greatly to our eventual relegation, so perhaps we are looking for some payback tonight. Some of you might have read the regular correspondence I have been receiving from former Bees and Watford striker

Richard Poole and I hope that he is anxiously looking out for the result tonight from his home in France, and I am pretty sure which team he hopes to win too! Games between the two clubs are invariably passionate and exciting and I expect nothing less tonight. I will be sitting on my hands in the Watford end accompanying a Hornets season ticket holder friend of mine. Let's just hope I can keep my mouth shut during the game or my enjoyment of the proceedings could be curtailed and end earlier than I would like!

League Table – 30/9/14

Position	Team	P	W	D	L	F	A	GD	Pt	Form
1	Norwich City	10	6	2	2	20	9	11	20	D W W D W L
2	Nottingham Forest	10	5	5	0	17	7	10	20	W D W D D D
3	Watford	10	6	2	2	19	11	8	20	W L W D D W
4	Derby County	10	5	4	1	19	10	9	19	D D W D W W
5	Ipswich Town	10	5	3	2	14	8	6	18	D W W W W D
6	Wolverhampton Wndrs	9	5	3	1	11	6	5	18	W W D D W D
7	Charlton Athletic	10	4	6	0	13	9	4	18	D W D D D W
8	Middlesbrough	10	5	2	3	14	8	6	17	L W W W D D
8	Sheffield Wednesday	10	4	4	2	10	7	3	16	L D W W L D
10	Reading	9	4	2	3	14	14	0	14	L W W W L D
11	Blackburn Rovers	10	4	2	4	16	18	-2	14	L W L W D L
12	**Brentford**	10	4	2	4	12	15	-3	14	W W L L W L
13	Cardiff City	10	3	4	3	13	13	0	13	D L L D W D
14	Leeds United	9	4	1	4	10	12	-2	13	L W D W W L
15	Bournemouth	10	3	3	4	14	13	1	12	D D L D W L
16	Millwall	10	3	2	5	10	13	-3	11	W L L D L L
17	Rotherham United	10	3	2	5	8	12	-4	11	L D L D L W
18	Brighton and Hove A	10	2	4	4	9	11	-2	10	D L L D D D
19	Birmingham City	10	2	4	4	11	17	-6	10	L D L D L W
20	Wigan Athletic	10	2	3	5	10	12	-2	9	W L D L L D
21	Huddersfield Town	9	2	2	5	9	19	-10	8	D L L D L W
22	Bolton Wanderers	9	1	2	6	7	15	-8	5	L L D W L L
23	Fulham	9	1	1	7	8	20	-12	4	L D L L L W
24	Blackpool	10	0	3	7	5	14	-9	3	L D L D L D

OCTOBER

I Hate Watford! – 1/10/14

I know, I really shouldn't have said that, it's a bit puerile and I should know better and be a bit more sportsmanlike and even-handed in my post-match comments. But, you know what, it is pretty damn hard to be calm and measured in what you write when you have just watched the Bees put in a wonderful performance against one of the Championship's promotion favourites and totally undeservedly end up with absolutely nothing. A point would have been a fair reward for all their efforts tonight, but yet another dubious penalty just before halftime and a world-class half volley from Vydra sent the Bees home empty handed. That was hard enough to accept, but I had to be on my best behaviour, sat, as I was, in amongst the Watford season ticket holders. They soon twigged that I was a Brentford supporter and took great delight in joshing and patronising me at every opportunity, acknowledging how unlucky we were at the penalty award and remarking constantly about what a decent team we were. At the final whistle I was told that we had really deserved a point. Abuse I can handle, and, indeed, it is something that I expect at away grounds, but half-baked compliments and condescension from opposition supporters who I know are inwardly rejoicing at my team's misfortune are just impossible for me to take.

Brentford replaced Pritchard with ex-Hornet Diagouraga, who joined Douglas in bolstering the midfield, but early on Brentford received a real chasing and were only saved from going behind by some desperate defending after a flurry of corners, and the ball rebounding off their crossbar from a close range header from Ighalo who was destined to have a far greater influence on the match later on in the half. The Bees slowly found a foothold in the game and went close through Douglas, who only half hit his excellent opportunity, before an electrifying run from Jota saw him dance inside from the left wing, leave two defenders in his wake and see his long ranger turned over the bar by Gomes. Judge then hit a searing volley just wide from thirty yards.

So nil-nil it was at the break – or it would have been had referee Graham Salisbury not given a really soft penalty right on the interval when Tarkowski and Ighalo clashed and the forward went down very easily and in instalments after the challenge. Who knows whether it was the linesman who signalled for the penalty as the referee took an age to make up his mind before belatedly pointing to the spot, almost as an afterthought. Ighalo made a total hash of his spot kick and insult was added to injury when he was fortunate enough to see the ball bounce off the diving Button which allowed him to plant the rebound into the net. Watford had deserved to be in front after all their early pressure, but Brentford were by far the better team in the latter part of the first half and the goal came as a hammer blow at a time when they were dominating the game. Mark Warburton described the penalty award as *shocking* and *appalling* and it was just one more in a catalogue of decisions that have gone against Brentford so far this season.

Brentford continued to press after the break and twice the ball flashed across the home goal without anyone getting the crucial touch. Gray's shot was comfortably saved and Jota shot wide. Finally, the equaliser came after ten minutes of Brentford pressure, and what a beautifully worked goal it was. Odubajo came inside off the left wing and passed the ball beyond Douglas to Judge. Douglas continued his run and Judge's instant pass inside the defender was perfectly weighted for Douglas to take in his stride and from a difficult angle place his shot just inside the far post despite the best efforts of Gomes to push the shot wide.

Celebration!

The Bees were now in total control and a low cross almost found Gray in space at the far post. Surely the goal was about to come, and come it did - for Watford! Out of the blue and from their first shot of the second half when a cross from the right was half cleared and headed by Douglas seemingly out of the danger zone, but the ball was returned with interest by Vydra with an incredible and unstoppable half-volley from just outside the penalty area.

Brentford took time to recover and the final twenty minutes were more even. Odubajo's trickery found him space as he turned inside but he blazed an acceptable chance high over the bar. The ball never seemed to fall Brentford's way in and around the home penalty area and moves constantly broke down in the last third. Pritchard replaced Diagouraga and Proschwitz came on for Jota without noticeable effect. Watford ran the clock down and wasted time with impunity before they were reduced to ten men in injury time when Pudil held back Gray as he ran through on the right flank. Button was up for the free kick, which resulted in a full length save from Gomes from a well-placed

Bidwell header. So near for the youngster who is still waiting for his first ever competitive goal for the Bees. Watford then caught us out on the break and almost scored a third goal which would have been so cruel on a Brentford team that looked visibly distraught and crushed at the final whistle, worn out as they were by their efforts.

This was a frustrating evening as we could, and indeed should, have got something out of the game. Mark Warburton will need to lift the squad before Saturday's tough match against Reading. Most of them looked out on their feet at the final whistle and it may well be that some changes will be necessary to rest some tired legs. In a day or so I will be feeling happier about the quality of our football and overall performance, but for now I am totally resolute in my view that I hate Watford.

A Great Day Out – 3/10/14

There are some days that will live long in the memory and always bring a smile and a warm glow when you think about them. Yesterday was such a day. Like most Brentford supporters I was aware that former favourite, Paul Shrubb, has been suffering from Motor Neurone Disease for quite a while and when another long-term fan, Paul Hewson, suggested that Paul might enjoy reading the book I co-authored - *The Big Brentford Book of the 80s* - in which his exploits are highlighted, I jumped at the opportunity to deliver a copy personally. There was an added bonus when Paul mentioned that Andy McCulloch, who he knows extremely well, would also be there given that he is Godfather to one of Paul's daughters.

So I turned up at Paul's beautiful home in Ash not quite knowing what to expect, but from the moment I arrived I was made totally welcome and spent a couple of hours chatting and laughing and relaxing in the company of some of the nicest and most pleasant people I have ever met. Neither player, of course, needs any introduction to any Bees fans who remembers the late seventies and early eighties. Paul began his career at Fulham, played one first team game and, then, much to his disgust, was released just after the 1975 FA Cup Final. He then spent two years playing out in South Africa, before returning to England and joining Brentford in March 1977.

After scoring on his debut as a midfielder, he moved back into the defence and formed a successful partnership with Pat Kruse, which helped the Bees to promotion in 1978. He was an absolute fans' favourite and made almost two hundred appearances during his five years at the club, before moving on to an equally successful spell at his local club Aldershot, where he is also revered. Shrubby was a very skilful footballer, quick to see a through pass and with the ability to score from long range, but more importantly he could be relied upon to give absolutely everything he had for the team's cause. He never gave up, never hid, never shirked a challenge, and was always there to help and support his colleagues. He sacrificed his own abilities for the sake of his team and was loved and respected by everyone for doing so.

Nothing has changed today. He looks extremely well and his legs remain strong. There is not an ounce of self-pity in him and he takes pride in the fact that he is about to commence his ninth year with an awful wasting disease that normally takes its terrible toll well within that time period. Not only is he surviving, he is thriving and acts as a source of inspiration to other sufferers from MND, visiting them in the local area and encouraging and supporting them through his own personal example. He is fortified and succoured by a close and loving family in whom he takes great pride, joy and comfort and he appears to be a person with great inner strength who is totally at peace with himself. He is also a man of steely determination who stated that because he was so small he was used to fighting for everything in his life and that nothing had changed and he would never give up.

He was full of stories about his time at Brentford. It was a real family club where everybody mixed well. He remarked with pride that every member of staff at the club, from the manager to all the players, and also the back room team, took the time and trouble to attend his eldest daughter's Christening. That was just the way it was done in those days. He mentioned the time when he partnered Steve Phillips up front at Southend, neither of whom were the tallest of men and Paul acted as the target man – a more unlikely one would be hard to picture – but he got one over his morose strike partner when he scored and Phillips didn't!

Before his Brentford debut, skipper and team inspiration Jackie Graham gruffly advised him to just get on with his game but offered to *help him out* if any of the opposition started to pick on him – not that Paul needed any assistance as he was never a soft touch and his opponents certainly knew that they had been in a battle. He regretted that he never won the Player of the Year award but he did collect it once at the presentation at The Winning Post when the actual winner, Andy McCulloch, was unable to attend. He is still friendly with Paul Priddy and Trevor Porter and was responsible for bringing Porter, another former Fulham colleague, to the club when Len Bond was injured in a car crash and reserve keeper Graham Cox was suspended after being sent off in a preseason friendly.

Andy McCulloch was also an absolute delight to spend time with. Relaxed, witty and urbane, he looked lean and fit and he too spoke fondly of his spell at the club and acknowledged that Brentford had sold him far too cheaply to Sheffield Wednesday, although that meant he could ask for higher wages in compensation! Ian St John, Jack Charlton's assistant had tapped him up whilst he was lying on a stretcher following an injury sustained in a match when he was being scouted by Wednesday. His knee was a total mess when he joined Brentford after botched treatment at Oxford United, but Director Eric Radley-Smith, a noted knee expert, eventually got him right and Andy became the perfect striker. Tall, fearless, great in the air, strong on the ground and excellent in front of goal.

He spoke of his battles with the massive centre halves of the time like Millwall's Barry Kitchener and Aldershot's Joe Jopling and was most interested to learn that his former nemesis still owned a pub nearby, and remarked that he might pay him a visit! He well remembered what happened at Aldershot back in 1977 when Jopling feigned injury and the referee bought it and sent Andy off for an alleged headbutt. Seeking revenge after the match, Andy tried to get into the home dressing room but was fought off by Jopling's wife brandishing an umbrella.

His mother came to watch him play for Cardiff one afternoon at Craven Cottage. The team left the dressing room reluctantly as the Grand National was just starting. Andy scored after thirteen seconds, was sent off a minute later for telling the linesman what he thought of him, stalked off the field, apologising to his Mum as he went for her wasted afternoon, and was safely back in the dressing room in time to hear the commentary of the rest of the race. He enjoyed playing with Gordon Sweetzer who he felt was far too brave for his own good and also recalls playing at Luton where their Chairman, Eric Morecambe, would always visit the away dressing room before the game, go through his repertoire of jokes and facial expressions and do his best to put the opposition off. These and many other stories made the minutes and hours flash by and a great time was had by all.

Paul Hewson suggested that Shrubby should attend the Brentford versus Fulham match next month and ideally come onto the pitch to be introduced to the crowd. Paul thought about it for a moment then, his face wreathed in smiles, said that he would take great pleasure in doing so and would wave at both sets of supporters and he then demonstrated exactly the gesture he would employ towards the Fulham fans given that his opinion of that club is exactly the same as ours. Paul, we salute you as a brave and exceptional man who is an example and inspiration to us all. Thank you for letting me into your life.

A Long Time Coming! – 5/10/14

Revenge is a dish best served cold and yesterday's three – one victory over Reading provided Brentford with some element of belated payback for the misery Reading inflicted on us back in 2002 when promotion was snatched out of Brentford's grasp by Jamie Cureton's heartbreaking late strike. Closure is certainly cathartic and good for the soul, and there was much rejoicing amongst Brentford fans about the fact that we had finally managed to allay that particular ghost from the past and put a painful memory to bed. Looking back is all very well but I would prefer to reflect on what yesterday's terrific victory means for us here and now.

We beat a team that for all their recent financial uncertainty has a budget far in excess of our own. Their squad was jam-packed full of players with vast experience not only at this level but even higher in the food chain. We also managed to beat the conditions as a morning downpour had saturated the pitch and made us change our normal short passing game from the back. Most importantly for me, whilst there were times yesterday, particularly in the final quarter, when we demonstrated our by now familiar and customary slick, close passing style of play, we really won the match through the good old-fashioned virtues of guts, passion, organisation and defensive solidity.

Make no mistake, this was a truly excellent team that we were playing, who at one time or another during the afternoon fielded strikers of the calibre of Glenn Murray, Nick Blackman, Simon Cox, Jamie Mackie and Pavel Pogrebnyak and yet we managed to hold them at bay. Normally this season we have dominated possession but, again, yesterday was different as we only had the ball for thirty-nine percent of the time. Mark Warburton mentioned after the match that we had been careless in possession and given the ball away too easily and, whilst he was correct in his assessment, Reading pressed us high up the pitch forcing Button to kick the ball long and given the paucity of targets and his over-clubbing the ball on occasions, this meant that possession was ceded far more easily than normal.

This was possibly one of the reasons why Nick Proschwitz replaced a tiring Andre Gray with thirty minutes still to play. We certainly dominated proceedings far more after his arrival and he provided us with a focal point and some aerial strength up front which enabled us to get a toehold back into a match that at one point in the second half looked as though it might be slowly slipping away from us.

Brentford welcomed back Alex Pritchard, who replaced Toumani Diagouraga despite his excellent display at Watford, but Alex of the twinkling toes and instant control was to play a massive part in our victory. He hit the post in the first minute with an angled shot and for once it was the Bees who started well, but Button was forced into an excellent low save from Blackman to keep us level. Lots of early excitement culminated in Brentford's quickest goal of the season when Jota slotted home from close range after eleven minutes. Moses's magic kept the ball alive wide on the right and McCormack's incisive cross fell perfectly for Jota after Gray's challenge for the ball with Hector. A well worked and well taken goal indeed, and Brentford maintained the initiative before doubling their lead on the half hour.

The Harpo Marx lookalike, Aaron Kuhl, dwelt on the ball and had his pocket picked by the marauding and relentless Jonathan Douglas. Reading were caught on the hop and an instant pass set Gray though on goal. He turned his man with ease and then totally missed his kick but Pritchard was following up and slotted the ball with precision through Federici's legs and beyond the two covering defenders. A bit of additional payback too for those with long memories, as the Reading player whose error caused the goal was the son of Martin Kuhl, a rampaging and, frankly terrifying, midfield player who left his calling card on many Brentford players when playing for the likes of Portsmouth and Bristol City a couple of decades ago.

Reading changed their tactics in the second half, reverted to 4-4-2 and went long. Their efforts were rewarded early on when Cox got in behind the defence and flicked home a harmless looking shot from Mackie. Game on! The next twenty minutes were torture for us as the ball was seemingly never out of our half. Corner followed corner and the pressure was intense but the Bees never buckled. We kept our shape and the back four defended like Trojans and were all heroes, putting their bodies on the line. Douglas was everywhere mopping up in front of them and Diagouraga replaced the impressive Jota to add even more cover for the defence. And yet, for all their possession, Button had surprisingly little to do apart from one excellent plunging save from Mackie and some impressive anticipation and handling. The Bees it was who came closest when Tarkowski's header from a corner was hacked clear off the goal line by Mackie.

Then the tide turned as we had weathered the storm. Holes started to appear in the visitors' defence as they poured men forward and we had the pace and nous to take full advantage as Judge, Pritchard and Moses drove us forward. Judge danced around the keeper but took an extra step and failed to finish with a coup de grace. Pritchard made us all coo with appreciation and amazement when he instantly controlled a high ball coming down with snow on it before twisting away from a challenge and firing just wide. Moses shot across the face of the goal before forcing a sharp near post save from Federici.

And then, miracle of miracles, came our first set piece goal of the season when Pritchard's perfectly placed curling left wing corner was met by Douglas rising high to leapfrog on the back of his covering defender to head the ball home powerfully via the crossbar. As the crowd went into shock, stunned by the sight of Brentford actually scoring from a corner, the referee ignored the vehement protests of the Reading defenders and awarded the goal. A narrow squeak indeed, and one that might well have gone against us on another day, but now it was game over and time for our party pieces.

The Bees saw out the remaining minutes comfortably enough and could even have extended their lead when the ever-willing Proschwitz hit the post from close range before the game ended with some beautiful possession football, which carved Reading open before the ball was hoofed away close to the goal line. Exhilarating stuff indeed and Brentford had won what I feel was perhaps our best victory to date in a season that promises so much. After Norwich, and you know how close we came to beating them, Reading were by far the strongest team we have faced at Griffin Park and we beat them fair and square.

It was heartening to see that the team can scrap and battle with the best of them and that, combined with the excellence of our football when we do things right, will be more than enough for us to thrive for the remainder of the season in these exalted circles. We now go into the international break bursting with confidence, in a strong and totally merited position in the Championship and with two weeks now to heal and rest some tired bodies and minds. Happy days indeed!

Then And Now – 7/10/14

The international break is a bit of a double-edged sword. On the one hand I, like I would suspect most other Brentford fans, will miss my football fix for a fortnight, but isn't it wonderful to sit back and relax for a while and just luxuriate in how well the Bees have done to date?

A brief resume of our achievements is as follows: We sit comfortably in tenth place in the Championship with seventeen points. We have won five of our first eleven games, three at home and two away. We have been competitive in all bar one of our opening matches. We have already played against several of the so called *bigger* clubs and anticipated promotion challengers in Brighton, Leeds, Reading, Norwich, AFC Bournemouth, Middlesbrough and Watford and have only looked out of our depth against Middlesbrough. We could quite easily have drawn against AFC Bournemouth, Norwich and Watford and beaten Birmingham City, which would have put us on top of the League!

We have scored fifteen goals so far, the ninth best record in the League. Only six teams have conceded more than our sixteen goals. So called lower division journeymen such as Alan McCormack, Jonathan Douglas and Tony Craig have adapted to the higher level like ducks to water. New signings like Alan Judge, Andre Gray, Moses Odubajo, Alex Pritchard and Jota have settled into their new home and are performing exceptionally well on the pitch. The younger players such as James Tarkowski, Harlee Dean, Stuart Dallas and Jake Bidwell have not been overawed by their new surroundings.

The team is being well managed and supported off the field and any gaps in the squad are quickly filled. We have looked totally comfortable and the quality of our football has already received much favourable comment. Clubs are beginning to alter their normal style of play in an attempt to counter our approach. We are beginning to cause a stir as the football world takes note of our achievements. The fans are responding and crowds are higher than anticipated with four consecutive five-figure home attendances.

Complacency will be fatal and we only need to look back at our last season spent at this level of the game back in 1992/93 to see just how badly things can turn out after a promising start. It is highly informative to go back twenty-two years in order to re-examine exactly what went wrong. We didn't play our eleventh league game until the seventeenth of October 1992, as by this stage of the season we had also played an additional four Coca-Cola Cup ties against Fulham and Spurs as well as two Anglo-Italian Cup Preliminary ties against those well known Italian teams, Swindon Town and Oxford United. A packed schedule indeed. Our league record was patchy in the extreme as we only won two of our first eleven matches, against Southend and Portsmouth (who else remembers the incongruity of Ashley Bayes crouching behind the goal and coaching Gary Blissett and Neil Smillie's googly header deceiving Alan Knight) and lost five of them, amassing a total of ten points. We had scored eleven goals yet conceded only thirteen.

Things were to improve dramatically, as between the middle of October and the end of the year we took twenty-three points from our next twelve league games, winning seven of them, and the New Year began with the team sitting comfortably in tenth place. It is easy to see now where the cracks were forming and that we were really in a false position even when we were congratulating ourselves at the turn of the year. A small squad was decimated by injuries and began creaking ominously given the pressure of the eight additional Anglo-Italian Cup matches. Players were played out of position and the gaps were not filled from outside. The New Year began with a horrendous run of results with one win and a draw and eleven, yes eleven, defeats in thirteen games which dropped us into the relegation zone from where we never really escaped.

Despite a mini revival which coincided with the return from injury of Terry Evans and which brought eight points from four games, four defeats in the last six matches brought about an inevitable conclusion and relegation was confirmed on the last day of the season after a shameful capitulation at Bristol City.

Why did we go down? It is difficult to know exactly where to start. We committed hara-kiri by selling our prime asset in Dean Holdsworth and replacing him appallingly, firstly with the ineffable Murray Jones and then with the one dimensional Joe Allon. A deadly combination of the cheap solution not working, before being followed by a panic buy – welcome to the world of *old* Brentford. Our general recruitment policy was flawed and slapdash in the extreme, and none of our signings made much of an impact. Despite losing Chris Hughton in December to a career ending injury, no real replacement was signed until March by which time the rot had well and truly set in. Mickey Bennett flattered to deceive and was a one game in four merchant, Detzi Kruszynski had an aversion to training and hard work, Shane Westley was slow, clumsy and agricultural and both Alan Dickens and Kenny Sansom were pedestrian, disinterested and well past their sell by date. Only Paul Stephenson impressed but he was signed far too late in the day to make a real difference. As for the loanees, Gerry Peyton was an excellent replacement for the injured Graham Benstead, but the less said about Paul Mortimer the better.

It is illuminating to note that we only managed to obtain a transfer fee for one of our 1992/93 signings in Joe Allon, the rest disappeared without trace and with no recompense to us in return for the investment we made in them. We basically had a strong Third Division squad minus two of its best players in the departed Dean Holdsworth and the injured Terry Evans, desperately trying to hold its own in a far higher standard of football. Our tactics were crude in the extreme and were mainly based on lumping the ball upfield to Marcus Gayle and Garry Blissett and hoping that the evergreen Neil Smillie might create something out of nothing. Blissett performed heroics in scoring over twenty league goals but nobody else managed more than six, and a grand total of fifty-two goals scored all season in forty-six league matches highlighted where the main problem lay. Once Detzi Kruszynski left the club, our midfield was bypassed wherever possible with hard tacklers such as Billy Manuel and Simon Ratcliffe employed mainly as ball winners and to help the ball on.

In other words, there was barely a creative bone in the entire squad, and a limited team employing basic tactics with a threadbare support staff and uninspired management, did pretty well to secure as many points as they did. No wonder we lost ten games at Griffin Park as our shortcomings were ruthlessly exposed when we tried to take the game to the opposition. The most embarrassing but enlightening moment of the season was watching a nine-man Swindon team running rings around us, and totally out-footballing us to such an extent that, despite our two man advantage, we were left clinging on desperately for a point.

The differences between then and now are many and obvious. We are now in an extremely fortunate and favourable position given our modern and scientific approach, and enlightened management structure, but it does us no harm to look back and learn from the mistakes made in an earlier era, which resulted in a massive opportunity to establish the club at a higher level being thrown away so quickly and carelessly. Given how far we have evolved I honestly cannot see history repeating itself!

International Bees – Part Two – 10/10/14

Previously, I started to tell the tale of some of the Brentford players who received international honours over the last fifty years or so and I thought that I would continue on that theme and discuss our internationals of the 90s, who certainly were a varied and eclectic bunch.

Brian Statham served the club well after joining Brentford from Spurs, where he had won three England Under 21 caps as an exciting young attacking fullback. He enjoyed a five-year stay at Griffin Park but never really fulfilled his early promise. Injuries certainly didn't help him and hampered his progress throughout his career that ended with him only playing around two hundred first team games. He broke his leg at Bournemouth at a time when a new contract was negotiated but not signed, but the Bees acted very well in honouring the contract despite his injury. He will perhaps be best remembered for marking his first ever appearance at Griffin Park by being sent off when playing as a loanee for Reading, receiving his marching orders in his last game for the Bees, at Wembley in the playoff final against Crewe, and then marking his return to the club as a Gillingham player the following season with yet another red card for a needless stamp on Ijah Anderson that also brought about the award of a penalty kick. Brian recently recalled his spell at Griffin Park with fondness:

The club I would say I had the most success at would have to be Brentford. I played there for five years and was part of some really good sides and worked under some good managers. I played at Wembley for Brentford and won the Third Division title in 1992. Looking back I had some really good times there.

Chris Hughton was a cool, calm, experienced and composed left back with fifty-three caps for the Republic of Ireland who helped get us over the line in 1992 as he signed for us at a time when our promotion dreams were stuttering. He lasted until the following Christmas when he broke down with a knee injury in the pre-match warm-up before the Derby County match and unfortunately never played again. If I remember correctly, Grant Chalmers had to be summoned down from the stands with a freshly eaten hot dog still digesting in his stomach, to sit on the bench as a last minute replacement! That story, apocryphal or not, just about sums up our levels of professionalism at the time! The Bees were having a good run until Hughton's injury but sank like a stone immediately afterwards as his influence was sorely missed. His eventual replacement was Kenny Sansom of whom the least said the better, as the experienced England international, a veteran of eighty-six England caps, was totally out of his depth and past his prime as he appeared to coast through his eight games for the club. Another Eire international, the thirty-six year old Gerry Peyton, a former old enemy at Fulham, had two excellent spells in goal as a loanee when Graham Benstead was injured, and did his utmost to save us from relegation but without success.

Relegation saw David Webb clear out the more experienced and expensive players and he built up a vibrant young team that should have been promoted twice in his first four seasons, but that is a story for another day! Nicky Forster was a wonderful signing for a club like Brentford, who were pretty much on the crest of a slump, but his agent, *Monster, Monster* Eric Hall made it clear that he saw Brentford as an ideal stepping stone for his star client. Nicky gave us two and a half seasons of excellent service and he amazed and frustrated us in equal measures. He had blistering pace but poor close control, and he often seemed to fail to take the ball with him. His finishing was clinical, except when he had time to think, and particularly when he was left with a clear run in on goal. I well remember the exciting Charlton FA Cup tie at The Valley when we lost bravely by the odd goal in five, but Nicky was particularly profligate that evening and let our opponents off the hook after he missed a procession of gilt-edged chances that his own pace and anticipation had created for himself. Nicky won four England Under 21 caps, scoring once, before his move to Birmingham City for £700,000 in January 1997. Brentford were firmly ensconced at the top of the league when he was sold and surely on the way to promotion. No replacement was forthcoming, the goals and victories dried up and the Bees finally limped into the playoffs and eventual embarrassment at the hands of Crewe Alexandra.

I was definitely in the minority in rating Gus Hurdle. He established himself in the team as an overlapping right back who was really comfortable on the ball. Defending was certainly not his forte but I felt that Micky Adams gave up on him far too early and he drifted out of the game, but not before winning a couple of caps for his native Barbados. Gus is really one of the nicest and warmest people I have ever met in the game and I am delighted that he has carved out a successful career for himself in television and the media, an area ideally suited to his sunny personality.

There was general excitement and anticipation when Paul Davis, veteran of over three hundred and fifty appearances for Arsenal, joined us in September 1995. He was a gifted creative midfielder who had won eleven Under 21 caps and he was expected to be the fulcrum of a renewed promotion charge after the disappointment of the Huddersfield playoff defeat. Davis managed the grand total of five appearances for the Bees and performed like a duck out of water and looked as if he would have preferred to be anywhere other than standing around in our midfield watching the ball fly over his head. This was a major lesson learned about the danger of signing experienced players who had no previous experience of, or apparent appetite for, playing at our level of the game.

Marcus Bent was another striker who had a long and successful career without perhaps reaching the heights that at one time looked likely. He showed wonderful potential in his early games and was a total breath of fresh air as his pace and strength presented a real threat to opposition defences. He was still developing and improving when David Webb surprisingly sold him to Crystal Palace before his twentieth birthday. The eventual fee of three hundred thousand pounds was also very low for a player of his potential and ability. Marcus won two England Under 21 caps but instead of becoming a star, his career stood still and he became a footballing nomad who played almost six hundred games for fourteen different clubs and his numerous transfer fees totalled over ten million pounds.

Manager, Eddie May, did his best to make bricks without straw after seeing his squad decimated by David Webb in the aftermath of the Crewe playoff defeat. His efforts to bring in new blood were thwarted at almost every turn but he managed to sign two decent loanees in Welsh international midfielder Gareth Hall from Sunderland and Chelsea's Republic of Ireland international keeper Nick Colgan. Both performed adequately amongst the shambles surrounding them, but their stays were short. Former Scotland Under 21 international defender Graeme Hogg was one of the very few players to emerge with credit from that appalling season as he gave everything to the cause, as well as being a potent attacking threat at set pieces. Niall Thompson came and went in the blinking of an eye in 1998 and the Canadian international striker made little impact apart from on a Carlisle United defender when he was sent off for a stamp in our rare victory at Brunton Park.

The arrival of new owner Ron Noades brought about a new recruitment policy with a series of eager, keen young players brought in rather than the journeymen employed by the previous regime. Danny Boxall, Robert Quinn and Martin Rowlands earned twenty-one Republic of Ireland Under 21 caps between them whilst at the club and all flourished at Griffin Park. For all the anger generated by his departure from the club and subsequent provocative behaviour when celebrating at the end of a QPR versus Brentford derby match, Rowlands was a wonderfully talented midfielder who was equally effective on the right hand side or down the middle. He got the last laugh over Brentford when he returned to Griffin Park in 2013 with Leyton Orient, scored with a scorching long-range free kick and, to add insult to injury, then ran the length of the pitch in celebration. An Adebayor-like action that did nothing to heal the rift between him and the Brentford supporters!

Tony Folan was gifted with immense talent and scored goals against Peterborough and Cambridge United that almost defied belief and should have been set to music. Four Eire Under 21 caps were scant reward for his ability, but his career was ravaged by injury and he faded from the scene far too young – a real tragedy. Midfielder Gareth Graham was another of the former Crystal Palace contingent to follow Ron Noades to Griffin Park. He never managed to establish himself and faded out of sight but not before winning five Northern Ireland Under 21 caps. Scott Marshall and Patrick Agyemang earned international recognition for Scotland Under 21 and Ghana respectively but had indifferent spells at Brentford, although Agyemang showed some indications of the quality he would develop later on in his career.

The decade ended as far as international recognition was concerned with Brentford's Icelandic contingent. Hermann Hreidarsson was signed out of the blue from Crystal Palace for a club record three quarters of a million pounds, and started slowly before showing his immense talent, not least when gallivanting up the field to support the attack. He scored a memorable match winner to settle a tight promotion clash against Cardiff City and was never going to stay too long with the club. He was far too good for us! He eventually earned us a fee of two and a half million pounds when he left a year later for Wimbledon having won a Championship medal and twelve full caps for Iceland during his stay at the club.

His international teammate Ivar Ingimarsson joined Brentford just after his departure and also proved a revelation once he moved to centre half where he gave the Bees excellent service, memorably going throughout the entire 2001/02 season as an ever-present without picking up a single booking, before joining the exodus after the Cardiff playoff defeat in 2002. So, the 90s saw a variety of international players pass through Griffin Park, some on the way up, perhaps more on the way down, and a similar trend was to continue into the next decade, as we will see when I am able to update this article.

Happy Birthday Brentford! – 12/10/14

Let me join the torrent of well-wishers celebrating our beloved Brentford's one hundredth and twenty-fifth birthday, a heady milestone that was reached a couple of days ago. There is so much water that has flowed under Kew Bridge since that momentous day back in October 1889 when the decision was taken by a narrow margin to form a new football club. Much of it has been captured perfectly in the wonderful *100 Years of Brentford Book* which is as comprehensive and fascinating a read today as it was the day that it was published in 1989. In the time since its publication, the Bees have been promoted four times, relegated on three occasions, lost two Associate Members' Cup Finals and suffered through seven, yes seven, unsuccessful playoff campaigns. The events of the past quarter century are pretty much a microcosm of our beloved club's topsy-turvy existence since its foundation where we have climbed ladders and descended snakes with apparent impunity. Now I can see massive parallels between the events of today and those of our halcyon days of the 1930s. For Harry Curtis who led us from the Third tier to the promised land of the First Division, read Mark Warburton, for legendary Chairman and Life Vice-President of that period Louis P. Simon, read Matthew Benham. The similarities might be eerie but they are also totally apparent to me. Given a fair wind and head of steam, and the luck that every successful team requires, I can see no reason why our momentum and phenomenal rate of progress cannot be maintained over the coming years.

These are exciting times to be a Brentford supporter and quite frankly, we are entering new and unexplored territory for many of us, inured as we are to the disappointments, inadequacies and lost opportunities of previous decades. I think I am writing in this vein today as I spent much of yesterday going through what are the final proofs of the forthcoming *Brentford 125th Anniversary Book* which is about to be sent to the printers in time for its publication and launch in the middle of next month. You all have an absolute treat in store! It contains almost three hundred pages of pure nostalgia, and I am sure that every reader will be captivated and mesmerised by the selection of old photographs, cartoons, caricatures, match reports, interviews, editorial comments and memorabilia that Mark Croxford and Dave Lane have managed to unearth. Most of the items had not seen the light of day for many years and were totally new to the three of us.

Even though the language and tone of voice changes, what the book tells me is that there is so much that remains the same and unchanged between different generations, as the Brentford supporter of say, the nineteen twenties and nineteen sixties in many ways faced similar concerns and frustrations as we do today. They just expressed them in a different manner. Hooliganism too reared its ugly head, although one notorious incident in October 1921 when a Brentford fan, Percy Sands, actually jumped the barrier and physically assaulted a Charlton player was explained away in court by mention of the assailant's shell shock suffered in the Great War. You will find many similar snippets of trivia and information all the way through the book and it was not until we researched it that I totally understood how big and successful a club Brentford really was in the four years leading up to the Second World War and quite how tumultuous and dramatic was our fall from grace once football resumed after the end of hostilities.

Just as the Brentford supporters from that era were taken on a wonderful and intoxicating magic carpet ride from the third tier of English football to almost the top of the tree, through the efforts of Harry Curtis and his band of men, I feel that the fans of today similarly have so much to look forward to. Who knows what fresh achievements will be recorded in a mere twenty-five years time when we come to celebrate Brentford's one hundred and fiftieth anniversary? It promises to be an exciting and exhilarating journey and I, for one, cannot wait!

Uwe Rösler – 16/10/14

We are now coming towards the end of the international break and our thoughts are naturally turning towards Saturday's match when the Bees return to the fray, hopefully refreshed and reinvigorated after a fortnight's rest and recuperation. Brentford will be playing away to a Wigan Athletic team which is stuttering, not firing on all cylinders, and which appears to be suffering a hangover after the disappointment of falling at the final hurdle in last season's playoffs. Wigan are currently down amongst the dead men in twenty-first position, a mere three points away from the dreaded relegation zone, a position which comes as a total surprise given that they were fully expected to challenge for honours again this season, and have a large and expensive playing squad oozing with Premier League and international experience.

The natives are getting pretty restless and there are already murmurings, which are rapidly growing in intensity, about the future of their manager, Uwe Rösler, who has presided over a run of only six victories in his last twenty-six matches despite spending expansively on recent signings such as Oriol Riera, Adam Forshaw and Andy Delort. And yet it all started so well for Rösler last December after he took over from the busted flush that was Owen Coyle. Rösler provided the impetus and leadership that saw Wigan not only reach the playoffs but also come within a hairsbreadth of beating Arsenal in the FA Cup semi final. He rightly received broad recognition for his achievements, which were truly excellent but, in my view, should have been even better.

I watched him put out a team that contained only one striker in their home playoff match against Queens Park Rangers, and it certainly appeared that the summit of his ambition was the nil-nil draw he ended up with. Wigan came out of the traps quickly in the second leg at Loftus Road, went a goal up but then sat back, totally gave the initiative to the home team, attempted to soak up their pressure and rely on breakaways, and eventually lost the game and the tie. Yet more playoff heartbreak for Rösler to follow on from the previous season's excruciating defeat for Brentford in the Wembley Final against Yeovil.

Now Rösler is no longer the fans' favourite at the DW Stadium. Their complaints centre upon his perceived lack of consistency in team selection, regular changes in formation, his innate caution, negativity and over-analysis, and his overriding reluctance to take the handbrake off. Now where have we heard some of those accusations before? We would be lying if we just said that this was merely another match for Brentford, as there is obviously added spice to the proceedings on Saturday given the presence in the Wigan ranks of Uwe Rösler as well as Adam Forshaw and our former Head of Performance, Chris Haslam. All three of them formed the Brain Drain from Griffin Park as they left Brentford to supposedly better themselves in their new home in the North West of England.

I see no reason for Brentford to change anything in either their approach or style of play on Saturday. Warburton gives due attention to his opponents and how they are likely to set up against him but is far more concerned about what damage his Brentford team can inflict upon the opposition, rather than vice versa. Surely a healthier and more positive approach than Rösler's cat and mouse efforts to out-think and perhaps over-analyse the other team? Warburton's Brentford are proactive and dynamic and are always looking to seize the initiative, Rösler's Brentford were reactive, constrained and cautious. Perhaps I am over generalising but I think I have assessed the two men's style pretty accurately.

That is not to rewrite history or diminish Rösler's achievements at Brentford. His overall record was truly exceptional. He oversaw one hundred and thirty-six competitive games in all during his two and a half seasons at the club, was unbeaten in seventy-three per cent of them, and had a forty-three per cent win ratio. Impressive figures indeed, but the feeling persists that it could and perhaps should, have been even better. So many away games saw a similar pattern emerge. Brentford would dominate possession, play pretty and intricate football with very little or no end product and then attempt to hold on to what they had for the last quarter of the game.

So many memories remain, so many opportunities missed: We played Doncaster Rovers, the eventual champions, off the park one October Saturday, but failed to put them away and lost ridiculously to two late goals having dominated the entire proceedings. A defeat that ultimately had a massive effect on the final league table. The same thing happened at Orient on a match shown live on Sky Television. Total domination in possession, no penetration and a loss to a spawny, late and offside goal. Playing three centre halves on the opening day of the season at Bury and allowing a poor team to escape with a draw. A late concession to Scunthorpe after running the entire game and missing yet another penalty. And please do not get me started on penalty kicks and the opportunities we threw away from them over his entire period at the club.

Rösler was a leftfield appointment by Matthew Benham, which nobody saw coming, and he certainly laid impressive foundations at the club and instigated a revolution in terms of the off field support team which were second to none at our level of the game. He improved our football, and with the help of Warburton and an enhanced playing budget, brought in far better players and almost took us to the playoffs in his first season, until we blew it on a ridiculous afternoon of low comedy and frustration at Stevenage. But never mind, everything was in place for a promotion charge the following season. As you all know, despite all of us doing our best to forget, it finally ended in tears.

Last season saw a poor start culminating in the defeat at Stevenage and the now famous behind-closed-doors meeting in which a lot of home truths were apparently expressed on a variety of concerns, including Uwe's insistence on rotating his players as well as his overall management and tactical approach. With the air cleared and a far more consistent selection policy employed, the Bees went on a long unbeaten run that continued until the point when Rösler was approached by Wigan and decided to jump ship. His relationship with the Brentford fans had deteriorated after a couple of intemperate outbursts after victories against Colchester and Bristol City, and the feeling persisted that perhaps the time had come for a parting of the ways. A point of view heightened by the success achieved by Mark Warburton once he succeeded Rösler and managed to put his own stamp on the team, and changed their approach towards the game.

Rösler too seemed to be revitalised and reinvigorated by his new challenge at Wigan, which brings us back to where we started. I wish Uwe well and thank him for taking Matthew Benham's vision for the club on board and coming so close to finishing the task of getting Brentford into the Championship. Uwe's alleged actions since he joined his new club and appeared to want to spirit away a succession of players and back room staff from Brentford, whilst a real compliment to our quality, have further hardened attitudes towards him. I hope he learns from his roller coaster experiences over the past couple of years and that he makes an ultimate success of his managerial career. Ideally he will adapt his approach, become more positive and less analytical and far less fearful of the opposition. If he manages to do so then he will throw off the *Nearly Man* tag that is beginning to follow him around. As for Saturday, let's just play the team and not the man and in that case there is every chance that the Bees will not return home empty handed.

We Have Come A Long Way – 19/10/14

A mere couple of years ago it would have been hard to imagine Brentford playing a competitive match against Wigan, separated as they were by the chasm of two divisions. Our paths had last crossed in 2003, and in the years since then Wigan had climbed to the heights of the Premier League where they seemed to have established themselves, won the FA Cup, and also competed in Europe. Yesterday saw the two teams meet at the DW Stadium on equal terms, and it is testimony to how far we have come that the general mood in the Brentford camp is one of acute disappointment that we came away with only one point after a nil – nil draw, rather than the three that our performance probably merited.

Football people are generally pretty guarded in their post match interviews, particularly if they have been given time to allow their emotions to calm down, but it is easy to read between the lines when listening to the thoughts of Mark Warburton, Tony Craig and David Button to understand that there was more than normal riding on yesterday's match, and that the Bees felt that they had let their illustrious hosts off the hook. As it is, Brentford remain firmly ensconced in tenth position and Uwe Rösler's Wigan are hovering uneasily just one point above the relegation zone and the knives are now out for the Wigan manager. There was a marvellous turnout of well over a thousand Bees fans at the game, some of whom, no doubt, adopted the role of tricoteuses revelling in the problems that Uwe is currently facing.

I wish Uwe no ill. We were good for him as we gave him the platform, infrastructure and support to act as the stepping stone to the prime job he eventually earned back home in the North West, and he helped to lay the foundations which enabled Mark Warburton to step in and take us to our current position, something that the majority of Brentford fans feel would probably not have taken place had Rösler remained in charge. Rösler had an immediate impact at Wigan, leading his new team to the playoffs and FA Cup semi final but last season ended in heartache for him and his expensively assembled squad are now struggling to keep their head above water.

Yesterday was their seventh match without a win, and for all their possession Wigan barely made David Button break into a sweat. Of course, exceptional players like Shaun Maloney, Callum McManaman and James McClean don't become bad ones overnight and they did cause Brentford some problems with their ability and movement, but tactically Brentford did a job on their opponents and stifled their threat. Wigan too were boring and negative in the extreme, totally lacking in confidence and relying alarmingly on a strange hybrid-quasi-long-ball approach which saw a plethora of sideways and backwards passes at the back being followed by a series of aimless thumps upfield which were easily dealt with by an organised and largely untroubled Bees back line. Adam Forshaw was totally wasted playing in a deep defensive role in front of his back four and the threat of two reputed Brentford preseason transfer targets in Oriol Riera and Andy Delort was easily snuffed out.

Ironically it was Forshaw who almost cost his new team the match when, dawdling on the ball, he slipped and was robbed by the marauding Jonathan Douglas who sent Andre Gray away with a clear run in on goal, but his lob, greeted with a banshee howl by the effervescent Billy Reeves on Bees Player, landed on top of the unguarded net rather than in it. I read two comments this morning that rather sum up the view of many of the Wigan faithful on their message boards today. One said that Forshaw was supposed to be Brentford's best midfield player whereas he saw three far better ones out on the pitch yesterday wearing the yellow shirt of Brentford. There was also bemused admiration for our always keeping three men upfield at Wigan corners in comparison with Uwe's customary all eleven men back policy.

Alan Judge, as always, playing with his head up and probing for an opening.

Yes, we were also patronised by the Wigan fans who felt that it was a bit beneath their dignity to be playing a team as small as Brentford, and that they should only need to turn up to beat us, but there was also some grudging acknowledgment of the quality of our football on the day. Moses, Jota, Douglas and Pritchard all went close, but not close enough, and one point was our reward when perhaps three were within our grasp. The fact that Scott Carson, the Wigan goalkeeper was by far and away their best player also speaks volumes of how well we performed. We were a team, Wigan a disorganised and demoralised rabble that, like Leeds United, are going nowhere at present. I have no wish for Uwe to lose his job, but perhaps it is time for another behind-closed-doors meeting, similar to the one at Stevenage last season, so that some home truths can be discussed and perhaps the air cleared, as it is plainly obvious that they are not a happy camp and have a disunited dressing room.

Another Tough Test – 21/10/14

Sheffield Wednesday come to Griffin Park tonight and, like everyone else so far this season, are sure to present Brentford with a stiff test. They have only lost once away from home so far, against Cardiff City, and have an effective blend of brawn, pace, height and no little footballing ability too. What's more they will be smarting after having their backsides tanned by Watford who won convincingly at Hillsborough on Saturday.

Matches between the Bees and the Owls are invariably exciting and end-to-end, and ever since the reign of Martin Allen there has been a friendly, respectful and enduring relationship between the two sets of supporters. This all began one cold Saturday December afternoon in 2004 when Allen took his team to Hillsborough, where nearly twenty-two thousand spectators were fortunate enough to witness an amazing game of football. Martin Allen is one of football's great motivators and his management that season was almost exemplary as he moulded a team of journeymen, has-beens and promising youngsters into a cohesive unit that fought and battled their way through the back door into the playoffs. There was experience in abundance with Stewart Talbot and Chris Hargreaves competing for everything in midfield. John Salako defied the years with some dazzling displays on the left wing, and some less glorious ones at left back, and Isaiah Rankin and Deon Burton were skilful and clever, if none too potent or energetic up front. Jay Tabb provided the class in midfield and there was a mean defence with Andy Frampton and Kevin O'Connor solid at full back and Michael Turner and Sam Sodje forming a raw but talented central defensive partnership. Behind them Stuart Nelson was still establishing himself in goal and delighting and frustrating supporters in equal measures with some up and down displays.

The potential jewel in the crown was young Alex Rhodes. He started his career with Eastern Counties League side Newmarket Town, where he scored twenty goals in the early part of the 2003/04 season. That earned him a move to Brentford and he became an instant fan favourite when he scored a wonderfully taken goal on the final day of the season which ensured that *The Great Escape* was successfully concluded and that the Bees would avoid a relegation that at one time appeared to be inevitable. By the time of the Sheffield Wednesday match, Rhodes was still trying to establish himself in the team as a left winger or central striker and he was to have a massive impact upon the outcome of the game.

The Bees were under the cosh from the start and were soon caught square and the onrushing Steve MacLean was caught from behind by the trailing Michael Turner.

Penalty, red card, goal – à la Tony Craig against Birmingham - was the immediate result and the Bees went behind when MacLean converted the spot kick with ease. Frampton moved into the middle, and the over-matched Andy Myers struggled to cope with the marauding Jon-Paul McGovern on the Wednesday right flank. Alex Rhodes also came on for Ben May and Brentford's sole threat was Deon Burton who seemed to be competing against Wednesday's clutch of immense defenders on his own. He was afforded absolutely no protection by the referee, Mark Cowburn, who penalised him with monotonous regularity and eventually seemed to take a little bit too much pleasure in booking the Brentford striker. Rhodes did ghost in from the left to smash a volley onto the underside of the home crossbar but that was the only time the Bees threatened in a totally one sided first half. Nelson was a hero, plunging in amongst the bodies to save time after time and then doing his best to spoil things by gifting possession back to the home team with a series of appallingly sliced and shanked clearance kicks.

The dominant David Button punching clear against Sheffield Wednesday.

Martin Allen was everywhere, directing and encouraging his team, changing their shape and exhorting them to greater efforts, until his frustration at the referee boiled over and he seemed to make a gesture at the official, which resulted in him being sent off from the technical area. A decision greeted with wild applause by the home fans who could tell how much influence he was having in keeping our heads afloat and yet appreciated his antics. Martin decamped in high dudgeon to the Directors' Box, and given that he did not have his mobile phone with him, tried to shout his instructions down to his assistant, Adrian Whitbread, standing alone on the bench far below. This didn't seem to be working so Martin's teenage son, George, was repeatedly despatched by his father down the Boardroom stairs to the touchline with a series of scribbled instructions for the bench.

Eventually the opposition cottoned on and an aged jobsworth attempted to stop young Master Allen from making any additional forays – a state of affairs that was not well received by his father. The home crowd by now didn't know what to watch, the action on the pitch, where Nelson was playing Wednesday on his own, or the other struggle playing out in the Directors' Box.

Somehow, as if by osmosis, Allen's instructions began to slip through the net and Brentford continued to change formation like an infantry battalion on the parade ground. Nothing seemed to work until finally, with ten minutes left to play, Allen played his final card and Alex Rhodes was moved up top to play alongside the ever-willing but totally exhausted Deon Burton. Fate finally decided to smile down on Brentford, as a rare corner was forced which led to an almighty goalmouth scramble and Rhodes hammered home a totally unexpected and unmerited equaliser. A precious point, rather than the expected thrashing, now looked an outside possibility. Affronted by the indignity they had suffered, Wednesday poured forward, left gaps behind them and were immediately caught with a sucker punch. Rhodes picked up the ball well within his own half, put on the afterburners, and scythed through the ungainly home defence. A clever sideways pass saw Burton left clean through. He mis-controlled, and time appeared to stand still but he recovered to chip the ball over the helpless David Lucas.

The last eight minutes, plus as much injury time as the referee dared to add on, seemed to last an eternity but Brentford somehow held out for the bravest and most unexpected victory I have ever witnessed and one received rapturously by the Bees supporters lucky enough to have witnessed this comeback. This was a win earned by guts, tenacity, sheer bloody-mindedness and, of course, brilliant management. A fact sportingly recognised by the home fans who shook off their disappointment and incredulity at the larceny they had witnessed, by applauding the entire Brentford team off the pitch, with a special ovation reserved for Martin Allen, who milked the moment, and fully deserved to do so.

Deon Burton had made an indelible impression on Sheffield Wednesday, aided of course by his blistering volleyed goal in the return match at Griffin Park, and eventually joined the Owls and enjoyed a successful stay there. Alas, the future for Alex Rhodes wasn't as glittering, as his horrendous collision with Paul McShane of Walsall, a mere few weeks later, brought about the serious knee injury that had a terminal effect on his career, as he lost his acceleration and was never the same player again. A terrible waste of an exceptional talent. As for the supporters, a bond between the Brentford and Sheffield Wednesday fans was created that unforgettable December afternoon which has lasted to the present day, and a warm and competitive, but friendly atmosphere is expected at Griffin Park tonight.

Silence Is Goalden – 23/10/14

Brentford supporters of all ages will be greatly saddened by the announcement yesterday of the death of George Francis. Francis was a Brentford legend who, with his lifelong friend Jim Towers, formed one of the truly great Brentford goalscoring partnerships and one that is never likely to be matched. George scored one hundred and thirty-six goals for the club, second only to Jim Towers who ended up with one hundred and sixty-three.

Amazingly, neither player cost Brentford a penny to sign as they were both local boys, Jim from Shepherds Bush and George from Acton, and *The Terrible Twins* terrorised Third Division defences throughout the nineteen fifties and early sixties.

George started as he was to continue, scoring a late equaliser on his debut at Walsall in February 1955, when only twenty-one years of age. The partnership with Jim Towers was launched the following season and the pair of them dominated the Brentford goalscoring charts year after year throughout a decade when the Bees were the *nearly men* coming so close on a couple of occasions to recovering their Second Division status. George seemed, at times, to play second fiddle to Towers, who possessed a cannonball shot, but he was a star in his own right, chasing lost causes and never allowing defences to settle. Perhaps his proudest moment came in October 1959 when he put local rivals Queens Park Rangers to the sword with a match-winning hat trick at Loftus Road. He couldn't stop scoring that season and, ever present, he notched up an incredible thirty-one goals in forty-eight matches.

In today's world of pre-match meals and early team get-togethers it is hard to picture the more relaxed and less organised and scientific regime of the 1950's when players were simply expected to report for home matches an hour or so before the kick off and conducted their pre-match warm-up sitting on the toilet smoking a Woodbine. George, in fact, missed the home match against Brighton in 1956 after not waking up from his late afternoon nap in time to get to Griffin Park before the kick off, a state of affairs that would be quite impossible to contemplate nowadays but, at the time, was simply shrugged off after his sheepish apology!

As George himself explained:

I like a nap before the game and left instructions to be woken up. But my mother-in-law woke me at the time I should have been at the ground. I couldn't get a taxi and was caught in the crowd, so that when I arrived the lads were going out onto the field.

No alarm clocks or mobile phones in those days then!

After the removal of the maximum wage in 1961, the Brentford board and management surprised nobody by deciding to pull in their horns and cut costs to the bone. A disastrous decision, which saw both Francis and Towers sold together, amazingly, to Queens Park Rangers, of all people, for a meagre eight thousand pounds in total, a giveaway fee for a pair of proven and established goalscorers, not far past their prime and both still only in their late twenties. Such a boggling decision was rewarded, quite inevitably, with relegation at the end of the season, as a toothless team denuded of its only goal threat subsided without much fight into the bottom division. Interestingly enough Brentford manager Malcolm MacDonald claimed at the time that Francis and Towers had in fact insisted on the move and that he would never have been responsible for transferring them both.

So confusion reigns over the cause of the transfers, but what is not in any doubt is the grudging tribute to the pair of them who were airbrushed out of existence and received a peremptory single line in the club programme, merely thanking them for their past services. How's that for gratitude after almost three hundred goals between the pair of them? Shoddy work, indeed, by the club, which smacks of the feudal attitude that existed in those days between the masters, who owned and ran the clubs, and the players - their serfs.

George made a brief return to Griffin Park, but the magic was gone and he finished his Football League career, alongside Jim Towers yet again, at Gillingham where he went out in a blaze of glory, leading the Gills to promotion in 1964, before ending up at the customary elephants' graveyard for Brentford players, Hillingdon Borough.

So what sort of player was George Francis? The best and most qualified person to answer that key question is surely his long-term partner Jim Towers:

George was very quick around the box, he chased the ball down and forced defenders to make mistakes, and because of that he scored a lot more goals than me inside the area. He was a real nuisance too and made a lot of goals for himself, whereas I would wait for the right pass or cross and I scored with a lot of shots from outside the box too.

George was a very modest man though. He would describe himself as a bit of a poacher and say things like, "I just used to hang around the goalkeeper and wait for them to drop the ball so I could tap it in". But he was a far better player than he would let you believe.

George Francis was, not before time, inducted into the Brentford FC Hall of Fame in March this year and died at the age of eighty from bowel cancer. When conducting our research recently for a potential *Big Brentford Book of the 60s*, Dave Lane, Mark Croxford and I discovered to our concern and disappointment just how few Brentford players from the late 50s and early 60s remain with us, and George's passing has seen that number decrease yet again. I am sure that the club will mark his passing with suitable ceremony and I would make the fervent and heartfelt request that they announce a minute's silence to take place before the next home game against Derby County. Silence, if properly observed, seems a much more fitting and appropriate tribute than applause, and the supporters at the recent match against Reading, with an immaculately observed silent and moving tribute to murdered local schoolgirl Alice Gross, proved that they can be trusted to behave properly.

Let's hope that this gesture is repeated a week on Saturday to mark the passing of a true Brentford great and local legend. Rest in Peace, George Francis and I hope that your partnership with Jim Towers is renewed in Heaven.

Not The Best Day! – 26/10/14

Sometimes you just get the feeling that absolutely nothing is going to turn out right. Yesterday was a perfect example. Yet it had all started so well. There were five of us sharing a lift to the match at Bolton and we were enjoying each other's company and making excellent time until we hit the car park that was the M6. Then things began to go downhill and never really recovered. Our estimated arrival time of just before one o'clock soon went by the board and, as one traffic jam morphed into another, our spirits fell and the chances of our arriving before the kick off began to fade. The anticipated three and a half hour journey took well over five hours but our driver, Gary, desperately urged on by all of us, made a final herculean effort and got us to the stadium just as the teams emerged from the dressing rooms, and we managed to watch the entire match.

Given what was to follow, perhaps that was no real blessing as Brentford gave an insipid, careless and fairly lifeless performance in subsiding to a three – one defeat to a home team that had been struggling for points, but was boosted and re-energised by playing its first home match under the leadership of new manager, Neil Lennon. As this was the third game that Brentford had played in a week, accompanied by two long trips to the North West of England, it seemed surprising that Mark Warburton kept an unchanged team from Tuesday, although Tommy Smith returned from his hamstring injury and replaced the invisible man, Betinho, on the bench. Harlee Dean was rewarded for his fine performance against Sheffield Wednesday by keeping the eligible again James Tarkowski out of the starting lineup. Good man management in my opinion, as if you get hold of a shirt you should keep it for as long as your performances merit it.

The first half ended goalless, but the nagging thought remained that we had let a golden opportunity slip through our fingers. The home team was nervous, laden with expectation and totally lacking in self-belief, and if the Bees had put their foot down on the gas a bit more, exerted some real concerted pressure and scored a goal they would probably have folded. As it was, after almost falling behind within the first thirty seconds, Brentford created some decent half-chances which were missed by Jota, Pritchard, Judge and Bidwell but they played far too much on the back foot and never took the game by the scruff of the neck and seized control. Given the home team's diamond formation which matched us up, there was plenty of space on the flanks which we never took full advantage of. The home team huffed and puffed, pressed us high up the pitch and had four monsters at the back who dealt fairly easily with the pretty non-existent threat provided by the isolated Andre Gray.

We were reasonably satisfied at the break but felt that perhaps we had let Bolton off the hook, and so it proved. As it was, Brentford did show more ambition and determination at the start of the second half, but apart from a mishit cross by the excellent Harlee Dean that forced a stretching save from Lonergan, no real chances were created. Brentford then self-destructed in a terrible quarter-hour spell that saw them repeatedly turn the ball over to Bolton, who took full advantage with two totally avoidable goals. The home crowd, which had been growing quieter by the minute, was revived by Brentford's careless attitude and lack of ball retention, and finally came alive.

Bolton were allowed to advance unchallenged down their left and the ball was played inside to Neil Danns, thirty yards out. Pritchard made a half-hearted effort to close him down and none of his colleagues helped him out and Danns hit a powerful shot inside Button's far post before the keeper was able to react. Could he have done better? Probably, as he looked a little bit slow to react. Was he helped out by his defence? Not in the slightest.

As if that was not bad enough, Alan McCormack who had been a subdued and peripheral figure finally made a typical surge down the middle of the field and was sandwiched by two Bolton players. He remained ominously still on the ground and was stretchered off. His injury looked serious and before the Bees could settle they went two goals behind. Recently arrived substitute Mark Davies made an instant impact, picked the ball up on the left before Odubajo, who had moved to full back, could react, slalomed into the penalty area, went past a feeble challenge by an off-balance Tony Craig who seemed terrified of bringing him down and slotted the ball beyond Button. An excellent goal to savour if you were a home fan, but a terrible one to concede.

Game over? Well it would have been had it not been for the almost singlehanded efforts of substitute Jon Toral who replaced the anonymous Alex Pritchard. After Douglas had forced Lonergan into his only strenuous save of the entire afternoon with a well-placed header, the Bees stirred themselves with a rousing but belated recovery, and Tommy Smith's excellent cross went over the head of a straining defender and was instantly controlled by Toral who scored emphatically from close range. Game on at last, and for the final ten minutes Brentford took control and should have equalised when Odubajo, who seemed to provide far more of an attacking threat when coming forward from right back than when he had played further forward, found space and put a perfect low cross into the six yard box for Gray, but he criminally delayed his shot and, he who hesitates is lost, and Brentford's final chance had come and gone. To add insult to injury, Bolton, who were clinging onto the ropes and praying for the final whistle throughout the seven minutes of injury time caused by the lengthy treatment received by McCormack, had the cheek to score a *Comic Cuts* and misleading third goal when they broke away unchallenged from a late Brentford corner and, with Button stranded upfield, Craig Davies found an empty net and became the third substitute to score a goal.

The journey home from yet another soulless out of town stadium was easier, shorter, fairly introspective and pretty uneventful apart from an encounter with a very friendly and well-spoken Oldham Athletic player at Stafford Services. He expressed amazement that his former colleague Tarky had been left out of our team and was keen to discuss the differences between Division One and The Championship, all the while scoffing down his Burger King Whopper. Whilst commenting that his body was evidently his temple, I neglected to mention the importance of diet to a budding young athlete who aspires to reach the top of his profession!

A long, exhausting and frustrating day finally came to an end, one that was enlivened only by some good companionship. The long journey did, however, allow sufficient time for some analysis and introspection on the match and how we performed. I am well aware that if it ain't broke then don't fix it, and we are doing exceptionally well so far and have probably far exceeded most expectations. But you have to keep examining yourself and continually look for ways to improve lest you either stand still or go backwards. The unpalatable truth of the matter is that we have lost three of our last four away games and drawn two of the three seemingly winnable matches that we have played over the last hectic week. Certainly the margins have been extremely narrow and we were an assistant's flag and a goal line clearance away from beating Sheffield Wednesday and should have beaten Uwe Rösler's Wigan too.

The goalkeeper and back four are absolutely fine. I fully expect Tarkowski to earn his place back shortly but I am happy for either him or Harlee to partner Craig. I do expect the central defensive positions to come under review in January as a bit more pace and composure would not go amiss. Jake Bidwell just does his job every week without much comment or recognition. He is a consistent seven out of ten and nobody has given him the run around so far this season. His attacking forays are well timed and menacing and he has adapted brilliantly to the higher level.

First reports suggest that Alan McCormack has twisted an ankle, but if he is out for a spell, then I would hope that Moses Odubajo is moved back to take his place. He defends well, can head a ball, and of course, as he showed yesterday, he can get forward quickly to support the attack. He has been a pretty peripheral figure wide on the right lately and might find it easier to face the play rather than looking to be fed possession. I am very concerned about our five man midfield, not that I expect Mark Warburton to change it as he commented recently that we need to execute Plan A better rather than switch to a Plan B. The problem is, in my opinion that we have been spluttering recently and not firing on all cylinders.

I exempt Jonathan Douglas from any such criticism as I doubt if he has ever played better at any point throughout his long career. He is everywhere, at one moment shielding the back four, the next leading the forward press. He is also making a habit of slipping late and unnoticed into the opposition penalty area and presents a real goal threat, particularly with his head. He can do no more than he is already doing and is an inspiration to his teammates. Alan Judge is, I feel, trying to do too much and taking on too much responsibility and, as a consequence, not achieving as much as he can. He tracks back, he runs at defenders, plays incisive passes and is a threat from long range with his powerful shooting. It just has not come off for him as much as he and we would like over the past week and hopefully a week's rest will bring him back to his best.

Jota and Alex Pritchard are both luxury players and can only merit their place if they get on the ball and make things happen. I am going to be controversial here and say that away from home we cannot afford both of them, as on the evidence of the past few games their contributions going forward have been spasmodic and erratic, and for all their efforts, defending, covering, pressing and tacking are alien to the pair of them. Jota did his best but conceded a free kick in a dangerous position and Pritchard drifted in and out of the game and was an uninvolved bystander when Danns took possession before scoring the crucial opening goal. This is not to denigrate them as they are both potential match winners but can we afford both of them together, particularly away from home? Toral has been champing at the bit and now fully deserves a start, which will surely come next week. He is tall, strong, puts his foot in and has a wonderful touch on the ball. I believe we have a potential gem there and that he will establish himself in the team.

Given that we are at home next Saturday I would play Douglas behind a middle four of Judge, Toral, Jota and Pritchard and hope that Toral's presence will enable Jota and Pritchard to spend more time and find space on the ball to open up the Derby defence. Dallas too is well on the way back to fitness and will challenge for a place soon, and we certainly improved when Tommy Smith came on yesterday, as he has great vision and experience and does the simple things extremely well. Toumani Diagouraga, for all his assets, should not be the first substitute employed as has been the case recently, as he is a neutral influence at best and should ideally be used to help run the clock down when we are winning.

The real problem is up front where for all his pace and tireless, unselfish running, Gray is becoming more and more isolated and is getting bullied and swamped by four defenders. The ball does not stick and we are denied the chance to give our defence a rest, as it seems to come back at us far too quickly. Given that Button has been forced to kick far more regularly too, we need somebody that might win the odd high ball and retain possession. Perhaps once or twice a match Gray manages to time his run perfectly and gets behind the defence, but there is rarely enough support for him to take advantage of the situation he has created. It is easy enough to pinpoint the problem, but far harder to solve it. I believe in the five-man midfield for the time being, but there might well come a time when Gray will be given some support up front. This would however put more pressure on the midfield and the defence which would be diminished in numbers; so for every positive there is an accompanying negative too. I think it is time for Gray to be given a rest, mainly for his own good. He has more than surpassed expectations but he is beginning to snatch at his chances, a sure sign of diminishing confidence, and he needs to be taken out of the firing line for a brief spell.

Given the enigma that is Betinho, who seems totally out of the reckoning, either for the time being or permanently, that means that there are three options, two serious and one that should not be followed. Montell Moore is one for the future, but the future is not now and he should be left for the time being to develop his formidable talent outside the first team arena. Tommy Smith played alone up front for much of the second half at Blackpool but that was on an emergency basis, which leaves Nick Proschwitz. I honestly do not know what to make of him as he has hardly had sufficient game time for us to come to a considered opinion. He has scored a goal from an easy chance at Rotherham and missed two decent late opportunities to become an instant hero by winning the Sheffield Wednesday match. He is awkward and ungainly, but given his track record and the money previously expended on him, he surely must have something about him. The only way to find out is to give him some proper game time and I would suggest that he is given a start next Saturday to see what he can do within the current system that we employ.

I still think that we are doing better than expected, but it would be ridiculous to ignore and not to address the weaknesses that have become self-evident in recent matches. Mark Warburton is a wily bird and, whilst his hands are tied by the makeup of the squad he currently possesses, I am sure that is well aware of what needs to be done and that some changes are imminent.

Ooh Betty! – Part One – 28/10/14

Has anybody here seen Betinho? The young Portugese striker, whose arrival on transfer deadline day caused such a stir, seems to have dropped off the radar and disappeared entirely from sight. The Brentford brains trust needed to take speedy action as soon as Scott Hogan suffered his horrific season-ending injury at Rotherham. Given that there were only a couple of days remaining before the end of the transfer window, there was really no time to waste, and they are to be applauded for getting a transfer over the line so speedily.

Goals win matches, so inevitably good strikers are notoriously difficult and expensive to capture, particularly for a club like Brentford who have languished for years in the nether regions of the game, and are only now building a justified reputation as a progressive, ambitious club, and one becoming a far more attractive proposition to potential signings.

Over the years we have generally had to settle for strikers who were a little shop soiled, who had a few extra miles on the clock, who were perhaps in their golden years, or trying to make their way back from injury, as well as some real gambles from the lower reaches of the game. Ian Benjamin, Steve Kabba, Carl Cort or Matthew Metcalf anyone?

In the interests of fairness I will also put forward the names of Clayton Donaldson and DJ Campbell. Purely on the law of averages we had to get it right occasionally! Not since Nicky Forster arrived in 1994 had we managed to bring in a real prospect who was also coveted by many other clubs far higher up the food chain. Scott Hogan and Andre Gray had both broken the mould as they were promising and much sought after youngsters who had shown immense promise at a lower level and were keen to take the chance we offered them to prove that they could thrive in the Championship. As for our other new striker, Nick Proschwitz, he was a different kettle of fish, as his career had stalled at Hull City and he was simply looking for an opportunity to re-establish himself and demonstrate that he had what it takes.

The loan signing of Betinho came totally out of the blue and not been anticipated by anybody. Like his fellow countryman and former Brentford loanee, Joao Teixeira, he had come to Mark Warburton's attention during the Next Gen series where he had apparently scored for fun. At twenty-one he had a highly impressive goal scoring record for both his club, Sporting Lisbon, at youth and B Level, as well as for the Portuguese international teams at all age levels, up to and including the Under 21 team. And not just any old goals, a trawl of YouTube revealed eye-catching strikes of all shapes and sizes. You name it, he could do it – volleys, overhead kicks and diving headers alike. From the sparse evidence gathered, Betinho appeared to be a classic goal poacher, someone who came alive in the penalty area.

After the recent arrival of Jota, signing another foreign player known only by a nickname seemed to be yet more evidence that Brentford were joining the big time! Like every other Bees fan I was salivating at the prospect of watching Betinho play, and felt that he would more than likely provide the goals that we needed to help cement our position in the Championship. The scene was set for him to take us all by storm, and after the inevitable delay required for his international clearance to come through, we eagerly waited for him to make an immediate impact.

And that really and frustratingly is where the story currently remains. Betinho made his debut as a late substitute in a losing cause against Norwich City, played for the final thirteen minutes, created an opportunity that was blazed over the bar by his fellow substitute Nick Proschwitz and has never been seen again. Those few sparse minutes represent the sum total to date of his appearances for the club at first team level. He has sat on the bench ever since, like a wallflower awaiting an invitation to dance, until last Saturday at Bolton, when he wasn't even named in the eighteen man squad. What is more galling and mysterious is that our goals have largely dried up and no forward has scored for us since Betinho became eligible to play. Since his arrival our entire ration of goals have been provided either by our midfielders or full back Alan McCormack.

Andre Gray has been worked to the bone and ploughed a lone furrow up front without scoring since the Brighton match early in September, and Nick Proschwitz who has also not troubled the scorers lately, and in all honesty, rarely looked like doing so, has invariably replaced him late in every game. There have been several times recently, like in the away game at Watford, when we desperately needed a goal, the game had become open and totally end-to-end and it seemed like the perfect opportunity for Betinho to get his opportunity. He has never received the call and when youngster Montell Moore was also named as a substitute last week we all wondered if he might get on before our foreign import. In the end neither was required.

So the burning question remains unanswered – why has he not been given any further opportunities to play? I have given the matter a lot of thought and I now firmly believe that we supporters should recognise and acknowledge that our initial expectations were both ridiculous and totally unfair on a young boy leaving his country for the first time to play in a totally strange, unknown and alien environment. When examining his playing record in more detail, it also becomes evident that he had barely played a first team game at the top level in Portugal and, for all his promise and potential, was totally inexperienced. How could he be expected to come into such a competitive and tough environment as the Championship and contribute from day one? How hard must it be for somebody of his age to move away from home and have to deal with the problems of climate, diet, accommodation, language, homesickness and loneliness as well as having to adapt to a totally different style of play. However much the club, Player Liaison Officer, Peter Gilham, and indeed his new Iberian colleagues such as Jota, Jon Toral and Marcos Tebar have tried to help him settle down, it must be a daunting and indeed difficult prospect for him to become acclimatised, without even taking into account the additional problems of fitting in with his new team mates on the field too.

And that is where I suspect the explanation to this enigma lies. Brentford have adopted a new 4-1-4-1 playing system this season which relies upon fast midfield runners to get forward in support of a lone striker who is supposed to work tirelessly both in and out of the penalty area, to show and make space for himself, run the channels, hold the ball up until his colleagues arrive, win the ball in the air whenever keeper, David Button, is forced to kick the ball long, press the opposition when they are in possession and, of course, finish clinically whenever a chance does come along. I am exhausted simply typing that out and can only imagine how tough an ask and how demanding this role must be for any player, let alone such a young and inexperienced one who has probably never been asked to perform in a similar manner before.

Andre Gray has taken up the mantle willingly and without complaint, and he has shown enormous levels of energy, skill and commitment, but he is now looking drained and badly in need of a break. I suspect that Betinho is used to a totally different style of play back home, one that is far slower and less frenetic, where his team dominates possession and he plays off another striker who does a lot of the donkey work for him. He is probably used to playing off the shoulder of the last defender and concentrating his energy simply on taking his chances as they are presented to him. With Brentford he will probably be shattered from all the required hard work and running before he even gets a sniff at goal. He has therefore had a lot to cope with and in retrospect we should have looked at the small print before we all got so excited at his arrival.

Betinho did play in a Development Squad match last month and scored a typically well-taken goal against Sheffield Wednesday, and he is also expected to play tonight at

Crystal Palace. Hopefully he will be given the time to develop over the coming months and perhaps he will be able to contribute as the season progresses. Ideally Betinho will speak well of the treatment and help he has received since his arrival, and how the Brentford coaches and support team have improved his game, and his will be merely the first in a series of future loan deals between Brentford and Sporting Lisbon.

That is all very well but our goalscoring problem and lack of available bodies up front still remains, and there has been much talk and speculation of a far more experienced striker, Sunderland's Danny Graham, arriving imminently on a loan deal. Hopefully that is a story that has legs. As for Betinho, for all his promise it would appear that he is perhaps a player for tomorrow rather than today. The season is still young and I hope that his time will come at Griffin Park, but the need still remains for immediate help up front, assistance that I believe will have to come from elsewhere.

Ooh Betty! – Part Two – 29/10/14

Well, Betinho did play a full ninety minutes in the Development Squad last night, partnering Nick Proschwitz in a rare two-man attack as Brentford employed a diamond formation. Unfortunately, they subsided to a three-one defeat to an impressive Crystal Palace team and early reports would suggest that neither Brentford striker made much of a case to press for a starting position in Saturday's crunch match against Derby County. From what I have gleaned from spectators at the game, they appeared listless and presented little goal threat.

The good news from last night was that Sam Saunders played for the entire first half and apparently came through his first match for nine months with flying colours. His effervescence and *joie de vivre* have been sorely missed, along, of course, with his peerless ability at set pieces and it would provide a wonderful fillip to the entire squad if he were to work his way back into contention for the first team before Christmas.

The news also broke yesterday that the proposed Danny Graham loan move had broken down for unspecified reasons, which potentially leaves Frank McParland and Mark Warburton scrabbling around if they are to be successful in bringing in a new loan striker in time for Saturday. I really don't envy them their task in what is a total seller's market.

As for Betinho, I gave chapter and verse previously on why I felt he had not been a success to date. I was therefore fascinated and delighted to receive the following comments from former Brentford striker, Richard Poole. His words provide much food for thought as he went through the exact same situation as Betinho nearly forty years ago, and experienced similar problems to our Portuguese loanee. Let Richard explain in his own words:

I can look back from my own personal experience from when I moved from Watford to SC Toulon in the French Second Division when I was only twenty years of age. I firstly had to adapt to the incredible heat, as it was twenty-five degrees by the early morning.

The language barrier was tough and I also had to adapt to a totally alien style of football. Remember, I came from Brentford and Watford who had their own particular way of playing, and now I had to get used to a team which never hit a long ball but instead relied on a quick passing game. It took me well over six months to adapt, with a lot of problems on the way. It helped that my wife was French and came from not far away from Toulon, but it really wasn't easy for me.

I moved in July and it was March before things were starting to come together for me. Then I had my injury that finished my career, and it was all over. So let's hope that Betinho comes through this difficult settling in period and hopefully he will receive all the support he needs from us fans, right up to the Boardroom. Though in today's world, patience is in short supply and time is rarely given.

Wise and salutary words indeed, and he has provided some insights that we should all think about very carefully before we rush to criticise a young player who currently appears to be far out of his comfort zone, and struggling to adapt to an environment totally different to anything he has previously experienced.

Jeepers Keepers – Part One – 30/10/14

I was reading through some old Brentford programmes from the 60s the other day and saw a note congratulating Gordon Phillips on making his debut for the club in an FA Cup match against Margate. Nothing really out of the ordinary, apart from the fact that the article revealed that after the arrival of Joe Crozier in 1937 Brentford only played nine different goalkeepers between then and the mid 60s.

A quite remarkable record when you consider how regularly teams change players, as well as how often goalkeepers get hurt. For the record, throughout that thirty-year period the Bees fielded Joe Crozier, Ted Gaskell, Reg Newton, Sonny Feehan, Alf Jefferies, Gerry Cakebread, Fred Ryecraft, Chic Brodie and Gordon Phillips. What is even stranger is that the last four named keepers played in successive games in 1963. How often can a club have had different goalkeepers in four consecutive matches? I certainly cannot think of any other examples and wonder if anybody else can?

Joe Crozier was unobtrusive and a model of consistency and a key part of the Brentford team that took the First Division by storm in the late thirties. What a bargain he was, as he cost only one thousand pounds. He played three wartime international matches for Scotland, conceding eight goals against England on his debut, and yet he kept his place for the next game. Shades of Frank Haffey at Wembley in 1961 perhaps? After his retirement from football Crozier became managing director of Cory Lighterage and a Freeman of the City of London.

Gerry Cakebread, meanwhile, combined a career with the Admiralty with his football commitments. He was the undisputed first choice for nearly a decade, and played one hundred and eighty-seven games in a row between 1958 and 1963. In 1955 Gerry was named as reserve goalkeeper in the England Under 23 squad to Coventry City's Reg Matthews. Two players from the Third Division were recognised as the most promising young goalkeepers in the country. It could never happen today. Reg went on to win full international caps, but, hindered perhaps by his part time status, Gerry did not, but many supporters think that he was the finest goalkeeper they have seen play for the club. Remarkably, in his last season at Griffin Park, with his career winding down, Gerry was allowed to take a leave of absence of nearly a month to visit Russia for an extended business trip. Can you see any manager granting a player similar permission today? He also had a long and successful career after football and was awarded an OBE in 1995 for his work on Hydrographics at the Ministry of Defence.

Fred Ryecraft was Gerry Cakebread's patient understudy from 1959-1964 and from the look of him he would appear to have spent much of his spare time eating and training in the local Wimpy Bar rather than in the gym, as he was a portly figure to say the very least, and was known to eagerly accept, if not solicit, sweets proffered by young supporters standing behind his goal. He is the nearest that Brentford have ever come to *Fatty* Foulke, and quite how he ever managed to get his massive frame off the ground hardly bears thinking about. He certainly filled the goal but, in truth, loyal deputy that he was, he wasn't really up to the standard required and drifted off to Gravesend where he was also known to play at centre forward.

He wasn't alone in that feat as Luton goalkeeper Tony Read was converted into a striker during the 1965/66 season and scored an impressive twelve goals in only twenty games, including a match-winning hat-trick against Notts County, before he ran out of goals and was moved back to his original position. Talk about lack of gratitude!

Chic Brodie was a wonderful servant to the club and was calm and composed in everything he did on the pitch. He was an old style goalkeeper, nothing ruffled him, and he was consistent and totally lacking in flamboyance. He was also one of the last goalkeepers I can remember who rarely, if ever, seemed to wear gloves. Those were the days when keepers simply spat on the palm of their hands and hoped that the ball would stick. Misfortune seemed to follow Chic around throughout his career. He is best remembered for conceding nine goals to a rampant Ted MacDougall when playing for Margate, and, of course, for the notorious incident when a stray dog ran full tilt into his knee at Colchester practically ending his professional career. Ted MacDougall has a clear recollection of poor Chic Brodie:

The keeper always said he thought he was the unluckiest goalkeeper in football. He said one day he went to put his flat cap on for a game because it was sunny and he found a hand grenade in it. Then when he was playing for Brentford a Jack Russell ran on the pitch and smacked him on the leg and nearly broke it. Then, during another game, the crossbar broke and fell on his head. And then to top it off, I scored nine goals against him.

Chic suffered his final tragedy when he died far too young, but he was a skilled craftsman and, ever vigilant, he will always live long in my memory.

Gordon Phillips was a local prospect who was initially behind Brodie in the pecking order given his age and lack of experience, but he made the goalkeeping position his own in 1966 for a couple of years, and he and Chic vied for the first team spot in the late 60s, with first one coming out on top, and then the other, and it was not until Chic's retirement that Gordon became the undisputed first choice. Given our customary lack of resources, Gordon was also named as an outfield substitute at Crewe in September 1970, but his services were not called upon on the night. Gordon was an ever present in the 1971/72 promotion team and enjoyed a wonderful season, but things soon turned sour with Brentford suffering the ignominy of relegation at the end of the following season and Gordon's time at the club was over. Where Chic was solid and consistent, Gordon was smaller, slighter and more dynamic in his approach. Given his lack of height, he struggled with crosses, but he compensated with his speed of thought and reaction, acrobatic shot stopping and his ability to snuff out danger by diving fearlessly at opponents' feet.

Another local boy, Paul Priddy, still an amateur, succeeded Gordon, but after an up and down couple of years he was replaced by Steve Sherwood who achieved the rare feat for a loanee of being ever-present in the 1974/75 season and also being voted Player of the Year. We apparently made a pretty feeble effort to sign him on a permanent basis, but Watford outbid us by shelling out a mere five thousand pounds. Instead of buying a promising young keeper who would end up playing in the Football League until he was forty, we ended up taking a four thousand pound gamble that unfortunately did not pay off and totally backfired. That was Brentford to a T!

Bill Glazier had a long and distinguished career at the top level, playing over four hundred and fifty games for Crystal Palace and Coventry City and three times for the England Under 23 team. He was only thirty-two when he was persuaded to put off his retirement and sign for Brentford, but he seemed to be far more interested in running his hotel in Brighton than in keeping the ball out of the Brentford net. He was distracted, commuted from the South Coast, and seemed to lack interest and commitment. His performances were poor, culminating in an appalling and costly fumble that led to Brentford conceding a soft equaliser at Old Trafford just when it appeared that the Bees might be on the verge of pulling off a massive League Cup giant killing. He soon shuffled off into retirement and Paul Priddy seized his opportunity and played for a couple of seasons without ever totally convincing either his manager or the supporters that he was the long term answer to our goalkeeping problem. He had one unforgettable afternoon at Vicarage Road when he was unbeatable and touched by genius, saving two penalties and single-handedly earning Brentford a rare victory at Watford. On other days he was less authoritative and consistent and Bill Dodgin, perhaps harshly, released him in 1977. Another local boy who so nearly made it, but not quite. Paul wouldn't take *no* for an answer and even managed to sneak back for a third spell at the club as reserve goalkeeper in 1981, playing one farewell match against Chester, when he signed off with a clean sheet, before having a long and successful career as a well-respected goalkeeping coach.

The chequebook then came out and Dodgin paid Bristol City eight thousand pounds for Len Bond, and he repaid us with three good years of consistent and brave goalkeeping, before falling out with Fred Callaghan and leaving the club. We made a profit on him, but his leaving was a real shame as he was still in his prime, and he subsequently had a long spell at Exeter, but he was stretchered off to massive applause on a return visit to Griffin Park before being the largely blameless recipient of Brentford's seven-goal salvo at Exeter in 1983.

Brentford's last goalkeeper of the 70s was Trevor Porter, a last minute emergency replacement when Bond was injured in a car crash, just before the start of the 1978/79 season. Porter was an old friend of Paul Shrubb, and had also played under Bill Dodgin at Fulham, and we rescued him from oblivion at Slough Town for a fee of seven hundred and fifty pounds. He lasted for a couple of seasons and did a steady, unobtrusive job when called upon, and, when he wasn't, he kept up his previous career as a window cleaner.

So, Brentford fielded a variety of goalkeepers in the 60s and 70s, some good, some indifferent, but the only real shocker I can remember was Garry Towse, a talented all-round sportsman in his own right, but an average goalkeeper at best, who signed for the club from Crystal Palace and was in goal on that sad October afternoon in 1973 when Brentford conceded four goals in the opening seventeen minutes at Scunthorpe, and sank to the bottom of the Football League for the first, and hopefully last, time in their history. The only way from there was up and I will reminisce about Brentford's goalkeepers from the 80s and 90s in the near future.

Nothing Changes – 31/10/14

I really love reading through old Brentford programmes from years gone by. I can wallow in nostalgia and read about the exploits of my heroes from the past. You never really know what hidden gems you are going to find. However, one fact can be taken as read: nothing really changes. Time after time you read the same Pravda-like excuses, rewriting of history, and half-truths from the programme editor and team management alike.

- *The ball never ran for us.*
- *The referee gave us nothing.*
- *We are riddled with injuries.*
- *Our luck is certain to change.*
- *We have hit the post five times this month.*
- *Now we can concentrate on the League.*

Previously, I mentioned the grudging, feudal and half-baked send-off given to the *Terrible Twins* George Francis and Jim Towers, when they were peremptorily sold off to Queens Park Rangers. Almost three hundred goals and years of devoted service between them merited no more than a terse single line of farewell in the next home programme. Then I saw something really interesting in a Brentford versus Southampton programme from November 1956: Mr. Brentford, Ken Coote, had dramatically missed a potential match-winning penalty with five minutes to go in a local derby with Crystal Palace, which eventually ended all square.

Nothing changes there then, but the next paragraph really made me sit up and take notice: *Some spectators (after the kick had failed, of course) declared that the penalty should have been entrusted to Bragg or Towers, conveniently forgetting that neither of those players converted his last penalty kick for the League side. It was Brentford's third penalty miss of the season, but this was the first one to make any difference to the result.* Sounds familiar? Now where have you seen or heard that before? Remember the mini-fracas and pow-wow that took place before Marcello Trotta finally took that fateful season-defining spot kick against Doncaster, with Clayton Donaldson and Bradley

Wright-Phillips both interfering and hindering Kevin O'Connor in his efforts to do what had previously been agreed, and take the penalty kick? Who knows what would have happened had fate and his teammates not intervened.

I am quite certain, however, that Kevin would have slotted the ball away calmly and accurately low to the keeper's right as Neil Sullivan dived the wrong way and given the season a fairy tale ending. I have it on extremely good authority that in the week leading up to the Doncaster game, Kevin had studied footage of every recent penalty kick faced by Sullivan and discovered that he invariably flopped to his left. He therefore spent hours practising taking spot kicks against Richard Lee, always placing the ball to the keeper's right hand side in preparation, should the need arise on the big day. We all know what happened next, although thankfully promotion was merely delayed for one more year, and I think most fans would agree that we are better equipped for the demands of the Championship now, than if we had been promoted, as we surely should have been, under Uwe Rösler in 2013.

Ironic that it was finally another penalty kick, taken by Alan Judge, that cemented promotion the following season. Fortunate indeed that he actually managed to score the one that really mattered, rather than following the example of the other three he took last season, which were all frittered away.

I have written about Brentford's totally appalling, unacceptable and catastrophic record with penalty kicks in recent decades, and it is illuminating to note that by the end of October 1956 we had already missed three penalty kicks that season, all taken by different players. Evidently we were just as poor at taking penalties back in those days as we are now. As they say, nothing changes!

That leads me back nicely to the present day and the question as to who will actually take Brentford's next penalty kick? We are currently finding goals pretty hard to come by and can hardly afford to be as profligate as we were when James Tarkowski put our last spot kick into orbit against Leeds United. Mark Warburton quite predictably, and correctly, fully backed his young defender afterwards, and stated that despite his miss, he retained full confidence in James's prowess from the spot. I'm glad he did, because I can assure our normally astute and perspicacious team manager that his confidence is shared by precisely none of our supporters who, as one, gasped in astonishment when the gawky defender strode up to the spot, and unfortunately all of their worst fears were realised.

Tarky is currently on the bench after his suspension, and, assuming he is not on the pitch when we are next awarded a penalty, and given the idiosyncrasies of most of the referees that have been inflicted upon us to date this season, that could be quite some considerable time, who will be entrusted with the kick? Alan Judge did score in the penalty shootout earlier this season at Dagenham and maybe the job will revert to him, although I would prefer Jota, Alex Pritchard or Andre Gray to be entrusted with the responsibility. All of them are confident on the ball and have the ability and temperament to select a corner, not change their mind, and find it with aplomb. Alan McCormack, when fit, could also be an outside bet given his successful penalty in the FA Cup last season against Staines. Not the best of penalties, it must be said, but at least it went in.

Interestingly enough, Nick Proschwitz has a powerful and accurate shot, which he regularly demonstrates in the pre-match shooting practice and perhaps his time will also come. Given the two powerful and accurate spot kicks that he smacked home in shootouts against Swindon and Dagenham, *Captain Fantastic*, Tony Craig, also has his supporters and maybe we could do worse than give him a shot at the job that nobody really seems to want. I have now got to the stage that whenever Brentford are awarded a penalty kick I automatically assume the worst and, like Jonathan Douglas, hardly even bother to watch any more, and wait for the cheers or groans from the crowd.

Apparently, back in the 50s, regular penalty kick taker, Jim Towers, used to hit his spot kicks so ferociously that they would either result in the keeper flinching as the ball seared past him into the net, grateful that he hadn't got his body in the way of it, or every so often the supporters behind the goal were placed in clear and present danger of decapitation. As they say, nothing much changes!

League Table – 31/10/14

Position	Team	P	W	D	L	F	A	GD	Pt	Form
1	Derby County	14	7	5	2	24	12	12	26	W W D W W L
2	Watford	14	7	5	2	26	15	11	26	D W D W D D
3	Norwich City	15	7	5	3	24	13	11	26	L D L D D W
4	Wolverhampton Wndrs	14	7	5	2	21	15	6	26	D L D D W W
5	Bournemouth	14	7	3	4	28	14	14	24	W L W W W W
6	Middlesbrough	14	7	3	4	19	12	7	24	D D W W L D
7	Nottingham Forest	14	5	7	2	23	16	7	22	D D D L D L
8	Blackburn Rovers	14	6	4	4	21	20	1	22	D L D D W W
8	Charlton Athletic	14	5	7	2	16	15	1	22	D W D L W L
10	Ipswich Town	14	5	6	3	20	16	4	21	W D D D L D
11	Cardiff City	14	5	4	5	18	17	1	19	W D L W W L
12	Sheffield Wednesday	14	4	7	3	11	11	0	19	L D D L D D
13	**Brentford**	**14**	**5**	**4**	**5**	**16**	**19**	**-3**	**19**	**W L W D D L**
14	Reading	14	5	3	6	18	23	-5	18	D D L L L W
15	Millwall	14	4	5	5	14	16	-2	17	L L D D D W
16	Rotherham United	14	4	5	5	15	18	-3	17	L W D W D D
17	Huddersfield Town	14	4	5	5	19	25	-6	17	W W D W D D
18	Leeds United	14	4	4	6	14	18	-4	16	L D D L D L
19	Wigan Athletic	14	3	6	5	14	15	-1	15	L D D D D W
20	Fulham	14	4	2	8	19	25	-6	14	W W L W D W
21	Brighton and Hove A	14	2	7	5	13	16	-3	13	D D D L D D
22	Bolton Wanderers	15	3	2	10	14	26	-12	11	L L W L W L
23	Birmingham City	14	2	5	7	12	28	-16	11	L W D L L L
24	Blackpool	14	1	3	10	8	22	-14	6	L D W L L L

NOVEMBER

Ram Bam! – 2/11/14

I have been wracking my brains over the past twelve hours or so but I have yet to recall a better and more important overall performance than the one the Bees put on yesterday against league leaders Derby County. Yes, in recent years in one-off cup matches we have beaten Premier League opposition in Sunderland and Everton, and also given Chelsea a bloody nose, but yesterday we took on a team that is regarded as odds on for promotion and which has one of the deepest and most talented squads in our division. And we beat them – fair and square! We went head-to-head with Derby County, took everything they could throw at us, which was quite a lot in the first half, stayed in the game through our grit, determination and organisation and, then, when we finally clicked into gear, our footballing ability took over and they could not live with us.

There is now a marked and significant difference between past Brentford teams and the current squad. Previously if we beat, or even put on a good show against a better and more expensive team it would be seen as a giant killing, as little Brentford over-performed and strained all their sinews to bring off the unexpected. The current squad has pace and pure quality in abundance, and when you add that to our organisation, fitness and team spirit and also stir in a portion of self-belief, the ingredients all combine to form a heady and intoxicating brew which is fully capable of beating any team in the Championship. What is more they are finally beginning to realise just how good they are.

Mark Warburton made two changes from the team that lost at Bolton last weekend. Alan McCormack missed out through his ankle injury and Alex Pritchard, weakened by the aftereffects of flu, reverted to the bench. As expected, Moses Odubajo moved to right back, Jon Toral made his full debut and, to general surprise, Toumani Diagouraga was also named in the starting line-up. This was to turn out to be a masterstroke, as he was easily the best player on the field, giving his finest ever performance for the club. He acted as a shield and support to the ever willing Jonathan Douglas, and harried, tackled and won the ball back tenaciously and effectively and, most crucially, he never gave the ball away and ensured that we maintained possession. In fact we ended up with more possession overall than our visitors, which was an astonishing achievement.

The first half was dominated by Derby, whose machine clicked effortlessly into gear, and they played slick, confident and effective football with Chris Martin acting as their fulcrum, holding the ball up beautifully and bringing his colleagues into the game. Brentford pressed and harried but were hurried and careless with the ball and created little. Gray was isolated up front and the ball rarely stuck. Our best moves came when Toral and Jota broke forward menacingly but the final ball was never on the money and Jack Butland was totally untroubled in the Derby goal. The key was to stay in the game, and that we succeeded in doing, given the herculean efforts of the whole team, defending from the front, denying space and putting their bodies on the line. For all their first half possession, Derby created very little. Dawkins shot into the side netting and Button saved from Forsyth before, on twenty-seven minutes, Brentford attempted a quick break, Judge was dispossessed in a dangerous position, and with the overlapping Moses Odubajo caught upfield in support of the anticipated attack, Derby took full advantage of the space on their left flank and Forsyth's low cross was expertly turned in at the near post by Martin. A goal that they fully deserved at the time.

Brentford kept fighting and trying to play their football and managed to get to halftime without further punishment. The general mood at the interval was one of resigned acceptance. We were doing our best but were simply being outplayed by a better team. Somebody obviously refused to tell the Bees, as after the break they came out a totally different team. Immediately the fans could sense that the momentum was shifting as Brentford gave it a real go and finally realised that they had to impose themselves on the game rather than show too much respect to their illustrious visitors. Moses Odubajo finally threw off his defensive shackles and started to maraud forward with immediate effect. Forsyth could not live with him and another quick break ended with a clever pass from Moses into the feet of Andre Gray who had found a yard of space inside the Derby penalty area. His response was instantaneous and devastating as his first time shot raged into the corner of the net. George Francis, watching from above would surely have approved!

Confidence and self-belief now coursed through the veins of the entire team and Derby were on the rack. Slick incisive football was met with a barrage of fouls and body checks in an effort to halt our progress. David Button then hit a sublime eighty-yard pass to Alan Judge who turned outside his defender and put in a perfect chip that the straining Gray headed onto the post. So close to a goal. Derby tried to slow the game down and the introduction of the gifted Will Hughes helped them regain some semblance of control, but Mark Warburton also made two exceptional substitutions. Jon Toral had run himself out but made a real mark with one double shimmy in the area almost opening up the Derby defence. He and Jota were replaced by Alex Pritchard and Stuart Dallas, returning unexpectedly from his thigh injury. They both impressed from the start, Pritchard's dribbling and passing ability giving Brentford time and space and Dallas showed his power and running ability and gave excellent support to the tiring Gray.

Another Derby substitute, Jordon Ibe, also caught the eye and his tussle with the equally speedy Odubajo was one of the highlights of the last quarter of the game. The game ebbed and flowed with Button saving well with his legs from Ibe who had slalomed through the home defence. The pantomime villain was Chris Martin who moaned and dived his way throughout the match without any response from the referee before assaulting Tony Craig off the ball; amazingly he escaped with only a yellow card when red was surely called for. A point for each team seemed the likely outcome but Brentford maintained their pressure and finally their reward came well into the four minutes of allocated injury time. Moses made yet another forward run and passed square to Alan Judge. He centered hard and low and Stuart Dallas from the far left of the area, sent an awesome and unstoppable right footed volley into the roof of the net. The roof came off Griffin Park as the ground erupted and a famous and, in the end, totally deserved victory had been won.

Every home player was a hero. Button did what little he had to do exceptionally well. Some of his clearances were right on the money, others less so but that is the way we are going to continue to play and the sooner some isolated elements of the crowd accept and support it the better. The back four were brilliant. Moses won his personal battles and also was our most potent attacking force and I just hope that he is put in cotton wool until Wednesday when he will face another speedster in Michail Antonio of Nottingham Forest. Jake Bidwell was his normal unflustered self, never hurried on the ball, always there in both defence and attack and the two centre halves won everything. James Tarkowski is perhaps the most promising player in the squad, but he will have to wait his turn as Harlee Dean was a commanding figure and also used the ball well. Douglas and Toumani played a major role in keeping us steady when we were on the rack but the entire midfield worked hard and kept passing the ball. That is our mantra, pass, pass, pass and keep moving into space, and in the second half we did this to perfection and Derby could not cope with us.

Brentford United!

Could We Lose Mark Warburton? – 4/11/14

As already mentioned, Richard Poole is still a fervent supporter of Brentford and keeps a close eye on things his home in France. Like all Brentford fans, he took great pride and delight in the victory over Derby County, but also gave a salutary warning:

Well I saw the goals on Sky here in France, and it seemed a great win, but looking deeper at the various comments I heard both on television as well as from some people I still know in the game, I do not know what players will come and go but I do think that what the Bees have got to worry the most about is trying to keep hold of a very good manager. That might well be the real key to both staying in the Championship and then perhaps pushing on even further.

Richard also provided memories and brief descriptions of some of his teammates at Griffin Park from around forty years ago and started off by recalling the goalkeepers he had played with:

In my four years at Brentford I played with five goalkeepers: Gordon Phillips, Paul Priddy, Garry Towse, Bill Glazier and Steve Sherwood. As for Chic Brodie, his son was also at Brentford as a youngster. Gordon Phillips used to stay behind to help us apprentices when we needed a goalkeeper and I had a lot of shooting practice against him. Paul Priddy was quite a good keeper and even though he was pretty tall, in those days football was extremely physical and goalkeepers needed either to be as agile as a cat, like Steve Death of Reading or Peter Bonetti at Chelsea or big and strong. As for Bill Glazier, well yes it was the end of his time when he came to Griffin Park, but he was a nice bloke.

I played with Steve Sherwood at both Brentford and Watford. In the victory against Bradford City, which saved us Bees from re-election, our two goals both came from his big kicks up the field on to my head. I set up Dave Simmons who scored our first goal and the second goal was similar, with Dave this time helping me to score, and my first goal for Watford was nearly the same, coming from a massive kick up field from Steve. Though Steve Sherwood was a shy person off the field, on it he really imposed himself and you could always tell he was going to go far and, yes, I never could understand why Brentford didn't keep him, but, as you say, that was Brentford in the 70s.

I remember as an apprentice I babysat for Jackie Graham and his wife, well I had to earn some extra money given how little Brentford were paying me at the time! Jackie was exactly what he seemed to all you fans, he was hard but fair and with a never say die attitude. He was always there to encourage his teammates and really was Mr. Brentford for my generation.

As for Paul Bence, though he was a bit slow, he was a good player who performed well for the club until Mike Everitt arrived. Paul was not his type of player and I remember the last game of the season at Gillingham where I played up front with Dave Simmons. Paul said goodbye to us on the coach that day but he was very good friends with John Docherty and came back into the fold when Docherty was made manager. I know the Bees fans loved John Docherty, but it seems funny that not many seem to mention him any more given how long he served the club.

What a player Dave Simmons was, and he helped me so much. I remember in the changing room just after that Gillingham game, where we had lost 1-0, he apologised to us because the player he was marking had scored from a corner. What more can you say about someone? He was sold, if I remember correctly, by Mr. Docherty although he was a Mike Everitt signing. He was a real blood and thunder type of player, like a lot of Mike Everitt's signings.

I was a fan of Roger Cross, such an elegant player but not, I think a player to go to places like Rochdale or Scunthorpe, but that's just my opinion. Barry Salvage was a ball player with so much ability, and he was untouchable on his day, but I don't think he was best suited for the bread and butter of the Fourth Division, but he was another great bloke and I think another one let go by Mr. Docherty. You asked me about Nigel Smith who was a really classy player signed by John Docherty, but who was very young like me. I don't know why he fizzled out although he played far more games for Brentford than me.

In passing I would like to mention two other goalkeepers I knew at the club. Firstly, Graham Cox, and also Neil Oliver who signed as an apprentice a year after me. He would have been a great keeper but, well, he wanted more from life than being an apprentice footballer. I mean, at that time we were paid £10 a week (I've still got all my contracts) and nights out were not allowed. We had to make a choice if we were going to be serious about trying to become a professional footballer.

It wasn't at all a glamorous life back then but I would still have made the same choices today if I had the opportunity. There were lots of youngsters my age who were far better than me but then the sacrifices you had to make were huge. When I signed at 15 for Brentford my Dad said, look son you're working now (but to me it was a total joy, not a job) you can come home at night whenever you want, but each morning when you go to work you do your best. I always remembered his advice and tried to do just that, so that when after training and then doing the menial jobs like cleaning the changing room and washing the baths I could honestly say I'd done my best. I had my nights out like everyone else, but football was the most important thing to me.

When I look at my first team debut you remember it was only the year after Brentford restored the reserve team. I came straight from playing for Brentford Juniors to first team football in the fourth division and there were some hard old B…….. in the other teams! Well I hope I made my parents proud of me and the Brentford fans as well. To this day I keep them all close to my heart. I just wish I'd had the chance to give more to those Brentford fans who in my eyes mean far more to me than the supporters of bigger clubs like Chelsea or Manchester United. Well that's enough of me babbling on for now!

Joy! – 6/11/14

I wrote just the other day that I could not recall a better and more important overall performance than the one the Bees put on last Saturday against Derby County. Well, I was wrong. Brentford's excellent display against Derby was totally surpassed last night when we went to the City Ground and played Nottingham Forest off the pitch, and came away slightly disappointed at only scoring three goals when we should have netted at least six. The performance personified everything that Mark Warburton's Brentford team stands for. Passion, pace, positivity, movement, grit, determination, confidence on the ball, running at opposition players, accurate passing, pressing and a total lack of fear. All that was missing and what prevented us from notching a cricket score was more conviction in front of goal.

Brentford came of age last night, going head to head against one of English football's big names and they left the former European Cup holders chastened and with a bloody nose. This was by no means a giant killing when an underdog, inspired by the occasion, raises its game on a one-off basis to pull off a major shock, but further evidence, if more were indeed needed, that our style of total football (a term I haven't used since the halcyon days of the great Dutch teams of the 70s) is too much for many of our opponents to handle. The near one thousand travelling Bees fans also had a night to remember, outshouting the shell-shocked home supporters and memorably serenading them with exuberant shouts of *you should have gone to the fireworks!* Good advice, indeed, that they would have done well to follow, as their team, nervous as kittens after a long run without a win, initially bared their teeth but then stuttered and collapsed under the Brentford onslaught, contributing to their own downfall with a series of defensive frailties and schoolboy errors that contributed to two of the goals.

Alex Pritchard replaced Jota in the starting line-up and played his best game to date for the Bees. With the ball seemingly glued to his feet he was a master of vision and movement, finding the gaps in the hapless home defence. No show pony either, as he played a full part in all the necessary unfashionable and dirty work required to win a game away from home, covering, tackling back and pressing and he might also be said to have earned his spurs by receiving a booking when his desperate attempts to dispossess an opponent on the edge of our box resulted in a yellow card, a true badge of honour, and proof that he too is beginning to understand and become part of the team ethos. Forest didn't help their cause with a bemusing team selection which saw the dangerous Antonio played up front as a lone striker with Mancienne, normally a defender, playing the Jonathan Douglas role in front of his panicky back four. Brentford were therefore allowed to seize the initiative, and, in their customary fashion, piled men forward and began to cut huge swathes in the home rearguard.

The home fans were already making their growing sense of unease and disbelief known when Odubajo streaked down the right, played an incisive ball into Gray, lurking with menace in the box and when Moses went for the rebound he was unceremoniously taken out by Hunt. Rather than wait for the whistle, Toral reacted quickest and fairly lashed the ball into the roof of the net for a stunning finish which totally took the wind out of the home team, who visibly deflated. Hunt's ill-disciplined lunge was followed by an aerial assault by Lansbury (now there's a real show pony) on Dean, which resulted only in a generous yellow card when he might have seen red. Hunt managed to injure himself and there was poetic justice when his replacement, Lichaj, split the defence with a perfect through ball, but unfortunately for him it was at the wrong end, and Gray, took full advantage of the gift, rounding Darlow and scoring with ease. Behind the far goal we blinked with amazement and our eyes welled with tears of pride as our team was dismantling a side that on paper was far superior to ours. The difference was that we were a team in every meaning of the word, a well honed and drilled unit playing as one, whereas Forest were a disorganised rabble without a real clue or apparent plan of attack.

From time to time gifted individuals like Antonio or Ince caused us problems with their sheer flair and ability, but given the lack of team focus we easily snuffed out the threat. The only disappointment at the break was that we had only scored twice. Toral, who marauded forward with menace, a potent mix of skill, determination and aggression, almost scored with a close range header from Judge's perfect cross. Judge himself fired narrowly wide before Brentford spurned two great chances right on halftime. Douglas poked the ball wide from close range with the goal gaping after Brentford had sliced the home team apart with some beautiful short passing, and Forest tried to commit suicide yet again when Gray latched onto another appalling back pass but Darlow blocked his effort.

We were all a bit concerned at the break. Had we let them off the hook? Surely the paint was being stripped off the Forest dressing room wall by Psycho Pearce who would now throw on the likes of Britt Assombalonga? The home team could not be as inept as they had been in the first half? The former Peterborough striker formed a new three-man attack but Brentford took the wind out of the home team's sails by scoring a game-clinching third goal straight after the break. Gray ran at the defence and was pulled down by Wilson for as clear a penalty as you could ever see. Pritchard picked the ball up without any discussion and calmly slotted the ball home as the keeper dived the wrong way. Interestingly enough in his post match interview, Alex said that he had been totally unaware of our recent problems and adventures from the penalty spot, and calmly stated that he had always been confident of scoring. Long may he continue taking them with similar results.

Penalty kicks? No problem! Alex Pritchard shows exactly how it should be done.

With the job apparently done, Brentford sat far too deep, and, as a result, allowed Forest to come back into the game and they dominated the last quarter as they sought to regain some self-respect. Button came into his element making three excellent saves and dominating his penalty area. Craig and Dean put their bodies on the line and won everything as well as never resorting to the panicky, booted clearance. Pass, pass, pass is the mantra that has been driven into the head of every Brentford player, and last night it really showed as we kept playing our way out of trouble. Eventually the pressure told, and Antonio sent a wonderful long range drive screaming past Button. Even so, the best two chances were created by Brentford, Gray driving into the box past two terrified home defenders, who waved him past before Darlow managed to push his shot away and Judge, the orchestrator of so many of the good things that we did, curled a beauty inches beyond the far post with the keeper merely an interested and helpless bystander.

This was a famous triumph for the team and management alike, and one that now sets the benchmark for how well we can perform. We totally out-thought and outplayed Forest, and we were a potent combination of skill, movement and tenacity and left our illustrious opponents trailing and gasping in our wake. Douglas and Diagouraga were heroes, yet again, although another booking means that Jonathan will be sitting out Saturday's blood and thunder local derby at Millwall, but we will cope – we always do. Moses too seemed to flourish facing the play and terrorised the home team with his pace and attacking brio as well as dealing calmly with a tricky customer in Burke, until he was forced off by a knock, but emergency right back Stuart Dallas coped admirably with a totally unexpected role and looked comfortable in his new position.

I have left Andre Gray until last. He was a man inspired, and Forest just could not cope with his pace, power, strength and movement. He could have scored three goals and the penny finally seems to have dropped with him as he realises that he is more than good enough to thrive at Championship level, and, in the future, maybe even higher.

On a personal level, the day was a total joy as I spent the entire afternoon with my daughter who is studying in Nottingham. I allowed her to run amok with my credit card in *American Apparel* before enjoying a wonderful relaxed dinner with her in town. The game was merely the cherry on top and she was also totally caught up in the excitement and the atmosphere that she wants to come and see us play again. Another convert, and not before time! Today I feel tired but I have a satisfied smile on my face. This is a great time to be a Bee and, given the evidence of what we were privileged to see last night, the best is yet to come.

Memories are made of this. Celebrating with Becca!

Managers – Who's The Best? – Part One – 8/11/14

There has been a lot of discussion lately amongst Brentford fans concerning who they feel is the best Brentford manager of all time. Given how well the current incumbent Mark Warburton has performed since his appointment almost a year ago it is hardly surprising that many fans voted for him. How though can you compare him to, say,

Harry Curtis or Malcolm MacDonald, who both also had marvellous spells at the helm and maintained their success over a period of many years? Curtis took the Bees from the very depths of the Third Division to near the top of the First, as well as managing us to a War Cup Final victory at Wembley. How can anyone else match that? But, out of sight, out of mind, and there are very few people remaining who have first hand memories of his incredible achievements.

What about Jimmy Sirrel and Frank Blunstone whose records bear comparison with any of their successors and surely merit extra kudos given the financial constraints under which they worked? Time and distance often provide a sense of perspective and enable the emotions to die down and a more reasoned and objective analysis to be made than was perhaps the case at the time. In retrospect, the achievement of Wally Downes in keeping the Bees in the third tier of English football, avoiding relegation and also leading us to the fourth round of the FA Cup in 2003, despite working on a shoestring and relying on a ragtag and bobtail of untried kids, the remnants of Steve Coppell's nearly men of the previous season, journeymen and loanees, merits far more praise than he actually received.

I can only comment on those managers who I have seen at work over the past forty years or so, Frank Blunstone became the club's tenth post-war manager when he left his role as Chelsea's junior team manager to take over at Griffin Park in December 1969 to succeed Jimmy Sirrel. He narrowly beat John Bond to the job but soon put his own stamp on things. We just missed out on promotion in his first season with a team that gave little away at the back but also struggled for goals. But for the width of the post and a referee's benevolence we would also have beaten Hull City the following season and found ourselves in the last eight of the FA Cup. Blunstone brought defensive solidity and organisation, and his contacts at the top level of the game enabled us to bring in real talent such as Roger Cross and Stewart Houston. He also spotted the potential in a raw, young and temperamental striker playing at Wimbledon and brought out the latent ability in John O'Mara and turned him into a potent threat who spearheaded our promotion drive in 1972. Blunstone was far more ambitious than his board of directors, who restricted him to a squad of just fourteen players but, incredibly, he overcame all the obstacles to win a promotion based on the goals and aerial ability of O'Mara, the flair of John Docherty and Bobby Ross, Jackie Graham's industry and a tough uncompromising defence that gave little away.

The Board unforgivably, but not unexpectedly, failed to invest after promotion was won and could not wait to sell major assets in Cross and O'Mara. The replacement of John O'Mara by Stan Webb bore an eerie resemblance to the Dean Holdsworth/Murray Jones scenario twenty years later and was an equally imbecilic decision. Relegation in 1973 was inevitable and Blunstone, worn out from having to make bricks without straw, had had more than enough and resigned. He soon fell on his feet at Manchester United and their gain was certainly our loss as an enormously talented young manager was allowed to walk away.

Blunstone's replacement was Mike Everitt, a largely inexperienced player-manager at non-league Wimbledon who polarises opinion. He was undoubtedly a cheap option and received little support from the directors (now where have we heard that before) and did his best with a wafer thin squad. His approach did not go down well with some of his players and he brought in a number of tough bruisers. Under his management, Brentford declined rapidly, fell to the bottom of the Football League and barely escaped the need to apply for re-election.

With the club at probably its nadir, he lost his job in January 1975, to be replaced by John Docherty, who, at thirty-four years of age was a three-time former player and crowd favourite. *Doc* had only one full campaign in charge and left in September 1976 at the end of a disappointing stay. He did his best to bring in youngsters who he had developed during his coaching spell at Queens Park Rangers and Nigel Smith, Micky French and Gordon Sweetzer were promising talents, but it just didn't fall into place for him.

After a couple of unsuccessful appointments, the club finally got it right with Bill Dodgin, an experienced coach and manager with four promotions under his belt, and a man whose father had managed the club in the 1950's. He took over a club at a low ebb and going rapidly into free-fall. Gradually he imbued the team with confidence and introduced an attractive style of play underpinned by the dynamism of Jackie Graham in midfield and the hard running, bravery and innate goal scoring ability of Sweetzer. He began to bring in talented young players who could pass the ball, such as David Carlton and, a real favourite of mine, John Bain and he hit the jackpot when he stole a surly disaffected underachiever from his former club, Northampton Town.

Steve Phillips repaid the derisory fee paid for him with thirty-two league goals and his partnership with a rejuvenated Andy McCulloch, with the pair of them fed chances by the ebullient winger, Doug Allder, ensured that promotion was won to the Third Division. Dodgin was a football purist who was worshipped by his players who he treated like grown ups. They were allowed to slip the leash from time to time and rewarded him with their devotion and unstinting efforts on the pitch. He was unorthodox and often backed a hunch. A rampant Gordon Sweetzer ran amok one Saturday afternoon and scored a hat trick against Torquay. We all shook our heads in amazement when he signed the Torquay centre half the following week, but Pat Kruse became a Brentford legend, a footballing centre half despite being well under six feet tall, he formed an effective defensive partnership with the even smaller Paul Shrubb, who read the game brilliantly.

Dodgin had an eye for a player and his signings were generally on-the-money with the exception of one major aberration when the tiny Tony Funnell was brought in at vast cost to spearhead our attack, a task totally beyond him. After a slow start to the 1978/79 Third Division campaign, a superb second half of the season raised hopes of another promotion to follow and Dodgin rejected an offer to join Chelsea as assistant manager, in retrospect a massive mistake on his part. Although the new season started in great fashion, results declined after Christmas to such an extent that in March 1980, with relegation looking distinctly likely, the board gave Dodgin leave of absence and dispensed with his services a few weeks later. A poor reward for such an excellent servant to the club. Ironically, it was the misfit, Tony Funnell, who finally came good and scored the winner against Millwall that kept the Bees up.

What a Week! – 9/11/14

Today I would like every Brentford fan to try and recall some of the more recent disasters and horror shows in our history. I will start you off with a few that remain etched indelibly in my mind.

1. Bristol City away in 1993
2. The Dean Holdsworth/Murray Jones fiasco
3. Our seven, yes, seven, unsuccessful playoff campaigns
4. Not turning up for the three Cup Finals against Wigan, Port Vale and Carlisle
5. The Queens Park Rangers, David Webb and Ron Noades sagas that threatened to kill our beloved club
6. Conceding seven goals at Peterborough

Please take a few minutes to fill in the gaps and add your own *favourites* to my initial rogues gallery – offloading is healthy and good for the soul. There certainly have been many occasions when we have justifiably felt cursed as Brentford supporters and we have certainly had much to bemoan our lot about. Then comes a week like the one that has just ended when you realise that in reality we are totally blessed in our choice of football club.

Seven days ago, the doubts were beginning to creep in after a run of three games without a win. Granted, we should have won at Wigan, and the Sheffield Wednesday game was an even tussle that could have gone either way, but we had just come off a listless and disorganised performance at Bolton where we had got precisely what we had deserved – nothing, and with the prospect of three ridiculously tough matches in a seven day period against Derby County, Nottingham Forest and Millwall, the prospect of our slight dip in form turning into a slump loomed menacingly over our heads. We really shouldn't have worried. This is *New Brentford* we are talking about.

As for yesterday, Brentford simply shrugged off the loss through suspension of Jonathan Douglas, recognised by Millwall manager Ian Holloway as our best player, and totally dominated the first half of the game. Toumani Diagouraga is a man reborn, in fact he seems to have switched identities with the Patrick Vieira of a decade ago. He was everywhere. Protecting the back four, winning a series of crunching tackles, using the ball simply and effectively, but he has added a real confidence and even swagger to his game which he demonstrated by beating players and pulling off some perfectly weighted longer passes which have never before been seen in his armoury. This is what self-belief can do, he is a totally different player who has improved five-fold over the course of the past few weeks and this can only be down to his own hard work and dedication as well as the efforts of the manager and his coaching staff. From being a peripheral figure, on the verge of leaving the club, he is now our undisputed first pick and is rapidly becoming indispensable. Maybe a new contract might be in the offing, or perhaps it is best to keep him hungry for a little while longer?

It was instructive and illuminating to watch the first half from behind our goal as it enabled us to appreciate our pattern of play, the way in which play developed, and how our midfield switched positions and kept possession of the ball. The opening forty-five minutes saw us put on a footballing masterclass. Orchestrated by Pritchard and Judge and with Toral playing just behind Gray, we threatened to run amok and tear huge swathes in a poor Millwall back line with the lumbering Shittu and Beevers struggling to keep up with the electric pace of the turbocharged Andre Gray. Bidwell and Jota combined elegantly, Moses petrified them with his speed moving forward and the aforementioned Toral has taken to the Championship like a duck to water, an astonishing achievement for a player so young and inexperienced. He is going to be key to our success as he develops throughout the season and will soon make us forget all about Adam Forshaw. Signing both him and the rapidly improving Alex Pritchard is probably a pipedream, but they are both adding immeasurably to our team.

Whilst Toral seems to enjoy a hard tackle and putting his foot in, the penny finally seems to have dropped with Pritchard, who in addition to his silky skills, is now covering, pressing and tracking back like a demon. Jota promised more than he delivered and the final ball was often a tad too ambitious, but that will come. However, what pleased me the most about his performance yesterday was the moment when he tracked back early in the second half, supported Bidwell and dispossessed the Millwall right back down by our corner flag, before setting us off on the attack again. His teammates fully appreciated and acknowledged his efforts and he is rapidly becoming integrated into the squad. Alan Judge played a more central role yesterday and was always buzzing around and it was his perfect through ball that set up Gray for the second goal.

Despite all their first half domination, the opening goal would not come and indeed, it was the home team, who had been totally second best and unable to maintain any meaningful possession, given the quality of our covering and pressing, who came the closest but Button made an exceptional blocking save from a close range Martin effort. Finally, it all came good and Moses, Diagouraga and Pritchard combined perfectly, and Alex's cleverly disguised pass put Gray through and he shrugged off the limpet-like Beevers, desperately hanging onto his shirt, to finish emphatically. We had the lead and it was no more than we deserved. Millwall slunk off the pitch at the interval shell shocked by our superiority and with the boos of the home supporters ringing in their ears. They had worn a special commemorative kit to mark Remembrance Sunday, but they were more invisible than camouflaged.

They are not used to being totally outplayed at home, but there was more to come in the second half when Judge seized on a loose ball thirty-five yards out (after more careless play by the home team) and Gray scored his second coolly and calmly as he ran in unopposed on goal. Perhaps we took our foot off the gas and relaxed, but the game immediately turned on its head for no apparent reason as Millwall raised themselves from the dead to score twice in the blink of an eye. The first was a strange one, Shittu's slow, looping header from beyond the far post seemed to be merely catching practice for Button but, perhaps distracted by the close attentions of Gregory, he dropped the ball on to the striker from where it rebounded into the goal. Game on, and then came another hammer blow when the ball was laid back to Dunne on the edge of the area and his instant shot found the bottom corner. It could have been even worse when Judge dallied on the ball in midfield and had his pocket picked. Millwall had a man over on the left wing and the totally unmarked Gregory hit the post with a free header when he should have scored. Five minutes of total madness and further evidence, if it was really needed, of just how tough every opponent can be in this division.

Millwall had been hanging onto the ropes, now with the crowd revitalised they threatened to take control of a game that they had never really been in. This is where we showed our organisation and sheer guts. Craig and Dean ensured that we coped with the constant barrage of high balls launched like mortar shells into our box and Diagouraga and Judge wrested back control of the midfield. We weathered the storm and started to probe again. Gray's instant twenty-yard volley was fumbled by Forde and trickled just past the post before Toral's perfectly weighted pass sent Gray away on the right flank and his low cross was bundled home by a combination of Shittu and the straining Harlee Dean. A goal that was received with thunderous celebration by the packed ranks of Brentford supporters who knew we had survived the worst of the Millwall onslaught.

Warburton made three important substitutions as Toral, Pritchard and Jota had run themselves into the ground but the changes re-energised us with Dallas using his pace and power to stretch and occupy the Millwall back line, Smith holding the ball and making space and, best of all Sam Saunders came on for his Championship debut after ten months of injury hell. He was simply Sam - coolness personified. He was everywhere, winning the ball, using it, dribbling past opponents and even having a trademark long range shot. Welcome back Sam. We have missed you. He will add so much experience and composure to our squad.

We held on comfortably enough although Button redeemed himself with a couple of brave blocks and Gray was only denied a hat trick by the assistant's flag. A famous and totally deserved victory earned by our skill on the ball, composure, devastating finishing ability and non-stop pressing. Gray has now scored four goals in a week and is rapidly demonstrating just how good he is and I suspect we have barely scratched the surface with him.

Ian Holloway was magnanimous enough to recognise and acknowledge our ability and in his immortal words we are no longer *Little Old Brentford*. No, we most certainly are not!

Under The Radar? – 11/11/14

It's happened, the cat is finally out of the bag. Last night on Sky Sports' *FL72 Review* Show, presenter George Gavin uttered these fateful words:

You see, as a neutral it would be great to see Bournemouth and Brentford in the Premier League. That would sort them out at the top level, wouldn't it?

George, go and rinse your mouth out with cold water, we really do not want to hear such spurious nonsense spouted by anybody, least of all a respected soccer pundit like yourself. Brentford have advanced stealthily, sneaking under the radar as their rise to the top six of the Championship table has, up to now, gone practically unnoticed and unremarked upon. Managers of teams defeated by us have dismissed the result as a mere aberration and have barely deigned to remark upon our quality, or indeed, in some cases, mention us at all. Stuart Pearce and Sami Hyypia, I am particularly thinking about the pair of you and how mean-spirited, grudging and even condescending your meagre comments were about the mighty Bees.

Up until last weekend we were seen as no more than a team buoyed by the impetus of promotion last season, who had simply managed to maintain its progress and hold its own in the Championship. Three wins in a week, over tough and established Championship teams in Derby County, Nottingham Forest and Millwall have changed perceptions and finally seen people sit up and take notice and, not before time, start to analyse exactly what is happening behind the scenes at Griffin Park and why it is working so well. Then came Millwall manager Ian Holloway's heartfelt, eloquent and insightful post match tribute to the Bees:

I must congratulate Mark, his staff and Brentford for the way they have metamorphosed into a wonderful football establishment. We have got a long way to catch up with the knowledge, understanding and the group that he has developed there. Fair play to them, I knew how good they were by watching them. He's (Warburton) about three or four years ahead of me in what he wants to do, and I'm giving the credit to Mark because he must have been doing a job above their last manager, setting things up, and their players know exactly how to close, who to close, when to close. They lost their best player in (Jonathan) Douglas, but I knew they were going to pick our pockets.

Everybody should start looking at what a fantastic job they're doing. I'm a little jealous because their players know how to press and when to press. They've lost one of their best organisers and they can still do that. They're ahead of us. Well done to them, and they aren't Little Old Brentford any more. It's their structure. They've invested in the academy and put that way of playing into their players. They have put a way of playing in place that the lads know, with or without the ball. I guarantee they are doing it from the academy all the way up. Yet every one of their players knew exactly what they were doing and got their distances right, apart from the time we gained a bit of the ascendancy and shocked them and scored two. What their right centre back did, and the centre midfielder – I know that's a higher level than I'm used to and as high a level as I've come up against.

Their bloke (Warburton) has had five years. I think their manager deserves a medal the size of a coalbunker lid. He was putting in place this structure before Rösler went. It was a fantastic appointment by their owner. There are a lot of brains about what Brentford are doing. That's what I think, and the stats will show you. You've got to have a structure to play to and a way of doing it, and they're as good as anybody. Their downfall will be whether they believe that.

Now that is praise indeed from a wily and experienced football manager, an ex-Bee too, who is therefore well aware of how our club has traditionally been run - on a shoestring, and a wing and a prayer, and fully recognises just how far we have come in so short a space of time. What Holloway is saying comes as no surprise but the Millwall manager is the first opponent who has gone public and acknowledged that he fully understands what is going on at our club

When You've Got It, Flaunt It! – 13/11/14

I have suggested that the less recognition Brentford receive for their incredible start to the season the better, and that it would be far more beneficial for us if we remained firmly under the radar. Several of our early opponents seem to have totally underestimated us and have ended up with a bloody nose for their trouble. I was concerned that forewarned is forearmed, and we might well find the going tougher in the future once teams become less complacent, and begin to recognise that we are by no means a soft touch.

Given how cautious, superstitious and reactionary I thought most long-term Brentford fans to be, I fully expected that my comments would be well received and that the overwhelming majority would vote to tick the box for no publicity. Not a bit of it! I certainly misread the prevailing mood as quite a few of the responses I received certainly came from the Max Bialystock school of *When you've got it, flaunt it* and Eric Taylor, writing from Somalia, best summed up that viewpoint:

We are Brentford fans. Very few individuals are given that privilege. We support the best team ever and few people could possibly argue against that. This month we are sixth in the Championship. As the best and most real football club in the division (real in being we have no glory fans – nobody supports Brentford unless they are blessed) we're destined for promotion to the Premiership.

How can you fail to smile and nod your head in agreement with his comments and positivity? Peter Herman was slightly more constrained and conflicted in his opinion and seemed to be betting each way:

I am still finding it all a bit hard to believe after so many years of disappointments, interspersed with a few short-lived triumphs. It sounds crazy, I know, but now I am actually beginning to worry about the possibility of our being promoted before we get to Lionel Road! But as a Bees pessimist, my next thought is that we have still have a long way to go before we can even be sure of staying up.

Patrick Sutton is another one struggling to come to terms with the Brentford of today, but happy to accept things at face value:

For me as a supporter of forty-six years I feel it is vital that I remain prepared to shed many more tears for my beloved Brentford, and that, in my humble opinion, is why I believe that as a club, first of all, we are now in a stable and healthy position thanks to Mr. Benham's shrewd business head, and secondly as a football club we have come so far, so let's skip being under the radar and simply forget who is watching and talking about little old Brentford.

As a parent I get such a buzz every home game when I watch how excited my seventeen year old son is about travelling from our home in Wimbledon to watch the Bees, an excitement I have seen grow on his face since he was six years old. I guess my point is though excited, blessed and proud to be a Brentford supporter I will always take it one game at a time and no matter how far up we go or how far down, I will always be a Brentford man and, in return for the way we are now, I can look back and say that all the tears in the past were well worth it. Hope that all made sense.

Andre Rettelet too sums up some of the confusion and ambivalence felt by so many of us:

I'm torn. I'd obviously accept promotion at the drop of a hat. But I wonder whether it would be in the longer-term interest of the club if it happened this year. Griffin Park is totally unsuitable for Premier League football and the new stadium won't be ready until 2017 according to current estimates. We'd have to negotiate a groundshare, pay for the privilege, and lose income as a result of being tenants elsewhere. Inevitably resulting in less atmosphere and no fortress Brentford. This is not an old fashioned and reactionary "nah, they don't want to go up" kind of comment. But I'd rather hear about Brentford's three-year record in the Premier League against Manchester United, Arsenal, Spurs and Chelsea rather than experiencing one season of crash and burn. However, even that is better than nothing at all.

There's no way of telling what the future will bring.

I'll happily take the opportunities if they come. Hence my confusion. With hindsight, losing to Doncaster and Yeovil turned out to be a good thing, however much it hurt at the time. We are so much better prepared for the Championship this year. But of course, we now know what happened the following year. At the time, we could only feel the pain. I can't help feeling that the prospect of promotion this year scares the bejesus out of me.

But before then, there's the small matter of picking up those twenty-three points for safety, and sixteenth would still be fine and dandy, just as it was at the beginning of the season, although on the evidence so far, we're much better than that. What am I thinking of? The mere fact that I'm worrying about the prospect of playing in the Premier League, rather than wondering about what Conference football might be like, all in the space of seven years, says it all. What progress. Carpe diem. Being promoted too early is such a luxury problem! But let's get those twenty-three points first.

I still have to pinch myself when I stop to think about how far we have come in so short a period of time. Do you remember the days, not so long ago, in truth, when we fielded the likes of Simon Brown, Lee Thorpe, Craig Pead and John Mackie? Honest journeymen professionals they all most certainly were, but how can you compare them to the turbocharged thoroughbreds we are so fortunate to be watching nowadays?

As for the Premier League, is it a mere pipe dream, could it become a reality or are we in danger of becoming guilty of hubris and perhaps laying ourselves open to the prospect of nemesis? I have no idea but, you know what, I am becoming far more comfortable at the prospect of outsiders recognising and commenting about our achievements. It makes such a pleasant change from being patronised and ridiculed.

Lessons to Be Learned But Will Uwe Take Heed? – 14/11/14

So, Uwe Rösler has left Wigan. A disastrous run of only three wins from seventeen league games, which saw the team plummet into the relegation zone, was more than enough for trigger-happy owner Dave Whelan who duly acted as judge, jury and executioner yesterday and fired Rösler after less than a year in charge. When the dust has settled and he has finished licking his wounds Uwe will doubtless look back at his short spell in charge and wonder what on earth went wrong and how things changed so quickly for him.

The Wigan job ticked all the boxes for him:

1. A club based practically on the doorstep of his family home in the North West of England
2. A higher salary
3. A Premier League quality stadium in which he could strut his stuff
4. A squad jam-packed with experience and talent that would surely challenge for an immediate return to the top level
5. A generous playing budget augmented by the parachute payments that the club was receiving
6. An owner who would back him with all the resources he needed to win promotion

It all so nearly went totally according to plan last season, with Rösler accorded near-hero status for orchestrating a magnificent FA Cup run which saw him return in triumph to his old team Manchester City and then take Arsenal to extra time in the semi-final at Wembley, before losing a heartbreaking penalty shootout. The first glimmers of doubt came after the unsuccessful playoff campaign, which fizzled out in frustration and disappointment against Queens Park Rangers. An over cautious approach in the home leg left his team hamstrung, with only one striker named in the team and the match duly ended goalless – a massive opportunity wasted. After taking an early lead in the return Uwe refused to go for the jugular but characteristically funnelled his team backwards in the hope of clinging on to the narrow advantage, and handed the initiative back to a home team who had been on the ropes and eventually subsided to a two-one defeat. A seemingly certain victory magically turned into defeat owing to his innate caution and over-theorising.

The season therefore ended in a series of might-have-beens rather than in actual achievement, but surely the foundations had been laid for an assault on the Premier League this time around? His squad was weakened in the summer when key midfielder Jordi Gomez joined Sunderland on a free transfer and James McArthur moved to Crystal Palace for seven million pounds. Long-term injuries to Chris McCann and Ben Watson further diminished his options, but Whelan fully supported his manager in the transfer market, and this is surely where Rösler came unstuck. He was given the majority of the McArthur money to play with, but bought badly and at the top of the market, and none of his expensive captures have stepped up to the plate.

Much-vaunted striker Andy Delort joined with massive expectations and at great expense from Tours, former Barcelona B striker Oriol Riera arrived from Osasuna for two million pounds and after a long and debilitating saga, midfielder Adam Forshaw finally completed his move from Brentford.

Delort and Riera have contributed only one goal to the cause and, rather than becoming a vibrant and positive influence, Forshaw has been an invisible and peripheral figure, shunted backwards to play in a defensive role in front of the back four, where his creativity and energy has been stifled. A poor return indeed for such a heavy investment.

At Griffin Park, Rösler headed up an experienced and comprehensive back-up team who provided massive support in the key areas of player recruitment, analysis and preparation. Despite all his efforts, he was only able to bring Chris Haslam with him from Brentford as Head of Performance and ended up working with the existing coaching team of the grizzled veteran Graham Barrow and Eric Black. Rumours and scuttlebutt filtered back to Brentford ears regarding Uwe's apparent concern at the lack of quality of the infrastructure and backroom staff that he inherited, and I believe that it was in these crucial areas that things really started to go wrong for him. Uwe did not have his own men like Alan Kernaghan and Peter Farrell with him, and was left to fend for himself, and I suspect found himself out of his depth, particularly when it came to player recruitment.

There is also a natural hangover after playoff failure, as Brentford know all too well to their cost, but with the level of talent he inherited and also brought in, surely Wigan should have performed far better? There did not seem to be a regular and consistent pattern of play and players were moved in and out of the team. It was particularly illuminating to watch his last game in charge, the local derby at Bolton Wanderers. A solid if mainly counter-attacking first half display did not receive the reward it deserved, but Wigan were a different and far lesser team after the break, their heads went down after a couple of quick and easily avoidable home goals, and they disintegrated into a spineless, shapeless and demoralised rabble who could not wait to scuttle back down the tunnel at the end of the match.

Always the most demonstrative of men, Uwe went puce on the sidelines, apoplectic at the lack of organisation and desire, unforgivable in any game, but particularly in a local derby. His team appeared to have disowned him and he them, as his post match comments made clear, and it sounded as if he had as good as signed his own death warrant, and a parting of the way appeared inevitable. I have previously written in great detail about Uwe and his time at Brentford and do not intend to go over old ground, but it would appear that nothing has really changed with him.

Wigan supporters complained about his constant tinkering in team selection, regular changes in formation, his innate caution, negativity and over-analysis, and his overriding reluctance to take the handbrake off. Most Brentford supporters, who felt exactly the same way about him, could just as easily have written those comments a year ago. Rösler has performed at his best when he is the underdog, and is quite brilliant at setting his team up to defend, draw the sting out of the opposition and then hit them on the break, as Chelsea, Manchester City and Arsenal have found to their cost. He has, however, proved to be totally out of his comfort zone and left floundering when he is expected to set the tone and take the initiative and the attack to the opposition.

Can he recognise his shortcomings, learn from them and adapt? That is the key question, and why I said at the beginning of this article that a period of introspection and self-analysis is surely required. Andy Scott lost his job at Brentford because his approach had stopped working both on and off the pitch and he had been rejected by his players. So what did he do next? When given another excellent managerial opportunity at

Rotherham, he apparently proceeded to repeat everything that he had done at Brentford, with identical results, and was sacked in under a year. Leopards find it extremely hard or even impossible to change their spots.

Uwe is now slightly damaged goods but he is an immensely talented manager with some character flaws and will be in immediate demand. If he can recognise and address his shortcomings and reinvent himself, perhaps at a club with more limited ambitions than Brentford and Wigan, then he will thrive, as indeed I hope he does. If he allows history to repeat itself yet again, then he is doomed. It is totally up to him.

Bees Player – 16/11/14

I thought I would give it a couple of months for the dust to settle before I commented on the Bees Player situation. Like all Brentford fans, I am delighted that, not before time, matters were finally sorted out satisfactorily between the club and the commentators and that normal service was resumed. Well almost, as Luis Melville is no longer a member of the Bees Player team, at least for the time being, and I only hope that time will heal all wounds and that he will eventually return to the fold, as he is sorely missed. Not least for the massive amount of preparatory work that he would undertake in terms of preparing stats, background information and the running order before every match. All the necessary grunt work that makes the difference between the show being a success or an also-ran. Without betraying any confidences and revealing behind the scenes information, I would simply state that I hope that everybody has learned a lesson from what happened at the beginning of the season, that the impasse between the two sides is never repeated and that all necessary budgeting and negotiations are concluded well in advance in the future.

Bees Player Matchday Live is a Brentford institution, and is a unique service, prepared and delivered with love and dedication added to massive levels of knowledge, preparation and utter professionalism. The entire team fits together like a glove and every individual adds his or her own individual skills and quirks to the whole. It just works and everybody is to be congratulated. Mark Burridge is the glue that holds everything together and he is aided and abetted by Natalie Sawyer, Mick Cabble, Dave Morley and Alan Denman in particular. Injured squad players such as Richard Lee, Sam Saunders and in past seasons, Kevin O'Connor and Scott Barron provide valuable insight with their expert analysis and we are blessed to have so many intelligent and articulate footballers at Brentford who straddle the line perfectly between indiscretion and vacuous blandness, and their contribution adds immeasurably to the proceedings.

When the main team isn't available Billy Reeves takes over with his eccentric, passionate and inimitable style of commentating. He is a breath of fresh air and his enthusiasm is contagious if sometimes over applied, when, despite his banshee howls of celebration, the ball doesn't quite go into the opposition net as anticipated - ah well, nothing comes easy to us Brentford fans and it is good for us to suffer! Chris Wickham and Mark Chapman also do an excellent and understated job when called upon.

It wasn't always like this though, as in the deep and distant past things were done on a much more informal and ad hoc basis. Every Brentford home match used to be filmed by

Newsonic Video Productions, a small husband and wife-run company that provided the same service for one of our major rivals, and commentary was generally provided by a local journalist and radio broadcaster, Phil Mison, who, if the truth be known, was, and remains, a rabid Fulham fan! He did a decent job but when his other commitments meant that the position became vacant I seized the opportunity. I started doing the Matchday Video commentaries, as they were known at the time, on Sunday the third of December 1989, a date indelibly etched in my memory, when, as a season ticket holder in D Block, I noticed that there was no longer anyone filling that role.

Fifteen minutes before the massive local derby against Leyton Orient I approached the camera crew, asked them if there was a vacancy and lied my head off when questioned about any relevant experience I might possess. Well, I had watched *Match Of The Day* since childhood, and one brief conversation later, I was on the air there and then. I was very fortunate in that my first game was the ultimate clichéd seven-goal thriller with the Bees finally coming out on top. Neil Smillie had the dubious honour of scoring the first goal that I celebrated on air and I also had three penalty kicks to remark upon. All in all, not a bad introduction to the job!

Well, from that day on I took over the commentary duties, which I eventually shared with Ian Westbrook, and we were forced to learn on the job – no media training for us I am afraid. More is the pity as I could really have done with some expert advice, help and constructive criticism but was forced to soldier on and probably repeated the same errors every match. What I hope came over was my total enthusiasm for the job and all things Brentford, and that I gave the role the hard work, dedication and respect it deserved, as I had the ultimate responsibility of being the eyes, ears and voice providing information and insights that would eventually be shared with Brentford supporters all around the world.

Working conditions were appalling as I was wedged into a seat situated high up in D Block directly behind the video camera. I had to avoid being distracted by ignoring the constant and relentless barrage of advice, comments, abuse and non-sequiturs coming from everybody who was seated near to the commentary point, and there was really no escape or hiding place from them. It was also well-nigh impossible to read the illegible numbers on the back of the shirts of some club. Who else can remember that appalling early 90s kit of Stockport County which resembled a psychedelic disaster where the numbers were tiny and merged into the pattern on the actual shirt? Kevin Francis was easy to pick out, but as for the others... I also remember every match having to peer into the Bermuda Triangle down by the right hand corner flag at the Ealing Road end, which was never in clear view of my commentary position, and trying to guess what was happening.

I worked hard to show my support and encouragement for the Bees whilst also maintaining some sort of balance and perspective and although I certainly did not jump for joy when the opposition scored, I hope that I gave them some credit when it was due. I also tried to be honest. Viewers can't be fooled and they know when the game or performance they are watching is unacceptable; you cannot defend the indefensible. I always did my homework so that I was able to talk with some degree of knowledge and insight about every player on the opposition team. I also realised that my bon mots or, more likely, inanities and inaccuracies, would only be heard by fans who actually bought the video of the match I was commentating on, as well as by all the purchasers of the end of season highlights tape.

Please excuse my self-indulgence at this juncture as I did have so much fun at the time, and hopefully some of my occasionally more inspired descriptive terms and expressions remain in vogue even today: My personal favourites were:

It's raining goals at Griffin Park when Terry Evans scored the winner in that incredible opening day four-three victory over Leyton Orient in August 1991 and *Another nonsense from Ashley Bayes* as the poor, hapless young keeper committed yet another offence against reason and belief against Spurs. Apparently I found it all too much when Brentford threw away a vital promotion clash against Bradford City in 1992 and was heard to utter on air: *Oh Brentford, what have you done?* but I confess to having no memory of that one! Richard Cadette was always *The Wriggler* as he squirmed his way through opposition defences, but that is more than enough and I just hope that some of you appreciated my efforts and forgave me for my errors.

I kept going until the 1997/98 relegation season when the games were generally appalling and were like watching paint dry. It also became totally impossible for me work up any enthusiasm for them, particularly as there was so much else going on off the pitch at the time and I found it hard not to be able to make mention of them on-air. I therefore thought it was time to lay down the microphone and let someone else have a go. A decision that was totally justified by what has subsequently happened, which is light years ahead of the service that I could offer. Congratulations to everyone involved with Bees Player today, it is quite brilliant and I just hope that I was a worthy predecessor.

Fred Callaghan – A Decent Manager Who Missed His Big Chance – 18/11/14

Continuing my review of the Brentford managers from the last forty years, we pick up the story in March 1980 when four consecutive defeats in a disastrous fortnight meant that the Bees were in free fall. With confidence shot to pieces, they looked more than likely to plummet back down into the bottom division, and the writing was on the wall for manager Bill Dodgin. The final straw was a listless one-nil home defeat to Rotherham marked by Steve Phillips's remarkable fourth spot kick miss of the season. Missed penalties seem such a recurring theme throughout every decade for the Bees. This was too much for Chairman Dan Tana who gave Bill Dodgin leave of absence. Tana accepted that it had been a hard decision for him:

The supporters had been demonstrating in the forecourt at Griffin Park prior to his departure and I'd spoken out on behalf of the manager, telling people that he'd been good enough to get us up and I thought he was good enough to keep us up too. Bill and I spoke about the situation and he'd told me not to worry as he had every faith in being able to turn things around. But after the Rotherham game Bill came over to my house and we analysed the whole situation. Bill was no longer convinced that the team would escape the drop, so we came to a mutual decision that he should step aside. I didn't sack him. Bill was a very good man.

This was a sad and ignominious end to his spell at the club and simply reinforced the maxim that however successful a manager might be, memories are short when things start to go bad and there is only ever one inevitable outcome. Fred Callaghan was Tana's choice to replace Dodgin, who surely deserved better and was certainly a hard act to follow. Callaghan had recent history at the club and was an obvious and easy choice as the new manager.

He had been a long-serving, dependable and popular fullback for Fulham, who played nearly three hundred games for the Cottagers before a serious back injury forced him into retirement at the end of the 1973/74 season. A Fulham fan memorably described his style as both a player and a manager:

What he lacked in finesse he made up in shovel loads of panache. Chin jutting out he would steam down the left flank in attack, and in defence he was a no prisoners taken left back.

After retirement he soon moved into coaching and enjoyed a successful spell with Enfield before he moved to Griffin Park in February 1977 to assist Bill Dodgin with coaching duties. His initial stay coincided with an outstanding run of results and performances as the team soared up the table and at the end of the campaign he left to become manager at Woking. Tana might well say that his decision to replace Dodgin was more than justified as the impetus and influence of the new man in charge revitalised Brentford, who escaped relegation after a fine late season run of results.

Callaghan was a tough taskmaster who soon set out to show who was boss and quickly put his own stamp on things. It was certainly his way or the byway! He instigated a mini clear out which saw the departure of firm fan favourites such as Len Bond, Dean Smith, Steve Phillips, John Fraser, Barry Tucker and David Carlton. He wanted his own men in situ, ideally hungry young players with everything to prove, and, assisted by scout extraordinaire John Griffin, he brought in some of the finest prospects seen at the club for many years. David Crown, Terry Hurlock and Gary Roberts were all inspired bargain buys from non-league clubs. Mark Hill and Barry Silkman were less successful purchases but David McKellar proved to be a calm and safe replacement for Len Bond after some eccentric displays from another inexperienced youngster in Paul McCullough who had singularly failed to impress.

Callaghan tightened up the defence and stabilised the club in his first full season before putting together perhaps Brentford's finest midfield since the Harper, Greenwood, Hill combination when he swapped Crown for Chris Kamara and took a gamble on Stan Bowles who had been seemingly drifting towards oblivion at Leyton Orient. Bowles sliced opposition defences apart with his precision passes, Kamara was tireless and did his running and covering for him and also had the energy to get into the box to finish off his chances, and Hurlock was *like a caveman carrying a sledgehammer* according to Francis Joseph, the Incredible Hulk, an impassable barrier who could also play the game as well as intimidate. An unbeatable combination.

The team was beginning to gel although they were more dangerous on the counter attack, with a far better record away from home than at Griffin Park, where they struggled to break teams down. Callaghan made a costly and catastrophic blunder with the signing of an average centre half in Alan Whitehead for a ridiculous tribunal assessed fee of seventy-eight thousand pounds but the Chairman's and crowd's frustrations were allayed when his Midas touch returned with the signings of strikers Francis Joseph and Tony Mahoney which appeared to put into place the final pieces of the jigsaw. Mahoney came from the scrap heap at Fulham and provided the strength, hold up play and aerial ability and Joseph was a potent combination of pure pace, bravery and finishing ability. The 1982/83 team was so nearly an exceptional one as was evidenced by the totally deserved victory over First Division Swansea in the League Cup.

Callaghan's squad was lopsided; it incorporated the best strike force and midfield in the league but was, unfortunately, backed up by one of the worst defences and goalkeeper. Almost as fast as Joseph, Mahoney and Roberts scored at one end, Messrs Roche, Wilkins and Whitehead threw them in at the other. Fifty goals were scored at home and forty-nine conceded away – a strange and unusual symmetry, and the soft underbelly coupled with the tragic loss of rejuvenated striker Mahoney with a broken leg, whose crack I can still hear to this day, ensured that only four games were won away from home, and the team finished an insipid and disappointing ninth when a promotion berth surely beckoned given the quality under Callaghan's control. A massive opportunity squandered through ill luck and under-performance, and Callaghan's chances of glory had gone.

The decline continued into the following season as players no longer seemed to respond to his approach and the football became ragged and uninspired, with Terry Bullivant a totally inadequate replacement for the retired Stan Bowles and Ian Bolton an even slower centre half than Whitehead. Perhaps the playing budget had been cut, but his signings were no longer up to the mark. Our Third Division status was beginning to look under threat, and when the team collapsed spinelessly in the FA Cup at Gillingham, and a three-one lead was squandered in a twelve-minute horror show, which saw four goals conceded, the writing was on the wall for Callaghan. His brusque manner did not help his cause and Chairman Martin Lange fired him in February 1984 after almost four years in the post. Lange had some misgivings over his decision:

I thought Fred was a good man and a decent manager. He had some faults but was a good football man and a terrific judge of a player and knew the lower leagues well. That was borne out by the calibre of the players he brought in like Terry Hurlock, Gary Roberts and David Crown. Fred was a good first manager for me and it took a lot of soul searching when I decided it was time for him to go. In my heart of hearts I do sometimes look back at that decision and wonder if I should have given him a little bit longer, but his departure was down to my inexperience and I was getting a lot of flack from the fans and took the easy way out.

Brentford were in decline once again, relegation beckoned and a new saviour was needed to help ensure that, at a minimum, our Third Division status was maintained…

Bees Up! – Fulham Down! – 22/11/14

I have finally woken up this morning but feel as if I am still in dreamland. Did we really win our fourth consecutive Championship match last night, the first time we have achieved that feat almost since there was a King on the throne over sixty years ago? Is that us, little Brentford, sitting comfortably in fourth place in the league, a mere point off the top? Was that really Brentford who came back seemingly from the dead, with two goals in the final ten minutes of a pulsating match, to win a game that we looked like losing despite totally dominating from start to finish? Was that Griffin Park, ram packed to the gills with the roof seemingly coming off as the stadium erupted at the final whistle? The answer to all these questions is an emphatic YES!

This has been a seriously good few days for the club as we begin to come of age. Over six hundred guests celebrated the landmark 125th anniversary at a glittering dinner held on Thursday at the Hurlingham Club in SW6 where Brentford took over Fulham. The team repeated the feat last night, playing their illustrious visitors off the park and their sumptuous football provided yet another feast this time for the spectators at a sold out Griffin Park as well as the viewers of the live broadcast on Sky Sports.

The two teams were renewing a rivalry that flourished and grew in the 80s and came to a head on that glorious Sunday morning in April 1992 when the visitors were demolished by a four goal first half onslaught by the Bees. Since that unforgettable day Fulham, buttressed by Mohamed Al-Fayed's millions, roared ahead and left Brentford trailing far behind in their wake, and seemed to have firmly established themselves in the Premier League until they imploded last season and were relegated with ignominy after a thirteen year stay at the top level. Under Kit Symons they have been recovering from an appalling start to the season and although they fielded a team packed full of top level international stars there still seemed to be a sense of entitlement surrounding them; they gave the firm impression that they felt it was all a bit beneath them to spend a Friday night slumming it against their poor relations at their dilapidated shack of a stadium.

Back in the day, one of my clients, Ericsson, sponsored Queens Park Rangers, and by virtue of my job I was sentenced to five years' hard labour where I was expected to attend most matches at Loftus Road. At that time, just like Fulham, QPR had been relegated from the Premier League and mistakenly pulled out all the stops to retain most of the overpriced so-called prima donnas and superstars who had totally under-performed and got them into the mess in the first place. Excellent players, like Trevor Sinclair, slept-walked their way through the season, making it patently obvious by their inertia and reluctance to sweat that they had no real interest in playing at a level they felt totally beneath them and only gave their all on the big occasion in an effort to attract a new club. For Trevor Sinclair read Brian Ruiz last night. Fulham were a mirror image of that lamentable QPR team – *all fur coat and no knickers*, as the old expression goes.

Brentford took the game by the throat and totally outplayed their visitors in a first half of utter domination. Brentford's incisive and pleasing to the eye short passing style contrasting with Fulham's prehistoric long ball assault. The Brentford midfielders interchanged with alacrity. Pritchard's magic feet opened gaps in the Fulham defence, the rampaging Jonathan Douglas and the revitalised Toumani Diagouraga won every loose ball and passed it impeccably, the live-wire Alan Judge was at the centre of everything good we did and Toral showed further evidence that he is coming of age as a first team footballer. All that was missing was a goal, but thanks to an inspired display from the marvellous Marcus Bettinelli in the Fulham goal we were somehow denied the two-goal cushion which was the least that our first half display merited. He stretched like a languid cat to foil Toral's low header aimed into the corner, tipped over Craig's header, acrobatically pushed Judge's curling free kick over the bar and best of all, made a save from Toumani's carefully sidefooted volley that defied gravity and belief. It was a goal all the way until the keeper somehow stuck out a strong left hand to save his team. *If Toumani scores, we're on the pitch* goes the chant and it was so nearly put to the test.

David Button was a virtual spectator, but showed his sharpness when he plunged to his left to deny the dangerous Rodallega, who should have buried a close range header when set up by his partner Ross McCormack. Games at this level are settled by such narrow margins, as for all their domination and effervescent, mesmerising football, Brentford could actually have come in at the break trailing, despite having played perhaps their best forty-five minutes of the season. Football is such a strange game sometimes! Andre Gray had led the lumbering giant Dan Burn a merry dance and he escaped his attentions yet again before being foiled by the keeper who smothered his close range poke. Button too was called into action as Fulham finally roused themselves from their apparent deep torpor and made a sharp save to deny Rodallega.

But the Colombian would not be denied, and just before the hour, Brentford's well-oiled machine developed a kink in the engine as Dean's slovenly short pass was intercepted by Williams, and ten seconds later the ball was in the Brentford net as McCormack unselfishly set up Rodallega, the man over, who finished calmly and effectively. There were many similarities to Norwich City's first goal at Griffin Park in September, also donated by a generous home defence guilty of overplaying. Tarkowski was the culprit on that occasion, Dean on this, but he simply rolled his sleeves up and determined to make amends, which he did in quite spectacular style.

As is normally the case, Mark Warburton's substitutions revitalised us. Jota and Dallas gave us fresh legs and renewed impetus, and Proschwitz finally looked the part when he replaced the exhausted Gray. We survived a difficult fifteen minute spell when we dropped too deep as Fulham gained in belief, and surely thought that they were on the way to a smash and grab victory that would have been totally against the run of play. We recovered, found a second wind and started to play our football again. There was space on the flanks where Pritchard, Jota and Dallas tormented their defenders and Odubajo and Bidwell were tireless in their overlapping support. The Fulham defence creaked but the door remained firmly shut until Dean decided to become a hero.

He picked the ball up near halfway, saw no obvious pass, and, like a modern day Beckenbauer, strode majestically into the Fulham half. He found Dallas on the left wing, who performed miracles to hold off three straining defenders and conjure up a low cross from the touchline when the ball seemed destined to go out of play. Parker stretched to clear, but the ball fell to Dean near the edge of the area, who leaned back and struck a glorious right foot volley beyond Bettinelli and the helpless defender covering on the line. The net bulged and Griffin Park erupted. Game on, and a shell-shocked Fulham did not know whether to stick or twist and got caught between two stools, as they did neither. They forced another sharp save from the excellent Button but were caught upfield in injury time when Judge bounced the ball off his head like a performing seal, shook off a tired challenge, turned and pinged yet another perfect fifty yard pass straight out to Jota stationed on the right wing. His control was instantaneous and perfect, he cut inside his defender and there was only one thing on his mind. His shot from just outside the penalty area was hard and well directed and kissed the outstretched and seemingly beseeching arm of Burn diving in a vain effort to block the shot, and the deflection took the ball into the corner of the net. Cue disbelief and wild celebrations as the roof came off Griffin Park.

Fulham had a muted penalty shout ignored by the excellent David Coote, who officiated calmly and without fuss, and Proschwitz and Jota both forced sharp saves from Bettinelli as the Bees comfortably played out the remaining minutes of added time. The whistle went to roars of appreciation as the players, management and fans were united as one in celebration of a famous and merited victory. It is now time for everyone to believe and accept that we are quickly developing into an excellent team, with players who possess skill, pace, verve and confidence. The balance of power is shifting in West London. The Bees are on the rise!

Happiness is beating your old rivals, Fulham.

Day Off! – 23/11/14

What a lovely, peaceful and satisfying day I had yesterday. After a long lie in to sleep off the excess celebrations from the night before, I woke up with a smile on my face as I realised that the incredible and momentous events of Friday night had really happened and weren't merely a dream. In fact, the reality was far better and more satisfying than anything I could have ever dared hope for. Brentford had beaten their old enemy in the most satisfying of circumstances and sent them scurrying back to SW6 whining and moaning with their tail firmly between their legs.

Even more than that, Brentford had risen to the challenge and massive expectations of their fans and put on a performance that will live long in the memory, one that must also have thrilled, surprised and amazed everyone watching the live broadcast of the local derby on Sky Sports. The days of us crumbling and choking on the big occasion seem firmly behind us and the team seemed to relish the challenge and enjoy the opportunity to strut their stuff before a national audience. I have to confess that I watched the entire programme twice, once when I came in late on Friday night, and again, just to check that it wasn't a figment of my imagination, on Saturday morning. I was right the first time, we really had put on a notable performance that had even the hardened Sky pundits waking up and taking notice and appreciating our style, approach and quality. Griffin Park, too, looked at its best, resplendent and sparkling in the glare of the floodlights and the scene was set for a magnificent game of football where the presumed underdogs and no-hopers seized the initiative from the off, and bloodied the nose of their illustrious and wealthy opponents.

I was suffused with pride watching the events unroll on-screen yet again. How Ross McCormack, danger that he was, could have been named as Man of the Match was a decision so ludicrous that I simply laughed in disbelief. Was I being paranoid or was this simply more evidence of media bias against Brentford? The fact that the studio pundit, Billy McKinlay, was a former Fulham coach might have had something to do with it, but if a Fulham player had to be chosen, then the blindingly obvious candidate was their goalkeeper Marcus Bettinelli, the elastic man, whose series of wonderful saves kept the Cottagers in the game and almost led to them pulling off a totally unmerited victory against the odds. Perhaps they had simply been unable to pick out one Brentford player when in truth all fourteen shone equally on the night? Whatever the circumstances, the choice of McCormack highlighted the danger of making such a decision well before the end of the game, as I firmly believe that the Man of the Match had been selected at a time when Fulham were still winning the game. I take my hat off to Ross who was magnanimous when interviewed after the game, looked fairly sheepish and embarrassed when accepting his award and conceded that Brentford had been by far the better team and fully deserved their victory.

The *Daily Mail* published a full and effusive report on their website but otherwise our achievement went largely unnoticed in yesterday's media. Good, let's stay under the radar for as long as we can! A long day now stretched in front of me without the normal stresses and concerns of a Saturday in the football season. The Bees had more than done their stuff, the pressure was off and I could simply relax, smug in the knowledge that whatever happened we were certain to end the day still firmly ensconced in the Playoff zone.

I watched the Huddersfield versus Sheffield Wednesday no-score bore draw at lunchtime and whilst you have to make allowance for the passion of a local derby, there was so little quality on display from either team; the Bees looked light-years ahead of both of them on the evidence of that game. I awaited the other results with keen interest but felt totally confused and conflicted. Should I be looking at the teams at the top or bottom of the league? Did I want Derby or Blackpool to lose? With the innate caution and pessimism ingrained in a Brentford supporter of long standing, I was first drawn to the relegation zone and noticed with relief and satisfaction that we are now thirteen points above Rotherham who sit uneasily in twenty-second place. Can they make up the gap on us, are we going to be okay and avoid the dogfight at the bottom of the league?

Panicky thoughts such as these flashed through my mind until I took a deep breath and began to analyse the situation more objectively. We have now played eighteen of our twenty-three opponents, and yes, we are likely to find it harder when we play everybody for the second time, as forewarned is forearmed but a cataclysmic collapse like the one we experienced back in 1993 just isn't going to happen again. We really do have so much more quality and are so much better equipped for the gruelling demands of the Championship both on the pitch and behind the scenes. That is not to say that we will not experience some good hidings between now and the end of the season given the calibre of some of the opposition and players who will be facing us.

Mark Warburton turned up as a guest on *The Football League Show* last night. In his calm, understated manner he talked total sense, gave credit where it was due and his sharp analysis contrasted with the bumbling inanities and clichés spouted by the ineffable Steve Claridge, who he totally outshone. Mark advised caution and hoped that we would remain out of the spotlight for as long as possible. Most of me hopes that he is right but I really feel that the cat is out of the bag as is evidenced by this comment from Sam Lewis's match report in today's *Football League Paper*:

While rivals Fulham were parading themselves in the Premier League and playing in a European final, envious Brentford were pottering around in the bowels of the Football League in a half-empty stadium. How the tide of the Thames has turned in West London. It's taken sixteen years for the clubs to collide in the league, but what is it they say about good things coming to those who wait? Brentford are flying high in the play-off places. Their new stadium is coming and if they keep this up, so are United, City, Liverpool and Chelsea.

How I wish I had written those wonderful words! Just to cap a perfect day, the phone rang at about seven o'clock and it was Paul Shrubb ringing to say what a fantastic time he had had at the match, how welcome he had been made to feel and how incredible it was to walk onto the Griffin Park pitch once more to receive the acclaim of the Brentford supporters. Days don't really come much better than this.

Jota - in the last minute!

Hall Of Fame – 25/11/14

Brentford's 125th Anniversary Dinner last week saw another welcome milestone when five former players were inducted into the Brentford FC Hall of Fame. Bob Booker, Peter Gelson, Keith Millen, Alan Nelmes and Danis Salman are all true Brentford legends and are worthy and deserving additions to an elite club. With their arrival there are now fifteen members of the Hall of Fame and I would like you all now to try and see how many of the other ten inductees you can remember. In order to give you sufficient time to allow you to search the recesses of your memory so that you can work out their identities, I will reminisce for a moment about the five new inductees.

Bob Booker simply epitomises everything that is good about Brentford and what the club represents. Never the most gifted player in the world, he made the most of what he had, gave everything to the cause, never caused a moment's trouble – except to the opposition, and played in every position apart from goal. He scored an unforgettable hat trick against Hull City and I also remember an accomplished display as an emergency centre half against Fulham. His never-say-die approach endeared him to supporters and he overcame a career threatening knee injury to revitalise his career and earn a transfer to Sheffield United where he also became a club legend and First Division regular. Who else can recall the excitement when the news was leaked in November 1991 that the Bees were on the verge of signing a First Division star – and after much speculation it was Bob who eventually materialised for a final spell at Griffin Park, but we forgave him everything!

Peter Gelson was a loyal one-club man who served the Bees with dignity and pride for more than a decade and played well over five hundred games, second only to Ken Coote, as a rugged and reliable centre half. He was not the tallest of defenders but timed his leaps perfectly and won everything in the air and was a seemingly impassable barrier, except against his nemesis, Jack Howarth, who always gave him the run-around, and once scored an awesome hat trick of headers for Aldershot at Griffin Park. Peter remarkably scored twice with punts from inside his own half of the field, and less memorably, hit a late and potentially match saving penalty kick against Aldershot onto the inside of the roof of the old Brook Road terrace and caused the occupants of the Royal Oak End to be showered with years of accumulated rust. Then, just to add insult to injury, Aldershot broke away following the goal kick, and scored a match clinching fourth goal. Peter remains a season ticket holder at the club to this day, and he can be seen at every match in Braemar Road where he is rightly treated with the affection, awe and respect accorded to a true Brentford icon.

Keith Millen played against Wigan at Wembley as an eighteen-year-old teenage prodigy and developed into a consistent and gifted centre half who formed outstanding defensive partnerships with both Terry Evans and Jamie Bates, and Brentford were so fortunate to have three such talented defenders to choose from. He simply got on with his job calmly and efficiently and read the game so well that danger was generally snuffed out before any damage was done. It was a disappointment to all supporters when he fell out with David Webb and, after flirting with a possible move to Spurs, which never finally came to fruition, he was transferred, when still in his prime, to Watford where he also flourished.

Alan Nelmes took time to settle down to the rigours of league football after he joined Brentford in 1967 from Chelsea but he grew into the role and became a quick and underrated defender who proved to be the perfect foil to Peter Gelson. He only scored two goals for Brentford, once when playing as an emergency centre forward at Notts County, the other, a last minute winner from a corner against Scunthorpe at Griffin Park after he lost his marker, Kevin Keegan, who was ball watching. Unfortunately he was far more deadly at the other end of the pitch and signed off with a trademark own goal, a real beauty, in his testimonial match against Chelsea in 1978.

Danis Salman made his Brentford debut against Watford at the age of fifteen years, eight months, and three days and still holds the record as the Club's youngest ever Football League player. Danny was tall, quick and strong and played at right back or centre half and was an ever present danger when he overlapped down the right flank. He also scored one of the softest and most bizarre goals I have ever seen when his weak thirty yarder somehow spun through keeper Nigel Batch's hands and legs and barely had the pace to cross the goal line, but it was enough to gift us a victory over Grimsby. He spent eleven years at the club and made three hundred and seventy-one appearances before joining Millwall. I always felt that Danny rather missed the boat and stayed with us a bit too long as, with his ability, he could and should have played at a far higher level.

All five were wonderful players and are also real gentlemen who remember their time at the club with pleasure and pride. Anyway, it is now time to discover how many of the other ten members of the Brentford FC Hall of Fame you have managed to remember.

They are as follows:

- Malcolm MacDonald

- Dai Hopkins
- Joe James
- Phil Holder
- Dean Holdsworth
- Jackie Graham
- Alan Hawley
- Bobby Ross
- George Francis
- Terry Evans

Did any of you get all ten names correct? I doubt it, I certainly didn't. Worthy though they all are of their places in this august gathering. I spoke yesterday to the club's Deputy Head of Media and Communications, Mark Chapman, about the Hall of Fame and remarked that there were some obvious omissions from the current list of former players and managers already honoured. Mark stated that he was well aware of this but that it was the club's policy to first honour players who were still alive and, in that regard, it is likely that there will be another name announced very shortly who will be a very popular and deserving addition to the Hall of Fame. Exciting news indeed!

That is not to say that the pre-war giants and others who are sadly no longer with us, such as Jack Holliday, Jim Towers and of course, Harry Curtis, have been forgotten, and Mark assured me that their time will definitely come, once the most appropriate and fitting way to celebrate their memory has been decided upon.

Hopefully once Lionel Road is completed there will also be a space reserved in a club museum to pay suitable homage to the wonderful achievements of our former greats. Thanks to Mark, who with his knowledge, passion and respect for the past is a totally appropriate custodian for the Hall of Fame.

Much Ado About Nothing – 28/11/14

Well, that was a bit of a damp squib wasn't it? The loan window closed last night at Griffin Park without anybody either jumping in or being defenestrated. In truth, no real surprises there as Mark Warburton had already made it crystal clear that he was more than happy with both the quality and depth of his squad and was fully content to make do with what he has until the transfer window opens again in January. When interviewed at the training ground, yesterday, he seemed blithely unconcerned about the ticking clock and rapidly approaching deadline and, when asked if he expected any movements in or out, merely commented without an apparent care in the world that Frank McParland was dealing with all transfer matters back at the club today and would let him know if anything happened. Not a major priority then!

Would I have liked a new loanee? The answer is a qualified *yes*. We have cover in pretty much every position and there is now a plethora of talent unable to even claw a seat for themselves on the substitutes' bench. Nico Yennaris, Sam Saunders and Marcos Tebar are now fully recovered from injury, add further depth to the squad and are all challenging for their place. Montell Moore is also performing exceptionally well in the

Development Squad and is a real talent whose time might surely be coming fairly soon. All that being said, and agreed, I would still have been happier if a new striker had been brought in who could cover for our existing trio of Andre Gray, Nick Proschwitz and Betinho. I do not intend to go over the why's and wherefore's of the quality of each of them, and what they bring to the party, as I have done it to death previously, but I simply feel that we are going into a packed Christmas programme and another option up front would be extremely helpful as a contingency should injury or another misfortune befall one of our strikers, who we will need to wrap up in cotton wool.

The problem of course, is finding somebody who is available, affordable, fits in with and adds value to the squad and, in our current situation, with Gray excelling and our only playing one striker, is prepared to accept that he will be unlikely to start any, or many, games.

Those are hard boxes to tick and I suspect that we were unable to find someone who matched that exacting bill. Danny Graham, for example, who is likely to play against us on Saturday, would have cost us top dollar and expected, quite naturally, to have come in as first choice. That was not going to happen at Griffin Park given Andre's recent performances where he has excelled. Previously, I have suggested that the best option would be a young and unproven talent from the Premier League, but on reflection I can see what a risk that would have been, as, whilst there are certainly such players around, whether they would be able to step up to the plate in the Championship is highly open to doubt given the quality and physical demands of the competition.

Rhys Murphy anyone? Saido Berahino certainly had the ability in front of goal and was a precocious talent, but he fell short in other areas, and, given the unity of the current squad, and how well things are going, we cannot afford to take any chances. To be honest, I am delighted that Mark gave such a public show of confidence in his current squad and am also fully aware that last minute arrivals are never generally the best planned and can sometimes reek of being panic buys.

The squad is certainly talented enough, as has been shown by our wonderful November which has so far seen four straight wins, two over major promotion hopefuls, ten goals scored, a rise to an unprecedented fifth place in the table, the emergence of Andre Gray and Toumani Diagouraga as match winners and major influences, plus a growing awareness that there really is something incredible happening at Griffin Park under the noses of an unsuspecting football world. Mark Warburton is certainly well in the running to be Manager of the Month for November, and the two aforementioned players will also have a good shout of being nominated as Player of the Month too.

How Others See Us – 29/11/14

As we prepare to climb yet another mountain this afternoon and take on the challenge of Wolverhampton Wanderers at Griffin Park I thought that it might make us all feel a bit calmer to read what other people are saying about us at the moment. Sky Sports Football League pundit Peter Beagrie was asked this week to explain our amazing start to the season and to come up with the secret for our success. His comments should be nectar to our ears, which will surely be burning with pride:

The secret of their success is continuity. It's a squad that has grown together over the last few years with a few quality additions showing the same desire and work ethic and creating the consistency required to do well in any division. Mark Warburton has carried on the great work and structure Uwe Rösler put in place, maintaining the principles and professionalism the German demanded. He was a brilliant choice and it was not a gamble to put the former stock market man in charge having worked closely on the recruitment side studying players' character as well as their ability to maintain unity and harmony in the dressing room.

Plenty of pace and energy, and a mix of young and hungry players, with a couple of experienced heads, make Brentford a tough opponent for anybody, especially now mentally they all feel they belong among some of the more illustrious company in the Championship. Bournemouth are their direct comparison in size and stature and showing what you can achieve when you build a team over a few seasons. I fancied Brentford to do well and not only survive but possibly get a top-ten finish, and at the moment they are well ahead of schedule. It's refreshing to see a club and staff embrace the division above, playing without fear and being allowed by their manager to express themselves, long may it continue.

Just how good does it make you feel to read an impartial viewpoint like that from an experienced former player who knows precisely what he is talking about and has become a well-regarded, knowledgeable and thoughtful commentator on the game? Steve Claridge – eat your heart out!

Wolves midfielder and former Brentford loanee George Saville played a key role in last season's promotion team and has an in-depth knowledge of what makes us tick:

It's no surprise at all to see them doing well – they've got a good manager, a great set of players and good individuals. The owner there is very ambitious from talks he gave us last year and they're on the up, so it's a good place to be at the moment.

Wolves manager Kenny Jackett also had some good things to say about us:

Brentford are in a great position in the league, they have a new stadium coming and they've built well. Maybe they'd say they were in League One a year or two longer than they'd have liked because they were close to getting up, but perhaps that allowed them to build and to grow. They've just won four on the trot, which shows you that it can be done. They've brought in a new front four and have options off the bench as well – maybe Judge is the only one still around playing out of their front four. The options they have for that front four are good and they have kept it similar behind. They've been settled and started very well and, looking at the Fulham game on Friday night on television, they looked a threat right the way through and looked like they can score goals.

It might be sensible for us to take some of his words with a pinch of salt as it is customary for a football manager to big up his opponents before he plays them as a possible face-saving exercise, but, reading between the lines, he obviously rates us and is worried about the threat we pose his team.

I next scanned some of the Wolverhampton Wanderers message boards and amongst the normal hyperbole, gibberish, ignorance and blinkered views I read the following comment from Young Wolf with great interest:

They are in a rich vein of form at the moment, and they do play some lovely football, but if we can sort ourselves out quickly (and I trust Kenny to do so) I think we do have a better midfield and are a better side.

That is what they call being damned with faint praise, as there was certainly a sting in the tail, but hopefully we can turn the tables on Wolves and ensure that it is payback time for the convincing defeat they inflicted upon us last season.

Greg Dyke, Chairman of the Football Association, can hardly be called impartial given that he is a long-suffering fan and a former Chairman of the club, but distance lends perspective and he recently had this to say about how the long-suffering Brentford supporters have finally and not before time changed their tune:

Yes, we are the absolute world champion club in snatching defeat from the jaws of victory, something we have been doing since about 1947 when I was born. If we were three - nil up with five minutes to play, ask any Brentford fan if we would win the game and ninety-nine percent would still be uncertain. Having said that we are playing some great football now, the best I've seen in years. Is it an impossible dream? No, it isn't, let's see where it leads us.

When self-doubt strikes, as it undoubtedly will, simply cloak yourself in the comments you have just read above and believe!

Bees In Dreamland – 30/11/14

Brentford 4-0 Wolves. Yesterday's victory was never quite as convincing as the score suggests but our finishing was devastating and, as normal, we were fitter, better organised and totally out-passed and outworked the opposition. Mark Warburton unsurprisingly started with an unchanged team, with Fulham match winners Dallas and Jota remaining on the bench, but they would have a similar impact yesterday when they were finally called upon to enter the fray. Wolves sat back early on and allowed us to play in front of them and we kept possession easily and comfortably without ever managing to hurt our opponents.

The only one hurt was skipper Tony Craig who took an unseen and unpunished elbow from Sako in an aerial challenge, which stained the Griffin Park pitch red with his blood. It was Wolves, in fact, who came the closest to scoring. Bakary Sako, who had taken his ridiculous celebratory Swarovski crystal-encrusted boots off after the warm-up, bent a long range free kick narrowly over Button's crossbar with his more prosaic un-bejeweled pair of Nike's and the tricky van La Parra got away from Bidwell's close attentions and his centre beyond the far post was brilliantly met by the straining Danny Graham and his header went – well, nobody really knows quite where. It hit the underside of the bar and bounced down, over the line according to Wolves, but the man who counted, the assistant referee, was unconvinced and play continued. A narrow escape and maybe a let-off for Brentford, and this was a massive turning point, as Wolves came into the game on a poor run of form and an early goal would surely have revitalised their flagging spirits.

George Saville returned to his old stamping ground, almost literally at times, and he thrashed around the midfield like a human combine harvester and received his customary early booking for an agricultural scythe into Alan Judge. His influence waned like that of the setting sun, subsequently, on what was a quite beautiful mild November afternoon. For all their possession, Brentford created nothing until they scored. Finally, on the half hour, Toral picked Evans's pocket after a Wolves throw in and his persistence was rewarded when his slide rule pass sent Judge in on goal and he sashayed between two defenders at pace before flicking the ball almost contemptuously with the outside of his right foot beyond the helpless Ikeme. Incredibly, it was the Irishman's first goal of a wonderful season where he has been a massive influence with his nonstop energy, vision and skill. It was a goal of rapier-like deadliness, which skewered the Wolves defence and took the wind totally out of their sails. Button had one sharp save to make his with legs from Sako but Brentford were now in total command.

Wolves changed their approach in the second half and started pressing us high up the pitch, which resulted in them pinning us into our half for the first twenty minutes without creating much apart from an Edwards effort which went narrowly wide of the near post. Brentford were playing well within themselves and the introduction of Dallas for Toral resulted in us regaining the initiative and simply changing up into a higher gear, which Wolves simply could not live with. Odubajo finally won his crucial battle with Sako and with Golbourne off injured he could eventually find the opportunity and space to rampage forward, and, as Kenny Jackett ruefully admitted after the match, the more Wolves attacked, the more it was Brentford who looked like scoring. We sent men pouring forward into the space left behind the advanced Wolves players pressing for an equaliser, and we simply tore them apart with incisive close passing and our pace on the break.

Pritchard and Judge combined menacingly and a Hoddle-esque volleyed pass from Dallas sent Judge rushing into the area, and his lobbed volley was acrobatically turned over the bar by the keeper with Gray screaming for a square pass. The imperious Harlee Dean then won the ball deep in his own half, rampaged upfield, just as he had done against Fulham, and found Pritchard, who, with the ball seemingly tied to his foot, made space for himself, and played the ball across the area for the unmarked Dallas to score calmly and without fuss. Harlee has rapidly become a massive influence both in defence and as an auxiliary attacker and, on current form, will take some shifting from the first team. Wolves's heads went down and their challenge evaporated. Brentford now went for the jugular and Judge picked out Gray with a perfectly weighted long pass and the former Wolves youngster took the ball across the edge of the area, shrugged off three defenders and buried a fearsome low strike beyond Ikeme into the far corner. His was a goal of breathtaking quality, which emphasised the gulf in confidence between the two teams. Wolves stood off and just watched and tried to react whilst Brentford ran rings around them and made things happen. Gray retired to a hero's ovation, he now believes in his own ability, and with five goals in as many games, is fast becoming a massive threat and is an immense prospect. His recent progress just goes to show how well a player can perform when he is given the time and support to grow into an unfamiliar role.

Jota came on for the last few minutes and put the cherry on top with a typical party-piece goal which simply emphasised the gulf between the two teams. Judge it was who won the ball back and slipped him through, and Jota's angled finish from the edge of the six-yard box was perfect as he threaded the ball through the eye of the needle into the goal. Even from the kickoff Brentford kept pressing, ingrained as they are with good habits even when the match had long been won. So this incredible month is coming to an end with a fifteen point haul and every Brentford supporter must wish that it could continue ad infinitum.

Mark Warburton must surely be named as Manager of the Month given his perfect and unblemished record although Ipswich's Mick McCarthy could run him close given their four wins and a draw over the same period. Gray too and maybe Toumani Diagouraga, who was imperious yet again yesterday, might also come into contention for Player of the Month honours. To receive either or both awards would be wonderful as this is New Brentford, and we no longer worry about tempting fate, but in our heart of hearts we know just how good we are and hopefully the run will continue. We are certainly good enough to achieve great things this season.

League Table – 29/11/14

Position	Team	P	W	D	L	F	A	GD	Pt	Form
1	Derby County	19	10	5	4	35	19	16	35	L L W W W L
2	Ipswich Town	19	9	7	3	28	19	9	34	D W W W D W
3	**Brentford**	**19**	**10**	**4**	**5**	**30**	**24**	**6**	**34**	**L W W W W W**
4	Bournemouth	19	9	6	4	37	20	17	33	W W W D D D
5	Middlesbrough	19	9	6	4	28	14	14	33	D W W D D D
6	Blackburn Rovers	19	8	7	4	30	26	4	31	W W D D W D
7	Watford	19	8	5	6	31	22	9	29	D W L L L L
8	Cardiff City	19	8	5	6	24	22	2	29	L W L D W W
8	Nottingham Forest	19	7	7	5	30	25	5	28	L L L W W L
10	Charlton Athletic	19	6	10	3	20	19	1	28	L D D W D L
11	Norwich City	19	7	6	6	29	24	5	27	D W L L D L
12	Wolverhampton Wndrs	19	7	6	6	22	29	-7	27	W D L L L L
13	Sheffield Wednesday	19	5	10	4	14	15	-1	25	D D L D D W
14	Reading	19	7	3	9	25	30	-5	24	W L W L L W
15	Leeds United	19	6	5	8	23	26	-3	23	L L D W L W
16	Fulham	19	6	4	9	30	34	-4	22	W D D W L W
17	Birmingham City	19	5	7	7	17	30	-13	22	L D W D W W
18	Bolton Wanderers	19	6	3	10	22	28	-6	21	W L W W D W
19	Huddersfield Town	19	5	6	8	25	32	-7	21	D W L L D L
20	Millwall	19	4	8	7	21	26	-5	20	W L D L D D
21	Rotherham United	19	4	7	8	16	26	-10	19	D L L D L D
22	Brighton and Hove A	19	3	9	7	21	25	-4	18	D L W D D L
23	Wigan Athletic	19	3	8	8	20	25	-5	17	W D L L D L
24	Blackpool	19	1	6	12	13	31	-18	9	L L D L D D

DECEMBER

What A Bargain! – 4/12/14

Don't you find that everything is getting so much more expensive nowadays and the extra cost just seems to creep up on you insidiously? Deep in the mists of time, way back in the late 70s, I can still remember taking my girlfriend out to dinner and spending what seemed to me (back in my student days) the eye-wateringly enormous and extravagant sum of five pounds a head for a slap up dinner for the two of us in Chelsea. You can barely buy a small cup of tea and a sandwich for a fiver today. I bought one of my favourite Freddo Chocolate bars yesterday and was horrified to discover that it now cost a princely twenty-five pence when I can still remember buying one for ten pence not so very long ago. Mind you it tasted great and is still value for money even at the new price!

That reminds me that if you look hard enough there are still bargains to be had, and one of them can be found at Griffin Park. Next time you are wandering around the Braemar Road concourse with a few moments to kill before a match I would strongly suggest that you seek out and visit the Brentford Programme Shop which is tucked away in a small cupboard-like room situated underneath the main stand. Just keep looking and eventually you will find it. There you will receive a warm welcome as you enter an Aladdin's cave of riches with hundreds of programmes on display from Brentford home and away matches over the past decades as well as a smattering of programmes featuring other clubs. Interesting though they all are, what I am referring to is their selection of Bargain Bundles. For a mere one pound, yes, one pound, you can buy a shrink wrapped lucky bag selection of fifteen Brentford home programmes, all from matches played over the last thirty years. You have to take pot luck as, given the packaging, it is quite impossible to tell which games have been included in each bundle, bar the ones on either end, but whatever you end up with I can guarantee that it will be money well spent. And, to be frank, what else can you buy nowadays for the same paltry sum that provides as much satisfaction and stimulation?

I have to say that it is rare for me not to visit the shop at every home game and emerge with at least one packet of programmes, which I will savour later on. Occasionally there will also be a bundle of programmes from away matches on display but these are particularly highly prized, and are a rare and special treat, which do not remain unsold for long given the fact that there is a long queue of aficionados eager to snap them up. I find it enormous fun to sit back at home during the following week and read through these treasures, which remind me of past matches, players, managers and key incidents and happenings otherwise long-since forgotten. Sometimes too you read something which makes you challenge your own memory or even probe and question the current accepted truth of an incident that took place in the deep and distant past. I just thought that I would illustrate my point by noting down some of the things that I found particularly interesting or noteworthy when perusing the latest batch of programmes, which I purchased before last Saturday's match against Wolves.

Roger Stanislaus's long range Exocet of an equaliser against Fulham in the Littlewoods Cup in 1988 has long since entered Brentford folklore and the distance from where he unleashed his shot has increased with every telling until he was practically in another postcode. The Brentford programme for the Second Leg tie against Fulham put paid to these exaggerations and firmly states that the actual distance was nearly thirty-five yards.

A match report of the Brentford versus Cambridge Sunday morning match in 1993 brings back memories of that notorious and frankly bizarre incident when referee Roger Wiseman, having first booked our nemesis Steve Claridge for having his socks rolled down in trademark fashion, then sent off Cambridge midfielder Paul Raynor for arguing too aggressively with his own centre half, Mick Heathcote. Shades of Darren Powell and Karleigh Osborne at Bournemouth in 2009, perhaps? Anyone who has seen Raynor's more than animated behaviour on the bench alongside Steve Evans at Rotherham will not have been too shocked at this incident. Oh, and by the way, despite the man advantage, Brentford still lost thanks to a goal scored by another former Bee, Steve Butler.

I enjoyed reading a report of a seven goal win over Welling United in a Capital League match in October 1995. A surprising score line in itself, but what stood out was our first goal, scored by our new exciting, all-action midfielder, Paul Davis. Now whatever happened to him?

The chaotic manner in which the club appeared to be run was highlighted by the following news snippet in October 1997: Dean Holdsworth's big money move to Bolton Wanderers didn't earn Brentford any money because there was no sell-on clause in his £720,000 transfer from Griffin Park to Wimbledon. However if Marcus Gayle ever moves on then Brentford will receive twenty percent. So that's all right then! Gary Alexander was asked in 2012 which one player he would sign from our division and replied: *Bradley Wright-Phillips from Charlton*. Gary obviously has a future as a scout when he finally hangs up his boots. Phil Holder was a guest of honour for the home game against Exeter in 2012. Remarkably, this was his first visit to Griffin Park for almost nineteen years since he was sacked after relegation in 1993. Time does eventually heal all wounds. I will let you know if I unearth any more gems in the near future and hope to see some of you in the programme shop in due course.

Double Celebration for Brentford! – 5/12/14

What a wonderful way to start the day with a massive double celebration at Griffin Park! Brentford Manager Mark Warburton has been named Sky Bet Championship Manager of the Month for November and, just to round off the celebrations, striker Andre Gray has also become the Sky Bet Championship Player of the Month. These magnificent achievements are simply further examples of Brentford's progress this season being acknowledged and recognised by the football fraternity.

On the face of it, Brentford's five consecutive victories last month over tough opposition (aren't they all!) in Derby County, Nottingham Forest, Millwall, Fulham and Wolves with fourteen goals scored, culminating in the club shooting up to third place in the Championship table, a mere one point behind the leaders, would have appeared to make Mark Warburton a shoo-in for the award but, just like most things in life, it wasn't quite as simple as that.

He faced, and had to overcome, some tough opposition in fellow nominees Gary Rowett of Birmingham City, Mick McCarthy of Ipswich Town and Neil Lennon of Bolton Wanderers. Rowett has made a fantastic start at his new club where he took over following the debacle of an eight-nil home defeat to a rampant Bournemouth, and his ability to right the ship so quickly is a Herculean achievement. The experienced Mick McCarthy has presided over Ipswich Town's surge into the promotion frame after four wins in the last month, and, as Brentford found out to their cost in October, Neil Lennon's arrival has revitalised Bolton Wanderers, particularly at home.

Thankfully, the judging panel which comprised Chris Hughton, Sky Sports' pundit Don Goodman, Football League Chief Operating Officer Andy Williamson, the League Managers' Association Director Olaf Dixon, and Sky Bet Football Trading Manager Paul Lowery, sifted the evidence, and came up with the correct answer in choosing Mark as the winner. Their comments also bear testimony to his achievement: Chris Hughton, a fellow manager who chairs the Sky Bet Manager of the Month judging panel said:

For a team that won promotion last season Brentford have made a fantastic start to the new campaign. To record five straight wins in the Sky Bet Championship is a wonderful achievement and Mark Warburton is thoroughly deserving of this award.

Goodman was equally complimentary:

Brentford continue to impress in their first season in the second tier for twenty-one years. Securing their fifth straight Championship win with a four-nil demolition job of Wolves, Warburton will be dreaming of a repeat of last season's promotion heroics.

Paul Lowery then added his two-penn'orth:

For me there was no other contender for this month's award. Brentford have been breathtaking under Warburton during November.

I have already written much about Mark, his background, approach and achievements and there is no need for me to repeat my words. I will simply let his record since becoming Brentford manager almost exactly a year ago, speak for itself. After succeeding Uwe Rösler, Warburton was in charge for the last twenty-seven League games of last season which saw seventeen wins, six draws and only four defeats and an incredible haul of fifty-seven points obtained. In that time we scored forty-three goals and conceded only twenty-four. We finished in second place in the league with a massive ninety-four points. He was also undefeated in his first eleven matches of which the first six were won.

His Midas touch has continued this season with Brentford winning ten of the nineteen matches played to date, including the current run of five consecutive victories, the best run in this division for the club since 1935, and we start December in the playoff places. Today's award is exceptionally well timed as Brentford have now played an exact season's worth of forty-six league games under Mark, and the combined record of last season and this makes stunning and almost unbelievable reading: *Played* – forty-six, *Won* – twenty-seven, *Drawn* – ten and *Lost* – nine. *Goals For* – seventy-three, *Goals Against* – forty-eight. *Points* – ninety-one.

We are one measly point short of averaging two points per game over an entire season and he has an overall winning percentage of well over fifty percent. I have not checked and don't have the time or energy to do so, but I would be amazed if this record has been matched or surpassed by many other teams around the world, let alone just in this country. This is Mark's second such award since his appointment, as he was also successful in December 2013, his first month in charge, and he was also nominated in January and March of this year. Mark would be the first to admit that Brentford's ongoing success is not simply about him, but he is the catalyst, the glue that binds us together and makes us far better than the sum of all our individual parts. Brentford fans will all join me in saluting his achievement today and long may it continue.

If that was not quite enough then there is also the equally amazing achievement of Andre Gray to celebrate. He scored five goals and assisted in two more as Brentford won all five of their Championship matches in November. This represented an amazing transformation for the young striker who had previously gone eight matches without a goal. Brentford were also reportedly looking to bring in another experienced striker to take the weight off Andre when suddenly everything changed. Mark Warburton and his coaching staff had highlighted the need for him to become more forceful and try and impose himself more on the game and Andre certainly took notice of his instructions.

Suddenly everything fell into place and he started to bully defenders who had previously dominated him, and his pace and power, instant shooting and clinical finishing ability, all aided and abetted by a newly developed sense of self-belief, transformed him into a formidable opponent who is now treated with caution and respect by defenders who have started to drop off him slightly, worried as they are by his electric pace. His goals were all valuable and breathtaking in their variety and he impressed with his calmness and the deadliness of his finishing. A wonderful first time effort against Derby, clinical finishes against Nottingham Forest and twice at Millwall were followed by a rampaging run and venomous shot against Wolves where he held off the challenge of three defenders before scoring. With a modicum of luck he could have scored at least as many times again and notched hat-tricks at both Forest and Millwall. He also provided two assists as well as becoming an excellent focal point in attack, holding the ball up well and bringing his team-mates into the game. All in all a month to remember for a young player who, it must be noted, was playing in the Conference last season and has taken the rise of three divisions in his stride. He has eight goals to his name so far this season, with the prospect of many more to come.

The judging panel chose Andre ahead of fellow nominees Blackburn Rovers striker Rudy Gestede, Leeds United midfield player Alex Mowatt, and Birmingham City goalkeeper Darren Randolph. Fellow striker Dan Goodman said:

Gray's goals have been pivotal in Brentford's recent run, with the centre-forward running defenders ragged throughout the month.

Mark Warburton believes he has the talent to make the step up to the Premier League. Who are we to disagree? Who indeed as the season just gets better and better. This is a wonderful time to be a Brentford fan and let's just enjoy it. Oh, and as for the so-called curse of the Manager of the Month, we can totally discount it as we are New Brentford now.

All Good Things Must Come To An End As – Shock Horror – Brentford lose! – 7/12/14

Well it couldn't last forever. Brentford's incredible, unforgettable and unprecedented run of five consecutive wins ended on a cold, raw, Huddersfield December afternoon when the wind whipped across the Pennines and the scoreline was as bleak as the conditions and surroundings, and Brentford subsided to a narrow and perhaps slightly undeserved defeat by two goals to one. It was a match that highlighted the importance and accuracy of so many of Mark Warburton's maxims and truisms about how to succeed at Championship level. Taking them in no particular order:

- Take care of the football – we didn't, we were careless in the extreme, as despite having fifty-nine percent of possession we gave the ball away with monotonous regularity, often in highly dangerous positions.
- Be clinical with your chances – we weren't, as demonstrated by a tally of twenty-two shots at goal with eight on target, and only one goal scored.
- Games at this level are decided by fine margins – absolutely, as we came within a hairsbreadth of equalising on so many occasions late in the game and the referee's eccentricity and inconsistency certainly assisted the home team.
- Drop your standards and you will get punished – we did and we were.

We came into the game bursting with confidence and left shaking our heads in disbelief at how we had gifted the points to a home team totally lacking in confidence and out of form after a poor run of no victories in their previous four games. I was also concerned to hear a comment from a disgruntled Bees fan leaving the ground remarking that we should not be losing to a team like Huddersfield given our respective positions in the league table. Arrogant, ignorant and dangerous talk, indeed, as we are tyros and neophytes and have much to learn about this level. We still have our L Plates on, and Huddersfield are a Championship team on merit and therefore possess an abundance of talent and players who are highly experienced at this level and can really hurt you if you allow them the time, space and opportunity to do so.

Alex Smithies must have been wearing a Superman top under his goalkeeper's jersey so often did he foil us, Mark Hudson was an impassable barrier in central defence and Nahki Wells, Sean Scannell and Grant Holt led our defence a merry dance and at times threatened to tear us apart. An unchanged Brentford team took the game to Huddersfield early on and our confident, slick passing and approach work regularly opened up the home defence, but we failed to capitalise upon some glaring chances. Toral set up Judge who fired narrowly wide, Odebajo's deep cross found an unmarked Douglas who, unforgivably, headed wide of the gaping goal when it appeared easier to score, and Smithies readjusted brilliantly to turn Judge's deflected shot over the bar.

There was an early warning for Brentford when Wells twisted clear to shoot wide of the near post but, just as had been the case at Bolton, the game was there for the taking early on, but we spurned our opportunities and paid a heavy price when Huddersfield finally got their passing game together. They worked the ball from their right to left where Robinson, in acres of space with Moses caught infield, crossed low to Wells who beat Dean to the ball and his low pass across goal was hammered home by Scannell. It could have got worse as our performance levels dipped, we were second to every ball and stood off the Huddersfield attackers and allowed them space to turn. Holt systematically beat up and bullied Tony Craig, aided and abetted by an indulgent referee who allowed him to get away with all his tricks, and Bidwell seemed hypnotised by Scannell like a snake by a mongoose and backed off the winger with disastrous effect. Wells too ran in behind our defence on numerous occasions but thankfully had left his shooting boots at home. This was a bad period for the Bees as the crowd roused itself from its torpor and got behind the home team who responded well. We recovered and came again before the break and created more excellent chances, with Bidwell's long range volley being turned round the post, Gray just unable to force in a loose ball and when the clever Pritchard weaved his way into space his shot went inches wide of the upright. A curate's egg of a first half ended with our fine attacking play let down by poor final passes, loose finishing and by our allowing the home team space and time to hurt us.

Surely things would change in the second half, and they certainly did, as we got even worse. We started slowly, forgot to track the runners, played for a non-existent offside, allowed Robinson to cross from the left flank, and, just to cap it all, Bidwell chested the ball into his own net when Scannell missed the cross. A litany of errors that resulted in our now having to chase the game and having the proverbial mountain to climb. But climb it we did. We pushed men forward and inevitably left even more gaps at the back. Holt was left criminally unmarked from a long throw and his clever overhead kick inched past the post. Wells missed yet again when Craig's error let him through but Button saved brilliantly and was rewarded for his efforts by being stamped on by the forward in his follow through.

Dallas gave us more power and a threat on the left flank and had an effort saved, before Tommy Smith, who, not for the first time, made a massive difference when he came on, capped an intricate move from a throw in by slipping a clever pass into Douglas, whose late run left him with the space to score with a nonchalant outside of the right foot flick into the corner. Huddersfield dropped deeper and went into panic mode, wasting time with impunity as the referee looked on and did nothing. We battered them for the last quarter of the game with Moses and Bidwell pushing on and creating havoc. Chances came and went but were not taken. Pritchard and Judge argued over a free kick in front of goal and Alex had a mild hissy fit when his entreaties were rejected before Smithies arched backwards to tip Judge's effort over the bar. Dean set up Smith for a careful side-footed effort that was turned round the post before Judge's centre was headed back by Dallas and the ball fell for Douglas five yards out.

This was the moment, and time seemed to stand still as Dougie set himself, took aim and hit the ball powerfully with his left foot. Surely this would be the equaliser, but the ball hit a defender on the line and squirmed clear. It wasn't going to be our day, a realisation which was confirmed when, deep into injury time, Proschwitz went down on the edge of the box. No penalty was the inevitable decision by the referee who, to add insult to injury, penalised the stricken striker for handball.

Tommy Smith – always a calming influence off the bench.

It was a quiet and reflective group who shared a car back to London, lost in their own thoughts regarding what they had witnessed that afternoon. This was a game that we would probably have won comfortably if we had scored early on when we cut through their defence seemingly at will. Equally, it was a match that could have drifted further away from us if Huddersfield had taken advantage of the numerous chances created by their trickery and pace up front, combined with our careless defensive play. If we had equalised late on then perhaps the home team would have collapsed and allowed us a late victory. If… if… if! The fact is that we lost and contributed greatly to our own downfall. This season is simply a series of learning curves and Brentford were taught some hard lessons yesterday and they will need to do their homework on the training ground next week.

Did The Manager of the Month Curse Strike Again? – 8/12/14

There have been a few mutterings and imprecations since Saturday's defeat at Huddersfield about the curse of the Manager of the Month Award, particularly as the loss ended our perfect run of five consecutive victories. Frankly I put very little store on such superstitions and I would rather put our defeat down to our own failings and, indeed, the good play of our opponents, rather than to any supernatural occurrences. We are penned in behind the goal at the majority of away games and our view of the game is therefore limited, particularly when the play is at the other end and you are as myopic as I am. It is amazing how different a perspective you get when you watch the television or Bees Player recording of the match.

Sometimes it seems that you were, in fact, watching a totally different game. Those shots that in real time appeared to whistle inches past the post were, in reality, miles wide and sometimes the ebb and flow and pattern of the game bears no resemblance to what you think you saw live at the stadium. But in this case nothing I saw on *The Football League Show*'s in-depth coverage of the match changed the impression that I had formed whilst huddled and freezing behind the goal at Huddersfield on Saturday afternoon. It was a strange match that we could have won by a couple of clear goals, lost by the same margin, or even drawn, rather than ending up losing by the odd goal in three. And, no, I am not sitting on the fence either. Control fluctuated throughout the ninety-six minutes of hell-to-leather, nonstop action. Like two boxers exchanging blows, Brentford had twenty-two efforts on goal and Huddersfield nearly matched us with eighteen.

Both keepers made important saves, Button from Wells when the nippy striker got in behind the straining Tony Craig, and Alex Smithies, the India rubber man, saved his team on no less than four occasions, from Judge's deflected effort, Bidwell's long range volley, Judge's curling free kick and, finally, Smith's late angled shot which looked for a glorious moment as if it was going to sneak in at the far post. It was simply just one of those games. We had our chances early on to deflate a nervous home team desperately looking for a win, but failed to capitalise, and then went behind to an exceptionally well-crafted goal from Huddersfield that came totally against the run of play. Our game then fell apart for a spell as we defended poorly and stood off our opponents and we were fortunate not to concede again. Another belated revival saw us regain the initiative and miss more chances just before half time. We stood and admired the second goal just after the break and it looked for a while as if we were on the ropes, but we came again after the substitutions and dominated the final twenty minutes without quite managing to make up the two goal deficit.

So, all in all, it was a magnificent game of football, which both sides will think that they deserved to win, and we simply have to learn from, and not repeat, our mistakes rather than worry about curses and similar mumbo-jumbo. Richard Poole summed it up perfectly:

Let us not forget that even though we lost, these are the kind of games where everyone SHOULD learn a lot. It's these types of matches against teams below us in the table where we learn the most, and if we manage to take everything on board this defeat will help make Brentford a more solid team. The heavy grounds and the winter months ahead will also help highlight our team's true quality and just how good we are. These coming games will show our true strength and sort the men out from the boys.

Many keyboard warriors on the message boards are advocating throwing skipper Tony Craig under the bus after what they feel were two indifferent games from the Brentford captain. Grant Holt certainly won his battle on Saturday and dominated Craig, who appeared to be knocked off the ball all too easily. The referee allowed Holt total freedom to exploit the dark arts with several late challenges, which should surely have been penalised, but all in all, it was not one of Craig's better games. Danny Graham also worried him in the first half last week with his strength, anticipation and movement and gave Tony a particularly difficult opening forty-five minutes, but he persevered and eventually came out on top of a tricky and experienced opponent.

There was talk under Uwe Rösler of our bringing in a beast of a defender – a Dan Burn beanpole type who would be expected to win everything. Martin Taylor of that ilk had a reasonable loan spell with us early last season, but nothing else materialised until the eventual arrival in January of the far more cultured James Tarkowski. Andre Gray showed that Burn, for all his aerial prowess, is vulnerable on the floor when he led the Fulham defender a merry dance recently, and given Mark Warburton's determination to play a style of football that demands that every player is comfortable on the ball and able to pass it accurately and fluently I cannot see us being in the market for that type of player. Craig is calm and composed in possession, with the ability to switch play with accurate long passes to the right wing, and I do not think that he will easily be jettisoned by the management, particularly given his left-footedness, which helps provide us with more balance at the back. Harlee Dean has been playing out of his skin throughout November and although I felt he was sub-par on Saturday as Wells and Holt got the better of our central defensive duo, it would be harsh in the extreme to recall James Tarkowski quite yet. James and Harlee played together earlier in the season after Craig's suspension but their partnership did not look the equal of the Dean/Craig or indeed the Tarkowski/Craig combinations. A difficult conundrum for Warburton and David Weir to mull over throughout the coming week.

They might also look to refresh the midfield area where Stuart Dallas, Jota and Tommy Smith have all mightily impressed when coming off the bench recently and are clamouring for a starting position. Sam Saunders too is looking for some increased game time. Given how impressive the men in possession, Douglas, Diagouraga, Toral, Pritchard and Judge, have been, I am also scratching my head over all the possible permutations and whether, indeed, we need to freshen things up. Has Toumani's magic spell ended and is he returning to the ranks of the mere mortals? Does young Jon Toral, who has punched well above his weight since his recent introduction to the first team, need a rest and to be taken out of the firing line for a brief period? Could Jota replace Alex Pritchard for a game or two, particularly at home? Will Alan Judge try too hard next Saturday to impress his former employers at Blackburn Rovers? Does Jonathan Douglas need the odd day off in order to retain his sharpness?

Does Mark Warburton simply leave well alone as Saturday saw Brentford play an unchanged team for the third game in a row? This will certainly be an interesting week at the training ground and I await next Saturday's team announcement at quarter past two with keen anticipation.

Toums – 10/12/14

Good news indeed yesterday in that Toumani Diagouraga has signed a new contract at Brentford, potentially extending his stay at the club until 2017. Yet up until a few short weeks ago it looked very much as if his time at Griffin Park was rapidly drawing towards its conclusion with not too many supporters regretting his likely departure. He had enjoyed a successful loan spell last season at Portsmouth before regaining his place in the Brentford first team for the promotion run-in, but it seemed very much as if the Championship would be a step too far for the elegant, long-legged and combative midfielder.

As expected, Toums started the season very much on the periphery of the team and it appeared that he was no more than bench fodder at best. Coventry City were rumoured to be sniffing around him and it would not have come as any surprise if he had joined them, as Division One seemed to be his level. After impressing in training he was recalled, to everybody's surprise against Derby County, and Toumani enjoyed a November to dream about as he quarterbacked the team to five consecutive wins. He exhibited a newfound ability on the ball, a renewed confidence and appetite for the game that made him stand out from his teammates.

It would be easy to dismiss his exceptional form as a mere flash in the pan but for me the crowning glory was his display at Millwall where he dominated the match from start to finish and ensured that the absence of the suspended Jonathan Douglas was barely noticed. Cynically, one could simply attribute his recent brilliance to the spurt traditionally put on by a player rapidly coming to the end of his contract and doing his best to stay in a job the following season, but a closer examination of Toumani's performances highlighted a very real and significant improvement in his game. Suddenly he was attempting and pulling off a variety of skills that had previously seemed way beyond him. The list seemed endless – defence splitting passes made with the outside of his foot, changing the direction of the attack with accurate long balls to the opposite wing, sending the opposition the wrong way with a perfectly executed dummy, even forcing a brilliant save from the Fulham goalkeeper with a rasping shot.

Shooting, as we all know has never been his forte and he, like the former Arsenal midfielder, John Jensen, picked up a deserved reputation for endangering the fans in the top tier behind the goal rather than the goalkeeper when winding up for a shot. Everything he tried in November came off without a hitch as Toumani was suddenly transformed into a clone of Patrick Vieira. A meat and potatoes type of journeyman player renowned for his dependability, hard tackling, non-stop running and harrying and accurate short passing, but plagued by inconsistency, Toumani seemed to have found his level. Suddenly, though, the ugly duckling has become a swan and he has deserved his new contract as well as becoming one of the first names on the team sheet.

It is rare indeed that a player of twenty-seven improves as dramatically as Toums has and much of his success is simply down to how hard he has worked. But in my opinion there is far more to it than that. Toums is merely one of many Brentford players who have demonstrated a staggering improvement in their overall game this season. David Button has played like a man possessed and has developed into a goalkeeper as good as you will find at this level of the game. He suddenly seems to have found confidence and a belief in his own ability after so many years as a reserve or stopgap loanee. Central defenders Harlee Dean and James Tarkowski are now as comfortable on the ball as any of our multitude of midfielders and Harlee's beautifully weighted pass with the outside of his right foot to Alex Pritchard that split the Wolves defence and led to our second goal will live long in the memory. Let's be frank, Harlee has traditionally been an uncomplicated win the ball and thump it type of defender and yet suddenly he has turned into Beckenbauer, striding forward with the ball, selling dummies, making runs into the opposition penalty area and scoring brilliantly against Fulham (giving him instant hero status). What is going on?

Alan Judge was excellent as a loanee last season, but has achieved new heights now that he has taken over the mantle of the departed Adam Forshaw and been given the responsibility of becoming our main playmaker. He covers every blade of grass and his long passing is a joy to watch. He too has added to his game. Alan McCormack has combined his customary tough defending with well-timed rampages up the field and most remarkably, thirty-three year old Jonathan Douglas, at a stage of his career when players generally begin to let their standards slip, has very much gone the other way and massively improved all aspects of his game. No longer a mere destroyer, he has displayed a subtlety in his use of the ball that first became apparent in the preseason friendly against Crystal Palace when he was fed the ball at an angle just inside the penalty area. Bringing the ball instantly under control, he looked up and curled it perfectly, well beyond the reach of an admiring Julian Speroni for a goal of awesome quality that he would never have attempted in previous years, yet alone carried off.

I would put the credit for his players' improvement in technique, confidence and self-belief firmly at the door of Mark Warburton. Empowerment is a term that is grossly overused nowadays, and it has become an irritating buzzword, but for me it perfectly sums up his entire management ethos. He has simply taken away the fear element from the game and encouraged all of his players to try the unexpected, be positive, take the game to their opponents, attack relentlessly and never be afraid of making mistakes. I never fail to marvel and take delight at the sight of gnarled and cynical Championship defenders on their way up for a corner looking anxiously and with stunned bemusement over their shoulder at the sight of three Brentford attackers hovering with menace on the halfway line just waiting for a quick breakaway. They just haven't come across a team like us before and currently the league is finding it hard to deal with us. We play with just one striker yet pepper the opposition goal with shots from all distances and angles, further evidence of Warburton's determination to take the attack to the opposition and let them worry about us. Warburton's policy of positive reinforcement has brought massive dividends and Toums is simply one of many Brentford players to have benefited from this approach. He has received his reward and fully deserves it.

Manager of the Month – 16/12/14

After our 3-1 victory over Blackburn Rovers, I began to think about the Manager of the Month once again and wondered… what other Brentford managers had previously won this award. So, I consulted the oracle, Mark Croxford, co-author and inspiration of the *Big Brentford Book* series. Mark has voluminous records of everything that has happened both on and off the field in and around Griffin Park for the past forty-five years. Nothing, however seemingly inconsequential, escapes his eagle-eyed attention and everything is recorded for posterity – or indeed, the next Big Brentford Book.

How many times have Brentford managers won the prestigious Manager of the Month Award? Five, eight, twelve, fifteen times, perhaps? Well I was staggered when I added up the numbers. Mark Warburton's selection in November was the twenty-second time that a Brentford manager has won this coveted award.

Frank Blunstone won twice, both times during the momentous 1971/72 promotion season, in September 1971 and again in March 1972. September saw Brentford win three out of five matches and hammer Hartlepool and Peterborough at Griffin Park with eleven goals scored in two memorable home games, and March included a promotion-clinching run of five consecutive victories inspired by the return of John O'Mara from his harsh five-week ban. John Docherty took over the manager's job from Mike Everitt in early 1975 and revitalised a struggling team. His efforts were recognised in April when, with Roger Cross and Micky French scoring eight goals between them, the Bees won four times to finish in an excellent eighth place in the league table. Bill Dodgin's team played wonderful football throughout the 1977/78 season which was deservedly rewarded with promotion and what is surprising is that he only won the Manager of the Month award once, but then again, he faced tough competition as Watford, under their own inspiration, Graham Taylor, finished eleven points clear at the top of the table! Dodgin won in March, which saw eight matches crammed into the month and Brentford rose to the challenge with six victories.

Over a decade was to pass until a Brentford manager again caught the eye of the selection panel and the reigns of Fred Callaghan and Frank McLintock passed without recognition, as, unsurprisingly, did that of Mike Everitt in the early seventies! Callaghan might have gone close in his first month in charge, April 1980 when his new team went on an undefeated run of four matches before results deteriorated but even in his most memorable season of 1982/83 when his team scored eighty-eight league goals, their results were far too inconsistent for him to have come into serious contention for the award. The mid-eighties were a time of mediocrity when an average team played unmemorable football in front of poor attendances, and apathy ruled.

Momentum was restored under Steve Perryman, who was the next Brentford manager to win the award in January 1989. This was a wonderful month, which saw seven matches pass undefeated and Walsall and Manchester City defeated in the FA Cup. I will pause for a moment now and ask the question, which Brentford manager has won the Manager of the Month award the most times? Given where I have got to in my narrative I suspect that most of you will have guessed that the correct answer is Phil Holder, but what is even more praiseworthy is that he won the award four times in his three seasons in charge. He first won the award in December 1990 when an unbeaten run of five matches saw Brentford begin their challenge for the playoffs. Brentford fell for the first time in the playoffs that season but the following season saw the Third Division title won and Holder's magnificent achievement was recognised twice, in November 1991 and in April 1992. November saw a cagy draw against fellow promotion aspirants, Birmingham City, a four goal hammering of a poor Wigan team and the amazing come from behind recovery from a two-goal halftime deficit to beat a Swansea team inspired by *The Flying Postman*, John Williams. April saw a procession of five victories including the unforgettable mauling of Fulham, as an inspired Brentford team totally delivered at the business end of the season and strode triumphantly towards the title.

Holder's overall managerial record at the club was highly impressive as he won fifty-nine out of one hundred and thirty-eight league matches over three seasons. There were many factors other than poor management that caused our relegation in 1993 and his achievements deserve massive credit. Indeed Holder even won the Manager of the Month award in our relegation season, in December 1992, when the Bees went undefeated for five matches and ended the year in a comfortable mid-table position, looking upwards towards the top of the league rather than down towards the bottom. Unfortunately our optimism was to be misplaced given how the season ended. Holder's successor, David Webb won the award twice, in January 1995 and in August 1996. Both seasons were to end in playoff disappointment, but January 1995 was capped with a scintillating six-nil thrashing of Cambridge United, which saw all the goals scored in the last twenty-five minutes as the opposition, down to ten men after ex-Bee, Billy Manuel saw red, finally capitulated. August 1996 was a time of renewed optimism as our dynamic new front four of Nicky Forster, Carl Asaba, Bob Taylor and Marcus Bent threatened to steamroller the opposition, and the month ended with Carl Asaba scoring the club's fastest ever hat trick in eight minutes at Shrewsbury. Unfortunately, the season turned sour after the sale of Nicky Forster and after shooting ourselves in the foot we limped into the playoffs and an eventual Wembley embarrassment by Crewe Alexandra.

1997/98 was a horrible season marked by fan disaffection and revolt, the exodus of our best players and a fully justified relegation to the bottom division. Amazingly, new manager Micky Adams, replacing the doomed Eddie May won the award in March 1998 when he inspired his strugglers to three wins and an undefeated five match run. Too little, too late. 1998/99 saw an immediate promotion and the appointment of multi-tasking Owner/Chairman/Manager Ron Noades whose arrival was generally welcomed given that the truth about his *investment* in the club had not yet emerged. He won the award in August 1998, one of the few times when a manager won the award in his first ever month as a Football League manager, a feat, of course, matched by Mark Warburton in December 2013, as well as by a more unexpected name in Wally Downes. Noades and his support team built a vibrant, young team packed full of hungry, talented players from non-league and promotion and the title was won in a canter.

Steve Coppell came within a hairsbreadth of leading Brentford to promotion in his one season in charge and he won the award in October 2001, a month of breathtaking achievement when the Bees won all five matches, including wonderful away wins at two of the eventually promoted teams, Brighton and Reading. Wally Downes inherited a sinking ship, a team denuded of its best players who left the club after the playoff defeat to Cardiff and he had to make bricks without straw as he had no money to play with. Despite these handicaps, it all began so well for him and he won the award in August 2002 when he motivated a team of kids, loanees and journeymen to a six match unbeaten run. Unfortunately, there was only one way for him to go after such a wonderful start and he never threatened to win the award again.

Martin Allen's arrival undoubtedly saved the club from another relegation and he led the club to two marvellous FA Cup runs to the fifth round and two unsuccessful playoff campaigns. He won two Manager of the Month awards in September 2004, after three wins and a draw, and again, in February 2006, a month which saw a thrashing of Paul Merson's sleepwalking Walsall team who had thrown their manager overboard and an excellent win over league leaders, Southend. Andy Scott turned the club around after the disasters of the Leroy Rosenior, Scott Fitzgerald and Terry Butcher eras, and led the Bees to the title in 2009. His achievements were recognised in April 2009, a month in which the Championship was finally won. Heroes can turn into dunces so quickly in football and Andy Scott went from winning the Manager of the Month award in October 2010 to the sack after the Dagenham debacle in early February 2011.

That leads us onto the reigns of Uwe Rösler and the current incumbent, Mark Warburton. Uwe won the award in November 2013, which saw five consecutive victories, and after his unexpected departure to Wigan, Mark Warburton simply took over the mantle and ensured that the award remained at Griffin Park as he oversaw four wins in December 2013. Phil Holder has set the bar extremely high with four awards, can Mark Warburton equal or even surpass him? All will be revealed over the coming months and years but I fully expect that he will eventually achieve this momentous feat. One final thought. What a shame that such an award was not in existence during Harry Curtis's long and successful reign at the club. He would surely have set new records for the number of times a manager received this award!

The Manager of the Month Curse – True or False? – 18/12/14

So we now know that Brentford have won Manager of the Month twenty-two times. But, as SavvyBee subsequently asked:

...of course the real statistic we want to know is how many times did we lose the next game after the Manager of the Month trophy was awarded?

Frank Blunstone won the award twice, firstly in September 1971, which he celebrated thereafter with an unforgettable six-one thrashing of Northampton Town. This was a strange match. The prolific Dixie McNeil, a wonderful lower division striker, scored after just thirty-eight seconds, and with Peter Gelson limping on the wing, the Bees were struggling. Gelson it was who epitomised the marvellous team spirit by ignoring the pain to head home an equaliser before the interval and the Bees then ran away with it and scored five more times with our own goal machine, John O'Mara, notching a hat-trick. The news wasn't so good after Frank's next award in March 1972 as the Bees put in an inept display at bottom of the table Crewe Alexandra and lost by two goals to one with

O'Mara withdrawn at half-time, after what was reported to be a monumental row in the dressing room which ended with the manager being pinned to the wall. Truth or apocryphal – who knows? Fortunately, this defeat proved merely to be a blip and the Bees marched onto promotion.

John Docherty won the award in April 1975 and there were no fixtures remaining, but the first game of the following season in August resulted in a hard fought one-one draw at Bradford City where the Bees unveiled a new all-green away kit that didn't last long. Bill Dodgin celebrated his award in March 1978 with a comprehensive three-one win at Huddersfield where Steve Phillips scored a hat-trick which helped cement his award as *Evening Standard* Player of the Month soon afterwards. Brentford played out a drab nil-nil draw at Gillingham immediately after Steve Perryman won the award in January 1989 and Shrewsbury were put to the sword by three clear goals in the first game after Phil Holder won in December 1990. He then won the award twice in the 1991/92 title winning season and the matches following his awards in November 1991 and April 1992 were both memorable for different reasons. We drew one-all at Torquay in a tempestuous match marked by Gary Blissett's aerial collision with home defender John Uzzell which caused him to incur serious facial injuries and ended in a red card and subsequent court case. Marcus Gayle also saw red, but the nine men escaped with a draw in a horrid game that is probably best forgotten.

Brentford played only one match in May 1992 and that was the title clinching victory at Peterborough. There has been so much written about this game and there is really very little to add. My own memory is of having to buy a ticket in the home end, failing to keep my allegiance quiet and revealing my identity as a Bees fan when Blissett scored the only goal right in front of me. I feared verbal abuse or even worse, but all was well as the home fans were appeased by also reaching the playoffs and I escaped relatively unscathed. Phil Holder's celebrations for winning the Manager of the Month award for a club record fourth time were cut short when Brian Statham was sent off and Brentford's rigid and Neanderthal route one approach was totally exposed by a Leicester City team which cruised to a three-one victory and put the first doubts about our survival prospects into our minds..

David Webb drew one-all at Brighton following his first award in January 1995. We were under the cosh but it looked like we would bring off a smash and grab victory until we were denied by a Jamie Bates own goal and a ridiculous decision to disallow a last minute header from Barry Ashby. Nearly twenty years on I am still bemused by the decision. The Bees won by two goals at Chesterfield in September 1996 in a match marked by a rare Kevin Dearden penalty save. All Brentford fans will be really saddened by the news that Kevin has just resigned after seven years as goalkeeper coach and chief scout at Leyton Orient, apparently for *personal reasons*. The club, under new Italian ownership, seems to be in turmoil and Kevin looks as if he is just another victim of all the upheaval. I wish him well and hope that Kevin, with his massive experience allied to his cheerful and sunny disposition, finds a new employer very soon.

Micky Adams led his relegation-bound team to a surprising two-two draw at Wrexham and the Bees won a thriller by the odd goal in five at Hull, helped by a horrendous error by home keeper Steve Wilson, to ensure that Ron Noades also went undefeated after his award in August 1998. Steve Coppell went one better after winning the award in October 2001 as Blackpool were beaten in the next match, Brentford's seventh successive league win, equalling a club record. As you can see, the so-called curse of the Manager of the Month award has rarely reared its ugly head at Griffin Park, and even Wally Downes led his inexperienced team to a draw against Luton, Martin Allen won both of his matches immediately after winning his two awards and Andy Scott also celebrated with a win and a draw. Uwe Rösler didn't even put the curse to the test as he left the club immediately after his award was announced but Warbs managed to beat Oldham anyway in his first match in charge. Mark Warburton won the award in his own right in December 2013, which was followed by an epic performance at Peterborough where we totally outclassed the home team.

Only two previous Brentford managers, Frank Blunstone and Phil Holder ever lost their next match after winning the Manager of the Month award until Mark Warburton added to that unfortunate list by losing narrowly and unluckily at Huddersfield, ending a run of five consecutive victories. But three out of twenty-two isn't bad. So, as far as Brentford is concerned, the Manager of the Month curse barely exists, and roll on our next award!

Jeepers Keepers – Part Two – 19/12/14

I meandered down memory lane a little while ago revisiting some of the Brentford goalkeepers from the 60s and 70s. Players like Chic Brodie, Gordon Phillips, Steve Sherwood and Len Bond were all technically gifted goalkeepers who served us extremely well and were firm crowd favourites. The 80s were a different kettle of fish as nobody made the position his own for very long and a bewildering number of players, fifteen in all, wore the green jersey.

With Len Bond falling out of favour after failing to agree a new contract, and Trevor Porter released, Fred Callaghan was looking for a replacement keeper for the 1980/81 season. He managed to bring in a callow youngster in twenty-year old Paul McCullough who arrived from Reading on a free transfer. Paul had no league experience and was totally untested and he was intended to act as cover, but fate dictated otherwise. Callaghan was unsuccessful in signing a more experienced goalkeeper and failed in bids for the likes of Terry Gennoe at Southampton and Glen Johnson at Aldershot. Gennoe it was who played so well against us for Blackburn in all three memorable cup matches in 1988/89 and I would have also welcomed the balding Johnson, whose rotund Dearden-esque figure did not prevent him from keeping us at bay whenever we came up against him.

So McCullough started the season in goal and it soon became apparent that he was just not up to the job. His bravery was unquestioned whilst his tendency to hurl himself at the feet of onrushing forwards led to him earning the unflattering nickname of *The Kamikaze Kid*. He lasted for nine long games, which saw him concede seventeen goals, and he made costly errors against Charlton, Reading and Fulham as well as being lobbed by his own defender, Mark Hill, at Walsall for a memorable own goal that must have caused great hilarity amongst the television viewers later that night. This state of affairs couldn't go on any longer, he needed to be taken out of the firing line, and eventually Callaghan got his man in Dave McKellar. As for the unfortunate McCullough, who can hardly be blamed for being thrown into the lions' den, he disappeared without trace at the end of the season after conceding thirty-two goals in eighteen reserve games and never played senior football again.

His replacement was the real deal and well worth waiting for, and is generally regarded as being one of Brentford's best goalkeepers of recent times. Dave McKellar had a twenty-year long professional career beginning at Ipswich and ending with a year at Glasgow Rangers. In between, he played for Derby County, where he had extensive First Division experience, Carlisle, Hartlepool, Hibernian, Newcastle, Hamilton, Dunfermline and Kilmarnock, as well as, of course, the Bees. Fred Callaghan plucked Dave from Derby reserves for what turned out to be a bargain fee of £25,000 and he soon established himself as an automatic first choice. He was calm, unruffled, totally unflamboyant, utterly reliable and, unlike his predecessor, he filled his defenders with confidence. You never really noticed him and I can't recall any individual saves that he made, but he never let you down and you knew it would take a special effort to beat him. His record confirmed this as he kept thirty-one clean sheets in his ninety-two games for the club and conceded just over a goal per game. One minor quibble, if I have to be picky, is that he never managed to save a penalty kick in nine attempts! He was the best goalkeeper I had ever seen play for the Bees and I am not sure if we have had anyone better since.

Fred Callaghan was not the easiest man in the world to deal with – he was certainly not one to turn the other cheek, and he managed to fall out with McKellar, just as he had with Len Bond, and this argument cost us an exceptional player who could well have played for us throughout the remainder of the decade. Total madness, in my opinion. Let Dave McKellar take up the story:

Petar Borota was given a free by Chelsea and came to Brentford. He had no intention of signing as he subsequently played in Portugal, but Fred played him in the preseason friendlies. It didn't make sense as it prevented me getting match fit. We had words and I left. It was sad as I loved it at Brentford. My family was settled and I was looking forward to a long stay.

Oh, in passing I almost forgot to mention that Paul Priddy sneaked back for yet another spell at Brentford as cover for McKellar and made a farewell appearance in November 1981, against Chester, his first game for over five years (deservedly bowing out with a clean sheet). As mentioned, Petar Borota played in the preseason League Trophy competition in August 1982 before leaving us high and dry on the eve of the first league match. Callaghan was left desperately scrambling around trying to find a new goalkeeper and his scouring of the free transfer list was rewarded when he signed the experienced Eire International Paddy Roche from Manchester United a mere two days before the season began. Lots of time for him to develop a relationship with his new back four then! Roche had spent nine seasons at Old Trafford without managing to displace Alex Stepney and the jury was out on him given his propensity to commit howlers.

He settled down quickly, played in every game and was part of a dodgy defence that did its best to undermine the efforts of a wonderful midfield and potent strike force by conceding seventy-seven goals. In truth, he did far better than we supporters expected, and was probably a better goalkeeper at thirty-one than he had been at any previous time in his up and down career. He was still prone to costly errors and after making an elastic penalty save against Portsmouth, an effort which earned him a fusillade of golf balls from the frustrated Pompey fans congregated behind his goal, he then frustratingly fumbled an innocuous shot to gift the visitors a late equaliser.

Fred Callaghan decided to bring in some competition for Roche and after failing to capture Iain Hesford from Blackpool, Martin Thomas from Bristol Rovers and the wonderfully named Perry Digweed from Brighton, it was fourth time lucky when he signed the experienced Trevor Swinburne from Carlisle, with McKellar going the other way as part of the deal. As has so often been the case, Brentford got the thin end of the wedge as McKellar inevitably went on to prosper and Swinburne, so often impressive in the past for Carlisle at Griffin Park, played more like a player rapidly coming to the end of the road and merely hung on for a couple of seasons, initially sharing the jersey with Roche, before fading out of contention the following season. He played one unforgettable match when he temporarily regained all his former powers and inspired the Bees to a one-all draw at Bristol City but at other times he appeared to be no more than a mere shadow of his former self and he was replaced in December 1984 by Gary Phillips.

Phillips had impressed at Barnet and had helped the non-leaguers hold Brighton to a goalless FA Cup draw. This attracted Frank McLintock's attention and he was signed for a bargain £4,000 fee, initially remaining as a part timer combining football with landscape gardening. He made his debut in a spineless three-nil home defeat to Bristol Rovers on Boxing Day 1984 but soon established himself before crowning his debut season with a losing appearance at Wembley in the Freight Rover Trophy Final. Phillips soon became a crowd favourite and missed just a handful of games over the next three and a half seasons. When he did, Richard Key, Tony Oliver and the mysterious John Power who materialised for two matches from Kingstonian at the back end of the 1986/87 season and then just as quickly disappeared, filled in for him adequately. Gary was a spectacular shot stopper and saved four out of thirty-one penalties faced in his one hundred and seventy-one matches.

Let's just look at that figure again for a moment – Brentford managed to concede thirty one penalty kicks in less than four years, which means we gave away around eight penalty kicks per season – an enormous number. Gary wasn't the most dominating or consistent of goalkeepers but he was more than good enough to hold a job in what frankly was no more than a mid-table third division team. I am not sure that Steve Perryman was ever totally convinced by him and after a contractual dispute he was sold to Reading before eventually returning to Barnet where he helped them win promotion to the Football League. Perryman was looking to build a promotion challenging team and wanted to upgrade the goalkeeping position. Not unnaturally he looked to sign a player whom he knew well from their time together at Spurs and Tony Parks arrived in return for a frankly staggering £60,000 fee as Chairman Martin Lange unlocked his wallet in a preseason spending spell that also saw Richard Cadette and Neil Smillie join the club. Parks had been the penalty saving hero in the 1984 UEFA Cup Final but had never managed to establish himself in the Spurs goal.

Small in stature, he struggled with crosses but read the game well and performed consistently for two years and he made some crucial saves in the 1988/89 FA Cup campaign against both Manchester City and Blackburn. He was injury prone and that gave brief opportunities to a variety of deputies and loanees. John Smeulders, a loan signing from Bournemouth made a match-winning penalty save in the last minute against Blackburn Rovers in the Littlewoods Cup. England youth international Jeremy Roberts was signed from Darlington as reserve goalkeeper and kept an impressive six clean sheets in his nine games before surprisingly being released and disappearing seemingly off the face of the earth – shades of Paul McCullough! Keith Branagan and young Colin Scott also filled in for a few games in 1989/90 and then, on the twentieth of March 1990, seventeen year old Ashley Bayes made his debut against Preston North End. All was going swimmingly, with the Bees coasting to a comfortable and seemingly impregnable two-goal lead, until poor benighted Ashley made a catastrophic unforced error just before halftime, completely missing his kick as he rushed out of his goal. The game was drawn and this was merely the first in a catalogue of costly errors by a young keeper who was thrown into league football far too early!

What A Game To Miss! – 21/12/14

Well at first I was going to Cardiff, and then I wasn't. I have a few football friends, travelling companions and fellow Brentford fanatics who I generally accompany to away matches, but one by one they cried off during the week. Some didn't want to spend the money in the week before Christmas and wanted to keep their cash for minor necessities and trivialities such as food and heating. One was shopping, another decided to spend the weekend with his wife, and man flu claimed a couple of others. It looked like I was on my own, not a state of affairs that has stopped me in the past, but somehow this time I just didn't fancy a long solitary drive there and back in a day, and on Friday I made my mind up to give this one a miss.

What a mistake, as I missed yet another Bees triumph and a first half performance of pure class with the invention, pace and movement that you have come to expect from a Brentford team rewarded with three cracking goals. Whilst those far more committed than I dined out on the sumptuous feast laid on for them at the Cardiff Stadium, I was left to make do with the bread and water diet of a cold blustery afternoon spent shivering on an exposed touchline watching my local Ryman League team Wingate & Finchley. It wasn't a bad match, I have to say, as they edged to a narrow one-nil win over a tough Grays team, and there was plenty of skill and effort on show from both sides, but that was little or no consolation as the text, Twitter and *Griffin Park Grapevine* updates I received throughout the afternoon made it perfectly clear to me that I was in the wrong place and had made a terrible decision.

There was some very minor solace as I was back at home well in time to watch the final of *Strictly Come Dancing* with my wife, but as I tried to concentrate on the dancers pirouetting and preening through their choreographed routines, my mind kept wandering and, instead of admiring their pyrotechnics, I found myself instead picturing the twinkle-toed Jota and Alex Pritchard performing a perfect *pas de deux* as they danced in unison and glided through the Cardiff defence with the ball tied to their bootlaces, and I knew exactly where I should have been on Saturday afternoon.

From what I have seen on the scandalously brief highlights on *The Football League Show* I would have been far more like Len, Bruno and Darcey and less like Craig and given them both straight Ten's for their routines which touched the heights of perfection. I spoke briefly to Mark Burridge and Mick Cabble too, who kindly filled me in on our display and the pure theatre of the entire afternoon's proceedings, as in front of a crowd of nearly twenty-two thousand, the biggest of the season so far, Brentford didn't freeze on the big day but simply rose to the occasion and put a massive team to the sword. This time last year, Cardiff were competing in the Premier League.

Yesterday was probably the zenith of a half-season already littered with massive achievements, with the promise of many more to come. Mark and Mick are both sound, experienced and keen observers of all things Brentford and do not easily get carried away, but they were both drooling at the utter brilliance of the first half display and the sheer resilience, guts and organisation displayed after the break, when quite naturally, the home team, their pride dented and their ears burning from a halftime rollicking, finally abandoned their suicidal four-four-two formation and matched us up in midfield, went for our throats and with the encouragement of an early second half goal, put us under the cosh with an aerial bombardment that made us defend for our lives to hold onto a fully merited victory. Good to see that we managed to withstand the onslaught without the second half presence of colossus and inspiration Jonathan Douglas and hopefully his exit at the break was purely precautionary rather than a serious problem as we will need him in the packed holiday programme. Harlee Dean went down as if poleaxed in the first few minutes of the game, and for quite a while it seemed as if his afternoon would be over almost before it had begun. However, the sight of James Tarkowski eagerly stripping off his tracksuit top, ready to sprint onto the pitch was apparently more than enough to revive him, and Harlee went on to have an impressive match at the heart of our defence!

From what I understand, Alex Pritchard was the star of the show. His early finish for our first goal was predatory and eye-catching in its simplicity and perfection as the ball was threaded through the eye of the needle straight into the bottom corner of the net well out of the reach of the diving David Marshall. The ball was hit with pace, accuracy and power and with his wrong foot too. Praise too to Jota who put in a determined challenge in the opposition penalty area to help ensure that the ball fell perfectly at the feet of his colleague just waiting to strike. Pritchard is so quick to see and select the best option and his instant, incisive and perfectly weighted pass put Andre Gray through on goal, just as he did at Millwall, and unlike at Wigan when his finish plopped frustratingly onto the roof of the goal, this time the lob was judged to perfection and the ball dropped unerringly into the net for his tenth goal of a massively productive season. Pritchard also had a foot in the third goal when he ran unchallenged from his own penalty area, threaded a short pass to Jota and waited in vain for a return as the elegant Spaniard bewitched a horde of helpless and bovine defenders and sent them and the entire crowd behind the goal the wrong way with a drop of his shoulders and a swivel of his hips before he delicately placed an unstoppable curling left-footed shot into the far top corner of the net from the edge of the penalty area. Len and his fellow judges would surely have approved!

The synchronised dance pair of Alan Judge and Alex Pritchard celebrating Pritchard's goal at Cardiff.

The Olés resonated around the stadium and from what I have been told, the Brentford supporters were not the only ones that wondered at and applauded Jota's trickery, mastery of the ball, precision, and perfect technique. That being said, the denizens of the Cardiff message boards vented their incoherent and semi-literate spleen at the perceived shortcomings of their own team and manager after the match, which were, in truth, many and varied, without bothering to praise us for our performance or give any thought as to how and why we had defeated their team. Typical of the comments was this pre-match boast:

Today will go down in history as the day we beat a team by ten clear goals.

Followed by an in-depth analysis soon after the final whistle:

And none of their players are good enough to play for us, as they were League One players about six months ago.

As Cardiff fans we aren't going to accept signings that poor.

God, please give me strength at such hubris, ignorance and arrogance. Although having given it some further thought, the more we are ignored, underestimated and belittled the more I like it and the better it is for our prospects. Leroy Rosenior, however gets what we are trying to do and is a big fan. His comments on last night's *The Football League Show* were as succinct as ever, but he got straight to the nub of the issue:

Brentford have a small squad but great spirit and I am not sure if there are clubs around with as much quality.

So apologies to those who were perhaps expecting a full and detailed match report, but I wasn't there, so I can only give you my second-hand impressions of a wonderful day for the club which provided further evidence, if more was indeed required, that our promotion challenge is for real. Anyway, this is not a mistake I intend to repeat and my tickets to Wolves and Brighton have already been booked and are safely stashed away in my desk drawer. Now if I can just find somebody to go with…

Who Are Yer? – 22/12/14

I went to a family party last night still on a high following Brentford's wonderful win at Cardiff, but I was soon brought crashing down to earth. There were several guests there who purported to be serious football fans, so naturally I gravitated towards them to exchange gossip and perhaps even bask in the glow of our recent achievements. Surely they would be up to date about our progress and be full of admiration and praise? To my surprise and disappointment any mention of Brentford – or *Brentwood* as some clown insisted on calling us – produced shrugs of dismissal and total ignorance and disinterest.

The nation, or certainly this small cross-section of it, has not taken much or, indeed, any note of our progress to date, and to those few who had heard of us at all we were plainly still *Little Old Brentford*. Nobody I spoke to had any idea which league we were playing in let alone how we were taking the football world by storm. When I started to put them straight I saw their eyes glaze over and smug little patronising smiles appear on their faces. They had little or no interest in discussing or even finding out about anyone or anything that existed outside the cloistered and hallowed halls of the Premier League. Football at a lower level did not register with them and in their eyes did not even count, or exist.

Whilst the overwhelming majority of the people I approached scuttled away from me as fast as their legs could carry them, relieved at their close call, a few stopped to listen after I succeeded in cornering them and cutting off their escape route. I fully realise that I shouldn't have expected anything different, but their comments were totally demoralising and merely highlighted their indifference to our mere existence:

Aren't you the club with a pub on all four corners of the ground?

Now what league do you play in?

Brentford Nylons isn't it?

Doesn't that German bloke manage you?

Has Trotta taken any more penalties for you?

And best of all:

How's Ron Noades doing these days?

Nobody I spoke to had any conception of the club we were developing into or our massive growth and progress over the past couple of years. Initially I was innately depressed by what I had heard, but on further thought I think it was all to the good. We are like a stealth bomber, flying deadly but undetected, well under the radar, or the outsider making a late run to come home on the rails. Nobody knows, or even cares who we are or where we are going, and they are totally unprepared for what we Brentford fans know will happen over the coming years – or maybe even months! Our momentum appears to be unstoppable – and so few people outside our rapidly growing fan base have any idea what is actually happening under their very nose!

That being said, seeing is believing. I have done my best to show my missionary zeal by trying to convert a few of the sceptical, ignorant and uninitiated to the true faith. This season I took a Liverpool supporter to the Brighton and Sheffield Wednesday matches, an Arsenal fanatic to the Derby County game, a Queens Park Rangers supporter to the Fulham local derby (I smuggled her into the ground under a vow of silence) and finally, a West Ham season ticket holder accompanied me to witness the thrashing of Wolves. None of them had ever visited Griffin Park beforehand and I had not given any of them a big build up about the team, its style of play, and what to expect.

I could see their bemused and irritated expressions when they had to fight their way through the packed crowds in the Braemar Road forecourt to get hold of a tepid cup of stewed tea and I had to apologise repeatedly for the long, snaking queue for the toilets which resulted in some desperate leg crossing on the part of some of my guests. They were all used to the modern facilities of The Emirates Stadium and Anfield and were taken aback by the grassroots reality of the matchday experience Brentford-style.

The Griffin though did merit universal approval as they appreciated the chance to enjoy a pre-match drink and mix safely with supporters from both teams, something that is unheard of nowadays in the anodyne, segregated sterility of the Premier League. What all my guests also shared in common was a sense of utter disbelief, amazement and appreciation at the quality of the fare that they were privileged to watch. Brentford's positive approach, total attacking policy and the sheer quality on display came as a real surprise to all of them. None of them believed that football of this quality was on offer outside the Premier League – or indeed, too often within it!

Alex Pritchard recently commented that we played in the same manner and nearly as well as Spurs and you could almost see some of my guests nodding their heads in agreement. Andre Gray, Alex Pritchard and Jota in particular were all picked out as potential Premier League stars, not that you need to be a super-scout to predict their likely futures. They were nonplussed when I remarked we had many more of that ilk currently bubbling under and coming nicely to the boil in our burgeoning Academy. The West Ham fan said that he had seen more efforts on goal in one match than in the entire season to date at Upton Park. Surprisingly, what they all commented upon was our policy of leaving a minimum of two players in attack when we were defending a corner, something that none of them had ever seen before and they admired our chutzpah, without really appreciating that we are, in fact, more dangerous from opposition corners than our own.

The atmosphere generated by ten thousand roaring Bees fans was also commented on by my guests who acknowledged how intimidating a packed Griffin Park was to the opposition. They all left the ground wreathed in smiles and excited at the level of pure entertainment they had been fortunate enough to witness. What's more they have all expressed an interest in coming again before the end of the season, so real progress is being made. We are pathfinders and proselytisers and each of us has the responsibility of educating our friends about just how good we are. Not that many of them are ready, or have the interest or imagination, to really care.

Griffin Park – A Part Of My Life – 24/12/14

News broke yesterday that an agreement has finally been signed with developers Willmott Dixon to deliver the new Lionel Road stadium and its associated facilities, as well as to convert Griffin Park into a residential development once the new stadium is completed. The clock is now ticking as we prepare for the eventual move from Griffin Park, our spiritual home since 1904, and the scene of so many milestones, triumphs and disasters in the club's long and chequered history. This is wonderful news but it is also tinged with sadness.

We all know that progress is inevitable and that we have outgrown Griffin Park and its dilapidated facilities. We need the room to accommodate the new wave of supporters that cannot fit into Griffin Park, and we have been hamstrung by the lack of corporate facilities, which has resulted in our commercial revenue being seriously restricted. Lionel Road, once completed, will ideally be the answer to all our hopes and dreams and, most crucially, we are rapidly developing a team whose marvellous, incisive football is so successful, attractive and easy on the eye that it could well enable us to fill the new ground to its twenty thousand capacity. That is for the future and, for the time being, Griffin Park remains the present.

I have been going there for far more years than I really care to remember – in fact next February it will be fifty years since my Dad took me there for the first time to see us thrash Queens Park Rangers by five goals to two. Given that I have been watching Brentford regularly since 1966, save for three years spent in New York, when even then I managed a couple of visits per season, I would estimate that I have been to well over one thousand matches at Griffin Park, and the ground has played an integral and important part in my life. Even the journey has become part of the ritual. Should I chance taking the North Circular to Hanger Lane and risk getting snarled up in traffic chaos around Brent Cross or Park Royal? Would it be better to take the back doubles through Willesden and Acton? Much less direct but generally free from congestion until the inevitable and dreaded logjam in Tubbs Road near Willesden Junction. Swings and roundabouts, as on a good day I can get to the ground in about twenty-five minutes, but on a bad one, the journey can seem interminable.

Even coming home can be fraught with peril, particularly when Transport for London arbitrarily decides to close the Brent Cross flyover without the courtesy of providing any advance warning to us unsuspecting drivers. There is nothing worse or more annoying and frustrating than getting caught in an unexpected traffic jam at ten o'clock at night, particularly after a home defeat. Even when I get there I still have to decide where to park. There was a time when I could roll up with impunity at a quarter to three and find a space without any trouble within sight of the turnstiles. Now, with five-figure sold out crowds being the rule rather than the exception, you need to arrive a good hour and a half before kickoff if you expect to park in the same postcode as the ground. And no, I am not going to let slip where I still generally manage to find a convenient parking spot before most matches. Do your own research!

I never fail to get an anticipatory buzz of excitement whenever I turn the corner into Braemar Road. Going to Griffin Park is just like being back at home. I feel safe and happy there and it has become a major part of the fabric of my life. I have laughed and cried there, smiled and frowned, cheered and jeered, made long-lasting friendships, vowed never to return and yet found myself steering a path back there a fortnight later. Griffin Park is seared into my soul, as are the memories, sweet and sour, of matches long since passed, of players good, bad, indifferent, and now, maybe even great!

I have calculated that over the course of the past forty-nine years I have spent over one hundred days of my life in and around the stadium, firstly anticipating the match about to begin, then moaning, groaning, criticising, encouraging, celebrating and commiserating during the course of every match, and finally rejoicing or mourning on the walk back to the car - a mere skip and a jump away when celebrating victory, a seemingly endless trudge following a defeat.

For a few unfortunate years, a decade or so ago, I was inveigled into buying two season tickets for Arsenal as a means of entertaining some clients and contacts of mine. God forbid that I tried to entice them into attending a match at Griffin Park, the Bees were then in the nether regions of the Third Division and it was a hard, if not impossible, task to sweet talk business contacts into watching them. To be candid, I also wanted my company to be seen as a Premier League outfit rather than a third rater. Given the vagaries of the Premier League fixture list there were surprisingly few fixture clashes between the two clubs, as they existed in totally different stratospheres, and I was rarely faced with the difficult decision about whether to watch Arsenal or Brentford. I enjoyed visiting both Highbury and The Emirates Stadium as there was always a sense of occasion, and the lush, padded leather seats at Highbury found great favour with my son, but the atmosphere at both grounds was always sterile and could not compare in any shape or form with the febrile excitement of a packed Griffin Park. Whilst I wanted Arsenal to win, in truth I didn't really care about the result, matches never stirred my emotion as they did and still do at Griffin Park, and I certainly never lost any sleep or gave a second thought should they lose, something that has happened on many occasions after a Brentford catastrophe.

Over the years I have changed my allegiance from D Block in Braemar Road, to the Paddock, to Ealing Road, then to New Road and finally back to Braemar Road. Each area has its own individual characteristic, idiosyncrasy and identity, however I made my decision to return to where I started given that it provides the best and most complete overall view of the pitch, has the Programme Shop close to hand, and enables me to *kibitz* and gossip with all and sundry. There is, and will be, far more to say about Griffin Park over the coming months and even years as the clock runs down, and in the meantime I shall relish what time we have left at this iconic edifice as when Griffin Park dies, so too will die a small part of me. I am sure it will for most of you too.

Stuffed! – 27/12/14

I promise that the title to this section will be the only seasonal Christmas reference that I make, but I am afraid that it sums up what happened to us at Griffin Park yesterday. We were taught a massive lesson by an excellent, robust and organised Ipswich Town side that came to Griffin Park with a game plan and did a real job on us. Expectations were certainly at fever pitch before the game as Brentford fans in a sold out Griffin Park settled down for the match fuelled with the knowledge that a victory would enable us to sit proudly at the top of the league – at least until the results came through from the later kickoffs. But it wasn't to be as the day turned into a damp squib.

Ipswich had done their homework and they pressed us high up the pitch and hassled us relentlessly. We weren't given the opportunity to play through the press and develop attacks from the back, as is the norm for us. With the short throw to a defender generally cut off by the ever willing Murphy, Bishop and McGoldrick, David Button was forced to go to his Plan B, the measured kick to Bidwell on the left touchline near the halfway line. Mick McCarthy recognised this threat and stationed the giant Luke Chambers, normally a centre back, in that position and he won every aerial challenge. We were choked and stifled, found it hard to get out of our own half and, for all our possession, we rarely got into dangerous positions and were second best for most of the match.

It is all very well having a plan and whilst they often work well on paper and on the training ground, McCarthy must have been surprised that his paid such dividends within a mere nineteen seconds of the start. We played the ball around the defence straight from the opening whistle but were forced back and instead of playing the ball to the waiting Craig, Button kicked the ball down the middle where it was easily picked off well inside our half. Two incisive passes later, with Craig still out of position, the predatory Daryl Murphy was left with a clear sight of goal and his instant finish flew past the helpless keeper.

Our heads went down after conceding the fastest goal of the Championship season to date and Ipswich were buoyed by their early and unexpected success. The first half saw a continuing pattern. Lots of possession for the Bees, but little incisiveness and few chances created as we struggled to recover from the early hammer blow. Jota had a quick poke at goal which was fumbled by the nervy Bialkowski, who also knew little about an Andre Gray header that hit him, and the striker's instant control and clever layoff almost allowed the rampaging Jonathan Douglas a clear sight of goal before he was crowded out. Ipswich, for their part, were happy to soak up what little pressure there was, Berra and Smith won everything in the air and snuffed out any danger we posed.

Given our terrible start, we were nervy and hesitant at the back and Ipswich threatened carnage every time they came forward, we were cut open twice more soon after the goal. Jay Tabb should have marked his return to Griffin Park with a goal but shot wastefully over with the goal gaping and Murphy turned Craig far too easily before the prehensile Button shot out a long arm and saved the day. The second goal wasn't too long in coming when a hoof forward saw the Bees caught upfield and Murphy left one-on-one with Craig. No contest, and the striker shrugged Craig off and strode on to round Button and score easily for his sixteenth goal of a wonderful season. It looked as if the defender had had his heels clipped as he lost his balance but the referee gave nothing, apart from the goal.

Worse was to come as Dean headed the ball wastefully straight to Tabb when he should have played it into touch and his low centre saw two Ipswich players eagerly competing for the right to score, and it was Anderson who put the game far beyond Brentford's reach. Three defensive errors had resulted in three goals, as we had been out-thought, also to a large degree, outfought, and we certainly contributed to our own downfall with so many unforced and costly errors.

At the interval a few optimists recalled that incredible recovery from a three goal deficit against MK Dons but Ipswich were a far tougher proposition and did not exhibit any signs of weakness or a soft underbelly. They simply sat back, compact and smug, soaked up what we could throw at them and tried to pick us off on the break. Judge, Pritchard and Jota were tireless in their efforts to get us back into the game but most of our shots were from distance, and for all our pressure and clever approach play we never really hurt Ipswich, who looked as if they were going to see the game through in comfort and unscathed. As normal, Mark Warburton's substitutions made a real difference.

Judge, Gray and Douglas were all taken off, probably with Sunday's match in mind, and Toral, Saunders and Proschwitz gave Brentford a fresh impetus. Toral showed real strength and skill, he is so composed and is almost impossible to knock off the ball. What a prospect he is and he will have so much to contribute in the second half of the season. Jota weaved his magic; mesmerising defenders as he came inside from the left, and it was his slick pass to Toral that saw the ball laid off to Sam Saunders whose deflected shot put us back into the match. Game on with ten minutes to go?

It should have been, but, instead, we self-destructed and demonstrated our soft centre yet again within two minutes when we failed to defend a corner properly. Odubajo and Proschwitz were both guilty of half-hearted and tentative tackles and former Brentford loanee Tommy Smith was unforgivably allowed the time and space in a packed penalty area to turn inside and curl a delicate and impudent finish into the top corner and finally end the match as a contest. That was the killer blow and the one that annoyed me the most as it denied us the chance, slim though it was, of piling pressure on our visitors for the last few minutes. As it was, we scored a second and totally irrelevant goal just on the whistle when Jota made the space for Bidwell to cross low for Proschwitz to comically mishit a close range effort which was poked in by the effervescent Sam Saunders.

Ipswich returned to East Anglia with three thoroughly deserved points and the Bees were left with much to ponder over. We need to keep things into context as we remain on an incredible run of seven wins in nine games, but there are still key lessons to be learned from yesterday's defeat. We will and must not change our style but the key to continued success as opponents become more aware of our threat, is to be more careful with the ball in our own half of the field and minimise the costly mistakes when possession is handed to the opposition in dangerous positions. Our central defence has been creaking lately and both Dean and Craig have been guilty of unforced errors and of being knocked off the ball too easily. Clubs now realise that we can be bullied and Daryl Murphy yesterday joined the ever-growing list of strikers such as Kenwyne Jones, Grant Holt, Rudy Gestede and Cameron Jerome who have been far too strong and powerful for our defence to handle. There is no shame attached to this as we are talking about experienced, and in many cases, international class players who have far more top level experience than our two defenders, who were both playing in the third tier last season. Maybe we will see a couple of changes in personnel tomorrow at Wolves with Tarkowski returning to the fold and perhaps Toral starting again.

Yesterday we had a bad day at the office at a time when we could least afford it, and were taught a harsh lesson by an experienced and well-drilled team who were fully prepared for what we had to throw at them and took full advantage of our shortcomings. We simply need to learn from our mistakes, try not to repeat them and move onwards and upwards.

Sleepless Night – 29/12/14

It is long past my bedtime but sleep won't come. It was a tiring journey to Wolverhampton and back but I was in congenial company, the motorways were mainly free of traffic and everything about the day went smoothly and like clockwork with the exception of what took place between three and four fifty-five pm when Brentford somehow left Molineux pointless, after losing by the odd goal in three. I have been sitting here for a while reflecting about our defeat and have concluded that it really came about due to three key moments in the game where the luck went totally against the Bees on every occasion.

1. Jota's early shot which was pushed onto the post by Ikeme and bounced clear.
2. Dicko's opening goal for Wolves, which put us firmly on the back foot and was unquestionably offside by at least a couple of yards.
3. Andre Gray's header deep into injury time from an inviting curling cross from Sam Saunders, which clanged against the post and again, infuriatingly bounced the wrong way for the Bees.

On such narrow margins are the results of games decided. If any one of those three incidents had gone the way of Brentford then we would have certainly returned with something for our troubles. As it was, despite a decent performance in which we bossed proceedings, and had a remarkable sixty-four percent of the possession, we allowed the match to drift away from us and our efforts went unrewarded. Certainly for all our possession we didn't test Ikeme enough and so many of our moves fizzled out in the final third but, as always, we were easy on the eye and played some lovely football which did not bring about its deserved reward.

Rather than simply provide a match report I would rather focus upon some of the key issues that have emerged from the first half of what has been a quite remarkable season and all of which were highlighted in Sunday's match. Brentford have taken the Championship by storm, massively exceeding expectations from outside the club, and have fully earned their forty points from the first twenty-four games. In fact, without exhibiting any bias and being completely objective, that points figure could well have been increased by at least another ten if things had gone slightly differently. Our football has generally been quite slick and beautiful with the five midfielders interchanging at will, with all of them showing skill and vision on the ball, the ability to spot and make a pass, allied to movement off the ball and an eagerness to get into the penalty area and shoot at will. Sometimes, though, we over-elaborate and pass for the sake of passing and seem to share Arsenal's proclivity for attempting to walk the ball into the net, or score the perfect goal. Every goal counts the same – you do not earn style points, and we do need to become more clinical and direct at times.

It is not surprising that twenty-six of our forty league goals to date have been scored by our central and wide midfielders, an amazing figure, and over a goal per game. Alan Judge's goal scoring ability has temporarily left him but he has more than made up for that by becoming the fulcrum for much of what we create and has provided a remarkable eight assists. Jota, Alex Pritchard and Jonathan Douglas have more than taken up the mantle with fifteen goals between them, including five from Douglas who makes late runs and ghosts into goal scoring positions. Jota, for his part, is simply a marvellously gifted footballer who can do more with one foot than most players can with two. He appears calm and nerveless in front of goal and looks set to reach double figures. As for last season's midfield inspiration, Adam Forshaw, we managed a difficult situation perfectly and extracted a more than decent fee for him from Wigan, once he had made it clear that he wanted to leave. He has also not been missed which is perhaps the best compliment I can pay to our current coterie of midfielders.

Andre Gray has had to plough a lone furrow up front and when the midfielders fail to support him and get bodies into the box, he has sometimes appeared isolated, but he has learned extremely quickly how to play this demanding and exacting role, and with nine goals has far exceeded expectations given his lack of previous Football League experience. He has learned how to use his upper body strength and put defenders under pressure whereas earlier in the season he would often be bullied and easily knocked off the ball.

We attack relentlessly and never settle for anything less than a win, as is evidenced by a league low of only four drawn matches. There is little wrong with our attacking prowess apart from the lack of cover or realistic alternatives for Gray. Scott Hogan's season ending injury has hit us hard given that Nick Proschwitz has so far brought little to the table and much heralded Portuguese loanee, Betinho, has seemingly disappeared off the face of the earth and contributed a big fat zero to the team.

Forty goals is an excellent tally and totally endorses Mark Warburton's hell for leather approach, but it comes with a real downside. We are often too gung-ho and are left open and exposed at the back when moves break down and have conceded a whopping thirty-five goals. Our defensive personnel have remained largely unchanged from last season and as a unit we have found it harder to adapt to the higher level and the better strikers we have faced. David Button has proved to be an excellent goalkeeper and his quick and accurate distribution has been crucial to changing defence into attack. His shot stopping ability is beyond question but he often struggles on crosses, despite his size, and normally elects to punch, only sometimes effectively.

Before his long-term injury Alan McCormack had rampaged through matches in his inimitable fashion and whilst often being targeted as a potential weak link by opponents, he more than held his own. Moses Odubajo has proved to be a revelation as an attacking fullback but his sorties upfield have often left us short of cover when the opposition counterattacks, forcing a centre half to move out of the middle to cover for his absence. Jake Bidwell has also settled in well, is a tenacious marker and tackler, and finally scored his first league goal against Wolves. I know a defender deflected his cross beyond Ikeme, but try and take it off him at your peril!

The problem has been in central defence where we are not up to the mark. Tony Craig, James Tarkowski and Harlee Dean have all had spells in and out of the team and none of them has totally convinced or impressed. All of them have different attributes but we have struggled to find an effective partnership. They have also had to adapt to the necessity to play out from the back, which has sometimes put them under more pressure and led to mistakes. Teams are also trying to bully us more and we have not stood up to the battle well and our defence has creaked alarmingly, none more so than against Ipswich when we totally contributed to our own downfall, allowing four soft goals.

We threaten to score in every game, but we also look likely to concede and have only managed to keep five clean sheets. Frankly we need to improve in this area when the January transfer window opens later in the week and import some extra height, pace and strength, none of which will come cheap or be easily found. As far as most football managers and coaches are concerned, the opposition never scores a good goal and the fault for every goal conceded can always be laid at the feet of a specific individual.

I have spent the last couple of hours revisiting the tapes of all our matches so far this season – no wonder my head is aching, and my eyes closing. Of the thirty-five goals we have let in, I could only find six where we made flagrant errors that led directly to the goals being conceded. Button flapped on the opening day of the season against Charlton and allowed himself to be beaten to the punch from a simple near post corner. Craig got on the wrong side of his former team mate, Birmingham's Clayton Donaldson and clumsily brought him down for a penalty kick and red card. Tarkowski and Dean overplayed in dangerous positions against Norwich and Fulham respectively with disastrous consequences. Button took his eye off Shittu's simple looping header and allowed himself to be distracted by Gregory at Millwall and finally, Craig was outmuscled by Ipswich's Daryl Murphy for the second goal on Boxing Day at Griffin Park.

In addition, we have conceded six goals from outside the penalty area, against Brighton, Norwich, Middlesbrough, Watford, Bolton and Nottingham Forest. Whilst Button might have done better with Neil Danns's effort at Bolton and perhaps we could have closed a couple of the players down quicker, most were simply unstoppable. Referees have also cost us dear with Robert Madley's series of appalling decisions in the Birmingham match, the clear penalty against Norwich that wasn't given, the non-penalty against Watford that was awarded against us and, finally the Wolves offside goal on Sunday. Hopefully we will benefit similarly in the second half of the season.

I am being deliberately critical as I am simply trying to highlight where and how we can improve and I am certainly not trying to minimise our fantastic achievements to date. With a little bit of minor tinkering with personnel and tactics (I know we don't have or really need a Plan B!) I see absolutely no reason why we cannot maintain our impetus and challenge for a playoff position. And now, as the clock reaches four AM, it is time for bed, to dream of victories and new signings.

More Stats! – 30/12/14

I burned the midnight oil the other night turning over in my mind the reasons for our defeat at Wolves and outlining the lessons, good and bad, that we need to learn from the opening half of the season, and what we need to do in order to maintain our progress and impetus. Subsequently, I spent an interesting and illuminating half an hour watching all of our forty goals once again, and most entertaining viewing it was too.

Having surveyed our goals, the first stat to emerge was how many goals have we scored from headers. The answer is a bit shocking. We have scored the grand total of two headed goals all season, both by Jonathan Douglas, against Brighton and Reading respectively. Oh, I almost forgot, Harlee Dean also scored with a late header against Dagenham, but that came in a cup match. Given his height and build, Andre Gray is by no means an aerial threat and he has managed to hit the post twice with close range headers, against Derby County, and frustratingly, in the dying seconds against Wolves.

I then went on to break down our goals even further. It won't surprise many of our supporters to learn that we have scored from only two set pieces, a corner against Reading and a Pritchard penalty at Nottingham Forest, plus that Dean header from a Bidwell free kick at Dagenham. That is a quite frighteningly poor record given how crucial set piece goals are to a team's armoury, and it is an area that we need to improve over the remainder of the season. Our delivery is often not the best, particularly in the absence of Sam Saunders, and none of our players seem to attack the ball in the manner, say of the two Ipswich centre halves, Berra and Smith who this season have scored eight goals between them. I fondly remember the days of Terry Evans, thundering in like a rampaging bullock at the back post, who presented an enormous threat to our opponents with his aerial presence and feel that we are certainly missing a trick.

Over the past few months I have often remarked flippantly that given our speed on the break, we are far more dangerous from opposition corners than our own, and the more I think about it, the more certain I am that that statement is entirely correct. We have also scored only three goals from outside the penalty area, Alex Pritchard's at Cardiff and the two wonderful Jota specials against Fulham and Cardiff, and maybe we could improve that record too given Alan Judge's prowess from long distance. Brentford have become justifiably renowned for the quality of their football, and we have been treated to some really special goals this season, which totally encompass our pass and move philosophy, with Jonathan Douglas's effort at Watford, Jota's awesome goal against Leeds, and Andre Gray's first strike at Millwall being my personal favourites.

The Wolves performance on Sunday, however, did flag up some concerns as despite our massive sixty-four percent possession we only managed a mere five shots on target, an extremely poor return. Perhaps we should listen to the guru, Pep Guardiola who doesn't want to be associated with tiki-taka any more and commented in a recent book about him:

I loathe all that passing for the sake of it, all that tiki-taka. It's so much rubbish and has no purpose. You have to pass the ball with a clear intention, with the aim of making it into the opposition's goal. It's not about passing for the sake of it.

Don't believe what people say. Barça didn't do tiki-taka! It's completely made up! Don't believe a word of it! In all team sports, the secret is to overload one side of the pitch so that the opponent must tilt its own defence to cope. You overload on one side and draw them in so that they leave the other side weak.

And when we've done all that, we attack and score from the other side. That's why you have to pass the ball, but only if you're doing it with a clear intention. It's only to overload the opponent, to draw them in and then to hit them with the sucker punch. That's what our game needs to be. Nothing to do with tiki-taka.

Wise words indeed and ones perhaps that we should take heed of as we pass the ball relentlessly backwards and from side to side. Yes, we certainly need to probe for weaknesses but there does come a time when we need to take the bull by the horns and play an incisive ball into the penalty area or try a shot. Patience is certainly a virtue but sometimes action speaks louder than words!

League Table – 30/12/14

Position	Team	P	W	D	L	F	A	GD	Pt	Form
1	Bournemouth	24	14	6	4	54	25	29	48	D W W W W W
2	Ipswich Town	24	13	8	3	41	22	19	47	W W D W W W
3	Derby County	24	13	6	5	46	23	23	45	L W L D W W
4	Middlesbrough	24	12	7	5	38	17	21	43	D W W L W D
5	Watford	24	12	5	7	43	26	17	41	L W W W L W
6	**Brentford**	24	12	4	8	40	35	5	40	**W L W W L L**
7	Norwich City	24	10	7	7	44	29	15	37	L W W D W L
8	Wolverhampton Wndrs	24	10	7	7	28	33	-5	37	L L W D W W
8	Blackburn Rovers	24	9	8	7	35	33	2	35	D L L W L D
10	Sheffield Wednesday	24	8	10	6	18	21	-3	34	W W L L W W
11	Nottingham Forest	24	7	10	7	33	33	0	31	L D D D L L
12	Cardiff City	24	8	7	9	32	35	-3	31	W D L L D L
13	Charlton Athletic	24	6	13	5	24	28	-4	31	L D D L D L
14	Birmingham City	24	8	7	9	27	37	-10	31	W L W W L W
15	Bolton Wanderers	24	8	5	11	26	31	-5	29	W D D W W L
16	Reading	24	8	5	11	30	40	-10	29	W D L L D W
17	Fulham	24	8	4	12	35	43	-8	28	W L W W L L
18	Huddersfield Town	24	7	7	10	31	42	-11	28	L W L L D W
19	Rotherham United	24	5	11	8	21	30	-9	26	D D D W D D
20	Leeds United	24	6	6	12	25	36	-11	24	W L L D L L
21	Brighton and Hove A	24	4	11	9	26	32	-6	23	L L L D D W
22	Millwall	24	5	8	11	24	40	-16	23	D L W L L L
23	Wigan Athletic	24	4	8	12	24	31	-7	20	L L L L W L
24	Blackpool	24	2	8	14	18	41	-23	14	D W D L L D

JANUARY

Managing Bees – Part 1 – 2/1/15

The recent news of Chris Hughton's appointment as Brighton manager and the realisation that there would now be a familiar face in the opposition dugout on Saturday sent me scurrying to the record books in search of the answer to the question that I am sure is on all of your lips, namely, how many other former Brentford players have become managers in recent times? Before I start, I wonder if anyone would like to hazard a guess? No, I thought not. I did and I found that I was miles out with my answer.

I didn't have too long to spare for my research so I decided to make the arbitrary choice of 1970 as my start date, and I hit paydirt straight away.

John Docherty had an incredible five spells at Brentford, three as a player, one as manager and finally, as assistant to Frank McLintock. His most successful times as a manager came away from Griffin Park, firstly at Cambridge United where he performed near miracles on a shoestring budget and, after leaving Brentford for the final time, he and McLintock bizarrely swapped roles with Doc taking over as manager at Millwall with Frank as his number two, and together they led Millwall into the top flight for the first time in their history. A truly remarkable achievement given their resources. Docherty's next stop was at Bradford City, in March 1990. He was neither popular nor successful there and I remember murmurings against him after Brentford won there with a late Neil Smillie goal in 1991. He eventually returned for a second spell at Millwall before leaving the game for good.

Brian Turner is best remembered for hitting the post late on in *that* FA Cup match at Hull in 1971, but there was far more to him than that as he earned over one hundred caps for New Zealand and later became national team manager. I can still picture the elegant striker Roger Cross, resplendent in his white boots, and he had a long and distinguished career within the game as youth team manager at Millwall and as a coach at Queens Park Rangers and Tottenham Hotspur, where he was also assistant manager to Gerry Francis. He then went back to where he started, at West Ham, as coach and chief scout. Other stalwarts from the 70s in Paul Bence, Jackie Graham and Terry Scales managed non-league clubs at Wycombe Wanderers, Staines Town and Hoddesden Town respectively.

Stewart Houston was perhaps one of the biggest managerial names that Brentford have produced. He coached at Plymouth Argyle before becoming George Graham's assistant during Arsenal's successful spell in the early 90s and he twice held the caretaker reigns at Highbury, leading the club to the final of the European Cup Winners' Cup, where the Gunners lost to a last-minute freak goal – *Nayim from the halfway line!* Perhaps unfairly, he became known as *The Cone Man*, a title apparently dreamed up by Ian Wright but QPR were impressed enough with his credentials to name him as their manager in 1996. I got to know him at that point as I worked closely with the club managing Ericsson's sponsorship. To call him dour might perhaps be a tad harsh but I certainly did not find him the most expansive of personalities and any conversation beyond football was strictly limited, until one day, stuck for something to say to him and with the silence lengthening, I somehow started burbling on about a show I had just seen, and suddenly Stewart came alive. He was passionate about musicals and from that day on we had something in common and a point of contact! His time at Loftus Road was not a success and after the inevitable parting of the ways he had further spells coaching at Ipswich Town, Tottenham Hotspur and finally at Walsall, before returning to Arsenal as a scout.

Alan Murray came and went quickly at Griffin Park, ending up as top scorer with a miserly total of seven goals from midfield in our dreadful 1972/73 relegation season, testimony indeed to the folly of the Board of Directors' decision to sell John O'Mara without allowing the manager to bring in an adequate replacement. Murray began his management career at Hartlepool United in 1991 when, with boss Cyril Knowles battling against a brain tumour, Murray made the unusual shift from chief executive to manager.

He then moved to Darlington before working for Graeme Souness at Southampton, and then as assistant manager at Newcastle. David Court was also long past his peak and came and went in a blink of an eye, but lasted for years back at Arsenal as Assistant Academy Director and Assistant Head of Youth Development. Keith Pritchett also had a short stay at Griffin Park before impressing at Watford under Graham Taylor. Eventually he emigrated to New Zealand where he managed the New Zealand national team, taking charge for the first time in June 1996. New Zealand won two, drew one and lost eight of his eleven games in charge.

Ironically, the player with almost the shortest playing record for Brentford has had one of the longest and most successful managerial careers! Harry Redknapp lasted a mere thirty-eight minutes as a trialist at Aldershot before suffering an injury and leaving the club following the arrival of Bill Dodgin as manager a few days later. He cut his managerial teeth at Bournemouth and survived a nine-nil trouncing in his first match as caretaker manager at Lincoln in December 1982. It was an icy day, and Bournemouth could not afford Astroturf boots, so they could barely stand up and Lincoln slalomed past them at will. After the game, Harry was asked if he was disappointed and apparently complained bitterly that the seventh goal was offside. Things could only get better after that and Redknapp has now been in the hot seat for over thirty years at West Ham United, Portsmouth (twice) where he won the FA Cup, Southampton, Tottenham Hotspur and Queens Park Rangers as well as being widely touted at one time as England national team manager. His record certainly bears scrutiny as he has achieved a creditable forty per cent success rate in over thirteen hundred matches in charge.

Tony Burns had a decent loan spell at Brentford in 1977 and the former Arsenal keeper went on to manage Tonbridge three times as well as Gravesend & Northfleet. He was Millwall's goalkeeping coach for fourteen years and was appointed joint caretaker manager of Millwall for a month in April 2006. Remarkably, at the age of seventy he joined Gillingham in July 2014 as senior goalkeeping coach where he works with Stuart Nelson, still impressing in the Gills goal. Neil Smillie finished his long career with two years at Gillingham as player/coach, including a spell as caretaker manager, before moving on to Wycombe Wanderers as youth team coach and later becoming first team manager. He always struck me as being far too nice and decent a man to succeed as a manager in the cut-throat world of professional football! Barry Lloyd is also a survivor as after managing at Yeovil and Worthing, he took over at Brighton as long ago as January 1987. He guided them to promotion in his first full season and they also reached the Second Division playoff final in 1991 before money got tight and he eventually resigned in 1994 just before the roof fell in. He took the well-trodden path into scouting and has been at the club for the past seven years as Chief Scout.

Bob Booker is a rarity as he has become a folk hero at no fewer than three clubs, Brentford, Sheffield United and finally Brighton, where he became assistant manager and continued to serve the Seagulls in a variety of roles for over a decade, including two spells as caretaker manager. Ron Harris parlayed his experience of playing over seven hundred games, predominantly for Chelsea, into a brief term as player-manager at Aldershot but he soon tired of football management and turned to property development and after dinner speaking. *Gasping* Gary Roberts was a firm favourite at Griffin Park, apart from with Francis Joseph, who always complained that the winger was far too greedy and never passed to him in front of goal! Maybe Gary knew what he was doing as he managed to score sixty-three goals for the Bees, including a hat trick scored in four amazing minutes against Newport. He has combined his new career as a policeman with over eleven years as a successful manager at Cambridge City where he remains today.

Chris Kamara led Bradford City to promotion before not doing as well at Stoke City and correctly coming to the conclusion that television punditry was a better and more secure way to spend his time. Striker David Kemp only played a handful of games for the Bees as a loanee before injury struck and he has managed and coached for nearly thirty years as the number one at Plymouth Argyle, Slough Town and Oxford United as well as having a plethora of jobs as assistant manager, including spells at Wimbledon, Millwall, Portsmouth, Stoke City and then back at Crystal Palace where he became technical coach in 2014. He has worked extensively with Tony Pulis and will doubtless be following him to West Bromwich Albion. Full back Les Strong was far too sensible to enter the dog-eat-dog life as a manager in England, but instead spent three years as manager of the Anguilla national team in the West Indies. I spent my honeymoon there and it is simply paradise on earth. Midfielder Terry Bullivant took charge at Barnet and Reading, where he signed Carl Asaba from us, before he returned to Griffin Park in 1998 as a member of Ron Noades's title-winning coaching staff and he stayed for almost three seasons before quitting in April 2001 and having spells at Crystal Palace, Watford and Birmingham City.

In March 2008, he made a third return to West London as assistant manager to Andy Scott and once again helped the team to a championship success before teaming up with Scott again at Aldershot Town where he remains today, and I watched his team give Conference leaders Barnet a tough match yesterday afternoon.

Steve Wignall started his managerial career at Aldershot Town before taking over at Colchester United followed by shorter spells at Doncaster Rovers and Southend United. His autobiography is well worth reading and reveals much about life at the bottom of the football league. I shall end matters with the amazing tale of Rowan Alexander, whose underwhelming stay at Griffin Park soon came to an end and he returned to Scotland with Greenock Morton where, ironically, he rediscovered his shooting boots, before moving into management with his first club Queen of the South. He then moved to Gretna where he benefited from the largesse of Brooks Mileson and enjoyed huge success and led the tiny club to the promised land of the Scottish Cup Final and the Premier League before the money ran out. So many former Bees who became managers in recent years, and yet, I have barely scratched the surface, as will be revealed…

Maybe It's Time – 3/1/15

I wrote just the other day expressing some mild frustration and concern about the times when Brentford are guilty of overplaying, our long spells of possession come to nothing and we frustratingly lose games where we have had the lion's share of the ball.

I need to preface those remarks by stating that I remain massively supportive and appreciative of the overall style of play we have adopted, as well as our customary 4-1-4-1 or 4-2-3-1 formation, and am happy to accept our occasional defensive shortcomings as a natural result of our total commitment to exciting, positive and vibrant attacking football.

I was therefore delighted to receive the following thoughtful and detailed comment from another fervent Brentford supporter in Paul Grimes. His view is rather different, and perhaps far more pragmatic than mine, but rather than prejudge, I would prefer that you all make up your own mind once you have read what Paul has to say, and very interesting it is too:

I wondered what exactly the title of this guest piece should be and I looked at "To try something different," "To play all three centre halves," "To surprise our opposition" and, more controversially, "For Mark Warburton to take some of his own advice." I settled for "Maybe it's time to think outside of the box?" So what am I advocating exactly and are there any clues in the other prospective titles that ended up in the waste paper basket? Well, yes, in a nutshell I think now is the perfect opportunity to play all three centre halves together and to tinker a little with our possession and footballing philosophies that have got us this far. Why change, you might ask? But for me it's evolving not changing, for me it's learning something now that we will definitely try next season if this season ends up in disappointment. By "disappointment," of course, I am not talking about relegation, or finishing in the bottom half or even missing out via the play offs, all of which would have been viewed as much more likely than…. disappointed that we did not get promoted to the Premiership having given ourselves such a good chance!

It's madness to even talk about it but the fact remains that little over a fifty per cent win ratio from our last twenty-two league games would see us in the Playoffs from the position in the league where we are now.

So if we have done so well to get here why am I advocating using a different system? Well first of all it's more technical than just that change, because I am actually saying let's use it only for specific games starting on Saturday with Brighton in the FA Cup. A team rejuvenated under an interim coach over their last three matches and with a new manager that all of their players will be looking to impress. They will have had us watched and will also remember us beating them earlier in the season using our current system. But they have their tails up and so we should beware.

Throughout this wonderful season, Mark Warburton has regularly repeated his mantra of "defeat is okay as long as the players learn from it" so maybe it is time also for Mark to learn from our experiences. For instance our home shots tally is just twelve higher than the total number of shots taken by our opponents in the first twelve matches. Without wishing to be stating the obvious but that is only one shot per game more than our opposition! Well it gets worse because Brentford and our opponents have managed to hit the target an equal number of times, sixty-six in total.

So are the forwards misfiring, or are we too open and allowing away teams to come on to us a little too much? Well, no, not really, because we have scored eight more goals than our opponents. Twenty-three to fifteen. Is it due to our preferred style of possession football or Tiki-Taka or Tippi-Tappa as my Dad calls it? I don't think so or more to the point the stats do not back that argument up, as we have only won once with possession above fifty-eight per cent, and that was against Fulham in a charged atmosphere in front of a near sellout crowd at home in a local derby.

No, it's about when we are NOT in possession, because despite strong stats in our favour in those twelve home games, we have only three times been on the wrong side of the dominant possession line and each of those three occasions have resulted in victories against Brighton, Leeds and Reading.

So instead of trying to work out how we can create more chances or score more goals, or increase the percentage of goals from those shots, maybe it's time to start thinking outside the box or outside of both penalty boxes if you like? But particularly outside our own box where we have in my humble opinion been a little too open and, if we want to take full advantage of our excellent start, this is where I feel we need to tighten things up. We need to be more defensively minded in the second half of the season, to concede less shots and less goals and to earn the right to win ugly at times. The player who drops out initially would be Toumani Diagouraga despite some excellent performances so far this season. Both wing backs will have even more freedom to bomb forward, Tarks will have licence to step in front and push JD up, who will in turn push Judge that bit further forward in support of Jota and Pritchard. On both flanks we would have options as Bidwell could tuck in at times and encourage Pritchard to go outside, Jota would no longer be as easy to read as he steps inside, as a marauding Moses up on his outside, or making an angled dash for the inside line would all be additional options, and all would pose problems for the opposition to cover and force them onto the back foot a bit more than has so far been the norm.

At the back we need defenders who can defend first and foremost, and the defensive positional cover play of each of our defenders needs to be paramount in their minds before they start thinking about where our next goal is coming from.

The defensive line should be curved and resemble half a revolving door. When the right edge is furthermost forward, the left edge is furthermost back, and vice versa, and the lines between our defenders or channels need to be narrower to stop teams getting in behind us, which is where we are vulnerable due to a lack of speed, height and strength. We do not need to buy another centre half, rather we need to play another centre half. Basically, it's time to grind out a few one-nil wins at home and to go away from home and come away with a clean sheet, something we have only achieved twice each this season home and away.

I have read Paul's comments carefully and can appreciate his main point that we need to tighten up at the back. If we carry on at our current rate we will finish the season conceding seventy goals and it is hard to envisage us achieving much if that turns out to be the case. In Tarkowski we have a decent defender but also a gifted footballer in every sense of the term, and Paul's belief is that he could also act as the first line of attack as well as defence.

It is illuminating to look at the arcane world of statistical analysis in order to discover interesting insights into the game, and Mike Forde, formerly Chelsea's Performance Director, hit the nail on the head when he stated:

If you look at ten years in the Premier League, there is a stronger correlation between clean sheets and where you finish, than goals scored and where you finish.

Chris Anderson is a well-known author who specialises in football statistics and analysis and he totally agrees with Forde:

Forde is right on the money. Clean sheets on average produce almost two and a half points per match. And even only one goal allowed still gives a team slightly more than one and-a-half points on average. But by the time we get to two goals allowed, the point value rapidly declines. And once the other team scores three or four times, the point value declines to zero. Compare this with offensive production. You might think that scoring at least one goal will help you as much as not letting one in. You'd be wrong. Scoring one goal only gives you about one point from a match, on average. Compare that to one and a half points for allowing one goal only.

So the point value of one goal allowed is fifty per cent greater than the point value of one goal scored. Another way to think about this is to ask how many goals a team needs to score to produce the points produced by a clean sheet. The answer for the 2009/10 Premier League season is slightly greater than three. So a clean sheet produces about as many points for a team as scoring three goals. Keeping a clean sheet significantly increases your chances of winning a match and going from not having a clean sheet to having one, increases the average team's odds of coming away with three points from .20 to .72 – a staggering difference in the probability of winning of .52.

So maybe Paul Grimes is onto something. Given our own dedicated team of analysts, I am certain that Mark Warburton is well aware of the figures quoted above and it will be interesting to see if the second half brings about a minor shift in emphasis or approach, or if we simply concentrate on executing Plan A better.

What A Waste! – 4/1/15

It is not too much of an exaggeration to say that we tore Brighton apart for much of yesterday's first half but so much possession resulted in so few real chances. But we should have made far more of what we did create. Jota was untouchable, as none of the Brighton defenders could get close enough to him to make a tackle. His early shot was pawed away by Stockdale straight to Gray, who had two attempts to score from close range, but somehow managed to send the ball all the way along the goal line without it actually entering the net when surely it was easier to score? Jota it was who then danced through the entire Brighton left flank before setting up Toral for what seemed the formality of scoring, but he could only force a solid smothering save from the keeper.

Brighton were light years behind us in terms of imagination, movement, pace and use of the ball but they defended in numbers, rarely allowed us to get behind them and simply clung onto the ropes with few thoughts beyond surviving until halftime. Their craven policy deserved far less reward than it actually got, but we did not take advantage of our opportunities. Brighton reformed after the break and the match became more even and open with Jack Bonham, given his first start since the Derby League Cup fiasco last season, impressing as he came under increased pressure. Toral sliced over the bar before the game turned on the Andre Gray horror show. Having missed badly in the first couple of moments, his day went from bad to worse as the ball went everywhere apart from its intended direction. The ball fell invitingly to him from a cross, weakly spooned to him by Stockdale, but he shanked the ball horribly wide. Two more close range headed chances were spurned before he sped through on the left after a quick break from a Brighton corner, unforgivably ignored the three colleagues lined up unmarked and onside in front of a gaping net and sliced the ball towards the corner flag. Odubajo too let Brighton off the hook when roaring past his man into the box, but he too lacked composure in front of goal and blazed high, wide and not at all handsome.

Brighton then made an inspired substitution, with the burly Chris O'Grady at last giving them a decent out ball. Brighton gained in confidence as ours dipped and we decided to give our visitors a helping hand or two. Three times we gave the ball away criminally just outside our penalty area, twice by Tarkowski and once by Moses. Unlike us, who struggled to get a shot close to goal, Brighton seized on our generosity yet somehow we escaped as March and O'Grady both hit the post and Bonham half smothered O'Grady's second effort which slithered right through him and went tantalisingly close to spinning inside rather than outside the unguarded post. If you can't win a game then surely the next objective is not to lose it but, almost on time, we conceded a dubious free kick which was floated in and Dunk's touch beat the straining Tarkowski and the ball flew into the bottom corner of the net. We never looked like recovering and a naive offside trap was caught out before O'Grady left a floundering Tarkowski flat on his backside before finishing emphatically for a fully deserved goal.

I really am not too sure how to react to this defeat. I so wanted a victory yesterday, firstly in the hope of gaining a lucrative draw in the next round of the FA Cup which would ideally see us given the chance to test ourselves against a Premier League team, but, more importantly, to arrest a minor slide before heads drop and it becomes a mini-slump.

Gray surely cannot have such an appalling match again and I shudder to think how the supporters would have reacted had it been the unfortunate Nick Proschwitz who had been so profligate in front of goal. Given how well he has done, it is hard not to forget that, like so many of his colleagues, Gray is a work in progress and has barely got his L Plates off. The crowd stayed with him and indeed the rest of the team and they are fully aware that we will have bad days as well as good.

The Brains Trust – Warbs and Weir.

Managing Bees – Part 2 – 6/1/15

I recently covered the first batch of former Bees who had gone onto become managers since 1970, and the list can now be completed. And a very long one it is too.

Goalkeepers only rarely seem to go on to become managers and Gary Phillips joined their number when he took over as player-manager at Barnet in 1993 before being replaced by another goalkeeper in Ray Clemence. He subsequently managed at Aylesbury United and Hemel Hempstead Town but quit after just seventeen games. After a number of coaching roles, he was appointed as manager of Grays Athletic before returning to Hemel Hempstead Town. He has since worked as a goalkeeping coach at both Barnet and Stevenage.

Robbie Cooke often ploughed a lone furrow as a Brentford striker in the mid-80s but he thrived after retirement and had a long spell as David Moyes's chief Scout at both Everton and Manchester United before recently being hired by Burnley.

Keith Millen remains well in the public eye given his recent spells as caretaker manager at Crystal Palace, and it is good to hear that Alan Pardew will keep him on now he has taken over as the new manager. Keith is an experienced coach and also had a year managing Bristol City.

Andy Sinton was mentioned in despatches a couple of times as a possible Brentford manager, given his illustrious spell at Griffin Park as a player, but it remained a pipe dream. He became manager of Isthmian League Division One outfit Fleet Town in summer 2005, having spent the previous season as the club's Football Development Officer and stayed there for five years before being appointed as manager of AFC Telford United in the Conference North. In his first season, he won promotion to the Conference via the playoffs, and he remained in charge until January 2013, when he left after a sixteen match winless run, the worst in the club's history.

Ian Holloway had an unhappy time at Griffin Park and was never really able to demonstrate his full ability on the pitch owing to illness but he has had a long and chequered managerial career experiencing the highs and lows of managing at all levels of the game at Bristol Rovers, Queens Park Rangers, Plymouth Argyle, Leicester City, Blackpool, Crystal Palace and Millwall. He is a bubbly, eccentric and effervescent character who is as crazy as a fox and far more astute than he is generally given credit for. Steve Perryman could well have become a Brentford managerial legend had he not decided to quit in mysterious circumstances on the eve of the 1990/91 season, apparently when he was refused permission to sign Fulham left back Gary Elkins. Let Steve tell the story in his own words:

I'd done my homework and found out Fulham would let him go on a free. The chairman didn't want to sign him . . . in one conversation he said one reason he didn't want me to sign Elkins was because Terry Bullivant had told Lange that he thought the Fulham player had "shifty eyes!" What the chairman was inadvertently telling me was that he'd rather trust the judgement of one of his players than his manager, not based on footballing ability, but facial expression.

That was the end of his reign at Griffin Park on a point of principle, just when it appeared that he had finally built a squad that was on the verge of a promotion push. A terrible waste, although Phil Holder succeeded him and certainly put his own stamp on things, but it was a team largely made up of Perryman signings that won the league in 1992. Steve went on to manage Watford and enjoy success in Japan as well as having a brief stint back at Spurs as assistant manager before becoming director of football at Exeter City.

Ex-Brentford loanee Paul Merson (did he play for anyone else?) had an unhappy spell as manager of Walsall which ended one cold February afternoon in 2006 when his team visibly gave up on him and subsided gently to defeat to a Brentford that was not made to work very hard for their five goal victory. Colin Lee will never be forgotten for his four-goal debut for Spurs in a nine-nil victory over Bristol Rovers. He made his name as a youth coach but had managerial spells at Watford, Wolverhampton Wanderers, Walsall, Millwall and Torquay. Graham Rix had a wonderful loan spell at Brentford and he inspired a run towards the playoff positions, which tapered off, after his departure. He had brief but unsuccessful spells as manager at Portsmouth, Oxford United and Hearts.

Paul Buckle started well as a manager, leading Torquay to promotion from the Conference and then to the League Two playoffs, and was touted as a man to watch. It all turned sour for him at Bristol Rovers and after getting the plum Conference job at Luton Town he quit and moved to the United States in order to accompany his wife. He is now trying to restore his managerial reputation at Cheltenham Town.

Dean Holdsworth had a very successful reign at Newport County, before having a two year stint at Aldershot Town. His team mate, Marcus Gayle, has just lost his job at Staines Town, where he at least had the consolation of taking them to a First Round FA Cup tie at Griffin Park last season.

Steve Perryman did not make one of his more inspired signings when he spent a lot of time, effort and money in bringing Maltese international John Buttigieg to the club. His obvious skill and ability to read the game as a sweeper did not fit in with the manager's chosen style of play and he was too often left on the sidelines. He returned to his homeland with Floriana and Valletta after which his coaching career reached its zenith when he became Maltese national team head coach between 2009 and 2011. Eddie May was another highly priced disappointment and gave the impression that he could not wait to scuttle back over the border to his native Scotland, and as soon as he did his career was miraculously resurrected. He then had a short spell as manager of Falkirk.

Brian Statham's career was severely restricted by injury and he will best be remembered for his two red cards against Brentford, for Reading and Gillingham and for being sent off in the Wembley playoff final disaster against Crewe. He combined a career working in the City with managing Heybridge Swifts and Billericay Town.

Chris Hughton ended his long and illustrious playing career when injuring his knee in the warm-up for Brentford before the Christmas match against Derby County. This resulted in Grant Chalmers, who thought he was not going to be needed, having to sit on the bench whilst still digesting the pie he had just consumed. No wonder the substitute was substituted! Chris led Newcastle United back into the Premiership before being surprisingly sacked just months later and becoming the boss at Birmingham City and then Norwich City, before his recent appointment at Brighton, where he led his new team to an FA Cup win at Griffin Park, costing us a plum home tie to Arsenal!

Shane Westley was a panic buy replacement for the injured Terry Evans in 1992 and never really looked the part, being agricultural in the extreme. He did well at Lincoln City, and led them to promotion before eventually leaving the game to become a personal trainer. Tricky winger Paul Stephenson, who never made do with beating two men when he had the chance to take on a third, had a spell as caretaker manager at Hartlepool and is now First-Team Coach at Blackpool. Nicky Forster could yet make a successful return to management, as after the sacking of Andy Scott he was Matthew Benham's surprise choice to take over the reins. He gave the team a new impetus and confidence, aided as he was by Mark Warburton – now what on earth happened to him?

He enjoyed a successful three-month spell in charge and led the team out at Wembley in the JPT Final. He was not retained at the end of the season before having an unsuccessful spell at Dover Athletic.

Andy Scott is still in the game as manager of Aldershot but it might so easily have been so much better for him. He replaced Terry Butcher in 2007 and had an immediate impact, righting the ship when it was listing perilously close to the choppy waters of Conference football, before winning the title in his first full season in charge. At one time being touted for higher profile jobs, he apparently came within a whisker of being appointed at another one of his former clubs in Sheffield United before it all turned sour for him and he was sacked in February 2011. He then won a plum job at Rotherham which also ended badly before taking over the reins at Aldershot Town as the club dropped into the Conference.

Micky Adams is also one of football's survivors and is seen now as a lower division fire-fighter but he has achieved much in his long career and is unfortunate not to have made a bigger name for himself. He started off well at Fulham before being unceremoniously dumped for Kevin Keegan and after a bizarre thirteen-day stint as boss at Swansea City he was appointed Brentford manager in November 1997 before leaving the club when Ron Noades took over. His managerial career continued at Nottingham Forest as caretaker, two spells at Brighton, Leicester City, Coventry City, Port Vale and his boyhood team Sheffield United. He then returned to Port Vale where he achieved the fourth promotion of his career as he led the club out of League Two. He is now trying to keep Tranmere Rovers in the Football League.

Scott Fitzgerald was handed a poisoned chalice when he took over a poor and dispirited squad from Leroy Rosenior and was peremptorily sacked as soon as the inevitable relegation was confirmed, before returning to youth team management at Gillingham and Millwall. Chris Hargreaves was an honest toiler and midfield dynamo and is currently struggling to return Torquay United to the Football League. Steve Claridge came and went in the blink of an eye, and that was maybe too long for some people, as he was well over the hill when Martin Allen surprisingly signed him in late 1994, and he and Deon Burton formed a totally ill-matched strike duo of waxwork dummies with neither prepared to run the channels. He eventually had a thirty-six day spell as manager of Millwall in the summer of 2005 and was sacked before a ball was kicked in earnest. He is now the media pundit we all love to hate but could well return to the dugout next season at the reformed Salisbury City.

As you can see, many former Bees have ventured into the managerial hot seat after ending their playing days, with many of them being ejected fairly quickly.

I started my review in 1970, but I would be remiss if I did not end with a brief homage to Ron Greenwood, perhaps the most successful former Bee to become a manager. He enjoyed three great years at Griffin Park as a cultured centre half and his thirteen years in charge at West Ham saw the Hammers gain a deserved reputation for style and elegance. He led his team to FA Cup and European Cup Winners Cup victories in successive years and ended his career with a successful spell as England team manager before being replaced by Bobby Robson. Let's hope that one day another ex-Bee can emulate his success, Kevin O'Connor, perhaps?

Billy Reeves Speaks! – 8/1/15

Every football club has its fair share of characters and personalities associated with it. Brentford is no different in this respect, and one of the most popular is Billy Reeves, who is well on the way to becoming a legend in his own lifetime! Billy is a born performer and made his name initially in 1996 as the founder and leading light of Britpop group, Theaudience. Fronted by the inimitable Sophie Ellis-Bextor, their one self-titled album reached number twenty-two in the UK charts, with two of four singles released also reaching the Top 40. His musical career was cut short by a near-fatal car crash in 2001 and after recovering from his injuries he has reinvented himself as a talented and well-respected producer and broadcaster on *BBC London 94.9* where his unique, quirky and engaging style of broadcasting and witty repartee has won him a host of listeners and admirers.

He is the voice of Brentford FC on local radio and is also a long-term fan of the club.

I caught up with Billy the other day and he expressed some perceptive, heartfelt and trenchant views on the club and his profession in general – so please sit back and prepare to be stimulated and entertained:

1. Music v Travel v Sports Reporting – discuss

In the UK we are somewhat uncomfortable with the "portfolio" career; but I am jack-of-all-trades, master of none, which I is why I do it. Traffic reporting is about empathy. I used to be a lorry driver and I have a degree in Broadcast Journalism – combine the two and I can make agenda-decisions (what to say) and understand why I'm saying it. If you're stuck on the M25, we feel for you at BBC London 94.9, we're there for you! I'm not a sports reporter as such; I've tried but the only sport I know anything about is football.

It's been very interesting following one club; I have learned much about the football industry. Playing music (as I did in my teens and then again in my early thirties) is much more about showing off. There are similarities between the music business and the football business; both take a risk on talent. I've got to know a lot of DIY musicians of late and it seems that you can make a living outside the traditions of venture-capitalist record companies, I wonder if this can be done in the football industry?

2. Developing your own voice – being yourself as a broadcaster plus any influences you had

We're left to our own devices at BBC London, which is nice; if there's a 'house style' it's one of slight irreverence. My biggest influence is Mark Burridge, no one's commentated on more Bees games than he.

3. Sophie Ellis-Bextor or Jota – beauty personified?

Sophie is a friend, but Jota I admire from afar. No other manager would've signed him, he's slight, never really made it in Spain, his English is minimal, and he'd never tracked-back in his life. (Sophie's never tracked back either, mind you.) The Brentford Beatles – Matt, Mark, David & Frank – are geniuses for getting him to come to London and turning him into one of the most useful players at this level. I like his new haircut.

4. Living for today, the only policy? – Intimations of mortality

I assume this is a reference to my near-death experience? Bizarrely it was fascinating. Watching NHS professionals dealing with horrendous working conditions has made me a rabid supporter of their rights. I became a brave soldier, planning the ten things I'd do once I got out of hospital. Coming to Griffin Park for the first time after the crash, barely being able to walk was the point where I knew I'd be OK. (6th April 2002. Bees 3 Huddersfield 0 – three up at half time.)

5. What is so special about Brentford as a club?

The fact that we're not special. There's no overriding sense of a golden era that hangs over us as a reminder of better times. There's no trouble. There's a sense of community where the club's been in financial peril. There are no posh seats in the stadium. We have the West London moral high ground, surrounded as we are by the gruesome threesome.

6. How far can we go?

As far as our imagination. It'll be how we deal with any decline that will make us or break us over the next ten years. Once we get to the Prem, we must check our sense of privilege and not do what Charlton or Fulham did.

7. Tiki-Taka – do we take it too far?

No. We're working to a budget. We develop ball-players at the expense of muscle and brutality. Football clubs need to understand branding. FC St. Pauli has it. I want us to be known as the ball-playing, attack at all-times, develop young talent, nice, friendly, modern football club. I'd much rather we play this way. It's brilliant.

8. Mark Warburton and empowerment and positive reinforcement – is it the best policy?

Warbs/Weir is still in the experimental stage. The Brentford Beatles are intelligent individuals backed up by a big-for-this-level analysis department. So far, so good. Too early to say.

9. Working with players and management

Everybody has to be nice to me; I'm wearing a BBC pass. Footballers and backroom staff know how to behave. There's a sense of propriety. I'm grateful that at the all-new modern Brentford that I'm made welcome at the training ground, the inner sanctum. But I'm acutely aware that I must keep a "journalistic distance". I represent the fans. Uwe and Scotty understood that perfectly, I was their conduit to the supporters when they had the hump. Whether you support the club you're reporting on or not, there's a licence at a local level to want the team on your own patch to win. It makes gathering audio afterwards easier. I am not the pet of the club, however – my duty is to the listener and the supporter, I get to ask questions on their behalf.

10. Interviewing players and managers – do's and don'ts

As mentioned, reporters must never think they have a relationship with the manager. The representatives of the club understand they're using exposure in the media as PR to promote the club. Reporters therefore should understand this and give them a hard time, ask the difficult questions. It's the managers that understand that batting back awkward questions, asked immediately after games, is what makes them look good, or bad. Managers are now bigger stars than ever, watch the TV coverage – they get plenty of screen time (to help us understand what just happened on the pitch, as we couldn't work it out for ourselves) – last term it was drinking from water bottles (Arsène being, seemingly, the thirstiest). This season it's all about note-taking...

Anyway... Players are much more intelligent than people give them credit for. They are on their guard, so are careful about what they say, so this is why they often slip into the comfort of the football lexicon. It's up to the interviewer to steer them away from cliché. Tommy Smith, Alan Judge and Sam Saunders are all excellent. Richard Lee will make a good reporter, he understands what's required and, as he has said, punditry needs a goalie.

Perception v Reality – 11/1/15

I have just spent a fascinating four minutes and forty-five seconds listening to the post match thoughts of Rotherham manager Steve Evans after Brentford's hard fought and narrow one-nil victory yesterday. Perhaps it would be best if I simply note down what he said in an interview that took place very soon after the final whistle, admittedly at a time when emotions were still running high and there had not been a cooling off period or any time for any serious reflection or reasoned analysis of the game beyond the immediate evidence of his own eyes. We can then attempt to look at his comments more objectively and I will try and dispense with my innate Brentford supporting bias when I reflect on the truth or otherwise of his assertions.

1. Everyone in the ground knows that we should have been three-nil up at halftime.

Rotherham had the strong wind in their favour in the first half and we tried to play a high line and our offside trap let us down on several occasions. Matt Derbyshire was mobile and lively for the visitors and timed his runs well to get in behind our defence, but he had one major drawback for a striker – a total inability to hit a barn door with his shots on goal. He looked nothing more than what he is, a striker totally bereft of confidence who has scored the grand total of one measly goal in the League Cup all season.

He dithered and let Button smother at his feet, allowed Tarkowski to dispossess him far too easily when in on goal, shot wastefully over and then passed to nobody when he had the opportunity of a close range shot from a tight angle. Smallwood also broke the offside trap after a well-timed run, and had a wonderful chance but failed to put his foot through the ball when totally unmarked and directly in front of goal, and the ball dribbled through embarrassingly to a relieved Button. That was a lucky let off!

Several other long-range efforts threatened the crowd behind the Ealing Road goal more than the Brentford keeper.

Brentford were second best for the first half an hour of the game, slow to react and lacking in energy, tempo and confidence. Their normal slick passing was conspicuous by its absence and they sorely missed the spark and vision of the injured Alan Judge.

That being so, from time to time our passing combinations and skill on the ball created holes in the Rotherham defence. Moses Odubajo, who mesmerised the visitors for the entire game, breezed past two defenders and his cross was met by Stuart Dallas, whose header might have been goal bound but hit Jonathan Douglas and inched past the near post.

Alex Pritchard's trickery and skill on the ball took him past a defender and gave him the space for a measured lob which went narrowly over the crossbar, and his late free kick whistled past the post with Adam Collin a mere spectator. Andre Gray did have the ball in the net from Jota's pass but was just offside. So, on the balance of play, Rotherham did create the better chances in the first half and Smallwood should have gobbled up his opportunity. A one-nil scoreline in their favour would not have flattered them but it was obvious as the half progressed that the Bees were growing into the match.

2. They got a fortuitous goal coming from the goalkeeper shanking a ball.

Firstly, let's give Steve Evans some credit as he admitted that it was a great strike by Stuart Dallas, and he is also correct in that David Button hit a hasty clearance under pressure which went low and hard straight to the feet of Jake Bidwell just over the halfway line. So, yes, the pass was fortuitous but let's face it, Brentford had quite a lot to do to score from there and they did it extremely well. Bidwell, Pritchard and Dallas exchanged slick passes down the touchline and the full back's centre was met by Jota whose low volley was blocked by a defender straight to Dallas who had anticipated cleverly and made ground to the edge of the area, and his instant falling right footed volley from twenty yards was beautifully struck and far too good for Collin who managed to get a despairing hand to the shot which was perfectly placed into the corner of the net.

Rotherham then had several opportunities to defend against the goal but were outsmarted by our skill, movement, passing ability and the eventual lethal strike from Dallas who has now scored six goals this season in all competitions and deserves far more credit than he gets.

3. It was the save of the season for me. If he makes one like that then he would not be playing for Brentford would he?

Making allowances for his tangled and tortured English, the message is clear. Evans feels that his team was robbed of their just desserts by David Button's fantastic late save from a close range Paul Green header that seemed bound for the roof of the net before the giant keeper arched backwards to tip the ball over. It certainly was a wonderful reflex save and the ball seemed as though it had gone past him before he managed to stretch out a long right arm and turn the ball over the crossbar in less time than it takes to write this sentence. But save of the season? Not for me as I think it was easily bettered by his miraculous tip over from Lee Novak of Birmingham, who had a free header at goal from almost under the cross bar. Button has improved dramatically over the course of the season and we have almost got to the stage where we expect him to pull off seemingly impossible saves as a matter of course.

4. They've had a bit of a football battering today. We've out-passed them and outplayed them and dominated the game for long spells.

Well, I would agree that we were tentative and immobile early on and Rotherham were sharper in the challenge and created the better chances in the first half, but it was a different tale after the break. After we scored, confidence flooded back and Brentford spurned many chances for a match-clinching second goal. Andre Gray was put clean through and fired wastefully against the keeper's knee before Jota, forced onto his right foot, amazingly spooned the rebound over the bar with the goal gaping. Douglas was denied a tap in by a brilliant Wooton clearance close to the goal line, Pritchard hit the post with a bobbling long-range effort with the goalkeeper nowhere, and Douglas had a late effort cleared off the line. Rotherham huffed and puffed but created very few clear chances and Brentford should have been well out of sight before Button's late match winning heroics from Green's header.

Perhaps we should simply let the match statistics speak for themselves: Brentford had a massive 66% of the overall possession, although previous defeats have demonstrated that it is what you do with the ball rather than possession for its own sake that wins matches. Over the course of the ninety-five minute match, Brentford played a total of 612 passes with an impressive 78% passing success rate compared with Rotherham's 319 and 58% respectively. Brentford managed fifteen shots with five on target and Rotherham had seventeen with only four troubling Button. Those figures illustrate quite clearly that Brentford more than edged proceedings – they dominated them, and after the tentative opening minutes of the game when Rotherham failed to make their chances count, the home team was well on top.

5. Look at the three players we have pulled from the wilderness, Adam Hammill, Danny Ward and Jack Barmby. They'd play in the Brentford team, every one of them.

Would they indeed? Adam Hammill is an established Championship player who has had a spell in the Premier League at Wolves but has failed to settle anywhere, has a conviction for assault, and at twenty-six is unlikely to get much better. No thanks.

Danny Ward is more intriguing as he is a highly talented left-winger who has so far failed to show his true potential. He looked a world-beater when on loan at Swindon five years ago and at twenty-four he could still possibly justify the near one million pound fee that he commanded from Huddersfield, but again, I would pass. Jack Barmby is far more of an unknown quantity. The son of Nick, he obviously comes from wonderful football genes and earned a place at Manchester United before moving to Leicester City after a decent loan spell last season at Hartlepool. He looked clever on the ball and troubled us early on with his movement. Of the three, he would be the one I would possibly take given his youth and development potential, but I do not think he would be anywhere near our first team at present.

6. His movement caused carnage in the Brentford defence.

Amazingly, Evans is referring to Matt Derbyshire who I have commented on earlier in this article. It must be said that he did lead the line effectively and took up good positions, made good runs and got behind our back four on several occasions. But carnage? Come on Mr Evans! I would refer you to a dictionary, which defines the word as *the slaughter of a great number of people.* Did I miss something yesterday or is Steve Evans simply engaging his mouth again before exercising his brain?

7. Brentford are a quality side and have spent £10 million on transfers and we have outperformed and outplayed them for long spells.

I would refer you to answer four concerning the second part of that assertion, and as for the first… words simply fail me. Transfer fees are notoriously hard to estimate as they are largely undisclosed nowadays, but I have had a quick stab on the back of a fag pack and I have gone through the entire squad, not just this season's signings, and also included Will Grigg. My figures are entirely based on guesswork and rumours in the press and on social media, and I have no idea how accurate they may be. I have come up with a figure of around £5.5 million for the entire squad, but that includes fees paid in previous years for the likes of Tony Craig, Will Grigg, James Tarkowski, Toumani Diagouraga, Jake Bidwell and David Button. Obviously, there are loan fees, agents' fees, and signing on and relocation fees to add on top but it is clear that the figure plucked out of the air by Evans yesterday is wildly exaggerated. Brentford have also brought in substantial sums from the sales of Adam Forshaw, Simon Moore and Harry Forrester, which have greatly reduced our net outlay.

Perhaps if Steve Evans had concentrated more on quality rather than quantity and not embarked on a wild trolley-dash that has seen him bring in well over twenty players this season he would not be sounding so bitter and envious about Brentford's recruitment policy.

The famous Brentford corner kick routine!

A Director's Role – 14/1/15

Donald Kerr first made his name as a Planning Director at advertising behemoths, JWT, and in recent years the long-term Brentford supporter has played an ever increasing role behind the scenes at Griffin Park, firstly as a hard working Director of Bees United then as their representative on the board of Brentford FC six years ago. He is now Vice Chairman of the club. Given his advertising and marketing background and his deep involvement with Brentford's award winning Community Sports Trust, Donald is well qualified to describe exactly what it is that a director does at the club as well as taking stock of where the club is now and how it compares with many of our rivals:

The first thing to say about being a director of BFC is what a huge privilege and pleasure it is to represent the Club in any capacity. Even in bad times this would be true, but over the last three or four years that have seen us climb the Football League and play increasingly entertaining football, it has been especially enjoyable. My involvement in the club became more formal with my election to the BU board and, as one of the less busy directors, my selection by that board to be one of the Trust's representatives on the Club board. This all coincided with the increased investment and subsequent takeover by Matthew Benham, and, in turn, the departure of Greg Dyke to the FA and his replacement by Cliff Crown as Chairman.

We have a relatively small board of directors, but with a fairly good spread of different experience and expertise, and, with the focus on making sure the business is well run and successful in commercial terms, the board meetings are similar in structure to those of companies in other sectors. We are in the midst of developing a long-term strategy for the Club and this process mirrors others in which I have been involved in my previous pre-football business life. But it would be crazy to say that it isn't more exciting because it is such an exciting, dynamic and high profile industry.

As the business has expanded over the last few years, and the issues facing the board have increased, the football side has taken up proportionately less time in the meetings. Frank and Mark Warburton attend for anything up to an hour, depending on the time of year, with the transfer windows determining that more than anything. Mark keeps us informed on first team issues, and Frank covers all other aspects of football matters. Academy Director Ose Aibangee submits a report as part of the board pack we receive before each meeting and he attends meetings on an occasional basis to ensure we monitor developments on that key area of the Club.

The board meetings are very lively and, as we cover the whole range of the business, quite lengthy and intense. In the past few years they have followed on from the Lionel Road board meetings and so it makes for a fairly long day for those of us on both, but Lionel Road is so fundamental to the future sustainability of the Club that it has made it vital to keep them closely linked. I have to defer to those with much more financial expertise than me when we get involved in that side of things, but Cliff has introduced ways of presenting the figures which make the finance more easy for those less expert to understand and to contribute. Dave Merritt and I ensure that BU's voice, and by implication, those of the fan in general, is heard in the meetings, and, as a trustee of the Community Sports Trust, I report on that side of things too. I suppose my expertise, such as it is, lies in the marketing area, and so I tend to get more involved in those issues more than others. With Mark Devlin being elected to the Football League's commercial sub-group and my position on the Football League Trust board, we are able to keep track of wider industry issues too.

As regards other commitments, I attend the quarterly Football League Trust meetings in Manchester, which are chaired by Gordon Taylor and attended by FA and PL representatives, as well as Andy Williamson, COO of the FL. And I sit on their small but active marketing group as we attempt to raise the profile of the work done in the community by all FL clubs nationally. Cliff attends the quarterly FL meetings with Mark Devlin, but, when he was unavailable, I substituted for him in October, which provided a fascinating insight into the workings of that body at both a general and specific league level.

One of the more pleasurable parts of being a director is visiting the boardrooms of other clubs and meeting the people who run them. Over the last three seasons I have missed only a few away games and so have enjoyed the hospitality of clubs all over the country. It is rare not to get a really warm welcome and, particularly among the smaller clubs we played, a strong sense of all being in the same struggle to be as commercially successful as possible or, for a few, just to keep heads above water. What immediately struck me, as someone who worked in a fiercely competitive business where few business details would be shared with the opposition, was the frankness and openness of the conversations over the pre-match meal. But of course, we share many common issues; trying to recruit the best talent possible, trying to increase attendance at games and maximise on and off field revenue, trying to contain the constant upward pressure on player salary costs, and trying to meet the often wildly unrealistic expectations of the fans.

Like any away fan, directors pay their own way, but I am acutely aware that on arrival we are fed and watered, usually in very comfortable surroundings, before every match. I have huge admiration for the Bees away support and their amazing resilience particularly on the tougher trips like the long journeys to Carlisle for the Cup last December, or to Hartlepool at the end of the previous season, or to Boro' at the beginning of this one. It's not easy to remain good humoured in a boardroom after a game where we've dominated and taken nothing away, but we've equally had the satisfaction of seeing others wish us all the best as they've left Griffin Park empty handed.

I try to split my time at home matches between using my season ticket in Block D (or whatever it's called now) and representing the Club in the boardroom. We have a good reputation for being a warm and friendly bunch and for more than making up for the limitations of our facilities with the hospitality we provide. On a personal level, it is fascinating to host our boardroom which, in addition to welcoming owners and directors from other clubs, and their distinguished guests, often also has managers who have no games that Saturday or who are currently "resting", and players from other clubs who may be injured or just out of favour.

We are extremely informal at GP, but there is huge variance in the style adopted by other Clubs, from those who like us all to mix, one or two preferring to sit everyone round one table, to those that leave us to our own devices, greeting us, ensuring we are looked after, but seating us separately and keeping pretty much to themselves. Clubs generally put a limit on the number of people who can attend the boardroom. Usually, there are no more than four or five of us travelling, with Cliff, Mark Devlin and myself being almost ever present, although on a couple of occasions in the past I have found myself outnumbered ten to one by the opposition. Frank joins us if he isn't travelling on player business and Matthew comes to several away games too, although not always joining us in the boardroom.

Uniquely and rather charmingly, Uwe Rösler used to pop into the opposition boardroom to update us prior to the game on his team and reasons behind his choice. It was always a surprise to the host directors that he did so, and, as you can imagine, it transmitted a very strong and, to some, enviable signal of unity at BFC.

Like visiting someone's home, spending the match in the board room occasionally gives you an insight into how things are going on behind the scenes, how united the other club appears to be, or how genuinely supportive they are of the team management or style of play. As a result, the subsequent news of a takeover or of a team manager's departure is sometimes slightly less of a shock. If I was asked for my biggest surprise as a visiting director it would be the trip to MK Dons last Easter Monday. When we arrived, as usual about 1.30pm, I met their manager, Karl Robinson, as I was picking up my ticket from reception. He overheard me announce that I was a visiting director and spent ten minutes congratulating me on Brentford's promotion the previous Friday and discussing the prospect of our new stadium. He confessed that Griffin Park was an extremely horrible place for visiting teams and managers to visit (he didn't say extremely!) and that he hoped we retained that aura when we finally moved. When I finally reached the boardroom, their Chairman, Pete Winkelman was standing there, complete with a tray of champagne, demanding that everyone toasted our success. He also spent some time addressing the room, singing our praises as a club that was doing things the right way and one that deserved the promotion we had just achieved. I know that as a Trust Director I should perhaps take a different view of MK Dons but it was difficult not to admire the style with which they accepted another disappointing season for them, and by contrast our success.

I remember only too vividly the last season we spent in the Championship, and to my shame recall setting off for Bristol City on the last day of that awful campaign and then, not far from home, turning back because I sensed we had no chance of getting the win we needed, and I couldn't face the prospect of another and terminal miserable defeat. I never envisaged that we would struggle in the same way this season, and, having the privilege of inside knowledge of our pre-season planning, which started well before the end of last season, I was confident we would do more than just survive. However, even if I was allowed to place a bet, I couldn't have guessed that we would be in the top six at Christmas or that we would be playing the sort of football we are seeing home and away almost every week. Thinking back to the game at Middlesbrough, I feel that their dominance of that game was what I expected we might experience much more often than has been the case. And, with the exception of the Ipswich game on Boxing Day, we haven't since repeated that experience of being well beaten.

As directors, we generally don't hear about players being scouted or potential transfer targets until shortly before names are more generally known, and that I feel is exactly as it should be. We have enough off field matters to deal with, and that is where our expertise, such as it is, is best exercised. But we are keenly aware of the work being done by Frank McParland and those who support him, and the extent and reach of the scouting system. And, long before the season started, we knew that the players being signed had been subject to close scrutiny, and that the club's ambition was to compete rather than simply to consolidate. Notwithstanding that, I think it is astonishing how quickly Andre, Moses and Jota have adapted to the demands of the Championship, and how our own League One promotion winners have also thrived at the new level. Toumani has been like a new signing, and Stuart Dallas is developing exactly as we were promised when we first signed him. Of course, the worst moment of the season so far was the terrible injury to Scott Hogan at Rotherham.

Beyond the first team, I have tried to see a couple of youth and development squad matches this season and there are some encouraging signs of players finally breaking through from our own academy. We are investing a lot of time and money in that area and, as directors, we are constantly looking at the timescale of potential return on that investment. The recruitment of Lee Carsley is a real coup in this respect and I know he feels there are one or two stars in the ranks below the first team squad. There can't be any fans that don't want to see Montell Moore make that final step up, and it is great to see Alfie Mawson doing so well at Wycombe too. One of the clues to the potential in the Academy is the selection of players for teams above their natural age group and we have several earning that right at the moment. Maybe we'll see them in pre-season games next summer.

It is so encouraging to hear from Donald that things are going so swimmingly off the pitch as well as on it. The club is in good and safe hands, and there appears to be a well thought through and realistic strategy being applied and followed. My own brief experience of the Brentford board was totally different. I was invited to join it by Eddie Rogers shortly after the Southampton FA Cup tickets fiasco in 2005 with the specific remit of trying to improve the professionalism of the club's communication with the supporters and media alike. This shouldn't have been too difficult a task given the low base from which I was starting, as the club was rarely either positive or proactive in this crucial area. I was then asked to liaise with the team manager at the time as well as pave the way for the recruitment of a new Chief Executive.

For various reasons all of my plans were stymied and the goalposts changed completely, and I felt it impossible to remain a member of the board as it was organised at the time. This was a terrible shame as it had long been my ambition to become a member of the BFC Board and ideally use what knowledge and expertise I had for the benefit of the club and its supporters. But, it wasn't meant to be and that is something that still causes me some sadness and regret nearly a decade later. That is quite enough of my self-indulgence, and I am simply delighted that the club I love so much is now in such safe yet knowledgeable and ambitious hands.

Half Term Report – 17/1/15

I have been putting this article off for a couple of weeks or more but the penny finally dropped that if I didn't get it done this week then there really wouldn't be any point in writing a half term report on every Brentford player given that the second half of the season would already be well under way. As it is, we have now played twenty-six of our forty-six league matches, so I will simply tell you how I think each player has performed to date and what I believe might be in store for them for the remainder of the season.

1. Richard Lee. The mystery is why at the age of thirty-two, Richard Lee, a goalkeeper of proven ability who is also a great student of the game, has made less than two hundred first team appearances in his entire career. The answer is that he has been plagued by bad luck and a series of long-term injuries, generally at the wrong time, and has also had to deputise for keepers of the calibre of Ben Foster. This season has been no different. His chronic shoulder injury has prevented him mounting a serious challenge to David Button and his lack of fitness has meant that Jack Bonham has also overtaken him in the pecking order. His decision to retire at the end of the season is as measured and thoughtful as everything that he does and has come as no real surprise. Given his personality, drive, intelligence and enquiring mind he will have no problem in finding fresh challenges beyond football and it was fitting that his last appearance in a Brentford shirt, assuming there is no farewell cameo later in the season, saw him make two trademark swooping penalty saves to win the Dagenham & Redbridge shootout.

2. Kevin O'Connor. Kevin's influence has moved from the pitch to the dugout and training ground as he has grown into his new role as Player/Coach and succeeded in gaining his B License. He made what is almost certainly his farewell appearance in a Brentford shirt at Dagenham and signed off perfectly with the winning penalty in the shoot out, taken without fuss and with metronomic accuracy into the bottom corner – as he would doubtless have done had fate not intervened and he had taken the crucial spot kick against Doncaster. Kevin has now made five hundred and one first team appearances for the club and is fourth in the all-time appearance chart, a mere fifteen matches behind Peter Gelson, in third place. His place in the Brentford pantheon is assured and he hopefully still has much to offer as a coach given the respect he engendered as a player.

3. Jake Bidwell. What's there not to like about Jake Bidwell? At twenty-one he has played over a hundred games for the club, is an ever present this season, doesn't get injured or suspended and simply goes about his business efficiently and without fuss. I feel that sometimes he is taken for granted and supporters don't realise just how far he has come so quickly, and quite how good he really is. He is cool and calm in defence, does not make expensive errors, uses the ball simply and accurately and his ability to overlap and cross is crucial to the team's shape and pattern of play. He has assisted on three goals so far and I am surprised that he hasn't tried to claim that goal at Wolves when his cross was deflected over Carl Ikeme. Perhaps he is waiting to break his duck with a real thunderbolt. He isn't blessed with lightening pace and he was shown up by Scannell at Huddersfield, no disgrace there as he is a fast and tricky customer, but it is rare that he gets the runaround, he has never looked out of place in the Championship, and he still has much improving to do. Jake has had an exceptional first half of the season with the best still to come and he is an appreciating asset for us.

4. Lewis Macleod. The arrival of the Rangers wunderkind is a signal of pure intent and heralds our ambition to climb even further towards the top of the football tree. The tide has finally turned as it was ever the case that clubs further up the food chain cherry picked our best prospects and signed them for peanuts with us seemingly doffing our cap and proffering our thanks for the crumbs off the rich man's table. Andy Sinton, Paul Smith and DJ Campbell anyone? Now the boot is firmly on the other foot as *Little Old Brentford* just waltzed into Glasgow Rangers, one of the most famous teams in the United Kingdom, took advantage of their straitened circumstances and divested them of their jewel in the crown, as is confirmed by the following comment on a Rangers message board: *Twenty years ago we were buying players from Barcelona, now we're selling them to Brentford!* At twenty years of age the whole world lies before him and we await his debut with baited breath. I fully expect that he will be given the time he needs to regain full fitness and settle down in a strange new city far away from home and I have no doubt that he will make an enormous impact before the end of the season. Class will out.

5. Tony Craig. TC has had a slightly inconsistent and up and down campaign to date. On the one hand his coolness, anticipation and ability to read the game and leadership ability has shone through, his left-footedness helps brings balance to the team and he has also developed an accurate long pass to switch the play to the right wing, however he has also been caught out from time to time on the wrong side of attackers, which has proved costly. His red card against Birmingham, and Daryl Murphy's second goal for Ipswich are prime examples of this worrying trait and he has also been bullied and overwhelmed by the likes of Grant Holt, Danny Graham and Murphy. Tony has fully earned his contract extension and he has the experience we need at this level but I do wonder if we will need someone with a little bit more power, height and strength as we continue to improve and upgrade our squad.

6. Harlee Dean. Harlee has been in and out of the starting line-up as we are still searching for our best central defensive partnership. He replaced Tony Craig after his red card against Birmingham and immediately impressed, but lost his place after the insipid display at Middlesbrough where he was by no means the only player to disappoint. His next opportunity arrived after James Tarkowski's suspension kicked in and Harlee more than seized his chance. His confidence on the ball and willingness to adapt to our new system of playing from the back was evident. He made a costly error against Fulham through overplaying, but had the character and determination to recover and made amends with a glorious buccaneering equalising goal. He has shown signs of increasing maturity both on and off the pitch and his strength and aerial ability is more than welcome, but the jury is still out as to whether he will remain as first choice given the challenge he faces from Craig and Tarkowski and any potential new arrival.

7. Sam Saunders. Sam's 2014 provides a great example of the topsy-turvy life of a professional footballer. Riding high as League One Player of the Month for December 2013 and fresh from a spell of four goals in as many games, Sam was struck down with a serious knee injury which, after a couple of false starts, kept him out until early

November when he returned to the side with a cameo appearance at Millwall, where he managed to calm the nerves and help the team hold out for a hard fought victory. He has sat on the bench since then and shown his threat with two well taken, if fairly meaningless late goals against Ipswich. What reassured me more about his potential value to the team was that wonderful swerving cross from wide out on the left, which Andre Gray should surely have converted for an injury time equaliser at Wolves. Sam definitely retains his magic with the ball at his feet and it did not come as a shock when he was offered an extension to his contract, but I was certainly surprised that he accepted it given that he could certainly take his pick of pretty much every leading Division One team and play every week for them. I suspect that Sam realises that it has been a long haul for him to reach the Championship from his humble beginnings in the Southern League and Conference South and he intends to relish this opportunity for as long as possible. He is a good influence in the dressing room and Sam will also pay Mark Warburton back for his continued faith in him.

8. Jonathan Douglas. Something amazing happened soon after halftime in the preseason friendly match against Crystal Palace. Marcos Tebar took possession from a throw in and slipped the ball to Jonathan Douglas who ran into the penalty area, dribbled past a lunging defender and then curled a gorgeous shot way beyond Speroni into the far corner of the net for a sublimely well taken goal which demonstrated that given self-belief and good coaching it is possible for a footballer to continue to improve even at the advanced age of thirty-three. JD is the heart and soul of the Brentford team, stationed just in front of the back four, he anticipates and snuffs out danger before it can threaten our goal. But that isn't all, as Douglas has licence to roam and he has also developed the ability to make devastating late runs and sneak unseen into the opposition penalty area where he already scored five valuable goals as well as setting up a couple more. He has only missed one league match so far this season and Toumani Diagouraga ensured that he wasn't missed too much that day, but he is a massive influence and he remains the most important player yet to sign a new contract for next season and beyond. He has been one of our most consistent players so far this season and I fully expect that he will maintain his sharpness. Hopefully he will get a new deal that is acceptable to him and also realise that he is unlikely to find as good a situation elsewhere as he has at Griffin Park.

9. Scott Hogan. The one major disappointment of the season was Scott Hogan's season-ending anterior cruciate injury sustained totally accidentally and innocuously on his league debut as a late substitute at Rotherham when he went down as if shot with nobody near him. I was very excited when we signed Scott as he had scored nineteen goals for Rochdale last season and appeared to be a real footballer as well as a natural goalscorer. Scott was given the coveted number nine shirt too and was expected to become our first choice striker until fate intervened before he was able to get started. As of yet he has not been replaced and we remain shorthanded in attack, and we live in hope that a white puff of smoke will signal the arrival of a new striker any day now before the transfer window closes. Scott has been rehabilitating in America and will hopefully recover in time for the start of next season. He has all our best wishes for a speedy and full recovery.

10. Moses Odubajo. Moses was probably Leyton Orient's best player last season and scored a goal in the playoff final at Wembley that simply oozed class. There seemed to be a lot of competition for his signature and it came as a bit of a surprise when Brentford managed to capture him for what was rumoured to be our first ever seven-figure transfer fee. Moses took a few games to settle but offered us pace and width on the right flank. He became an almost instant hero when he scored a massively important late equaliser against Birmingham that earned a point against all the odds and helped us gain some necessary self-belief, and also impressed when he took Alan Judge's wonderfully weighted long pass into his stride to score emphatically against Brighton. For the most part, though, he flattered to deceive with an insufficient end result for all his trickery. His season turned on its head when Alan McCormack suffered a long-term injury at Bolton and Moses looked a different player when he was moved back to play as an attacking right back. Not only has he defended well but he has provided far more of an attacking threat when running from deep as he terrifies defenders and seems far more comfortable when he is facing the play. He provided a memorable assist for Andre Gray's equalising goal against Derby County as well creating chances in almost every game he plays. It will be interesting to see what happens when Alan McCormack returns to fitness in the next month or so as Moses has added a new dimension to our game when attacking from deep.

12. Alan McCormack. Moving Alan from midfield to right back proved to be a masterstroke early last season and his defensive calmness and solidity as well as his excellent use of the ball played a key role in our successful promotion campaign, but despite that, some supporters were concerned that he might not have the pace or know-how to cope with the Championship. Opponents too seemed to target him as a potential weakness but Alan has proved as indomitable as ever. No winger gave him the runaround, he scored an excellent goal against Leeds and his curling crosses proved to be a constant threat. His only aberration was a ridiculously wayward throw which almost set up Andrew Crofts of Brighton for an early gift goal. He looked totally his old combative self when given a rare start in midfield against Norwich where he would have scored but for the brilliance of Ruddy. Alan received an ankle ligament injury at Bolton but is now back in light training after his operation and should be challenging for his place within another month or so, and his return will provide us with another option and could allow us to move Moses Odubajo back to the wing. This will be another welcome selection headache for Mark Warburton.

14. Marcos Tebar. The Summer arrival of an established La Liga midfielder from Almeria excited most Brentford supporters and his performances in pre-season highlighted his skill on the ball and the way in which he seemed always to find time and space. He played alongside Jonathan Douglas and the two of them formed an instant partnership and dovetailed to perfection with one sitting and the other venturing forward. However, when the league began in earnest Tebar did not look quite so unflustered and the games seemed to pass him by. He soon dropped out of contention despite impressing in a late run out as a substitute against Leeds United. He then suffered an injury and has only just regained his place on the substitutes' bench. Hopefully there is far more to come from him as the jury is still out as to whether or not he can cut it in the Championship.

15. Stuart Dallas. Rodney Dangerfield was a famous American comedian and actor best known for his catchphrase *I don't get no respect!* and I can imagine that Stuart Dallas might well agree entirely with his sentiment. Whilst I am certain that his contribution is valued by his manager and team mates, many supporters seem to give him short shrift and totally underestimate him despite his massive achievements to date this season. Never an automatic first choice, Stuart has scored four vital goals in only seven starts plus eleven appearances from the bench. The winning goal at Blackpool when he chased a lost cause and panicked the defender into an error, an incredible right footed volley into the roof of the Derby net which came out of nowhere and gave us a win that set us off on a long run of victories, a perfectly placed side footed goal which sealed the win against Wolves and another classic volleyed winner against Rotherham. Add to that the assists for Harlee Dean's equaliser against Fulham and Andre Gray's winner at Brighton and you can see just how much he has contributed to the team's efforts this season. He also looked very comfortable when moved to an emergency right back role at Nottingham Forest. Stuart is a right footer playing on the left and is a constant danger when cutting in onto his favourite foot. He is good in the air, powerful and far quicker than he looks. He needs to track back more and support Bidwell better but for a youngster who has started a mere handful of league matches he is a quick learner and has shown that he is more than good enough to contribute at this level of the game. I expect him to become a regular starter.

16. Jack Bonham. Jack Bonham has quietly just got on with learning the game out of the spotlight of public scrutiny and has done enough on the training ground and in the Development Squad games to earn a three year contract extension, proof indeed of the faith that the management team has in him and his potential to develop into a Championship calibre goalkeeper. The consistency of David Button has made the position of reserve goalkeeper a thankless one this season but, with the imminent retirement of Richard Lee, it is crucial that Brentford have somebody ready and capable of stepping in when the need arises as well as keeping the pressure on Button. Button's massive improvement over the past year can partially be put down to the competition he faced from Richard Lee to keep his place and Bonham will need to do a similar job. Bonham was given a rare start against Brighton in the FA Cup and looked like a carbon copy of Button in terms of his desire to release the ball quickly and accurately to his defenders. He made a couple of decent saves, held onto a difficult cross under extreme pressure and also nearly made a hash of an effort from O'Grady that he failed to stop cleanly but the luck was with him as it inched past the upright. He looked exactly what he is, a player of raw potential who still needs a lot of seasoning. It will be interesting to see if he sits on the bench for the remainder of the season or if a more experienced keeper is brought in which would then allow Bonham to go out on loan and get some games under his belt.

17. Jon Toral. I remember thinking when we managed to sign Steve Sidwell on loan from Arsenal back in 2001 that it was a sign that we were a club on the rise and one to whom the big clubs would entrust their emerging talent. I had exactly the same feeling when Jon Toral arrived from the same club, but there is a key difference. Arsenal never really thought that Sidwell would make it at Highbury whereas The Gunners still have high hopes for Toral. As soon as he arrived at the club I spoke to an Arsenal fan about him. This was at the time when the Adam Forshaw transfer saga was being played out. It was obvious that he would leave Griffin Park, and it was simply a question of ensuring that we were properly recompensed. *But how is Toral going to replace him?* I asked and was immediately told that he was going to be even better than someone who had just been voted Division One Player of the Season. A likely story, I thought, until I saw Toral play. At nineteen he has everything going for him as he has height, strength, skill on the ball, finishing ability, the ability to read the game, some pace and a little bit of devil in him too. He is mature beyond his years and it is no coincidence that our results became far more consistent after he had forced his way into the team at the end of October. He has scored two well-taken goals, entered Brentford folklore with a howler of a miss at Brighton that will merit disbelieving replays for years to come and, more importantly, he has become an important cog in the wheel. We are good for his development and he is certainly good for us. Maybe, just maybe, we can sign him on a permanent basis, but I suspect that that is simply my wishful thinking rather than a view based on reality.

18. Alan Judge. Football is a game of opinions but I still find it hard to believe that Blackburn Rovers made the judgement call that Alan Judge wasn't good enough to play regularly for them and allowed him to join us for a fee that has been estimated to be around £250,000. What a bargain, and he has been without a shadow of doubt our best and most influential player this season. Alan had a wonderful loan spell with us last season when he mainly played out wide on the left flank and he contributed greatly to our promotion with his goals, energy and accurate crosses, if not his penalty taking! Everything changed with the departure of Adam Forshaw and Alan was switched to a more central role to fill the gap, and he has taken to his new responsibilities with total aplomb. He is a human dynamo who never stops running and harrying, a terrier in human form, who inspires and chivvies his teammates in equal doses. Alan's long passing is accurate and incisive, as evidenced by Moses Odubajo's goal against Brighton and Andre Gray's against Wolves when he split the opposition defence wide open. Something has to give and Alan's goal tally has fallen away with only one goal scored to date, but eight assists and his energy and ability to keep the ball moving and to switch the focus of the play is more than compensation. Alan took a knock against Brighton a fortnight ago and we all hope that he is not out of action for too long as despite our last two victories he is already sorely missed.

19. Andre Gray. Let's review our striking situation in more detail. The three main strikers from last season, Clayton Donaldson, Will Grigg and Marcello Trotta, whose goals helped us win promotion, have all left the club on either a temporary or permanent basis, two of our new signings aimed at filling the gap have barely featured owing to a combination of long-term injury and an inability to fit in to our system and our third new striker had played a grand total of four league games back in 2009 for Shrewsbury, in one of which he replaced Nathan Elder. And yet here we are with a highly respectable forty-two goals under our belt and the unknown striker has now reached double figures for the season. Talk about a gamble paying off! Andre Gray has been nothing less than sensational, as he has seized the opportunity provided to him by Scott Hogan's injury and established himself in the team. Strong, rangy and pacy, he showed his striking ability in preseason with well-taken goals against Nice and Crystal Palace. He took time to settle down and learn how to play the lone striker role demanded of him and cope with being bullied by giant defenders, but it all clicked into gear in November, and he has scored eight times in his last twelve league games. Of course, he misses a lot too, as Brighton can attest, but he is sharp and predatory and a constant menace to defences. His goals against Derby and Millwall bear testimony to his coolness in front of goal and clinical finishing. Our initial investment of around £600,000 now looks as if it is an absolute bargain, and he can be as good as he wants to be, given how much he has improved and progressed since the season began. The predators are already sniffing around him, but Andre is sensible enough to realise that he still has much to learn but that he is in the perfect place to develop and express himself.

20. Toumani Diagouraga. The verdict was in on Toumani, who was perceived at the start of the season to be no more than a decent squad player who often flattered to deceive and had probably found his level in Division One. It looked for a while as if he was even going to be sent to Coventry and I doubt if there were many Brentford supporters who would really have mourned his leaving. He had served us well, but perhaps his time had come and our progress had overtaken his capabilities. Toumani decided to fight for his place, kept his counsel, worked hard in training and when his chance came he took it – and, boy, did he do so. He has been our best player by far over the past three months, playing alongside Jonathan Douglas, winning the ball, covering, harrying, running with the ball and providing an impassable barrier to opposing runners. What has changed, though, is his use of the ball. He has a newfound confidence and rather than always making the simple five yard pass to a colleague he has now added longer more ambitious passes to his repertoire. He seems liberated by our policy of moving the ball swiftly and changing the direction of the play. His shooting is still laughable but we can live with that. Indeed, it simply adds to his charm. Toumani is Vieira reborn. He ensured that Douglas was barely missed at Millwall and he might yet replace him should Dougie not be with us next season. His level of improvement has been staggering and his influence shows no sign of waning.

21. Alex Pritchard. I hated Alex Pritchard when he played against us last season. A preening show pony who dived and moaned his way through Swindon's narrow victory over us but I also took note of his quick feet, two footedness, vision and rapier like ability to split a defence with one pass. When we followed our customary practice of signing Swindon's best player I welcomed his arrival, but saw him more as a left-winger. Little did I know that he was going to become a central midfielder who is becoming an increasing influence in every game he plays. Naturally, not everything he tries comes off and he needs to learn that sometimes the simple pass is the best option without having his imagination and sense of invention stifled, but he is becoming more influential and less likely to drift out of games. He also made a lung-bursting run to cover for Jake Bidwell, who had been caught upfield and made a perfect tackle on a Blackburn attacker deep in the Brentford half. It was at this point that I realised that he was coming of age as a footballer and was fully integrated into the team. Four goals is a reasonable return so far, but he has the ability to reach double figures. Alan Judge's absence might mean that he now gets the chance to take free kicks and his goal with a curling effort against Nice shows that he has the ability to capitalise upon them. He also scored from the one penalty he took at Nottingham Forest. It wasn't the most convincing spot kick I have ever seen but it went in and hopefully he will maintain his successful record when next called upon. We have Alex for the remainder of the season and it is a deal that suits all parties. Let's simply enjoy him whilst we can; he is only going to improve. We can worry about his longer term future, and whether it might be with us, at a later date.

22. Betinho. Scott Hogan's serious injury, incurred on 30th August, left the club little time to replace him before the end of the August transfer window and it is to their credit that they managed to do so. However, the gamble of signing Betinho has certainly not paid off. He initially came to Mark Warburton's attention during the Next Gen series where he had impressed as a regular goalscorer, and at twenty-one he had a highly impressive goal scoring record for both his club, Sporting Lisbon, at youth and B Level, as well as for the Portuguese international teams at all age levels, up to and including the Under 21 team. At first glance, he appeared to be a classic goal poacher and a reasonable choice to replace Hogan, particularly at such short notice. Betinho made his debut as a late substitute against Norwich City, played for the final thirteen minutes, and then disappeared from the reckoning never to be seen on the pitch again at first team level. He sat on the bench for a month or so but was never called into action. I think the reason why is fairly straightforward. Our initial expectations for him were totally unreasonable and unrealistic for a young, inexperienced player leaving his native land to play in a strange and unfamiliar environment. In addition, he was asked to play an entirely different role at an exceptionally high level of football. I seriously doubt if he had ever been played as a lone striker before, and the concept of tracking back and pressing, a prerequisite for a Brentford striker, would have been entirely alien to him. No wonder it hasn't worked out as we all hoped and anticipated and it really hasn't been his fault. We made a rushed decision that hasn't paid dividends apart from giving Andre Gray the extra pitch time required to prove that he is a star in the making, so some good has come out of this situation. I hope Betinho returns home shortly and becomes a star and that our coaching and the care lavished upon him will have paid some small part in his development.

23. Jota. I just love it when the Bees sign players known by only one name like Betinho and, of course, Jota, or José Peleteiro Ramallo, to give him his full name, who signed in August from Real Club Celta de Vigo for an undisclosed fee rumoured to be well in excess of a million pounds. Jota is another indication of Brentford's ambition and aim to be in the big time as he is a wonderfully talented inside forward who has a left foot that could open a tin can. The ball appears to be glued to his foot as he brings it under instantaneous control - already on the move, head up, looking at the options he can choose from. He is a wonderful proponent of the lost art of dribbling as he glides past opponents with effortless ease. Mainly playing in an advanced wide right role, he can move inside menacingly and shoot from distance with that wand of a left foot as Fulham can attest. His injury time winner against our rivals would have ensured him hero status in his lifetime even if he wasn't the most extravagantly gifted player I have ever seen wearing a Brentford shirt. He took a while to settle down in his new surroundings, Mark Warburton eased him in gently, and he also benefited from having other Spanish speakers around him in the squad, but it was quite obvious that he was a special talent and he introduced himself with a flourish by scoring a goal against Leeds of quite stunning quality, when he killed the ball instantly, somehow found space in a packed penalty area, dropped his shoulder, left two defenders on their backside and carefully found the roof of the net, all in less time than it has taken me to describe his achievement.

He has already scored six times in only eighteen starts and his long-range effort at Cardiff where he found the top corner of the net with unerring accuracy was another eye opener and was greeted with a stunned silence by the home fans. Tackling and pressing were anathema to him but he has learned quickly that there is no such thing as a luxury player in the Brentford team and he now does his fair share of the necessary dirty stuff off the ball. His determination to chase a lost cause towards the corner flag led to Brighton's Lewis Dunk losing his cool, pushing the Spaniard to the ground and fully earning his second yellow card. Yes, he can drift out of games and run out of steam soon after the hour mark, but Jota is becoming a greater influence on matches and now attracts the close attention of his opponents, thus providing extra room and space for his teammates. Alan Judge has monopolised free kicks close to goal up until now with Alex Pritchard generally in close attention waiting to pounce, but I suspect that Jota might also have something special to contribute in this area. He is already the most skilful player I have had the privilege of watching play for Brentford.

24. Tommy Smith. Tommy is the epitome of the good pro. A player of vast experience with over 550 games to his credit mainly at Premier League and Championship level, at thirty-four year of age he has been brought in as much for his off field influence and as a good example, as for what he can contribute on the pitch itself. He has only started one match and probably played a bit less than he either wanted or expected but he has made several valuable contributions when coming on as a late substitute, none more so than his late deflected equaliser on the opening day of the season that saved Brentford from what would otherwise have been a demoralising home defeat by Charlton. He has also made goals for Jon Toral and Jonathan Douglas. He might have lost a little pace but he is still an exceptionally canny and clever player who reads the game well, makes intelligent runs and does not give the ball away cheaply. He is the perfect player to bring on to help hold onto a lead and close the game out. He is exactly what we need this season, a player who has vast experience and knows the Championship inside out and understands what is expected of him. He has played his role to perfection.

25. Raphael Calvet. Given his pedigree one would have hoped that he would have earned an opportunity by now, but it hasn't happened for the young French defender as of yet, although he did well in the preseason games. He is not yet twenty-one and time is on his side. Calvet is tough and skilful but needs to get the chance to demonstrate his ability and get some experience of the Football League. Ideally he will get the opportunity for a loan move and benefit from it as much as Alfie Mawson has done from his spell at Wycombe Wanderers.

26. James Tarkowski. The season hasn't really taken off for James Tarkowski as everyone, himself included, would surely have expected. He was a colossus in the second part of last season when his anticipation, strength and excellent use of the ball ensured that he cemented his position alongside Tony Craig and he started the season as first choice ahead of Harlee Dean. This season, he has played reasonably well but never touched the heights of last year and his performances were punctuated by careless errors and ill-discipline. He was guilty of overplaying against Norwich which helped contribute towards the crucial opening goal, he conceded an unfortunate penalty at Watford when he made a needless challenge, and his penalty kick against Leeds is probably still in orbit. He lost his place after being suspended for five bookings, some unfortunate, others a bit silly on his part and Harlee Dean seized his opportunity. James had to wait for two months to get back into the team and after a couple of rusty performances now looks as if he is getting back to his best form. We now have three excellent central defenders competing for two spots in the team, plus perhaps the possibility of a new face arriving before the end of the transfer window and James will need to be at his best in order to keep his place.

27. David Button. It has taken a bit of time but even the most grudging Brentford fans are finally realising just how good their goalkeeper is. Button has played every Championship match, kept seven clean sheets, and his shot stopping ability has come increasingly to the fore. Who can forget the reflex saves against Birmingham and Rotherham that helped win us crucial points and he has conceded very few soft goals. He could still command his six-yard box better and does not use his physique as much as he surely should and sometimes his punches are a bit weak and insipid. Where he really stands out is in his distribution. He sets the tone for our possession-led style and rarely kicks the ball long unless forced to do so, or if he can see the opportunity to set Andre Gray free with a quick clearance. He invariably rolls or kicks the ball short to a waiting defender and sets us on our way. From time to time it can misfire with disastrous consequences, as it did against Norwich, Fulham and Ipswich but more often than not we retain possession, probe for gaps and start an attack thanks to Button's initial clearance. Button has grown in confidence as he has finally established himself as a first choice keeper after a multitude of loan spells and his improvement over the past half season has been massive and he has become one of the most reliable keepers in this division.

28. Nico Yennaris. The season has been a frustrating write-off so far for the young defender as he was forced off with an injury early on at Dagenham and has barely been seen since. He took time to recover, scored an excellent goal at Swansea for the Development Squad and eventually forced his way back onto the substitutes' bench. He came on for a brief appearance as a substitute against Brighton in the FA Cup just long enough to admire the visitors' two goals. At twenty-one Nico still has plenty of time to stake his claim either as a right back or defensive midfielder but he would have hoped to be higher up the food chain after spending a year at the club.

33. Montell Moore. Montell made a memorable debut as an eighteen year old at Dagenham, scoring a well-taken goal from the edge of the penalty area and assisting on three others. He has also sat on the bench six times without being called upon. He is a quick striker with an eye for goal and he has earned a new three-year contract, proof indeed of the faith the club has in him. He has just been sent on loan to FC Midtjylland in Denmark where he will gain valuable experience and hopefully reflect on some poor off-field decisions. He is definitely one for the future.

39. Nick Proschwitz. German striker Nick Proschwitz was not rumoured to be our first choice but joined the Bees in August on a free transfer from Hull City just before the first game of the season. He has only started one match in the absence of the injured Andre Gray at Blackpool and has invariably appeared as a late substitute. He scored a late tap-in to clinch the win at Rotherham but has otherwise struggled to make a contribution and generally looked off the pace. He has failed to demonstrate any potency in front of goal or the ability to hold the ball up consistently and he missed two gilt-edged late opportunities to win the Sheffield Wednesday match. The jury is still out although it must be hard for him to make an impact when he is only given the odd few minutes to impress on the pitch.

Finally, a few words of praise for Mark Warburton, David Weir, Simon Royce, Kevin O'Connor and the rest of the back room staff. We have totally surpassed everyone's expectations except perhaps for theirs, and they have imbued the players with confidence and self-belief and simply encouraged them to play football and remain positive at all times. Long may they continue to do so and given good luck with injuries there is no reason why we shouldn't maintain our progress and success over the second half of the season.

No Regrets! – 25/1/15

Given the absence of an FA Cup tie, yesterday's planned Championship match at Norwich went ahead as originally scheduled, one of only four such games to do so. Our two-one victory (incredibly, our first in the League at Norwich since 1929) elevated the Bees to fourth place in the Championship and, more importantly, threw down the gauntlet to the rest of the division.

The highlights on *The Football League Show* clearly demonstrated our class and pedigree. Despite a bobbly atrocity of a pitch which seemed totally incongruent with Norwich's long established tradition for playing a passing game (but which made far more sense when the home team's game plan was revealed) it was Brentford who adapted perfectly to the conditions, whilst it was their hosts who hoofed the ball unceremoniously from back to front with monotonous and mind-numbing regularity and only really threatened danger on the few occasions when the will-o'-the-wisp Nathan Redmond was allowed to run at an exposed Jake Bidwell.

Despite the fact that they were flattered by the margin of their victory at Griffin Park earlier in the season, Norwich had impressed me on the night with the quality of their football with players running effortlessly off the ball into position and holding the ball whilst probing for opportunities, but they now seem drained of confidence and appear to have morphed into yet another long ball clone of a team, far removed from the heritage of the club, and we simply picked them off.

Mark Warburton is always saying that the players must keep believing in their own ability and realise that they are where they are in the league totally on merit and fully deserve to be challenging for promotion either automatically or via the playoffs. The players seem to be totally on message given the ease with which they rolled the ball around as if playing on a bowling green. They kept possession and took care of the ball for long spells and pulled their opponents out of position with apparent ease. I really have no doubts on that score, the penny has finally dropped and the players fully realise that they have every chance of achieving what at the beginning of the season was considered to be the impossible and unthinkable – return to the top division after an absence of nearly seventy years.

After yesterday's latest victory, Mark Warburton calmly stated that this time last year Brentford were playing against Gillingham, and who we play against at the same time next year totally depends on how far the players believe they can go.

Premier League – More Than a Pipedream! – 27/1/15

One of the many privileges of being involved with the recent *Brentford 125th Anniversary Book* was being able to read, at first hand, all the original press clippings about the club's incredible rise from the depths of the Third Division to the top of the First in what seemed no more than a twinkling of an eye. The parallels between then and now are eerie, as an enlightened chairman discovered a manager from far out in left field, invested his total trust and faith in him and gave him the support and wherewithal to rebuild his squad from top to bottom, initially bringing in unheralded players from footballing outposts such as Middlesbrough. A reborn and revitalised team then swept all before them and completed their triumphant journey with promotion to the First Division in 1935. Not content with that incredible achievement, they swept everyone aside and, over the next four seasons, they not only established themselves at the top level of the game but the Bees consistently challenged for the title playing a swaggering brand of attacking football with the team now buoyed by the arrival of a number of top international players who gelled into one of the best teams in the country.

There is a marvellous clipping in the book that discusses with total sincerity the possibility of the Bees achieving a First Division Championship and FA Cup double. Unfortunately it wasn't to be as the Second World War came at a time when Brentford were on the verge of greatness, with packed crowds at Griffin Park the rule rather than the exception, but by the time that peace was restored our time had come and gone. The money had run out and the team had grown too old to compete at that rarefied level again. The point to be emphasised is that Brentford have already created the precedent of rising from the third tier of English football to the top, albeit eighty years ago, and why shouldn't we repeat that feat this year, as we are currently threatening to do? Who knows whether we can maintain our promotion challenge, but here we are, twenty-eight games into the season and we find ourselves in fourth place in the table, after a run of three consecutive wins, two away from home, and with our previously disbelieving supporters finally beginning to accept that we are for real and that 2015 could actually be the year when history repeats itself.

All will be revealed over the next three months and let me just put things firmly into context by stating that whatever happens from now on this will still go down in history as one of the most amazing, incredible and memorable seasons in the club's long and august history. Over the course of the past couple of months there have apparently been some long and detailed talks between the club and the Premier League purely on a *what if* basis regarding the feasibility and suitability of Griffin Park hosting Premier League football should Brentford actually achieve promotion this season. Potential ground shares have also been considered however, despite there being no official announcement, I would guess that the club will decide to remain at Griffin Park if humanly possible should the unthinkable happen.

The last time we reached the pinnacle of the game Griffin Park was able to cram in almost forty thousand spectators, and contemporary photographs show quite clearly how densely packed the spectators were, with children passed down over the heads of other supporters to stand safely at the front of the terraces. The average attendance throughout our previous spell in the First Division was around twenty-five thousand, which put the club on a par with the majority of its opponents. However, given the diktats of health and safety and the fact that the standing accommodation at the ground has been massively reduced, the capacity at Griffin Park is now no more than around twelve thousand, a figure that would be reduced even further if we were forced to become an all-seater stadium, as would be the case in the Premier League.

Griffin Park would comfortably be the smallest stadium ever to host Premier League football with Swindon, Blackpool and Oldham Athletic the previous holders of this unenviable record. Oldham averaged gates of just over twelve thousand in the last two of their three seasons in the Premier League. The dressing rooms, floodlights, media and hospitality facilities at Griffin Park, whilst benefiting from recent upgrades and refurbishment, are totally in the dark ages compared with the majority of the top level clubs with their sleek and well-appointed new stadia and I am sure that the moguls at the Premier League preface their daily prayers with a special entreaty for the Bees not to darken their doors, at least until our new stadium at Lionel Road becomes a reality.

Personally I feel that our promotion would demonstrate that good football, positive management and careful planning can reap its justified rewards and I think that we would be a total breath of fresh air and revitalise what is so often a dull and predictable division, just as Blackpool did under Ian Holloway when they played an expansive brand of attacking football that embarrassed so many of their so-called betters and almost led them to survival on the last day of a momentous season.

If you examine the European football scene there are also precedents that should fill us all with hope and prove that the Promised Land is no chimera. You need look no further than Sassuolo and Eibar who are both thriving in the top division of their respective leagues despite their lack of resources and infrastructure. Sassuolo are funded by one of Italy's most prominent industrialists, Giorgio Squinzi, who first invested in them in 2002 when they were homeless and semi-professional. Under his direction his team, despite coming from a town of less than forty thousand inhabitants, has risen to Serie A with their success based on a tight knit group of young home grown players.

The Eibar story is even more astonishing. A tiny town in the Basque Country with a stadium holding just over five thousand supporters, they have been brilliantly managed by Gaizka Garitano and been promoted in just two seasons from the third division of Spanish football to La Liga. Despite a playing budget that would be sniffed at by many fourth tier teams in England they have built up a squad of mainly home-produced players and developed a close-knit sense of togetherness that has enabled them to defeat technically far better teams. They have also been assisted by some well-selected loanees, such as Jota, who helped earn them promotion last season by scoring eleven goals from midfield. Eibar are the smallest club to reach the top flight and only eight teams in

England's top four divisions had a smaller average attendance than the Spanish side's 2,901. Jota is quick to see the parallels between his current and previous club:

There are a lot of similarities with Eibar and Brentford. No one expected Eibar to go up and no one thought Brentford would be this high in the table. But, hopefully, we can maintain our form and repeat what we achieved at Eibar last season. It is not going to be easy to stay in the position we are in but we are capable of fighting for promotion.

So fairy tales can come true, as has been proved recently in both Italy and Spain, and maybe it will be Brentford who next turn dreams into reality.

The Grass Isn't Always Greener – 30/1/15

There might well be an old friend playing against us on Saturday but most likely Adam Forshaw will start the game on the substitutes' bench and it will be interesting to hear what sort of welcome and reception he receives from the aficionados on New Road. His move from Wigan to Middlesbrough was described to me this morning by another Bees fan as *just another rat leaving the sinking ship.* Harsh but maybe accurate as he played a mere seventeen matches for Wigan and remained there for only five months before moving on. It all looked so good for him when he left Brentford, but his dream move turned sour very quickly and he has explained his recent whirlwind state of affairs in an interview published on the Middlesbrough website today:

I had two great years at Brentford. We went very close in my first year there by getting to the playoff final. Unfortunately we missed out, but the following season we went one better and went up as runners-up. I know Brentford have a lot of good players but I am honestly surprised to see them doing so well this season. People keep saying they will fall off but they are not showing any signs of it, so all respect to them, including the staff and players and everyone there. They will be tough opposition on Saturday. Their home ground is a bit of a fortress to them, so we'll have to be really ready. They get about 12,000 fans and they are really close to the pitch. They are a good set of fans and they are a really good football team, but I am more than confident that we can go there and get a result.

Forshaw is just the latest player to join the brain drain or, less charitably, fire sale from Wigan and follows Callum McManaman, Roger Espinoza, Ben Watson and Shaun Maloney out of the exit door from the DW Stadium. Either they are clearing the decks and ridding themselves of all their prime sellable assets and top earners in preparation for a rocky road ahead and likely relegation to the First Division, or this is Malky Mackay's last gasp effort to build a team in his own image that will keep them in the Championship.

Adam Forshaw is one more in an ever-growing list of players who thought the grass would be greener away from Griffin Park. His departure gives some credence to the Griffin Park curse… but what about other recent leavers?

Simon Moore's career has stood still over the past couple of seasons and he has played far fewer games than his talent has warranted. He is more than young and good enough to come again but he needs to play regularly at Championship level, something that would have happened had he remained at Brentford. Harry Forrester is the saddest case of all as Brentford and Doncaster have passed each other like ships in the night and, despite his gifts, he is now no more than an injury-prone winger playing for an average First Division club who bursts into life and illuminates matches with his sheer ability far too infrequently. He made a cataclysmically poor decision to leave Brentford and it is one that I suspect haunts him to this day when he looks ruefully at how far we have progressed and how his career has gone backwards and become stymied.

A couple of months ago I would have added Clayton Donaldson to the Hall of Shame as both he and his new club, Birmingham City had started the season slowly, but the Blues have recovered under Gary Rowett's inspired leadership and Clayton has scored an impressive ten league goals and now resembles the dynamic, powerful leader of the line that we so enjoyed throughout his three years at Griffin Park.

The message to me is clear. Footballers have a short and unpredictable career and it is quite understandable that they seek to better themselves and maximise their earnings. But sometimes the seemingly obvious move is not in their long-term best interest and it is best to simply do nothing. I hope that our current crop of stars have learned that our increasing profile, the quality of the coaching they receive and the way in which we play the game, means Brentford is a fitting and appropriate place for them to hone, develop and show off their burgeoning abilities and that the grass is not necessarily greener elsewhere.

League Table – 31/1/15

Position	Team	P	W	D	L	F	A	GD	Pt	Form
1	Bournemouth	28	16	6	6	59	28	31	54	W W L W L W
2	Derby County	28	16	6	6	52	25	27	54	W W W L W W
3	Middlesbrough	28	15	8	5	43	18	25	53	W D D W W W
4	Ipswich Town	28	14	9	5	46	27	19	51	W W L W L D
5	**Brentford**	**28**	**15**	**4**	**9**	**44**	**37**	**7**	**49**	**L L W W W L**
6	Watford	28	14	5	9	56	33	23	47	L W L W W L
7	Wolverhampton Wndrs	28	12	9	7	33	35	-2	45	W W W W D D
8	Norwich City	28	12	8	8	50	34	16	44	W L W W L D
8	Blackburn Rovers	28	10	9	9	38	38	0	39	L D L D L W
10	Sheffield Wednesday	28	9	11	8	21	25	-4	38	W W W L D L
11	Birmingham City	28	9	10	9	31	39	-8	37	L W W D D D
12	Nottingham Forest	28	8	10	10	37	40	-3	34	L L L W L L
13	Cardiff City	28	9	7	12	36	42	-6	34	D L W L L L
14	Bolton Wanderers	28	9	7	12	33	39	-6	34	W L D W L D
15	Fulham	28	10	4	14	41	49	-8	34	L L L W W L
16	Reading	28	9	7	12	33	42	-9	34	D W D L D W
17	Huddersfield Town	28	9	7	12	36	47	-11	34	D W W L W L
18	Charlton Athletic	28	6	15	7	25	35	-10	33	D L L L D D
19	Leeds United	28	8	8	12	30	39	-9	32	L L D D W W
20	Rotherham United	28	6	12	10	26	36	-10	30	D D L L W D
21	Brighton and Hove A	28	6	11	11	30	36	-6	29	D W W L W L
22	Millwall	28	6	9	13	26	44	-18	27	L L L L D W
23	Wigan Athletic	28	4	10	14	26	36	-10	22	W L L D L D
24	Blackpool	28	4	8	16	22	50	-28	20	L D W L L W

FEBRUARY

How Did We Lose That Game? – 1/2/15

I was sitting on the sofa last night trying to read a book but, in reality, I was still trying to understand how we could possibly have lost that match against Middlesbrough yesterday lunchtime. A match that we totally dominated, having the lion's share of the possession, creating the better chances and yet somehow we came away with nothing. All the key moments were replaying on a loop in my mind. The chances we missed, particularly early on when we had the best defence in the league seemingly on the ropes, but we didn't put them away and ultimately paid a heavy price for our profligacy.

The ball always seemed to run Middlesbrough's way at key times of the match, in particular when Stuart Dallas's drive was pushed onto the post with Andre Gray and Jota waiting eagerly for a simple tap in from the rebound; fate intervened and the ball came back, hit the goalkeeper and somehow diverted away from our players directly to a Middlesbrough defender. Gray had earlier headed wastefully and haplessly wide when presented with a free header right in front of goal by Pritchard's perfect delivery and it was Alex who laid the ball to Jota from a cleverly-worked free kick and Konstantopoulos somehow pushed his shot over the bar when he really should have been given no chance. Tarkowski too had a flick from a corner blocked on the goal line and the ball again bounced Middlesbrough's way.

Middlesbrough were forced to funnel back and simply try to absorb our pressure and they relied on a series of long balls into our half simply to create some breathing space and allow their overworked defenders some respite from our non-stop barrage. Their negativity didn't deserve the reward it received right on halftime when the fates laughed at Brentford again when Harlee Dean, under no pressure, unaccountably allowed a harmless long ball from the left back to drift over his head and the predatory Bamford was in for the kill. Button, caught back on his heels, was expecting his defender to head the ball to safety, but Bamford touched the ball first before collapsing under the keeper's late challenge for an obvious penalty and a chance that Leadbitter was never going to spurn. This, incredibly, was Boro's first attempt at goal and the Bees left the field at halftime trailing by a goal instead of holding the two-goal advantage that their play and possession had fully merited.

Middlesbrough improved after the break and played a perfect cat and mouse game, breaking quickly from defence as we pushed forward and left inevitable gaps at the back. We were cut open by a beautiful passing move that led to Adomah letting us off the hook when left with an open goal. Adam Forshaw, the new pantomime villain, then came on to the inevitable mixed reception and his presence enabled the visitors to keep possession for longer spells and frustrate us. Stuart Dallas really should have bought a four-leafed clover on the way to the game as the Gods laughed at his immense efforts to score as he resembled nobody more than Sisyphus carrying his boulder up the hill before letting it drop at the final hurdle. On any other day he would have been celebrating a hat trick. After hitting the post before the break, he peeled away to the back post at a Jota corner and his twisting volley flew inches over, as did a twenty yarder that was hit like a shell. Right on time he had another perfectly hit volley blocked by former loanee Ryan Fredericks as it flew towards goal. It just wasn't his day.

Jota too had a long ranger well saved and Tarkowski could only hit the side netting from a tight angle. The final blow came in the dying moments of added time when Bidwell played a half-cleared corner back into the danger area and for once the ball dropped our way and Jonathan Douglas hit a close range effort that was heroically blocked by the keeper. How I hated that giant keeper Konstantopoulos when he, along with the towering Michael Nelson would so often prove an impassable barrier when playing against us for Hartlepool, and now he came back to haunt us yet again with another match winning display.

I watched the entire match again this morning and can now reflect on things in a calmer and more dispassionate manner. We really should take a deep breath and simply appreciate and take pride and delight in that we took probably the best and most organised team in the Championship right to the wire and both could and should have beaten them. We certainly missed Alan Judge and his speed of thought and trickery who would have moved the ball around quicker than we did but even without him, we created more than enough chances to win two matches. That we didn't win is really down to ourselves as we contributed to our unjustified defeat by shooting ourselves in the foot. It is a football truism that you have to score when you are on top, and in all honesty we totally dominated the first half with almost seventy percent possession. The chances we created were better than decent and at least two of them should have been put away. That would have forced Middlesbrough to come out at us rather than play on the break and we then could have done what they tried to do with us and picked them off.

More Haste Less Speed – 3/2/15

The Transfer Window shut late last night and there have been several murmurings on social media and the message boards that Brentford did not do enough and failed to address their major problems. In order to decide where the truth lies let's first try and put things into context. Here we are on the third of February, basking in the warm glow of achievement with Brentford currently sitting proudly in fifth place in the Championship, well in contention for a playoff place or even automatic promotion to the Premier League. How incredible an achievement is that when the most optimistic of supporters would have been more than happy with a season of consolidation? As it is, we have totally exceeded all expectations and are way ahead of the club's own ambitious plans for future progress.

Time is truly on our side. In my opinion, we have to reconcile two opposing points of view: firstly, more haste, less speed and then *carpe diem*. The club has planned for structured growth and whilst the Premier League is the ultimate goal, I am sure that nobody involved at Brentford even considered that becoming a serious possibility before the move to Lionel Road and having facilities appropriate enough for us to cope with the jump in status and capitalise upon the revenue opportunities provided by the Premier League. I will also remind you that only a year or so ago the stated hope of most Brentford fans was that we would be in the Championship rather than Division One when we moved to our new stadium, and now we are talking about the Premier League! How far have we come in so short a period of time!

The question is whether we should perhaps mortgage our future by gambling on expensive new acquisitions in the hope of going up this season or if, instead, we should take a more patient and measured approach? Opportunities need to be grasped and the fact that this season has gone so swimmingly is no guarantee that next year will be even better. It should be, given the sound foundations put in place, but you never know what the future has in store.

We all expected promotion last season as a natural progression after the Doncaster and Yeovil disappointments in 2013, and on the face of it we achieved this feat extremely comfortably with a triumphant procession to the Championship, and yet there was a tipping point, after the defeat at Stevenage in October, when we were floundering in mid table with confidence at a low ebb and disaffection within the ranks, and without the now famous post match discussion which totally turned our season around, who knows where we might have finished?

Let's now look dispassionately at what Brentford actually achieved in the January transfer window. For the glass half-empty brigade we did not lose any of our star assets. Who knows if there were any serious approaches for the likes of Alan Judge, Jota, Moses Odubajo and Andre Gray but all of them remain with us for the remainder of the campaign and any predators have been thwarted.

We also brought in four new players. Josh Laurent, a promising young midfielder arrived from our local rivals QPR and it has been highly amusing to eavesdrop on all the internal squabbling that his departure caused at Loftus Road where the club appears to be in total disarray. At first sight he is a typical Brentford player, comfortable on the ball, fast, strong and eager to prove himself. Chris Long has also arrived on loan from Everton, where he is highly regarded, to boost our attacking options. Of course he is young and untried but he is a raw talent who impressed in his initial outing at Norwich when he helped us over the line in his late cameo appearance. Lewis Macleod and Jack O'Connell are a totally different kettle of fish, though. Two young, promising players, bursting with ability and potential and yet we have managed to spirit them away from their previous clubs, taking advantage of their desperate financial straits.

It has been the case, going back over the years, that Brentford were robbed of their best prospects for derisory fees. Now the boot is firmly on the other foot – and doesn't it feel good! Lewis is slowly recovering from a niggling hamstring injury and will shortly be back in action and I believe that he will make a significant impact throughout the remainder of the season. Generally acknowledged to be one of the most promising players in Scotland and a member of the full international squad, his potential is frightening. The supporters at Rangers have still not really got over his departure to a supposed minnow like Brentford.

Yesterday, twenty year-old Jack O'Connell arrived from Blackburn for a bargain fee. Jack who? Was the question on the lips of most Brentford supporters, but fans of Blackburn Rovers and Rochdale, where he has had two highly successful loan spells, are well aware of his identity and ability. Here are some of the comments about him on the Blackburn message boards:

He's got a quality left foot, he's big & strong with pace.

He's very good in the air and is head and shoulders above both centre halves we have at the moment. He can actually pass a ball.

Our best defensive prospect in years,

The best prospect we have had since Phil Jones

This lad is quality

This one might come back to haunt us

Sky Sports also recently highlighted O'Connell as one of the most promising young players in the country and produced the following scouting report on him:

Jack O'Connell has been hugely impressive for Rochdale this season. Liverpool-born O'Connell is an unusual case, given that as a youngster he almost slipped through the net, and was not picked up by any club until he was 18 when he joined Blackburn. A year after signing, he was handed his first professional deal and months later he was making his league debut, but with Rotherham United, who he joined on a three-month loan. By this point O'Connell's displays for Blackburn's second string had also attracted attention from England's coaching team, and he was capped by the Under 18s. After returning from his spell with Rotherham he was snapped up by York City, where he spent five months and really emerged as a real prospect.

Rochdale agreed a six-month loan deal for O'Connell last summer, which was soon extended to the full campaign, and his displays at Spotland have not gone unnoticed. Indeed Keith Hill has also handed him the captain's armband, such has been his progress. He has also captained England's Under 19 side as he continues to be recognised at international level.

O'Connell is a cultured defender, and has a real touch of class about him as he often looks to bring the ball out of defence before looking to open up play. O'Connell, who is also capable of operating at full-back, has an excellent left foot and he uses it with great effect to often try and switch play from the back. Despite his inexperience, O'Connell has come on hugely in the past 18 months and he looks destined for a high level. He is an outstanding prospect, who has made great strides since joining Blackburn. Very much one to watch and already has a number of Premier League clubs monitoring him.

The Scout rating:

- *Shooting: 5/10*
- *Passing: 7/10*
- *Tackling: 7/10*
- *Heading: 7/10*

- *Pace: 6/10*
- *Vision: 6/10*
- *Current ability: 6/10*
- *Potential ability: 8/10*

OVERALL SCOUT RATING: 52/80

Current value: £500,000

Potential value: £8million

This is the player that we picked up yesterday for a fee rumoured to be less than a quarter of a million pounds. Not bad, and what's not to like about this move?

His arrival is just one more in a catalogue of recent arrivals who all share similar characteristics: young, talented, hungry, and eager to improve, and I am certain they will eventually take us to where we intend to go – the Premier League.

How long is it since the club possessed young players of the ability of James Tarkowski, Alan Judge, Moses Odubajo, Lewis Macleod, Scott Hogan, Andre Gray, Jota and now O'Connell? All of these players have been signed within the last year and they could be worth millions of pounds to the club as they are all appreciating assets of a calibre rarely seen before at the club. That is also without even mentioning the calibre of recent loanees such as Jon Toral and Alex Pritchard.

Yes, at first sight it would have been nice if we had blown an inflated fee on an experienced journeyman striker yesterday, but we all know the potential cost of such a move if it doesn't pay off, as has been the case to date with Nick Proschwitz (who scored a well-taken goal last night for the Development Squad). I am sure that we tried to buy a promising striker from abroad earlier in the window but our efforts were rebuffed.

We will continue to conduct our business in a calm, rational, measured and planned way. I am sure that when the loan window reopens shortly we might consider a short term deal for another striker if the need continues, or maybe even another central defender given that it is expected that O'Connell will go out on loan, but then again, that was the plan for Tarkowski this time last year too!

The name of Swansea's giant defender Kyle Bartley was also mentioned in despatches last night and who knows if he will arrive in a couple of weeks to bolster our squad?

We are in good and safe hands, we are well ahead of schedule and we will continue to do things in the manner that has been proved to work over the last couple of years. We are truly fortunate to be supporters of a club that is so well run and managed and has a clear blueprint for success.

No Complaints At All – 4/2/15

I wrote of our need to review the transfer window and the fact that over the course of the month Brentford had succeeded in bringing in four players and losing nobody. They had also resisted the temptation to bring in an experienced striker to support Andre Gray and instead decided to keep their powder dry should a short-term addition be required once the loan window reopens shortly.

I felt that the club had acted carefully and responsibly and simply kept to their tried and tested blueprint of improving the squad slowly but surely and concentrating on bringing in young players with huge development potential.

I waited for the fallout but I was gratified to discover that the overwhelming majority of the comments I received totally agreed with the club's actions. David Carney just seemed to wonder what all the fuss was about:

Spot on, of course, but far too much analysis by just about every Brentford supporter. The simple fact is that Matthew Benham has a clear vision for success and the creation of a dynasty. In setting out to achieve that vision, he has seen the absolute necessity to have the very best mix of minds that create an outstanding football club. Benham knew Mark Warburton before he worked at Brentford and knew exactly how his mind ticked AND what a wonderful technical football and people-motivating mind it is, alongside his understanding of Team Environment.

Add into the mix David Weir, Frank McParland, Mark Devlin, the other coaches, medical staff, academy, etc, and there is a unit that is the equal to, if not better than, any other football club in the UK. Everyone outside that select group running Brentford FC is unaware of the detailed planning and strategies being implemented, cost pressures, personal player issues, competition from other clubs, etc. All we know is that this is one hell of a trip and very few football supporters at any club experience the development of a dynasty on their doorstep as we are witnessing now. I first saw Brentford in 1954 and there has never been anything like what is happening now – so just enjoy the ride, enjoy the wins and do not become an instant expert. We have Benham, Warbs and the rest of the team to do all that for us. Our role is simply to support and enjoy.

I wish it was so simple David and that all of us were as phlegmatic as you appear to be! We all live and breathe Brentford FC and it is hard not to scrutinise, *kibitz* and even criticise simply because we care so much and are desperate for things to work out as we believe they can and will. Mike Rice also felt strongly that we need to remember how far we have come in so short a time and that we have kept to our pre-planned strategy without attempting to *live the dream* or run before we can walk:

Your remarks got me musing on when exactly did the change take place? Mark Warburton's arrival at the club was clearly highly influential, but my trip to Wembley, when he was assisting Nicky Forster, did little to change my "stated hope". Uwe Rösler also represented a sea change in attitude at the club, but as you say, there were still the "Stevenage talks". I have trouble with the chronology, of who arrived when and before whom, but I think two factors have played an enormous part: our ability to attract the likes of Adam Forshaw and Jake Bidwell on loan, and Matthew Benham's reticence to "splash the cash".

Ever since he has arrived at the club he has matched his generosity to the position of the club, and the ability of those running it to spend his money wisely. Nobody knows how much he is worth, but the money has always been there in sufficient quantities, but never more than necessary.

When Bees United took over, he stood back and injected the bare minimum to get by. That clearly wasn't going to work, so he took more of a stake in the club and spent a bit more money. Andy Scott was given just enough cash to get us out of League Two. We have never been at the top of the pile in terms of playing budget, but have had enough for an astute manager (and director of football) to bring in players, set up loans, adopt a playing style and achieve success. Not for Matthew Benham the Chelsea or Man City approach. He has never flung money at the problem. He has shown admirable restraint. How easy would it have been for him after the Doncaster/Yeovil season to throw money at the problem? And when we did get into the Championship, he increased the budget enough to make a few key acquisitions, all young and good investments for the future, but not enough to attract the attention of the media or our "biggers and betters" with their parachute payments. Of course, the FFP regs now come into the equation, but I bet Brentford, with some of the smallest gates in the league, do not fall foul of it.

Similarly, I bet Brentford's playing budget (and player expenditure) may put us in the top half of the money table, but by no means matches our league position. At this moment in time, I believe Brentford has the perfect combination of wise owner and loyal lieutenants in Mark Warburton, David Weir, Mark Devlin and Frank McParland, who all share the same vision for the club and fully agree the means of achieving it. This combination has worked so well that we are now ahead of the timetable. But that is no reason not to believe that all that has been achieved won't last. Indeed, while many including me scoffed at the idea of an Academy as being above our station or a bottomless money pit, I can now see it is all part of Matthew Benham's long-term plan. It will hopefully provide a steady stream of the kind of players we now take on loan or buy for £1 million. So getting back to when the change in my "stated hope" happened. I think it was the moment – after a first half in which we were the total underdogs – Stuart Dallas connected with the thunderbolt that put Derby firmly in their place.

Luis Adriano was far more vehement and bullish in his comments about how happy he is with how the club is being run and that we managed to keep hold of our prime assets:

Seriously, anybody whinging about our business in the transfer window needs to have a visit from the Ghost of Transfer Deadlines Past... Remember Nicky Forster? Remember DJ?... Some of the best business in these times is in simply keeping hold of the talent you already have. How would you feel if Harry Redknapp actually knew his stuff and spent his time on Monday chasing our talented youngsters rather than his usual preference for has beens like Adebayor? Or he wasn't too busy trying to get an exchange on his duff Christmas present from West Ham?

Just imagine that Crystal Palace had taken Andre Gray off our hands giving us a quick profit... Or if Jota had been snapped up by a Premier League or La Liga club willing to invest in his potential.

We have KEPT HOLD OF OUR VALUABLE ASSETS. HOORAH.

We got Long in on loan and he is clearly a talented boy. There's our cover up front in addition to "Big Nick" who actually scored a goal on Monday night. Some people don't know how good we've got it right now.

Also, would you rather we bought a modern day equivalent of Neil Shipperley? I'm sure there are plenty out there. That is NOT how we do things now.

Honestly, I read/hear people moan and can't help shaking my head.

It is also important that we don't just become satisfied with where we are. When we see the Ghost of Transfer Deadlines Future, I don't want it to be saying, "ah yes, 2015, that's the best you'll ever have it". I think we need to get the balance right of understanding where we came from and enjoying careful, steady progress.

I have every faith that there won't be a second season syndrome struggle if we don't go up this year. Just consider how much losing a playoff final can muck teams up. Look at Orient as the most recent of many examples. When I came away from our Yeovil game though, I knew we'd go up the following season.

Don't underestimate the intelligence of the people we have in charge and generally around the place these days. We have brought in players, staff with the correct mentality (as well as knowledge of the game) to succeed. This is why if we get close but no cigar again (I can't see us/anyone ever getting as close as a crossbar away), I'm sure we'll just continue to come back stronger. If we do go up to the Premier League, there is every possibility we'd come straight back down. Not a guarantee, just a fact of financial life. If we did, I'm sure we'd rebuild and just go up even tougher next time round.

So basically, enjoy where we are right now. There shouldn't really be any true Bees fan whinging these days. It's not been better in most of our lifetimes. We just haven't reached our pinnacle yet.

TRUST the people in charge. They know what they are doing and they will continue driving us on this wonderful journey.

There is absolutely nothing that I can add to those wonderful words. Thank you everyone – and thank you Brentford FC too!

Fathers And Sons – 8/2/15

Sometimes your day is touched with gold dust and you sit back the following morning and just bask in the happiness that is coursing through your entire being. This is how I am feeling today. My son, Nick, is twenty-three now, nearly three years out from graduating with a Politics degree from Leeds University, and he is making his way in the world. He is doing just fine, he has an admirable work ethic, is never one to give up, or complain too much, he is kind and thoughtful, his current success is well deserved and his future is bright. He is establishing himself in his career, has moved into a lovely new flat and has some decent and caring friends. He also manages to find some time in his frenetic schedule for his loving and proud parents, and yesterday was one of those days.

Replete from a wonderful Friday night chicken dinner, lovingly prepared by his incredible Mother, we waddled to the car and set off bright and early together for Leeds.

Don't think for one moment that Nick is a football fan, at best he tolerates it for my sake, but he wanted a lift to Leeds so that he could spend some time with his old University friends and the cost of the ride was to pass the day with me and watch Brentford play at

Elland Road. Nick used to come with me occasionally to Highbury where, as a teenager, he was tempted more by the plush leather seats and the wonderful archaic sweets kiosk outside the stadium: *Two for a Pound* was the stentorian cry, and I can hear it still resonating across the room as I write.

He had done his homework and the journey up passed in a torrent of conversation about his life and aspirations, *New Brentford* and the likely date for the move to Lionel Road. Nick is well clued up on transport and planning issues and was keen to pass on his thoughts and advice. The hours seemed like minutes as we flew up the M1 and the only mystery was why I never seemed to get a red wine gum whenever Nick passed me the packet as I drove – a real conundrum that will remain forever unsolved.

We parked beside the stadium at midday and decided to forgo the pleasure of a walk around the town centre but instead spent a lovely lazy hour or so in McDonald's, reading the papers, totally comfortable in each other's company with no need for constant conversation. A perfect morning! Frankly I would have been more than happy if the day had ended then after quality time spent with my son and a feeling of warmth, love and contentment, but there was to be no end to the delights of the day.

Little Old Brentford simply took over Elland Road, a dilapidated mess of a stadium, that, like its team and rabid fans has seen far better days. Jethro Tull's *Living In The Past* should replace the tired and creaking and faintly martial *Marching On Together* as the club's anthem. Their supporters, incandescent with rage, and fuelled with frustration and thwarted aggression, spent the entire match harking back to their past glories, and a time when they really were good. Despite their enhanced sense of entitlement, condescension and disbelief at the indignity of having to play the likes of Brentford, it was hard not to feel a little bit sorry for them given how they have been sold down the river by a seemingly never-ending series of unsympathetic owners.

Brentford just played their football as only they can do. It took time for them to gel and they were slightly off the pace in a goalless first half that saw Leeds, inspired by the skilful Cook and Murphy, two players in the Brentford mould, huff and puff and press us high up the pitch, but seldom threaten. We simply sat back, held the ball and probed for openings when we were finally able to beat the press. Pritchard's gorgeous flick sent Gray hurtling through the Leeds defence with a clear run in on goal. Bamba chased after him, his hot breath on his collar, and for an unworthy millisecond I hoped that the straining defender would catch Andre and bring him down for a certain red card and penalty but Gray held him off before only finding the keeper with his shot when he had to score. His overall hold up play and movement was as excellent as ever yesterday but he has lost his touch in front of goal and Mark Warburton could be seen on the touchline visibly encouraging his faltering striker. We can only hope that his fallow spell ends shortly before his profligacy costs us dear. I watched Callum Wilson score comfortably for Bournemouth at Wigan from two similar opportunities last night and that is the difference between a striker at the top of his game and a player still accustoming himself to the rigours of league football. It will come for him – it has to, if we are to maintain our exalted place in the Championship table.

Jota too missed horribly when he was left clean through and dillied and dallied on another occasion without getting his shot off. Pritchard was taken out by Cooper when running through and the defender saw yellow when red might well have been the verdict. We defended well when necessary and were troubled only when Morrison forced a comfortable save from an otherwise untroubled Button. Dean committed his one weekly error and sliced horribly past his own post and Moses tussled with Austin who was too keen to go to ground and we escaped without punishment.

We upped the tempo in the second half and Leeds could not live with us. Douglas and Diagouraga were an impassable barrier and Prichard's feet twinkled to good effect. We dominated without looking dangerous until Toral replaced the ineffective Jota and his physicality and tenacity gave us the impetus to break the deadlock. He charged down a clearance, ran menacingly into the area and slid Diagouraga through, and the straining Douglas thankfully missed his perfectly weighted low centre before Pritchard scored easily. We erupted with joy, the Leeds supporters reacted with fury – how could they be possibly be losing to the likes of us? It had to be someone else's fault, so they picked on the referee, Graham Salisbury, not one of my favourites from our previous encounters with him, including the JPT Final against Carlisle and the recent penalty incident at Watford. He stood firm, though, and protected our players from the brunt of the physical onslaught of a frustrated home team and denied them two penalty kicks after blatant dives from the overly aggressive Austin.

As always after we have scored, we looked for another, and Toral smashed a beautifully controlled volley against the post before Long, who put in an excellent shift, twice came close to breaking his duck, under-hitting a clear chance from in front of goal and then failing to beat Silvestri from a tight angle. As always, there was a sting in the tail and Sharp shot wastefully wide from an excellent opportunity before an almighty scramble in front of the Brentford goal saw last minute disaster averted through Bidwell's brave and brilliant defending.

So we won, and in all honesty our victory was far more comfortable than the score suggests. We were tight and organised at the back and stood up to considerable intimidation from a committed home team. We concentrate on playing the beautiful game but we are also not a soft touch anymore and Dean, Tarkowski, Bidwell, Odebajo, Douglas, Dallas and Diagouraga all put their bodies on the line and were resilient and committed. We are coming of age and wins like this show just how far we have travelled and the development potential that still remains within the entire squad.

Like the Bees, my son Nick is still a work in progress but he has already become a young man of substance, stature, charm and ability. He too is on a long journey and one that will, I am sure, end in happiness, fulfilment and success. I am delighted and proud to accompany both of them on their voyage of discovery.

Sour Grapes and Self-Delusion! – 9/2/15

Any impartial and objective observer would have agreed that Brentford fully deserved to win at Elland Road on Saturday. Their margin of victory was narrow and Brentford squeaked home thanks to a single goal from Alex Pritchard. The statistics, though, tell a totally different tale. Brentford dominated possession, attempted and completed far more passes than the opposition, committed fewer fouls and had more shots on target. David

Button walked off the pitch at the end of the game with his kit unblemished, so little did he have to do.

Leeds had appealed in desperation for three penalty kicks, one of which appeared to be a close call, but had otherwise only threatened in the last few minutes when they made a desperate late surge towards the Brentford goal and forced a few scrambles which might have gone their way had it not been for some resolute defending. The referee was strong and did not allow himself to be swayed by the baying hordes of home supporters screaming for free kicks and penalties.

Brentford held out for a comfortable win and their only complaint would have been that they had missed a number of gilt-edged chances to make their victory far more conclusive and less stressful right at the end. Leeds icon Eddie Gray fully agreed with this assessment and stated that the best team had won:

I don't think Leeds were unlucky to lose to Brentford on Saturday.

I thought we should have had a penalty kick in the first half and I thought the referee was very average. But most of the major decisions he got right. Neil Redfearn also thought we should have had a penalty in the second half but I didn't think that was a penalty kick and that's just opinions. But I thought we were second best in the game and Brentford deserved to win. Brentford are one of the better teams in the league and we're not at that level yet I don't think.

A perusal of the Leeds message boards quickly demonstrated that a mere handful of fair-minded home fans shared his viewpoint, but even then there was generally a patronising sting in the tail:

I hate reading that Brentford are better than us and we are still a long way behind them. Having supported Leeds United during the Bremner, Giles, Gray era it's very hard to accept that Brentford can be better than us. I know it's true but it just fills me with sadness. Let's hope we don't have to wait too long before Super Leeds are back where they belong.

I totally agree with you Eddie, Brentford, were the best side to visit Elland Road this season, they did their homework on Leeds and we did not force a single save from their keeper, but we were worth a point because of our gutsy performance.

There was a sense of disbelief that not only was it ludicrous that a team like Leeds, steeped in history and past glories, should be forced to sully their hands and demean themselves by actually having to play the likes of Brentford but that we should have then fallen down at their feet, paid homage to them and allowed them to walk all over us. Just read some of the other comments that more accurately reflected the sour, bitter and twisted mood of the Leeds supporters:

But it's an indication of where we are at the moment as a club that we can't beat Brentford.

We are Leeds, we are being victimised by referees.

That referee wants kicking out of football – Leeds players were kicked off their feet time and time again – he gave Brentford ALL the free kicks, Austin was thrown to the ground in the penalty area – and he gives Brentford a free kick. I lost count of how many blatant corners we SHOULD have had – the Football League is corrupt.

I never thought I would see the day when Brentford would take six points off us.

However, with the assistance of Mr Salisbury and his officiating team, Brentford couldn't really lose the game.

It wasn't just the clear penalty that Leeds were denied in the first half that made it an inept performance, but the referee's clear insistence in giving Leeds absolutely nothing, whilst gifting Brentford a free-kick almost every time a tackle was made.

Although they had possession United rarely troubled Brentford's keeper but we still didn't deserve to lose.

Is there any way that the performance of the officials can be examined and questioned by the Football League?

If Leeds were not allowed to play football and were constantly pulled back, then the Football League needs to look at the wider implications of that.

I have never read so much myopic and delusional drivel in my life. Their argument can best be summed up as: we are Leeds, we have a divine right to win and when we don't then it can only be someone else's fault, and by the way there is a conspiracy against us too.

Everything about Elland Road was living in the past: the aggressive and one-eyed home fans who bayed at the referee and the away fans throughout the game, the way we were packed away in a distant, dank and dark corner of the ground and ripped off for the privilege, the constant tape loop before the game of, admittedly, great goals from their far and distant past and the distinctly old-fashioned and faintly martial club song that resonated around the ground. Leeds remain in a time warp and are firmly stuck in the early and mid 70's, a period when they deservedly dominated the English game. It is easier and more comfortable for them to remain there, in their bunker, than take the tougher approach of self-examination and understanding why the world has passed them by. Their fans cannot and will not accept that they have fallen upon hard times through *living the dream* and abject mismanagement as well as the normal cyclical nature of good fortune and success.

They have a well-developed sense of entitlement and arrogance which was truly bemusing to witness in the flesh and then read about. And yet, in truth, loyal Leeds supporters deserve far more than they have received over the past decade and more, and their reaction to Saturday's defeat was simply their coping mechanism as they are totally unable to comprehend that the football world has moved on and their prehistoric tactics and approach have been superseded by a new breed with clubs such as Bournemouth and Brentford at the forefront. The fact that Brentford took six points from Leeds this season without conceding a goal or barely a shot on target speaks volumes and should be lesson enough for the Leeds fans, but there's none so blind as those who will not see.

A Day To Forget – 11/2/15

Football has a way of taking you to the heights and then allowing you to plummet to the depths and as good as Saturday was, with our triumphant day out at Leeds, Tuesday was ten times worse. In fact, I would go as far as saying that I cannot remember a day as depressing to be a Brentford fan since… I really do not know when, but I am sure another disaster will eventually come to mind.

The day started with the massive shock of experienced journalist Matt Hughes's exclusive story in *The Times* claiming that Matthew Benham has already made the decision to dispense with manager Mark Warburton's services at the end of the season and that clandestine talks were held in Spain last week with Paco Jémez, the Rayo Vallecano coach with a view to him taking over the reins at Griffin Park next season. The former Deportivo La Coruña, Real Zaragoza, and Spanish International centre back has impressed as a manager with an attacking, positive and progressive bent but no more so than Warburton, a true diamond in the rough who has led the Bees to promotion and a totally unexpected position in the Championship playoff zone. He has established a justified reputation as one of a new breed of modern forward-looking managers. He has operated on a rolling twelve-month contract since succeeding Uwe Rösler, and according to the article, he has apparently been told that it will not be renewed at the end of the campaign irrespective of what he achieves for the remainder of the season.

The club issued a verbose, vague and woolly statement that in essence did nothing to allay the supporters' fears. It merely confirmed that Warburton will remain in charge for the remainder of the season, that his abundant qualities have been noticed by other clubs and that Brentford FC is simply keeping its options open should the need arise. We are also a progressive club who do talk to other people within the game to learn about other ways of doing things, and to consider novel strategic approaches to the game.

What on earth are we supposed to make of that tortuous gobbledegook? Who on earth knows and only time will tell, but like many other supporters I felt that *New Brentford* were not like other clubs and did not shoot themselves in the foot nor wash their dirty linen in public.

The statement begs more questions than it provides answers to, and leaves me with the firm belief that the original article is pretty close to the truth and that our current manager's days at the club are indeed numbered. Who can tell who leaked the story to the journalist and I would only assume that nobody at the club intended for it to break at such a sensitive time in the season when we are poised to make our promotion push and that the statement is merely a quick response to a story that has broken unexpectedly.

From Mark Warburton's point of view, if the owner has in fact, already confirmed the bad news to him, does he stick or twist? Will yesterday's events make him even more keen to remain in situ until the end of the season when his contract expires and simply try and see the job through and lead Brentford to promotion, or will he seek to jump ship and find long term stability should another opportunity immediately present itself? No employee can be blamed for looking after his own interests and ensuring his own and his family's future. I think it will be the former and he will be more steely-eyed and determined than ever to leave at the apex of his success if his contract is indeed not going to be renewed.

As for an explanation for this shock decision, should indeed there be truth in it, I can only assume that Matthew Benham is looking to accelerate the development of the club which is already running far ahead of schedule and believes that just as Uwe Rösler was an improvement over Andy Scott, and Mark Warburton was a far better bet than Rösler, he simply wishes to upgrade yet again and is already looking to the future. He has made the dispassionate decision that by bringing in a foreign coach and allowing him to invest he will be in a better position than Warburton to attract high quality players from around Europe and build a truly cosmopolitan team that can sustain a place in the Premier League and allow Brentford to sup at the top table.

Benham has both the funds and the single-minded focus, drive and ambition to make his plans come to fruition and he is not renowned for making either hasty or irrational decisions or ones unsubstantiated by facts. His data and statistics-driven approach has been an unqualified success and I suspect that he sees himself playing a key role in shaping the club's overall strategy, recruitment policy and playing style and wants a manager who totally buys into his approach.

What about the club's fantastic and highly qualified back room staff? Will men of the calibre of David Weir, Frank McParland and the array of analysts and fitness coaches also be swept away with the bathwater and will any new arrival have to rebuild from scratch? There is only one person qualified to answer such questions and our reclusive owner is not speaking. As the sole owner of the club what Matthew Benham wants, Matthew Benham gets, and so far he has made very few mistakes.

Do I want a foreign manager and a team packed with continental imports – no, not really. I would ideally like a blend of foreign and homegrown talent as Spaniards such as Jota and Toral have made a fantastic impact and I certainly want us to continue improving, but not at the cost of losing our West London identity. I am certainly not a Little Englander but I want a sense of balance and proportion to reign and I hope that Matthew Benham bears that in mind when deciding how best to progress.

As if that was not unsettling enough, just to pile Pelion on Ossa, Brentford came across referee Keith Stroud at his enigmatic worst on Tuesday night as every major decision went against the Bees and led to an unlucky and contentious home defeat to promotion rivals Watford. Jake Bidwell's one-footed challenge was late and slightly high but the red card was instantaneous as was the decision to penalise Jonathan Douglas when the ball bounced off his shoulder, although the brilliant Button saved Troy Deeney's spot kick.

Stroud has so much previous against Brentford it is hard and pretty pointless to know where to start and I do not want to demean myself by resorting to pointless personal abuse. Just as Leeds moaned about Graham Salisbury on Saturday, we are doing the same about Stroud last night as he choked the life out of us. We subsided to a late and totally dispiriting defeat after fighting so hard and even having the temerity to take the lead when Andre Gray ran onto David Button's perfectly placed long clearance, shrugged off his marker who was hanging onto him like a limpet and hammered an unstoppable shot into the roof of the net. Brentford scoring a Route One goal is almost beyond belief but it inspired us and we so nearly hung on for a well-deserved point. But it wasn't to be as a last minute goal brought Watford the points and an unmerited double over the Bees.

Andre Gray holds off two Watford defenders.

But it gets still worse. James Tarkowski, so impeccable in everything he did, suffered at the hands of Deeney and limped off soon after half time. Let's hope that it is nothing more than a dead leg and that he will recover quickly. Barring the miracle of a successful appeal (although we did get Ricky Newman's Stroud-inflicted red card against Huddersfield rescinded back in 2006) we are struggling for a left back for the next three games. Stuart Dallas deputised valiantly in an unfamiliar role and Tony Craig, Nico Yennaris and Alan McCormack will all come into consideration at Charlton on Saturday, particularly as new signing Jack O'Connell, who has extensive experience at left back was yesterday loaned back to Rochdale for the remainder of the season. Maybe a decision that is now looking a little short-sighted and premature.

The season has been one of total pleasure and progress and yesterday was undoubtedly a major setback. What happens now is totally up to our owner and I suspect that Matthew Benham is not a man for turning.

What Next? – 12/2/15

So what has happened over the course of the past twenty-four hours in the Brentford soap opera? In reality, not too much new information has been made public. As you would expect, there have been public votes of support for Mark Warburton from players such as Harlee Dean, Tommy Smith and Richard Lee and the team made it perfectly clear how much they value and respect their manager by their choreographed and moving celebration with Warburton after Andre Gray's goal on Tuesday night.

Players are generally the last to be informed about off-field developments and are always best advised to stay out of club politics and shenanigans so I simply take their actions at face value: as a heart-warming demonstration of support for their beleaguered manager. There is no doubt of the depth of their respect for Mark as was made clear by Harlee Dean in his recent interview in the excellent *Thorne In The Side* fanzine when he described Warburton as: *someone who wants to do better himself and give that chance to those around him. He encourages all of us to succeed and wants everyone to be the best they can be.*

It is rare to read such a ringing and heartfelt endorsement of a manager's capabilities so if it is generally recognised and accepted that Mark Warburton is exceptionally good at what he does, why does Matthew Benham apparently want to replace him and his management team too? We will have to wait for the Brentford owner to make his reasons public and he hinted in two enigmatic tweets early yesterday morning that the last twenty-four hours had been very difficult for him, that he was acting in the long term interests of the club and that he would try to explain the situation more in the next couple of days.

So whilst we are waiting for further developments and revelations we can only speculate on what has been going on behind the scenes at the club. Given Mark Warburton's evident success and no suggestion that he has in any way passed his sell-by date, why should our owner allegedly wish to dispense with not only his services but also, as has been speculated, those of Sporting Director, Frank McParland, as well?

There was a clue in *The Times* yesterday, which reported that the manager had not wished to accept the offer of additional coaching resources, in particular a free kick coach and a sleep guru. These suggestions are so bizarre that they can only be true and are symptomatic of the owner's approach, which is to ensure that all avenues are explored, no matter how seemingly outlandish, so that we can exploit every potential advantage given that matches are decided by such small margins. A fact that we have discovered to our cost time after time this season.

Perhaps Mark Warburton was resistant to change and not as receptive to such novel ideas as the owner anticipated and expected, and Benham is looking for somebody who will embrace new ideas and philosophies and work hand in glove with him rather than against him?

Given that our record from set pieces this season is abysmal, you would have thought that any help in that area would have been welcomed with open arms, particularly given the proportion of goals that other teams seem to score from their set pieces.

Maybe we are not progressing as quickly as Matthew Benham desires, despite the generally accepted view that we are moving far faster than anticipated. In that regard there has been much speculation in previous months about the likely arrival of high quality foreign players and yet none of them have materialised.

Perhaps the owner wants to move quicker than the manager in terms of bringing in new players and he feels that Warburton is too loyal to his existing squad? Assuming we have made serious efforts to sign them then why have we not been able to get any of these deals over the line? Certainly we are now competing for a better class of player with teams with greater resources than ours who might well be playing at a higher level, and we all know that transfer deals are fraught with problems with so many parties appearing out of the woodwork claiming to represent any footballer of note. But that is why we have a Sporting Director in place and given that the media have reported Frank McParland's possible departure too, maybe his performances and perceived lack of results have also come under scrutiny by Matthew Benham?

A new manager might well take on board more of Benham's philosophies and buy into his proven data and stats-driven approach and allow the owner to contribute more fully. He might also be more receptive to an influx of higher quality players from abroad. Maybe, too, there is a potential cross-fertilisation of ideas and best practice from our association with Danish Superliga side FC Midtjylland that could be better exploited?

As for the leak in *The Times* the other day, I suspect that that is far more easily explained. There were reports a week or so ago from Spain that the club had apparently been in contact with Paco Jemez of Rayo Vallecano and these filtered through to the UK, and were indeed mentioned briefly on *The Griffin Park Grapevine*. Perhaps they were brought to the attention of Mark Warburton who, not unnaturally, approached Matthew Benham for clarification. Whatever actually happened, the result was inevitable and the cat was out of the bag.

As to who was responsible for the leak, I need do no more than refer you to the old Latin adage *cui bono* – or *who benefits* and let you make your own mind up.

So what happens now? The damage has been done and Matthew Benham's plans for what I am sure was intended to be a seamless if painful transition at the end of the season have been totally scuppered. The club has been holed beneath the waterline, morale has been shattered, the unique relationship and bond between club and supporters has been cast asunder and Mark Warburton is a dead man walking.

Mark Warburton is a man of great strength and determination and I can only hope that he remains totally fixed upon the task in hand – getting promotion, and remains in situ until the end of the season, assuming that no rapprochement can be reached between him and Matthew Benham, something that is highly unlikely to occur. Benham too is a totally focused and single-minded individual who is used to being proved right and to getting his own way. Assuming he has decided to make changes in the management structure then I am sure that is what is going to happen and when his mind is made up, he rarely if ever changes it. Whether he is proved right or wrong is for the future. He has made his decision, hopefully discussed it with his advisors and taken their counsel on board.

What cannot be questioned is his total commitment to and love for Brentford FC and his determination to do what is best for the club: improve us and never put our future in jeopardy. Maybe a truce can be brokered, wounds can be patched up and smiles, even if only a rictus grin, can return to peoples' faces? We can but hope. This has been a season of total triumph and it would be unconscionable if it should all fall apart because of the owner's leaked intentions.

The further complication is whether both parties will come to the conclusion that Warburton's position is now untenable or other clubs will swoop down on us and attempt to prise him from our clutches even at this late stage of the season. There are two Premier League clubs currently looking for managers with a third potentially having a vacancy in the near future. At least one of them is, I know, an admirer of Mark Warburton and what he can offer. Assuming that he has been advised that his contract will not be renewed at the end of the season, Mark has to look after his own best interests and consider all his options. The nightmare scenario is that he is offered and accepts another job, walks out with his entire back room staff and we are left high and dry and rudderless for the remainder of the season. That is a prospect that hardly bears thinking about, but is in my mind, a possibility.

I wish I could be more positive but we are now in a real pickle and the immediate future is totally unsettled. I can see a point at the end of the season when a new manager arrives from abroad, perhaps a name that will surprise and excite us, and we move on to greater things with an influx of high profile foreign stars. Such is the way of football. What concerns me more is the here and now is what happens over the next few difficult days and weeks. All, I am sure, will be revealed shortly.

Lull Before The Storm – 13/2/15

There was little new to report regarding the Brentford management saga on Thursday. Mark Warburton attempted to take the heat out of the situation with a trademark cool, calm and collected press conference where in his customary self-effacing manner, he attempted to pass the spotlight back onto his players rather than discuss and enlarge upon the stand-off between himself and the Brentford owner Matthew Benham. Warburton stated that the club would be releasing another statement within the next day or so, ideally before the Charlton match on Saturday, and we can only hope that this one sheds more light on situation and is also more measured and apposite than the club's last miserable and appallingly drafted effort earlier this week. It simply fanned the flames rather than dousing them.

Quite what the statement will say is open to debate, however in my opinion the options are strictly limited. For reasons that I have already written about at great length, and see no purpose in reiterating, I cannot believe that Benham will go back on his decision to change the management team and structure at the end of the season by introducing a new foreign manager more attuned with his way of thinking and desired approach.

That really leaves very little wriggle room for all parties. Mark Warburton will ideally accept that decision with as good a grace as possible - it being the owner's prerogative - and state that he will remain until the end of the season to see out his contract and do his utmost to lead his players to either automatic promotion or the playoffs. That would enable the club to see out the season with minimal disruption, at least above the surface, and the two parties could continue to work together like a polite separated couple forced to share the marital home before the divorce becomes absolute. That is certainly not an ideal solution but I cannot for the life of me see a better or neater one.

The nuclear options would see Warburton walking out perhaps into another managerial position, or Benham deciding that the situation has now become unworkable and coming to an agreement for an early termination of Warburton's contract. That would strike me as cutting off your nose to spite your face and suit nobody as the team would be left leaderless and rudderless given that David Weir would doubtless leave with his boss, and we could end up with the inexperienced Lee Carsley, Kevin O'Connor and Simon Royce acting as caretakers as we come into the business end of the season. A terrible solution, and one that would undoubtedly spell the end of our promotion challenge.

The only other possibility, slim though it is, would see Warburton and Weir agree to stay on next season, perhaps in a reduced and changed role, but probably reporting to the new manager or head coach, however he is titled.

I cannot see these two proud and talented individuals, who in the eyes of the overwhelming majority of the supporters, as well I am sure in their own, have done little or nothing wrong, acceding to such a retrograde or backwards step.

As for the players, it is up to them to continue to act in a professional manner and simply get on with the job of winning football matches to the best of their ability. Whilst there is no *I* in *team*, footballers are essentially playing for themselves and to ensure their future. Whoever is the manager next season, or indeed, for the remainder of the current campaign, there are contracts and bonus payments to be earned and once they have absorbed and got over the initial upset and distraction I fully expect that the team will just get on with things. Indeed, the current situation might well prove be a motivating rather than destabilising influence on them all.

As it is, they will be going into a tough local derby at Charlton without the suspended Jake Bidwell and with James Tarkowski and Alex Pritchard also trying to recover in time from injuries sustained on Tuesday night against Watford. The whole squad will need to pull together as one and I hope that they are up to the task.

I remain in no doubt that the mid to long-term future for the club remains a glittering one, however it is the immediate short term that really concerns me, and whatever is currently being debated and hopefully agreed behind closed doors will decide how matters will turn out. This week has shown the club in an extremely poor light with a number of own goals being scored and supporters left confused and bemused as they are seemingly being asked to choose between supporting Benham or Warburton, an impossible choice, when in truth both men are heroes and icons to us all. Now is the time for both parties to handle matters sensibly and correctly, restore the reputation of the club and get things back on track.

Hopeless! – 15/2/15

Over two thousand Brentford supporters travelled to The Valley on Saturday afternoon by car, bus, train and boat, all full of hope, if not expectation, that the Bees could put the troubles of the past week behind them and turn on a morale-boosting display. But the only team whose confidence was boosted was Charlton who ended their long run without a win and strolled to an easy and comfortable three-goal victory against a lethargic, dispirited and well under-par Brentford team.

Before the game, the talk was that the mood in the camp was positive and confident and that the team was both determined and well prepared to put on a performance that would demonstrate their support for beleaguered manager Mark Warburton and ensure that their playoff charge was not derailed. So much for good intentions and brave words! The body language did not look right from the off and a well below strength team lacking the presence of Jake Bidwell, James Tarkowski and of course, Alan Judge, started slowly and soon got worse.

Brentford's success this season has been based on a high tempo pressing game with the ball moved quickly and accurately from side to side of the pitch, maintaining possession for long periods whilst probing for an opening and when one appears for the pace to be increased suddenly so that we can take advantage. What we saw today was a team playing without belief and seemingly going through the motions. Their confidence and pace had been sapped, as if by an unseen force, as the ball was turned over with monotonous regularity, Gray was starved of support and resorted to niggly fouls, Pritchard and Jota were peripheral influences and Douglas and Toumani probed but to little effect. But for Button, Charlton would have scored far more than their one first half effort as the defence in front of him creaked ominously. Moses seemed to be wearing lead boots so seldom did he forage forward and he was often left trailing and left gaps in defence, Craig and Dean were willing but porous and poor Nico Yennaris was the sacrificial lamb at left back where he was hung out to dry with little support either in front or beside him.

No shots on target was a fair end result for an anaemic and witless first half performance and thankfully the tempo increased after the interval but although we maintained possession better and even ventured into the final third more often, we never threatened and Charlton scored another soft goal on the first occasion they threatened. Jota and Douglas seemed to bicker as we prepared to kick off and heads went down even further. We huffed and puffed and improved significantly when the invisible Jota as well as Diagouraga and Dallas were replaced by Long, Toral and the excellent Tommy Smith in a rare triple substitution which demonstrated the manager's displeasure with what he was watching on the pitch.

Charlton panicked when they realised that they were on the verge of their first win for three months and did their best to help us by funnelling back into two banks of four, inviting us onto them. Douglas and Pritchard forced comfortable saves from Henderson before we gave away a comic cuts goal in injury time, which simply highlighted how poor we were on the day. All three goals were totally preventable and the defence hardly covered themselves in glory, Dean in particular being responsible for two of the goals with Craig running him close in culpability.

This was not a true Brentford performance that we witnessed yesterday – or certainly not one that I had seen since the dog days of the Andy Scott regime. We looked listless, rudderless and played without passion, desire or organisation and our customary sense of togetherness seemed to have disappeared as players did not run to support each other, create space or help their colleagues out.

Charlton are to be congratulated as they fully deserved their win but it is not sour grapes when I say that they were a poor team who we made look far better than they are. What does that make us then? Hopefully a good team having a bad day at the office, weakened by injuries and suspensions and a lack of depth in the squad rather than a team whose spirit has been broken by the undercurrents and uncertainty that has reigned at the club since Tuesday when *The Times* broke the news of Matthew Benham's supposed decision to replace Mark Warburton at the end of the season. Hopefully this was a one-off rather than conclusive evidence that things are broken beyond repair.

So where do we go from here? That depends totally on what is said in the club statement that is expected to be released on Monday. Clarity, certainty, harmony and closure are needed if the club is not to be torn apart by the confusion and feeling of total negativity that currently reigns. Nobody at the club has covered himself in glory if the media stories, rumours and scuttlebutt circulating throughout the ground yesterday are correct.

Day Of Reckoning – 17/2/15

Now I know how it must feel to be one of massed crowd of supplicants in St Peter's Square waiting eagerly for the puff of white smoke that signifies the election of a new pope and I can well identify with their frustration when all they see, instead, is the *Fumata Nera*, or dark smoke that signifies that the necessary two thirds majority has yet to be achieved. What's all this got to do with Brentford FC, you might well ask? Well, along with every other Bees supporter I was hoping to see, on Monday, the long-awaited statement that promised to bring an end to an appalling week of indecision, muddled thinking and strife at the club that has prevailed ever since we learned of the supposed intention of Matthew Benham to replace Mark Warburton as manager of the club.

Everything turned to dust as the week progressed with no satisfactory explanation or resolution from within the club and Brentford's reputation became increasingly sullied with know-it-all commentators throughout the media treating our club as a laughing stock rather than as the ambitious, well run, ground-breaking and united institution that we supporters had thought it to be.

Since last June, I have written one hundred and seventy-five articles which have mainly been a paean of praise to the club. Over the course of over two hundred thousand words I have referred time after time to Brentford's forward thinking, vision, ambition and sense of community, how the club and its supporters connect as one, as well as the ground-breaking partnership of Benham and Warburton. For the last week, I have been doubting myself and my judgement. Did I get it entirely wrong? Recent years had seen a universal sense of wonderment and disbelief as an ugly duckling was transformed into a beautiful and elegant swan. Today I look back at some of the words I have written with bemusement and disbelief as the club that I love and admire is unrecognisable and seems almost to have returned to the bad old days and dark ages.

Just as the Roman Emperors gave their subjects circuses and gladiatorial shows, we supporters need to have our minds distracted from the current hiatus by the arrival of a centre half and a striker, and not more callow eighteen year olds still wearing their pimples with pride, but a couple of battle hardened and probably expensive professionals who will add value and contribute from the start of their stay at the club. Not easy to find, I grant you, but that is what a scouting department is for.

The season is balanced on a tightrope and can go either way. We can plummet to our doom or we can hold on tight and maintain our balance and equilibrium. I expect to know which way we will go within the next day or so.

The End of the Beginning – 18/2/15

Well, the long-awaited statement finally arrived late yesterday afternoon. Brentford supporters have been clamouring for information and clarification from the club ever since Matt Hughes's bombshell article last Tuesday. Supporters were confused, angry and disappointed not just at the proposed changes but also because they had been forced to wait for a week until the situation was confirmed. Personally, whilst I welcomed the statement which, in its carefully and well drafted nine hundred and twenty-four words, gave chapter and verse into the owner's thinking I thought that it had not arrived late but in reality it was three months too early.

I have absolutely no problem with what Matthew Benham is proposing as it demonstrates his vision, openness to change, uniqueness of approach, passion for the club and determination for it to progress and excel. I simply wish that his hand had not been forced prematurely and that the changes could have been announced and implemented as originally intended after the end of the season. Had that been the case then the ensuing uproar could have been handled and managed far better and the fallout would not have been as damaging as has been the case in the last appalling eight days which have seen the club mocked, pilloried and heavily criticised throughout the media and football world, and supporters turn on each other. Not just that, but two crucial matches have been lost, we have fallen out of the playoff positions and the players are naturally saddened, angered and confused at what has transpired as well as the lack of clarity.

The statement confirmed that Mark Warburton and David Weir will leave at the end of the season and Sporting Director Frank McParland has been put on immediate gardening leave. Again, their departures, harsh though they might appear, had not been intended to be discussed, formalised and announced until the close season and it remains to be seen if Warburton and Weir can maintain their focus and commitment to a club that they know will shortly dispense with their services and, crucially, manage to re-motivate and inspire the players to climb off the floor, redouble their efforts and ideally maintain our promotion challenge – a tall order indeed.

At least the players now know where they stand and the doubt and uncertainty has been removed. They know that they are playing for their future and for the right to remain at a club that for all the setbacks of the last few days, remains ambitious, progressive and determined to progress further. Getting to the crux of the matter, the players are also well paid and I understand that there is a highly lucrative bonus scheme in place that is worth significant sums to every squad member should we finish at or near the top of the Championship table. There now needs to be a show of unity and togetherness and Mattthew Benham needs to visit the training ground straight away and address the players face to face, look them in the eyes, discuss his plans with them and persuade them to get back onside.

Mark Warburton and David Weir will also be determined to leave on the highest possible note and ideally complete the job that they have both so ably started. They need to convince potential new employers that it is as much their management, coaching and motivational abilities as the structure and system employed at Brentford that has been responsible for the club's success. At a more basic level, there is the natural human reaction of wanting to show the world that Benham has made a massive error in his decision.

Not many Brentford supporters would disagree with the owner that the squad, admirably though it has performed, or even over-performed, needs strengthening both in numbers and quality to cope with tired legs and the pressure of the business end of the season. That opportunity was spurned in January, which, of course, led to the schism between Benham and Warburton and the fateful leak of the news of the owner's determination to make the changes in both approach and personnel. There is still a final opportunity to bring in loanees and I would hope that a new striker and centre half are at the top of the agenda. Who scouts or selects them now is open to question but the bottom line is that supporters and players alike would be reinvigorated by a couple of high quality, experienced players who could take the slack off some of the existing squad members who have been visibly wilting under the telling pressure they have experienced. Let's hope that something is being planned and implemented in time for the visit of Bournemouth and that two of the injured players, Alan Judge and James Tarkowski, are also fit to return. The eyes of the world are on Brentford and we need to respond on Saturday.

It is hard to know what to write about the situation facing Mark Warburton. So far, forty-two managers have lost their job this season and looking through the list of names and examining their individual records, it seems laughable that a man as obviously successful and gifted as Mark will soon be joining their number. I have written pages of praise about him over the past few months and even described him, accurately, I feel, as *The Renaissance Man of Football* given his overall record, approach, coaching and man-management skills. Despite his success, I am not quibbling with the owner's decision to move on. Benham wishes to remodel the club's management structure and employ and implement a system rare in the UK but far more common elsewhere in the football world. A Head Coach will be appointed to work alongside a new Sporting Director and he will rely upon a new recruitment structure using a mixture of traditional scouting and other tools including mathematical modelling.

Crucially, as a key part of the new recruitment structure, the Head Coach will have a strong input into the players brought into the Club but not an absolute veto. That, I am sure, was the main sticking point between Benham and Warburton and ensured his departure, given that they apparently disagreed over player recruitment last month and several deals failed to be completed - which brings us full circle as Warburton apparently does not buy into this approach and he therefore has to go.

Mark Warburton will depart with the sincere thanks and gratitude of every Brentford supporter as he has done an outstanding job and he now faces the biggest test of his career. He must ensure that the Brentford players do not merely go through the motions for the remainder of the season and risk throwing away the rewards of all their labour!

The Dust Settles – 19/2/15

Yesterday was one of contemplation when Brentford supporters reflected upon and considered the import of the statement issued by the club on Tuesday afternoon and their views differed as to how well they thought the club had handled matters and whether we were all now in a position to put things behind us, move on and concentrate on the football again.

Rebel Bee spoke for many when he admitted how conflicted, disappointed and sad he was about the situation and how it had been dealt with:

So after the week from hell and the arrival of a statement finally worthy of the name, we are left in the knowledge that it was indeed Times Journo 1 – BFC 0. That hurts as much as anything that has followed, and the thought of a previously disinterested media dining out on BFC's shortcomings fills me with rage. Whoever leaked the story, if it went down that way, had better stay clear of Griffin Park, they will not be welcome again.

Short lived though it was, the honeymoon period is now over. Since Mr. Rösler departed my bad days at work or troubles elsewhere have been soothed by the magnificent achievements of our club – unified and pulling together. My every moment has been consumed by this fine manager and his team, the growth of Brentford FC, and of course the incredible improvements off the pitch to boot. I honestly thought it could be dynastic, Warbs as our Shankly, Busby or alike. I knew he would move on one day, mad though it sounds, only to manage the national team! But it's all over now, and although I'll be there as ever cheering on my club, things will never be the same again.

Maybe I'm out of step, old school and lacking the vision and ambition that we need to progress, sorry – I can't help it. Mark Warburton has been treated shabbily in my eyes and I thought we were better than that. There seems to be a swing of opinion towards Matthew Benham now, and his money, his club and his ambition. Maybe his "Moneyball" formulas and apparent penchant for structure & foreign coaches will pay off, he may be right and I'll be first in line to commend him if it comes to pass. But for me we had it all, the full package – we were getting there anyway, and now have decided to change tack. He has my gratitude and support – not that he probably needs it.

They've been caught out and someone needs to provide checks and balances, more so now than ever. Blind faith support for the owner isn't healthy and if we as supporters form opinion simply through the fear of him bailing out on us, the slippery slope has begun. It would be great to see all of the non-playing staff reach out to us fans now and put this to bed, that would go a long way towards bringing us together again. So the games come thick and fast and there is all to play for, can Mark Warburton and the team regain focus and get back on track? What happens if they don't and defeats pile up – not a pleasant scenario for anyone concerned. Our next opponents will help to answer that one, if the Bees turn it on with a packed Griffin Park behind them AFC Bournemouth had better watch out, if not they have all the tools to pull out all the stitches on recent wounds – what then? We'll know soon enough.

John Hirdle too was wrestling with the happenings of the past week and how they had been allowed to come to pass and seemed resigned and cautiously optimistic about the outcome:

I think the thing I find most difficult to grapple with is why Matthew Benham has chosen this particular time to make these changes to the structure of the club when things were going so well under Mark Warburton and the present system. If we were struggling at the bottom of the table then it would be more understandable. Of course having put in the amount of money into the club he has, Benham has every right to go down whichever future avenue he wishes too and he deserves the trust and support of the fans until he proves to us otherwise. Being the dinosaur I am I can't say the talk of mathematical modelling and sleep coaches leaves me drooling but who knows? Benham may well be a complete visionary and in three to five years' time his success with such methods at Brentford may well have many other English clubs going down the same road.

For the here and now, whether Mark Warburton actually lasts the season out or not, we should all get behind him in the remaining games and show our appreciation of an excellent manager, and as the events of the last week have shown, a man of great integrity also. There will be no shortage of takers for his talents when he becomes available post Brentford, I am sure. The players as always are the key to everything and now we do at least have some clarity on things it is up to them to make the last couple of months of the season exciting. We know they have the ability and quality. The question is with all that has happened will they have the motivation? I guess we will find out Saturday.

Richard Poole from his eyrie in France gave the footballer's dispassionate viewpoint:

Well, if I read it right, the owner is looking to run the running of the club similarly to how we operate in France. I know this system very well as when nearly forty years ago when I signed for second division club SC Toulon it was the owner who wanted me and not really the coach. Then after six months I got injured and the coach was sacked as for the third year in a row we missed out on promotion by a mere couple of points. So in the end after changing the coach several more times the club finally got promoted in 1983.

But where are SC Toulon today? They exist only in the depths of non-league football and the owner's gamble did not pay off. Though I cannot see this happening to our Brentford I recognise that Matthew Benham, like lots of today's owners wants more say on the playing side of things and that's reasonable given that it is their money. How many of the teams in England have a similar system that works? Very few! Clubs like Chelsea and

Manchester United have strong-willed managers who, rightly I feel, would not let the owner meddle with the playing side, although I am not suggesting that this is the case at Brentford, but the line is very thin. I have some experience of managing in the lower reaches of non-league football here in France many years ago and I am totally old school in my approach. I think that the only thing we Bees can do is to stay behind our team and just hope that it all works out, although like many, I feel it was not just badly handled but quite un-professional and should have been dealt with near the end of the season.

In response to John and Richard I would simply say that things were not planned or meant to have been handled in the manner that transpired. The newspaper leak changed everything and meant that a difficult situation that was being discussed calmly, rationally and slowly behind closed doors between the owner and the manager, and was never meant to go beyond the club until the end of the season became public property and swiftly intensified until it got out of control with the ghastly results that we have all witnessed. It is also totally unfair to associate Matthew Benham with other interfering, megalomaniac and meddling owners. You all know who they are! He is not doing things on a whim and a prayer or by consulting the runes, totally the opposite. Everything he does is cold, clinical, measured and based on innovation, breaking the mould, best practice, intensive research, data analysis and statistics. He is not accustomed to making mistakes and every Brentford fan will hope that he has got it right again this time.

Someone close to the action remarked to me today that Mark Warburton's view of life is, *if it ain't broke don't fix it*, whereas Matthew Benham's is at entirely the opposite end of the spectrum and is far more akin to *it might not be broken but let's keep improving it*. Therein lies the difference between the two of them. Patrick Sutton was far more bullish in his views:

I am amazed at some of the fans' reactions to this decision and while I understand the support for Mark Warburton I am at a loss as to how and why folk can damn Matthew Benham. For his actions I am behind Benham 100%. To hear fans saying let's start a petition to get Benham out is outrageous and full of blind ignorance. The matter is now clear and if Mark does not see or agree with Matthew's philosophy on moving the club continuously forward that is his choice. I get the impression that both had an in-depth heart-to-heart and though different views were aired, an amicable parting was agreed. Now we as fans must focus on our bright future once again and see that managers like players, as we have witnessed over the last two seasons, come and go almost in a heartbeat.

We are lucky to have an owner who cares about the club, has a long-term vision and I'm sure a passion just as big as every other Brentford fan. The only thing I am not sure about is if he should have stayed until the end of the season, and I feel the swift appointment of a new manager would have been the better way for the club although I do see the negative side to this and how it might affect our style of play for the rest of the term. As sad as it is to see this outcome let's just remember how long we have waited to be in the position we now find ourselves………Onwards and upwards. It is not an option…………it's our destiny.

Back To The Football – 22/2/15

Sleep wouldn't come on Friday night so rather than simply toss and turn upstairs in bed I turned to the comfort of a holy relic and switched on my much watched and already badly worn tape of the Brentford versus Fulham match. Was it only three short months ago since that magic evening that symbolised everything good about Brentford? I rejoiced in the memories of a performance packed full of energy, skill, confidence, passion and commitment and was struck yet again by the sheer joie de vivre of our approach and the obvious bond and connection between the players, manager and supporters who all came together as one and became a seemingly insuperable force that left Fulham floundering in our wake.

Given the horrors of the past fortnight I wondered if the magic had gone once and for all and if the players and supporters alike would be able to regain their Mojo? On the surface, strenuous efforts had been made to paper over the cracks. Mark Warburton had done his imperturbable Zen Master impression, calmly and dispassionately towing the company line in all of his many media appearances. He talked about his gratitude to Matthew Benham for giving him the opportunity in the first place, and his absolute right to take the club in whatever direction he feels is best and how he felt it was better for everyone if he and David Weir were totally honest and parted company with the club at the end of the season if their philosophies differed in how they felt the club should be run moving forward. Who knows what his deep innermost thoughts really are, but he was totally on-message and won the PR battle hands down – not surprising given his extensive media experience obtained whilst running the NextGen series. Cliff Crown also succinctly and convincingly put forward the case regarding Matthew Benham and the Board's view of the future, and both owner and chairman had visited the training ground on Thursday and had spoken to the players and been grilled about their chosen path.

After last week's abject surrender against Charlton, nobody really knew how the team would react when there was also the little matter of a match coming up against league leaders Bournemouth, perhaps the best team in the league.

I shouldn't have worried as Brentford rose to the occasion and, totally re-energised, pulled off their most impressive, skilful, determined and passionate performance of the season, and their most important, and proved beyond doubt that they had regained their focus. Whether they were playing for the shirt, themselves, pride, the manager or simply to demonstrate how much they disagree with the owner's decision is open to question but matters not a jot as Brentford totally overwhelmed Bournemouth and fully merited their three-one victory on the day.

The Gods also decided that we had all suffered enough over the past torrid fortnight and things certainly went our way. Referee Mike Dean gave a performance of sheer Premier League quality, cracking down on our opponents' niggling and diving. We scored at exactly the right time too with Jonathan Douglas settling nerves by stealing in unnoticed at the back post to convert Alex Prichard's low centre to round off our first real attack. Bournemouth were left reeling as we seized the initiative and never let go for the

remainder of the first half. We had regained our touch and played the Brentford way –
retaining possession, playing the ball out from the back and probing for openings.

Alan Judge made his long-awaited return from injury and immediately demonstrated
how much we had missed his influence. He is a little pocket dynamo whose energy,
infectious enthusiasm and ability to see a pass and switch the focus of the attack gave us
an edge that we never lost. Alex Prichard too was a man inspired and was touched by
genius as Bournemouth couldn't get near him. He was everywhere, and his work rate and
commitment matched his undoubted skill. He was a total inspiration and match-winner
with a goal and two assists. Stuart Dallas was given the nod at left back and with the
recalled Tony Craig on his right talking him through the match, and Judge covering in
front of him, he rose to the challenge and so frustrated Matt Ritchie that the tricky winger
was extremely fortunate not to see red before he was removed for his own protection at
the interval.

David Button dominated his area and looked unbeatable but after Jota forced a good low
save from Boruc and Pritchard had lobbed a close-range chance just wide, Bournemouth
equalised well against the run of play when a hopeful ball forward was deflected over
Tony Craig by the straining Diagouraga and Pugh scored messily at the second attempt.
Would Brentford heads go down? Not a chance, as Dallas immediately played the
through ball of the match and set Andre Gray in behind the visitors' defence. He did
everything right, rounded Boruc, kept his head and his angled effort was heading for the
unguarded net when Cook appeared seemingly out of a hole in the ground to make an
incredible goal-line clearance.

It seemed as if for all Brentford's efforts they would go into the break level when they
deserved far more, but fate smiled on them again. Right on halftime, Wilson cynically
tripped Judge when the ball had long gone and Alex Prichard's free kick from over thirty
yards was well struck. The ball was moving in the air but it should have been a
straightforward save for the keeper, but Boruc had a brainstorm and merely succeeded in
flailing the ball into the corner of his own net instead of around the post and Brentford
went into the interval with their tails up and the initiative firmly in their grasp.

The second half was a different matter as Bournemouth were stung into action.
Substitute right-winger Fraser was a tricky customer and tormented the Brentford
defence. He combined well with the overlapping Francis and forced Button to push his
shot onto the post. That was merely the first of a number of telling saves that the keeper
made in order to allow a gritty Brentford team to hold onto their narrow lead. Wilson
also lobbed wastefully wide when given a clear sight of an empty net and Brentford put
their bodies on the line and defended like heroes with Tarkowski a veritable colossus.

The Bees deservedly weathered the storm and then the tide turned as Bournemouth
committed men forward in search of that elusive equaliser and we simply picked them
off on the break. Judge went off to a hero's reception when he had run himself out after
an hour but, no matter, Toral was an influential replacement who immediately dominated
the midfield. What a prospect that young man is and how I would love us to sign him.
Chris Long replaced the tiring Gray and Alan McCormack made his long-awaited return
to rampage around the midfield and put even more bite and steel into Brentford's efforts.

Jon Toral on the ball.

We quite simply have to be the fittest team in the league as we got stronger and faster and more dominant the longer the game went on, and I counted at least seven wonderful chances in the last quarter of the game as we created havoc in the visitors' defence. Long's angled effort was pushed around the post by Boruc, who was by now the busiest man on the field as he did his utmost to redeem himself and refute the ringing cries of *It's all your fault* from the merciless Ealing Road *tricoteuses*. Jota could have scored four in the last few minutes but somehow missed each time. He hit the bar with a screamer and failed twice when he could see the whites of the keeper's eyes before then hammering another effort inches past the post. Long also got into the act as his deflected drive clanged off the post. Prichard forced an excellent save from the overworked keeper and by now the game was deep into injury time and we all feared that there might yet be a sting in the tail as Bournemouth still retained the quality to hurt us. In a game of slim margins teams that fail to put away their chances are often punished late on, but not this time as we strode away yet again and Toral's clever pass put Prichard in space and his hard low cross was turned in exultantly by the ever-willing Long for his first league goal. He was mobbed and deservedly so and victory was ours. Bring on Blackpool!

Voices Of Experience – 24/2/15

I have just received articles from two Brentford supporters who both have many years on the clock. Larry Signy and Bernard Jackson have been following Brentford FC for more years that I suspect the pair of them care to remember and they have trenchant and heartfelt views about the current situation which they can put into context given the multitude of ups and downs they have both witnessed during their decades of loyal support. Here is what Larry has to say:

I have deliberately refrained from writing this until a whole week after the official announcement about the future of Brentford was released by the club. It has given me time to read all the many varying, conflicting, often wildly biased views – and to try and reflect my own opinion. And I have to say that I'm just as confused as ever I was when the whole sorry story first leaked out. The only clear thing is that Mark Warburton will leave at the end of the season – and we knew that already.

Please don't think I am taking sides in anything I now write – or that I denigrate anything that anyone has done to get The Bees where they are today. I am just baffled, and in trying to de-baffle myself am simply trying to put things the way they seem to me. We are told that club owner Matthew Benham wants a new-style "revolutionary" way of running the club – but so far, to my mind we have been given no proof of that. Changes – yes. A new title for the man running the first team (rather than a Manager, he's to be a Head Coach); a new Sporting Director whose job will be to find and sign new talent replacing a Director Of Football, whose job has been, ahem, to find and sign new talent; and a panel of experts to help find those new players replacing an existing panel of experts trying to find and replace new talents. That panel, we are told, will use statistics to find the best players for our club – as we have been doing since Matthew took control.

But even statisticians will tell you, statistics can be made to prove anything. For instance – does two and two equal four…or twenty-two? It's a system that may well work in a number of fields where there are definites (banking, insurance, etc) – but we are talking football here…a little matter of twenty-two human beings (and a referee) knocking the hell out of the statistics and what should happen. As I said somewhere else, does that mean if Joe Bloggs of Little Puddefoot FC keeps ten clean sheets in a row is he is a better 'keeper than England's Joe Hart who has only managed nine?

Oh yes, the new Head Coach will not have the power to veto players he doesn't want in his squad – and if he's presented with some players like that by the "new" selection panel he will possibly have to build his team with some players he doesn't fancy. To my mind, that's like asking Leonardo da Vinci to paint the Mona Lisa using only blue and red paint or telling Michelangelo he must carve the Pieta and David statues using house brick rather than marble. So far, things have gone well, very well, with the old system over a couple of seasons – with Matthew and Mark Warburton as a very good partnership. So I have to wonder why there needs to be change. No-one has yet explained that. Nor has anyone told us why Mark can't buy into the new idea (least of all the very diplomatic man himself). The various statements have apparently tried to clarify things – but as far as I can see, there is nothing revolutionary in any of it. To my simple mind, we have been fed a lot of words about looking to the future, the way things are going etc, etc, etc. Except – to my ill-informed and possibly ignorant-of-the-facts mind there is one big change. And that is what the announced changes might mean to the future of the club.

We have been told that there is a five-year plan to develop the club (abee has written about this recently and knows more about it than me) and were given to understand that Matthew Benham wanted (and I've put it in quotes although he may not have used these actual words) "a sustainable club in a new stadium at Lionel Road...established in The Championship." To attain that sustainability he wanted to develop the youth system so the club could find young kids, bring them through the various youth levels to the development squad, and then into the first team where they would eventually be sold at a profit to allow the next batch to come through. That was the successful old Crewe Alexandra way – and, I believe, the way Barcelona go about things.

Now, apparently, we are looking at paying (big?) money to bring in new first team players – probably from overseas, and either senior ready-to-use names or youngsters who can be trained up in the Brentford style – so we can become a top Premiership club. We don't exactly know that's the way we'll be going because we just haven't been told. We are, we are told, going for a more continental style of running things – but it's interesting to note that Barca, again, has a manager rather than a Head Coach – like Real Madrid, and the English Euro League giants Manchester City, Chelsea. Alex Ferguson didn't do too badly in sole control either.

But now? Well, will the existing youth set-up change under the new regime (what statistics do you use for a six-year-old who loves playing football?) Will the existing medical team stay? How will BFC be set up in the future? I don't know, and my reaction to it all? Well... I am not taking sides between new way and the old way – I can't, because to my mind I still don't know – and I still wonder just where is this big revolution? Perhaps somebody will eventually tell me – and other fans. What is planned for the future? Will it all work? Only time will tell, and I can only sincerely hope that the Championship table statistics at the end of this season prove successful.

Factually, I believe that Luis Enrique is actually titled Head Coach rather than Manager at Barcelona but Larry makes his points clearly and cogently. Bernard Jackson also has his doubts in his mournfully titled *Bees Lament*:

Having seen the Bees lose five or six times in a Wembley/Cardiff cup final I have decided not to attend if they should reach a Championship playoff final this year. What a really tough decision for a supporter to make and strange for someone supporting since 1947! My grandchildren's schoolmates are "supporters" of Premier League teams whom few of the youngsters have ever seen live. Having a grandfather with allegiance to the Bees is strange but also interesting and unusual. So here is a granddad in his eighties and doubtless a member of a small group still alive, who saw Bill Gorman, Joe Crozier and Dai Hopkins playing at GP. What can I make of current events? Sadness, pride and expectation. Sadness that arguably the best manager we've ever had, has decided to leave at the end of the season. Pride that the team has achieved its present position and reputation and expectation that things ain't gonna be the same as they were!

Matthew Benham's involvement and money has brought the club to where it is today. The reputed investment of £90 million earns the incontestable right to make the decisions which he considers best for Brentford Football Club. Whether he is correct in those decisions remains to be seen but I foresee changes at the club I've supported for the last 67 years. The clapped-out old stadium will go along with the memories of clapped out old teams and results which caused many miserable Saturday nights for me (and my family!). There will be a recruitment strategy relying on mathematical modelling which may bring an unexpected manager and players to the club. The new manager, new players and new stadium are signs that there is a future model for Brentford Football Club which old blokes like me will just have to get used to. I suppose I'll still apply for a season ticket in the new place and hope for regular success...but it ain't gonna be the same. That's progress I suppose.

I appreciate and well understand that our supporters have reasonable doubts about the way forward and the current uncertainty. Indeed, I share some of these concerns and look forward to more clarity about what is proposed. I worry about the immediate future but remain highly optimistic about our medium to long-term prospects.

I spoke to an experienced, highly informed and connected national football journalist yesterday who also knows the people involved with running the club. I asked him where he thought Brentford would be in three years. He paused, cogitated for a moment and said: *"Good question! Before the current shenanigans I would have said lower half of the Premier League given the way the club has been run and structured and the high levels of team spirit, self-belief and morale. Now.... who knows?"*

Back In The Game! – 25/2/15

A week is a long time in football and things have moved on dramatically from the turmoil of the previous couple of weeks. The past seven days have seen Mark Warburton's future clarified, if not to everyone's satisfaction, and clear notice given regarding Matthew Benham's intended strategy and future direction for the club. Tempers and emotions have finally cooled as all parties have remained firmly on message and emphasised their determination to work together for the remainder of this tumultuous season. Not before time, the attention has returned to matters on the pitch rather than in the boardroom.

The response of the manager and players has been utterly beyond reproach and they have responded to the uncertainty with two decisive home wins that have fully restored confidence and optimism. Two games that could not have been more different, as we overcame differing challenges from both ends of the spectrum. Bournemouth were defeated through a combination of grit, determination and organisation, allied, of course, to some pulsating and scintillating football – it wouldn't be Brentford otherwise, would it?

Last night was an entirely different kettle of fish as a performance of total dominance culminated in a comfortable four-nil win over a demoralised, hapless and toothless shambles of a Blackpool side that barely went through the motions and went down almost without a fight. Frankly, the team were shown up by their long-suffering supporters who displayed far more effort and commitment, and demonstrated a black humour and resignation to their fate that was entirely to their credit.

This was, by some distance, the most one-sided game that I can recall. It is no exaggeration to state that with a little more steadiness in front of goal, an understandable failure to retain focus and keep their foot on the peddle for the entire ninety-four minutes, and less concentration on walking the ball into the net, Brentford could easily have eclipsed their record nine-nil victory against Wrexham.

The statistics bear this out as Brentford made 666 passes, managed an incredible 74% possession and 87% pass accuracy rate and an outrageous 42 attempts on goal, almost one every two minutes. This is easily a record for the Championship this season and, but for some profligate finishing and the sheer pride, ability and bloody mindedness of the overworked Joe Lewis, who was determined to stave off total embarrassment for his beleaguered team mates, we would have needed an abacus rather than scoreboard to keep count.

Despite the six points gained and seven goals scored over the last two matches, the only disappointment is that Brentford still find themselves just outside the playoff zone, but they are now firmly ensconced in a thirteen match promotion dogfight with eight teams seemingly competing for the prize, and he who is bravest, best prepared, organised and the most positive will ultimately prevail, especially if favoured with a little bit of good luck. Why shouldn't it be us given the turnaround and change of fortune and the fact that we have players returning from injury who can provide fresh impetus and legs at a time when minds and bodies are becoming jaded?

Compared to where we were as we emerged shell-shocked from The Valley a mere ten days ago, this is progress indeed, and who knows what the next ten weeks or so will bring, but what is certain is that we are back in the game and have a fighting chance of playing with the big boys next season. Something that looked highly unlikely a mere fortnight ago.

What transpires in the close season is for the future and everyone needs to put that prospect totally out of their mind for the time being as it is now imperative that total focus and concentration is maintained as well as a continuation of the renewed bond and unity within the camp, without allowing any distractions to further sabotage our efforts.

I often bemoaned the fact that in last season's promotion triumph there were really no easy games and we supporters could never afford to relax as the outcome was in doubt until near the end. Even our best win by five clear goals over Crewe was no stroll in the park as we didn't break the deadlock until a minute before the break. Last night was a rare example of a match being over almost as soon as it had started owing to the immense gulf and chasm between the two teams. It was lovely to watch a game where it was clear that we were going to come out on top but, strangely, I have to confess that I missed the cut and thrust of a tightly-contested game, as I am sure the remaining fixtures will be.

The outcome was never in any doubt last night once the marvellous Jon Toral, a total unsung hero, struck twice in a two-minute spell on the quarter hour to alleviate any nerves and tension in the stands if not on the pitch, and it was then simply a matter of how many more we were going to score. Blackpool could barely get out of their half and David Button was totally untested and surely deserved a game off after his heroics on Saturday. That being said, given the levels of concentration maintained by all goalkeepers, I am sure that he was mentally exhausted at the end of the game last night despite his almost total lack of involvement in the proceedings.

Tarkowski and the recalled Dean snuffed out what little threat Blackpool offered and Odebajo and the immaculate Stuart Dallas were able to rampage up their respective wings and play as auxiliary wingers. Alan Judge had frustratingly picked up a knock on his return against Bournemouth and wasn't risked last night, but he was hardly missed as Toral, Pritchard and Jota weaved intricate patterns and cut vast swathes in the visitor's defence. Diagouraga and the buccaneering Douglas ensured that possession was regained on the few occasions that Blackpool managed more than one consecutive pass and it was the skipper, slipped in by Jota who set up Toral for the opener with the ball swept through the keeper's legs as he advanced in vain. Toral it was, again, with a rare far post headed goal when picked out by Gray's immaculate cross.

Blackpool visibly subsided like a pricked balloon and concentrated on damage limitation. They didn't even try to press or knock us out of our stride but appeared resigned to the inevitable. Gray hit the keeper when put clean through and Pritchard found increasingly ingenious methods not to score when given clear sights of goal. Blackpool's cause was further diminished when Dunne's crude challenge on Jota was immediately punished by a red card, flourished seemingly in sadness by a thankfully subdued Andy D'Urso who did not otherwise influence the proceedings.

A comparative rarity – Harlee Dean going close from a set piece.

The second half was a procession and there were loud cheers when Blackpool finally got the ball into the Brentford penalty area late on in the game, but otherwise it resembled nothing more than a game of three-and-in with the visitors funnelling back to the edge of their area and forming a human barrier aimed at keeping the score down.

There was a relentless barrage of shots which rained in on their goal from all angles and distances. Some threatened the crowd massed behind the goal, others were blocked or forced excellent saves from Lewis. Gray beat him with a deflected effort from the rebound after the keeper made a wonderful parrying save from a fierce volley and, after spurning a number of opportunities, Toral bobbled in a last minute fourth to notch the first Bees hat trick since Gary Alexander's in 2012. Saunders, Long and Smith were given run outs to rest Douglas, Gray and Jota for the crucial visit to Birmingham on Saturday and simply emphasised the strength and quality of the Brentford squad.

This has been a wonderful, restorative and recuperative few days for the Bees and we go into the final run in revitalised, confident and in great heart and with as much chance of success as all of the so-called bigger names that are also jockeying with us to reach the promised land.

League Table – 31/2/15

Position	Team	P	W	D	L	F	A	GD	Pt	Form
1	Derby County	34	19	8	7	66	35	31	65	W D D W W L
2	Middlesbrough	34	18	9	7	50	24	26	63	W W D L W L
3	Watford	34	19	5	10	69	42	27	62	W W W L W W
4	Bournemouth	34	17	9	8	67	37	30	60	W D D L L D
5	Ipswich Town	33	17	9	7	54	34	20	60	D L W W L W
6	Norwich City	33	17	8	8	64	37	27	59	D W W W W W
7	**Brentford**	**34**	**18**	**4**	**12**	**53**	**44**	**9**	**58**	**W L L W W L**
8	Wolverhampton Wndrs	34	16	9	9	47	40	7	57	L W L W W W
8	Nottingham Forest	34	13	11	10	56	48	8	50	W W D W W W
10	Sheffield Wednesday	34	11	13	10	30	32	-2	46	D L D L W W
11	Blackburn Rovers	34	11	12	11	43	44	-1	45	L W D D L D
12	Charlton Athletic	34	9	15	10	37	43	-6	42	L L W W L W
13	Birmingham City	34	10	12	12	39	50	-11	42	D L D L L W
14	Huddersfield Town	34	11	9	14	44	56	-12	42	W L D D W L
15	Cardiff City	34	10	11	13	39	45	-6	41	D D D D W L
16	Leeds United	34	11	8	15	36	45	-9	41	L W W W L L
17	Bolton Wanderers	34	11	7	16	42	53	-11	40	L W L L L W
18	Reading	34	11	7	16	36	52	-16	40	W L L W L L
19	Fulham	34	11	6	17	46	58	-12	39	D L L D L W
20	Brighton and Hove A	34	8	13	13	38	43	-5	37	L D D W W L
21	Rotherham United	34	8	13	13	34	50	-16	37	W L D L L W
22	Millwall	34	7	10	17	30	53	-23	31	L W L D L L
23	Wigan Athletic	34	6	10	18	31	47	-16	28	L L W L L W
24	Blackpool	34	4	10	20	29	68	-39	22	L L D D L L

MARCH

A Wasted Journey – 1/3/15

I hadn't written anything in the buildup to Saturday's game as I was trying my hardest to resist the temptation to vent my spleen and list the reasons why I so heartily dislike Birmingham City. *Don't do it,* my inner voice kept telling me, *you're better than that, accentuate the positives and look forward, rather than merely hark back to the past.* Somehow I managed to take my own advice and stayed away from my computer keyboard but I am afraid that things have changed, and I now feel that reminding everybody of all the slights, real and imaginary, that we have suffered at the hands of the Blues is entirely merited and, more importantly, will enable me to delay, albeit for a few minutes, describing our abject performance at St Andrew's Stadium yesterday afternoon. So here we go, and please feel free to add anything that memory and the mists of time have caused me to forget.

- Denying us a day out at Wembley in 1991 when they beat a weakened Bees team one-nil at Griffin Park to seal a place in the Leyland DAF Final with a three-one aggregate victory. Oh, and what about Trevor Aylott and his headband?

- The shenanigans in the final game of the 1992/93 season which led to Birmingham sealing a late and highly controversial win over a disinterested Charlton Athletic team to bang the final nail in our coffin and seal our relegation.

- Doing the double over us in 1994/95 and Barry Fry and Co making a big noise about it and gloating at every opportunity. We bottled it in the massively important promotion-clinching match at St Andrew's on 26th April 1995, a date etched indelibly in my memory. We were three points above the Blues at the top of the Second Division and it was effectively the title decider. Goals from a hobbling Kevin Francis and Liam Daish gave the Blues a 2-0 victory in front of over twenty-five thousand howling banshees, as well as the advantage at the top, on goal difference with a game in hand, that they just about held to the season's end. Nicky Forster also has vivid memories of this fateful match: *Only the team who finished top of the league got automatic promotion that season, so it was a massive game. We had been neck and neck with Birmingham and whoever won it, won the title. The atmosphere was the most intimidating I have ever played in. We had a young team and most of us had never known anything like it. We didn't do ourselves justice. We let the crowd get to us, and Birmingham bully us. We were just overwhelmed on the night and it was a big learning curve for us.*

We never turned up and allowed ourselves to be systematically bullied and intimidated in the most important match of the season. I too was the most scared that I have ever been at a Brentford match in fifty years of watching the club as the threat of violence was never far from the surface – and I was sitting in the Directors' Box! A truly horrible evening and I well remember the long and terrifying walk back to my car, surrounded by a hideous, gloating, baying mob of seemingly sub-human low-lives. God knows what would have happened had we had the temerity to have won, but that was never on the cards as, not for the first or last time on the big occasion, Brentford folded without much of a fight.

- Losing our star players such as Nicky Forster, Martin Grainger, DJ Campbell and, more recently, of course, Clayton Donaldson to a club who naturally consider themselves far bigger and more important than us. Not replacing Forster and Campbell adequately contributed heavily to blown promotions in 1997 and 2006.

- Our paths then didn't cross until 2010 when a scrappy and totally undeserved injury time goal from Kevin Phillips got Birmingham out of jail in a memorable League Cup tie where Sam Wood's volley seemed to have given us a well merited win. We then lost the penalty shootout with Craig Woodman missing the final crucial kick.

- Allowing a poor Birmingham team to take four vital points off us this season.

That brings me full circle and has allowed me the time and breathing space to calm down and consider what happened yesterday in a more rational, dispassionate and less emotional manner than would have been the case had I dashed into print as soon as I got home, tired, weary and very frustrated and with the Blues's anthem *Keep Right On To The End Of The Road* still reverberating through my brain as if on a tape-loop.

There is not a lot to say about the match. Conditions were poor with a bobbly pitch and a strong wind making it difficult to play our pass and move game. We dominated possession and retained the ball for nearly 70% of the game but did absolutely nothing with it. There was no penetration, no final killer ball and we were far too static and careless with our passing. Our set pieces lacked imagination or quality and we rarely beat the first man with our efforts. Birmingham's game plan was embarrassing in its simplicity – funnel back, frustrate, pack the final third so that there was little space for Brentford to exploit, and then pick us off on the break. What was far more embarrassing was that it worked perfectly, and even with their limited possession, the home team created several wonderful chances which should have brought them further reward.

The team selection was, frankly, baffling. We have now played different central defensive pairings in each of our last five games and yesterday saw no exception, with new loanee Liam Moore brought in to partner James Tarkowski. There was much muttering in the tea bar before the game about this move, but in my opinion Moore is supposed to improve us, and his presence enabled Tarkowski to revert to his more natural right hand side so I was happy to see him play. I was not so content by the end as Clayton Donaldson, playing the lone striker role with aplomb, totally dominated the two of them and was the fulcrum of Birmingham's victory. Everything went through him, he chased lost causes, won most things in the air, held the ball up and could have had a hat trick. His very presence on the near post panicked Tarkowski into scoring the own goal that turned out to be the winner and he forced a quite brilliant save from Button with a perfectly placed glancing header.

It is impossible not to compare him with Andre Gray, even if it is a little bit unfair as Andre is admittedly a tyro, who is still learning the game at this level. However, he accomplished nothing on the day, running into blind alleys, hammering the ball high, wide and not at all handsome when given a rare sight at goal, carelessly letting the ball slip under his feet when in good positions and generally displaying a poor and negative demeanour. We have missed Clayton terribly this season and I am not ashamed to admit it. Gray has real promise and can terrify defences when the force is with him, but all too often he fades into insignificance and offers very little threat. He has been played too much too soon, and appears to be both physically and mentally exhausted. The manager's failure to provide an adequate alternative striking option, such as all our promotion rivals possess, demonstrates a totally baffling and inexplicable blind spot in his judgement that could well ultimately cost us a playoff berth. Chris Long is also highly promising but is still in nappies, and Clayton clearly demonstrated what we are really lacking – an experienced pro who has been around the block a few times, who is strong, quick and powerful, knows the game and can make much out of very little and who demands careful attention at all times. Clayton was the key difference between the two teams yesterday and I salute him for his crucial contribution to their victory.

Most of the home team's danger came down their right flank where the overlapping Caddis combined cleverly with the ever-dangerous Cotterill. They both put a number of dangerous crosses into the Brentford penalty area and it was a Caddis cross that led to the winning goal. Cotterill too generally cut inside onto his favourite left foot and forced a top-notch save from Button with a rasping long-range effort. It was total madness in my opinion to keep Jake Bidwell, available again after his suspension, on the bench and leave the inexperienced Stuart Dallas to cope with the threat of Caddis and Cotterill. For all his effort and energy, he was totally unable to do so and the match was lost. Bidwell finally came on far too late with the stable door firmly bolted.

Loyalty is an admirable and praiseworthy characteristic, but blind and misplaced loyalty to players who have admittedly performed well, when there are better options available, is a worrying weakness, and I wonder if in retrospect Mark Warburton would have made a different decision when deciding upon his team. Alan Judge, recovered from injury, also came on but for all his energy was unable to unlock a tough, packed and uncompromising home defence in which our former loanee Rob Kiernan impressed.

Randolph was totally untroubled in the home goal, making two routine saves from long range efforts from Pritchard and watching attempts from Judge, Toral and Tarkowski sail wastefully wide. Our massive opportunity came and went on the stroke of half time when the otherwise anonymous Toral put the ball right onto Douglas's head eight yards out, but he headed over. Maybe he was flagged offside, which would let him off the hook, otherwise it was an unforgivable miss, as an equaliser at that juncture would have turned the game on its head and sent us out revitalised after the break with the bit between our teeth.

We huffed and puffed in the second half and knocked on the door, but never threatened to burst it open. Our commitment, thankfully, was never in doubt but we lacked guile and penetration and were blunt and toothless, and fortunate not to concede a second goal on the break. The defeat was annoying and demoralising but not terminal. Many of our rivals also dropped points so yesterday can go down as a missed opportunity that must not be repeated. Three points on Tuesday against Huddersfield are now a priority, and we owe them payback after our narrow defeat in the reverse fixture in December. It is worrying though that we have barely threatened to score in our last two away games and allowed two teams in Charlton and Birmingham to end long waits for a victory. Are we becoming a soft touch away from home? I can only hope that the last two matches were blips and we will soon be back on track.

More encouragingly, I watched Derby County, Middlesbrough and Bournemouth on *The Football League Show* last night and they all put on abject performances, so it is imperative that we do not overreact and keep things in perspective. It is a nervous time of the year and we have to retain our unity and self-belief. A new striker with some nous and experience wouldn't come amiss too, as he would help provide us with the fresh impetus required to help get us over the line. Wishful thinking perhaps, but a totally necessary move in my opinion, however it is one that for whatever reason seems highly unlikely to come to fruition. Let's hope that our inactivity does not come back to haunt us over the coming weeks.

Normal Service Resumed – 4/3/15

Victory in last night's clash with Huddersfield Town was an imperative if Brentford's promotion push was to get back on track after Saturday's minor derailment at St Andrew's, and the Bees stepped up to the plate and totally overwhelmed their opponents with a victory that was entirely as comfortable as the four-one scoreline suggests. Huddersfield had defeated Brentford in the reverse fixture in December so some element of revenge was also on the agenda and Brentford paid them back with interest, dominating the proceedings with sixty-eight percent possession and twenty-three shots at goal. More importantly, the win took Brentford back into the top six and leaves them in good heart for the dog-eat-dog promotion clash at Ipswich on Saturday.

Brentford needed to come out of the blocks quickly last night and they started well with Chris Long looking eager from the off. His first moment in the spotlight came as early as the fourth minute when he received the ball from Jonathan Douglas with his back to goal, turned quickly, left Wallace for dead, ran in on goal and his effort from just outside the area scorched past Smithies before the keeper could react. Not a bad way to celebrate your first start for the club. With any nerves settled, Brentford tore gaping holes in the Huddersfield rear-guard and Douglas missed a sitter and Smithies then saved sharply from Long when Diagouraga put him clear on goal, but the angle was tight, the keeper quick and brave and Brentford spurned their chances to increase their lead. The only danger to Brentford came from James Vaughan and Harry Bunn and, seemingly out of nothing, the two combined well for Bunn to turn outside the straining Odubajo, who was caught on his heels, and the finish was angled perfectly past Button into the bottom corner. A goal totally against the run of play that, yet again, highlighted what is always likely to happen in the Championship if you do not take your chances.

Bunn and Vaughan joined together in a preening and taunting celebration in front of a distinctly unimpressed horde behind the Ealing Road goal and were lucky to escape censure for their actions that reeked of arrogance and incitement. Bunn had once been a Brentford loan target but his behaviour last night demonstrated that despite his obvious talent, his maturity left a lot to be desired. As for Vaughan, he seemed to enjoy throwing his weight around and was totally indulged by a weak referee in Lee Collins who gave him at least three last warnings as his personal foul total totted up, yet incredibly the striker ended the game without receiving the yellow card that his antics sorely deserved.

Brentford should have been home and hosed by the interval but thankfully started the second half brightly and their efforts were rewarded early on when Jota tormented and bamboozled the hapless substitute Carroll and dribbled along the goal line before attempting to set up Long. The pass was half blocked but Jota was not to be denied, and showed great persistence in winning the ball back. The ball fell perfectly to the feet of Long who drilled the ball home from close range, with the Spaniard narrowly avoiding decapitation as the ball flew past his head en route to the back of the net. Huddersfield visibly wilted and funnelled back in damage limitation mode and, with the initiative given back to them, Brentford simply took over, played their football, and tore the visitors to shreds with Douglas and Diagouraga selflessly fetching and carrying which enabled Jota and Pritchard to indulge in their party pieces. Dallas too played an important but selfless role shuttling up and down the left flank and ensuring that he was always there to help Bidwell deal with Sean Scannell who had dominated proceedings in the first match between the two teams. His threat was totally snuffed out and he suffered the indignity of being substituted late on.

Brentford's pressure paid off when Diagouraga found Pritchard in a pocket of space just outside the box, he turned perfectly and his right foot effort hit a defender and was deflected perfectly into the top corner. Alex has now scored eight times this season and he is a potent goal threat as defenders have become increasingly wary of his ability to turn them inside out and drop off him, thus giving him the extra time and space he needs to shoot. Huddersfield gave up at this point and the game meandered to a close enlivened only by a thunderbolt into the bottom corner by substitute Jon Toral. Brentford were by no means flattered by their three-goal margin of victory and had they taken their chances or really gone for the jugular then Huddersfield would have received a real thrashing. As it is, our young loanees scored all four goals. Were the signings of Long, Pritchard and Toral initiated by Benham's stats or Warburton's contact book? Who knows and it really does not matter. That is a discussion for another time… ideally after the end of the season.

I would mention in passing two telling comments from a Huddersfield message board which highlight the chasm between the two teams last night: *Brentford are everything we are not, slick, fit, comfortable on the ball and incisive. Their keeper passed the ball better than any Town player.* We also out-passed them by a vast margin with a massive eighty-three percent of our six hundred and four passes being on the money. There were no real downsides to last night's performance. Button was totally untroubled but swept up in his normal vigilant manner and the back four looked a cohesive and confident unit. Liam Moore is beginning to bed in and James Tarkowski was his usual peerless self. He is still a work in progress but that work is likely to turn into a masterpiece. Andre Gray was long overdue a rest and he looked sharp and eager when he came on near the end to replace Chris Long who had been our real match winner on the night. We have all bemoaned the lack of an experienced striker but on the evidence of last night Gray and Long are certainly lively and good enough to provide us with a potent goal threat in the last quarter of the season. I still feel a third striker is a necessary precaution should injury or illness lurk, but that is a decision for Mark Warburton. Alan Judge is also nearing full fitness after a stop-start return to the side and his influence will surely be required at Ipswich. Our place in the top six might well be short-lived given that Ipswich play tonight and will overtake us should they get anything at Leeds and we could also do with Wigan doing us an unlikely favour at Norwich but we must not get distracted by the results of others. Our sole objective is simply to take care of our own business. Should we continue to do so and play with the vigour, vim and sheer excellence that we exhibited last night then this season could still end up with our winning a prize beyond our wildest expectations.

International Break – 5/3/15

Given that we are now in the Championship, I thought that I would simply follow the example of the team and go off on my own international break. I will be away for just over a week, missing the trip to Ipswich and returning home just in time for the Cardiff match. Isn't it an amazing stroke of good fortune that my holiday dates do not clash with a Brentford home game – I wonder how that happened as I, of course, had nothing to do with making all the arrangements necessary to bring this trip to fruition. I have a big birthday coming up later this month and my long-suffering wife decided to whisk me away for a week to an unknown destination. She did an incredible job of covering her tracks and I had no idea where we were going until we actually stepped onto the airplane.

Anyway I am now far away and relying on a dodgy and intermittent WiFi signal in order to remain in touch with news from home. I have managed to hear the amazing scores from Elland Road and Carrow Road respectively and later on I will be toasting our newfound friends at Leeds and Wigan for services rendered. I remember being in Thailand last February and waking up to similar good news when a Simon Moore inspired Bristol City team managed to win at Brisbane Road and enabled us to sneak ahead of Leyton Orient as their promotion challenge began to unravel.

We are now on a rollercoaster and our emotions will continue to veer from the highest of highs to the lowest of lows as every result counts and we now enter the business end of the season. I thought that our chances of promotion had pretty much gone as I emerged sullen and ashen faced from The Valley and I was also distinctly unhappy on the drive home from Birmingham, but three convincing home wins have kept us in the game and we remain in control of our own destiny.

Results are really all that matter now but it was particularly pleasing that we have also put on three excellent and pulsating performances in a row at Griffin Park, which have reinvigorated the fans as well as significantly improved our goal difference. Last night clearly demonstrated that the formbook means nothing and we simply need to follow the hoary old chestnut, *Who Dares Wins!*

Our style of play is totally based on being brave, patient and positive and we just have to remain true to our principles. If we do so and do not allow ourselves, both on and off the pitch, to get caught up in the emotion of the situation then I am certain we will prevail. Can we do it? Of course we can! Our defence is now more settled, pacy and cohesive, our midfield threatens goals from every quarter and Chris Long has emerged from the shadows and clearly demonstrated his promise as a potent and vibrant goal scorer who can provide us with an injection of talent and fresh enthusiasm just when we need it, at a time when minds and bodies can otherwise become paralysed with tension and fear.

We need Alan Judge to regain full fitness, and ideally see Lewis Macleod restored to good health and pushing for a place on the bench, but our squad is strong and probably the fittest in the entire league. Given some luck with injuries, the bounce of the ball and the idiosyncratic whims of megalomaniac referees I quite honestly feel that our fate is totally in our own hands. That is my own measured opinion and is as objective as I can make it. The difference between success and failure can be a hairsbreadth. Derby and now Norwich have had their seemingly serene and unstoppable progress towards the Premier League jeopardised by unforeseen injuries to key strikers and fate is sure to play its part in what will ultimately be decided over the last few weeks of what has already proved to be an unforgettable season.

I shall, of course, miss Saturday's titanic clash against Ipswich. Let's just hope that it is payback time and we do not repeat the defensive suicide we committed on Boxing Day. I will be waiting on tenterhooks for the news from Portman Road, but whatever happens on Saturday, I am certain that there will be several ladders to climb and snakes to slither down before our fate is decided.

Another's View – 9/3/15

As most of you know I am away at the moment being pampered and utterly spoiled by my wife as we celebrate my forthcoming birthday. Over the last few wonderful days, I have taken the advice of more sensible people than me and done my utmost to switch off and I have paid very little attention to what is going on in the outside world. Saturday afternoon, or mid-evening, given the time difference, was a rare exception, and after an early dinner I came back to the room, switched on *Star Sports* and was regaled with live coverage of the QPR versus Spurs match and took massive delight in watching our local rivals subside to yet another damaging home defeat. Wouldn't it be quite amazing if we manage to avoid playing them next season for the best of all possible reasons – our promotion and their relegation? Stranger things have happened.

Simultaneously, I started fiddling desperately with my iPad with no real expectation of success, and to my surprise and pleasure I was soon graced with the dulcet tones of Mark Burridge ably assisted by Scott Barron, and was able to listen to Bees Player's excellent coverage of the Ipswich match. It is sheer torture having to rely on someone else describing the action and you feel totally helpless as you wait for confirmation of what has actually happened. After ninety-six minutes of torment we finally emerged with a potentially crucial point which I celebrated long into the night along with Mark Warburton's selection as *London Manager of the Year* and Clayton Donaldson's unexpected but very welcome late, late show at Derby. I am totally unqualified to provide a first-hand report of the happenings at Portman Road so I am really grateful to fellow Bees fan Stephen Burke who has provided the following excellent match report. Thank you Stephen for taking the time and trouble to do so and for getting me off the hook!

It wasn't the greatest game of football played by Brentford this season, but the one-one draw at Ipswich was one of the most compelling and tense Bees matches I have seen. And it was Brentford's first draw since October (surely a club record?), and only the fifth this season. After Ipswich's comfortable win at Griffin Park on Boxing Day, I was nervous before the game. And the nerves got greater in the first twenty minutes. Ipswich were all over us, pressing high up the pitch, denying us space. Button had no one to pass out to and we resorted to the head tennis that is Ipswich's forte.

It was no surprise that Ipswich took the lead after nine minutes, inevitably through Murphy, albeit a soft goal following a corner when Moore was out-jumped and the ball fell kindly to the predatory striker. We just couldn't get our normal passing game going and Ipswich chased and harried us all over the pitch, which was poor and bobbly. Gradually we got into the game and one of our better moves led to the equalising goal with Douglas heading in after twenty-five minutes following good work by Gray, Judge and Dallas. Gray and Judge also both came close to giving us the lead before the interval.

Again we were very slow off the mark at the start of the second half and Murphy amazingly missed the sitter of the season when it was surely easier to score than miss. He was also denied when clean through but Button made one of a series of great saves. The Bees got stronger and started to win the second ball, which we had failed to do early on. Toumani, Douglas and Pritchard began to run the game although Judge naturally looked rusty after his long lay-off and was replaced after the hour. Credit must go to Tarkowski who will be feeling it on Monday morning as Murphy and Sears (and then Wood) were niggly, tough opponents who really made him work. Moore, however, was out of his depth and struggled throughout. Moses too found it particularly difficult dealing with the Ipswich challenge down the left from Parr and Mings.

None of our substitutions changed the game. Jota struggled to get into the game when he came on for Judge while Gray had worked his socks off with little reward before giving way to Long. Dean however did well, replacing Moore for the last twenty minutes as we finally tightened up at the back. The Bees held on and a draw will have been welcomed by both teams, particularly given the results elsewhere. At the end of the game both sets of fans were left breathless as they headed home. Two very different styles had in effect cancelled each other out. Ipswich's long ball game forced Brentford to adopt a similar approach at times, much unlike our normal patient passing game. Ipswich just didn't give us the time to play, on occasions supported by a referee who let them foul away with apparent impunity. But we stood up to them and all credit to the Bees for earning the point in a real game of Championship football.

It was also great to see Jay Tabb ("he's a Brentford fan," went the chant) again and he was central to a lot of Ipswich's more creative play. He returned the respect, acknowledging the Bees fans and not milking a couple of hard challenges on him. So ten matches left and with five points covering the top seven teams, it's still anyone's promotion.

Perfect technique from Toumani Diagouraga.

Mark Burridge – Part One – 13/3/15

I have just returned from a wonderful relaxing break courtesy of my wonderful wife, Miriam where I simply did what every self-respecting exiled Bee does on match day – tune into Bees Player.

Mark Burridge, Chris Wickham and special guest, Scott Barron, transported me from my exotic climes to the more prosaic surroundings of Portman Road. I shut my eyes and it was as if I was there in the stands alongside them. As always, they did a quite magnificent job, acting as they do as the eyes and ears of all Brentford supporters who, for whatever reason, are unable to attend a match. From personal experience I know just how hard it is to make sense of what is happening on the pitch below you and how difficult it is not to let your emotions and bias run amok and somehow manage to provide a balanced, coherent and accurate description of the match as it unfolds.

Mark Burridge is the consummate professional, with a wonderful relaxed tone of voice. He paints vivid verbal pictures and yet he knows exactly when he needs to bring in his co-commentator or player summariser. Having listened to some of the efforts from other clubs far more exalted than Brentford, I just have to say how blessed we are with the whole Bees Player operation which is streets ahead of the service provided by the overwhelming majority of our rivals. I caught up with Mark recently and over the next couple of articles I will let him tell you all about Bees Player, how it came about, and what it means to him. Thanks also to Chris Wickham for his help in providing this information.

Why Brentford?

My father has always been a staunch Bees fan . When he was a table tennis international, he trained with the Brentford players. He also helped set up the Junior section many years ago in Frank Blunstone's days. I believe he was the first Chairman, or President, of Brentford Juniors. At one time he was invited on to the Board but declined due to having taken up golf and didn't want to be committed to watching us play home and away each week. I have no idea what my first game was, probably around 1965. I remember the Cup games at Cardiff and Hull. We went back with the players on the coach to the station. I have probably only missed ten home games in the last thirty odd years. It's fair to say most people who know me realise Brentford is massively important in my life.

Bees Player – a potted history

It started off as Bees World in the 2001/02 season as a free service for two seasons. We used the same rota and team that commentated for the blind supporters. It then became a subscription service for commentary, then came all the other additions such as interviews, etc. With Bees Player as a whole there is so much content for subscribers as well as the match commentary. We started off doing this either talking through a standard old-fashioned phone, at many away games doing it on a mobile phone. At Cambridge United, in 2001, I was sat amongst the home supporters, trying to relay the action. It was a bit strange, as were the looks we were getting! Long-time subscribers will know that over the years it has changed from starting a few minutes before the kickoff to being a full MATCH DAY LIVE programme, where listeners have a programme that runs from 2.30pm, right through to 5.30pm, including buildup, pre-match discussion, half time interviews with various guests, and the post-match thoughts of the manager and key players with interviews from Billy Reeves.

When Chris (Wickham) was involved on the commentary side he was keen to get players involved as summarisers where possible and that takes the experience for fans to a whole new level. Not only does Richard Lee work as our summariser at home games (if available) we've also enjoyed the wisdom of Alan McCormack, Sam Saunders, Kevin O'Connor, Harlee Dean, ex-players Paul Gibbs and Glenn Poole plus Ben Burgess at games in the North West. We must also pay homage to Luis Melville who was the ultimate professional for me when working on MDL, his enthusiasm and attention to detail helped take the whole programme to another level.

So the product has come a long way from the early days and a lot of preparation goes into trying to put on a good match experience for subscribers. Fans can also get their own thoughts across via Twitter (@brentfordfc #beesplayer). It's the next best thing to being there is how we like to describe MDL, so fan interaction is important to the listeners and us. Further emphasising the progress of the whole experience, Brentford have invested in state-of-the-art equipment in recent seasons to ensure we deliver the same sound quality as you would enjoy on mainstream radio broadcasts. With the addition to the media team of Sean Ridley (Video Content Manager) subscribers will have seen added extras this season such as the 30-40 minute-long highlights footage less than twenty-four hours after the game, synchronized with our "live audio" commentary. This is really useful for long-distance fans who don't get to see the players in action very often, and it has been very pleasing to hear how much subscribers love this additional service this season. Sean works through the night to get this ready on time and the Club continues to increase its spend in all the highest spec equipment to make sure our fans get the most comprehensive portfolio of essential Bees viewing. Seeing more of it up close this season, it's fair to say the thorough professionalism of the media team as a whole is a testament to all the hard work that goes on in the week and on match days, whether it's covering Youth Team, Development Squad or First Team games.

Helping the disadvantaged keep in touch?

The Blind Commentary Scheme at Griffin Park has a long and proud history. Brentford were only the second English Club to introduce such a scheme which started back in August 1951 with Eric White and Peter Pond-Jones covering the game against Rotherham. As hard as it is to believe, Bees manager Jackie Gibbons assisted them throughout the match with his own contributions. Brentford won 2-0!! Alan Denman, who still assists in some home matches each season, has been a contributor for around forty years and others such as the late Mary Farley, Alan Rogers, Geoff Buckingham and Steve Leggett have given their valuable services freely over the years to enable this proud service to flourish.

Through the generosity of The Brentford Lifeline Society, our blind and visually impaired supporters (and visiting fans) can hear the commentary through a UHF Radio system, which operates anywhere within the stadium up to a range of two hundred metres. Not only is this available at Griffin Park, our fans can also pick up the full MATCH DAY LIVE service at away games too. We had four blind fans at MK Dons last season who were able to pick up Brentford commentary on the day, rather than a "home club" service.

Apart from the huge privilege to be involved in bringing the game to our blind fans we have been fortunate to get to know some of them personally too, many having come to GP for several years. I've driven Andy Godfrey to several away matches and anyone who knows him will say the same, that he is non-stop entertainment and fun, is blessed with an incredible memory of Bees games from yesteryear and football in general. Andy has also come across quite a few Bees fans over the years as he is a schoolteacher in languages – I wish he had been mine as I'm sure I would now be fluent in French and German! Brentford still actively encourage new blind and partially sighted fans to come along so if anyone reading this knows of someone who could benefit from the club's service with a match day visit to Griffin Park, the scheme will offer them a great welcome.

Best and worst working conditions?

Bramall Lane is excellent, high up, plenty of room, a proper long gantry. Plus you can stand, which I far prefer. Basically the higher up and more central you are, the easier it is to see what is happening. Bolton's this year was very good and from seasons ago Reading's gantry view was impressive so I'm looking forward to going back there soon. Wembley is, as you would expect, just amazing, a great experience plus a great meal beforehand! Shame we haven't yet turned up as a team. Maybe this year? The old Saltergate was a nightmare, simply no room at all, a real hazard, to be brutally honest. Anywhere behind a glass enclosure isn't good as you don't get the atmosphere, although we have not had any this season.

What does Griffin Park mean to you?

Well it's a spiritual home for all of us. Even if I'm simply driving into London I get a buzz from passing it, tinged with disappointment I'm not going to a game! I've seen all the changes over the years and, like many others, a big part of me doesn't want to leave, yet we know it has to happen.

Finding your own voice and style?

I guess we all have professional commentators we like and don't like. The best radio commentator for me is Alan Green. He has this ability, like no other, to bring listeners the goal as it happens. His timing and tempo is different class. My view is simple – the excitement is when a commentator can work up to "a chance" that split second when you know a player is going for goal and you wait for the crowd to erupt to know it's in the back of the net. Listeners want to know the basics first and foremost - where's the ball on the pitch, are Brentford attacking or defending? If there is an attempt on goal then tell the listeners straightaway what's happened. So basically, I will try and get a good tempo for the game and keep with it. Remember you are "painting a picture in words."

Be honest. If Brentford are playing very poorly, say so. Our fans respect that far more. They won't want to read message boards after a game and discover those at the game said we had played badly whilst we were relaying all throughout game that Brentford were matching the opposition. That's a sure way to lose trust of your subscribers. Be fair and respectful to the opposition. As fans we are, naturally, pro-Brentford but give credit where it's due to our opponents. Also, try and be light-hearted and have good banter with your co-commentator. Some effort at humour does mix it all up for listeners.

There will be more gems from Mark shortly.

Sh*t Happens! – 15/3/15

Apologies for the directness and bluntness of today's title. It really wasn't what I'd originally had in mind. My initial intention had been to write a piece themed around the idea of catching up with all the news, rumours and scuttlebutt in and around Griffin Park after returning from my trip abroad, but my plans were rather overtaken by the ultimately frustrating events of yesterday afternoon, which have necessitated a total change of emphasis.

Things had started so well with a lovely relaxing lunch at The Weir followed by the post-prandial passeggiata stroll through the splendour of The Butts and the nearby maze of terraced houses, then past The Griffin, and finally inside the ground where I eagerly sought out the company of some badly missed old friends.

I had been far away for over a week and really needed a fresh fix of all things Brentford. How had we played at Ipswich? Was there any transfer gossip? Who should start this afternoon in central defence and upfront, Liam Moore or Harlee Dean, Andre Gray or Chris Long? How fit is Alan Judge? I needed the answers to these and many other pressing questions from established Brentford sages such as Billy Reeves, Mark Burridge, Paul Briers, Matt Casey, Phil Coffey, Dave Morley and Ian Townsend. I paced up and down the Braemar Road forecourt and into various byways and boltholes in order to seek them out as I needed to reconnect with them, hear their opinions and even argue the toss with them. Some I found, others I didn't but, overall, my endeavours were rewarded, as by the time the two teams emerged I felt replenished and reinvigorated, really back where I belonged and totally re-immersed in the DNA of my beloved club.

Three points against a mid-table and seemingly disinterested Cardiff City team that appeared to be going through the motions in a first half totally dominated by the Bees seemed to be a formality and Brentford should have been leading by more than a single goal at the interval. For all their possession, imagination and energy, Brentford did not create as many chances as they should, but after Jonathan Douglas had a goal ruled out after he challenged ex-Bee Simon Moore in the air and Stuart Dallas miscued badly after a dazzling run by the mercurial Jota, Andre Gray tapped in from close range after Moore could only paw away a long range free kick by Alex Pritchard, reminiscent of his recent effort against AFC Bournemouth.

Cardiff were totally outthought and outplayed and time wasted shamelessly almost from the outset without interference from a weak and benign referee. Morrison and the moody Macheda both saw yellow for niggly fouls and Brentford let the visitors off the hook by not going for the jugular and securing the second goal that would surely have sealed victory and left the visitors dead and buried.

The second half started as the first had ended with the Bees on top, and only a sharp low save from Moore prevented Gray from scoring at the near post. And then, having been under no pressure whatsoever Brentford, not for the first time this season, exposed their soft underbelly and self-destructed. This time the unexpected *kapore-hun*, or *scapegoat* for those of you who do not speak Yiddish was goalkeeper David Button, so often our salvation this season, who now showed his less positive side when he spilled an easy ball when he collided with the covering Harlee Dean and Macheda was left with an open goal. Dean was the innocent fall-guy in this instance but Tarkowski was also beaten far too easily in the air by Alex Revell in the lead up to the goal. Unusually, heads seemed to go down after this bolt from the blue and another gift was soon in the offing when Macheda played the ball in behind an advanced defence, Button came, then stopped, left himself exposed and high and dry in no-man's land, and was easily lobbed by Revell. Two goals from two chances and both were easily avoidable and came from totally inexcusable defending. Even more galling was that they were Cardiff's only efforts on target throughout the entire match.

Brentford came back strongly but for all their dominance in possession and flurries in the box, created very little. Jota and Pritchard schemed in vain but ran into blind alleys and even when Judge came on to add his energy and change of pace not too much fell our way as we were smothered by the sheer weight of numbers. Tarkowski and Toral headed wastefully over. Moore tipped over a lame header from Bidwell and that was it until Cardiff were reduced to nine men with former Brentford loanee Kadeem Harris dismissed for a high tackle on Judge which probably looked worse than it was, and Macheda receiving a long overdue second yellow card for a raised foot on Tarkowski.

The last ten minutes saw Cardiff under siege but Brentford lost their heads, stopped playing their football, went Route One and played into Cardiff's hands with a series of aimless crosses which were meat and drink to their huge defenders. Smith's deflected volley went just wide and a heated late appeal for handball were the closest that we came to an equaliser.

This was a tough but not necessarily mortal blow to our promotion prospects as we beat ourselves and allowed a horrible, sly and negative team to walk away sniggering with three totally undeserved points. Once again, we gave away soft goals through failing to do our job and defend properly. We have to work so hard to score ourselves and yet we are so profligate at the other end. No wonder we appeared so demoralised once we had conceded the first goal. At the other end, some of our passing was a joy to watch but the final ball rarely fell kindly or was often overhit.

For all our possession and clever, intricate play, Simon Moore was rarely extended and we only tested his supposed weakness from long range once and hit the jackpot when he spilled Pritchard's free kick. Surely an opportunity wasted and a mere five shots on target from twenty-four attempts tells its own sad story.

This season has been so exciting and successful that it almost appears carping to criticise but we really should not be repeating the same errors at both ends of the field in March as were being made in September. Margins are so slim and there are certain to be many more peaks and troughs over the last crucial nine games, but today was a massive missed opportunity and our prospects of automatic promotion now look slim. We simply need to regroup, put today down as just one of those games and ensure that we do not return empty-handed from our long, tough trip to a resurgent Blackburn Rovers on Tuesday night. We will certainly need to defend far better than yesterday and snap up whatever chances we manage to create. Ipswich and Wolves are breathing down our neck and we need to ensure that sixth place at a minimum remains ours. We deserve no less after our incredible exploits this season, but we certainly make life hard for ourselves sometimes, and yesterday was a prime example.

Mark Burridge – Part Two – 17/3/15

Brentford play a quite crucial match away at Blackburn Rovers tonight, and they face no easy task against a team bang in form and justifiably full of confidence after three league wins in a row and a meritorious draw at Anfield in the FA Cup. The Bees, on the other hand, must still be smarting after Saturday's ludicrous self-inflicted defeat to Cardiff City and need to get back on track immediately if they are to retain their limpet-like hold onto that crucial final playoff place in the Championship table.

A midweek away game in Lancashire, particularly on a work night, is too tough an ask for most of us and I salute all of those rabid Bees supporters, heroes each and every one of them, who will shortly be setting off on their long and hopefully rewarding journey to Blackburn. I am sure that I will not be alone in keeping in touch with events as they unfold at Ewood Park by tuning into Bees Player and listening to Mark Burridge describe all the action in his normal calm and professional manner. Which leads me on to the second part of my recent interview with Mark, where he expounded on all things Brentford and shed further light on the role of Bees Player.

How honest can you be?

Very. All of us just say what we see and feel. The media team has always been good with us that way, and we are trusted to say it how it is. Common sense has to prevail in certain areas, if there's a player who is having a poor game you should say, everyone has a bad day at the office, but being completely disrespectful to our own players is crossing the line.

How did you get the gig in the first place?

I saw an advert at the back of a fanzine for volunteers to commentate for the blind supporters back in 1997. The first game I did some commentary on we beat Gillingham 2-0 and the first Bees goal I had the pleasure to call was by Bob Taylor. By 2001/02 when clubs were encouraged and expected to cover away games too (in the trial period) Gary Hargraves asked me to commentate at Newcastle for the League Cup game. I sat about three yards from Newcastle legend Malcolm Macdonald and they couldn't get us a phone line, so we had to use Gary's phone. I gave out my own number in case anyone wanted a message read out. At half time I discovered there were thirty-eight texts to read! The Bees were one up through Owusu's early goal and it was a great experience.

Gary then asked if I could do the away games that season and I did all but three, covering away games with Mark Chapman. It was a great season, tremendous fun and we so nearly gained promotion. I am not sure exactly how many games I've been involved in commentary for Brentford over the years but I'd estimate it's been around six hundred.

The Bees Player team of commentators and analysts

Our current squad comprises Billy Reeves, Alan Denman (over forty years with both the blind scheme and Bees Player) and I on commentary, our summarisers include Chris Wickham, Mark Chapman, Ciaran Brett, Dave Morley, Natalie Sawyer and Mick Cabble, plus players when they are available.

Working with players and guests – do's and don'ts

Be respectful and have fun. With players you simply cannot ask them to criticise their team mates, or even a fellow professional who is guilty of a very bad challenge. Try and bring them in as much as possible and if the opportunity arises take the topic off the game for a few seconds. The players can come up with some enlightening and lighthearted stories about their team mates, all in good humour, of course!

Unforgettable games – good and bad!

So many memorable ones, particularly this season. I loved Forest away, total domination by Brentford. The first half at Cardiff away this year was mesmerising. The win against Derby, Preston and Peterborough away last year, that first away game I ever covered at Newcastle. All were very memorable. Bradford City at home on a rain sodden pitch with Nathan Elder's late winning header in the title-winning season. Blackpool away in 2002, with a brilliant opening goal from Lloyd Owusu in a superb and important win.

Mind you, nothing will ever match Sheffield United away in 2013 will it? Keith Stroud, four penalties, three reds, numerous yellows (was it nine?) and a late equaliser from us too. Two-two and we felt robbed. Anyone who was there will never, ever forget that night.

Bad ones? Well nothing was more painful than the last fifteen minutes of the Reading home game in 2002. It was like being punched in the stomach when Cureton scored. I only got over it last year with our three-one win against them!!

As for football of a quality I hope we never see again, the very word "Macclesfield" can send shivers down my spine, the one-nil loss on a Tuesday night there under Terry Butcher was about as difficult to commentate on as I can remember. Morecambe at home too with a one-nil loss. In both games, the football was as bad as I can remember -we were fifty shades of diabolical!

Best Interviewees and analysts?

I think it's fair to say all are good in their way. We've added "Fan Interviews" to half/full time, which seem very popular and it's great to try and hear how different supporters came to follow the Bees. Of the players we've worked with there's no doubt Richard Lee and Sam Saunders have a potential career in media, indeed they've both already worked for Sky. Richard has a brilliant radio voice and I wouldn't be surprised to see him on Sky's Soccer Saturday at games next season. Hopefully it's decent media training for players anyway, if they are injured/suspended, to get involved with a live game and express their thoughts.

"It's raining goals at Griffin Park!" – Discuss

Up there with "They think it's all over!" Even the very best of commentators are lucky if they come up with one gem in their career. You have yours Greville. It's in Brentford folklore. I do use it, tongue in cheek, if there's a goal rush at Griffin Park.

How far can we go and how quickly?

Well, we can get to The Premier League next season. Nine games left and eight great teams going for two automatics and four playoff places. Our run in looks fairly good compared to others but it's about standards and keeping them high, as Mark Warburton always says. Such is the quality of this League that if you only play to around 60% of your best then you'll get beaten. It's going to be a tremendously exciting six weeks. Personally, I'd love sixth place right now! What an achievement that would be for Matthew Benham, Mark Warburton and everyone at the Club – and I'd fancy us in the playoffs for sure! Next season? Well who knows – there are going to be a few changes and it would be a brave or wise man to say at this stage. I am neither brave, nor wise!

Bees Player – the legacy

Whichever way the service goes I do hope we keep it "in house" as having a slightly biased commentary does make fans feel more connected with the service. At present the listeners appear to like the way it all knits together, though with ever-changing technology we must adapt to what the fans desire. Speaking for myself, though, I'm sure all the others in our team echo this sentiment. It's been a joy to work on Bees World/Bees Player as I've met some great people, made strong lasting friendships through this experience with both fans and colleagues and if the media team are happy with what we do and the supporters enjoy the service, then I'm happy too. After all we are one big family in every way and that's what makes us proud to support Brentford Football Club.

To catch all the commentaries and interviews plus up to date news, you can subscribe to Bees Player for less than 10p a day at **www.brentfordfc.co.uk**

BBB At Blackburn – 18/3/15

I worked late last night and then, just to cap it all, had to sit through a boring committee meeting that dragged on interminably. I kept sneaking looks at my watch and after a couple of earlier failed attempts that brought down a cascade of dirty looks on me from my colleagues who seemed more than happy to spend the entire evening chewing the fat, I managed to slip out of a side door almost undetected accompanied by a few last gasps and hisses of disapproval, and with a sigh of relief, rushed home where a far more urgent and pressing appointment awaited me.

It was almost kickoff time before I was able to switch on Bees Player and my Herculean efforts were immediately rewarded when I was able to catch the last moments of the pre-match build up so expertly provided by Mark Burridge and his guest summariser Ben Burgess. Ben has established a niche for himself as a lucid, knowledgeable and entertaining contributor to the coverage of Brentford matches in his native North West of England, and, as always, he did not disappoint. Big Ben Burgess, or Triple B, as he became known, almost singlehandedly transformed our fortunes when, as a callow and unknown teenager, Steve Coppell brought him in on loan from Blackburn Rovers in August 2001. Finally we had a dual threat up front and someone to take the weight off Lloyd Owusu who had been forced to plough a lonely furrow for far too long.

Scott Partridge, so elusive and effective on his arrival, had been found out at the higher level and his threat snuffed out, and, as for Mark McCammon, his signing was an aberration – another bad joke inflicted upon us by Ron Noades. I was just this morning speaking about McCammon on the telephone with a friend of mine, a fellow Brentford fanatic, who interrupted my stream of consciousness with the terse, pithy and heartfelt description of him as: *that useless lump!* I couldn't have put it better myself. Poor Mark certainly looked the part and had pace, power and strength in abundance, but whilst he was certainly an athlete, he was never an effective footballer at our level of the game. The ball clanged off him, he always arrived just a millisecond too late to capitalise on chances and for those of you who wonder how lethal he was with the ball in the air, I would just refer you to his glaring missed headed chances in the Cup Final against Port Vale, and even more crucially late on at QPR when he managed to bounce a simple late headed chance down into the ground and over the bar from almost under it. If that had gone in, as it surely should have done, then our history might have been rewritten, as we would only have needed to draw that fateful last game of the season against Reading. He tried hard and never shirked, but whilst the flesh was willing he never justified the fee reputed to have been paid for him, and we would surely have been far better served by the elusive Trevor Benjamin who teased us by seeming to be on the verge of signing for us for the best part of a season but somehow always evaded our desperate clutches.

Ben Burgess made us all stand up and take notice when he announced his arrival with a precocious and beautifully taken goal to clinch victory against Port Vale with a twenty-yarder curled perfectly into the bottom corner, and he immediately looked the part. He was well built, strong, powerful, deadly in the air and impossible to knock off the ball. But he was far more than a mere bruiser as he had a subtle left foot that could open a can of peas and he also had an excellent eye for a pass. He formed a deadly partnership up front with Owusu, and but for Noades's parsimony we would surely have obtained automatic promotion. Coppell was forced to manage with one hand tied behind his back and late on in the 2001/02 season had to sell important squad members in Paul Gibbs and Gavin Mahon. Crucially, he was apparently not allowed to bring in a loan replacement when Burgess damaged his hamstring when playing for Eire Under 21s. Echoes indeed of the fateful injury suffered by Owusu when playing in a friendly for Ghana against an obscure German team, which cost us his services in the promotion run-in in 2006 and contributed heavily to yet another promotion choke.

After incurring his injury, Burgess was little more than a passenger, forced to limp through the remainder of the season, playing like a stork on one leg. His goal threat was seriously diminished and he scored only once more – unfortunately at the wrong end, deflecting a free kick into his own net in the Playoff final against Stoke City. Once promotion was lost our squad was dismantled and the next couple of years were a desperate struggle, ironically with McCammon becoming our number one striker by default, initially partnered with another young loanee in Rowan Vine, an indication of how far we had fallen so quickly.

As for BBB, there was never a chance of our signing him on a permanent basis and he went on to have a career at Stockport, Hull and Blackpool that, whilst decent enough, due to a series of niggling injuries never touched the heights that once looked so likely. He came close to notching twenty goals for us and left us with some indelible memories, in particular that unforgettable, acrobatic, overhead volleyed goal in our televised four-nil victory against Brighton, where he demonstrated an almost balletic beauty that totally belied his bulk.

As for last night, Burgess revelled in Brentford's skill on the ball as well as their dogged determination not to be defeated despite conceding two goals, which were largely due to poor defending, lack of concentration and giving the ball away cheaply in dangerous areas of the pitch. He would have been particularly impressed by Jota's delightful solo equalising goal when he ran unopposed over half the length of the pitch with Long's clever decoy run creating the space and room for the Spaniard to slot the ball unerringly into the corner of the net from just outside the penalty area. On second thoughts, I can't imagine Ben ever choosing to run fifty yards if there was any other viable alternative! Ben would also have taken great pleasure in Brentford's other two goals last night. Chris Long provided further evidence of his determination to shoot on sight and received his just reward when his shot was deflected over the helpless keeper. Substitute Andre Gray scored the winner with a close range predatory finish from Jota's half-saved shot and proved that he was Johnny-on-the-Spot for the second match running.

Sheer delight! The happiness of a late winner.

Last night's hard-fought three-two victory has given a massive boost to our playoff aspirations and will have restored confidence after the disappointment of last Saturday. All in all, I had a great night's listening at home with the exception of my disappointment at the slovenly early goal conceded and I had barely finished celebrating Long's equaliser when, given the presence of my wife in the room, I had to stifle my fury at the concession of a second goal immediately afterwards. But all's well that ends well and there is now everything to play for as we enter the home stretch, and victory on Saturday against Millwall is a prerequisite given that Ipswich and Wolves both won last night and are hot on our heels. Bolton's tattooed striker Craig Davies has never been a particular favourite of mine, and he went even further down in my estimation last night when he missed a point blank header that would have given his team a last minute equaliser at Ipswich. He proved far less deadly in front of goal last night than he had been when he scored unerringly against us last year into an empty net from way out on the right wing. That being said, it is simply up to Brentford to keep on the front foot and win as many of their games as they can without paying too much attention to our rivals as they hopefully keep taking points off each other.

As for Ben Burgess, it was such a pleasure to listen to him and last night brought back so many splendid memories of his past performances. Bob Taylor shared many of the same attributes as Ben. But with the exception of Marcello Trotta who possesses some of his languid skills, we have seen nobody quite like him since he left us thirteen years ago. BBB Mark II would be a magnificent addition to our ranks next season.

Brentford Quiz – 20/3/15

Tomorrow's match is looming ominously ahead of us and given the fact that so many of our rivals are playing against each other, a victory and three points against a Millwall team fighting for their life at the bottom of the table is an absolute imperative. Like every other true Brentford supporter I have total faith in our team to produce the goods when it is necessary and I am very confident that not only will we put on a decent performance tomorrow lunchtime but we shall also come away with the points. Given that we are fast approaching *squeaky bum time* as it is so inelegantly called, I thought that I would do my best today to take our collective minds off what is certain to be a nervous encounter tomorrow and instead I am setting you all a Brentford Quiz. Apart from the tie-break, every question concerns Brentford players and matches since 1970 so there is really very little excuse for the vast majority of you not to be right on the money with all your answers. So here we go:

1. How many appearances has Kevin O'Connor made for the club?

2. What did Kevin O'Connor do with his last touch of the ball to date in a Brentford shirt?

3. Who are the top five goal scorers for Brentford since 1970? One of them did score for the club before that year.

4. Who has been shown the most red cards for Brentford since 1970, and how many times has he been sent off? Who are second and third in the list?

5. Which current Brentford player has been sent off three times for the club?

6. How many Brentford players has Keith Stroud sent off – so far?

7. Which Brentford player has missed the most consecutive penalty kicks since 1970, and how many in a row did he miss?

8. Who has scored the most penalty kicks for Brentford since 1970?

9. Name the eight Brentford players who have a 100% success record from the penalty spot and have taken more than one penalty for the club?

10. Who was the last Brentford loanee to score two goals on his debut for the club?

11. Who was the last Bee to score four goals in a game?

12. How many hat tricks did Lloyd Owusu score in 1998/99 and which club did he score two hat tricks against that season?

13. Which loan goalkeeper was ever-present, named Player of the Year and conceded under a goal per game for Brentford?

14. Ashley Bayes played twelve games for the Bees. How many goals did he concede?

15. Name five Brentford outfield players who have played in goal after the first choice was sent off or injured?

16. Who never missed a game and played 157 consecutive league games before he left the club?

17. Who was sent off in the twelfth minute of his Brentford debut and never played for us again?

18. Name five players who were nominated as team or club captain?

Tiebreak Question: Which Brentford personality was involved in the 1933 FA Cup Final between Everton and Manchester City?

Good luck to everyone!

One Point – I'll Take It! – 22/3/15

With barely five minutes left on the clock in Saturday lunchtime's clash with our neighbours, Millwall, it looked as if it would all end in tears. Particularly *Chez Waterman* where my wife was waiting on tenterhooks for the result of the match, knowing as she did – and I didn't – that she was planning a surprise birthday dinner for me on Saturday evening and she didn't want the so-called guest of honour sulking in a corner and reduced to a series of monosyllabic grunts.

I was surprised and delighted when my son, Nick, unexpectedly asked to accompany me to the match as normally he is a more than reluctant attendee, but I didn't twig that his presence had a more nefarious purpose. He seemed to spend the entire ninety-four minutes with his head buried in his iPhone rather than concentrating on what was happening on the pitch and little did I realise that he was sending my wife a constant series of texts updating her not only on the score, but, more importantly, a barometer on my state of mind and my likely temper later in the day.

There was a time when I would allow a defeat or poor performance to spoil my evening. I would allow myself to fall into a deep funk and replay the horror show on a continuous mental tape loop, and woe betide anyone, friend or family member alike, who had the misfortune to have to spend time with me for the next twenty-four hours or so. Now things have changed, maturity and old age have finally kicked in – not before time I would add – and I no longer allow results on the pitch to interfere too much with the rest of my life. I am delighted to say that despite the events at Griffin Park yesterday we all had a wonderful time last night, with much merriment, eating, drinking and good conversation which lasted well into the early hours of Sunday morning. So please excuse me if today's article is not as polished as I would like but I am a bit bleary eyed and not thinking too straight.

On reflection I am extremely pleased that last night I was able to take my mind off matters at Griffin Park as yesterday's performance was disappointing in the extreme and Brentford were more than fortunate to emerge with a point from a match where, despite their customary overwhelming amount of possession, they gave further truth to that old adage, *It's not what you have, it's what you do with it.* Millwall proved to be tough and resilient opponents who came with a game plan which worked perfectly for them. They packed their defence, pressed us high up the pitch and then funnelled back denying us space and room in the final third where the visitors were more than happy to show us outside onto both flanks where we were impotent and created little danger. We played a constant series of passes, but mainly backwards and sideways. Gray was left isolated in the penalty area and when on the rare occasions he did manage to escape the close attention of the giant Jos Hooiveld his finishing was wild and inaccurate.

We started the game slowly as if finding it hard to adapt to the early lunchtime start and our customary skill on the ball and clever runs into space were rarely evident as we lacked our normal tempo and were reduced to slinging a series of wasteful balls into the penalty area which were meat and drink to their tall defenders. Apart from an excellent header from Jota that dipped onto the junction of post and crossbar and a long range effort from Odubajo straight down the keeper's throat, we seldom threatened and were put onto the back foot by Millwall's other tactic – one which we should be more than used to by now, as they were the latest in a series of teams who have clocked our Achilles heel. They simply played a series of long balls over and behind our central defenders in an effort to find space and make them turn. Gregory and O'Brien were a pair of eager and pacy runners who caused Dean and Tarkowski no end of problems, if not running them entirely ragged. The alarm bells had been ringing well in advance of Millwall's opener when Upson played the ball over the top of our non-existent defence, Button came out, more in hope than expectation, but was easily beaten to the ball by Gregory who had escaped Dean's attention and slotted home. Yet again we had fallen for a sucker punch, just as we had against Cardiff, twice, and Blackburn.

It could have been worse when Gregory fired over before we finally woke up and came to our senses, managed to string some passes together and forced four excellent saves from Forde who stretched backwards to tip over a beautifully executed Dallas lob, then denied Douglas and Dallas again from close range before pushing a long-range Pritchard free kick round the post. These were crucial saves that denied us the fillip of an equaliser before the interval. As it was, we pressed forward early in the second half and Gray had two early sights of goal which he spurned. Millwall were playing deeper and more cagily but received a massive boost when Dean lost possession and we were swiftly punished with Douglas the only Brentford player attempting to prevent Woolford standing up a perfect cross which took Button out of the game and allowed the gangly O'Brien to nod in from almost on the goal line. Another terrible goal to concede and one that was totally preventable, and but for a brave block from Tarkowski it could have been three shortly afterwards. As it was, we looked shell-shocked and impotent and despite the presence of Judge who gave us fresh legs, imagination and impetus, we did little with the ball which would invariably progress up either wing where Moses and Jota on one flank, or Bidwell and Pritchard on the other would eventually run into a blind alley and the chance would evaporate.

Smith and Toral came on as we went to three at the back but despite another sharp save by Forde from a Jota effort the game seemed to be ebbing away from us until finally the tide turned. Judge ran along the byline with the ball seemingly tied to his bootlaces and invited Woolford to lunge into him and he suitably obliged. An obvious penalty which Pritchard calmly converted. Now it was panic stations at the back as Millwall tried desperately to hold onto the win that their bravery and organisation fully deserved, but in injury time Pritchard jinked, dropped a shoulder and his low cross was only half cleared by the straining Nelson and Odubajo buried the chance low into the corner. There were three minutes remaining but we lost our shape and discipline as we poured men forward in a Kamikaze attempt to force an unlikely victory and there was almost a sting in the tail when the Sumo-like Gary Taylor-Fletcher showed strength and subtlety in bursting past Bidwell and cleverly used Tarkowski as a screen before curling the ball inches wide.

One point is better than none but we were poor yesterday and fell far below the high standards we have set over the course of the season. We looked tired and flat, lacked our normal pace and invention, ran out of ideas and our defence creaked ominously whenever Millwall attacked. I am not sure if all the blame should be laid at the door of Dean and Tarkowski who were both unimpressive in the extreme. Perhaps they lacked cover and were left far too exposed as we pressed forward, but they were both a mistake waiting to happen and perhaps we now need yet another new defensive partnership. The truth remains evident, we have become a soft touch and have conceded six goals in our last three games, all of which were totally avoidable. We now come into the final international break of the season and we find ourselves outside the playoff places for the first time this year. Perhaps this might take some of the pressure off and be to our advantage, or maybe I am merely clutching at straws? But games are rapidly running out and over the course of the next twelve days we have to rest tired legs, recover our poise and composure, and, most importantly, our defensive solidity before we go into the final countdown. Goals have never been easy for us to come by this season given the formation we employ and we cannot keep having to overcome the need to score three times to win a match. There is no more time for excuses or learning curves, now is the time when we need to perform or the season will end on a whimper rather than the crescendo that we deserve.

Jeepers Keepers – Part Three – 25/3/15

Watching David Button's goalkeeping masterclasses this season reminded me of some of the other excellent keepers that have played for us in past years, so I thought it was time to continue my review of Brentford goalkeepers and go back in time to the 90s. The decade began with Graham Benstead who was signed by Steve Perryman to replace Tony Parks for the 1990/91 season. Parks had been decent but he wasn't the dominating type of keeper that the manager wanted. Benno cost a massive £70,000 from Sheffield United, at the time a record fee paid by the club for a goalkeeper, and most fans were questioning the wisdom of that investment when he conceded six goals to Chelsea in a preseason friendly at Griffin Park – shades of Richard Lee, twenty years later who similarly introduced himself to the Brentford faithful by conceding five goals to neighbours Fulham in Kevin O'Connor's testimonial match.

Like Richard, Graham recovered and ended the season in a blaze of glory by winning the Supporters' Player of the Year Award. Graham was tall and agile if a bit gawky in stature and had the ability to inspire his teammates by making the seemingly impossible save look commonplace. He performed miracles by saving three consecutive Wrexham penalty kicks in a shootout, eerily, another feat matched by Richard Lee against Charlton in the same competition, and he was largely responsible for a hardworking team, but one that had major weaknesses at left back and upfront, where Dean Holdsworth struggled all season with injury, overachieving and reaching the playoffs. Graham more than maintained his standard for the next two seasons but missed several matches each year through niggly injuries which allowed Perry Suckling and the evergreen Gerry Peyton to prove that they were both highly impressive deputies. Peyton was so good at the advanced age of thirty-six that we even forgave him for having been a Fulham favourite for so many years.

Ashley Bayes was the reserve goalkeeper at this time and was also called upon to deputise twelve times, conceding a massive thirty-four goals, and never looking like keeping a clean sheet. He was patently unready, unprepared and undercooked and whilst it is easy to point fingers at him and make him a figure of fun and derision I blame the manager and coaches who exposed him to the spotlight and allowed him to become an Aunt Sally. In truth, he was always a mistake waiting to happen and would intersperse saves of real quality and agility with a series of catastrophic and costly errors that sometimes beggared belief. Benstead withdrew late from the season opener against Leyton Orient in August 1991 with a hamstring strain, and I was horrified to see Ashley warming up in goal. We won a nail biter by four goals to three and he was sensational, making a series of saves from close in efforts by Nugent, Burnett and Sayer that saved our bacon on a sizzling afternoon when rampaging winger Ricky Otto tore poor Simon Ratcliffe to shreds.

Ashley was also more than decent in a narrow League Cup defeat at White Hart Lane but reverted to type in the second leg where he proved to be a one-man fifth column that reduced a certain commentator to despair! He reached his nadir when with Brentford clinging onto a narrow one goal lead against fellow strugglers Luton Town, he arched backwards like a dying swan and, under no pressure except perhaps from within himself, punched Chris Kamara's wayward cross into his own net for an equaliser of spellbinding ineptitude. Horrified by his example, his team mates downed tools and we subsided to a late loss which proved crucial at the end of the season. On another day, striker Gary Blissett was forced to replace the injured Benstead against Southend and I still have a vivid mental picture of Ashley kneeling behind the goal coaching Blissett through the game to assorted cries from the crowd of *Don't listen to him Bliss!*

Football is all about opinions and new manager David Webb made it clear that Benstead, always awkward with the ball at his feet, was not to his taste, substituting him at halftime at Rotherham and it was evident that he was on borrowed time. Dean Paul Williams, not to be confused with the equally anonymous striker Dean Anton Williams, was his exceptionally average short-term replacement before Webb pulled a rabbit out of the hat by signing Kevin Dearden from Spurs. Just like another former Tottenham goalkeeper, David Button, Dearden had trawled around the lower league circuit and he had had loan spells at nine clubs. Rejected, dispirited and broken, he was apparently on his way to sign for Kettering when the fateful call came from Webb. Finally, the Ugly Ducking had found a home. Known as the *Flying Pig* just as Liverpool's Tommy Lawrence had been before him, Kevin looked like Fred Rycraft's slightly thinner younger brother and was short, stubby and rotund. He looked more like a Sunday morning parks player than a professional footballer, but in his case looks were totally deceiving. Grateful for his opportunity, Dearden rewarded Webb for his trust in him with countless performances of true quality, bravery and agility that belied his shape and size and he was justifiably rewarded with the Player of the Year Trophy at the end of his first season with the club. Kevin played more than two hundred and fifty games for the club and conceded little over a goal per game, testament indeed to his ability, consistency and the level of understanding he developed with his defenders. Yes, he was caught out from time to time by his lack of stature, particularly by Andy Booth in the playoff semi final second leg in 1995, but we supporters loved him and forgave him everything because he represented Everyman and gave further proof to our sad misconception that we could all have played professional football given half a chance.

Young Tamer Fernandes, who had changed his surname from Aouf, initially deputised well for Dearden when required but indelibly blotted his copybook when he fumbled a harmless low cross into his own net against rivals Fulham. Nobody could recover from a gruesome error of that magnitude and he retired soon afterwards and became an estate agent. Dearden was then challenged for his place by loanees Nick Colgan and Mike Pollitt who were both highly competent but he fell out of favour when Ron Noades took over. He brought in the experienced Jason Pearcey who was calm and unobtrusive and did little wrong but Noades remained sceptical and splurged £100,000 on Northampton's Andy Woodman.

At the time, I was delighted and excited by his capture as he had been a model of consistency for many years, but for some reason, despite a return to his London roots, Woody never really convinced nor was he widely accepted by the supporters who were unimpressed by his reluctance to leave his line and, on the rare occasions that he did, his flapping at crosses. This was surprising as he had demonstrated that he was a real talent but it never came together for him at Brentford apart from on the one day when it really mattered when he was unbeatable in the winner-take-all clash at Cambridge United on the last day of the 1998/99 season when his saves broke the heart of the home team and striker John Taylor in particular and Lloyd Owusu's goal brought the title to Griffin Park. The magic soon faded, however and the decade ended with an unexpected hiatus in goal with Woodman out of favour and exiled on loan, Pearcey forced into retirement after a seemingly innocuous injury against Wigan proved to be far more serious, and journeyman Jimmy Glass acting as a short term stopgap. Who would answer the call and fill the gap? All will be revealed!

"Agent Lee" As Fifth Columnist leaves for Fulham? – 28/3/15

Well the loan window slammed shut on Thursday afternoon with barely a whimper from Griffin Park. As expected, no fresh blood arrived as Mark Warburton has made it patently clear on many occasions recently that he feels that his current squad is quite strong enough and fully capable of winning promotion from the Championship to the Premier League and deserves to be allowed to finish the job that has been started so effectively. There could still be an addition to our numbers given that, finally after a three month injury hiatus, the so-called Invisible Man, Lewis Macleod, is expected to make his long-awaited debut for the club today in the Development Squad fixture against Nottingham Forest and if he can prove his fitness in that game as well as in a behind-closed-doors friendly arranged for early next week, he might yet come into contention for first team selection. Fresh legs, ideas and enthusiasm could prove vital at this crucial stage of the season when minds and bodies are feeling increasingly tired and jaded and he might just produce the spark that we require to climb back into, and then cement our position in the top six.

Alan Judge looked far more like his old self when he came on in the second half against Millwall last Saturday and he produced an outrageous piece of skill that brought about the penalty award for the first goal, and revitalised us when it appeared as if we were bashing our heads against a brick wall and perhaps running out of ideas. Our form since Christmas has been patchy at best and there are many reasons for that, however the absence of Alan Judge who missed seven weeks of action through injury has perhaps been the biggest hurdle that we have had to overcome as he is the man who keeps Brentford playing, the inspiration for so much that is good about our play.

He is a total dynamo who combines energy and nonstop running with the vision and skill to both see and execute a long range pass and change the direction of the attack in an instant. I can still picture that rapier-like thrust to the heart of the Brighton defence when he cut it open and sent Moses Odubajo darting inside their left back to score a sorely needed and confidence-boosting opening goal. All the olés have understandably gone to Jota for that magnificent last minute, game winning finish against Fulham, but who was it who had the energy to win one final midfield battle and fight off the tired challenge from his opponent, bounce the ball seal-like on his head and then ping the ball unerringly fifty yards to Jota lurking unseen on the right wing? Alan Judge, of course! He was rushed back before he was fully recovered from his injury and we have had to nurse him carefully, and hopefully the international break will have enabled him to rest up as well as strengthen his knee, as a fit Alan Judge could be the difference between our gaining a Playoff spot or narrowly missing out. We also had a nasty shock when it was reported that Everton were considering recalling Chris Long, given injuries to two of their other strikers, but, thankfully, this has so far proved to be a false alarm and the Bees will rely on Long and Andre Gray to share the load upfront and hopefully score the goals that we need over the course of the next seven, or Please God, ten matches.

Our remaining conundrum is to decide the makeup of our preferred central defensive pairing, given that we have conceded six totally avoidable goals in our last three games and we cannot continue to donate goals as if we were a charitable foundation. Harlee

Dean and James Tarkowski are the men in possession but Tony Craig is breathing down their neck and perhaps his experience and leadership might be just what we need to get us over this period of defensive instability? Liam Moore is off with the England Under 21 squad, played for them last night, and is not around at the moment to challenge for his place. He has pace in abundance, an asset that his rivals do not possess and I just wonder if his time will come again, as it seems really strange that a player considered good enough to start for his country cannot establish himself in the Brentford team. I fully accept that his performance at Ipswich was ghastly in the extreme and the manager was entirely correct to take him out of the firing line, but given how porous we have remained, perhaps we now need to reconsider? I'm glad that this is Mark Warburton's decision and not mine as I am totally bemused and perplexed at this problem and really am not sure what the optimum solution is.

Whilst nobody arrived at the club, two more went out of the exit door to join the ever-growing phalanx of Brentford players plying their trade away from the club on loan. Manny Oyeleke has joined Lionel Stone at Woking where they will both benefit from facing the pressure of a Playoff assault. Oyeleke has impressed every time I have watched him play but I can honestly see no real future for him at Brentford and I just hope he can get himself fixed up for next season and beyond. The other move came out of the blue and surprised everyone. Richard Lee, who recently announced his retirement at the end of the season has moved on loan to our neighbours and rivals, Fulham. Supporters greeted his move with some degree of annoyance and disappointment on social media and he came in for some unnecessary criticism and personal abuse, but my view is totally different. You are a long time retired, and if Richard sees this as a final chance to stay involved and maybe even play a last couple of first team matches before the curtain comes down on his long and distinguished career, then good luck to him. He cannot play against us and given that he was seemingly confined to Bees Player duties at Griffin Park, then how can anybody deny him this opportunity?

Sam Saunders and Nico Yennaris have also extended their loan spells at Wycombe Wanderers until the end of the season. They can be recalled to Griffin Park should the need arise, although I think it highly unlikely that the services of either player will be required. I watched eight current and ex-Bees play in the televised clash between Luton and Wycombe on Tuesday night and it was a slightly surreal experience – the ghost of Christmas past. Saunders ran the whole game and always seemed to find time and space in what was otherwise a frenetic promotion clash. Yennaris was good on the ball but was often caught upfield and easily bypassed in defence. Another Brentford player, Alfie Mawson, has been at Wycombe all season and he scored a wonderfully inventive winning goal on Tuesday and also looked very comfortable on the ball. Whether he can defend to the standard required in the Championship is another question and a decision will shortly need to be made on his future given that his contract expires at the end of the season. Like Aaron Pierre who defended stoutly on the night, and Luke Norris, he might well decide that he needs to move on but I hope that we manage to persuade him to extend his contract so that we can send him out on loan again next season and see how good a player he can become. Former Bees Paul Hayes, Marcus Bean, Sam Wood and Fraser Franks were also involved in the match and Hayes and

Bean in particular showed their experience and ability and were highly instrumental in Wycombe's victory. Hayes even managed to score with a perfectly placed penalty kick!

Jack O'Connell has been quietly impressive since he rejoined Rochdale on loan in January and it is clear that we have a major asset in the tall, blond defender who has also proved to be a massive danger in the opposition area at set pieces, an attribute that our current incumbents would do well to copy. He too could be recalled if Mark Warburton feels that a fresh face is required but he is probably one for next season, when I fully expect him to make his mark. Nick Proschwitz remains at Coventry City but seems to have disappeared into a black hole as he has not been seen in recent games for the Sky Blues following an apparently gruesome open goal miss that cost his new team a crucial victory against Bradford City. Well the die is cast, there is no more room to manoeuvre and Mark Warburton now has to play with the cards that he currently holds. Will they be strong enough or will we fall just short? I can hardly wait to find out!

Brentford Quiz – The Answers – 30/3/15

1. How many appearances has Kevin O'Connor made for the club?

Kevin has made 501 appearances (420 in the League, 31 FA Cup, 20 in the League Cup and 30 in other games). He is fourth on our all-time appearance chart behind Ken Coote (559), Jamie Bates (524) and Peter Gelson (516). He is highly unlikely to play for us again and for all his wonderful achievements he must be a little bit frustrated that he will probably end up only a season and a half short from topping the list. So near – yet so far.

2. What did Kevin O'Connor do with his last touch of the ball to date in a Brentford shirt?

He calmly slotted away the winning penalty kick in the shoot out at Dagenham in August 2014 beating former Bee Liam O'Brien low to the keeper's right hand side, exactly where he would surely have placed the ball had he been allowed to take that fateful penalty kick against Doncaster Rovers in 2013.

3. Who are the top five goal scorers for Brentford since 1970? One of them did score for the club before that year.

Gary Blissett – 105 goals, Lloyd Owusu – 87 goals, Roger Cross – 79 goals, John Docherty – 78 goals, Dean Holdsworth – 76 goals.

4. Who has been shown the most red cards for Brentford since 1970, and how many times has he been sent off? Who are second and third in the list?

Jamie Bates was sent off eight times, Martin Grainger, six times, with Brian Statham in third place with five. Statham also managed to get himself sent off twice against Brentford too, playing for Reading and Gillingham.

5. Which current Brentford player has been sent off three times for the club?

Tony Craig who was sent off by Keith Stroud (see the next question) at Sheffield United. He has also seen red twice at Griffin Park, last season against Carlisle and against Birmingham City this season.

6. How many Brentford players has Keith Stroud sent off – so far?

A quite ridiculous six! Ricky Newman for an alleged stamp against Huddersfield in 2006, Stuart Nelson in the 2006 Playoff match at Swansea, James Wilson at Wycombe in 2009, Tony Craig and Clayton Donaldson in THAT match at Sheffield United in 2013 and Jake Bidwell recently at home to Watford. Of the six, Newman's red card was expunged on appeal and Nelson, Craig and Donaldson were dealt with extremely harshly by a referee who always appears to be extremely quick on the draw.

Jake Bidwell – a model of consistency all season.

7. Which Brentford player has missed the most consecutive penalty kicks since 1970, and how many in a row did he miss?

Steve Phillips scored eight of the first ten spot kicks he took and generally succeeded in placing the ball unstoppably in the top corner of the net. Then it all went wrong for him and he totally lost his touch, missing his last four penalty kicks in 1979/80, although it has to be admitted that he did score from the rebound after the keeper saved his initial effort at Southend United.

8. Who has scored the most penalty kicks for Brentford since 1970?

Kevin O'Connor has scored nineteen out of the twenty-four kicks he has taken. Leaving aside shoot outs, the last penalty he took for us was that majestic last second equaliser in the playoff semi final at Swindon in 2013 when in a high pressure situation he took the best penalty kick I have ever seen by a Brentford player, giving vent to the anger and frustration that I am sure he felt after the Doncaster fiasco.

9. Name the eight Brentford players who have a 100% success record from the penalty spot and have taken more than one penalty for the club?

As we long suffering Brentford fans well know, the award of a penalty kick is generally no guarantee of a goal with a success rate far lower than we would prescribe for our galloping pulse rate. Mark Croxford has informed me that since 1970 we have in fact been awarded 269 penalty kicks of which 194 have been scored and 75 spurned. In other words, we have scored just under three out of every four kicks. If it is any consolation when reading through match reports in old Brentford programmes from the 30s and 50s, guess what? Yes, every penalty kick was an adventure even back in those days. We just are not very good at taking them and nothing seems to have changed over the years.

Terry Johnson, Joe Allon, Roger Cross, Barry Tucker, Warren Aspinall, D J Campbell, Paul Gibbs and Alex Pritchard (I hope I am not tempting fate here) are the only Brentford players who have a 100% success rate from the penalty spot and have taken more than one kick for the club.

10. Who was the last Brentford loanee to score two goals on his debut for the club?

The answer is John Bostock who scored twice against Millwall, including a goal scored direct from a corner and I might well ask in my next quiz who else has managed to achieve this rare feat? At one time it looked like he would become a worldbeater and at only twenty-three years of age, time is still on his side however he is now playing in the Belgian second tier at Oud-Heverlee Leuven which seems a level far below his ability. He started like a house on fire at Griffin Park but struggled to show consistency or impose himself on games.

11. Who was the last Bee to score four goals in a game?

This was also a no-brainer for all of you. Mike Grella scored four times in that amazing six-nil thumping of, it has to be said, a pretty lethargic and disinterested AFC Bournemouth team in a JPT clash in November 2011. Incredibly, those were the only goals he scored for the club in a less than distinguished stay.

12. How many hat tricks did Lloyd Owusu score in 1998/99 and which club did he score two hat tricks against that season?

Lloyd took the division by storm after we plucked him from non-league obscurity at Slough Town. He scored three hat tricks in 1998/99, two against Southend United and one at Rotherham.

13. Which loan goalkeeper was ever-present, named Player of the Year and conceded under a goal per game for Brentford?

Another one that fooled nobody. Steve Sherwood was brought in to challenge a faltering Paul Priddy and proved to be a massive success. He had two highly successful loan spells and conceded only 45 goals as an ever present in 1974/75 and was an easy choice as Player of the Year. We then shilly-shallied over signing him on a permanent basis, lost out to Watford and ended up with Bill Glazier in goal – go figure!

14. Ashley Bayes played twelve games for the Bees. How many goals did he concede?

I have written more than enough about Ashley so I will simply state without further comment that in twelve games he conceded a total of thirty-four goals, an average of 2.83 goals per game.

15. Name five Brentford outfield players who have played in goal after the first choice was sent off or injured?

This flummoxed most of you and me too I think! The ones that I can recall are: Paul Shrubb, Jim McNichol, Gary Blissett, Andy Scott and, most recently, John Mousinho.

16. Who never missed a game and played 157 consecutive league games before he left the club?

Steve Phillips played in 157 consecutive league matches between February 1977 and May 1980. He was a substitute in his last match against Millwall. He also played ten cup matches, making a total of 167 games.

17. Who was sent off in the twelfth minute of his Brentford debut and never played for us again?

Poor Wally Downes was forced to scrape underneath the barrel when it came to player recruitment in 2003 and a seemingly unfit Puffing Billy named Peter Beadle, way past his peak, was given the opportunity to play up front. He lasted twelve minutes on a blisteringly hot day at Tranmere, received what was generally acknowledged to be a harsh red card and never played for us again.

18. Name five players who were nominated as team or club captain?

Take your pick from a vast choice including: Bobby Ross, Alan Hawley, Gordon Riddick, Paul Bence, Jackie Graham, Terry Hurlock, Chris Kamara, Wayne Turner, Keith Jones, Terry Evans, Jamie Bates, Paul Evans, Michael Dobson, Ricky Newman, Kevin O'Connor and Alan Bennett.

Tiebreak Question: Which Brentford personality was involved in the 1933 FA Cup Final between Everton and Manchester City?

Denis Piggott, the long serving club secretary, was a ball boy at the 1933 FA Cup Final!

League Table – 31/3/15

Position	Team	P	W	D	L	F	A	GD	Pt	Form
1	Bournemouth	39	21	10	8	82	40	42	73	D W W W D W
2	Watford	39	22	6	11	78	46	32	72	W W D W W L
3	Middlesbrough	39	21	9	9	59	30	29	72	L W L W W L
4	Norwich City	39	20	10	9	76	43	33	70	W L W D D W
5	Derby County	39	19	10	10	69	43	26	67	L L D D L L
6	Ipswich Town	39	19	10	10	59	43	16	67	L L D L W W
7	**Brentford**	**39**	**20**	**6**	**13**	**64**	**52**	**12**	**66**	**L W D L W D**
8	Wolverhampton Wndrs	39	18	11	10	56	45	11	65	W L D D W W
8	Nottingham Forest	39	15	12	12	62	54	8	57	W L W D W L
10	Blackburn Rovers	39	14	12	13	51	50	1	54	D W W W L L
11	Charlton Athletic	39	13	15	11	48	50	-2	54	W W W L W W
12	Sheffield Wednesday	39	13	14	12	36	40	-4	53	W L W D L W
13	Leeds United	39	14	10	15	43	47	-4	52	L W W D W D
14	Cardiff City	39	13	12	14	48	50	-2	51	L W L W D W
15	Birmingham City	38	11	14	13	43	55	-12	47	L W W D D L
16	Brighton and Hove A	39	10	15	14	43	46	-3	45	L W L D D W
17	Bolton Wanderers	39	12	9	18	46	57	-11	45	W D L W L D
18	Huddersfield Town	39	11	11	17	48	67	-19	44	L L L D D L
19	Reading	38	12	8	18	42	61	-19	44	L L D W L L
20	Fulham	39	12	7	20	50	68	-18	43	W L L D L W
21	Rotherham United	39	9	13	17	40	60	-20	40	W L W L L L
22	Wigan Athletic	39	8	11	20	35	52	-17	35	W W L W L D
23	Millwall	39	7	12	20	33	64	-31	33	L L L L D D
24	Blackpool	39	4	11	24	30	78	-48	23	L L L L L D

APRIL

How Much Longer? – 3/4/15

It really isn't too long now! Like every other Brentford supporter I am anxiously and impatiently counting off the hours and minutes before today's crucial and potentially season-defining local derby clash with Fulham. Who knows whether it really will be a Good Friday for the Bees. In reality my brain is pretty scrambled at the moment and I am making little sense whenever I try and analyse how we are likely to approach the game and, more importantly, whether it will all end up in tears of joy or disappointment. All I know is that it is well past midnight now and sleep will not come too easily tonight.

There is so much riding on the result. Local pride and bragging rights are at stake. For so many of our supporters a double over our near neighbours and close rivals, Fulham, would be the crowning glory of what has already proven to be a magnificent season. I will certainly be celebrating and screaming as loud as everybody else should we prevail but victory for me, however wonderful it would be, isn't the be all and end all, but would merely be a means to an end and help us on our way to our final objective – namely winning promotion.

With seven games to go we are now entering the home stretch and there is no longer any margin for error. The Bees have fallen out of the top six for the first time in over four months and need to get back on track at Craven Cottage. A minimum of four points is surely a prerequisite from our next couple of matches if we are to have a realistic chance of going up.

The international break came at just the right time for us as it gave us the chance to rest tired legs and regain some equilibrium as well as pick up some additional kudos from the excellent performances produced by Stuart Dallas, Alex Pritchard and Moses Odubajo whilst they were all on international duty. Thankfully they all returned to Griffin Park unscathed and should be bursting with confidence for today's match. Dallas, in particular, so often the unheralded and unsung hero whose contribution often goes largely unnoticed, clearly demonstrated that he fully belongs at the highest level as he starred for Northern Ireland against both Scotland and Finland and Alex Pritchard contributed much to England Under 21's excellent wins against the Czech Republic and Germany. Moses Odubajo also made two sparkling appearances for England Under 20s and is tipped for even greater honours should he maintain his level of performance. Pace terrifies and unsettles opponents and Moses possesses pace in abundance.

The conundrum for Mark Warburton will be choosing a team from what is practically a fully fit squad. Lewis Macleod did finally make his much awaited debut for the club last Saturday in the Development Squad's defeat by Nottingham Forest but simply proved that the road to recovery and full fitness is a long and tortuous one and he surely has much work to do before he can mount a serious challenge for a first team place. I suspect that his time will come next season rather than this. We are blessed in midfield where we have a plethora of talent and the problem is more who to leave out rather than who to select. How on earth can you pick five from Douglas, Diagouraga, Pritchard, Jota, Judge, Toral and Dallas? You can make a serious and credible case for all of them to start and I do not envy the manager his task.

I forgot to mention that earlier tonight I also tried to still my beating heart and fortify my spirits for the morrow by watching the Brentford versus Fulham clash at Griffin Park and I almost wore out the remote control playing and replaying Jota's magic moment. How many of you remember that both Dallas and Jota started that match on the bench and that they came on to help revitalise us and recharge our batteries midway through the second half at a time when, unimaginable though it seemed, Fulham looked as if they were going to commit highway robbery and emerge with three points from a match in which they were decidedly second best? Happily all's well that ends well and the good guys deservedly came out on top, but certainly would not have done had it not been for those substitutions. Okay, for once, Nick Proschwitz also contributed when he came on too!

As I said, Mark Warburton has much to ponder over when deciding upon the makeup of his midfield as Fulham are no slouches in an area where the game will more than likely be decided. Chris Long was also on international duty but apparently returned early for treatment on a dodgy hamstring and I will lose more sleep later on tonight wondering if he will be fit enough to participate, even if only from the bench. Andre Gray provided a passable impersonation of Road Runner when he gave a lumbering Michael Turner the runaround and led him a merry dance at Carrow Road back in January when he was still playing for Norwich and I hope that he can ideally repeat the performance later this afternoon. Talking of strikers, perhaps the best news of the week so far was the fact that Scott Hogan has returned to training after his sickening injury at Rotherham way back in August. He has been much missed and given a full recovery will provide an exceptional addition to our firepower next season.

We haven't even mentioned our central defence yet where chaos and confusion remains. Dean and Tarkowski have resembled a pair of bears dancing on ice lately and we have been leaking goals given that the otherwise impeccable David Button has also started to look fallible at just the wrong time. Liam Moore has returned to Leicester after a horribly unimpressive loan spell and I still find it hard to reconcile the fact that a player apparently good enough to represent his country at Under 21 level looked so out of place in our defence. Go figure! Jack O'Connell has been recalled from Rochdale where he was quietly impressive and the question remains unanswered as to whether he is merely seen as defensive cover or if he might have far more than a bit part to play over the remaining few games. He certainly has the ability and from what I have seen and heard he also seems to have the temperament required. Could he be the joker in the pack and help revitalise what has become a porous defence?

So what am I looking for this afternoon? Three points, certainly, are paramount, and I would go down on bended knee for them, but I am also feeling greedy and would like far more than just a victory. I would also ask for the team to put on a real performance, one that on the one hand fully restores our confidence but one that also puts the football world on notice that Brentford will not buckle to the pressure of their current situation but will rise to the challenge, just as we did a year ago. Good Friday 2014 was unforgettable; can we make Good Friday 2015 a worthy successor? Not long to go now!

Jota – In The Last Minute! – 4/4/15

As all my friends and family know I am a bit anal about timekeeping and invariably turn up far too early for every appointment and come out in hives at the prospect of being late. Thus it was that I arrived at Putney Bridge station at around one o'clock yesterday with a lot of time to kill. I have always been a sucker for secondhand bookshops and my spirits rose when I saw one just around the corner from the tube. Food was out of the question as my stomach was churning with a combination of anticipation, excitement and fear at the prospect of the match looming up ahead and how much it meant, and I thought that a few minutes of quiet reflection and browsing might take my mind off the football and help me regain my equilibrium. No such luck, as amongst all the dog-eared thrillers and faded Johnny Haynes biographies, what did I see in pride of place in the front window but a bright yellow coloured copy of something entitled *A World Without Bees*. I did a quick double take, as I wondered if my eyes were deceiving me or had I really seen what I thought I had? I grabbed the book with a sense of fear and foreboding in order to read the blurb inside the front cover and was relieved and gratified to learn that the tome was in fact a scholarly discourse on the mysterious decline of the honeybee and what that means for us all, rather than a polemic or diatribe by a disaffected Fulham supporter jealous of our success this season. I tramped through Bishop's Park towards the ground reflecting on whether or not this was a good omen.

The answer was soon to become apparent as Brentford demonstrated a winning combination of organisation, steely-eyed determination, effervescence and pure skill to steamroller a poor and dispirited shambles of a Fulham side to register an awesome four-one hammering of their local rivals and, crucially regain a place in the playoff positions. Perhaps I am being a tad harsh as Fulham played some slick passing football from time to time, particularly early on, but they only really threatened to hurt us after being gifted a non-existent penalty by an indulgent referee which allowed them to regain a foothold in a match which seemed to have totally slipped away from them. They then discarded all their footballing principles by bringing on the Big Lump, Matt Smith, going Route One and looking for the knockdowns. They looked more like a reincarnation of Wimbledon circa 1988 than a traditional Fulham short passing team and for ten minutes or so they overpowered us and threatened an equaliser. My mind kept replaying images of the match at Millwall in November when, after looking in total control, we buckled under an rabid aerial assault at about the same point in the second half and but for a narrow squeak when Smith lobbed just wide and then the referee thrust his arms almost out of their sockets to dramatically deny them a second penalty after an appeal which in truth looked far more credible than their first after Tarkowski baulked Smith, we weathered the storm and simply went down the other end to score two more goals to blow the opposition away and seal the points.

With over six thousand supporters in attendance, our largest away league following in living memory, Brentford seemed to have taken over Craven Cottage and the entire neighbouring area. The noise was deafening and the backing total. You could almost sense the team growing in confidence and becoming even more inspired and determined to prevail when they emerged from the tunnel to warm-up and glimpsed the fervent red and white hordes assembled behind the Putney End goal. It sounded more like a home game and just as was the case at Orient last season, Fulham surely blundered in allowing us to obtain such a foothold within their stadium. Our supporters were our Twelfth Man and more than played their part in securing the victory. Well done to each and every one of them who was in attendance.

Mark Warburton also deserves great credit for his team selection. I wrote yesterday about the boggling number of potential permutations that he had at his disposal throughout the team, but quite obviously he hadn't read my column as he fielded an unchanged team, and was proved totally correct in doing so. I am sure that he fully realised that Alex Pritchard, Moses Odubajo and, in particular, Stuart Dallas had been inspired by their international appearances over the previous fortnight and that they should all start and play until they ran out of steam. I have previously written about Dallas being an unheralded and unsung hero and I really do not think we quite realise what a gem we possess. He is tall, quick, strong, can beat a man, is versatile and can play in several positions on both flanks across the front line and at full back. He also possesses a howitzer of a shot. Not a bad combination of skills in one player and it is also quite evident that he just loves to play football and his attitude is first class. Rather than look at him as a squad player who can fill in where necessary we should recognise that he has metamorphosed into a fully-fledged international footballer who deserves to be one of the first names on the team sheet.

After surviving Fulham's initial pressure thanks to an excellent Button save, we gradually inched into the game and found joy on our left side where Bidwell and Dallas dovetailed to perfection and found space in the home rearguard. After an early sighter that was easily saved, Dallas tried again from just outside the area and his effort seared into the bottom corner. Pritchard pulled all the strings with Douglas and Diagouraga both inspirational.

It was Douglas who won the ball early in the second half, strode forward and sent a perfect lobbed pass to Gray who held onto the ball, turned and laid it back beyond Pritchard to Dallas who advanced unchallenged and hit an absolute screamer into the top of the net from almost thirty yards. I was seated close to its trajectory and felt scared as the ball flashed towards me and I now know what it must have been like to face a fusillade of cannon balls in Napoleonic times. His shot would have taken my head off if it had missed the goal. Thankfully it didn't and we celebrated in style. In my report of the first match between the two teams at Griffin Park, I believe that I referred to Fulham as being *all fur coat and no knickers* and that disparaging description would also aptly sum up the way in which they shirked their defensive responsibilities. They were not prepared to put their bodies on the line by attempting to block either shot by Dallas.

Pritchard's job was done and Judge replaced him and he gave the home team no respite as he did his Duracell Bunny impression, but his energy was matched by his guile and he made a massive contribution to our ultimate victory. We then tore Fulham apart and a goal of the season candidate was denied us when Jota and Odubajo combined perfectly to set up Gray for a tap in, but he decided to try and break the net instead and his effort raged into the crowd.

Get In! Stuart Dallas celebrates at Fulham.

Fulham were out on their feet until the referee gave them a helping hand when Diagouraga's perfect sliding tackle on Husband was ludicrously adjudged to be a foul and then the excitement started. Dean and Tarkowski stood firm and we survived, not without some alarms, but the sting in the tail was to come from the Bees as, with Pritchard safely off the pitch, Judge was allowed to take a free kick from the edge of the area and scored brilliantly and unstoppably off the underside of the bar. We were now in total ecstasy but the day had still more to give us, as deep into stoppage time six thousand Brentford supporters and the few remaining Fulham fans were treated to the sight of Judge speeding towards the corner flag and with the defenders fully expecting him to see out the final few seconds, he did the unexpected, turned towards goal and centered low for Jota to run towards the near post undetected and thrash the ball into the roof of the net.

Jota In The Last Minute roared the Brentford supporters almost in unison as we floated out of Craven Cottage after a perfect day which had seen us do the double over our illustrious neighbours for the first time since 1992 (I wonder what happened then?), to secure West London bragging rights and regain our place in the top sixth. Now all we need to do is win our last six games too. A tough task awaits us, starting on Monday when we face the challenge of Nottingham Forest but We Are Bees, and we *can* do this!

Back On Track– 5/4/15

It is quite impossible to exaggerate the importance of Brentford's stunning victory at Craven Cottage on Friday and the effect it has had on us. It has provided a massive confidence boost to us all, supporters, players and management alike and has put us firmly back on track for promotion. After some recent up and down results and performances and slipping out of the top six for the first time in over four months we were seeing some understandable signs of self-doubt. But now the Bees find themselves back in the playoff zone and their ultimate fate remains in their own hands. You cannot really ask for more than that at this stage of the season. The victory itself was paramount, but what made it even better was the manner in which it was achieved.

After a stuttering start when the Bees seemed to forget how to press and challenge and simply sat back and admired the pretty patterns being weaved in front of them by a Fulham team long on style but thankfully short on penetration, reality finally kicked in and we began to compete. Once we did so, our superior organisation and skill on the ball allowed us the time and room to take control. Pritchard was the catalyst for everything good that we did in the first half, always finding little pockets of space and the subtle pass that opened up the home defence and almost put Jota in on goal was a joy to behold.

We took the game by the scruff of the neck and totally dominated proceedings after the initial nervous quarter hour and were seemingly coasting with a two goal cushion until Simon Hooper decided to emerge from the shadows – where referees belong and should always remain – and put his stamp on proceedings by gifting the home team a penalty after a sliding tackle so perfectly timed by Diagouraga that there was barely an appeal for a spot kick. We creaked under the pressure for the next quarter hour but we held firm under an aerial bombardment more reminiscent of the The Blitz than a football match before reasserting our control with two late and brilliant goals.

No victory is easily earned and this was no exception. We defended well and stoutly with the much-criticised central defensive partnership of Dean and Tarkowski standing firm and resisting almost everything that was thrown at them. We regained our faltering trust in them and we will need them to maintain their form, and more importantly, concentration over the torrid weeks ahead of us. Craig and now, O'Connell are there as cover but we really needed our current pairing to come good and they certainly did so on Friday.

After receiving fully justified paeans of praise for his effervescent performances for Northen Ireland, Stuart Dallas is finally beginning to realise just how good he is and I believe that there is so much more yet to come from him. He has grown into his paws and is now a potent weapon and a massive part of our armoury. He can go for the byline and cross the ball hard and low into the danger zone, or cut in onto his favoured right foot and give the ball a hell of a whack. In a team that can be frustratingly elaborate and which consistently tries to walk the ball into the net it is so refreshing to have a player who is totally uncomplicated and is prepared to shoot on sight. He combines power with accuracy and his two goals on Friday were both perfectly executed and sizzled into the net.

Alan Judge also proved that he has finally recovered from his long-term injury as he took the game by the scruff of the neck when he came on for the tiring Pritchard. Fulham must surely have breathed a collective sigh of relief when they saw the back of Pritchard but there was to be no respite for the tiring Cottagers who were then led a merry dance by Judge who offered us a fresh dimension with his nonstop running, accurate passing and shoot-on-sight policy. What a relief to us all to see him do so well as he is our talisman and inspiration and we know that he will be determined to lead us to the promised land. The only cautionary note is the need to curb his enthusiasm as both he and Jonathan Douglas have picked up eight bookings and must ensure that they keep their noses clean in at least one of the next two matches if they are to avoid what would be an enormously costly and badly timed two match ban.

I have deliberately refrained from any gloating, up until now at least, but it has been quite wonderful to sit back and simply luxuriate in the fact that we have beaten and totally outplayed Fulham in both Championship matches this season. Their message boards have also gone quiet and there has barely been a repetition of the patronising and ignorant comments that followed our first win at Griffin Park late last year. We are now a better-managed and run club than Fulham. We have a set of players who have totally invested and bought into what has been asked of them because they know it works and will get results. We have a clear strategy and plan for the future and I would be prepared to bet a large sum on Brentford steaming way ahead of Fulham in terms of our onfield achievements over the years to come.

Saturday and Sunday could have been horrid days full of negativity, regret and foreboding if we had lost, as we would surely have been contemplating the prospects of promotion slipping through our fingers. Now we are perky and positive and eagerly looking forward to the next challenge.

It was in the reverse fixtures against Derby County and Nottingham Forest last November when we first realised just how good this team could be and our performance at Forest was in my opinion by far the best of the season. We totally dominated them, should have been five up at the break, and played with a freedom of expression that left the home team and supporters totally nonplussed. I hope that Mark Warburton takes Andre Gray to one side and reminds him of just how well he played that night as he terrified their defenders and could have scored four goals instead of the one he managed. A repeat performance at Griffin Park would be extremely welcome.

Who would ever have thought that we would find ourselves at Easter with still so much to play for? The pessimists amongst us might have feared that we would now be immersed in a relegation struggle, but here we are, with six games to go, realistically contemplating the prospects of the Premier League next season. Heady times indeed and dreams really do not come much better than this! Oh and by the way, a final pointer for the commercial staff at the club: suitably inscribed *Jota In The Last Minute* T-shirts would be a surefire winner and top seller!

Be Afraid – Be Very Afraid! – 6/4/15

I was having a quick lie down yesterday afternoon, reduced to a torpid stupor by the utterly appalling and unwatchable Sunderland versus Newcastle non-event, when through eyes half-closed and gummed with sleep I happened to glance at a preview of today's clash against Nottingham Forest. And there it was, staring me in the face, the name of one of the Assistant Referees – Mathew Buonassisi. In an instant, I was restored to a state of complete wakefulness and I discovered to my amazement that I was in a cold sweat.

Mathew Buonassisi – how can the mere sight and sound of that name reduce me to such a condition? Well the answer to that question is pretty obvious when you look back at his chequered history when officiating Brentford matches. I will refrain from describing his appearance but he bears an uncanny resemblance to a well-known Hollywood actor, and no, I am afraid it certainly isn't George Clooney! Anyway, looks are totally superficial, it is how you conduct yourself and do your job that really matters.

My first sight of him was on Sky Sports in October 2011 when they covered our Johnstone's Paint Trophy tie at Charlton. We won comfortably by three goals to nil and Toumani Diagouraga scored our third goal, but then the assistant referee got involved, trying his best to get the referee to disallow it even though the ball clearly rebounded to Toumani off a home defender. Fortunately, the referee had seen what had happened and correctly awarded the goal. Guess who that assistant referee was? The first time I saw him in the flesh was at the midweek match against Shrewsbury Town in October 2012. A match of stultifying boredom, ineptly controlled by referee Tim Robinson and enlivened only by two highly controversial incidents described below by Teamtalk.com:

Uwe Rösler's side survived a late penalty scare. Defender Tony Craig was adjudged to have handled in the box and the referee pointed to the spot, only to reverse the decision after consulting his assistant. Seconds later Brentford's Paul Hayes had the ball in the net after a Forshaw cross, but was denied by the offside flag.

For what it is worth Marvin Morgan blasted a shot against Tony Craig from point blank range and the referee, far from the action, nonsensically decided to award a penalty kick but was persuaded to consult an assistant referee (not MB!) before sanity prevailed and his original decision was changed to a corner kick. What I am referring to came at the other end, late on, in a match which saw a stuttering Brentford team barely threaten. With time running out, Adam Forshaw jinked inside from his position on the left wing (don't ask me why he was playing there, ask Uwe) and from the edge of the area shot towards the goal through a crowd of players, and there was substitute Paul Hayes to cleverly divert the ball from close range into the opposite corner of the net for what we thought was a late and totally undeserved winner. We rose in celebration but our delight was quickly stifled by a late-appearing flag from the assistant – Mathew Buonassisi. Even though it was clear that Hayes had judged his run perfectly, the decision stood and we were denied. Buonassisi had already irked us all night with a hapless performance when literally, and I do mean *literally* every time we got the ball into the Shrewsbury half after the break, according to him it was either a foul by Donaldson or offside. This was the crowning glory.

I quickly marked him down in my mental notebook as one to watch, for all the wrong reasons, and thankfully we did not see him again until the FA Cup Third Round tie at Southend. We drew a tough match after leading at one stage by two clear goals and it was Barry Corr's equalising goal that stuck in the craw, as the Brentford website recalls:

Kevan Hurst delivered a free kick from the right and Brentford stepped out en masse, leaving the Southend attackers offside, however, assistant referee Mathew Buonassisi kept his flag down and Corr headed home from 12 yards. Brentford appealed, justifiably claiming their move up had left the attackers offside, but the goal was given.

We can only assume that Buonassisi was sleeping on the job as the Brentford defence, expertly marshalled by Sam Saunders, appeared to time their advance perfectly, leaving Corr stranded and apparently yards offside, but the man who mattered disagreed and the goal was given. According to Uwe Rösler he apologised after the game but in the manager's opinion this was not good enough. I share this viewpoint. What annoyed me more is that before the match, when the referee and his two assistants were warming up, it was Buonassisi who engaged in some lively banter with the Brentford fans behind the goal, even kicking the ball into the goal and clapping and waving in response to some of their ribald chants. He was drawing attention to himself and I feared the worst, as here it seemed was an official who craved the spotlight, and my concerns were eventually justified when he made his fatal error in the second half.

The last time he appeared at Griffin Park was in late October last year when we played Sheffield Wednesday and my stomach lurched when I saw that familiar figure lurking on the Braemar Road touchline. This time he struck early:

The Bees thought they had taken the lead in the 10th minute but Andre Gray's side-footed finish from Jota's cross was ruled out for offside. Mark Warburton commented: "We believe Andre was onside when he scored and the video backs that up, but there is little we can do about it after the event."

Jota had turned the Wednesday defence inside out and sold them an outrageous dummy that had the entire crowd on their feet before crossing low for Gray to surely run past the last defender to score. But Mathew Buonassisi knew better; the flag was raised triumphantly and we were denied yet again.

Perhaps I am bring unreasonable, perhaps he is simply doing his job to the best of his ability and I am certainly not so paranoid as to suggest that he has something against Brentford, but it is fair to say that he has a lot of previous with us and that we have never benefitted from one of his decisions. I will do my best to ignore him this afternoon and maybe, just maybe, the game will pass without incident. But somehow I doubt it!

Go Figure! – 9/4/15

I've been examining the statistics from the Nottingham Forest match on Easter Monday and they make for fascinating if salutary reading. I still find it impossible to understand how Brentford failed to win a match in which they had a massive 74% possession of the ball. Remember too that this wasn't Blackpool or a bottom of the table no-hoper or also-ran that we were playing, but an expensively assembled team who were early season pacesetters and promotion favourites and who were packed full of talented and experienced players of the calibre of Michail Antonio and Henri Lansbury. And yet we totally dominated possession by a quite ridiculous margin.

Not only did Brentford keep hold of the ball for the majority of the game, but they also created a plethora of chances and had a massive thirty-three shots on goal of which nine were on target. The Bees scored twice and forced Karl Darlow, who proved to be an almost impassable barrier in the Forest goal, to make lithe and agile saves from Jota on a couple of occasions – including an exquisite Zola-esque near post flick from a corner – as well as Andre Gray, Alex Pritchard and Stuart Dallas. Pritchard and Tommy Smith also saw excellent efforts shave the crossbar. Brentford scored their customary two late goals but in reality their pressure and quality of approach play merited at least double that number.

With Mancienne sweeping up and protecting a back four who only ventured forward for set pieces, Forest were restricted to breakaways, but despite far less possession they managed three shots on target and also scored twice from a third of the number of shots managed by Brentford. Our overall superiority is also reflected by the fact that we successfully completed a highly impressive 82% of the 572 passes we attempted throughout the match. In comparison, Nottingham Forest made 208 passes of which just over half were on the money.

It is even more illuminating when you take a look at our statistics from the season as a whole and several clear trends soon begin to emerge. Brentford manage an average of 15.7 shots on goal per game which is a figure bettered only by Bournemouth and Norwich, and Jota, Gray and Judge are the Bees players who take the most shots per game. Our shooting accuracy is the second best in the Championship with 5.7 on target and we take just under seven shots each match from outside the penalty area. This is more than any other team in the league and bears testimony to the attacking prowess and eagerness to shoot of Jota, Pritchard and Judge. So far so good until you look at the other side of the coin, which reveals that we have less than one shot per game from within the six-yard box. This is a truly awful figure, one of the worst in the Championship which clearly demonstrates the downside of only playing one striker and highlights how hard it is for us to get men up in support of Andre Gray who is often left totally isolated within the penalty area.

We are certainly one of the fittest and quickest teams in the league and our tactic of leaving three up at opposition corners has certainly paid off. We have scored five goals from counterattacks, more than anybody else, and have also scored an incredible twelve last minute or injury time goals; testament indeed to our refusal to give up and the relentless pressure we exert on teams and the manner in which we wear them down. Our set piece record is appalling with only eight goals scored, a record that twenty-one Championship teams have bettered. A set piece coach next season anybody? All in all, despite all the moans and groans, we have scored a healthy seventy league goals so far this season with another five games still to play, which is surely far more than we all expected before the season commenced.

Where we excel is in ball possession and passing accuracy. Many pundits remark upon our close resemblance to Bournemouth in terms of our style and approach, and the figures certainly endorse this view as we are second to them with our average of 56% possession per game. Our passing accuracy of 78% is one of the highest in the league. Where we struggle though is in winning aerial challenges where we have the worst record in the league and only five teams give up more than our 14.4 shots per game. No wonder we have conceded fifty-five goals to date, but you really cannot have everything and the way in which we play with defenders pouring forward to initiate and support attacks certainly leaves us wide open to quick counter attacks and balls played over the top. You really cannot beat Brentford matches for excitement with there being over thirty shots per game – or one every three minutes. We also concede only 8.9 fouls per game, far less than anyone else and yet we have had 70 bookings which means that we are either tactically astute at choosing the most advantageous times to foul, something that I certainly haven't noticed, our, more likely, referees for some reason seem to penalise us more heavily than most other teams.

Alan Judge, Alex Pritchard, Andre Gray and Jake Bidwell have accumulated the most assists and it is surprising that for all his ability to open up defences, Jota has only provided the final pass for two goals to date. Can any of you guess who makes the most passes per game? Well, the answer truly amazed me and further opened my eyes about the way we are encouraged and set up to play. James Tarkowski makes 47 passes per game on average, closely followed by Jonathan Douglas. We might well criticise Tarkowski for some of his defending but he is crucial in terms of getting our attack moving and playing through the initial opposition press. It will also surprise few of you to learn that Toumani is our most accurate passer of the ball closely followed by Tommy Smith who I feel is an invaluable asset to have coming off the bench. This is further evidenced by his pinpoint cross over the straining fingers of Darlow and right onto the coiffured head of Jota in the ninety-fifth minute on Monday.

So to sum up, what do the statistics show about Brentford's traits and characteristics as a team? Our strengths and style of play can best be summarised as the following:

- Counter attacking

- Attacking down the right flank

- Taking long shots

- Creating chances through individual skill

- Accuracy from direct free kicks (as has been demonstrated lately by Judge and Pritchard)

- Coming back from losing positions

- Defending set pieces

- Possession football

- Short passes

- Controlling the game in the opposition's half

Where we are weak is in:

- Defending against long shots

- Aerial duels

- Making individual errors

- Defending counter attacks

- Conceding too many chances

I firmly believe that our strengths greatly outweigh our weaknesses and with five games to go we remain in a strong position to at least extend the season.

Pride And Tears – 12/4/15

I could not go to Derby yesterday and was reduced to watching the live coverage on Sky Sports on account of a long-standing social commitment last night. Well, in case you were wondering, let me just say that I was no company at all, and wandered around all night in a catatonic trance, replaying the entire match in my head, still rendered speechless by the total and utter unfairness of Brentford's result at the iPro yesterday lunchtime.

Without mincing words we ran rings around Derby, played the home team off the park, totally dominated possession with some beautiful and characteristically precise and incisive football and created more than enough chances to win three matches. Not just half chances either but truly massive opportunities that we really could not afford to spurn without risking a sting in the tail.

As it was, we were quite comfortably holding onto the lead given to us by Alex Pritchard's exquisitely struck curling twenty-harder and waiting for the final whistle when deep into injury time a scuffed mishit long range effort which could have gone anywhere from a player fortunate still to be on the pitch after a horror show tackle on Tommy Smith, fell at the predatory feet of Darren Bent six yards out with only Button to beat and he did not miss.

Unfortunately, the same could not be said about Andre Gray who missed three gilt-edged second half chances to seal the points. His control let him down twice at the crucial moment and prevented him from getting his close range shots off quickly enough to escape the attentions of the covering defenders, and on both occasions he sliced wastefully wide. With his third effort, he could not grow enough to get over a Dallas cross and head into a gaping net. Jonathan Douglas too should have scored but his close range poke after Jota had opened up the Derby defence like a can of beans, was underhit and allowed a defender on the line to hack it clear.

Derby had started the faster of the two teams with Ince shooting narrowly wide from a free kick before forcing an excellent save from Button, but just as had been the case at Fulham, the Bees grew into the game and then took total control. The midfield dovetailed perfectly with Douglas and Diagouraga breaking up the play and driving us forward relentlessly with Pritchard, Jota, Judge and Odubajo cutting vast swathes in the home defence. Derby could hardly get a kick as Brentford probed for openings. Moses pinged a shot into the ground from where it rebounded clear off the keeper's chest and Judge shot just wide from a free kick before a quick break saw the ball played to Pritchard in space who cut inside and with Bidwell's brilliant decoy run distracting the defenders, the ball was curled thrillingly just inside the far post for a quite wonderful goal of Premier League class. The remainder of the first half saw total domination from Brentford with Jota, Tarkowski and Pritchard threatening a second goal that never quite arrived.

Jonathan Douglas winning an aerial challenge at Derby.

Derby couldn't cope with Brentford's movement and relentless pressing and the second half was comfortable for the Bees with Tarkowski and Dean confident and dominant and Button largely untroubled apart from a well timed dive at the feet of Bent and a sharp tip over from Whitbread. Then nemesis struck and two precious points were thrown away.

In everything bar the finishing this was by far our most impressive performance of the season as we totally silenced nearly thirty thousand home supporters, the largest league attendance since I started to watch the Bees, with the quality of our football, accuracy of our passing and tenacity of our tackling and pressing. We looked massively composed and this was almost the complete team performance.

Before I start carping over where and how we fell short at the final hurdle yesterday, we would do well to reflect on just how far we have come, the fact that we are disappointed and aggrieved at not winning at Derby, a Premier League club in all but name, as well as the fact that we are playing football of a quality and sophistication unseen at Griffin Park in living memory. As Leroy Rosenior commented on *The Football League Show*:

It was almost the perfect away performance, the most perfect performance I have seen all season in the Championship. They dominated the game from start to finish. I can only echo his words.

I would say that we shot ourselves in the foot, but on the evidence of yesterday we would probably have missed. There are a couple of truisms that bear repeating given their relevance and appropriateness to what occurred yesterday – goals win matches and never give a sucker an even break. In fact, those wise words should be etched into the subconscious of every Brentford player as they reflect on how they let the game slip.

It is a knee jerk reaction and far too easy to heap the blame on Andre Gray who ran tirelessly for the cause, as in legal terms he is part of a joint enterprise with all his team mates and they are all equally responsible for what transpires on the pitch and must share the bouquets and brickbats when they win or lose. That being said I am afraid his failings and inadequacy in front of goal cost us dear, and I sorely doubt that Bent or Chris Martin would have been quite so profligate had they been presented with identical opportunities at the other end.

We have now scored over seventy goals this season with three players in double figures, but we have let far too many teams off the hook with our wayward finishing. We are deadly from twenty yards out, but far less so from five. Gray has massively over performed and exceeded expectations with fifteen league goals in his first season in the Championship, but I am sure that there will be much backbiting, grinding of the teeth and second guessing about our lack of cover and options up front should we ultimately fail to reach the playoffs. There was again no striker available to sit on the bench with Long still injured. This is a ludicrous situation that has cost us dear and should never have been allowed to occur.

Who knows where we will end up after another day of topsy-turvy results with Ipswich sneaking into the final playoff place after narrowly beating doomed Blackpool and Wolves finally losing in a hard fought local derby at Birmingham City. There is still everything to play for but we aren't half making it hard for ourselves. Will we finish in the top six, will all our hard work recover its merited reward or will we fall just short? All will be revealed in the next three tumultuous weeks.

We so deserve to make the playoffs given how well we have played, the effervescence and style of our approach and the consistency we have shown for the past six months, but there is still so much room for improvement and I shudder to think just how good we can become next year as our players grow in experience and confidence and we become more clinical. I will naturally be desperately disappointed if our season ends on the second of May but would still look back with utter pride and joy at what we have been privileged to watch this season. Mark Warburton, the catalyst and inspiration for all that is so good about us, I salute you.

Out Of Our Hands Now – 16/4/15

I have always made it a rule never to write a match report immediately after the final whistle. With good reason too. It is all too easy to go off on a poorly considered and ill-judged rant and tear everybody and everything to shreds without allowing for tempers and emotions to calm down and for a more measured analysis to be made in the cold light of day. I have therefore taken a day or so to reflect on where Tuesday night's disappointing one-nil defeat at Sheffield Wednesday has left us and why we find ourselves in our current position.

Let me start off by saying that even after mulling things around my head and analysing Brentford's performance in forensic detail, I'm still frustrated, furious and fuming at what happened at Hillsborough and I am not going to pull my punches.

As ever, we totally dominated proceedings, but I am sounding like a broken record as that is invariably the case nowadays both home and away. We had 59% possession and were accurate with 71% of 491 passes, which, it has to be said are all fairly low figures for the Bees. The telling statistic, and the one which highlighted where the match was lost is the fact that we managed fourteen shots of which a miserable three were on target.

The pitch resembled a cabbage patch, being bumpy and bobbly and almost denuded of grass and it has to be said that Brentford managed to play as much football as was possible on such a terrible and uneven surface.

Wednesday were more than happy to sit back and defend in numbers, draw us in and then hit us on the break, relying on a tall, tough and well-drilled defence to keep us at bay. Their game plan worked perfectly as they kept their record-equalling seventeenth clean sheet of the season and scored from one of the few opportunities that they created, albeit one that we did our utmost to set up for them.

After our customary slow start, we finally got a toehold into the game and created four excellent first half opportunities that should have put us out of sight and ensured that the points would be travelling down South. Gray did brilliantly to conjure up two chances out of practically nothing, each time bursting past his marker who was utterly out-powered by his strength and determination, but faced only by the goalkeeper, Westwood, albeit from a tight angle, he failed to finish off the job either time and the ball drifted wide on both occasions. It is hard to criticise a young player who is left isolated game after game and who creates most of his chances for himself given that he is left to forage largely on his own, but his finishing has quite literally been hit and miss and far less than clinical for half a season now.

Jota was well marshalled but finally escaped the clutches of his marker before running into a blind alley when he could have shot. And then, just before half time, came the key moment of the match. Gray's clever back-heel put Judge clean through straight down the middle but with the goal gaping, he thrashed the ball onto the top of the bar and over with the referee generously adjudging that the keeper had touched the ball on its way into the massed ranks of relieved home supporters, well aware that they had been let off the hook. Judge's lack of composure was telling and was perhaps symptomatic of the fact that with the inspirational Alex Prichard out injured, he was trying too hard to put his stamp on proceedings.

Gray was guilty of yet another glaring miss soon after halftime when Diagouraga's exquisite through ball gave him time and space to pick his spot from fifteen yards – *cometh the hour, cometh the man*, surely, but Gray once again fluffed his lines and shot unerringly a foot wide of the goal.

Having survived so many chances for us to win the match and yet being let off the hook time after time, Wednesday were reinvigorated and finally roused themselves from their torpor and began to probe us on the break as we pushed players forward in desperate search of the opening goal. Toral replaced Dallas and just as had been the case at Leeds in early February he turned the game and set up the match-winning goal – unfortunately, this time at the wrong end. He took Button's slightly overhit clearance onto his chest in the centre circle but slipped and carelessly allowed the ball to run away from him. Wednesday seized on the gift and with players caught upfield, were left with a man over and a low cross saw Tarkowski block the first shot but Lee snaffled up the rebound to score a soft and totally unearned goal.

We were stunned by this self-inflicted body blow but fought back well and created two more chances. Jota finally forced Westwood into a save with a bouncing long range effort that was scrambled away, before Judge unforgivably ballooned over from close range after Jota had put him in on goal. The Brentford fans were already beginning to celebrate as the ball dropped to Judge in time and space, but their anticipation turned in a split-second to groans of disbelief as he snatched at the ball when he could have brought it down and then shot way over the bar. That was our final chance and the game slipped away from us. Three points gift wrapped and thrown away given the excellent opportunities that were wasted.

The defeat leaves us in a position where we are no longer in control of our destiny and we surely need to win our final three matches, all of which are on paper eminently winnable, as well as rely on a couple of snookers from Ipswich and Wolves if we are to reach the playoffs. With two draws and a defeat in our last three matches we have nobody else to blame but ourselves. All three should have seen comfortable victories and whilst you can bemoan our misfortune at Derby the statistics tell their own story of our shortcomings. We have averaged over 60% possession in the last three games, had sixty-four shots of which only eighteen were on target and scored a measly three goals. We allowed the opposition thirty-two efforts on goal with ten on target and four finding the net. We scored from one in twenty-one of our efforts, the opposition were far more clinical, scoring with one in eight of their shots.

Mark Warburton has pretty much said the same thing and repeated the identical mantra in every post match press conference:

- We must be more clinical in front of goal

- We must take more care of the ball

- We must stop making unforced defensive errors

Unfortunately, the players seem totally unable to take these messages on board and these constant errors at both ends of the pitch are more than likely to cost us very dear come the end of the season. I appreciate the youth and relative inexperience of many of our squad but a genuine promotion-chasing team simply gets the job done at the business end of the season, as have several of our rivals who have now sprinted way ahead of us whilst we have struggled to get over the line.

There are also questions that have to be asked about the depth and quality of our squad, despite the manager's continued refusal to accept that we are anything other than fully equipped for every challenge that awaits us. Tuesday saw us without the services of Long and Pritchard and today we have learned that Chris Long was recalled by his parent club, Everton to play in an Under 21 fixture this afternoon as they felt he had not been starting recently for Brentford. To add insult to injury, or in this case should it perhaps be the other way around, he scored and was then taken off with a gashed thigh that required stitches. This is a strange one as it had previously been reported that we had sent him back to receive treatment as he hasn't been able to feature in our last three match day squads, yet he was fit enough to play for Everton yesterday. Where does that leave us? Will we see him again or are we going to end up playing our last six Championship matches with one fit (and I use that term advisedly) striker in the case of the drastically overworked Andre Gray?

I would share the view of Gary Blissett, when he recently expressed on Facebook, that now is the time to get behind and support the team unconditionally as we still have a mathematical chance of reaching the playoffs. There will be more than enough opportunities for analysis, praise and even recrimination once the season ends. Hopefully that will not be for a few weeks yet. Victory on Saturday against Bolton is essential. There is no margin for error. Let's hope we can get at least one of our injured players back as we continue to try and get ourselves over that finishing line.

Warburton's Words – 21/4/15

I do so enjoy reading Manager Mark Warburton's regular article in the *Bees Review* match day programme. They are invariably measured, thoughtful, pithy and to the point, just like the man himself and are quite evidently self-penned and not the work of some anonymous hack or ghost in the media department. He takes the time and trouble to open the dressing room door ajar and allow supporters to sneak inside the secretive, arcane and cloistered world of professional football, and he generally provides a deep and personal insight into some fascinating aspect of the club, playing squad or, indeed, the team behind the team.

I particularly like the courteous way he welcomes the opposition manager by name and remarks how much he is looking forward to sharing a drink with him after the game. For me, at least, his words conjure up vivid images of a convivial gathering with the two of them sitting down at a table covered with a spotless white starched tablecloth, napkins around their neck, with David Weir serving a selection of carefully sliced triangular cucumber sandwiches and cutting up the Battenberg, and Kevin O'Connor pouring cups of tea all around.

I am sure that the reality is somewhat different and far more akin to the Liverpool Boot Room with the two managers drinking a can of beer together and quietly reflecting on their respective fortunes in the hard fought game recently finished. Just in passing I must try to unearth my dog-eared copy of the Rotherham programme from January 10th and see if Warburton extended the same hospitality to Steve Evans as not only would he undoubtedly have hogged all the food on offer but also Evans (in his customary full-on post-match hectoring and hyperbolic rant mode) would surely have turned out to be a most unwelcome, loudmouthed and unsavoury guest and that nasty Paul Raynor would also have been asked to wait outside the door!

I read Mark's article in Saturday's programme with particular interest as he took the belated opportunity to look back three months in time and comment in great detail about his perspective on what happened, or perhaps more specifically what didn't, in the January transfer window.

Firstly, let's review the facts. We managed to bring in four players and, perhaps just as crucially, we lost nobody from our squad. We signed a promising young midfielder, Josh Laurent, from QPR, spent heavily on one of Scotland's top prospects in Rangers starlet Lewis Macleod, bought highly rated left-sided defender Jack O'Connell from Blackburn Rovers for a reported quarter of a million pounds, and signed England Under 20 international striker Chris Long on loan from Everton.

Our three permanent signings share similar characteristics in being young, inexperienced and highly talented and they all appear to have the potential to develop into exceptionally valuable long-term assets for the club. Unfortunately what is far more pertinent at the present time is that none of them have contributed in the slightest for us yet at first team level or have even played one minute's football in the Championship. We did have high hopes and expectations for Macleod but he arrived as damaged goods and has been a permanent sick note ever since, managing a grand total of forty-five eminently forgettable minutes for the Development Squad a few weeks back. He has now been put back into cold storage for next season when we can but hope that he manages to get himself fully fit and earns a place in our revamped midfield.

O'Connell was sent straight back on loan to Rochdale, where he really impressed in a team challenging for the Division One playoffs and justifiably earned a recall to his parent club. Despite our continued problems and adventures in central defence he has yet to be given his opportunity, although he has looked the part sitting on the bench! Next season perhaps? Laurent has no Football League pedigree but is an educated gamble for the future. Long is also short on experience but has impressed with his enthusiasm and eye for goal when given an opportunity, however he has been plagued with injuries and illness and has only made ten appearances including a mere two starts. Four goals is a more than decent return, but the overall feeling about our January signings is one of frustration and disappointment at their overall lack of contribution. Frankly they looked more like signings for January 2016 rather than this year and have done little or nothing to either strengthen or assist us in our promotion push.

One possible inference from the lack of immediate impact of our new arrivals in January is that they really were intended for the future rather than the present, and that the management were more than content with what they already had in terms of the strength, make-up and chemistry of the squad and were simply looking to tinker rather than make radical improvements.

Warburton's explanation is totally different in that he claims that key players were targeted both at home and abroad who would have added quality and depth to the squad, but for a variety of reasons every deal fell through. He mentioned player or agent financial demands that did not represent good value for Brentford or the requirement that potential loanees had to be automatic starters. Warburton categorically denied turning down any high quality players who were within our grasp and who would also have improved us.

Certainly it was rumoured at the time that funds were available and that strenuous efforts were being made to sign players of the calibre of giant Colombian central defender Bernardo from Sporting Gijon and top Austrian striker Marco Djuricin from Sturm Graz. Despite our apparent efforts, Bernardo remained at his present club and Djuricin allegedly snubbed us in favour of a move to Red Bull Saltzburg where he gone on to win a full international cap for Austria. Whilst it is impossible to be categoric, given their quality, they or their ilk would probably have made a massive difference to our fortunes had they arrived at Griffin Park and settled down to life in London.

Hindsight is always twenty-twenty, as Billy Wilder so memorably stated, and it is very easy to look back from our position today, outside the playoff positions and anticipating the increasing possibility of a massive missed opportunity, and assert that we made a huge error in not strengthening in January. But if we are to take Warburton's words at face value, which of course I do, then it wasn't for the want of trying.

What really surprised me was the timing of his remarks and that Warburton chose to raise this subject now, months after the event, when the season is approaching its climax, rather than wait until the postmortem after the season ends next month. Conspiracy theorists have been hard at work with their convoluted explanations for why we failed to bring home the bacon in January, so perhaps Warburton simply wished to rebut them, but it is difficult to reconcile oneself to the sight of Harlee Dean acting as our sole emergency striker in a *must-win* game on Saturday after the withdrawal of Andre Gray. A promotion chasing team should not have allowed itself to be reduced to such straits at this crucial stage of the season.

I have invariably found Mark Warburton to be open and honest in words and deeds alike, and this article is no exception, but the fact remains that our promotion rivals succeeded in January where we failed and the cost is likely to be high.

Jeepers Keepers – Part Four – 23/4/15

The New Millennium began with Brentford desperately looking for a new goalkeeper. Andy Woodman had not been the success that we had expected and was on his way out of the club and Jimmy Glass was no more than a short-term stopgap. Ron Noades certainly pulled a rabbit out of the hat and bemused us all when the identity of the new goalkeeper was announced. Noades apparently followed the recommendation of Hermann Hreidarsson and signed his Icelandic International colleague Olafur Gottskalksson from Hibernian. Tall, slender and athletic, he had an exceptional first season before suffering a chronic shoulder injury which affected his confidence and mobility and he rapidly lost form, went walkabout on several occasions, conceding costly late goals which threatened to becalm our promotion drive. He was unceremoniously dropped and replaced by young Paul Smith. He retired late in 2002 but reappeared a couple of years later at Torquay and made a surprise return to Griffin Park in the notorious Leon Constantine hat-trick game on Boxing Day 2004 before fading away and later receiving a couple of prison sentences for violence back in his native Iceland.

Paul Smith first came to our attention playing as a young unknown trialist for Crawley against the Bees and soon after he signed for us. He made a massive impact replacing the injured Gottskalksson against Southend in the LDV Vans Area Final when he made a series of brave and brilliant saves against Southend. Ironically he conceded six goals at Swansea on his full debut but he soon proved that he was an exceptional young goalkeeper in the making once he took over as first choice in January 2002. He was calm and unflustered and scouts were soon sniffing around him. Given the club's financial woes, his departure was a foregone conclusion and it was simply a question of getting the highest possible fee for him. Eventually Southampton offered £250,000 plus a series of lucrative add-ons that barely came to fruition as he failed to seize his opportunity on the South Coast, moved onto Nottingham Forest and ended up at Southend United. What looked at one time likely to be a glittering career ended in anticlimax. Smith made a glorious return to Brentford when he played us seemingly single-handedly in a FA Cup Third Round replay early in 2013 and more than earned the standing ovation that he received.

Alan Julian was the obvious replacement for Smith as the former Junior had impressed in his few opportunities, including one incredible match-winning performance at Rushden & Diamonds but he was far too erratic and inconsistent to make the position his own and eventually embarked on a long career in the lower divisions and upper echelons of non-league football that has just seen him winning the Conference South title with Bromley.

Wally Downes settled on another untried youngster in Stuart Nelson and this time the gamble paid off. Nelson made an unwanted impact on his debut, seeing red for a foul outside his penalty area at Brighton but he soon made the jersey his own and went on to concede an excellent 1.32 goals per game throughout his stay at the club. At first glance Nelson really did not look the part with his shirt perpetually out of his shorts and an eagerness to engage with opposition supporters when he was barracked. He had his weaknesses and often came flying out of his goal to little effect. He was not the best in dealing with crosses and his kicking often defied belief with a constant series of shanks and slices into touch. But for all his shortcoming and eccentricities he was reliable and more than got the job done. He was agile and brave and it was rare that he let in a soft goal. His temperament was sound and he scored a crucial penalty kick in a shootout at Swindon and also had a goal controversially ruled out when his long clearance found the net at his former club, Doncaster Rovers. Nelson was a favourite of Martin Allen for whom he also played at Notts County and Gillingham, where he remains to this day.

Josh Lennie made his one and only Bees appearance as a halftime substitute in a long-forgotten LDV Trophy game against MK Dons before drifting into non-league. He memorably describes himself thus on Twitter: *London born & raised washed up ex-pro footballer for Brentford, Wimbledon and Chester, now full-time coach and scout in Connecticut.*

Ademola Bankole, a giant Nigerian international keeper who had previously played at Crewe Alexandra, was brought in as Goalkeeping Coach and also played a few games as a back-up for Nelson. He was tall, spider-like and gangly and, for a coach, worryingly seemed to have no appreciation or understanding of where his penalty area started and ended. He memorably punched away a cross when jumping way outside his area and somehow escaped a red card against Nottingham Forest and was thankfully not seen too often again in the first team.

Clark Masters was given the opportunity to replace the suspended and then injured Stuart Nelson at the start of the 2006/07 season and it was a case of too much too soon as he was patently unready for his premature promotion and leaked goals like a sieve. He played well on his debut against Blackpool but luck was never on his side as he suffered a harsh sending off against Gillingham and conceded seven goals despite impressing when replacing the sent-off Simon Brown at Peterborough. He proved to be out of his depth and his once-promising career never recovered and he soon dropped into non-league football where he remains today. Had he been given more time to develop then who knows how his career might have panned out... We might even have had another star on our hands.

2006/07 was an appalling season which culminated in a fully deserved relegation. By Christmas 2006 it was plainly obvious in which direction the team was irrevocably headed and Scott Fitzgerald tried to plug the gap in goal by signing Nathan Abbey from Torquay. He was exactly what we needed – calm and reliable, uninspired but competent and someone who rarely made an unforced error. He performed excellently and conceded a mere 1.25 goals per game despite having an awful defence in front of him. Despite his efforts he was released at the end of the season and his replacement did little to inspire confidence.

Simon Brown had started out at Spurs and had several years as first choice at Colchester United before moving to Scotland where he played for Hibernian. He was the second goalkeeper to join the Bees from the Edinburgh club but he was never the keeper that Oli Gottskalksson had been and his stay was undistinguished. He rarely looked the part, losing his place to loanee Ben Hamer before being offloaded on loan to Darlington. Hamer arrived on the eve of the season from Reading when Brown suffered a late injury and he was to have four loan spells at Griffin Park making seventy-five league appearances in total. Confident to the point of cockiness he played a massive part in the Championship winning team of 2008/09, missing only one game. He dominated his area, had a vast prehensile reach and kicked the ball huge distances. It came as a surprise when his own poor judgement and recklessness cost him a red card, and the Bees a defeat in a televised FA Cup tie at Barrow. He was also the only Brentford player to successfully hit the crossbar in Soccer AM's Crossbar Challenge. Ben returned for a fourth loan spell in 2010 as part of the beauty parade of goalkeepers auditioned by Andy Scott but his late arrival for a midweek match against AFC Bournemouth provided Scott with the excuse he needed to play his Cup goalkeeper Richard Lee in the league and Hamer drifted out of contention. He subsequently had a good spell at Charlton and is now at Premier League Leicester sporting a quite ridiculous bushy beard!

We are nearly at the end of our journey, which will be concluded soon!

Staying Alive! – 26/4/15

Brentford's promotion dream is still alive and kicking after a fairly comfortable two-nil victory at hapless Reading, which in conjunction with the Ipswich and Derby results, ensured that the battle for the final two elusive playoff places goes into what is certain to be a heart-stopping last day of the season next Saturday. Given that Ipswich eventually managed a late cruelly deflected winner against a determined Nottingham Forest team and Derby also got out of jail close to the final whistle at Millwall, who were fighting for their Championship life, matters are now out of Brentford's hands. One thing though is for certain, Brentford need to do their bit and defeat Wigan at Griffin Park next Saturday, in itself no formality, and hope results involving Ipswich or Derby go in our favour. We will go into the match in seventh place in the table with a meaty seventy-five points, two behind sixth-placed Derby and three less than fifth-placed Ipswich who have a superior goal difference of three over us.

Assuming we do the business over what is likely by then to be a relegated Wigan team, then we will have to rely upon Blackburn Rovers doing us a favour and beating Mick McCarthy's team. Hopefully the predatory Jordan Rhodes will want to turn it on against the team that disposed of his services so carelessly – we can but hope. There is one other potential route into the playoffs should Derby fail to pick up a point against a demoralised and uninterested Reading team that clearly demonstrated yesterday afternoon that they are already on the beach. If all that is not enough we will also have to keep a weather eye on Wolves who are tucked in right on our coattails with the same number of points but they would have to make up four goals on us and they will be facing Millwall who might still have something to play for.

Enough of all that for now as otherwise I shall have absolutely nothing to write about throughout the next week as we nervously prepare for Wigan and the final showdown. That being said, when the fixtures were announced way back in June last year, I am sure that when we saw that we would be facing Wigan at Griffin Park on the last day of the season the majority of our supporters expected that we would probably be looking to spoil Uwe Rösler's promotion party rather than seeing the boot firmly on the other foot – such is the joy and unpredictability of being a football supporter!

Back to yesterday's game, Brentford were always a little bit sharper and more committed and dare I say, better organised defensively than the home team who almost equalled us in terms of possession but were toothless upfront and squandered the chances that they either created, or, on a couple of occasions, we gifted them.

Brentford were unchanged and Mark Warburton's policy of keeping faith with his regulars was emphasised by the fact that no fewer than eight of the team that began the match yesterday also started the season's opener against Charlton and the others, Craig, Dallas and McCormack were on the bench at Reading. Given the likelihood that, subject to injuries, the team that Warburton names for next week's final league match will also be either identical or extremely similar to yesterday's, I was going to wait a week before making this point but I thought that I would mention it in passing now in case it slips my mind given all the anticipated excitement of the next few days.

Given the turnover of footballers, and indeed managers, I suspect that this is an extremely rare feat that can be looked at in two ways, firstly that the eleven regulars have shown great consistency and have also largely stayed injury-free, but on the other side, perhaps in some key positions there has been a lack of competition for places and an opportunity to freshen things up might not have gone amiss. We can look at this again when we come to review the season next month.

Any nerves were settled by a well-worked early goal. Dean sent a measured long pass to the feet of Gray wide on the right, who slipped his man, initially looked in vain for a colleague in the penalty area and then timed his curling near-post cross perfectly to coincide with the arrival of Judge who had made a late lung-bursting run to meet the ball and sweep it into the roof of the net. Reading were caught ball-watching and defended poorly but were undone by our movement and accurate use of the ball. The home team responded well, but were powder-puff in attack and barely threatened. Pritchard was wasted in the first half, playing out wide on the left wing but eventually moved inside to become a massive influence on the game. Near halftime his instant left footer from Jota's pass was seemingly bound for the bottom corner until a late deflection took it wide. Gray played his customary party trick of creating a massive opportunity for himself by turning his defender and racing clear early in the second half but it was Groundhog Day as he allowed the advancing Federici, who was cruelly taunted by the Bees fans following his Wembley *faux pas*, to close him down and throw out his right foot to deflect the ball wide of the post.

That would have given us some breathing space and Reading threatened down the flanks and forced Button into a couple of decent saves and had an apparent equaliser correctly ruled out for offside. The game was drifting in the sunshine until something remarkable and almost unprecedented happened – Tarkowski scored with a stooping header from a Judge free kick after making a clever late run. The free kick came after a cynical throat-high assault on Jota, more akin to GBH, after a defender had been skinned by his trickery on the ball. This was the first time a Bees defender had scored from a free kick since Harlee Dean's late face-saving equaliser at Dagenham eight months ago and highlights another area where drastic improvement is necessary.

The game appeared over, but it was at this point when our bad old habits revealed themselves either through complacency or an understandable desire to keep pushing forward for more goals. As it was, we left the back door wide open. Button had been far more circumspect with his distribution from goal kicks with the Bolton horror show still fresh in his mind and Dean played his best game of the season, being tough, strong, composed and sensible with his use of the ball. Tarky too had been excellent until he suddenly lost his head and concentration, made bad decisions and twice lost possession deep in his own half but thankfully Button saved his bacon and we did not suffer from his aberrations.

Tarkowski quite simply has to learn to differentiate between the times when he can and should play football and situations when the ball just has to be cleared upfield or played into touch. I have written exactly the same thing on so many occasions throughout the season and he really has not yet learned his lesson. He is a marvellously gifted player and his passing and dribbling ability are crucial to the team but it is a question of balance and judgement as his first job is to defend and not set up chances for the opposition on a plate. We were extremely fortunate that a poor home team did not take advantage of the gifts we lavished on them but other teams have been far more clinical. Reading gave up near the end and we had late chances to boost our goal difference but Toral hit the post and Judge missed horribly when clean through.

Tarky pointing the way to victory at Reading.

The win was crucial and we did our job competently and professionally and it was encouraging to see us beat a team so comprehensively despite our not firing on all cylinders. One further bonus was the appearance of Stuart Dallas as a late substitute for Gray and he performed excellently as a makeshift central striker. Another string to his bow for this impressive young player and another option for us even though it is expected that Chris Long might be fit for selection next week. A word of praise too for referee Andy Madley who was excellent and unobtrusive yesterday and proved that there is at least one decent referee bearing the Madley name!

A long week awaits us as the anticipation grows for next Saturday's day of destiny. Oh, and in passing many congratulations to Alex Pritchard, named today by his fellow professionals in the PFA Championship team of the season, the only Bees player so honoured, and he thoroughly deserves this accolade.

The Journeyman Footballer – 28/4/15

Surely you remember Ben Smith? You don't? Well I still have a clear memory of a sunny late April afternoon back in 2008 when all-conquering Hereford United stomped all over a weak Brentford team and thrashed us three-nil to secure a promotion slot to Division One. Their raucous supporters took over an otherwise morgue-like and desperate Griffin Park and in midfield Watford loanee Toumani Diagouaraga and the aforementioned Smith dovetailed perfectly and ran rings around us, creating chance after chance for the predatory Gary Hooper. Whilst Hooper has gone on to fame and no doubt fortune in his subsequent career at Celtic and Norwich City, Ben Smith never succeeded in touching those heights.

He had high hopes when, as a callow, cocky young Essex boy he started off as an apprentice in the hallowed marble halls of Highbury, marvelling at the skills of the likes of Dennis Bergkamp, and dreaming of the day he would play alongside his hero, but it wasn't to be and he was soon shipped out to begin his long odyssey around the lesser reaches of the football world.

He became the epitome of the journeyman footballer, surviving, if not always thriving, for no less than seventeen years in a sport that mercilessly weeds out the weak and unfortunate and established himself in such outposts of the game as Yeovil, Hereford, Crawley and Swindon.

His marvellous autobiography, *Journeyman: One man's odyssey through the lower leagues of English football,* is published today. No tales of the Champions League or Baby Bentleys here – instead, what you get is a gritty, fascinating and indeed salutary tale as Smith is searingly honest, opens himself up to criticism and scrutiny and spares nobody, least of all himself. He looks back with the perspective of a now mature adult at some of the naive, immature and frankly daft decisions and mistakes he made that condemned him to the life of a lower league journeyman rather than a Premier League superstar.

Ben certainly had the raw talent to play at the top level as he was skilful on the ball, read the game excellently and had the ability to open up a defence with one incisive through ball but he was never given the opportunity to prove it and when glimmers of hope appeared he was either cursed with bad luck, ill-timed injuries, the vagaries of unsympathetic management or indeed his own myriad shortcomings.

He now realises and admits that early on in his career, before the penny dropped, he squandered his ability through ill-discipline, abusing his body, which was hardly a temple, and a failure to knuckle down to self-sacrifice and the monastic lifestyle required to be a successful professional footballer.

He was left to scrabble around each year for one more contract, a club car, an extra fifty quid a week or an appearance bonus to help secure his future and delay the inevitable. This is what life is really about in the lower divisions where there is no job security and a footballer is simply a depreciating asset with the clock ticking, who is instantly replaceable by another identical clone and can be disposed of at the will and whim of despotic chairmen or managers who have their own agendas, play favourites, pay lip service to the truth and are always looking to find a way to cut the wage bill or slither out of their obligations.

Smith often falls foul of their machinations as he is despatched from pillar to post and learns the hard way about the perils of finding a new club and contract negotiations both with and without an agent. He leaves himself exposed to danger by agreeing to a potential new contract that only kicks in if he plays a set number of games the previous season, and is left to wither on the vine as his manager did everything within his power to avoid him reaching that milestone and get rid of him.

Not that he bemoans his fate as, throughout the book, it becomes quite clear that he was massively proud and grateful for the chance to play professional football for so long and to make over three hundred appearances at levels ranging from Division One to the Conference South. He was a craftsman, a survivor and he made some money, got the girl, won the odd promotion and title here and there, became a local hero and established a decent reputation in some of the aforementioned outposts of the game, enjoyed himself and most importantly, did not have to succumb to the drudgery of a normal nine-to-five routine.

As we have heard elsewhere this season, *football is a village* and in the course of his travels Smith meets up with so many incredible characters within the game both on and off the pitch; he is an excellent fly on the wall and has taken careful note of their strengths and weaknesses. He is a keen observer and paints vivid word portraits. He is sympathetic to the likes of Graham Turner, juggling the horrendous joint roles of Chairman and Manager at Hereford United but he has little time for and eviscerates Gary Peters and Steve Evans for whom he played at Shrewsbury Town and Crawley respectively. Peters comes over as a totally miserable and negative influence, playing a horrible brand of percentage long-ball football and a man far keener to carp, criticise and diminish rather than empower, encourage and support his players.

As for Steve Evans, the chapters on Smith's roller coaster ride at Crawley under the aegis of Evans are pure comedy gold and are worth the cover price of the book on their own. The man is obviously as crazy as a fox and he is a total loose cannon with the players never knowing which side of his Jekyll and Hyde character he will display from day to day – or even minute to minute. Players are screamed at, abused and sacked on a seemingly random and daily basis only to be reinstated quickly and quietly. But there is a method to his madness and, fawningly supported by his equally foul-mouthed yes-man number two Paul Raynor, Evans keeps the players on their toes, never allowing them to relax or feel secure and ever ready to indulge in a mad trolley dash to bring in replacements, but his unorthodox approach gets results. Smith found success at Crawley as they rose into the Football League and he played an important part in their incredible FA Cup run that saw them beat the likes of Derby County and Torquay United before the high-spot of his career, running Manchester United extremely close in a narrow one-nil defeat at a packed Old Trafford.

Brentford fans will be fascinated by the sympathetic descriptions of the likes of Toumani Diagouraga, one of the best midfield partners Smith ever played alongside, perennial good pro and nice guy David Hunt, and of course the immortal Martin Allen who plays a cameo role in Smith's story and orchestrates a hilarious meeting worthy of a Brian Rix farce with the Cheltenham chairman intended to earn Smith a contract at the club.

This well-written book should be required reading for every supporter of a lower league team whether it be Accrington or York as it tells it exactly how it is. Budding young footballers and their parents would also do well to peruse it in order to become aware of the traps and pitfalls that may well await them.

Ben Smith has clearly demonstrated that there is no shame in being described as a *journeyman*. Quite the opposite as he is to be applauded for writing what is surely the best book of this ilk since Garry Nelson's classic *Left Foot Forward*.

Jeepers Keepers – Part Five – 29/4/15

Today we will conclude our review of all the Brentford goalkeepers from the past forty-five years, and we pick up the story in 2008/09 with loanee Ben Hamer firmly in possession of the position.

His backup was Seb Brown, a self-admitted AFC Wimbledon fan who played once for us in the Johnstone's Paint Trophy and saved a penalty in a shootout victory over Yeovil before signing for his favourite team where his two penalty shootout saves against Luton helped them gain entry into the Football League. Young Lloyd Anderson also had his moment in the sun when he came on to replace Hamer when he was stupidly sent off at Barrow and he conceded two goals for his trouble before finally ending up as perhaps the only other Brentford player since Keith Hooker to play for both Brentford and Brentwood Town. Mikkel Andersen was another one-game-wonder, as one Reading loan goalkeeper replaced another when Hamer was suspended. Mikkel could not have chosen a more exciting game to play in and he really looked the part too in our last gasp victory over Bradford City in which he was named Man of the Match. Not a bad way to mark your only appearance for the club. Mikkel is still only twenty-six and was stuck on Reading's bench when we played them last Saturday, but I fully expect that he will eventually make his breakthrough and become an established top level goalkeeper.

With Hamer returning to his parent club, newly promoted Brentford were on the lookout for a new goalkeeper and they ended up playing four of them throughout the 2009/10 season. Andy Scott was apparently offered Everton's John Ruddy on a season-long loan but changed his mind at the last moment and signed Derby County's Welsh International keeper, Lewis Price instead. This was not one of the best decisions that he ever made given how well Ruddy has subsequently progressed and Price's inconsistency. Lewis did made a phenomenal last minute save from Morgan Schneiderlin to earn us a meritorious point at Southampton, but, looking far smaller and frailer than his claimed height of six foot three inches, he never really convinced and conceded a bizarre last minute equaliser at home to Millwall from a forty-yard free kick from way out on the left wing which precipitated his replacement, but more of that anon.

The Bees also made the surprise signing of Aldershot's Nicky Bull who, after being their undisputed first choice for many years, had decided to retire but quickly changed his mind and joined Brentford as back-up keeper instead. He spent a frustrating year largely kicking his heels after suffering a back injury but his rare appearances saw him go from the ridiculous to the sublime when firstly he dozily stepped over his own goal line whilst still holding onto Simon Francis's seemingly innocuous long-range free kick against Southend before saving a penalty kick at Leyton Orient. Bull was soon forgotten when Scott then totally redeemed himself by making perhaps the most inspired signing of his managerial career in young Arsenal starlet Wojciech Szczęsny.

Not yet twenty years of age but already a full international for Poland, he saved a penalty kick in his second match and it was immediately obvious that we had a star on our hands. He remained on loan until the end of the season, conceded just over a goal per game and his incredible all-round ability and sheer force of personality shone through. He put on goalkeeping masterclasses game after game and some of the saves he made against Norwich, Leeds, Carlisle and Bristol Rovers in particular beggared belief. Have a look on Youtube if you doubt me and I guarantee that you will be as astounded as I was. His ability was merely confirmed by the general bemusement amongst Bees supporters when he had a rare off day and played appallingly against MK Dons and was totally responsible for two soft goals, but as the old saying goes – *The defects of great men are the consolation of the dunces*. He received the ultimate accolade of receiving a fully deserved standing ovation from the home supporters when he was withdrawn for Simon Moore to make a brief debut just prior to the final whistle of the last game of the season so that he could milk their applause. We will not see his like again as he was precociously brilliant and light years ahead of anyone else we had watched at Griffin Park, in my memory at least.

How do you replace such an icon? Well Andy Scott seemed to have hit the jackpot when he brought in experienced Watford keeper Richard Lee, but he made a disastrous start and was rusty and unimpressive in his first two preseason appearances. Scott handled the situation poorly and instead of giving Lee, a keeper of proven ability and pedigree, the opportunity to settle into the role, he immediately banished him to the bench and gave young Simon Moore a brief chance before bafflingly auditioning two more loan keepers who further muddied the water. Alex McCarthy was yet another Reading goalkeeper who followed the well-trodden path to Griffin Park but he was soon on his way back after a tentative and stuttering loan spell which saw six goals fly past him in only three games. McCarthy has subsequently proved himself at Premier League level but he was distinctly below average for us.

Like a bad penny, Ben Hamer was soon back for his fourth loan spell at Brentford replacing his own teammate Alex McCarthy. Again he did nothing wrong but by this time the Bees had embarked upon successful runs in both the Carling Cup and Johnstone's Paint Trophy and Richard Lee seized his chance to establish himself as our

Cup Keeper with some phenomenal performances. He impressed in a narrow win over Hull City before earning his spurs with a superlative match-winning performance against Premier League giants Everton. Lee made save after save to help keep us afloat before becoming an instant hero when saving Jermaine Beckford's effort in the penalty shootout. Our Carling Cup run came to a cruel halt with a shootout defeat at Birmingham in the next round but it was in the Johnstone's Paint Trophy where Lee came into his own as the Bees won three penalty shootouts in a row against Orient, Swindon and Charlton on their way to a Wembley final appearance. I have written previously about Richard's Three Card Trick against Charlton when he emulated Graham Benstead's feat against Wrexham and made three consecutive, and indeed, outrageous penalty saves. Not surprisingly Lee soon took over in league matches, too, from the blameless Hamer who had become surplus to requirements. As if fate had not intervened enough, Lee's roller coaster season ended with him being named as Player of the Year but also missing out on a place at Wembley when he dislocated his shoulder making a brave save against Orient.

Poor Richard never had much luck with injuries and eventually his recurring shoulder problems forced him out of the reckoning far too early, and for good, and this enabled firstly Simon Moore and then David Button to establish themselves in the first team. He has remained in the background in a supporting role and as an overall good influence and will retire at the end of the season after a long and distinguished career that never quite rose to the heights that his undoubted ability suggested. Given his popularity and affability we will gloss over his recent short-term and career-ending loan at Fulham! His business nous and intelligence will surely provide him with a fulfilling and successful post-football career.

Goalkeeping Coach Simon Royce, a man who had already enjoyed an excellent career, deputised for Lee when he was sent off and subsequently suspended and clearly demonstrated in his brief appearances that it was time for him to pack up for good and concentrate on teaching rather than doing. Trevor Carson, a loanee from Sunderland, also made a brief cameo appearance at Sheffield Wednesday and was never seen again.

Simon Moore fought his way up from being an unheralded trialist from the Isle of Wight and, aided by Lee's injury battles, he became first choice and quickly demonstrated his exceptional ability. Unspectacular, calm and competent, he made few mistakes and picked crosses out of the air with consummate ease. Having secured his reputation as one of the brightest talents outside the top flight, he joined Premier League Cardiff City on the eve of the 2013/14 campaign for a substantial fee but his career has unfortunately stymied as he has so far been unable to displace David Marshall.

Unknown Frenchman Antoine Gounet emulated Gus Hurdle by walking unannounced into the training ground and earning himself a contract. He was small, agile and unorthodox and finally earned his opportunity when helping the Bees to an FA Cup replay victory over Bradford City before fading out of contention.

That leads us to the present day, and our excellent current pairing of David Button and Jack Bonham about both of whom I have already written extensively. We have been blessed with some exceptional goalkeepers over the past four decades or so and whilst comparisons are invidious, if pushed, my top ten in terms of a combination of talent and overall popularity would be as follows:

Ahead of the Game

- Chic Brodie

- Steve Sherwood

- Len Bond

- Dave McKellar

- Graham Benstead

- Paul Smith

- Wojciech Szczęsny

- Richard Lee

- Simon Moore

- David Button

David Button currently sneaks into my top ten, but I fully expect him to rise to near the top of the list over the next year or so should he continue to develop and improve to the extent he has this season.

MAY

Speechless! – 3/5/15

Brentford supporters are traditionally fatalistic as we have been taken almost to the heights and then let down all too often in the past for us to be anything other than negative in outlook and the scene was set yesterday for yet another massive letdown and I am afraid to confess that I feared the worst. With the last two playoff places still up for grabs it wasn't simply enough for us to beat relegated Wigan, not such an easy task in itself given our shaky recent home record, but, in addition, we also had to rely on one of our closest rivals, Ipswich and Derby slipping up, as well as keeping a beady eye on Wolves lurking in our slipstream. Ipswich had a tough looking match at a revitalised Blackburn Rovers and faced the awesome dual goal threat of Gestede and Rhodes but surely a draw, their minimum requirement, was well within their capabilities? As for Derby, all that they required was a point against a shambolic Reading team without a win for nine Championship matches and who had barely gone through the motions just a week ago against the Bees. Wolves too were at home with an eminently winnable game against relegated Millwall.

Nerves were certainly jangling at Griffin Park and early on we struggled to cope with a re-energised Wigan team who denied us space, pressed us high up the pitch and packed the midfield. The visitors had all the early play with the impressive Kim pulling their strings and the wonderfully named Bong overlapping menacingly. Button saved well from Fortune who also put the ball into the net but we were saved as the ball had drifted out of play before Bong had managed to get his cross in.

The news elsewhere was mixed. Ipswich, through the inevitable Murphy, roared into the lead at Blackburn but to counter that, Reading snatched an early goal at Derby. Wolves also got their noses in front before the Bees worked out how best to counter Wigan's threat. Slowly we grew into the game, Douglas and Diagouraga began to win possession and Pritchard flitted into space and began to probe menacingly. The breakthrough came from a set piece after Gray had turned the lumbering Maguire and was tripped for his pains. The free kick was thirty yards out and firmly in Pritchard territory and, not for the first time, he grasped the opportunity when his firmly hit drive caromed off the straining head of Chow in the wall and unerringly found the top corner of the net far out of the reach of Nicholls who dived in vain but could not get anywhere near the flight of the ball.

In an instant you could almost see and feel the tension drain out of Brentford fans and players alike. The game had turned on a moment of genius, aided and abetted by a piece of good fortune and from then on we never looked back. Pritchard and Gray missed excellent chances to stretch our lead as halftime approached but the news elsewhere was good and just kept on getting better. Two quick Blackburn goals turned their game on its head as Ipswich now needed to score as Derby were certain, surely, to recover and get the point they needed against Reading. So you would think on any normal matchday, but not today, as with the staccato tones emanating from radios being clearly heard above the crowd noise and with smartphones flashing in the sunshine and working overtime the news from the iPro Stadium was clear. Derby were huffing and puffing but not succeeding in blowing the house down and Darren Bent's gloriously missed penalty just on the interval made us believe for the first time that the unthinkable might just be about to happen.

The second half could not have gone better for us. Barely had we kicked off when an intricate move involving Moses, Judge and Jota saw a six-pass interchange which left Jota with a clear sight of goal. His instant shot was perfectly placed and provided us with the breathing space of the second goal we so desperately needed. Naturally it wouldn't be Brentford if we did not make it hard for ourselves. Wigan replied instantly and cut us open, the ball pinged around the home penalty area and Bidwell's deflection looked certain to reduce the deficit as Button plunged on the ball near the goal line. With heart in mouth as one we all looked at the assistant referee but thankfully he remained unmoved and we escaped. Wigan never threatened us again and it was now a case of simply how many we would score whilst still keeping an anxious eye on the scores elsewhere.

Wolves were home and hosed against Millwall but barring a late goalfest we were safe from their challenge and even so they would need Derby or Ipswich to recover and incredibly there was no sign of that happening. The news in fact just got better as Blackburn scored a third and even when Murphy reduced the arrears we were not too worried given that Reading, dear wonderful Reading, a team now close to my heart, scored a second and then third goal against a Derby team now reduced to a rabble. Wigan too had given up the ghost as we began to carve them apart. Judge saw an effort come back off the keeper; Tarkowski, so effective in defence alongside the impeccable Harlee Dean, hammered a close range shot against the crossbar before Jermaine Pennant sent a quick free kick unerringly straight to the darting feet of Jota on the halfway line. He made for goal and using Dallas as a decoy, gave the entire Wigan defence the eyes before caressing the ball through the eye of a needle to Gray who timed his run perfectly, stayed onside, and scored emphatically for a quite wonderfully worked goal.

We now knew that we were playoff bound and it was party-time at Griffin Park with late substitute Alan McCormack patrolling the midfield with menace. Unfortunately Tarkowski entered into the spirit a bit too much when he took responsibility for a last minute penalty after Judge was tripped. With Pritchard off the pitch there was a paucity of volunteers. Tarky stepped forward and mindful of his spot kick fiasco against Leeds, we all feared the worst. At least this time his effort was on target but it was powderpuff and Nicholls received some deserved reward for his labours by saving easily. Never mind, it is hard to quibble about anything on such a wonderful day although it still rankles that every penalty we win is an adventure in the extreme rather than the near certainty that it should be.

The final whistle sounded and we had stepped up to the mark and done everything that was required of us and our comfortable victory, allied to the defeats for both Ipswich and

Derby, ensured not only a playoff berth but also fifth place and a playoff semi final against a Middlesbrough team that will surely fancy their chances against us given their two victories against the Bees earlier in the season. There is time aplenty to contemplate the mouthwatering prospect of both ties during the week to come. Now, however is a time to celebrate, pay tribute, recognise the contribution and give thanks to a wonderful set of players as well as Mark Warburton, his team of coaches and support staff and of course, Matthew Benham who have all combined so brilliantly to get the reward that they so thoroughly deserve. I am almost speechless with pride and am honoured to be able to support this club. The dream continues unabated!

Caveat Emptor – 4/5/15

I was watching *The Football League Show* a couple of weeks ago in the wee early hours of Sunday morning and I thought that I really must have been dreaming as through eyes half closed with tiredness I saw a familiar looking lanky striker wearing Sky Blue dance around an opposition goalkeeper with consummate ease and even balletic grace and then with the empty goal gaping in front of him, he carefully and precisely rolled his shot onto the outside of the post from where it dribbled feebly wide. I sat up with a start and realised that it was no dream but what I had witnessed was the renaissance of Nick Proschwitz, recalled to the Coventry City team after an injury crisis which saw them otherwise bereft of strikers and seemingly left with no alternative other than pick somebody out of the crowd if they were not to select the Brentford loanee.

Nick signed for Coventry on loan a couple of months or so ago in an attempt to bolster their squad in their uphill fight against relegation from the First Division – a ridiculous state of affairs for a club of their stature and resources to find themselves in. Well, a win at Crawley on the final day of the season on Sunday allied to defeats for some of their nearest rivals ensured that it was mission accomplished as Coventry ended up in seventeenth place five points clear of the drop, but it was a close run thing.

Interestingly enough Nick signed for the club at a time when they were between managers as the sacked Steven Pressley had yet to be replaced by Tony Mowbray and it was joint caretaker manager, Neil McFarlane, who finalised the deal with Brentford. At the time he sounded as pleased as punch at the wisdom of the signing, commenting: *We're delighted to bring in a player we've been tracking at this club for a long time.* I would love to know whether they actually saw him play in one of his rare Development Squad starts or perhaps they were impressed with the manner in which he sat on the Brentford bench, or warmed up.

So how did he do in his new temporary home? In truth, not too well as he struggled to find form and fitness and to secure a regular place in a Coventry team that appeared to be nosediving inexorably towards the bottom division with little sign of stopping the rot. Proschwitz ended up playing nine times, six as a starter, and managed one well-taken headed goal, a late consolation in a dire home defeat by Crewe last week. He was guilty of some appalling misses at a time when every goal was crucial and yesterday was no different, as with Coventry needing just one more point to ensure their survival they were awarded a penalty just before halftime. Nick it was who was brave enough to take responsibility at such a key moment, and surely this would be his moment in the sun, but no, he scuffed his shot which was easily saved by Crawley keeper, Brian Jensen. He was replaced in ignominy and the local paper remarked after the game that it was inexplicable that Proschwitz did not hit the spot kick high as he had apparently been doing successfully in training all week – shades of James Tarkowski perhaps?

What happens to Proschwitz now? Brentford will certainly not want him back and he will be a free agent. Perhaps he can earn a contract for next season at Coventry, but from my outsider's vantage spot it would appear that he has not done nearly enough to convince the new management of his value and I would expect that they will also baulk at the salary he will probably be seeking. I suspect that his unhappy spell in this country has now come to an end and that he will be looking for a fresh opportunity elsewhere in Europe.

The tough but appropriate question that has to be asked is why so much money was wasted on a player who had never really achieved much at a decent standard? Proschwitz was brought to England by Steve Bruce at Hull City in 2012 whose interest had been piqued by his record in his homeland where he played for the second teams at Wolfsburg, Hamburg and Hannover before spending two seasons in Swiss football. He hit an impressive twenty-three goals in twenty-nine league games with Swiss Challenge League side FC Vaduz, then a further eight in thirty-one league games for FC Thun, the first time he had played in a country's top league, before moving back to Germany in the summer of 2011 to join SC Paderborn. He scored regularly there and was joint top scorer in the division, but again at a lower level of the game, in Bundesliga 2.

This was enough for Bruce who pounced and in July 2012 he lavished a massive £2.6m on a player who had accomplished very little at the top level of the game. Hull were promoted to the Premier League at the end of the following season but apart from a brilliantly taken late strike in the FA Cup against Leyton Orient and a vital equaliser at Cardiff in a last day of the season promotion clash he hardly contributed and indeed missed a late penalty in the same game that could have cost his team dear. He barely played in the Premier League and was loaned out to Barnsley for the remainder of the 2013/14 season where he scored a few goals was unable to save them from relegation from the Championship.

Hull were desperate to get rid of a player who had hardly proved to be value for money and the real surprise was that it was Brentford, so painstaking and analytical in their scouting and assessment of potential signings who surprisingly took him off their hands immediately before the start of the current season. That I suspect was the key to his signing for the Bees, as for all their sustained efforts throughout the preseason, Brentford had been unable to conclude an acceptable deal to bring in a third striker who would ideally start as first choice ahead of the inexperienced Scott Hogan and Andre Gray. Two days before the season opener against Charlton, with no other deal in sight, Proschwitz arrived, a body or *sparesie* as David Webb once so memorably stated of Mark Janney, to fill the gap, apparently at the behest of Director of Football Frank McParland. He signed a one-year contract with a further club option for an additional two years and manager Mark Warburton warmly welcomed him:

We have had a long search to find the right striker that offers us quality and a variety of weaponry. Nick is a very experienced player. He put in some fantastic performances in Germany before his move to Hull. He is an aerial threat and has very good technical ability. We think he will bring outstanding quality to the squad. We are delighted to secure him and look forward to him playing an important part this season.

I wonder how the manager would feel now when he reflects upon those words? Nick came on as a late substitute against Charlton and clearly demonstrated his ring rustiness given that he obviously lacked match fitness and sharpness, and, quite frankly, he has been struggling to catch up ever since. In all he made three starts for the club, only one in the Championship, away at Blackpool, never completed a full ninety minutes and came on as a late substitute on seventeen occasions. In total he played three hundred and forty-two minutes for the Bees and none of them were particularly memorable nor were there many highlights although the player could possibly argue that he was never given the time on the pitch or continuity of games to settle into his stride. He played well in the crazy twelve-goal thriller at Dagenham and he showed some neat touches on the ball and also worked hard that night but it was against lower league opposition. He was credited with a goal but in reality it was a definite own goal from a home defender, but who cares, he was off and running. His only other goal was a crucial one, a last minute clincher at Rotherham after Toral's trickery and low centre left Nick unmarked facing an open goal that not even he could miss!

I would love to read a scouting report on him as it is always enlightening to understand what it is that the professionals see that we supporters have failed to take into account. To my untrained eye he was slow, clumsy, had an appalling first touch, never got off the ground and consistently failed to win balls in the air despite his height. He showed little or no anticipation in the opposition penalty area and a reluctance to shoot. He also got in the way disastrously when apparently helping out defensively in our own area, as is evidenced by the unwitting part he played in setting up Ipswich's final goal at Griffin Park on Boxing Day. He was just on a completely different wavelength to his more technically gifted teammates and looked to be totally out of his depth. It has to be acknowledged that he was on the pitch when we scored twice in our incredible come-from-behind victory over Fulham but even then he played no part in either goal.

In truth he was a last minute panic buy who contributed little or nothing to us but I have no words of complaint towards Nick as it was plain that he was trying his best and giving his all. Indeed it was stated by many observers that he impressed in training and it was clear from the pre-match shooting practices that he had a shot on him that combined accuracy and awesome power, but we saw no evidence of this once the games had begun.

I wish Nick Proschwitz well for the future wherever he ends up. It is a salutary reminder of the insecurity of a footballer's career to see just how far and fast he has fallen. Or maybe it is equally surprising to see how high he at one time actually rose. I simply wonder how thoroughly he was scouted by all the teams that signed him as his utter lack of achievement in this country makes a nonsense of the huge fee that was paid for him by Hull and highlights the danger of taking on trust successful playing records from what are in truth minor European leagues.

The Dreaded "P" Word – Part One – 6/5/15

So it's to be the playoffs for Brentford, news that was greeted by every Brentford supporter with utter relief and jubilation which given our appalling playoff record over the past twenty-four years might appear on the face of it to be a strange and perverse reaction. The only positive thing that can be said about Brentford and the playoffs is that at least we are consistent – consistently awful in fact, as we have so far failed to win promotion through this route seven times in all. Amazingly enough there is one club, Preston North End, whose ineptitude makes our record look almost acceptable as having blown automatic promotion on Sunday they are about to embark, doubtless with fear and trepidation, upon their tenth playoff campaign with a one hundred percent failure rate.

If our past record wasn't bad enough we really have nobody else to blame apart from ourselves given that the playoffs were the bastard child invention of our former chairman Martin Lange back in 1987 when he saw them as a way of maintaining and extending interest on the part of clubs who would otherwise have seen their season fizzle out once their hopes of automatic promotion had disappeared. The playoffs have rightly been considered a complete success by armchair supporters as well as by everybody not specifically involved in them as they undoubtedly add a sense of theatre, occasion and excitement even though they represent pure torture to the nervous followers of the teams actually competing in them.

Our first experience of the playoffs arrived in 1991 when we crept into sixth place in Division Three on the back of a well-timed and frankly unexpected run of five victories in the last six games of the season. We had never really mounted a challenge for automatic promotion and were more than happy and gratified to have obtained a playoff spot particularly as a patently unfit Dean Holdsworth had fired blanks all season and we were totally beholden to Player of the Year Graham Benstead who had performed a series of miracles in goal.

The playoffs were entirely new to us, an unexpected gift and we were naive ingénues with absolutely no expectations and totally unaware of the devastation and horrors that a playoff failure could wreak on us. Tranmere awaited us, a team that had already defeated us twice that season, but we felt no fear as we were just pleased to be there. The first leg was at home and we totally dominated, scoring first through Terry Evans after a well-worked Wilf Rostron free kick and missing several other chances to put the tie well beyond our listless opponents. The match turned on its head after the break when Tranmere's previously anonymous striker Steve Cooper performed his party piece by rising as if on springs to head home two identikit goals from corners. Little did we know at the time that Steve had excelled as a gymnast as a youngster which probably helped him in his athleticism and ability to leap in the air to score his trademark headers. We were stunned and wondered if Cooper bore us a grudge as he had also scored four times against us for Newport County six years previously. We fought back from these body blows and eventually salvaged a draw when Kevin Godfrey lobbed a late equaliser past the static Eric Nixon. We travelled to Prenton Park more in hope than expectation and lost narrowly by a single scrambled goal in a game of few chances where we dominated possession but lacked incisiveness in front of goal. Given the novelty value of our situation I don't remember any real sense of sadness or loss immediately afterwards - that would come in good time after some of our subsequent playoff disappointments.

1995 was a case in point and I am still traumatised by how cruelly we were treated and what fate laughingly had in store for us. We had a vibrant exciting team inspired by the FT Index, Nicky Forster and Robert Taylor who managed forty-seven goals between them. We were tough and organised in defence and had a potent threat from set-pieces in marauding full back Martin Grainger. This was the one and only season when, owing to the reorganisation of the Premier League, there was a trickle-down effect which resulted in only one team receiving automatic promotion from Division Two. There are no prizes for guessing who finished second! Promotion was in our own hands and we let it slip. Without mincing words we choked in the last month of the season, scrambling a last minute equaliser at home to an abject Chester team, then losing meekly in a crucial midweek promotion clincher at our closest rivals Birmingham City who did the double over us before allowing a Bournemouth team seemingly doomed to relegation to beat us in our last home game.

This time we felt totally different as the cup had been dashed from our lips and faceless bureaucracy had denied us the promotion that was indubitably our just reward for finishing second. Surely we would right the wrong done to us by winning the playoffs, and cementing promotion at Wembley would be a wonderful way of doing it. I felt that our victory was assured as it was so obviously right and proper that we did so, but unfortunately nobody had informed Neil Warnock and his tough and driven Huddersfield team. We drew a hard-fought first leg away from home with Nicky Forster scoring a well-worked team goal and his strike partner Taylor improbably and almost unbelievably skying over an empty net with the goalkeeper already lying helpless on the floor for what was to become an iconic miss.

We scored early on at home through a cool, calm and collected Grainger penalty kick but we took our foot off the gas and were punished by Andy Booth after Dearden was surely impeded. Both teams became increasingly cautious and cancelled each other out, afraid to risk defeat by opening up and going for the winning goal. The dreaded penalty shootout arrived and Huddersfield blinked first when Dearden saved brilliantly, but Denny Mundee, who had scored twice from the spot against Steve Francis at Huddersfield the previous season blew the chance to put us two goals ahead when he was outguessed this time by the keeper. Jamie Bates too, criminally failed to put his foot through the ball and one kick later our season was over. We left the stadium in utter silence, disbelieving and devastated at the turn of events. Had we really witnessed what we thought we had seen? How could we have lost that tie? Was life really that cruel? Twenty years on and I still ask myself the same questions and, yes, it hurts even today to remind myself of that torrid evening when it all unravelled for us. Of all our playoff failures 1995 perhaps rankles the most given the circumstances although as we will see, 2013 comes close behind!

We needed a year to recover from the trauma of 1995 but we came again in 1996/97 when we again tanked promotion through our own inadequacies and mismanagement and were forced to rely yet again on the playoffs. Surely we should by now have known better? The new four-pronged spearhead of Forster, Asaba, Taylor and Bent inspired us to an eleven match unbeaten run at the start of the season and we were sitting pretty and coasting at the top of the league when the quite staggering decision was taken in January to sell Nicky Forster to arch-nemesis Birmingham City for a mere £700,000. He was never replaced, the prolific Carl Asaba was mysteriously shifted out wide to the left wing and the remaining seventeen league matches produced a mere eighteen points. We failed to score in ten of our last fourteen games and won only once at home after Christmas. We can all speculate as to why the management stood idly by and allowed our promotion challenge to disintegrate as we limped into the playoffs holed below the waterline.

Miraculously we recovered our Mojo for the tough-looking playoff semi final against Bristol City and surprised everyone, including perhaps ourselves by winning both legs and qualifying for our first ever playoff final against a Crewe team bursting with young talent and ideally suited for the massive Wembley pitch. Having been taken to the heights by the renewed confidence and organisation we displayed against Bristol City, we plummeted to the depths of despair and embarrassment by playing like a disorganised rabble at Wembley. We had Statham sent off, were totally outclassed and could easily have lost by six goals rather than the one that the opposition actually managed. Our Neanderthal long ball style could not cope with the short passing and clever movement of our opponents. Crewe outplayed and out-thought us, hit the woodwork three times and the heroic Carl Hutchings cleared the ball off our goal line on two further occasions.

I was left fairly unmoved by our defeat in 1991, and was distraught in 1995, but this time I felt humiliated and angry and was just glad to leave Wembley as fast as the crowds would allow. We lost a lot of fans that day when we capitulated and completely failed to compete. It is time to stop now, as I need to take a deep breath and have a break before I resume this tale of disaster and disappointment.

The Dreaded "P" Word – Part Two – 7/5/15

There was a gap of five years before the playoffs reared their ugly head again in 2002, and once more it was heartache for the Bees. I still find it hard to believe that a team that boasted the talent of players such as Ivar Ingimarsson, Darren Powell, Gavin Mahon, Martin Rowlands, Paul Evans, Steve Hunt, Steve Sidwell, Lloyd Owusu and Ben Burgess could not grab one of the top two places in the league table but Brighton and Reading proved to be just that little bit better, although we demonstrated our ability by doing the double over the eventual champions, Brighton, including that unforgettable four-nil thumping we handed out to them at Griffin Park on a magical night when Ben Burgess was utterly unplayable.

Unfortunately Owner Ron Noades had lost interest in us by then which resulted in the squad being weakened, and valuable assets in Mahon and Paul Gibbs were sold off at vital stages of the season without a hint of a replacement and the inspirational Jason Price was also allowed to leave at the end of his short-term contract. Worse still, Ben Burgess damaged his hamstring whilst on international duty and with no new loanee arriving on transfer deadline day, our most potent striker was forced to see the season through despite being unable to summon up a gallop and his goal threat unsurprisingly disappeared.

As always we seemed to be our own worst enemy and no wonder manager Steve Coppell called it a day at the end of his only season in charge. Mark McCammon frittered away a glaring late opportunity to earn us a vital win at Queens Park Rangers, so, shades of Doncaster in 2013, we went into the final showdown needing to beat Reading to go up whilst our visitors simply needed to draw.

The tension was unbearable as we could barely dare to watch what was happening on the pitch. After a first half of shadow boxing with Reading more than happy to slow the proceedings down, the game burst into life when Owusu's electric run down the left flank saw the ball pulled back to Martin Rowlands, at the time still a Griffin Park hero, who thrashed the ball low into the net. Reading finally decided to make a game of it given their need to score and we funnelled back and gave away the initiative hoping to hold onto what we already had. As is so often the case a one goal lead is a mere chimera and the ineffable Jamie Cureton secured a permanent place in our chamber of horrors by poaching the all-important late equaliser with a clever lob; time stood still as the ball dropped just inside the post.

So near yet so far. I confess to the ultimate heresy of leaving the game a few minutes early after Paul Evans had wasted a chance from a late free kick, I just could not bear to watch the blue and white hordes cavorting around the Griffin Park pitch and lording it over us whilst we were left jilted at the altar once again.

I contemplated the playoffs with as much enthusiasm as Sisyphus must have done, clutching his boulder looking up in anguish at the steep hill looming in front of him, but we rallied and finally did to Huddersfield what they had done to us back in 1995. It was payback time with a disciplined defensive performance away from home followed by a brave recovery from Paul Smith's early aberration at Griffin Park. Roared on by a passionate home crowd we scored twice through Darren Powell and then Lloyd Owusu to earn the right to play Stoke City at the Millennium Stadium.

The stakes were high, as this was the last chance saloon with promotion to the second tier on the one hand, the certain loss of Steve Coppell and the breakup of our squad on the other, should we lose. I am afraid that I made the long journey to Cardiff filled with trepidation as I felt that the dice were loaded against us and unfortunately I was proved correct. This was a step too far for a team that had been systematically weakened by niggling injuries and outgoing transfers. Death by a thousand cuts, indeed. We had peaked and could not compete on the day with a strong Stoke City team packed full of expensive imports. We subsided meekly to a two-goal defeat with the ultimate irony of BBB scoring the clincher into his own net when attempting to clear a free kick. The journey home was horrible, as we all knew that this was the end of an era and that the next few years were going to be extremely tough both on and off the pitch.

The following two seasons were simply about survival and avoiding relegation, and thanks to Wally Downes in 2003 and the ultimate Great Escape under new inspiration Martin Allen, we earned ourselves some much-needed breathing space. Allen rebuilt and patched up the squad on a shoestring and imbued them with his own passion and confidence. A team led by the experienced Stewart Talbot, Chris Hargreaves, John Salako and Deon Burton, buttressed with the youthful enthusiasm of the likes of Alex Rhodes, Sam Sodje, Jay Tabb and the elegant Michael Turner gelled together and had a remarkable season culminating in a totally unforeseen run to the fifth round of the FA Cup where we almost defeated Premier League Southampton as well as making a late charge towards the playoffs. It all looked like it was going to fall apart when we lost three consecutive games in April but we eventually fell over the line when Scott Fitzgerald's late winner at Wrexham earned us a surprise playoff place.

Could this be fifth time lucky as we sought to overcome a stuttering Sheffield Wednesday? Their recent home record had been appalling but instead of attacking them, Martin Allen for once misread the situation and played an ultra defensive lineup which gave a nervous home team the initiative, and we returned to Griffin Park facing a one goal deficit but with the feeling that we had squandered a real opportunity to take the tie by the scruff of the neck.

The second leg was far more even and the turning point came when Wednesday keeper David Lucas somehow kept out a Deon Burton effort that seemed bound for the back of the net. Our hopes ebbed away and two breakaway goals sealed victory for our visitors before a late consolation by Andy Frampton heralded a nonstop cacophony of noise from the Brentford fans who knew that the tie had slipped away from us but were simply celebrating and acknowledging the achievement of a team that had massively over-performed.

Promotion looked well on the cards the following season as DJ Campbell's arrival from Yeading at last gave us a real goal threat and the elegant Darren Pratley roamed around the midfield with a combination of grace and menace. Yet once again we let things slip through our fingers and contributed massively to our own failure. Campbell was sold to Birmingham on the back of his two brilliant goals that ensured us a wonderful FA Cup giant killing against Premier League Sunderland, and his replacement Calum Willock proved to be a total misfit who managed to go through almost half a season scoring only one goal. Lloyd Owusu tore his groin playing in a nondescript friendly match against Stuttgart for Ghana and our striking options were restricted to veteran Marcus Gayle and Isaiah Rankin.

Automatic promotion was still totally in our hands but, as always, Brentford found a way to seize defeat from the jaws of victory. Sam Sodje, such an inspiration at the back, self-destructed when his proposed move to Southampton fell through and, losing focus and concentration, became a defensive liability. We failed to win any of our last four home games and became paralysed by fear and apprehension whenever we scored first, funnelling back in a vain and desperate attempt to cling onto our lead. Victory at Bournemouth on the final day of the season allied to a defeat for Colchester at Yeovil would have been enough for promotion but it wasn't to be and we finished third in the table.

A Leon Knight inspired Swansea were given a helping hand when Referee Keith Stroud controversially sent off Stuart Nelson when Brentord were a Jay Tabb goal up and coasting in the first leg and we were pegged back by a cruel late deflected equaliser. Surely now we were in the catbird seat, but once again disappointment was to strike as a desperately poor performance from a toothless Bees team saw us subside to a two goal defeat. Zero for six and counting! I was pretty numb by now and expected little else than the loss that we suffered. We just did not seem to do playoffs and had developed a complex about them and our inevitable losses became no more than a self-perpetuating prophecy.

Our final playoff failure in 2013 is still too sore and fresh in the memory to need much retelling and I am certainly not going to rake over the coals by forensically deconstructing the Trotta penalty fiasco against Doncaster. We drew at Swindon thanks to Kevin O'Connor's brilliantly taken injury time penalty and the home tie remains one of the best and most exciting games I have ever seen. We were seemingly coasting with a three-one lead. Marcello Trotta was imperious and Clayton Donaldson a constant danger, and quite frankly, we could have scored at least six times but were pegged back with two late goals that highlighted our chronic weakness defending corner kicks.

A dreaded penalty shoot out in a playoff match surely represented two opportunities for heartache for Brentford, but we rose to the challenge with all five nominated kickers scoring emphatically and Simon Moore's plunging save followed by Adam Forshaw's perfect conversion of our last kick saw us earn a trip to Wembley. Surely this time? But no, a stunning Paddy Madden volley early on was like a dagger to our hearts, and the lumbering Dan Burn's header gave us a mountain to climb at the break. Talk of climbing, I was ready to leave Wembley by any method available at halftime and had to be persuaded to stay, given how deep I was in the depths of despair.

So near yet so far, as Harlee Dean's thumping header gave us false hope but we squandered a plethora of chances to allay our playoff bogey and it was to be yet another desperate tramp back to the car interrupted only by an unscheduled stop at a rubbish bin where I deposited my Clayton Donaldson autographed shirt which had more than outlived its potency as a lucky omen.

Given this tale of never-ending failure and despair, why then am I looking forward with relish to tonight's playoff match against Middlesbrough? Quite simply because this is a totally different and, indeed, unique situation. All our seven failures in the past were in the third tier playoffs. Now we are in uncharted waters for the first time and are actually on the verge of reaching the Premier League. Something that would have been quite preposterous to even contemplate a mere year or so ago.

I quite appreciate that Matthew Benham and his intrepid team of analysts had us down at Christmas to finish in sixth or seventh place this season and we have now met his expectations by reaching the playoffs. That being said I see this as being a free hit for us as hardly anybody outside the club really expected us to get there and even fewer now expect us to win the playoffs.

With the pressure off we can play with freedom and without the weight of pressure and expectation. It would really not surprise me if we beat Middlesbrough and then triumph at a packed Wembley against either Norwich or Ipswich. I have already visualised this happening in my dreams and imagination and I live in constant hope of it coming true.

Tonight is therefore a time for celebration and not apprehension. What has happened in the past should not concern or worry us. If we pull it off then it will be an astonishing achievement which will go down in the annals of the club's history. If not – this time I can live with it without my summer being ruined.

Cruel! – 9/5/15

What a fantastic game of football it was last night. It had everything - skill, passion, commitment, rip-roaring excitement, end-to-end drama and finally a nasty sting in the tail as Middlesbrough stole victory with an injury time decider. This was playoff football at its finest.

Fortunes fluctuated with Middlesbrough shading the first half and then the Bees took over after the break and a draw would certainly have been the fairest result, but it wasn't to be and now Brentford are up against it and have it all to do, knowing that nothing less than a win at Middlesbrough next Friday will suffice if their promotion dreams are to stay alive.

Of course I am desperately hurt and upset to see us lose a game in which we contributed so much and where, as normal, we totally dominated possession, but there were so many positives to take out of the match. We stood up to a seemingly never-ending series of downright dirty and intimidating tackles from a Middlesbrough team who found it hard to cope with our pace and movement and resorted to a series of tactical fouls intended to break up the play.

Six of the opposition were booked and Adam Forshaw undoubtedly should have seen red near the end for a truly horrible x-certificate flying lunge at Diagouraga. The referee, Mr. Moss, bottled out of what should have been a straightforward decision and, naturally, it was Forshaw who contributed to the move which led to an injury time corner which was beautifully converted by another late substitute, Amorebieta, helped by a favourable deflection off Bidwell, which took the ball unerringly into the corner of the net.

Even then we responded but Friend's deflection of Pritchard's raking low centre did not fall so favourably for the Bees, with the ball scraping past the far post with the lunging Smith just unable to turn the ball in for a last gasp equaliser.

Middlesbrough could play as well as kick and their game plan worked perfectly before the break. They pressed us relentlessly very high up the pitch and we were unable to break through and were forced to pass the ball around the back four without being able to beat the press and bring our midfield into play. Gray was a forlorn and isolated figure and we barely threatened except from a long range Judge thunderbolt, pushed onto a post by Konstantopoulos and a clever flicked header from Tarkowski which flew just over the bar.

As if that wasn't bad enough, the visitors were gifted a soft opening goal when Pritchard stood back and admired Clayton instead of closing him down and his curling centre flew over three Brentford defenders seemingly marking each other, and Vossen was left in splendid, but unforgivable isolation to head into the net. A poor goal to concede particularly on such an important evening, and worse could have followed but for two wonderful Button saves from Tomlin and Vossen.

Brentford finally managed to play the ball around far quicker after the break and soon forced the visitors back. Judge and Jota set up Gray who blazed a glaring chance over the bar but he soon redeemed himself when he chased a lost cause and took advantage of the keeper's dithering to seize possession just outside the penalty area and calmly roll the ball into the empty net.

The fans responded and the Griffin Park roar threatened to tear the roof of the stand off its moorings and, suitably inspired, the Bees went up a gear. Pritchard, Moses and Judge weaved their magic and played wonderful one touch football. Douglas and Diagouraga did the fetching and carrying and Gray relished the enhanced service and came within a whisker of scoring a second when he turned brilliantly in the box but shot over. Jota, though was a marked man and a little out of sorts. We improved when Dallas replaced him and added his strength and hard running to our attack.

We had no central striker on the bench given that yet again Chris Long was playing for Everton Under 21's yesterday rather than being part of our squad; a move that quite simply defies adequate explanation. This was our biggest game of the season and we missed him badly.

The initiative ebbed and flowed as the game drew towards its close. A quick breakaway saw Button fly as if on an invisible trampoline to turn Adomah's raging volley over the bar, a save matched by Konstantopoulos when he stretched up a massive paw to turn away a looping header from Douglas that had looked to have gone beyond him.

Patrick Bamford was a constant danger to us with his clever runs and strength on the ball and it needed all the concentration of Dean and Tarkowski to keep him in check. We wasted several opportunities to test the keeper from free kicks in and around the area and it seemed as if the game was set to finish as a draw, which would have suited both teams, until the injury time sickener from the visitors.

I was so proud of Brentford as the whole world watching the television coverage of a pulsating match could clearly see just how good we are, and enjoy the breathtaking quality and brio of our football. It was also obvious that we remain porous in defence and are, frankly, helpless babes in the wood when compared to the streetwise and cynical nature of Middlesbrough's approach. They know exactly how to manage games and officials and how to get the job done.

We are not so pragmatic and are too naive by far. Referees often remark on what a pleasure it is to officiate our games which is all well and good but there are times when we need to stand up for ourselves and be far more assertive. Last night was certainly one of them and the presence of the snarling Alan McCormack would have helped ensure that we had perhaps received a fairer crack of the whip.

We now face an uphill struggle as we have to go and win next Friday. Anything else and the season ends there and then. We are at our best when the chips are down and we invariably create chances away from home. Nothing less than our best will be good enough and it would be more than satisfying to overcome a Middlesbrough team whose bench and supporters made it quite clear by their over the top celebrations at the final whistle that they felt it was already mission accomplished. Let's just hope we can pull another rabbit out of the hat when it is most needed.

So close! A great save foils Douglas.

Groundhog Day – 18/5/15

So despite their best efforts Brentford's season came to its conclusion at the Riverside Stadium on Friday night. The Bees just couldn't pull back the one goal deficit from the first leg, conceded again halfway through the first half when Tomlin's long range effort received a helpful deflection off Harlee Dean which took it beyond Button's reach, and then carelessly lost possession twice after the break and were ruthlessly punished by breakaway goals from Kike and Adomah. A four goal aggregate defeat in the tie was cruel indeed on Brentford who deserved slightly better but it cannot be denied that we were comfortably second best overall.

For us to reach Wembley there were several prerequisites. We needed to be at our absolute best and to be brave and positive on the night. We also had to display the self-belief and confidence to play our own game and take care of the ball. We needed leaders on the pitch who would set a personal example and help encourage their team mates. Most crucially, we had to be clinical in front of goal when chances came our way. Unfortunately none of these boxes were ticked and we subsided to a comprehensive defeat.

We must give credit where it is due. Middlesbrough were everything that we weren't. Tough, big, strong, compact, organised, street-smart, determined, ruthless, comfortable on the ball, quick to turn defence into attack and deadly in front of goal.

Their game plan worked a treat. Firstly, just as had been the case at Griffin Park, they let us know they were there and knocked us out of our stride and never allowed us to build up a rhythm by committing a series of cynical and deliberate fouls whenever we threatened to break forward. They gambled correctly that the referee would not intervene early on and by the time Lee Mason belatedly decided to exert his authority and use his yellow card, it was far too late and the damage had already been done. We were nervous and tentative and never managed to break at pace as Middlesbrough funnelled back and denied us any space as soon as we reached the congested midfield area.

Leadbitter and Clayton chased and harried and snapped at our ankles from the first whistle. They were relentless and tireless in their efforts to snuff out danger before it developed and not to allow us the time and space we needed to hurt them. But they were both far more than water carriers and mere defensive spoilers as they demonstrated a real ability to read the game and to pass the ball accurately and with precision.

Both Jonathan Douglas and Toumani Diagouraga have been inspirational for the Bees this season but it was instructive to compare their overall effectiveness and impact upon the game with that of Leadbitter and Clayton who clearly demonstrated the difference between excellent players and the true elite at this level.

With our creativity stifled at birth, Jota, Judge and Pritchard flickered into life only intermittently and were never an influence on the game. Our chances were few and far between and there was no margin for error. We simply had to take our opportunities when they fell our way, but we let them all slip.

Early on, Jota shot weakly from outside the area and his effort was easily saved but our two key moments came either side of halftime. Judge's angled cross eluded the straining head of Ayala and Gray was left with a clear sight of goal but his weak headed effort was going nowhere when it hit a defender and was deflected straight to the keeper. We came out far more determined and positive after the break and straightaway the overlapping Odubajo's perfect low centre was somehow missed by Gray as he attempted to turn the ball in from right in front of goal. That could have been a turning point as if he had scored it would have silenced the crowd whose anxiety would doubtless have transmitted itself to the team. That was it until a sweet move opened up the defence near the end but substitute Chris Long was pressured into slicing his angled effort well wide of the goal. I doubt if we have ever created fewer chances in a match over the course of the entire season but you have to give due credit to the job that Middlesbrough did on us as well as acknowledge that we did not do ourselves justice on the night.

Harlee Dean was by far our best player closely followed by Moses Odubajo, David Button and James Tarkowski. Jake Bidwell appeared to be mesmerised by the pace and twinkling feet of Albert Adomah and was far too preoccupied with his defensive responsibilities to help support his ailing attack.

We did our best but it never really looked as if it would be enough and Middlesbrough finished up beating us four times in a row over the course of the season, scoring ten times with us managing one measly goal in reply, despite our knocking on the door so many times, particularly in our two home matches.

Could and should we have approached the game in a different manner? I would, in passing, refer you to Albert Einstein's definition of insanity: *Doing the same thing over and over again and expecting different results*. Mark Warburton and Plan A anybody? We basically played the same game four times against Middlesbrough with identical results on each and every occasion. It would certainly have been brave and maybe even foolhardy to have tinkered with, or even changed, a formula that had worked so well throughout the season and that had indeed been responsible for getting us to the playoffs in the first place. Managers are paid extremely well to problem solve and be flexible and imaginative where necessary but nothing changed and on Friday our limitations and shortcomings were yet again ruthlessly exposed.

Jota chased by the relentless Leadbitter.

It would be churlish indeed to carp and criticise given how wonderfully well we have performed all season and the amount of pleasure that Brentford have provided to all lovers of pure attacking football around the country. Mark Warburton's loyalty and commitment to his squad was also laudable and their sense of unity and togetherness certainly played a large part in our success, but our failure to strengthen in January when the opportunity apparently presented itself, meant that we were forced to rely on a small squad and there were precious few options available to freshen things up or make significant changes off the bench.

I still believe that the most illuminating statistic of the season is the fact that thirteen of the eighteen players in our squad on the opening day of the season on the ninth of August last year were still involved when the season finally drew to a close on the fifteenth of May. The five who fell by the wayside were Richard Lee, Marcos Tebar, Nico Yennaris, Montell Moore and Nick Proschwitz. They were replaced by Jack Bonham, Toumani Diagouraga, Jota, Jon Toral and Chris Long. So with the exception of Chris Long, who arrived in January, and Liam Moore who came and went in the new year, the squad remained almost unchanged for the entire season, something that I doubt has ever occurred in modern day football where there is invariably a high turnover of players who come and go and are seen as replaceable assets.

That was the way that Mark Warburton wanted to manage and it will be fascinating to see whether his ultimate successor favours a different approach next season in terms of squad size and rotation and, indeed, our overall formation and pattern of play.

That is for the future and now is the time simply to reflect on all the incredible events of the past nine months and salute the Bees and everyone involved with the club for providing us with such an incredible season that came so close to returning us to the top flight of English football for the first time in sixty-eight years. Friday's match ended in a cacophony of sound as the travelling Brentford supporters paid a raucous and heartfelt tribute to their team and its supporting cast of Mark Warburton, David Weir and Matthew Benham. The imminent departure of Mark Warburton and David Weir certainly marks the end of this chapter but the story has barely yet begun.

The Highlights Of The Season – 20/5/15

I have now just about recovered from the excitement of Brentford reaching the playoffs, if not the slight letdown of our defeat last Friday at the Riverside Stadium.

Whilst everything that happened last season still remains so clear in my addled brain I thought that I would like to pay my own personal tribute to everyone at the club by noting down a list of my most memorable and favourite moments from the past ten months or so of hectic activity. I am sure that you will all have your own preferences and personal highlights. I fully intend to come back to this list time and time again during the summer months without football and use it as an *aide memoire* and comfort blanket as I eagerly wait for the new season to begin. So here we go!

- Understanding for the first time how ambitious and sensible our recruitment plans were when we signed Andre Gray, Moses Odubajo, Alex Pritchard and Scott Hogan

- Watching Andre Gray in the preseason friendlies and seeing how deadly he could be in front of goal

- Moses Odubajo's incredible winning goal against Crystal Palace

- Seeing so many of Fleet Street's finest in the press box for the Charlton match

- Tommy Smith's late equaliser against Charlton. Starting the season with a home defeat would have been a real bodyblow

- That mad night at Dagenham when six goals were not enough for us to win

- Richard Lee signing off with two trademark penalty saves in the shootout at Dagenham

- The excellent performance in defeat at AFC Bournemouth when I realised for the first time that we would be able to cope with the demands of the Championship

- Signing a much-vaunted foreign player with only one name – and Jota really lived up to the hype

- Our first win of the season at Blackpool and the unique 4-6-0 formation we employed in the second half

- The brave and brilliant second half performance with ten men against Birmingham City when Warbs totally outmanaged Lee Clark, we overcame Mad Madley's best efforts to thwart us, and Moses kept his head to score late on

- Winning at Rotherham. Payback for the previous season's lacklustre surrender

- The beauty and incisiveness of Moses Odubajo's goal against Brighton after *that* defence-splitting pass from Alan Judge

- Walking away smiling and happy despite a three-nil home defeat to Norwich City

- Knowing that we could never play quite as badly again as we did at Middlesbrough

- Dispelling our fears and acknowledging the mental strength and determination of the team to recover from two debilitating defeats

- Easily beating and totally outplaying the faded glory that was Leeds United

- Knowing that we had been robbed of at least a point at Watford and that we were as good as them on the night

- Totally outplaying Uwe and Adam Forshaw at Wigan

- Jota's outrageous dummy against Sheffield Wednesday just before Andre Gray's disallowed goal

- The week beyond our wildest dreams when we beat Derby, Forest, and Millwall and shot up the table

- Stuart Dallas's last minute volleyed winner against Derby County

- Toumani Diagouraga's reincarnation as Patrick Vieira

- Singing in the rain in the post match lock-in at Millwall

- Ian Holloway's heartfelt praise of Brentford and how well our club was run. The first outside recognition of just how good we were

- *The Brentford 125th Anniversary Book* and working with Dave Lane and Mark Croxford to bring it to fruition

- Beating Fulham!

- Toumani almost scoring against Fulham

- Harlee Dean's run and blistering equaliser

- *Jota – in the last minute!* Against Fulham

- Alan Judge's perfect assist after his performing seal impression

- Pulverising Wolves without even playing that well

- Andre Gray's run and shot against Wolves

- A perfect fifteen point November

- Mark Warburton and Andre Gray winning the Manager of the Month and Player of the Month awards in November

- Making more so-called big names in Blackburn and Cardiff look ordinary

- The magical first half display at Cardiff

- Jota's goal at Cardiff and his interplay with Alex Pritchard

- Sam Saunders scoring two consolation goals against Ipswich Town

- Jonathan Douglas becoming a real goal threat, particularly in the air

- Jack Bonham proving against Brighton that he really is an excellent goalkeeper in the making

- Laughing at Steve Evans's ludicrous post match posturing and hallucinations after we beat Rotherham

- Feeling that we were finally being taken seriously by referees when we were awarded a well-dodgy penalty at Norwich

- Alex Pritchard showing nerves of steel by calmly converting the penalty that won us the game at Norwich

- David Button's elastic save from Cameron Jerome

- Outclassing Leeds at Elland Road and dismissing the whines of the home fans who could not accept losing to *Little Old Brentford*

- The whole team celebrating as one with Warbs after Andre Gray's solo goal against Watford

- The match of the season against AFC Bournemouth marked by Mike Dean's exceptional refereeing

- Total domination against Blackpool with forty-two shots and a Jon Toral hat trick

- Chris Long's youthful exuberance and clinical goalscoring ability against Huddersfield

- Enjoying Daryl Murphy's unbelievable miss for Ipswich Town

- Mark Warburton being named as London Manager of the Year

- Welcoming Simon Moore back to Griffin Park

- Jota's solo goal at Blackburn and Mark Burridge's euphoric celebration on Bees Player

- Stuart Dallas starring for Northern Ireland and not looking out of place on the international stage

- The sheer relief after Moses Odubajo's totally undeserved last gasp equaliser against Millwall

- Completing the double against Fulham watched by over 6,000 Bees supporters

- *Jota – in the last minute!* Again

- Stuart Dallas's two long range goals at Craven Cottage

- *Jota – in the last minute!* Against Nottingham Forest

- Playing Derby County off the pitch

- Alex Pritchard's goal at Derby – touched by genius

- A central defender scoring with a header from a free kick at Reading

- Everything about the Wigan match

- Giving thanks to Blackburn Rovers and Reading for services rendered

- Reaching the playoffs at the last gasp and finishing fifth in the Championship

- The fans' celebrations at Middlesbrough

- Saying *thank you* and *goodbye* to Mark Warburton and David Weir at Middlesbrough

- The team and management making us all so proud all season

- Watching the confusion we caused when we left three men up for corners

- The sheer brio, excitement and beauty of some of our football

- Playing without fear

- Rejoicing in the sheer ability of our players and at how Judge, Pritchard and Jota could all make accurate fifty-yard passes and bring the ball under control with effortless ease

- Watching Alex Pritchard and Moses Odubajo play and thinking that we could be seeing future full internationals playing for the Bees

- Seeing all our loanees and former players doing so well at Wycombe Wanderers

- Listening to Bees Player

- Enjoying matches with my family and taking my son and daughter to the Leeds and Nottingham Forest games

- Ex-Bee Richard Poole's comments and replies from France

- Matthew Benham's continuing vision and support of the club

- Seeing smiles on the faces of every Brentford fan interspersed with tears of pride and sheer disbelief at our transformation

The Lowlights Of The Season – 21/5/15

It was a lot of fun recalling all the highlights of the season and it really wasn't a difficult exercise. Now the boot is on the other foot as I go to the other extreme and note down the low points – all the things that saddened, angered, confused and upset me over the course of the past ten months or so. Given how exceptional last season was, I really do not want to nitpick so I very much hope and expect that this list will be a darn sight shorter than the previous one, but here goes…

- Transferring Farid El Alagui to Hibernian without our having the chance to say *goodbye* to an excellent pro and a really lovely guy who was prevented by a serious injury from showing us just how good he was

- Clayton Donaldson coming to the conclusion that the streets of Birmingham were paved with gold. I still wonder just how well he would have done for us last season in our new system.

- Promising local product Montell Moore falling foul of the law and being sent abroad for his own good

- Adam Forshaw deciding that money talked and helping to engineer his move to Wigan

- The Bees Player hiatus and the eventual loss – hopefully not permanent – of the irreplaceable Luis Melville

- Putting a brave face on it and trying not to show how disappointed I was when I heard that we had signed misfit Nick Proschwitz

- Seeing Nick Proschwitz play and realising that he was even worse than I had imagined

- Our non-existent defending at Dagenham – a total embarrassment

- Not getting the result we deserved at AFC Bournemouth

- Mad Madley and his eccentric refereeing performance against Birmingham City

- Clayton Donaldson wearing the blue of Birmingham at Griffin Park

- Losing a tepid Capital One Cup match to Fulham

- Scott Hogan's appalling injury at Rotherham, when he collapsed with nobody near him

- The initial excitement when we signed Betinho turning into complete bemusement when he totally disappeared from sight

- Tarky's misplaced pass against Norwich which led to their opening goal against the run of play

- The non-penalty against Norwich when Pritchard was flagrantly clattered in the area

- Getting *Middlesbroughed* – Part One

- Being told how clinical James Tarkowski was from the spot and then watching him put his penalty against Leeds into orbit

- Marcos Tebar becoming the invisible man

- Graham Salisbury's appalling slow motion penalty award against us at Watford

- Getting patronised by all the Watford fans sitting around me as we totally outplayed them - but lost

- Suffering through an interminable five hour journey to Bolton and then having to watch us subside to a tepid defeat

- Alan McCormack's long-term injury at Bolton

- David Button getting caught upfield in Bolton's penalty area as they scored their third goal from our corner kick

- Mathew Buonassisi disallowing yet another Brentford goal against Sheffield Wednesday

- Watching us standing around admiring Derby County in the first half without suspecting what was to follow after the break

- The journey home from hell from Nottingham with multiple M1 junction closures

- Harlee Dean's *faux pas* against Fulham

- Somehow losing at Huddersfield after dominating, and Jake Bidwell's classy own goal

- Gestede equalising for Blackburn right on half time after a cruel deflection by Harlee Dean

- The second half at Cardiff – seemingly the longest forty-five minutes in history

- Self-destructing against Ipswich Town

- The early and crucial offside goal at Wolves

- Jake Bidwell not claiming our goal at Wolves after his cross was deflected in

- Andre Gray missing from point blank range in injury time at Wolves

- Uwe Rosler getting fired at Wigan

- Andre Gray's horror show against Brighton in the FA Cup

- Alan Judge missing seven weeks through injury

- Jon Toral getting the ball stuck comically between his feet at Brighton after going round the keeper

- Andre Gray's shank in the first minute at Norwich

- Getting *Middlesbroughed* – Part Two

- Suspecting that it was, in fact, Patrick Bamford who called out for Harlee Dean to *leave it*

- Not strengthening the squad in January when we were still in contention for the top two and our needs were obvious

- *Timesgate* and how it became open season on us in the national media, a factor that threatened to blow our season apart

- The schism between Matthew Benham and Mark Warburton

- The appallingly drafted initial press release from the club – *Football is a Village*

- Keith Stroud – just who we needed to referee the Watford match

- Losing so cruelly in the last minute to Watford

- The terrible non-performance at Charlton

- Playing Stuart Dallas at left back at Birmingham

- Clayton Donaldson leading us a merry dance at Birmingham

- Liam Moore at Ipswich Town

- Throwing the Cardiff City home match away through two appalling unforced defensive errors

- Kenwyn Jones's great save in the last minute going undetected by the referee

- Two more soft and avoidable goals conceded at Blackburn

- Allowing Millwall to totally outplay us

- The joke penalty awarded against us at Fulham

- Yet more soft goals given away against Nottingham Forest

- Throwing away two points after our best performance of the season at Derby and feeling sick for the rest of the weekend

- The lethal combination of missing gilt-edged chances at Sheffield Wednesday before handing them the winner on a plate

- The Dancing Bears – Button, Diagouraga and Tarkowski's combined horror show from that goal kick against Bolton Wanderers

- Thinking that we had blown the playoffs

- The Chris Long saga

- Scott Hogan suffering another serious injury in training

- Getting *Middlesbroughed* – Parts Three and Four

- Watching us squander yet another corner or free kick

- Not getting enough players into the opposition penalty area

- Cringing at some of the unnecessary risks taken in our defensive zone

- Saying *goodbye* to Mark Warburton and David Weir

- Realising that the season was finally over

End Of Term Report – 24/5/15

Well, the dust has finally settled, I have reflected, and it is now time for me to give my brief verdict on the entire Brentford squad and how they performed last season:

1. Richard Lee. It is finally the end of the line for an excellent and popular goalkeeper who was plagued by a series of ill-timed injuries throughout his career. I have no concerns for his future given his eclectic interests and capabilities. He is a true polymath who is likely to be a success in anything that he puts his mind to. With his pathway to the first team firmly blocked at Griffin Park his last hurrah was a surprising short term loan move to Fulham but he was not called upon there. We will all remember him fondly, particularly for his sunny disposition and penalty saving prowess.

2. Kevin O'Connor. Another giant of the game whose influence on the pitch has waned but who I fully expect to have an important part to play in our future both as a coach and an exemplar of what the club represents and the values that it espouses. Kevin became the first person in history to be inducted into the Brentford Hall of Fame whilst still involved with the club, a fitting honour for a true gentleman and Brentford legend.

3. Jake Bidwell. Jake just gets better and better and has established himself as an excellent Championship-quality player who simply gives of his best every week, unobtrusively and effectively. He defends well, is tough in the tackle, good in the air, uses the ball well and is rarely embarrassed by his lack of genuine pace given his ability to jockey his opponents out of the danger zone. He is eager to overlap and his crossing is accurate and incisive. He is often taken for granted by our fans who fail to take into account his relative youth and the fact that he is likely to improve still further. We still await his first competitive goal for us – one that is certain to be celebrated in style!

4. Lewis Macleod. Well at least we still have something to look forward to next season given that the arrival of Lewis Macleod turned out to be a massive let down and damp squib. A lingering hamstring injury that was exacerbated by a bizarre accident incurred in training meant that he was restricted to an anonymous forty-five minutes in a Development Squad match. Our hopes were resurrected and our interest piqued when he made a surprise appearance on the bench for the home playoff match against Middlesbrough but he remains shrouded in mystery until the start of next season.

5. Tony Craig. Tony Craig lost his place in February and was never able to regain it or overcome the challenge of James Tarkowski and Harlee Dean. He remained an influential figure on the bench cajoling his team mates into greater efforts, but after three seasons of excellent service the top of the Championship is now perhaps a step too far for him. We certainly missed having a natural left-footed central defender but I suspect that TC might well be looking to move on and he deserves to play regularly given his age, experience and ability. Perhaps a return to Millwall and his old stamping ground might be on the cards for him?

6. Harlee Dean. Harlee had an up and down season and was never slow to speak his mind, but ended the campaign on a real high with several blistering performances where he combined his customary passion and aggression with signs that he was finally maturing and learning what it takes to succeed at Championship level. He became less impetuous and began to recognise when it was safe to play out from the back and when Row Z was called for. I had thought for a long time that he was likely to be on his way out from Griffin Park in the close season but I now suspect that he has shown sufficient progress and development potential to remain part of the squad for next season.

7. Sam Saunders. Sam barely featured for Brentford in the second half of the season and was allowed to move on loan to Wycombe Wanderers where he thrived and was an integral part of a swarm of current and former Bees that spearheaded their promotion push. Sam's season ended in total heartbreak when he was forced off the field after only two seconds of the playoff final. At least he is now part of Wembley folklore, but not in a way he either envisaged or wanted! His future with us is uncertain for next season but I fully expect him to be in massive demand and to be able to take his pick from the cream of Division One clubs. His last appearance for the Bees came as a second half substitute against Blackpool and Sam signed off perfectly with a last minute assist from a trademark perfect near post corner.

8. Jonathan Douglas. Jonathan Douglas maintained his consistency throughout the season and ended up with a career high eight goals. He was as competitive as ever, driving the team forward and he also developed the ability to drift late and often unseen into the penalty area where he offered a real goal threat. Who knows how differently the season might have ended up had the giant Konstantopoulos not somehow stretched to save his looping header in the playoff semifinal game at Griffin Park? JD has signed a new contract and is expected to maintain his enormous influence next season.

9. Scott Hogan. What can you say about Scott Hogan and the traumas he has experienced? He was signed as our first choice striker from Rochdale and we were all excited at the prospect of him leading our attack. Injury prevented him starting the season and he finally made his league debut as a substitute at Rotherham where he suffered a horrible anterior cruciate ligament injury in his left knee. Scott underwent reconstructive surgery and it appeared that his rehabilitation was going well and that he was even on-track for a return to full fitness in time for preseason training when in April he re-injured the same knee after catching his foot in the turf in training. He has had to have another operation and is now expected to be out for the rest of 2015. Life is so cruel sometimes.

10. Moses Odubajo. Moses can hardly have anticipated how well the season ended up for him. Alan McCormack's injury saw him switched from the right wing to right back and he never looked back. He has learned how to defend and his pace generally gets him out of trouble. His real strength is in going forward and he and Jota combined so effectively and formed a highly potent partnership on our right flank which was the source of much danger for our opponents. Moses has found himself in his new position, he is already an England Under 20 international and seems certain to play at the highest level as he possesses all the attributes required to play full back in the modern game.

12. Alan McCormack. Alan's season was ruined by his ankle ligament injury at Bolton in October as by the time he had recovered full fitness Moses Odubajo had established himself in his position at right back. Alan was a constant presence on the substitutes' bench from February onwards but was rarely called upon, which was surprising as he generally made a real impression when he came on, given his bite in the tackle, good use of the ball and his ability to act as an enforcer and ensure that our more subtle ballplayers were not subjected to intimidation by the opposition. He is another whose future is open to question, as at thirty-one he surely wants to play more regularly.

14. Marcos Tebar. Marcos dropped out of sight and was only called upon as an unused substitute on three occasions after Christmas. What is more, he was barely used in Development Squad matches either. There is no explanation for this mystery and it is hoped that he remains at the club next season and that the new Head Coach gives him another opportunity and a fresh start, as Tebar demonstrated in preseason that he is an enormously talented player who simply needed time to get used to a new environment.

15. Stuart Dallas. Stuart Dallas can look back with great pride at his season's accomplishments. He established himself in the Northern Ireland squad and looked fully at home in the international arena. He also played over forty times for Brentford, scored eight valuable goals, played on either flank as well as filling in seamlessly at centre forward and full back. Dallas was often a victim of the numbers game given that we possessed so many quality midfielders and was a real danger coming off the bench when he was often able to turn the match in our favour.

Strong, quick, direct, powerful, good in the air, and with a rasping shot, he is a manager's dream and he will go down in Brentford history for scoring two wonderful, unstoppable and unforgettable goals at Craven Cottage against the old enemy, Fulham.

16. Jack Bonham. Jack Bonham played only once last season and impressed against Brighton in the FA Cup and, more importantly, kept first choice David Button on his toes through his quality performances in training. He proved that he is developing into an excellent goalkeeper but at some point he will need to gain some Football League experience ideally through a loan spell away from Griffin Park.

17. Jon Toral. Another loanee who played with a level of maturity way beyond any reasonable expectations, given his total lack of experience before he joined the Bees. To end his debut season at the age of twenty with thirty-four league appearances and six goals, including a couple of magnificent volleys and a hat trick against Blackpool, was no mean achievement. Tall, rangy, comfortable on the ball, technically excellent, and with a few tricks in his repertoire, he has a glittering career ahead of him, hopefully at Griffin Park, if a suitable deal can be negotiated with Arsenal for whom he has signed an extended contract.

18. Alan Judge. He was the team dynamo, a nonstop bundle of energy, and our go-to guy who simply made us tick. His contribution was immense with three goals and a team leading thirteen assists and he was badly missed during his extended injury break early in 2015. He was always able to spot and then execute long range passes and create gaps in the opposition defence. His shooting was as powerful as ever even though his radar was often a bit off, but his perfect curling match-clinching free kick at Fulham was one of the moments of the season. His immense contribution was finally recognised when *The Irish Messi* won his first Republic of Ireland full senior call up on 12 May 2015, when he was named in the provisional squad for two matches the following month. Perhaps our most important and influential player overall.

19. Andre Gray. In his first season as a regular Football League player Andre Gray totally defied expectations by scoring eighteen goals and barely missing a game. All this whilst playing in a totally new position for him as a lone striker at a level three leagues above what he had experienced on a regular basis before. His overall contribution was absolutely staggering and some of his goals were eye-opening and quite brilliant in their execution - think of Derby, Wolves and Watford at home and Millwall and Cardiff away. No wonder that scouts were queuing up to cast their eye over him. Of course he showed his inexperience and was by no means a complete player. There is still much room for improvement and I think that he will perform even better when playing in a wider position supporting another central striker, but it remains to be seen if our new Head Coach will change our system and play with two strikers.

Andre *was* frustrating as he missed a ton of chances, but he created so many of them for himself, and ploughing a lone furrow was an exhausting and thankless task. Next season he will be even better.

20. Toumani Diagouraga. What a season from a player who had pretty much been written off at the start of the season. He simply got his head down and when his opportunity finally came he produced a series of brilliant performances and maintained his form until the end of the season. Dovetailing perfectly with Jonathan Douglas, with one sitting and the other playing in a more forward role, he was our ball-winner and quarterback who got us up and running and helped turned defence into attack with his unerring ability to find a man. His shooting was as appalling as ever but we really didn't mind and expected nothing more. His level of improvement and consistency was staggering.

Being totally objective, our eyes were well and truly opened when we saw how impressive Leadbitter and Clayton were for Middlesbrough playing in a similar role to Diagouraga and Douglas and that is the level that we need to aspire to next season.

21. Alex Pritchard. Quite simply, Alex Pritchard was absolutely brilliant for us and was one of the most influential loanees we have ever had. This was, however, a double-edged sword, as the better he played, the less chance we had of signing him on a permanent basis. He also established himself in the England Under 21 squad and will be welcomed back to his parent club, Tottenham Hotspur, next season with every chance of establishing himself as a Premier League player.

He scored twelve times for us, demonstrated that he knew how to take a penalty - a rare skill for a Brentford player, assisted on another seven goals and made eighty key passes from open play, more than any other Championship player. Alex made a massive contribution to us in the new year, scoring eight times, including a quite brilliant long range curling effort at Derby that had us all drooling and blinking in total disbelief, and he maintained an eye-opening level of consistency and commitment that was admirable in a young player and a loanee as well.

Alex always managed to find pockets of space in which to operate and he was mesmerising on the ball. To watch footballers of the skill and panache of Pritchard, Jota, Judge and Odubajo play together for Brentford was something totally beyond my wildest dreams and clearly demonstrates just how far we have come.

22. Betinho. Who? Why? Answers on a postcard please.

23. Jota. If I close my eyes and allow myself to daydream I can see a clear image of Jota dribbling down the right wing with the ball seemingly tied to his bootlaces. Head up, he looks for openings, cuts inside with the ball glued to his left foot, leaving defenders trailing in his wake bewitched by his twinkling feet, before ending up with a perfect cross or effort on goal.

We expected a lot given his background and the record fee we had paid for him, but Jota, or José Peleteiro Ramallo, to give him his full name, was even better than we could ever have envisaged, and he ended a remarkable first season in English football with eleven goals and a glowing and enhanced reputation.

Even if he had done nothing else, he would have lived long in our memory as *Jota - in the last minute!* To score a season-defining late winner against Fulham was enough to make him an instant hero but to repeat the feat by scoring again late on at Craven Cottage, followed by a last gasp equaliser against Nottingham Forest in the next match truly beggared belief.

It wasn't so much the number of goals he scored, although eleven was quite a tally for someone who played out wide, but the way in which he did so and the variety of goals he scored. A mesmerising dribble in a packed penalty area against Leeds, a close range tap-in against Reading, cutting inside and shooting from outside the box against Fulham, rolling the ball home through the eye of a needle against Wolves, a curling long range belter at Cardiff, finishing calmly and clinically against Blackburn, Norwich and Wigan, a brilliant near post volley at Fulham, running from his own half at Blackburn and picking his spot and a most unlikely header against Nottingham Forest. The pace of a long and exhausting season understandably seemed to take its toll in the last few games when he appeared to run out of steam and was less effective, but he did more than enough by virtue of his undoubted skill and bravery on the ball to attract the attention of Premier League predators. He will be even better next season as he becomes more attuned to the demands of the English game and I desperately hope that we can hang into him.

24. Tommy Smith. Tommy was consistency personified whenever he was called upon, generally as a late substitute. He always put in a shift, looking for the ball and using it sensibly and he was a valuable calming influence. He scored the opening goal of the season - a much needed late equaliser against Charlton, and contributed several assists, none more crucial than when he stood up a perfect cross in a packed penalty area that took out the goalkeeper and picked out Jota for his injury time equaliser against Nottingham Forest.

He more than justified his contract as he was also an excellent influence and example in the dressing room and he leaves with our thanks, admiration and gratitude.

25. Raphael Calvet. Never really challenged for a place and has been overtaken by others coming through the ranks. After two seasons without making any impact it is surely time for him to leave.

26. James Tarkowski. A stop-start campaign for James as he had to undergo a massive learning curve, experiencing Championship football for the first time. He ended up playing thirty-four games partnering a combination of Harlee Dean, Tony Craig and Liam Moore. Dean and Tarks ended up in firm possession of the shirts and gelled together well in the latter part of the season, but James had to cope with the extra handicap of having to play on an unfamiliar left side of the defence, and this caused him problems as he was sometimes caught in possession whilst trying to take an extra touch and get the ball onto his favoured right foot.

He was as comfortable on the ball as ever, striding forward, dropping his shoulder and advancing menacingly into the opposition half. He distributed it beautifully as well, and he played an important part in helping us break through the initial press and start our own attacks. Sometimes, though, he lost concentration and overplayed, costing us a number of goals, but he is still learning and improving and has more than enough ability to play at Championship level or even higher.

He also had a one hundred percent record at taking penalty kicks!

27. David Button. David Button had a wonderful season and was a Championship ever present in goal. He was very much our first point of attack as well as our last line of defence and his quick and accurate distribution played a massive part in our overall style of play and freedom of expression. He generally tried to play it short but would occasionally hit the ball long for Gray or Dallas and he was the instigator of Andre's brilliantly taken and confidence restoring goal against Watford - Route One football at its most effective.

He sometimes failed to deal effectively with crosses and he could also use his physique better as he is an enormous man, but he was utterly reliable and often quite brilliant and he won us numerous points with some incredible saves against Birmingham, Rotherham and Norwich in particular. You can count his blatant mistakes on the fingers of one hand and Button has developed into one of the best goalkeepers in the Championship with admirers from the level above. He is another who we will do well to hang onto this summer.

28. Nico Yennaris. His season at Brentford never got started and he only played once in the Championship, unfortunately in our worst performance of the season at Charlton, where he looked uncomfortable and exposed at left back. Nico had a successful loan spell at Wycombe Wanderers where he played at both right back and in midfield and ended his season at Wembley in the playoff final. Will he be back next season for another crack at establishing himself at Griffin Park or will he perhaps be searching for regular first team football elsewhere? Nico has real ability but he still needs to make his mark.

29. Liam Moore. Liam's return to Griffin Park for a second loan spell was generally welcomed given his pace and left sided bias but the England Under 21 international totally failed to seize his opportunity. He had mixed fortune in his three matches, struggling against Clayton Donaldson at Birmingham, coming out all square in a physical battle against James Vaughan of Huddersfield and looking weak and totally out of his depth against Ipswich's aerial bombardment. He was withdrawn from the fray at Portman Road and soon returned to Leicester allowing Dean and Tarkowski to develop an effective defensive partnership.

30. Josh Clarke. Formally a flying winger, Josh reinvented himself as an attacking fullback in the style of Moses Odubajo, and he impressed in his new position in the Development Squad. This was enough to earn him a contract extension and now it is up to him to prove that he has what it takes to forge a successful career.

31. Chris Long. Chris Long arrived in the January transfer window to back up and support Andre Gray and he more than did his job whenever he was fit. He scored four times in ten appearances including three in his two starts. He was what we had previously lacked all season, a goal sniffer and six-yard box predator. He would doubtless have played more games had he remained fit and he also made a couple of perplexing returns to turn out for Everton when we were desperate for him to play for us. I hope we make every effort to ensure his return to Brentford next season on either a loan or permanent basis.

32. Jack O'Connell. The tall, cultured, yet powerful left sided defender did not feature for the Bees beyond sitting on the bench after his January transfer from Blackburn Rovers but he is seen as a potential star of the future. He performed well whilst on loan at Rochdale and did enough to suggest that he will be challenging for a first team place at Griffin Park next season when his presence, if selected, would enable Tarkowski to revert to his more natural right side.

33. Montell Moore. Montell made an instant impact on his debut at Dagenham with a goal and three assists. He was named as a substitute on several occasions but never played again and unfortunately received a criminal conviction. It was considered politic and best for his development to send him on loan to FC Midtjylland in Denmark where he has since gained valuable experience. Let's see how he responds next season.

34. Daniel O'Shaughnessy. Daniel was a regular in the Development Squad who did not look out of place in the preseason friendlies but he was never close to earning a first team place. His future at the club might well depend upon whether Alfie Mawson decides to stay with Brentford or take his chance elsewhere. I suspect he will be given another season to prove himself and perhaps be sent out on loan.

35. Jermaine Udumaga. Nineteen year-old Jermaine Udumaga impressed as an attacking midfielder or striker whose goal tally reached double figures in the Development Squad. He was named as a substitute for the first team on four occasions but has yet to make his debut. He has signed a new one-year deal and will probably be competing for opportunities next season with Montell Moore.

39. Nick Proschwitz. Nick was a last minute purchase that reeked of uncharacteristic panic and poor judgement. He contributed little off the bench and never looked up to the standard required. He was offloaded to Coventry City where he had an equally unimpressive loan spell and he will not be back at Griffin Park next season.

Alfie Mawson. The tall central defender enjoyed a wonderful season at Wycombe Wanderers where he was named Player of the Year and he now has a tough decision to make. Does he accept Brentford's offer of a new contract or instead move to a new club where he can start as first choice? The central defensive position is in a state of flux at Griffin Park with at least two of the six current incumbents likely to move on, as well as there being perhaps one new arrival this Summer.

Mawson is unlikely to force his way into the first team squad next season but he could yet decide to sign a new deal with the Bees and go out on loan again, but my guess is that he will move on.

Will Grigg. Will enjoyed a sensational season on loan at MK Dons where he scored twenty-two times, helped them to promotion, won their Goal of the Season award and was named in the Northern Ireland international squad alongside Stuart Dallas.

He still has one year remaining on his Brentford contract and a decision now needs to be made on him. Should we give him a clean slate and see if he can force his way back into the reckoning at Griffin Park or sell him when his stock is at its highest? The key questions are whether we see him as a Championship striker and if we feel he can thrive in the system we are likely to employ next season. I suspect that in the event that MK Dons, or another club, meets our valuation of him then Will is likely to leave on a permanent basis.

The manager, Mark Warburton, his assistant, David Weir, coaches Simon Royce, Kevin O'Connor and the rest of the back room staff all made a massive contribution to the team's success as they filled the players with confidence, encouraged them to remain true to their principles and ensured that they continued to play positive, attacking football throughout the entire season.

Mark Warburton and Matthew Benham. An unforgettable partnership.

AFTERWORD

Looking Back & What The Future Holds – by Greville Waterman – 31/5/15

It was the best of times, it was the worst of times - having followed Brentford closely throughout the entire 2014/15 season I now finally understand what Charles Dickens was alluding to with that enigmatic comment.

The season that just ended took us on an unforgettable and breathless magic carpet ride that finished with the Bees falling just a fraction short of the Premier League. It was by far Brentford's best season since before the Second World War. And yet... and yet, it might have ended up even better had things gone slightly differently for us.

I still find it hard to talk about the Premier League, promotion, and the Championship playoffs in conjunction with Brentford despite how far we have come in so short a period of time. Even though promotion was gained with a real swagger from Division One last year, the Championship presented us with an entirely stiffer and, indeed, unknown challenge.

As the new season loomed ever nearer, we tried to take stock. We knew that we were good. We knew that we had an exceptional infrastructure in place behind the scenes and we knew that we had the Benham and Warburton partnership at the helm - but would it be enough?

The pessimistic streak firmly ingrained in all long-serving Brentford fans ensured that our expectations were minimal. Survival? Certainly. Mid-table mediocrity with perhaps the excitement of a cup run? Yes, that would do just fine. And of course it would also be fantastic if we could beat our old rivals, Fulham too. Surely this was not too much for us to ask for?

Inside the club though, I am certain that the bar had been set much higher. The owner, his analysts and stats gurus had run all of the numbers and the manager saw the evidence of our ability every day on the training ground. They knew that we definitely had what it took to take the league, if not by storm, but certainly by surprise and I suspect that the internal target set from day one was for us to do far better than consolidate and perhaps even challenge for the playoffs.

And so it proved. We had invested extremely wisely in a number of young, emerging, hungry and talented footballers. My eyes were opened when I heard about their arrival, and I wasn't the only one, as I well remember the Peterborough Chairman, Darragh MacAnthony, commenting on how well he thought we would do given the quality of our recruitment. His, though, was a voice in the wilderness as to the media and football world in general we were still *Little Old Brentford* and we remained completely invisible and well below the radar and were discounted, ignored or, at best, patronised.

It was the players and supporters who were initially unconvinced of our true capabilities, until everything changed after the second league game of the season when we ran eventual champions, AFC Bournemouth close, outplayed them for long periods, silenced the home crowd, and were desperately unlucky to lose by a single goal.

Finally, the penny dropped and our faces became wreathed in smiles. We were more than good enough to compete at this level. Our approach took other teams by surprise and most of them found it hard to cope with our pace, energy and non-stop attacking brio. Our defenders were actually attackers in all but name, and our goalkeeper passed the ball better and more accurately than most of our opponents. The midfield five passed, probed, ran, dribbled, shot and switched positions with total freedom and impunity and our lone striker was a constant threat.

We even shrugged off the loss of the previous season's Division One Player of the Year, Adam Forshaw, who decided that the streets of Wigan were paved with gold. That was a shame, and I take no pleasure in the fact that his move turned sour for him, but the presence of Jota, Alex Pritchard, Alan Judge and Jon Toral, who, in tandem, provided midfield strength and quality in depth, meant that even a player of Forshaw's ability was barely missed. This was *New Brentford*, a place where outgoing players were replaced even before they were sold and we no longer shot ourselves in the foot - or so we thought!

We were totally committed and extremely fit, everyone knew his role and we kept going relentlessly until the final whistle; many of our opponents finally cracked late on, exhausted and worn down by the constant onslaught that they had faced.

Mark Warburton was a positive and calming influence on the bench, almost Zen-like in his serenity; cajoling, praising and encouraging in equal doses and never criticising when his players did the right thing, even when it occasionally turned out wrong. We were often victims of our own naivety, impetuosity and nonstop commitment to attack and many of the goals we conceded were self-inflicted through unforced errors when players were caught out whilst trying to turn defence into attack, as they had been coached to do. His mantra after every game remained the same and gradually the players took at least some of his key messages on board:

- *We'll learn from this*
- *We need to take more care of the ball*
- *Plan B is to do Plan A better*
- *We need to be more clinical in front of goal*
- *We need to play without fear*

What best summed up our approach to the game was the way in which we invariably left at least two, and often three players lurking upfield with intent whenever we conceded a corner, and most opposing players and managers were totally nonplussed by this and did not know whether to stick or twist. As I have said many times over the past nine months, we were far more dangerous from opposition corners than our own, and we scored more counter-attacking goals than any other team in the Championship.

November was an incredible month when everything turned in our favour and we began our surge towards the playoff zone. Alan McCormack's ankle injury at Bolton left a yawning gap at right back and Warburton's decision to move Moses Odubajo back to fill the vacancy proved to be a masterstroke as his pace and flair provided us with a fresh attacking dimension. Five consecutive wins saw us roar up the table and the month ended in triumph with both Warburton and Andre Gray winning Manager and Player of the Month awards respectively.

December saw the upstart Bees comprehensively outplay two more former Premier League giants in Blackburn Rovers and Cardiff City and the Bees were almost unbelievably challenging for a top two place, but Ipswich knew a bit too much for us on Boxing Day and took full advantage of our defensive inadequacies. No matter, though, we ended the year firmly established in the playoff mix.

This is where the problems began. The tom-toms were sounding loud and clear about Brentford and our secret was finally out; teams were now wary of us and were at last paying us some respect. The second time around the league was certain to be far tougher as teams began to work us out and find ways to combat our threat.

For those of you who have not yet caught on I would suggest pressing us in numbers high up the pitch and preventing us from playing out from the back, playing a tall right back to cut off our other out-ball from Button to either Bidwell or Dallas and trying to get in behind us and turn our centre halves, or catch us on the break with half our defence stranded upfield.

The squad was tight-knit but thin in numbers after injuries to Hogan and McCormack, and we lacked cover and depth in key positions. This is when we needed to take stock and capitalize on the massive opportunity that had presented itself, unexpected though it might have been.

If we were to maintain our challenge and perhaps even flirt with the possibility of automatic promotion, we needed to take an educated risk, or even gamble, and invest wisely in the squad in the January transfer window by bringing in a couple of high quality recruits who could potentially improve us and challenge the current players for their places.

It really wasn't rocket science to see where we could do with some help and upgrading. Tarkowski, Dean and Craig had played pass the parcel with their shirts and we had not really established an effective central defensive partnership. A new left sided central defender with an injection of pace and strength would have meant that Tarky no longer had to play out of position and he and Dean could have competed for one place.

Andre Gray had not been expected to be the first choice striker before the season began but his impressive form, allied to the fact that he was pretty much last man standing given Hogan's injury, the total ineffectiveness of Proschwitz, and the demands of our favoured 4-2-3-1 formation, meant that he was forced to plough a lone furrow game after game. He had started slowly and peaked in November, but he was now running on empty and clearly needed some help and respite.

We waited patiently and expectantly for the anticipated reinforcements to arrive in January, but were seriously underwhelmed by the eventual new arrivals particularly in terms of what they were likely to offer us in the here and now. Lewis Macleod would have been an immediate and important addition to the squad but for his injury jinx, which prevented him from making his debut, and Chris Long was a promising young striker who could contribute from the bench and also spell Gray from time to time. Jack O'Connell and Josh Laurent were brought in with next season more in mind and it is illuminating to note that our four January recruits started only two matches between them.

Why was this situation allowed to occur given the strength of our position at the turn of the year? I am sure that neither Matthew Benham nor Mark Warburton had been taken totally by surprise by our success and they, and the rest of the football department, had had plenty of time to make plans for the transfer window so that we could ideally start the new year and go into the home stretch with the fresh legs, enhanced quality and the impetus required to sustain and cement our promotion challenge.

I am well aware of how difficult it can be to get transfers over the line nowadays given the demands of players and their agents and one can only surmise why we were unable to do so in January, assuming that the stories on social media were correct where it was claimed that funds had been made available and various major potential targets were identified.

There were claims, refuted by the manager, that he had refused to countenance any additions to his squad, as he feared that their team spirit and close-knit harmony might be jeopardised by new arrivals potentially upsetting the apple cart. What cannot be denied is that, for whatever reason, there were no major additions to the squad and we had to get by with what we had at a time when most of our rivals improved and strengthened for the final countdown.

It is easy, in hindsight, to say that this was a grave mistake and, indeed, Mark Warburton might well assert that the ends more than justified the means given our final league position but, *carpe diem*, as the phrase goes.

All eleven of the players who were in action for the opening match of the season in early August were also involved in our last game at Middlesbrough in mid May, a mind boggling statistic that - to me - highlights a massive positive as well as an equally huge negative. The squad was certainly united as one, gave everything to the cause, performed brilliantly and every player was totally behind the manager, but who knows whether a couple of top quality additions of the calibre that we were rumoured to be pursuing in January might have made all the difference. At the very worst they might have made us a tougher proposition in the playoffs and, who knows, their presence and influence might even have enabled us to compete for the two prized automatic promotion spots?

A big opportunity was squandered in January and our subsequent form rarely hit the pre-Christmas heights as our hopes of reaching the top two slowly faded away. The loss of the inspirational Alan Judge for seven long weeks also caused us to lose a step, but our confidence was restored by a highly professional performance and victory at Leeds

United before being totally shattered on the morning of the crucial home game against Watford.

This was when Matt Hughes's exclusive story was published in *The Times* claiming that Matthew Benham had made the decision to dispense with Mark Warburton's services at the end of the season and that clandestine talks had already been held in Spain with a potential successor, Paco Jémez, the Rayo Vallecano coach. All hell broke loose after this self-inflicted wound and our season threatened to go up in smoke. Suddenly Brentford were forming the news agenda and we did not come out well from the mauling we received in broadsheets and tabloids alike.

Many of the comments were ignorant, ill-informed and old school in the extreme, but there was a general feeling of bemusement as to why Benham wanted to rock the boat at a time when everything appeared to be going so well. One can only assume that, beneath the surface, things had not been going so swimmingly between owner and manager for quite a while but there had certainly been no intention of washing any dirty linen in public before the end of the season, even if a consensus could not be reached between them.

The leak to *The Times* ended any hope of keeping our business private and in-house and after an early abortive press release which simply muddied the water, made us a laughing stock and left me cringing with embarrassment, the club finally managed to get onto the front foot and control the agenda by redressing the balance the following week with a well thought through statement which set out clearly and concisely the way in which the club intended to operate in future years.

The departure of Sporting Director, Frank McParland, Mark Warburton and David Weir was confirmed with McParland going on immediate gardening leave. The management duo would be replaced by a Head Coach working alongside a new Sporting Director and the club would also rely upon a new recruitment structure using a mixture of traditional scouting and other tools including mathematical modelling, with the Head Coach having a strong input into the players brought into the club but not an absolute veto. Mark Warburton was not prepared to agree to the last point, which was fundamental to the successful implementation of the preferred system, and a parting of the ways became inevitable.

The team, naturally loyal to a manager who had been more than loyal to them, initially and understandably responded badly to the situation with the owner apparently receiving a frosty welcome at the training ground, and results suffered, before a confidence-boosting victory over Bournemouth in a quite fantastic game of football, got us back on track. The mini-slump was reversed and results fluctuated for the remainder of the season.

We won only seven and drew five of the seventeen games remaining after the leak on the tenth of February but the magic still remained from time to time, particularly when we thrashed Fulham on an unforgettable afternoon at Craven Cottage, thus completing the double over our neighbours and we then put on a season's best performance of style and class at Derby County which deserved far more than the draw that we finally obtained.

An unexpected defeat at Sheffield Wednesday followed by a sloppy defensive display against Bolton Wanderers put our playoff place in serious jeopardy, but we recovered just in time and did everything that was in our control by winning our last two matches.

For once the fates smiled down upon us with Derby and Ipswich stuttering on the final day, which meant that we reached the playoffs by finishing fifth, an incredible achievement that we totally deserved given the quality of our performances throughout the season and the way in which the squad had stuck together after *Timesgate*.

The schism between owner and manager was insurmountable, but Warburton had led the team to the playoffs and could justifiably assert that he had more than achieved what I believe had been his preset target.

However the question still remains - would we have done even better had fresh blood been brought in, as this would have enabled some tired legs to be rested, players to be rotated and fresh options to be tried out when the team remained practically unchanged for the last two months of the season?

Despite our attacking prowess, which remained a feature of our game all season, there were times when we became fairly predictable and perhaps a proper Plan B would not have gone amiss and would have presented the opposition with fresh problems to deal with. But, for all the quibbling, Mark Warburton did a fantastic job and leaves with our total gratitude, and it is a shame that he feels unable to work within the new structure and philosophy.

Middlesbrough knew too much for us in the playoffs, and as much as I mourned missing out on another Wembley final and the chance to end our playoff hoodoo (now zero for eight and counting), nobody was really too disappointed as this year was considered a free-hit and we know that our time will shortly come.

What does concern me is that we lost four times in a row to Middlesbrough and yet we seemed to have learned nothing and played totally the same way every time without attempting to vary our game plan. Confidence or inflexibility? At least the playoff matches clearly highlighted our shortcomings and where we need to strengthen, adapt and reinforce and hopefully our weaknesses can be addressed in the close season.

Our results against the teams in and around us also demonstrate quite clearly that we finished in exactly the right place in the Championship table. In the ten league matches we played against the five other teams in the top six, AFC Bournemouth, Watford, Norwich City, Middlesbrough and Ipswich Town, we won only two and drew once, a clear indication of why we fell just short and were not quite deserving of a promotion place - this season that is.

As for next, who knows? There will certainly be several additions to the playing squad and Brentford have already signed Georgian winger Akaki Gogia from Hallescher FC. The stats indicate that he is the best player in a team that competes in a division that is felt to be comparable in quality to the Championship. Will he turn out to be as good as Pritchard or Jota or will he be more like Martin Fillo? All will be revealed next season.

The immediate priority is to assemble the team behind the team and in that regard the chairman of the Danish champions, Midtjylland, has become Co-Director of

Football alongside Phil Giles, who is Head of Quantitative Sports Research at Smartodds, a company owned by Matthew Benham.

It will be their job to analyse and interpret the data and ensure that there is a constant supply of uncut diamonds brought in to replenish and enhance the playing staff. They both impressed when discussing our philosophy when interviewed recently by Billy Reeves, and it is clear that we intend to keep the best parts of last season's approach, maintain and indeed build upon the now trademarked Brentford brand of football, tinker and improve where necessary, and remain at the cutting edge of progress and innovation.

We now all await the puff of white smoke that will announce the imminent appointment of the new Head Coach. The key is for us to use our data to identify and headhunt somebody who has overperformed in his current position, and who is prepared to buy into the Brentford project and the way in which Matthew Benham intends our club to be run.

He will be given the total freedom to decide upon our tactics and pattern of play as long as they fit into the overall ethos of the club. He will also be able to decide which members of our current squad are surplus to requirements but, crucially, he will not have the final say on player recruitment.

I am informed on good authority that our first choice, Marinus Dijkhuizen, who guided Excelsior to fifteenth place in the Dutch Eredivisie this season after gaining promotion last year from the Jupiler League, will shortly be announced in the job. He has gained success on a minuscule budget and has gained a reputation for player development and also playing attractive football.

The new Head Coach will be taking over a successful and close-knit squad whose spirit and sense of togetherness played a significant part in their success last season. He will need to hit the ground running, quickly demonstrate and convince the players of his capabilities, put his own ideas across and build a relationship with them that ensures that everyone is working together and towards a common goal.

There is also the Mark Warburton factor to consider and Dijkhuizen (assuming he does take over) will have to cope with the shadow of his successful predecessor looming over him. Should the season hit some early bumps in the road there will be lots of know-it-alls both in the media and even amongst our own supporter base who will be eager and quick to jump on the *I told you so* bandwagon.

Warburton's stock is currently extremely high and he will be in great demand, and I am sure that I am not alone in hoping that it would be for the best if his next job is somewhere out of sight and out of mind like Glasgow Rangers, perhaps, rather than at another Championship team, particularly one just down the road which is rumoured to be interested in him!

Depending upon where he eventually ends up it is also not beyond the realms of possibility that Warburton will return to Griffin Park attempting to sign players and recruit staff, as was the case with his predecessor. Given Mark's frosty comments during the Adam Forshaw transfer saga, when he made it clear how unhappy he was with

Wigan's behaviour, I would fully expect that he, in his turn, will behave with dignity and integrity.

Brentford will no longer be underestimated and taken lightly by a long list of opponents who had their tails tweaked by us last season. To visit, outplay and defeat clubs with massively higher budgets and recent Premier League pedigree was an incredible achievement and next season the likes of Nottingham Forest, Cardiff City, Leeds United, Blackburn Rovers, Fulham and Reading will be far better prepared to take us on. I only wish I could add the name of Derby County to that list as we somehow failed to win the game in which we put on our most impressive performance of the season.

Our better players will also be in demand and we will probably have to fight off clubs higher up the food chain who are clamouring to take the likes of Button, Odubajo, Jota and Gray off our hands. Peradventure, we might even feel the need to sell one of our major assets to avoid the risk of falling foul of the demands of Financial Fair Play, but if we do so it will only be on our terms.

If the previous few paragraphs sound negative and full of foreboding then I apologise and will redress the balance by accentuating the positives, of which there are so many.

The opposition might well know what is coming their way when they play against the Bees, but that is still no guarantee that they can do anything about it!

I am confident that if we do lose a key player then somebody just as talented and full of promise will come in to replace him given the quality of our scouting. Our squad is young and brimming with talent and jam-packed with players experienced beyond their age who have already established and proven themselves at Championship level.

Brentford is now an extremely attractive option as players know that if they decide to join us, their ability will be showcased in a nurturing environment and that they will become part of a talented young team that is well-run and coached, brilliantly supported behind the scenes and that will always play a vibrant brand of attacking football.

We have attracted high calibre loanees such as Alex Pritchard, Jon Toral and Chris Long through the links we have established with leading Premier League clubs and I fully expect this state of affairs to continue next season as managers appreciate that their starlets will be well looked after and continue to progress and develop in the enlightened atmosphere that exists at Griffin Park.

We have also established our own development pathway from the Academy and it is anticipated that we will begin to see the benefits at first team level in the not-too-distant future. Montell Moore has already made his debut, Jermaine Udumaga has been a non-playing substitute and there are others like Josh Laurent, Courtney Senior, Aaron Greene, Gradi Milenge and Zain Westbrooke also bubbling under.

I fully expect that next season's team will contain more players from outside the United Kingdom, and the time they take to bed in will be crucial to our success. We also have to keep a sense of balance and proportion and ensure that there remains a core of homegrown talent to provide the backbone of the squad.

I look back at where we were this time last year and our progress is truly astonishing. I am more certain than ever that the best is yet to come. There may well be teething troubles ahead to endure and hopefully overcome - there generally are when major changes are made, and next season could well be a transitional one - but I remain more confident than ever that we will reach the Premier League sooner rather than later, certainly in time for the opening of Lionel Road, and that we are certainly way ahead of the game.

A Player's View – by Richard Lee – 31/5/15

Is there ever a dull season at Griffin Park?

A week after the disappointment at Middlesbrough, I've boarded a flight and I finally have the chance to gather my thoughts on what was another monumental season for Brentford FC.

It's hard to believe that this is the same club I joined in 2010. At that time we were a League One club in every way, shape, and form. The football we played was of a poor standard and there was very little evidence to suggest that we'd be climbing the echelons of English football at any time soon.

So what's changed between then and now? The answer is a simple one. There have been two men who have been instrumental in helping to shape this football club - Matt and Mark.

Upon first meeting Benham you wouldn't instantly associate him as someone who is a self-made multimillionaire. He's far from extravagant; from memory he drove a Ford Mondeo when I was first at Brentford and certainly wasn't dressed from head to foot in designer labels.

However, I would soon appreciate that Benham is a visionary.

Not only has he helped his boyhood club climb the ladder but he's doing it in such a way that is sustainable and very much from the bottom up.

With each day that has passed since I arrived at what was then a dated Jersey Road training ground I've witnessed innovation after innovation. The infrastructure in place now offers an environment for success.

Each morning now begins with the obligatory questionnaire, which is shortly followed by a urine sample and often blood tests before heading to the gym to do *pre-activation*. The gym itself is new with an array of expensive equipment, including an anti-gravity treadmill and Pilates Reformer. In fact, we now have a room dedicated to Pilates and another room specifically for pre-briefs and debriefs.

Something Benham did early on was to gradually build a highly educated staff that understood his vision and could help it become a reality. One of the first people he employed was Mark Warburton.

I've known *Warbs* for a number of years dating back to my days with Watford. His story is totally unique and one that I've told to many people. Another visionary who had the most unlikely of dreams, but if ever I needed proof that anything is possible then *Warbs* has certainly confirmed that.

The football world is very much about relationships and *Warbs* has travelled the world in his quest to build links at the biggest clubs and heighten his football knowledge. It took him ten years to graduate from working in the city to becoming the manager of Brentford FC and he's very much taken everything that he learned as the manager of a team in his city job into the football world.

He's someone I have so much time for. He's far from the stereotypical football manager. More an astute businessman who understands totally how to lead men and get the best from them.

Warbs has certainly taken on board the simple realisation that good communication, honesty and integrity can go a long way. Simply letting a player know he's been dropped and giving him the reason why seems simple enough, but that is a courtesy and practice rarely exercised elsewhere. Understanding when a player needs an arm around the shoulder or knowing when to kick him up the backside is often the difference between the good and great. Add to this a well thought out approach to the game of football and you soon have a recipe for success.

Warbs understands this and alongside Benham has put together a strategy for playing the game that shares similarities with that employed by some of the greatest teams in the world.

It isn't by luck that we play the way we do, it isn't by luck that we dominate games, and it isn't by luck that more often that not the players signed are successful. There is a groundbreaking combination of science and a trained eye behind every recruit at Brentford FC nowadays. They know things about players that not even the players themselves would know. It truly is a case of mathematics and football being in perfect harmony.

It concerns me that so many teams at Championship level are still reliant on a lucky break or good fortune as opposed to putting in place a solid foundation and then building on it. Constant reactive decision-making will at some point result in failure. A solid business that focuses on the small details, treats its staff well and is continually growing and improving will naturally outperform a rival that has no culture of success or self-analysis. The same is very much true in the football world.

It would be the dispute between the two key figures that would perhaps be the talking point of the season. There was quite a furore that surrounded the announcement that Mark Warburton would be stepping down.

Initially, we players believed it was simply an ill-founded rumour but when it emerged that it was true we were of course shocked and I'd be lying if I said that it didn't rock us somewhat. A couple of defeats followed the announcement, which at the time knocked us off track.

As with any announcement like this I'm sure it could've been handled better. Regardless of people's opinions about the overall situation, the way in which it played out in the media certainly didn't do anyone any favours – except, of course, for the teams around us.

My opinion is simply this - Mark Warburton is a superb manager who will go on to have huge success because he ticks every box. Matt Benham has a vision and will ensure that his vision is realised at Brentford.

Both Mark Warburton and Brentford FC have a superb future ahead of them, however I am very sad that it's not in unison and that their remarkable partnership is no more. It was such a good match. We'll never know exactly what happened and why it couldn't work but I refuse to take sides because there really isn't anything negative that any true Brentford fan can say about either man. Benham will continue to lead Brentford FC in a positive direction and *Warbs* will go with everyone's blessing.

So although there's a tinge of sadness that this season wasn't quite the fairytale that we believed it could be, for such a long period of time, this remains a very positive piece on what was a truly historic season for our fantastic football club and what promises to be an even more exciting future.

This season would also see the rise of several stars. Who would've thought that Toumani would scoop the Player of the Season award? I was delighted for Stuart Dallas who played an instrumental role all season and will forever be remembered for his part in the dismantling of Fulham. Alex Pritchard showed that stardom at Spurs looks inevitable. Dougie just continues to soldier on and lead the team and ensures that we all live up to his high standards. Andre Gray showed that the jump from Conference to Championship isn't perhaps as big as we had assumed.

Moses, Harlee, Tarky, Tony and Bidders were also superb at the back, and they all contributed to our attacking, free-flowing style of football too. Jota was a revelation and would soon be the name of the back of many a fan's shirt and I've no doubt we'll see more young Spanish talent arriving in West London next season.

Naturally the lads I was closest to during the season were the goalkeepers, both of whom had monumental seasons for very different reasons.

In a similar way to me, David Button has emerged from a slow start to his Brentford career to be a mainstay who plays the game exactly how I believe it should be played. When I say that I mean he has all the attributes that the goalkeeper of today requires. His distribution is superb; we take for granted the way in which he can fizz the ball perfectly fifty-plus yards at head height to Bidders in order to start an attack. He's also very calm in his demeanour and rarely flustered. I have no doubt that he will represent England providing he tidies up one or two small areas. He's a true gent too and deserves all the success that comes his way.

Jack Bonham's season was stunning for other reasons. I've got a lot of time for Jack. His first two games in professional football couldn't have gone much worse, in truth. The first of which resulted in a defeat to Leeds which ended hopes of promotion for Watford and the second saw him come off the bench to replace Butts only to then concede four times against Bradford City. This soon had the Brentford faithful questioning him and, combined with a few other issues, he was on the verge of exiting Griffin Park a mere twelve months ago.

Roll on a year and you now see a mentally and physically attuned athlete between the posts. He was at a crossroads and he got his act together. He refused to be a victim of circumstance and I was aware on day one that I had a fight on my hands to keep the number two spot, let alone become a number one.

Jack used what could have destroyed him to make him stronger and for that reason I'm really excited to see how his career pans out. He was able to give a glimpse of his potential in the one cup game he played in this season and we'll no doubt see more of him in the coming years. Without a shadow of a doubt he deserved to oust me this season. He's also got a top class goalkeeping coach in Simon Royce who will no doubt help him reach his huge potential.

Which leads me nicely onto my season, not that there's a great deal to speak of.

On a personal level I had approached the season with high hopes. I'd spent the summer break training hard with the dream that I could once more grace the Championship.

The issue that I've had personally over the past couple of years is simply a case of head versus heart. I approached the season with the dream of forcing my way back into the team. Upon doing this and having a successful season, then as an English goalkeeper playing at a high level, perhaps international recognition would be within touching distance etc. The reality was unfortunately very different.

Are my injuries bad enough to stop me playing football? No. Are they bad enough to inhibit me? Yes. I would follow a familiar pattern. Start to train, feel a sharp pain in one of my shoulders or knee and either pull out of training or continue begrudgingly. I'd often train with the knowledge that a familiar pain would accompany a full stretch save. My motivation levels dropped as a result and the joy that I found in my projects away from football soon eclipsed my fading enjoyment for a game that was becoming more and more painful and one that I was becoming less and less equipped for.

I also had other issues away from football that took their toll and before I knew it I was on the bench fearful of being called into action and also doubting that I was at the required standard in order to compete.

This culminated in playing my one and only game of the season, a game which would prove to be my last competitive appearance and what a game to go out on!

Prior to playing Dagenham I had never conceded more than four in any one particular game. Even that had only happened a handful of times, twice at the hands of Manchester United and in particular, Ronaldo, who put a few past me. Well Ronaldo wasn't on show for Dagenham but it felt like he was.

The game itself was like no other I've ever experienced. I made several saves, we won on penalties and I exited the pitch to the chorus of *England's number one*. Sounds great? Yet this was the game when I finally had clarity that enough was enough.

The game finished 6-6. I was at fault for two. It wasn't necessarily the fact that I was at fault for goals that made my decision an easier one; it was more to do with how I felt. I didn't enjoy the game one bit; I felt limited in areas of my game that I once considered to be strengths and had that realisation that my passion for playing football had vanished.

I didn't sleep that night and spent most of the early hours planning my exit strategy.

Soon after, I met the manager and was so grateful at how he dealt with the situation, although I expected nothing different from him. I told him in September but didn't tell anyone else until January.

The one other twist on a personal level came in the shape of a highly unexpected loan move to Championship rivals Fulham. Now some people will never understand this and that's fine. For me it was simply a case of knowing that by going there I had more of a chance of perhaps playing one more game. I knew it would cause a bit of a stir (and the Twitter antics didn't help matters!) but I chose to be selfish.

I believe I finished my career having played one hundred and ninety-nine times, I liked the idea I could maybe make it to two hundred and I couldn't see that happening at Brentford. As it turned out it wasn't meant to be as Bettinelli fought through a niggling injury to see the season out but I have no regrets in the decision. I enjoyed the experience and was treated really well by the Fulham staff and players.

Thankfully the large majority of Brentford fans understood too, which also didn't surprise me. I'll never understand why some players are liked and others aren't, but I was aware that the fans took to me after my early troubles. For that I'll always be so grateful.

As I reflect on what has been a solid career I'll always remember running out at Griffin Park and the injection of adrenaline I'd always get upon hearing the sound of *England's number one*, which is music to any goalkeeper, however my favourite chant will always be the one created about me to Bob Marley's classic *Three Little Birds*. Hearing that sung for the majority of the second half against Tranmere when making my comeback from my shoulder operation was one of the best experiences of my life. I was truly blessed and can't wait to come back as a fan.

So what now for the mighty Bees?

I am gutted that Mark Warburton won't be leading Brentford into both the new stadium and the Premier League however this won't stand in Brentford's way.

This is a club very much heading in the right direction and this is only the beginning.

And, as for me? Well I've just landed in America. Life after football starts now. Thanks for the memories.

Warbs: An Appreciation – by Billy Reeves – 31/5/15

If someone had offered you this at the beginning of the season, you'd have bitten their hand off.

If I had a penny for every time I heard this in 2015 I'd have enough money for a Griffin burger (fill in your own joke about similarity of flavour and/or texture). It's a revolting image, and, despite good intentions, a patronising one. I know of no Bees supporters who thought Brentford would struggle in the 2014/15 season, we knew all along that with a stable club, a good manager, a clever playing-style and a sassy recruitment policy that we would surprise the so-called *bigger clubs*.

On the way back from yet another impressive away performance, having dished out a footballing lesson to one of the many dysfunctional old-guard in Leeds United, the Bees Player commentating gang - mustering all the gallows humour football fans are well known for - started jamming ideas about how we were going to screw it up this time. No-one guessed that disruption in the relationship between owner and manager was just around the corner.

I'm agnostic about whether the schism between Messrs Benham, McParland & Warburton caused a downturn in form. We were flying at the time and were always going to find it difficult to keep it up. Warbs – the football man - was the one with the ear and mics of the press, so the *bitten your hand off* mantra we heard everywhere became: *crazy decision*. Pundits should know by now that football clubs are strange beasts. When wealthy men own them they bring in methods (and personnel) to the football club that have made them their money outside of it. There's PLENTY of empirical evidence that this doesn't normally work. But Matthew Benham's business IS relevant to a football club. In Matthew we trust.

To begin with, at Charlton away (the game after the news became widespread), there was much head shaking in the camp before the game (talk of *six coming in*), but Warbs kept his counsel – only using one word pre-game to describe the situation - *inappropriate*. The Bees were roundly beaten by a relegation-threatened side; players later told me that they had let emotions get to them that day.

In the end it mattered not. It may, indeed have helped galvanise the team. Warbs original line was: *of course I would bring in players if I thought it would add value to the side, it's nonsense to say I wouldn't*, later on in the campaign he said, *I want to put this to bed, attempts were made to bring in players in January but for a variety of reasons, agents, etc, this didn't happen.*

Meanwhile the patronising and hounding of Matt Benham in the press reached a nadir with Mark Clemmit comparing him in *The Times* to the villain in Austin Powers. Many of the *football people* in the media were content with an easy, smug soundbite and did not bother to do their homework on what Matt has said in the past about statistical and mathematical modelling: i.e. it's just that, a model, not reality, and he's keen on old-fashioned scouting too. This, I feel is typical of how the media treats anything outside the Premier League; it's all a bit wacky. The unusualness and uniqueness of the story caught them on the back foot. And, having seen Cliff Crown on *The Football League Show*, so many of the inhabitants of press boxes up and down the country got totally confused between Chairman (spokesperson) and Owner (decision maker). Got on my nerves, that did.

Warbs remained dignified. The team went though a couple of bad performances but kept about their business and stayed in the playoff hunt. He told me in a rare aside that he'd decided to be *a man about it*, clever, as it was crucial that the focus should be on the team. Although exasperated and discombobulated, Manager and Players stuck to the script both on and off the record. It was a shame the Manager was leaving, they said - but they accepted and respected Matt's plans. Warbs remained loyal to the team he'd built – whatever went wrong in January the Bees built up a team spirit you can't buy. They were brilliant, entertaining to watch and gave it their all. True Brentford legends.

Those of us who had done our homework and knew a little about Matt's methods had a feeling in our water that plans were already afoot. The day after the play-off defeat at Middlesbrough this was confirmed with the announcement of a two-man team to perform the role of all-powerful sporting director – in conjunction with the board. Almost like a team of selectors from the early days of the professional game. I hope we don't lose the *club* abstract of BFC, i.e. the relationship between the fans and the team. Warbs was very good at that, always keen to praise the supporters, to appear avuncular, never to *disrespect* other teams. If I had a penny for every time he praised his own team's achievement with the phrase *tough place to come* I'd have some cheese on my Griffin burger.

I'm a vegetarian. I don't want to sink my teeth into any flesh. But if you, dear and sensitive reader could somehow have manufactured a change of heart with Warbs staying then you could've popped a little tomato ketchup just south of your wrist and I'll have grabbed a bun. But we must get used to different, more exotic flavours now. Along with the sweet smell of success.

King Kev Hangs Up His Boots: A Tribute – by Jim Levack – 31/5/15

So, the day we've all been dreading but knew was coming has finally arrived.

Kevin O'Connor, as Brentford as Peter Gilham and loyal to the core, has hung up his boots. But, importantly, the new-look set up, with Rasmus and Marinus at its heart, has decided that he is very much a part of the club's plans going forward.

And that, in an instant, gave me hope that the very essence of the club we all love is still very much alive and well despite all the recent upheaval.

Rasmus, in a heartfelt welcome to the coaching ranks, said: *He is the perfect person to inform the new coaching staff about what sort of club Brentford is if they need it*.

Humility, awareness and realism all rolled into one… maybe the future coaching scenario won't be such a quantum leap after all.

Kevin will now be well aware that he has a critical role in the future of the club as an anchor to the past and a springboard to the future. And we should all count ourselves extraordinarily lucky that we have such a model professional and honest, down to earth bloke to fulfill that role.

Sure, some clubs will have the equivalent of King Kev, but he is ours… the kind of player we all looked up to and admired for his honest endeavour and one club mentality.

O'Connor was the kind of player who'd always be first on the team sheet. You knew what you'd get from him. He wasn't a game changer but was the kind of player who allowed the game changers to change games.

At his best just in front of the back four, he'd break up play effortlessly and then simply give the ball to someone who could turn defence into attack more effectively.

He knew his strengths and he knew his limitations, and his reading of the game made up for any shortage of blistering pace and he'd always be in the right place at the right time. Uncanny.

There were occasions when I'd watch him solidly for ten or fifteen minutes, and his positional awareness was incredible, always seeming to work his way into areas where the ball would drop loose several minutes later.

As the game became more obsessed with statistics – something we are now embracing to what, I'm sure, will be impressive effect – he was always an eight or nine with the best pass completion of them all.

Nicknamed *Shearer* in his early days at the club, he was a play anywhere, do anything kind of footballer with an eye for goal and a shrewd tactical awareness of the game that only comes with experience.

Just as importantly he was – is – a thoroughly nice bloke who is as passionate about his club as the fans who will always worship him.

When decisions have gone against us in key games this season and the blood has boiled, I've been heartened to see Kev in the face of the match officials at full time. Deep down he's a fan who has struck gold.

Down the years there have been many nice guys who have worn the Brentford shirt, but in my career as a journalist covering the club, few have come anywhere near Kevin O'Connor in ticking all the boxes of what a footballer should be.

My sons both idolise him just as Chelsea fans worship at the altar of Didier, because he epitomises what really matters to every true Brentford fan… loyalty, dedication and devotion – all attributes that, sadly, don't feature too much in the modern game.

Unlike Drogba and the embarrassing episode as he was chaired off in his farewell game, that's not the style of Kev O'Connor. He's the type who will move quietly on to the next phase of his career without a fuss – just like he played the game.

As a player I don't think we will ever see his like again… so it's just as well that he's now knitted into the very fabric of our club.

Thank you Kev for all the memories. Now, let the next chapter begin.

Graduation: Life Lessons of a Professional Footballer by Richard Lee

The 2010/11 season will go down as a memorable one for Goalkeeper Richard Lee. Cup wins, penalty saves, hypnotherapy and injury would follow, but these things only tell a small part of the tale.

Filled with anecdotes, insights, humour and honesty - Graduation uncovers Richard's campaign to take back the number one spot, save a lot of penalties, and overcome new challenges. What we see is a transformation - beautifully encapsulated in this extraordinary season.

Saturday Afternoon Fever: A Year On The Road For Soccer Saturday
by Johnny Phillips

You might already know Johnny Phillips. He is a football reporter for Sky Sports' Soccer Saturday programme and a man who gets beamed into the homes of fans across the country every weekend.

For the 2012/13 season, Johnny decided to do something different. He wanted to look beneath the veneer of household-name superstars and back-page glamour to chronicle a different side to our national sport. As Johnny travelled the country, he found a game that he loved even more, where unheralded stars were driven by a desire to succeed, often telling stories of bravery and overcoming adversity. People who were plucked from obscurity, placed in the spotlight and, sometimes, dropped back into obscurity again. Football stories that rarely see the limelight but which have a value all fans can readily identify with.

Small Time: A Life in the Football Wilderness by Justin Bryant

In 1988, 23-year-old American goalkeeper Justin Bryant thought a glorious career in professional football awaited him. He had just saved two penalties for his American club - the Orlando Lions - against Scotland's Dunfermline Athletic, to help claim the first piece of silverware in their history. He was young, strong, healthy, and confident.

Small Time is the story of a life spent mostly in the backwaters of the game. As Justin negotiated the Non-League pitches of the Vauxhall-Opel League, and the many failed professional leagues of the U.S. in the 1980s and 90s - Football, he learned, is 95% blood, sweat, and tears; but if you love it enough, the other 5% makes up for it.

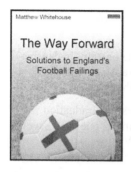

The Way Forward: Solutions to England's Football Failings by Matthew Whitehouse

English football is in a state of crisis. It has been almost 50 years since England made the final of a major championship and the national sides, at all levels, continue to disappoint and underperform. Yet no-one appears to know how to improve the situation. In his acclaimed book, The Way Forward, football coach Matthew Whitehouse examines the causes of English football's decline and offers a number of areas where change and improvement need to be implemented immediately. With a keen focus and passion for youth development and improved coaching he explains that no single fix can overcome current difficulties and that a multi-pronged strategy is needed. If we wish to improve the standards of players in England then we must address the issues in schools, the grassroots, and academies, as well as looking at the constraints of the Premier League and English FA.

Universality | The Blueprint for Soccer's New Era: How Germany and Pep Guardiola are showing us the Future Football Game by Matthew Whitehouse

The game of soccer is constantly in flux; new ideas, philosophies and tactics mould the present and shape the future. In this book, Matthew Whitehouse – acclaimed author of The Way Forward: Solutions to England's Football Failings - looks in-depth at the past decade of the game, taking the reader on a journey into football's evolution. Examining the key changes that have occurred since the turn of the century, right up to the present, the book looks at the evolution of tactics, coaching, and position-specific play. They have led us to this moment: to the rise of universality. Universality | The Blueprint For Soccer's New Era is a voyage into football, as well as a lesson for coaches, players and fans who seek to know and anticipate where the game of the future is heading.

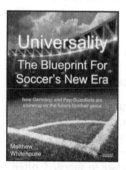

Conference Season by Steve Leach

Disillusioned with the corporate ownership, mega-bucks culture, and overpaid prima donnas, of the Premiership, Steve Leach embarked on a journey to rediscover the soul of professional football. His journey, over the 2012/13 season, took him to twenty-four different Football Conference towns and fixtures, visiting venues as diverse as the Impact Arena in Alfreton, Stonebridge Road in Ebbsfleet, and Luton's Kenilworth Road.

Encountering dancing bears at Nuneaton, demented screamers at Barrow, and 'badger pasties' at rural Forest Green – Steve unearthed the stories behind the places and people – it was a journey that showed just how football and communities intertwine, and mean something. Conference Season is a warm and discerning celebration of the diversity of towns and clubs which feature in the Conference, and of the supporters who turn up week-after-week to cheer their teams on.

Lightning Source UK Ltd.
Milton Keynes UK
UKOW07f1858030715

254602UK00011B/189/P